Sample *smb.conf*

NetBIOS computers are identified by a name and workgrou[...] Samba allows you to assign one or more *aliases,* or duplicat[...] can also assign a comment with the `server string` parame[...]

Samba logs important information to the specified log file, using a level of detail set with `debug level`. See Chapter 4.

You can bind Samba to just one network interface, and configure it to accept connections from only specified hosts. See Chapter 14.

Password security is critically important to Samba. With the `security` parameter, you can set Samba to use any of four security models and tell it whether or not to use encrypted passwords. You can also map Windows to Linux usernames, control guest access, and block certain users from connecting at all. See Chapters 14 and 15.

Samba can function as a network's *domain controller,* meaning that it handles logons for the entire domain, including home directory assignments and logon scripts. See Chapter 10.

The *master browser* compiles lists of computers for clients' use. Samba can fill this role, as described in Chapter 11.

NBNS, or WINS, is one NetBIOS name resolution system. Samba can fill this role, as described in Chapter 9.

Samba can share all available printers (via `load printers = Yes`), and can provide printer drivers to Windows 9*x* systems (through the `printer driver file` and `printer driver location` parameters). See Chapter 6.

The `include` parameter lets Samba load supplementary configuration files. The `%a` expands to a name for the client OS. See Appendix B.

Linux Samba Server Administration

Roderick W. Smith

SYBEX

San Francisco   Paris   Düsseldorf   Soest   London

Associate Publisher: Neil Edde
Contracts and Licensing Manager: Kristine O'Callaghan
Acquisitions Editor: Maureen Adams
Developmental Editor: Thomas Cirtin
Editors: Carol Henry, Pete Gaughan
Production Editor: Shannon Murphy
Technical Editor: Elizabeth Zinkann
Book Designer: Bill Gibson
Graphic Illustrator: Tony Jonick
Electronic Publishing Specialist: Nila Nichols
Proofreaders: Jennifer Campbell, Erika Donald, Nanette Duffy, Laurie O'Connell, Nancy Riddiough,
Nathan Whiteside
Indexer: Nancy Guenther
Cover Designer: Ingalls & Associates
Cover Illustrator: Ingalls & Associates

Library of Congress Card Number: 00-107350

ISBN: 0-7821-2740-1

To Catherine, whose absence from the East Coast is felt by all her friends.

Foreword

Microsoft Windows holds the lion's share of the desktop operating system market. The majority of clients connecting to a Linux server are Microsoft Windows clients. Effectively serving those clients is a major task for every Linux system administrator. Samba is an important tool for tackling that task.

Most of the network services provided by a Linux server are standard Internet services. Apache, DHCP, DNS, and `sendmail` are all topics covered in the Craig Hunt Linux Library and are all services built on standard Internet protocols. Samba is different. It implements the NetBIOS and Server Message Block (SMB) protocols that Microsoft uses for its proprietary networking. Samba integrates a Linux server into a Microsoft network almost seamlessly. This makes Samba an extremely important component of the Linux system administrator's toolkit.

In 1999, I attended two talks given by Andrew Tridgell at the Open Source Software Convention. Because I already knew I wanted to include a book about Samba in the Craig Hunt Linux Library, I was struck by something he said. Andrew, a leader of the Samba development team, said that people were always asking him to write a book about Samba but that he thought the best book about Samba would be written by a system administrator, not a software developer. I had to agree with him, and I was lucky enough to find an author with system administration skills who really knows how to write. That author is Rod Smith.

Rod is the author of several books, all of which focus on Linux. He has written about Linux hardware, Linux networking, and Linux applications, and all of his books are highly rated. I was pleased to find an author of his skill who also understands the importance of producing top-quality books for the Linux system administrator—which is the entire reason the Craig Hunt Linux Library was created. By the time I had finished his first chapter, I knew we had found the right person to write *Linux Samba Server Administration*. I hope you enjoy reading Rod's book as much as I did.

Craig Hunt
October 2000

Acknowledgments

A book doesn't just happen. At every point along the way from project beginning to finished product, many people other than the author have their influence. This book began with Craig Hunt's conception for a series of Linux system administration titles, and his influence on this book has continued through his comments and suggestions on each chapter. Maureen Adams, acquisitions editor, helped set the book on course at its inception. Tom Cirtin, development editor, guided the book's development, especially for the critical first few chapters. As production editor, Shannon Murphy coordinated the work of the many others who contributed their thoughts to the book. Editors Carol Henry and Pete Gaughan and proofreaders Jennifer Campbell, Erika Donald, Nanette Duffy, Laurie O'Connell, Nancy Riddiough, and Nathan Whiteside helped keep my grammar and spelling on track. Elizabeth Zinkann, the technical editor, scrutinized the text for technical errors and to be sure it was complete. Nila Nichols, electronic publishing specialist, transformed my plain manuscript into the beautiful book you are now holding. I am grateful to them all.

Roderick Smith
October 2000

Contents at a Glance

Contents

Introduction

Networking has transformed our world. From the rapid exchange of e-mail among individuals separated by thousands of miles, to the sharing of files between two computers on a simple home network, the capability to link computers together has influenced the ways in which we work and play. With the proliferation of networking, however, has come a proliferation in networking *protocols*. Just in the realm of file sharing among small computers, four protocols are in common use: Microsoft and IBM's SMB/CIFS, Novell's IPX/SPX, Sun's NFS, and Apple's AppleTalk. Each protocol is unique and incompatible with the others. In a mixed-OS environment, therefore, it can be difficult to maintain several protocols, especially when you need computers from different vendors to access the same files.

Enter Linux. Built by enthusiasts through a worldwide collaboration—made possible by the global Internet—Linux includes support for most network protocols in common use. In particular, Linux supports Samba, a package that allows Unix-like OSs to participate in the SMB/CIFS networking that's popular on networks of Windows computers. With Samba and Linux's other network protocols, a single computer can replace what might otherwise be two or more computers running two or more operating systems. In fact, the combination of Samba and Linux is so good that it's often desirable to use Linux in place of a Windows 2000 server—even on an otherwise all-Microsoft network! Linux and Samba afford enviable levels of flexibility and stability. This book will help you configure your Linux server to work with Windows, OS/2, or DOS systems on a network using the SMB/CIFS protocols.

A Linux computer running Samba can perform most of the functions of a Windows file server, and can do so well enough that your users might not know the difference between a Samba server and a Windows 2000 server. From an administrative point of view, the two systems are quite different, because Samba uses Linux filesystems and network administration features rather than Windows equivalents. These differences pose both challenges and opportunities. Samba contains extensive code to smooth over the challenges, such as features to automatically handle differences in filename requirements between Linux filesystems and the SMB/CIFS protocols. Opportunities present themselves in the ability to use Samba's fine-grained configuration options and Linux's networking and filesystem features to help improve the security and utility of your network server.

Who Should Buy This Book

This book is written for experienced Linux or Unix system administrators who have little experience with Samba. Perhaps you need to add Windows computers to an existing

Linux network, or take over server duties previously performed by a Windows NT server. If you're new to Linux but have Unix administration experience, you should have few problems with this book, or indeed with Linux in general. If you're completely new to the Linux and Unix worlds, however, you should supplement this book with another on Linux system administration, such as the forthcoming *Linux System Administration* volume of the Craig Hunt Linux Library (Sybex, 2001).

Linux Samba Server Administration contains all the information you're likely to need to configure Samba for a Windows network. It covers the basic concepts of SMB/CIFS networking, explains Samba configuration, and provides tips to help you keep your Samba network operating at its best.

How This Book Is Organized

This book is divided into four parts—How Things Work, Essential Configuration, Advanced Configurations, and Maintaining a Healthy System—and concludes with three appendices. Each part contains between two and six chapters, for a total of 17 chapters. If you're completely new to Samba, you can start with Chapter 1 and read through to the end to obtain a clear view of Windows file and printer sharing in general, and of how Samba fits into such a network in particular. If you already know a little about Samba, you may want to skip some chapters, particularly those at the beginning of the book. When a chapter relies heavily on material presented in another chapter, I say so at the beginning of the chapter, so you won't be caught unaware.

Part 1: How Things Work

Part 1 lays a theoretical foundation for the rest of the book. Its two chapters introduce the SMB/CIFS protocols as well as the underlying NetBIOS and NetBEUI protocols, and explain how Linux interacts with these protocols. You'll read about the development of these protocols and their relationship to protocols that are more common in the Unix world, such as TCP/IP and NFS. Differences between Linux and Windows present certain challenges when it comes to Linux's serving files to Windows computers, and these issues are introduced in Part 1. Many of the options described in later chapters relate to these challenges, and to the opportunities that arise from these differences.

Part 2: Essential Configuration

The five chapters in Part 2 cover the basics of Samba configuration. You'll learn how to install Samba, how to configure it via GUI tools and the smb.conf file, how to set up file sharing, how to set up shared printers, and how to use Samba as a client rather than a server. Since these are the core features of Samba, the five chapters of Part 2 should be enough to get you up and running with the software for many basic configurations. Unless your needs are extremely modest, however, I don't recommend you stop here, because subsequent chapters cover many important topics.

Part 3: Advanced Configurations

The topics covered in Part 3 are automation, Samba as an NBNS server, domains, browsing, Samba performance tuning, and Samba's interactions with other network protocols. Some of these topics may sound strange to anybody who's unfamiliar with Windows networking. Basic definitions are covered in Chapter 1, so don't be concerned if these terms are new to you. Although you can probably get a Linux computer up and running as a Samba server using only the material in Part 2, Part 3 will help you to fine-tune your Samba configuration. NBNS can reduce some unnecessary broadcast traffic, for instance, which can be quite important in large networks. Understanding domains and browsing will help you organize your network and your Samba server's place within it.

Part 4: Maintaining a Healthy System

Administering a network server involves more than just setting it up, and Part 4 is devoted to necessary maintenance and the preparation for such maintenance. The four chapters of this part cover the topics of security, account management, backups, and troubleshooting. Many Samba security issues are similar to those for other servers, of course; other matters, though, such as file ownership policies, can be handled differently in Samba than in other servers. Similarly, you may need to give some thought to how you create and manage user accounts on a Samba server, for reasons of both security and convenience. Since it implements a network file-sharing protocol, Samba can be used to back up other computers on your network.

Appendices

This book includes three appendices. The first is a reference guide to Samba configuration. This guide lists the options you can use in the `smb.conf` file and what they do. Appendix B covers Samba issues that are specific to particular non-Windows client OSs, such as OS/2 and BeOS. The final appendix includes the text of the GNU GPL, under which terms Samba is licensed.

Conventions Used in This Book

This book uses certain typographic styles in order to help you quickly identify important information, and to avoid confusion over the meaning of words such as on-screen prompts. In particular:

- A normal, proportionally spaced font is used for the bulk of the text in the book.
- *Italicized text* indicates technical terms that are introduced for the first time in a chapter. (Italic is also used for emphasis.)
- A `monospaced font` is used to indicate the contents of configuration files, messages displayed at a text-mode Linux shell prompt, filenames, and Internet URLs.
- *`Italicized monospaced text`* indicates a variable—information that differs from one system or command run to another, such as the name of a client computer or a process ID number.

- **Bold monospaced text** is information that you're to type into the computer, usually at a Linux shell prompt. This text can also be italicized to indicate that you should substitute an appropriate value for your system.

In addition to these text conventions, which may apply to individual words or entire paragraphs, the following conventions are used to highlight segments of text:

NOTE A Note contains information that's useful or interesting but somewhat peripheral to the main discussion. A Note might be relevant to a small number of networks, for instance, or refer to an outdated feature.

TIP A Tip provides information that can save you time or frustration and that may not be entirely obvious. A Tip might describe how to get around a limitation, or how to use a feature to perform an unusual task.

WARNING Warnings describe potential pitfalls or dangers. If you fail to heed a Warning, you may end up spending a lot of time recovering from a bug, or even restoring your entire system from scratch.

Sidebars

Like a Note, but longer, sidebars give you helpful information and advice that may not fit into the flow of the primary discussion.

Help Us Help You

Things change. In the world of computers, things change rapidly. Facts described in this book will become invalid over time. When they do, we need your help locating and correcting them. Additionally, a 600-page book is bound to have typographical errors. Let us know when you spot one. Send your suggested improvements, fixes, and other corrections to support@sybex.com, or go to the Sybex Web site at www.sybex.com. To contact Craig Hunt for information about upcoming books and talks on Linux, go to http://www.wrotethebook.com. Rod Smith can be reached at rodsmith@rodsbooks.com. He maintains a Web page devoted to this book at http://www.rodsbooks.com/samba/.

Part 1

How Things Work

Featuring:

- The Development of Windows Networking and Samba
- SMB/CIFS Terminology and Structure
- Integrating SMB/CIFS with TCP/IP
- Samba's Daemons
- Resolving Filesystem Feature Conflicts

1

An Introduction to SMB/CIFS

Samba was developed as a means of letting Unix computers offer the types of networking services used on IBM and Microsoft networks. Presumably you're reading this book because you want to do the same using a Linux computer. If you're already familiar with Windows networking, you can probably skip this chapter, or perhaps just skim it for information specific to Samba. You might not be familiar with Windows networking protocols, though—for instance, you might be a Unix administrator who must suddenly cater to a new group of Windows clients, or you might be trying to set up your first home network. In such cases, you should read this chapter carefully, because it lays down much of the theoretical groundwork for what follows in the rest of the book. Without an understanding of the core protocols and terminology in Windows networking, you'll have a hard time configuring Samba to fit into a Windows network.

This chapter describes the history and fundamental technologies behind Windows networking, specifically the *Server Message Block (SMB)* protocol, also called the *Common Internet File System (CIFS),* and its relationship to other network protocols such as TCP/IP. In this chapter you'll learn about the genesis of these protocols and how they've developed over the years. You'll also learn the most common terms used in discussing Windows networks, and how these terms correspond to equivalents in TCP/IP networking. Finally, I'll compare and contrast Windows networking protocols with some other common network protocols that you may already know.

> **NOTE**   Because CIFS is the new official name for the SMB protocol, you'll some-
> times see the protocol referred to by one name, and sometimes by the other.
> Through most of this book, I use SMB/CIFS to make it explicit that these two
> names are largely equivalent. In a few instances, I use one name in preference to
> the other, as when discussing pre-CIFS SMB development, or CIFS as used in
> Windows 2000.

Windows Networking and the Development of Samba

Windows has its own networking history, independent of the evolution of TCP/IP networking that's familiar to most Unix and Linux administrators. It's important that you
know some of this history as you're learning about Samba, because the initial SMB/CIFS
design decisions still have an influence today. Since the initial protocols were established,
Microsoft and others have expended increasing effort making them compatible with the
TCP/IP networking that's become dominant. This ongoing effort is part of what makes
Samba possible, but merging TCP/IP with Windows networking protocols isn't always
elegant.

The Basic Protocols: NetBIOS, NetBEUI, and SMB

In the mid-1980s, IBM wanted to sell networks to businesses. These networks were not
the globe-spanning networks that were beginning to emerge on mainframes and minicomputers of the time; rather, they were networks for small offices. These networks
offered basic office productivity services, such as file and printer sharing. On such networks, several computers could access files stored on a central server computer, or could
print to a single printer. The goal was to improve productivity by reducing the need for
moving files around on floppy disks.

IBM's desktop computer line of the time was the ancestor of today's $x86$ computer. Like
today's PCs, the PCs of the mid-1980s used a *Basic Input/Output System (BIOS)* to provide application programs and operating systems with access to machine resources. A
program or OS could make a BIOS call to read the hard disk, for instance, or to display
information on the screen. IBM's engineers saw the network as an extension of the computer's hardware, and so they called the basic protocols they developed *NetBIOS*. This
protocol suite was released in 1984. Today, NetBIOS is a series of protocols that can be
used in conjunction with various others. It sits in the middle of a stack of protocols used
by Windows networking, as described shortly.

NetBIOS by itself is largely inadequate as a networking protocol. Its extension is known as the *NetBIOS Extended User Interface (NetBEUI)* and was released in 1985. Although originally an extension of NetBIOS, NetBEUI today is often considered a lower-level transport layer in a network stack, as illustrated in Figure 1.1. NetBEUI now competes with the more common *Transmission Control Protocol/Internet Protocol (TCP/IP)* networking stack. The differences between these protocols are discussed later in this chapter in "SMB/CIFS and TCP/IP." For now, though, you should know that NetBEUI is a good protocol for use on small networks, but it doesn't scale up well. You can't use NetBEUI for a globe-spanning network such as the Internet because it supports only a limited number of computers (255), among other deficiencies. On the other hand, these very problems can sometimes be benefits. For example, if your Windows network uses only NetBEUI internally, the network is less likely to be invaded from the Internet.

Figure 1.1   NetBEUI resides between NetBIOS and the low-level networking hardware.

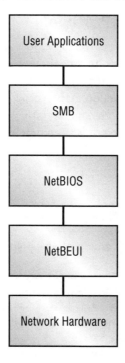

The final core protocol of Windows networking is SMB. In fact, it's from SMB that Samba takes its name. SMB provides high-level constructs atop NetBIOS. If you look at Figure 1.1, you can see that SMB falls between user applications and NetBIOS. This is analogous to the way DOS falls between applications and the BIOS for many functions.

DOS provides constructs and services, such as disk files and the ability to access them. Similarly, SMB/CIFS provides file-sharing mechanisms to allow one computer to access another's files.

To the average end-user, these details are largely unimportant. The typical user of Windows 98 or Windows 2000 today (or of Windows for Workgroups a few years ago) wants to click on network drive icons and access files. NetBEUI or TCP/IP, NetBIOS, and SMB operate in concert to allow this sort of action. As an administrator, however, you must know something about these protocols in order to evaluate alternatives and select the appropriate protocol and configuration for your network. Only in 2000 has NetBEUI support become available for Linux, from Procom Technology (`http://www.procom.com`). In most cases, you'll run Samba through TCP/IP rather than through NetBEUI, but you can use NetBEUI if you like. The implications of this configuration are discussed in more detail later in the chapter, in "SMB/CIFS and TCP/IP."

The Evolution of SMB Protocols

Windows networking has evolved over time, just as have other computer-related standards. Because any given network might contain a mix of clients and servers that support variants of the different SMB protocols, the initial connection between computers includes a negotiation of the level of SMB protocol to be used. Specifically, the client sends a list of the protocols it understands to the server, and the server replies with the most advanced protocol it understands from that list. The most important protocol levels are summarized in Table 1.1.

Table 1.1   SMB Dialects

Name	Description
CORE	Original version of SMB. No support for usernames or long filenames.
COREPLUS	More-efficient implementation of CORE.
LANMAN1	Modern implementation with support for usernames and long filenames.
LANMAN2	LANMAN1 with enhancements.
LANMAN2.1	Minor enhancement to LANMAN2.

Table 1.1   SMB Dialects *(continued)*

Name	Description
NT1	LANMAN dialect as implemented by Windows NT.
CIFS1	Minor modification to NT1 protocol, used by Windows 2000.

Samba understands all these SMB dialects, although as of version 2.0.7 Samba's support for CIFS is incomplete. (CIFS is discussed in the section "SMB/CIFS Terminology" later in this chapter.) You can therefore use Samba to serve shares to the oldest or most recent OSs that understand Windows networking protocols. In the case of very old SMB implementations, though, such as CORE and COREPLUS, you may need to adjust your Samba configuration so that it doesn't require usernames. Chapter 14, "Samba Security Considerations," covers Samba's security options.

The Emergence of Samba

Samba began life in 1991 at the Australian National University in Canberra. A graduate student, Andrew Tridgell, began a reimplementation of the SMB protocol. Tridgell had access to SMB servers running on VMS and Ultrix (a Unix variant for DEC minicomputers and mainframes), and he used packet sniffers and some ingenuity to deduce what the protocols did. The first release of Samba was in 1992, albeit under a different name (SMB Server). Two years later, interest in Samba began to grow, in part because interest in Linux was accelerating at the same time, and Samba proved to be a useful way to integrate Linux into Windows networks.

Over the years, Samba has grown to support many—but not yet all—of the features of SMB/CIFS as implemented on Windows computers. Samba's capabilities are compared to those of Windows later in this chapter, in the section "Samba's Capabilities."

As I write these words, the current version of Samba is 2.0.7. If you're using a particularly old Linux distribution that contains a pre-2.0 version of Samba, I recommend you upgrade Samba. Although much of this book is relevant for Samba 1.9.*x*, some of it isn't. Andrew Tridgell and others are actively working on future Samba releases. One of these currently goes by the name *Samba TNG* (for *The Next Generation*). This version implements features that help Samba operate in a Windows NT or 2000 domain environment, as described in Chapter 10, "Configuring Domains." Other changes are being made to the mainstream 2.0.*x* tree, expected to produce a 2.2- or 3.0-level release in late 2000. This release may incorporate some of Samba TNG's changes, but the exact nature of the release is as yet unclear.

With Windows 2000, Microsoft has changed the focus of its networking protocols. There are a number of new protocols, including *Active Directory Services (ADS),* a replacement for the *Windows Internet Name Service (WINS);* and the *Distributed File System (DFS),* a replacement for the core SMB/CIFS file-sharing protocols. On a network that contains nothing but Windows 2000 computers, SMB/CIFS as it's known today isn't used. In mid-2000, such networks are quite rare, however, so Samba remains useful. Support for Microsoft's new protocols will no doubt find its way to Linux, either through Samba or some other package.

SMB/CIFS in Various Environments

Today, SMB and related protocols are used mostly on networks dominated by Windows computers. Windows isn't the only OS to support SMB and related protocols, however. You can use these same protocols on a number of OSs, including the following:

Windows Windows for Workgroups, Windows 9*x*, and Windows NT (including Windows 2000) all support SMB "out of the box." Because these OSs are so popular, SMB and related protocols are often referred to as *Windows networking.* Indeed, I frequently use this term in the book.

OS/2 IBM's OS/2 4.0 and later comes with support for SMB networking. Configuration details differ from Windows, but the basic capabilities of OS/2 are similar. In addition, Samba has been ported to OS/2, so you can set up a Samba server on OS/2 if you don't like the way OS/2 handles the matter, or if you're using an older version of OS/2 that lacks SMB networking.

DOS You can obtain a client for SMB networking on MS-DOS from `ftp://ftp.microsoft.com/bussys/Clients/MSCLIENT/`. You need two files, `DSK3-1.EXE` and `DSK3-2.EXE`, both of which reside in the same FTP directory.

BeOS BeOS support for SMB exists but is still fairly new. In BeOS 5, you must use a component called WON for a BeOS computer to function as an SMB client. Samba has been ported to BeOS and allows a BeOS computer to function as an SMB server.

MacOS A third-party utility known as DAVE is available from Thursby Software Systems (`http://www.thursby.com`). DAVE functions for MacOS much as Samba does for Linux, providing both client and server functions. As of mid-2000, DAVE is available only for MacOS through version 9. MacOS X is based on a Unix core. It's likely that Samba will eventually work with MacOS X.

Amiga A port of Samba is available for the Amiga OS, providing it with SMB interoperability and particularly server support. Amiga SMB client support is weak, however.

VMS   VMS is an OS used mainly on DEC mainframe and minicomputers. Samba is available for VMS, allowing it to function as an SMB server. VMS client support is more limited.

Unix   Samba runs on just about all Unix computers, allowing them to function as SMB servers. Client operation is a bit spotty. All Unix systems can use `smbclient`, which is awkward. Some can use a package called `smbwrapper`, which simulates a filesystem mount.

Samba, of course, also runs on Linux. Building a Samba server under Linux is the focus of this book. Linux's SMB client support works differently from Unix's SMB client support. As of mid-2000, the `smbwrapper` package has problems with Linux's glibc, and so doesn't work with Linux. In Linux, the usual way to mount SMB filesystems is through a program called `smbmount`, described in Chapter 7, "Using Linux as an SMB/CIFS Client." In most OSs for which Samba is available, a program called `smbclient` allows you to access Samba shares using an interface similar to that of text-mode FTP clients. The use of `smbclient` is covered in Chapter 7, as well.

Of course, SMB is not the only network protocol used by these various operating systems. If you're an experienced Linux system administrator, chances are you're familiar with TCP/IP, and probably with file and printer sharing via the *Network File System (NFS)* and the *line printer daemon* (`lpd`). You may also be acquainted with Novell or AppleTalk networks, both of which use their own network stacks. Using your knowledge of these networks to compare them with SMB should help you understand Samba networking.

SMB/CIFS and TCP/IP

SMB/CIFS can operate over either NetBEUI or TCP/IP. Therefore, SMB/CIFS and TCP/IP aren't really alternates; rather, TCP/IP is one option for operating an SMB/CIFS network. Because NetBEUI has not traditionally been supported on Linux, Samba typically operates *only* over TCP/IP. Recently, however, Procom Technology (`http://www.procom.com`) has released a NetBEUI protocol stack for Linux. This stack works with Samba and thus allows Samba to participate in networks that use NetBEUI exclusively.

For some time, however, Microsoft has been moving away from NetBEUI and toward TCP/IP as a protocol stack. So in most cases there's no need to use NetBEUI on Linux. Some security-conscious administrators, however, are concerned that running SMB over TCP/IP might expose the SMB systems to Internet-based attacks. If you want to use a protocol that can't be routed across the Internet, you might want to consider NetBEUI instead of TCP/IP for your SMB/CIFS networking.

How Things Work

PART 1

The most popular "pure" TCP/IP file-and-printer-sharing protocols, particularly in the Unix and Linux world, are NFS for file sharing and lpd for printer sharing. Following are some of the critical differences between these protocols and SMB/CIFS.

Authentication   Both NFS and lpd operate on a *trusted hosts* model of security. Any computer that appears to be calling from an approved IP address is given a specified level of access to the computer. For instance, you can configure your Linux system to give access to the /home and /opt directories to the computer at 192.168.4.43. Although Samba can be configured similarly, the usual method of authentication in Samba (and in SMB/CIFS generally) is via username/password pairs—any user who has the correct username and password can gain access to a share. You can apply both methods to Samba, and this can increase Samba's security level. On the other hand, this model often ends up producing passwords stored on a variety of remote computers, which can itself be a potential security problem.

Filesystem Features   SMB/CIFS was created with the needs of DOS and, later, OS/2 and Windows filesystems in mind. As such, it includes features such as hidden and system bits for files, but not Unix-style ownership or permissions strings. NFS, on the other hand, is a Unix file-sharing protocol by design, so it includes Unix features, but not DOS/Windows features. As a general rule, therefore, NFS is the best protocol for file sharing between Unix and Linux computers, while SMB/CIFS is best in a Windows network. Samba goes to great lengths to make Linux work like a Windows system, and for the most part succeeds. With filesystem features passing through a DOS/Windows "filter," however, SMB/CIFS is a poor choice for most Unix-to-Unix file-sharing situations.

Monolithic Protocol   SMB/CIFS handles both file and printer sharing. In Samba, it can be configured completely through just one file, smb.conf. (You can also use auxiliary configuration files for various functions, though.) By contrast, Linux's native file-and-printer-sharing protocols are separate, and require separate configuration files. Further, SMB/CIFS supports a few extra network features that require separate protocols in Linux, including Messages and a time protocol for clock synchronization.

Implementation Completeness   Samba is a very useful tool, but it's not yet complete. As described in the later section "Browsing," features such as backup master browser functionality are missing from Samba. Linux's support for NFS and lpd are quite complete, however. To be sure, the gaps in Samba's support for SMB/CIFS are comparatively minor, but they might be significant on rare occasions.

Despite these differences, SMB/CIFS and NFS/lpd serve much the same functions. Which works best depends largely on your network. Networks dominated by Windows computers typically work best with SMB/CIFS; those with mostly Unix or Linux computers work best with NFS/1pd. You can mix both protocols, though. Indeed, one server can share the same files and printers via both SMB/CIFS and NFS/1pd. It's even possible to add Novell's IPX/SPX and Apple's AppleTalk to the mix; these protocols don't interfere with each other.

Contrasts to Novell Networks

Novell developed a set of networking protocols at about the same time IBM and Apple did, in the mid-1980s. The result is an entire suite of network tools that competes against NetBEUI, NetBIOS, and SMB/CIFS on the Windows side; and against TCP/IP, NFS, and 1pd on the Unix/Linux side. Following are some of the key components of a Novell network:

> **IPX** The *Internet Packet Exchange (IPX)* is one of the core protocols in Novell networking. It's roughly comparable to the Internet Protocol (IP) of TCP/IP networking.

> **SPX** The *Sequenced Packet Exchange (SPX)* protocol sits atop IPX, much as the Transmission Control Protocol (TCP) sits atop IP in a TCP/IP network.

> **NCP** The *NetWare Core Protocol (NCP)* is Novell's file-sharing protocol. In broad strokes, it's similar to SMB/CIFS or NFS.

Novell's networking scheme was developed with DOS in mind, and later Windows. As such, it doesn't include support for Unix-style permissions or file ownership. The Novell setup is very efficient, however; it's often possible to achieve faster file transfers using Novell networking than using SMB/CIFS or NFS.

Linux includes support for Novell networking protocols. To turn a Linux computer into a Novell server, you must use one of two packages: mars_nwe or lwared, both of which are available from ftp://sunsite.unc.edu/pub/Linux/system/filesystems/ncpfs/. Most Linux distributions ship with at least one of these packages. You can use Linux as a client on a Novell network by using the ncpfs kernel module. In both configurations, you must also include IPX networking support in the Linux kernel.

It's possible to bind SMB/CIFS to the Novell network stack, but only in Windows. Linux doesn't support this option.

Contrasts to AppleTalk Networks

In the mid-1980s, Apple developed a networking protocol for its Macintosh computers. Called *AppleTalk,* the protocol was originally designed to allow a network of Macintoshes to share an Apple LaserWriter printer, which was quite expensive at that time. Ethernet hardware was not yet as dominant as it is today, and so Apple used custom networking hardware. This hardware is now referred to as *LocalTalk,* although some early documentation used the term *AppleTalk* for both the hardware and the software. Since then, AppleTalk has been adapted to work over Ethernet hardware—a combination that's often named *EtherTalk*.

AppleTalk is composed of a network stack, much like the other office networking protocols. Its key components include the following:

DDP The *Datagram Delivery Protocol (DDP)* is at the core of AppleTalk. It's roughly comparable to TCP/IP or NetBEUI.

AFP The *AppleTalk Filing Protocol (AFP)* is the AppleTalk file-sharing protocol, roughly equivalent to NFS or the file-sharing components of SMB/CIFS.

PAP The *Printer Access Protocol (PAP)* is AppleTalk's printer-sharing protocol. It's similar to lpd or the printer-sharing components of SMB/CIFS.

In recent years, Apple has adapted AppleTalk to work over TCP/IP, just as NetBIOS can now be used over TCP/IP. Linux supports both the original AppleTalk (over Ethernet or, with rare LocalTalk hardware for *x*86 computers, over LocalTalk) and AppleTalk over TCP/IP. In most cases, you must compile DDP support into your Linux kernel. AppleTalk over TCP/IP works without this support, but you won't be able to browse Linux computers from a Macintosh's Chooser without DDP support, and printing doesn't work at all without DDP support.

You'll also need the *Netatalk* package, available from `http://thehamptons.com/anders/netatalk/` or from many Linux distributions. Netatalk lets your Linux computer function as a file and print server for Macintoshes, and lets you print to AppleTalk printers. As of mid-2000, however, support for using Linux as an AppleTalk client is extremely primitive and unreliable. If you need this functionality, you're better off installing NFS or SMB/CIFS support on the Macintosh, as discussed briefly in Appendix B, "OS-Specific Issues."

AppleTalk's file-sharing capabilities are similar to those of SMB/CIFS. For instance, AppleTalk operates through a username/password security model. Macintoshes also support filesystem features similar to those of Windows, such as hidden bits, but not Unix-style permissions or ownership. In addition, MacOS supports two *forks* for each file, a *data fork* and a *resource fork*. The data fork contains data such as ASCII text or spreadsheet data. The resource fork contains specialized information such as icons or program code. To accommodate forks, Netatalk creates a hidden subdirectory in each shared directory. The resource forks go in the hidden subdirectory under a name matched to the data fork file in the main directory.

Like a NetBIOS network, an AppleTalk network is basically two-tiered. AppleTalk supports the concept of *zones*, which are similar to workgroups or domains in NetBIOS. AppleTalk can't be further expanded in a way that's parallel to that of TCP/IP networks, with domains of ever-increasing size. If you use plain DDP-based AppleTalk, those packets won't be forwarded over normal TCP/IP routers, so DDP-based AppleTalk networks are comparatively safe from external attack, just as are pure NetBEUI networks.

To learn more about using Linux as an AppleTalk server, consult my book, *Linux: Networking for Your Office* (Sams, 2000).

Integration of TCP/IP and SMB/CIFS

The networking stack shown in Figure 1.1 is a fairly basic structure. One of the problems with this picture for cross-OS interoperability is that few operating systems support NetBEUI. Unix-like systems, in particular, have traditionally not supported this network stack. Instead, these OSs use TCP/IP networking, which is the protocol upon which the Internet is built. Because of the popularity of the Internet, Microsoft and IBM have added TCP/IP support to their OSs, and made it possible to bind SMB and NetBIOS to TCP/IP rather than to NetBEUI. The end result is a stack of network protocols that looks much like Figure 1.1, but with TCP/IP used in place of NetBEUI. This is often called *NetBIOS over TCP/IP,* or *NBT* for short.

Most Internet protocols are defined by standards documents known as *Requests for Comments (RFCs)*. NBT is defined by a pair of RFCs, 1001 and 1002, which outline methods of implementing NetBEUI-like functionality over TCP/IP networks.

One of the most important differences between NetBIOS/NetBEUI and TCP/IP is in the way computers are addressed. TCP/IP uses four-byte *IP addresses* to represent computers, as in 192.168.33.12. The host names with which users reference computers are converted to IP addresses, and the numeric addresses are used in the data packets sent over the network. NetBIOS, on the other hand, uses names more straightforwardly. In a NetBIOS/NetBEUI network, packets from or to a computer known as LARCH would use the address LARCH literally in the data packets. To run NetBIOS over TCP/IP, the NetBIOS name must be converted to an IP address before the data packet can be sent.

To bridge the gap between these two different and incompatible addressing schemes, NBT can derive an IP address from a NetBIOS name and register a NetBIOS name on a local network. There are actually two ways in which both name resolution and name registration may occur: broadcast and NBNS. On a broadcast network, a computer may broadcast a name to the entire network, either to register that name or to find out what computer uses the name. This approach is depicted in Figure 1.2. On an NBNS network, a computer can function as a *NetBIOS Name Service (NBNS)* server and handle all name-resolution functions on a network. This approach is similar to the typical TCP/IP practice of using a machine to handle *Domain Name System (DNS)* resolution requests, and is illustrated in Figure 1.3.

Figure 1.2 Broadcast name resolution or registration requires no central authority but consumes a great deal of network resources.

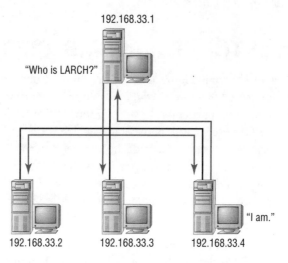

Figure 1.3 NBNS reduces the network load associated with name resolution but requires that a computer be devoted to the task.

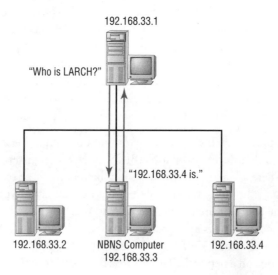

In both broadcast and NBNS networks, individual computers *register* their names. That is, rather than assign a computer a name from a central DNS server, the individual computers initiate the process and attempt to use a locally configured name. In a broadcast network, a computer can use the name if no other system responds that the name is already in use. In an NBNS-based network, the NBNS server approves or disapproves use of a specific name. These matters are explained in more detail in Chapter 9, "Samba as an NBNS Server."

> **NOTE** Even with TCP/IP, you configure a name locally on a computer, and the computer may use that name when it identifies itself to other computers in particular protocols. If this locally defined name doesn't match the name on the network's DNS servers, problems may occur. For instance, you might tell a computer that it's `larch.threeroomco.com`, but `threeroomco.com`'s DNS server might point to another machine as `larch` or might have no entry for that name. In this situation, when another computer tries to make a new connection to `larch`, that connection will fail. This problem won't, however, affect data returned to the computer that calls itself `larch` when `larch` initiates the connection.

Microsoft implements NBNS functionality in a service it calls the *Windows Internet Name Service (WINS)*. Samba, too, can be configured to function as an NBNS server, as explained in Chapter 9.

> **NOTE** Windows 2000 shifts the emphasis of name resolution away from NBNS or broadcasts. By default, Windows 2000 tries to use the computer's Internet hostname in name resolution. For instance, if you try to contact LARCH for SMB/ CIFS networking, Windows 2000 uses its assigned DNS server to try to find the IP address for LARCH. If this attempt fails, Windows 2000 falls back on broadcasts or an NBNS server, if it knows of one. Samba can be configured to operate in a similar way. Chapter 9 goes into more detail on this topic.

CIFS, the very latest version of SMB, is basically a formalization of the expansions to SMB that Microsoft has implemented during the nineties. In the middle of the decade, when much of the initial coding of Samba was done, the SMB protocols were not well documented. CIFS changes this state of affairs and turns SMB into a more official TCP/ IP-based protocol than previously. CIFS has been submitted as an RFC but (as of mid-2000) has not yet been finalized.

SMB/CIFS Terminology

It's important that you understand particular terms when reading about or discussing Samba and SMB/CIFS technology. Some of these terms will likely be familiar if you've worked much with other networking protocols. Others are unique to SMB/CIFS.

Clients, Servers, and Shares

You probably already know the terms *client* and *server* as used in other networking environments. Fortunately, these terms have the same meanings with respect to SMB/CIFS and Samba as they do elsewhere. In case you need a reminder, though, here's a summary:

- A *server* is a program that responds to network requests. Servers can either dish out existing data or receive data from a remote source, but as a general rule it's the remote source that initiates the transfer. Most of the functionality provided by Samba is on the server side, although the Samba package does include some client programs.

- A *client* stands at the other end of the data transfer from the server. The client initiates the data transfer, often under direct supervision of a human. For instance, in the case of Samba, a human typically uses an application program to load or save a file, print a document, or perform some other action. The SMB/CIFS client then takes that request and passes it on to the Samba server.

Client and server are defined with respect to individual transfers. In the broad scheme of things, two interacting computers can trade these roles, or even occupy both simultaneously. For instance, suppose a small network contains two computers, each of which has a printer that's shared via SMB/CIFS. If the user of one computer (let's call it LARCH again) wants to print to the inkjet printer attached to the other computer (MAPLE), then LARCH functions as the client and MAPLE is the server. If, at the same time, the user of MAPLE wants to print to the laser printer attached to LARCH, then the relationship is reversed. In that case, both computers function as both client and server, simultaneously.

Many small networks are configured in essentially this way—every computer can run both client and server versions of the same protocols. Such a network is known as a *peer-to-peer* network, because each computer is the equal of every other. Other networks are set up in a *client-server* configuration, in which some computers run predominantly client programs and others run mostly as servers.

The servers in a client-server network work as central clearinghouses for data storage, printing, and other functions. This design is superior for large networks because the centralized nature of the design makes administration easier. For instance, suppose a user leaves the company. In a client-server network, you need only remove passwords and accounts on the server computers, which are typically small in number. In a peer-to-peer network, you might need to remove passwords or accounts from every computer on the network.

The other side of client-server networking is that its centralized nature requires you to be extra careful about data integrity on the servers. If a server computer crashes, the problem is much more severe than if a single computer on a peer-to-peer network crashes. For this reason, the reliability of the OS used by server computers on client-server networks is of paramount importance. Fortunately, Linux has developed an excellent reputation for reliability, one of the factors that make it a good choice as a Samba server computer.

When you configure Samba to share resources, you don't give clients complete access to everything on the computer. Instead, you give access to specific directories or print queues. These resources are then called *shares*. (In Unix-style NFS networking, the term *export* is often used in much the same way.) For instance, you might provide access to the directories /home/samba/winprogs and /home/samba/shared-data, each of which is a separate share. The client computers can then access each directory separately. Furthermore, Samba gives you a great deal of flexibility to configure who can access each share. Perhaps everybody needs access to the /home/samba/winprogs directory, but you want only a selection of users or computers to have access to the /home/samba/shared-data directory. Those who have access to the latter share might be separated into two groups: those who can write to the share and those who can't. You can control all of this through the Samba configuration file or through Linux's built-in file permissions.

Workgroups and Domains

Windows networking has traditionally been built around the concept of a *workgroup*. A workgroup is a set of computers linked together to facilitate networking tasks. For instance, you might have a workgroup for your department. Every workgroup has a name, and when you open the Network Neighborhood window, Windows automatically shows the workgroup to which your computer belongs. (In Windows 2000, there is no Network Neighborhood icon; rather, there's a Computers Near Me icon accessible from the My Network Places window.) It's therefore easy to browse shares on one's own local network. You can still browse to other workgroups, but it takes a few more mouse clicks to do this; you have to open the Entire Network icon inside Network Neighborhood or My Network Places.

> **NOTE** Just how widely you can browse depends on a number of factors, such as the arrangement of subnets and routers on your local network, the presence (or absence) of master browser machines, and so on. Some of these factors are described briefly later in this chapter, and then in more detail later in the book—particularly Chapters 9, 10, and 11. Even if you can't use the Windows Network Neighborhood icon to browse a computer, you may be able to access its shares by using its Internet address. For this reason, a Samba server should be secured against unauthorized outside access, as described in Chapter 14.

Workgroups are fairly primitive networking structures. Essentially, they are merely groups of computers that announce themselves as having the same workgroup name. For instance, you might have a SALES workgroup on your network, consisting of computers in the sales department. If a couple of these computers are misconfigured with the workgroup name SALS, then you suddenly have a new workgroup called SALS on your network. No special infrastructure or central configuration is required to maintain a workgroup.

A *domain,* by contrast, is a workgroup with at least minimal centralized configuration. Specifically, a domain contains one or more *domain controllers.* The domain controller can be used to control user access to resources on the domain. (You can configure Samba to function as the domain controller.) Figure 1.4 illustrates the role of the domain controller in a NetBIOS domain. Every server hands over the right to perform its own authentication to the domain controller. This approach is quite convenient because it allows for centralized authentication of user accounts and passwords. Otherwise, domains and workgroups are much the same.

Figure 1.4 The domain controller provides user authentication, but individual servers can still block access to specific shares.

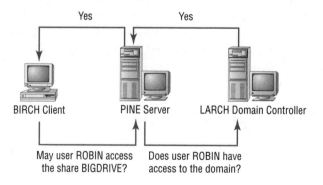

One point of potential confusion is the fact that the same word—*domain*—is used to describe both the Windows networking construct and an Internet construct. Although an Internet domain need not include centralized authentication, as a Windows NT domain does, similarities do exist between the two. An Internet domain is, like a Windows networking domain, a collection of computers. An Internet domain is a hierarchical naming system designed to provide unique names to a global network. The Internet domain name must be registered with central authorities, and it ends in an abbreviation such as .com or .net that denotes the domain's central authority. For instance, upenn.edu is the domain associated with the University of Pennsylvania.

> **NOTE** If you run a TCP/IP network that's not connected to the Internet at large, you may want to create a fictitious domain name to facilitate internal networking tasks. This name should end in a code that's not valid on the Internet as a whole, such as .invalid rather than .com or .net.

Because it is hierarchical, an Internet domain can be broken into *subdomains.* At the University of Pennsylvania, for example, psych.upenn.edu and cis.upenn.edu are the psychology and computer departments, respectively. A Windows networking domain cannot be broken into smaller sections or combined into a larger unit.

Both Windows and Internet domains can span more than one physical subnet—that is, routers or bridges can sit between various groups of computers on one network. The number of computers on a single Windows networking domain (or workgroup) is severely limited—to 255. An Internet domain, of course, can have potentially millions of computers.

As a general rule, a domain in this book means a Windows networking domain, not an Internet domain. An Internet domain is called specifically by that term. If you need to learn more about Internet domains, see *Linux DNS Server Administration,* Craig Hunt (Sybex, 2000).

How Things Work

TIP To avoid confusion, you may want to construct your network in such a way that your Windows domains correspond to your Internet domains or sub-domains. For instance, suppose you work at the Three Room Company, which has registered the Internet domain name threeroomco.com. You want to config-ure networking and set up subdomains to modularize your network configura-tion. You therefore set up three subdomains: room1.threeroomco.com, room2 .threeroomco.com, and room3.threeroomco.com. You can reuse these names and configure the machines in the same way for Windows networking, creating Windows workgroups or domains of ROOM1, ROOM2, and ROOM3. An individual computer could then have the Internet address of maple.room2.threeroomco .com and be MAPLE in the ROOM2 Windows networking domain.

Network Browsing

The term *browse* has appeared here and there in this chapter so far, and now it's time to define it. Most people think of NetBIOS browsing in terms of actions taken on a Win-dows client computer. Specifically, on Windows 9*x* or NT 4.0, you can double-click on Network Neighborhood to see a list of computers in one's workgroup, as shown in Figure 1.5. In Windows 2000, equivalent functionality comes from the Computers Near Me icon in the My Network Places folder. You can then double-click one of these com-puters to see its shares, or double-click the Entire Network icon (in My Network Places in Windows 2000) to see all the workgroups and domains to which your com-puter has immediate access.

Figure 1.5   Windows's Network Neighborhood lets you browse a network's resources much as you browse a hard disk's directories.

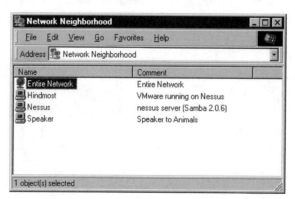

Network browsing works similarly to browsing a hard disk's directories, but there are some important differences:

- Any given computer may or may not give you access to its shares. In fact, depending on various configuration options, you might be able to use some shares but not others. You might even be unable to *see* some shares.

- You can browse to network printers. To use a printer, though, you must install a driver on the client computer.

- Computers can appear and disappear from the network as they're turned on and off, or as network problems come and go.

WARNING   Don't confuse browsing in Network Neighborhood with browsing the Web using a browser such as Netscape Navigator. Although there are similarities, the capabilities of these two types of browsing are quite different. For instance, file transfers are comparatively awkward and crude in Web browsing. On the other hand, you can access a much wider array of computers when you browse the Web using Netscape, assuming your computer has full Internet access. Recent versions of Windows blur the line between the two types of browsing, but the underlying network protocols and capabilities remain quite distinct.

The Structure of an SMB/CIFS Network

Now that you've covered some of the basic terms and technology underlying Windows networking, and some of the structures used in these networks, it's time to go a little deeper and get into some of the pesky but necessary details of Windows networking. This section covers NetBIOS computer and network naming, name-related network services, and domain control.

Naming of NetBIOS Computers and Networks

Just like Internet host and domain names, NetBIOS names have certain restrictions:

- NetBIOS names can contain upper- and lowercase letters, numbers, and the following symbols:

    ! @ # $ % ^ & ( ) - ' { } . ~

- NetBIOS names cannot exceed 15 characters in length.

As a general rule, it's best to avoid symbols in NetBIOS names because they can be confusing to users—especially the period (.), which has special meaning in Internet host names. Furthermore, it's generally a good idea to use the same name as both the computer's Internet hostname (without the domain name) and the machine's NetBIOS name. This practice can save a great deal of confusion as you attempt to maintain your network. Because only the hyphen (-) is a valid symbol in Internet names, using the same name for both environments takes all the other symbols out of the running as name components. The same rules apply to workgroup and domain names as apply to NetBIOS machine names.

As with Internet names, NetBIOS names are case-insensitive; LARCH, Larch, and larch all refer to the same computer. Many utilities display NetBIOS names in uppercase letters, although Windows's Network Neighborhood displays only the first letter in uppercase (see Figure 1.5). Internet names are generally expressed in lowercase, and that convention is used in this book, as well. (Because some companies promote their Web site names in mixed case, their URLs are reproduced here that way, too.)

A Named Hierarchy in a Flat Space

A complete Internet machine name (often called a *fully qualified domain name,* or *FQDN*) consists of several names separated by periods, as in larch.room2.threeroomco.com. The rightmost component (.com in this example) specifies the name of the *top-level domain.* Each top-level domain can have many associated domains. Each of these domains can be (but is not required to be) broken up into *subdomains.* The subdomains can be further divided, and so on, until you reach actual machine names. This logical hierarchy allows for a huge number of machines that bear the same names but are in different domains or subdomains. For instance, larch.room2.threeroomco.com need not be the only larch in threeroomco.com; there can be a larch.room1.threeroomco.com and even a larch.threeroomco.com. Of course, there may also be machines called larch in entirely unrelated domains, or larch could be a domain name or subdomain name. This hierarchical structure is part of the reason for the success of TCP/IP, because it's highly extensible. It also allows each domain to administer its own internal structure.

NetBIOS, on the other hand, uses a *flat namespace,* meaning that every machine on a network has one name, and there is no higher-level name construct such as a domain name. If you've read the earlier section on workgroups and domains, you may find this statement surprising, because Windows workgroups and domains were defined as groupings of computers, much like Internet domains. The structure of workgroups or domains is an illusion, however, as illustrated by Figure 1.6. Each computer simply knows to which workgroup or domain it belongs, and a network browser such as Network Neighborhood can use that information to provide the *appearance* of a hierarchical organization, albeit one with only two levels.

Figure 1.6   A truly hierarchical organization like that provided by the Internet (left) is much more flexible than the flat namespace provided by NetBIOS (right).

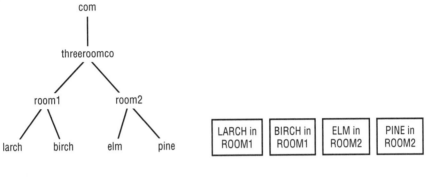

WARNING   You cannot give the same NetBIOS name to two machines on the same subnet but in different Windows workgroups or domains. If you do, you're likely to see only one of the two machines on the network, or you may see a bizarre admixture of the two, such as the comment field for one machine and the shares from the other. If you have an existing TCP/IP network with duplicated machine names in different subdomains, you may need to change one of the duplicated names, at least in NetBIOS.

NetBIOS is largely a local networking protocol, intended for use on small networks. This is particularly true of the NetBIOS naming rules and restrictions. Specifically, you're restricted from using duplicate names in two situations:

On a single subnet   When your network uses broadcast name resolution, the broadcasts can reach every computer on a single physical network segment, but no farther. If you use routers or similar network-joining devices between network segments, you can duplicate names on the various network segments. Such an arrangement usually works best when each network segment hosts a different NetBIOS workgroup or domain.

On networks served by a single NBNS server   Even widely separated networks can share a common NetBIOS workgroup or domain, and hence may encounter name conflicts, if you use an NBNS server for the domain or workgroup. If you maintain two separate workgroups or domains, however, each of which has its own

NBNS server, you can duplicate names for individual machines between domains or workgroups, but not within these structures.

As an example, consider the fictitious threeroomco.com. Suppose each of its three rooms contains a subnet, and the subnets are linked together through a router. In this situation, if the NetBIOS computers are configured to use broadcast addressing, then the same Net-BIOS name can appear on computers in each of the three rooms. Each room effectively hosts its own workgroup or domain, even if you use the same workgroup name or domain name. If one computer is set aside as an NBNS server, however, and if all the computers are configured to use that NBNS server, then each computer must have a unique name.

Factors other than naming play a role, as well, in this arrangement. Specifically, browsing and domain controllers often require special configuration to function in a routed network environment.

It is the fact that NetBIOS naming protocols require special configuration to be routed that prevents NetBIOS-created chaos from spreading through the Internet as a whole. The fictitious threeroomco.com can have a computer called LARCH, and this computer's name doesn't conflict with a computer of the same name at the fictitious pangaea.edu—because these two Internet domains are physically separate and haven't taken steps to join their NetBIOS networks together.

Resource Types

Earlier, in the section "Naming of NetBIOS Computers and Networks," I said that Net-BIOS names are 15 characters (that is, bytes) long. This isn't quite entirely correct. In fact, NetBIOS uses 16-byte names—but the 16th byte is used as a resource type code. (If necessary, the computer pads a shorter name to 15 characters by using spaces.) The computer can then use the same (15-character) name several times, once with each resource code that's associated with each resource the computer wants to register. In effect, the network sees the computer as several computers simultaneously, with names that are identical except for their type codes.

Table 1.2 explains the resource types for individual computers. Some of these values aren't used under Samba, as indicated in the table. The most important services are 00 (which is used by all NetBIOS-equipped computers) and 20 (which indicates that the computer offers one or more file *or* printer shares).

Table 1.2   NetBIOS Resource Types

Resource	Value (in Hexadecimal)	Function
Standard Workstation Service	00	Main computer name.
Messenger (WinPopup) Service	03	Person-to-person text transmission service, similar to `talk`. Described in Chapter 7.
RAS Server Service	06	A server that allows remote access to Windows via a modem. Not supported by Samba.
Domain Master Browser Service	1B	A computer that collects other computers' names for use by a client browser. Described in Chapter 11.
Master Browser Name	1D	Like a domain master browser, but limited in range to a single subnet. Described in Chapter 11.
NetDDE Service	1F	Network Dynamic Data Exchange. Used to share data across networked applications. Not supported by Samba.
File or Print Service	20	File or printer sharing. Described in Chapters 5 and 6.
RAS Client Service	21	A remote access client, not to be confused with resource type 06, the RAS server. Not supported by Samba.
Network Monitor Agent	BE	A tool and protocol for monitoring network performance. Not supported by Samba.
Network Monitor Utility	BF	Similar to Network Monitor Agent. Not supported by Samba.

How Things Work

PART 1

In addition to the resource codes associated with individual computers, codes are associated with workgroups or domains. Because computers register themselves with workgroups or domains, in practice these codes come from individual computers; the codes simply announce the group-related resources offered by the computer. See Table 1.3.

Table 1.3 NetBIOS Group Resource Types

Resource	Value (in Hexadecimal)	Function
Standard Workstation Group	00	Domain or workgroup name; used once by each client.
Logon (WINS/NBNS) Server	1C	Server that authenticates user for a domain. Described in Chapter 10.
Normal Group Name	1E	Group name used during browser elections. Browser elections are described in Chapter 11.
Group Name	20	Occasionally used as a duplicate of the workstation group value.

Like the resources for individual machines, not all the group resource types are used by all computers. Most computers will use the 00 (Standard Workstation Group) and 1E (Normal Group Name) entries. If a computer serves as a browse master, as described shortly, the 1C entry will be used.

A computer may also register a resource with the name of a user. This usually happens in conjunction with a code of 03, and is used for Messenger (WinPopup) services. When a computer allows Messenger service, it accepts messages that it immediately shows to the specified user.

> **NOTE** There is overlap in the codes used for machine, group, and user NetBIOS resources. For instance, a computer may register itself twice with the code 00—once to register its presence as an individual computer and again to register its presence in a domain or workgroup.

You can check on these codes in Windows or in Linux by using one of two commands, depending upon the OS. You might do this as a troubleshooting measure. For example, if you've configured a system to take on NBNS server functions but it's not working, you could check it and other systems in this way. Here are the commands you can use for this inquiry:

For Linux:

    nmblookup -SR *name*

For Windows:

    NBTSTAT -a *NAME*

The output of both commands is similar but not identical. In both cases, *name* is the NetBIOS name of the target computer. For instance, here's how to check the status of SPEAKER, from Linux:

```
$ nmblookup -SR speaker
querying speaker on 192.168.1.255
192.168.1.1 speaker<00>
Looking up status of 192.168.1.1
received 9 names
            SPEAKER          <00> -           M <ACTIVE>
            SPEAKER          <03> -           M <ACTIVE>
            SPEAKER          <20> -           M <ACTIVE>
            .._MSBROWSE__. <01> - <GROUP> M <ACTIVE>
            RINGWORLD        <00> - <GROUP> M <ACTIVE>
            RINGWORLD        <1b> -           M <ACTIVE>
            RINGWORLD        <1c> - <GROUP> M <ACTIVE>
            RINGWORLD        <1d> -           M <ACTIVE>
            RINGWORLD        <1e> - <GROUP> M <ACTIVE>
num_good_sends=0 num_good_receives=0
```

This output shows that the computer called SPEAKER has registered the name SPEAKER three times, using the codes 00, 03, and 20; it's registered .._MSBROWSE__. once, and RINGWORLD five times with codes 00, 1B, 1C, 1D, and 1E. The instances of SPEAKER register the computer itself, and tell the network that it can accept Messenger messages and offers file or print shares. (The name .._MSBROWSE__. is a special name that announces a master browser, described shortly, to a workgroup or domain. The periods in this name are actually nonprinting characters that NBTSTAT and nmblookup display as periods for convenience.) RINGWORLD is the name of the domain to which SPEAKER belongs. The five RINGWORLD codes register the machine as part of the domain (00 and 1E) and advertise it as offering browse services, including both subnet and domain master browser services (1B through 1D).

The Role of PDCs

A *primary domain controller (PDC)* is a computer that's able to handle authentication requests for a domain, as described earlier and shown in Figure 1.4. This term is sometimes restricted to login support for Windows NT networks rather than Windows *9x* networks. A *backup domain controller (BDC)* serves a similar function but exists, as its name implies, as a backup to the PDC. If the network operates flawlessly, the BDC is never called upon to serve this function.

NOTE Windows *9x* and Windows NT use different authentication technologies. Samba supported Windows *9x* authentication well before it supported Windows NT authentication. As of version 2.0.5a, Samba supports basic PDC functions for both Windows *9x* and NT. For more complete PDC support, you may need to use more recent versions of Samba. PDC configuration is discussed in Chapter 10. Samba's BDC support does not exist in version 2.0.7, but it is being added to development versions of Samba. If this support is important to you, you should either use Windows NT computers as both PDC and BDC systems, or look into the latest (possibly experimental) version of Samba.

The presence of a PDC is the key feature that distinguishes a domain from a workgroup, as described earlier in this chapter. As a general rule, domains are easier to administer than are workgroups. This is because domains use centralized password databases, so on domains it's easier to add and remove users, or change users' passwords, than on workgroups—particularly if users routinely use more than one computer. If configured properly, domains can also be more secure, because it's more practical to remove potentially insecure Windows *9x* password files from client computers. I therefore recommend configuring Samba or a Windows NT or 2000 computer as a PDC in most cases.

Samba's PDC support is rudimentary. It supports centralized logons, but Microsoft has implemented remote configuration tools that are poorly, if at all, supported by Samba. This is a focus of current Samba development efforts, however, so Samba is likely to improve in this area in the near future.

The Role of NBNS Servers

If present, the NetBIOS Name Service (NBNS, also known as WINS) server functions much like a DNS server; it fields requests from client machines for the IP address of a specified computer. NBT actually supports four methods of address resolution. These methods, described below, are called *node types,* in reference to the behavior of a computer (a *node*) that needs to locate another computer.

b-node The computer sends a broadcast to all the computers on a subnet to locate the target machine. This approach is roughly equivalent to walking up to an office building and using a megaphone to ask for somebody from a specific office to identify that office for you.

p-node The computer sends a request to the network's NBNS server to ask for the address of a given computer. This is akin to using a directory listing in an office building to locate an office.

m-node The computer sends a broadcast and, if that approach is unsuccessful, the computer sends a request to the NBNS machine.

h-node The computer sends a request to the NBNS computer. If the NBNS server doesn't know the name of the target computer, the requester sends a broadcast. Computers that use this approach are also known as *hybrid* nodes.

Most Windows clients are configured as h-nodes. Because broadcasts require every computer to do some work, they tend to be expensive in terms of network resources. Most computers don't actually respond to broadcasts, but they do *receive* them. Using an NBNS computer, by contrast, reduces the need for system resources because the name discovery process uses point-to-point communication. Particularly if your network uses switches rather than hubs, such point-to-point communication helps to conserve network bandwidth. Broadcasts also don't pass through routers, so you can't use broadcast name resolution if your network consists of several subnets. (There are workarounds possible with Samba, but it's usually easier to use NBNS.)

As with domain controllers, there can be both a primary and a backup NBNS machine for a domain or workgroup. Although Samba can be configured as a primary NBNS, it cannot currently function as a backup NBNS. (Both domains and workgroups can host NBNS computers.)

NetBIOS Browsing

Browsing may seem quite simple from a user's point of view when everything works as expected, but it can actually be quite complex from a network point of view. In order for browsing to function properly, one computer must serve as the *master browser.* This computer is responsible for maintaining a list of the other computers on the network, known as the *browse list.* The browse list contains only machines that are available, not each machine's shares. For instance, suppose a user wants to browse to the JENNIE share on the computer TURRILL. The client computer consults the master browser to obtain a list of computers, including TURRILL. When the user clicks on TURRILL, the client system consults TURRILL directly for a list of available shares, which presumably includes JENNIE. This approach minimizes network traffic and reduces the load on the master browser.

In fact, there are different types of master browsers available—specifically, *domain* and *local* master browsers. The local master browser handles browse requests on a specific subnet. A domain master browser handles browse requests for an entire domain, even if that domain includes multiple subnets. When a domain spans multiple subnets, each local master browser must be told about the other subnets in order to synchronize browse lists across subnets. These issues are discussed in greater detail in Chapter 11, "Local and Routed Browsing."

You don't normally specify a master browser explicitly. Rather, the computers in a network follow certain rules to determine which one is to serve as the master browser. This procedure is known as an *election;* elections take into consideration factors such as the OS on each machine, the amount of time each computer has been running, and (as a last resort) the name of each machine. You can rig a Linux computer to win (or lose) a master browser election, as described in Chapter 11. Linux can function as a local or domain master browser, but not as a backup browser (the computer that takes over browsing functions if the master browser goes down).

When a computer comes online, it's supposed to announce its presence to its local master browser. Similarly, when a computer shuts down normally, it's supposed to announce its unavailability to the local master browser. Of course, if a computer crashes, the latter notification won't happen, but the local master browser will eventually figure this out and remove the computer from its browse list.

Because of the way browsing occurs, it's possible for a Windows browse list to show inaccurate information, both on the master browser and on individual clients. When a master browser updates its list, it doesn't automatically notify all the clients of that change. Therefore, you may need to select View ➢ Refresh in an open Windows network browser to obtain the latest information from the master browser. When the master browser itself contains outdated information, this action may not be adequate. Even if a computer doesn't appear in a browse list, you can access the computer by typing its name directly into a window's Address field. For instance, if the computer TURRILL doesn't appear in a browse list, you can still access the JENNIE share on that computer by typing **\\TURRILL\JENNIE** in the Address field.

Samba's Capabilities

Samba can fill most of the major roles available in a Windows network, including the most critical ones of file server and print server (see Table 1.4 for a summary of Samba's capabilities). The chapters of Part 2, "Essential Configuration," cover the configuring of Samba for these two roles. Part 3, "Advanced Configurations," is devoted to the remaining roles and a few miscellaneous additional topics. If your goal is to integrate a Samba server into an existing Windows network, Part 2 probably covers most of the material you need.

Table 1.4   Samba's Windows Networking Capabilities

Network Role	Samba's Capability
File server	Yes
Print server	Yes
Local master browser	Yes
Domain master browser	Yes
Backup local browser	No
Windows 9x Primary Domain Controller (PDC)	Yes
Windows NT Primary Domain Controller (PDC)	Yes (version 2.0.5a or later required; limited capability)
Backup Domain Controller (BDC)	No
Primary NBNS/WINS server	Yes
Secondary NBNS/WINS server	No

WARNING   A Samba server can sometimes usurp the role of master browser on a functioning network. If this happens, with any luck the network will continue functioning normally. If you experience browsing problems on any computers after adding a Samba server, though, you can add the lines os level = 1, preferred master = No and domain master = No to the [global] section of your smb.conf configuration file. These options should ensure that Samba will never take on the role of master browser. For details, see Chapter 11.

Summary

The basic structures and protocols for Windows networking resemble, but are different from, those used by traditional Unix and Linux networking tools. Although it's possible to set up a simple Samba server without understanding the details of Windows networking protocols, it's imperative that you understand these details when your network is complex, or when you want the Samba server to take over critical but transparent services such as NBNS/WINS server functions.

The structures and components of a Windows network parallel those of other network types, such as TCP/IP, Novell, or AppleTalk. All networks require some means of name resolution, organization, and so on. Although the names and configuration details differ, your experience in configuring TCP/IP equivalents to NetBIOS structures can be useful in grasping the basics of what a protocol does. Be careful not to draw the parallels too closely, however, because there *are* critical differences. Those differences are discussed in subsequent chapters of this book.

2

Integrating SMB/CIFS into Linux

Linux, modeled after Unix, was not designed as a Windows network server. Although certain aspects of Unix and Windows are similar, the two differ in many details. Samba must therefore overcome these differences in order to serve files to a Windows network effectively. Considered strictly as a Linux package, Samba must integrate itself into the usual structure of Linux servers. This task is less daunting than the task of masquerading a Linux filesystem as a Windows filesystem, but it's still helpful to know something about Samba's internal structure as you configure the system. In mid-2000, Samba is undergoing changes; the 2.0.*x* versions of Samba follow one structure, but the latest development versions follow another. Both are covered in this chapter.

This chapter explains the basic principles for getting Samba to work with Linux. These include the integration of SMB/CIFS with TCP/IP networking, and an overview of the Samba daemons and the tasks they perform. In addition, we'll look at the differing assumptions about filenames and attributes made by Linux and Windows, and how Samba strives to bridge those differences.

SMB/CIFS over TCP/IP

As mentioned in Chapter 1, the typical method for using Samba in Linux is to use Samba at the top level of a TCP/IP network stack. In the past, Windows relied upon a competing network stack, NetBEUI, for linking Windows computers. Today, however, TCP/IP is a common—but not universal—network stack for using SMB/CIFS even on the Windows platform. This section describes the advantages and disadvantages of TCP/IP as a transport mechanism for SMB/CIFS, and the basics of integrating the two together.

TCP/IP vs. NetBEUI as a Transport Protocol

TCP/IP and NetBEUI both perform fundamentally the same tasks. Specifically, both are examples of *network stacks*. Generically, network stacks can be described by the *Open Systems Interconnection (OSI) reference model,* which is illustrated in Figure 2.1. The OSI model is a theoretical framework for any network stack—TCP/IP, NetBEUI, Apple-Talk, or anything else. In practice, the OSI model is often simplified in one way or another. For instance, TCP/IP is often described with only four layers, some of which are conglomerations of more than one OSI layer.

In Figure 2.1 you can see where Samba rests in this model. Although TCP/IP is shown occupying a subset of the OSI model, in fact TCP/IP can be thought of as occupying the entire model; it's just that, when used with TCP/IP, Samba and the hardware drivers become *part of* TCP/IP.

Figure 2.1 Data passes down the layers of the sending computer's network stack and then up the layers of the target computer's network stack.

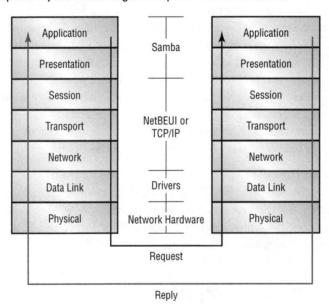

There are certain key differences between TCP/IP and NetBEUI:

Addressing TCP/IP uses four-byte *IP addresses* to identify computers. These numbers are typically expressed in *dotted-quad notation* as four decimal numbers separated by periods, as in 192.168.43.9. To link names to numbers, TCP/IP relies upon the *Domain Name System (DNS)*. NetBEUI, on the other hand, uses machine names directly for addressing. This approach is simpler in some ways because there's no need to convert between a name and a number, but reliance on a single name makes the system less expandable. NetBEUI networks are limited to just 255 computers, compared with about 4 billion allowed by the four-byte IP addresses of TCP/IP.

Routing Most any network protocol can be *routed*—that is, its packets can be transferred from one network to another. TCP/IP, however, was built with routing in mind, and in fact this capability is part of what makes the Internet possible. NetBEUI's addressing limitations mean that it's not as easy to route NetBEUI data. More precisely, the packets can be routed, but extra effort is required to do so. The 255-computer limit restricts the size of the network even for routing NetBEUI data. In practice, therefore, NetBEUI packets are seldom routed, and the protocol is often considered nonroutable.

High-Level Protocols In theory, you can build any number of tools atop either NetBEUI or TCP/IP. In practice, though, TCP/IP supports many more tools than does NetBEUI. Programs such as Web browsers, FTP programs, Telnet, and others run on TCP/IP but not on NetBEUI. For this reason, most networked computers support TCP/IP. The principal high-level NetBEUI protocol is SMB/CIFS, and this protocol runs on TCP/IP as well as on NetBEUI.

The addressing and routing characteristics of NetBEUI are usually considered limitations. In some cases, though, these "limitations" are beneficial. If you bind SMB/CIFS services *only* to NetBEUI, your computers cannot be attacked from the Internet by way of those services. By contrast, if you use SMB/CIFS via TCP/IP, a cracker from across the globe might be able to gain entry to your system via a bug in the SMB/CIFS implementation or through a weak password. This is the primary reason to at least consider the possibility of using NetBEUI for your Samba services.

NOTE The news media frequently use the term *hacker* to refer to computer criminals of various types. This term, however, has an older and more honorable meaning: A hacker is an individual who writes computer programs for the joy of creation. Many of the individuals who wrote Linux and Samba consider themselves to be hackers in this more traditional sense. I therefore use the alternative term *cracker* to refer to computer criminals.

Keep in mind that using NetBEUI for SMB/CIFS connectivity can't protect non-Samba services such as a Web server, Telnet login server, and so on. There are ways to secure your network without using NetBEUI, including

- Using a firewall to block unwanted access by outsiders to your SMB/CIFS servers
- Configuring your systems with good passwords, and changing those passwords frequently
- Using Samba's hosts allow, hosts deny, and other by-machine security features
- Not connecting a local network to the Internet at large

With the exception of the final option, none of these methods can guarantee that you won't be cracked through SMB/CIFS. Even the last option won't guarantee against theft of the computers or an "inside job" by a disgruntled employee.

For more information on Samba security, see Chapter 14, "Samba Security Considerations." I *strongly* recommend that you set up a firewall and take other measures to secure your network, and especially your Linux server. Two excellent network security resources are *Maximum Security,* 2nd Edition (Sams, 1998) and *Practical Unix and Internet Security,* 2nd Edition (O'Reilly, 1996).

Binding SMB/CIFS to TCP/IP in Windows

The default installation of Samba binds to TCP/IP in Linux. Because this is a common configuration in Windows, it's simplest to use TCP/IP for SMB/CIFS networking. If you have strong reasons to use NetBEUI, you can do so with the help of a third-party add-on from Procom Technology (http://www.procom.com). Procom's NetBEUI stack for Linux forces you to recompile both the Linux kernel and the Samba package, making installation of NetBEUI support tedious as compared with using the standard TCP/IP-based Samba.

To use the standard server setup with TCP/IP, you need to make sure that the clients are properly configured. SMB/CIFS may or may not be bound to TCP/IP on your Windows computers. This section tells you how to ensure that a Windows computer uses TCP/IP rather than NetBEUI. Incorrect binding of services can result in slow network performance (particularly when opening a share or starting to browse), or in extreme cases, complete inability to use the network services. It's therefore important that your Windows clients bind SMB/CIFS to TCP/IP correctly.

Windows 9*x*

Windows 9*x* automatically binds SMB/CIFS networking to TCP/IP, but this configuration can become undone. Also, if NetBEUI is installed, Windows may attempt to use it instead of TCP/IP, leading to poor performance or even inability to reach Samba servers on your network. Therefore, I recommend removing NetBEUI when you use NetBIOS over TCP/IP. Because NetBEUI isn't normally used by any other protocol, removing it won't create any problems if your entire network uses TCP/IP rather than NetBEUI.

> **WARNING**   If you use NetBEUI for SMB/CIFS networking, ensure that NetBEUI is installed, but *do not* remove TCP/IP. Doing so disables other networking protocols, including Web browsing and FTP.

To remove NetBEUI, open the Windows Control Panel and double-click the Network icon. You'll see a dialog box similar to the one in Figure 2.2. If you see a NetBEUI item, select it and click Remove. Windows immediately removes the protocol. When you click OK, Windows may prompt you to restart the computer.

Figure 2.2   Network protocols are listed in the Windows Network dialog box.

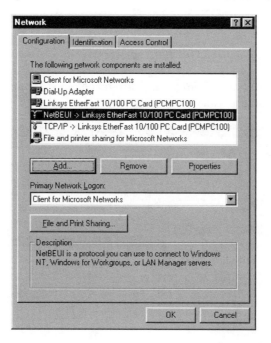

> *NOTE* Figure 2.2 shows that NetBEUI is linked to a Linksys EtherFast 10/100 PC-Card network card, which also appears in the list just above NetBEUI's entry. On your computer, you should see a linkage to whatever network card you have. If the network card's drivers aren't installed, install them. Consult the network card's documentation or a book on Windows for details.

If your Network dialog box (Figure 2.2) shows that the Novell IPX ODI Protocol or IPX/SPX-Compatible Protocol is installed, you can remove either protocol for the same reasons and in the same manner that you remove NetBEUI. Of course, all of these protocols—IPX ODI, IPX/SPX, and NetBEUI—should only be removed if they are not being used.

If your Network dialog box doesn't show a TCP/IP entry like the one below NetBEUI in Figure 2.2, add TCP/IP support to your computer by following these steps:

1. Click Add in the Network dialog box.

2. In the Select Network Component Type dialog box that appears, select Protocol and then click Add.

3. Select Microsoft and TCP/IP in the Select Network Protocol dialog box (Figure 2.3).

Figure 2.3 You can choose from among several network protocols, but only a few are in common use—including TCP/IP.

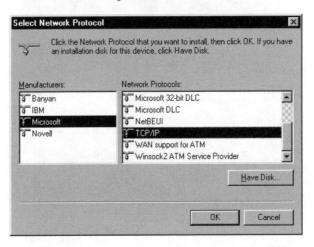

4. Click OK. Windows may ask for your installation CD. When Windows is done installing the TCP/IP software, Windows may reboot your computer.

Figure 2.2 shows that the computer hosts both the Client for Microsoft Networks and the File and Printer Sharing for Microsoft Networks protocols. These are SMB/CIFS client and server packages, respectively. If your Windows computer is to be only a client, you can remove the unnecessary package. (Client software is useful even on a server, so I recommend you leave it in place.) If you need to add a package, you can do so in much the same way that you added TCP/IP networking support. Instead of selecting Protocol in the Select Network Component Type dialog box, though, you select either Client or Service. You must then select the appropriate Microsoft packages. Once installed, these services should bind automatically to TCP/IP or NetBEUI.

To ensure that SMB/CIFS is bound to TCP/IP, follow these steps:

1. In the Network dialog box (Figure 2.2), select TCP/IP.
2. Click Properties to bring up the TCP/IP Properties dialog box.
3. Select the Bindings tab, shown in Figure 2.4. Ensure that the Client for Microsoft Networks item is checked. If your Windows computer is to function as a server, be sure that the File and Printer Sharing for Microsoft Networks item is also checked.

Figure 2.4   Bind clients and servers to TCP/IP from the TCP/IP Properties Bindings tab.

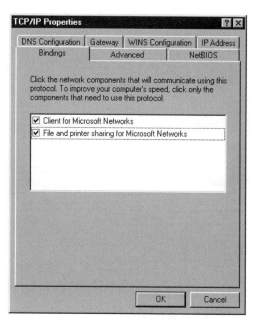

Windows NT 4

Windows NT 4 uses network configuration options similar to those of Windows 9x, but just different enough to cause confusion in some cases. As with Windows 9x, you can avoid several potential problems by removing the NetBEUI protocol, if it's installed and you don't need it. To do so, log on as the Administrator and follow these steps:

1. From Control Panel, double-click the Network icon to open the Network dialog box.

2. Click the Protocols tab to open it. It will resemble the one in Figure 2.5.

Figure 2.5   In Windows NT, you can add or remove protocols from the Protocols tab of the Network dialog box.

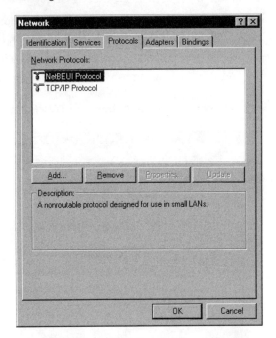

3. Select the NetBEUI Protocol item.

4. Click Remove. Windows asks for confirmation, then removes the protocol. Windows may prompt you to reboot your computer after this step.

If you need to add TCP/IP networking, you can do so from the same Network dialog box. Select the Add button rather than Remove, and pick the appropriate protocol from the list that Windows NT presents.

To ensure that the SMB/CIFS protocols are installed, click the Services tab in the Network dialog box and examine the list of available services. The service called Server provides SMB/CIFS server features; Workstation provides SMB/CIFS client functionality. You can safely omit the former if the computer will only be used as a client. If you need to add a service, click Add and select the appropriate protocol from the list. Windows may prompt you to reboot the computer after installing the new protocol.

If you install TCP/IP but not NetBEUI or IPX/SPX, Windows NT will automatically bind SMB/CIFS to TCP/IP. If you have multiple protocols installed and want to bind only one to the SMB/CIFS features, you can do so from the Bindings tab (Figure 2.6). Windows NT tries the protocols (TCP/IP or NetBEUI) in the order in which they appear for each service. You can enable, disable, or shift a protocol within the displayed order; select the protocol and click the appropriate buttons in the dialog box.

Figure 2.6   Windows NT gives fine control over the order in which the OS tries network stacks with SMB/CIFS clients and servers.

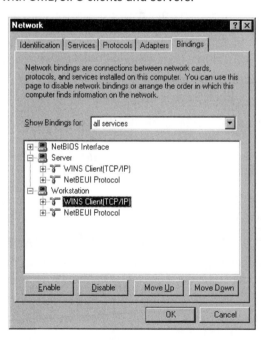

> **_TIP_** You can use Windows NT's bindings as a primitive means of access control. For instance, you might want to use TCP/IP under Workstation for accessing a Samba server, but disable TCP/IP on the Server side to reduce the risk of break-ins from the Internet, while leaving NetBEUI active on the Server to allow local NetBEUI-based access.

Windows 2000

By default, Windows 2000 uses TCP/IP for its SMB/CIFS networking. If your Windows 2000 computer has been configured for NetBEUI and you want to change this, follow these steps as the Administrator:

1. From Control Panel, open the Network and Dial-up Connections window.
2. Right-click the Local Area Connection icon and choose Properties from the pop-up menu. This produces the Local Area Connection Properties dialog box, which is similar to the Windows 98 Network dialog box shown in Figure 2.2.
3. Select NetBEUI Protocol from the list.
4. Click Uninstall. Windows 2000 asks for confirmation. Proceed with removal of the protocol.
5. Windows 2000 will probably suggest restarting the computer. Do so.

If you need to add either TCP/IP or NetBEUI support, use the Local Area Connection Properties dialog box. The procedure is similar to that described for Windows 9x or NT 4; you click the Install button, highlight Protocol, click Add, and select the protocol from the list that Windows 2000 provides.

If you have both TCP/IP and NetBEUI installed and you want to ensure that Windows 2000 uses TCP/IP for SMB/CIFS networking, follow these steps as the Administrator:

1. From Control Panel, open the Network and Dial-up Connections window.
2. Right-click the Local Area Connection icon and choose Properties from the pop-up menu. This produces the Local Area Connection Properties dialog box, which is similar to the Windows 98 Network dialog box shown in Figure 2.2.
3. Select Internet Protocol (TCP/IP), and click Properties.
4. In the Internet Protocol (TCP/IP) Properties dialog box, click the Advanced button.
5. In the Advanced TCP/IP Settings dialog box, click the WINS tab, which will resemble the one shown in Figure 2.7.
6. To use TCP/IP for SMB/CIFS networking, click the radio button for Enable NetBIOS Over TCP/IP.

Figure 2.7   The WINS tab primarily controls name resolution but also allows you to enable or disable NetBIOS over TCP/IP.

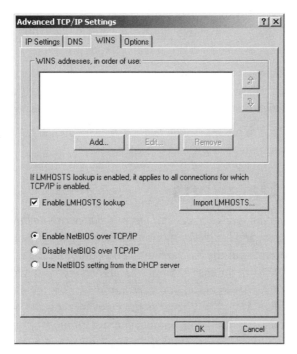

Linux Features Required for Samba

To use Samba in Linux, you must include certain features and packages. These include the following:

TCP/IP Networking   You must enable TCP/IP networking support in your Linux kernel, including support for your network card. All major Linux distributions' kernels come configured appropriately for TCP/IP networking.

SMB Filesystem Support   If you intend to mount SMB/CIFS shares on your Linux computer, the SMB filesystem support option must be enabled in your Linux kernel. In the Linux kernel configuration, this option appears in the Filesystems menu, in a Network File Systems suboption. All major Linux distributions come with this support enabled by default, but you'll need to attend to this matter if you recompile your kernel. You do *not* need to activate this support if you don't intend to mount SMB/CIFS shared directories, or if you only intend to use SMB/CIFS printer shares.

Samba All major Linux distributions ship with Samba, but the package may or may not be installed by default. If Samba isn't installed, or if you want to use a more advanced version than whatever comes with your distribution, you'll need to obtain and install the Samba software. Chapter 3, "Installing Samba," covers this matter in detail.

This book cannot cover all the details of basic Linux networking configuration. If you need more help with these tasks, consult the Linux HOWTO documents, which come with all Linux distributions, or a book on basic Linux networking, such as Craig Hunt's *Linux Network Servers 24seven* (Sybex, 1999) or my *Linux: Networking for Your Office* (Sams, 2000).

The Samba Daemons

Linux operates most network servers as *daemons*. The word *daemon* comes from a Greek word meaning *helper,* and Linux daemons help networks by providing services. Daemons typically run unattended in the background. You configure them through special configuration files (`smb.conf` in the case of Samba) and then set the daemon up to run when the computer starts. Once it's in place, you need not deal with the daemon directly. If it encounters a problem, it typically records the error in a log file, such as `/var/log/messages`. Most daemons, including Samba, can run for months on end without requiring attention, assuming the initial configuration is good.

Traditionally, Samba has used two daemons, `smbd` and `nmbd`, to handle all its server tasks. The latest development versions of Samba, however, split these daemons up into several smaller ones. Both schemes are described in this section, which offers an overview of the Samba daemons and their functions.

Instructions for starting and stopping Samba's daemons are not included here. For that information, read the section "Running Samba" in Chapter 3.

NOTE In addition to the daemons described here, the Samba package includes a daemon called the *Samba Web Administration Tool (SWAT),* which allows for remote or local Samba administration via a Web browser. SWAT is described in Chapter 4, "GUI Configuration Tools and the smb.conf File."

Samba 2.0.*x*

In mid-2000, the current stable release of Samba is 2.0.7. This version and other 2.0.*x* releases of Samba use two daemons: nmbd and smbd. Earlier versions of Samba also used this configuration. As a general rule, nmbd handles initial computer-to-computer identification, whereas smbd handles the core file-and-printer-sharing functions.

It's possible to run one daemon without running another, but if you do this, your system will lack important functionality. If one daemon crashes or doesn't start but the other works correctly, you may experience some strange connectivity problems. For instance, you might be able to see a computer in the Windows Network Neighborhood but not to log onto it; or you may be prevented from browsing the computer but can access its shares if you connect in some other way. For any such problems, check to see that both daemons are running.

The smbd program typically consumes about 1MB of RAM for each connection it maintains. This amount may go up as the connection is used. For each connection, smbd spawns a new instance of itself, so if you use ps to view your processes, it's not uncommon to see several instances of smbd running. Because of smbd's memory use, it's important that a Samba server have enough memory to service all its clients. In a large network with dozens or hundreds of clients, you may need hundreds of megabytes of RAM in a Samba server. In a small network with just a few clients, a server with 16–32MB may be adequate, although it's probably best to have at least 64MB even for a small server.

nmbd: The NetBIOS Name Browser Daemon

The nmbd program understands the NetBIOS **name** browser protocols; hence the program's name. These services are critical if a Samba server is to respond to broadcast NetBIOS name requests or if the computer is to function as an NBNS/WINS server. You can configure many details of nmbd's operation through the main Samba configuration file, smb.conf. Much of the rest of this book describes the details of this configuration.

Although nmbd is normally considered a daemon, its default operation is *not* to operate as a daemon. You have to use the -D switch to force nmbd to run as a daemon.

> **NOTE**   nmbd normally listens for connections on UDP port 137. You can override this behavior with the -p switch, but there's seldom any reason to do this because clients won't know to use the unusual port.

Following are some of the services supplied by nmbd:

Response to Name Broadcasts   As described in Chapter 1, when a Windows network does *not* include a NetBIOS Name Server (NBNS), client machines send broadcast messages to all computers on the network in order to locate a specific machine. For instance, if you configure a Windows computer to mount a share from LARCH, the Windows computer sends a broadcast to all the computers asking which one is LARCH. If nmbd is running and is configured to respond to that name, nmbd responds to this request.

By default, nmbd responds to the computer's TCP/IP hostname, but you can configure it to respond to other names. You'll need to edit the smb.conf configuration file, or pass the name with the -n parameter to nmbd.

NBNS Duty   You can configure nmbd to function as an NBNS computer and field requests to identify other computers. In this arrangement, if ELM wants to contact LARCH, ELM contacts the computer running nmbd and asks for LARCH's address. Then nmbd responds with LARCH's four-byte IP address. In addition, when configured in this way nmbd automatically compiles a mapping of NetBIOS names to IP addresses, so that the daemon can respond correctly when queried about a name.

NBNS Proxy   Sometimes you may want nmbd to function as a *proxy* for NetBIOS name broadcast queries. Suppose you have two subnets, as shown in Figure 2.8. Because they're separated by a router, NetBIOS name requests don't reach from one subnet to another. Using nmbd as an NBNS proxy, however, facilitates broadcast NetBIOS name queries by having a system on each subnet respond as a proxy for systems on the other. This arrangement is described in Chapter 9, "Samba as an NBNS Server." This feature is most likely to be useful if you have a large subnet that's already configured to use broadcast name queries, and you want to add a few machines from another subnet to a workgroup or domain on the main subnet. If the main subnet is configured to use NBNS to begin with, there's no need to set up a proxy.

Figure 2.8   An NBNS proxy lets you expand a broadcast-based network with minimal fuss.

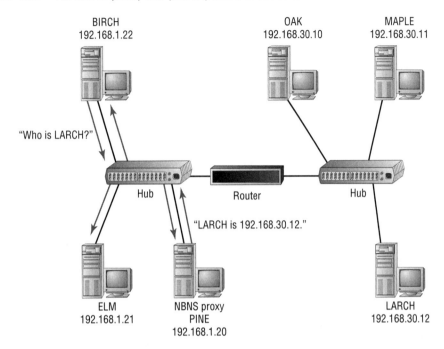

Master Browser Duty   nmbd can function as a master browser, either for the local subnet or for an entire Windows network. When it does so, nmbd maintains a list of SMB/CIFS servers on the network, and returns that list to any computer asking for it. This is different from NBNS functions. In NBNS, nmbd returns the IP address of a computer (itself or another computer); in master browser functions, nmbd returns a list of computer names.

Share Browsing   When you browse the shares on a specific Samba server, nmbd on that server is what returns the list of available shares to the client computer. This function is distinct from master browser functions, in which nmbd returns a list of computers on a network.

smbd: The SMB/CIFS Daemon

The daemon that does most of the heavy-duty file and printer sharing in Samba is smbd, the SMB/CIFS daemon. This program binds to TCP port 139 and responds to all requests for file or printer access. Its duties include the following:

Authentication One of the first tasks that smbd performs for any connection is authentication. If the requestor's username and password don't match what Samba is configured to accept, access is not granted.

File Sharing smbd provides all the file-sharing services—it accepts files from clients, sends files to clients, deletes files for clients, and so on.

Printer Sharing Printer sharing is quite similar to file sharing, from a network point of view. In printer sharing, the client sends the server a file, which is then printed rather than stored on disk.

Time Server Samba can function as a time server for Windows clients. In Windows, you can type **NET TIME *HOSTNAME* /YES /SET** to set the time of the Windows computer to the time maintained by the Linux computer called *HOSTNAME*. In Samba's smb.conf file, you must use the time server = Yes option to enable the time server function.

TIP You can use the xntpd package (http://www.eecis.udel.edu/~ntp/) in Linux to keep Linux's clock synchronized to an atomic clock signal from any of several sites on the Internet. If you then insert the NET TIME command in a Windows startup file, the Windows computers on your network will have reasonably accurate clocks, reset from your local time server every time they reboot.

Samba TNG

The Next Generation (TNG) is the name that's been applied to a development branch of Samba devoted to bringing improved Windows NT domain support to Samba. Because this is a development branch, it's not as stable as a mainstream Samba release, and so shouldn't be used in critical environments. Along with changes to Samba's domain support code, Samba TNG has split the work of the two Samba daemons among several additional daemons:

smbd	The file-sharing server. Run this at all times.
nmbd	The name browser server. Run this at all times.
browserd	Daemon to handle name-browsing functions. Run this if Samba may be a master browser.

`lsarpcd`	A logon security protocol. Run this if you use encrypted passwords.
`samrd`	Handles password changes from Windows NT. Run this if you use encrypted passwords.
`spoolssd`	Spool service for printing from Windows NT clients.
`srvsvcd`	Server service for browsing. Run this at all times.
`svcctld`	Service control daemon. Run this to start or stop services remotely.
`winregd`	Another password-changing daemon. Run this if you use encrypted passwords.
`wkssvcd`	Workstation service. Run this if you want browsing to work correctly.

In order to obtain full functionality of Samba TNG, you must start all of these daemons. As I write this, the Samba startup scripts included by most Linux distributions are inadequate, because they only start smbd and nmbd. You must therefore modify your old startup scripts or create new ones to support this explosion of daemons. (If Samba TNG's daemon model is used with a future final version of Samba and included with Linux distributions, no doubt this situation will change, and the distributions will start all the necessary daemons automatically.)

Why run Samba TNG? Here are the primary reasons at this time:

- You need advanced domain control features for a Windows NT network, such as remote control of Samba's services. Basic Windows NT 4 domain functionality exists in Samba versions 2.0.5a and later, however, so you don't need Samba TNG for that.

- You need to use Windows 2000 clients on a domain controlled by a Samba server. Although you can use Windows 2000 clients with a Samba server version 2.0.6 or above, Samba versions through 2.0.7 can't function as domain controllers for Windows 2000 clients. Windows TNG includes this support.

Before you try Samba TNG, I recommend you look for a more recent mainstream release. It's possible that some of Samba TNG's features will make it into a 2.2 or 3.0 release in late 2000. Whether the Samba TNG daemon structure will be used in that release remains to be seen. As of mid-2000, Samba TNG is still considered experimental, so I don't recommend you use it on a mission-critical server. If necessary, you can configure a Windows NT 4 or Windows 2000 computer as a domain controller, and use one or more Samba 2.0.x computers as file and print servers on this domain. (Chapter 10, "Configuring Domains," discusses domain controllers in greater detail.)

Resolving Filesystem Feature Conflicts

One of the difficulties inherent in using Linux to serve files to DOS, Windows, and OS/2 clients is the fact that these systems use various conventions for file naming and attributes. Linux follows Unix conventions. DOS, Windows, and OS/2 all derive from another tradition, and so use rules incompatible with Linux. Additional differences exist between these three major Samba client OSs, particularly with respect to filename length limits. Samba must therefore support multiple rules for translating filenames and attributes between filesystems derived from Unix and DOS.

WARNING   People sometimes dual-boot a computer between Linux and Windows (or some other OS) and want to share the same files from both OSs. It's also sometimes desirable to share a Zip disk, floppy disk, or other removable media from Linux, even when the medium uses a *File Allocation Table (FAT)* filesystem. In both cases, Linux filters the FAT filesystem features through its own filesystem features model, so you may lose certain features of the underlying filesystem. For instance, you'll lose the hidden and system bits of a FAT filesystem when you share that file through Samba. On rare occasions, this can be a significant problem.

Filename Length and Case Retention

One of the most obvious differences between OSs is in file-naming conventions. Length and case are the two attributes that are important in this respect. Different OSs and filesystems support filenames of various lengths. Linux's ext2 filesystem is capable of handling filenames of up to 256 characters in length. SMB/CIFS allows up to 127 characters for filenames, but some operating systems (notably DOS) have much more restrictive limits. Samba must find some way to convert long filenames to shorter ones or to simply drop long filenames when the client doesn't understand them.

In terms of case, OSs can treat the upper- and lowercase characters in filenames in one of three ways:

Case-Sensitive   When upper- and lowercase characters are treated as different characters, the filesystem is known as *case-sensitive*. On such a filesystem, the files BigFile.txt and bigfile.TXT are different files. Both can exist in the same directory, and entering one name when only the other exists produces a "file not found" error. Linux is a case-sensitive OS, although it can behave differently when it accesses files from other filesystems, such as FAT. A Samba server normally serves files from a Linux ext2 filesystem, however, and Linux always treats ext2 filenames in a case-sensitive manner.

Case-Retentive   In a *case-retentive* filesystem, the filesystem preserves the case of filenames but doesn't distinguish between upper- and lowercase characters. For instance, you can save a file as `BigFile.txt` and then retrieve it as `bigfile.TXT`. If one filename exists, you can't create a second file with the same name but in a different case. Windows and OS/2 both use case-retentive filesystems and treat SMB/CIFS shares in this manner, as well.

Case-Insensitive   A *case-insensitive* filesystem treats upper- and lowercase characters identically and converts to one case when saving files. For instance, you might enter the filename `BigFile.txt` in a File Save dialog box, but the computer will store it as `BIGFILE.TXT` or `bigfile.txt`. DOS treats file access in a case-insensitive way, as does OS/2 when it uses a FAT filesystem. In these situations, uppercase is used. When Linux accesses a case-insensitive filesystem (such as a FAT floppy disk or an ISO-9660 CD-ROM), Linux converts uppercase filenames to lowercase by default.

Samba includes a large number of configuration options to control how it converts between its 256-character case-sensitive filesystem and the shorter, case-retentive or case-insensitive filenames expected by its clients. These options are described in Chapter 5, "Configuring File Sharing."

FAT-Style File Attributes

DOS uses FAT as its only filesystem. Operating systems with a DOS heritage, including OS/2 and all versions of Windows, have added the characteristics of FAT filesystems to their more sophisticated filesystems, such as OS/2's *High-Performance File System (HPFS)* and Windows NT's *NT File System (NTFS)*. FAT filesystem attributes are each represented by a single bit that's stored as part of the file's description on the disk. Following are some of the attributes supported by FAT and other Microsoft and IBM filesystems. (The specifics of configuring the FAT-style attribute settings are in Chapter 5.)

Hidden Bit

If the *hidden bit* is set, the file is invisible to many programs. Programs actually have a choice of showing or not showing files that are configured as hidden, so a user can easily overcome the hidden bit in many programs. Linux, however, doesn't support the hidden bit. In Linux (and Unix generally), the equivalent effect is achieved by starting a filename with a period (`.`), as in `.bashrc`.

Samba can be configured to add the hidden bit to these so-called *dot files* when sharing a directory. (Samba does *not* apply the hidden bit to the `.` and `..` files, which refer to the directory and its parent, respectively.) Samba can also store the hidden bit as the world execute bit in the Unix-style permissions for the file, but this configuration can cause minor problems if the files are ever accessed from Linux. Specifically, if somebody tries to run a randomly selected file that was hidden by a Samba client, an error is likely—albeit not one that will damage the server or its files.

Archive Bit

The *archive bit* is used by the OS to signal when a file needs to be backed up. Normally, a program sets the archive bit whenever it modifies the contents of a file. Backup programs can subsequently use this bit to back up only those files that have changed. There is no equivalent feature in a Unix-style filesystem, but Samba can store the archive bit in the owner execute bit for the file. Like storing the hidden bit, this can cause a file that's not a program to appear executable in Linux, which can be confusing or cause error messages to appear if a user tries to execute the file.

System Bit

DOS and related OSs use the *system bit* to identify files that are required or have special meaning to the OS. Chances are you won't store files that use the system bit on a Samba server. If you do, and if you must preserve this bit, you can configure Samba to store it in the Unix group execute bit. As with the hidden and archive bits, setting the group execute bit can cause a file to look like a Linux program file, but trying to run the file just produces an error message.

Read-Only Bit

The *read-only* bit signals that a file can be read but not written to or deleted. This meaning is similar but not identical to the write permission supported by Linux. When the DOS read-only bit is set, the Linux write permission must *not* be set. Samba performs this translation automatically. More importantly, in DOS and its descendants, when the read-only bit is set, you can't delete the file. In Linux, on the other hand, the right to delete a file is considered a characteristic of the directory in which the file resides.

You can configure Samba to follow DOS-style handling of the read-only bit with respect to file deletions by using the `delete readonly = No` parameter in `smb.conf`. This setting is the default. Changing it to `Yes` sets Samba to follow normal Linux standards for file deletions.

Ownership and Permission

Unix systems, including Linux, support two features that aren't supported by DOS or Windows *9x*—*ownership* and *permissions*. If you're an experienced Linux administrator, your challenge is to understand how Samba uses these features internally. If you're new to Linux, your challenge is in learning how to use these concepts to increase security on your Samba server.

An Overview of Linux File Security

You can discover the security settings in a Linux file by issuing the `ls -l` command in a directory or on a specific file. The result is something like the following:

```
-rw-r-----   1 philkent users        1846 Oct 23  2000 title.txt
```

For understanding Linux file security, the first, third, and fourth fields of this line are important. The first field, `-rw-r-----`, is the *permissions string* for the file; it represents access rights granted to various classes of users. The third field, `philkent`, is the username of the file's owner. The fourth field, `users`, is the group to which the file belongs. These three strings determine who may access the file and in what ways.

As a general rule, the owner of a file is the user who created that file. The owner usually has superior access rights to the file, as described shortly. The group to which the file belongs is usually the primary group of the file's owner. Both of these characteristics can be changed in Linux with the `chown` command, or with the `chgrp` command in the case of the group. A file can have only one owner and one group.

The permissions string has four parts:

- The first character represents any special attributes of the file. For instance, a d as the first character indicates that the file is a directory. In the example string, `-rw-r-----`, the special attributes position is unoccupied (represented by a dash), meaning the file is an ordinary file.

- The second through fourth characters represent the read, write, and execute permissions, respectively, assigned to the file's owner. In the example, rw- indicates that the owner has read and write but not execute permission; rwx would indicate read, write, and execute permission. The read and execute permission bits have no counterparts in the FAT filesystem, although all FAT files are assumed to be readable.

- The fifth through seventh characters represent the read, write, and execute permissions, respectively, for members of the file's group. In the example string, r-- indicates that members of the group `users` may read the file, but not execute or write to it. Thus, if `symmes` is a member of the group `users`, `symmes` may read the file but not modify it.

- The final three characters represent the read, write, and execute permissions, respectively, for all other users of the system (often called *world permissions*). In the example, this string is ---, which translates into no permissions—people who are not `philkent` and who do not belong to the group `users` cannot access this file at all.

NOTE One exception to the world permissions rule is *root*, also known as the *superuser* or *administrator*. The superuser has full access to all files on the computer, no matter what their permissions.

The permissions string can also be expressed as three or four octal numbers, as in 640 or 0640. Each of the final three digits is the octal representation of the three permission bits for the owner, group, and world permissions. For example, rw- is a binary 110, which converts to an octal 6, hence the 6 in 640. Similarly, r-- is binary 100, or octal 4.

In a multiuser environment, it's possible to use Unix-style ownership and permissions to provide security on the system. If a company has half a dozen different projects underway, it can create six groups and assign employees to the appropriate groups. You can then set permissions on files and directories to allow or deny access to files based on group membership. Although a file can only belong to a single group, users can belong to multiple groups, so it's possible to grant members of two or more different projects access to both groups' files.

Using Linux File Security with Samba

At its core, Samba obeys Linux's file security model. Every individual who mounts a Samba share does so as a specific Linux user. Therefore, file accesses follow the permissions allowed to that user. For instance, consider again the example file owned by philkent, which belongs to the group users, with permissions of 0640. If philkent mounts a share, he can read and write the example file. On the other hand, the user symmes, who also belongs to the users group, can read the file but not write it. To symmes, the file appears to be read-only from a Windows computer. To another user who doesn't belong to the users group, the file appears in directory listings but cannot be accessed in any other way—Windows returns an "access denied" message.

An experienced Linux system administrator should have no trouble setting up a basic system of username-based security for a Samba server, particularly if that server is to be used mainly as a repository for individual users' files. Think of Samba as just another user program and you won't go far wrong. If you're less familiar with Unix-style file security, you must familiarize yourself with it to learn what it can do. Table 2.1 summarizes a few permissions and their possible roles.

Table 2.1   Linux Permissions and Their Uses

Permission	Meaning and Possible Uses
0666	Complete read/write access to all users. Useful for low-security shared directories.
0664	Complete read/write access to all users in a given group; read-only access to other users. Useful for collaborative projects in a low-security environment.
0644	Read/write access to the file's owner; read-only access to all other users. Useful in environments with little or no confidential information, and when access to other users' data is beneficial.
0640	Read/write access to the file's owner; read-only access to the file's group; no access to others. Useful in moderate-security collaborative projects.
0600	Read/write access to the file's owner; no access to others. Useful for high-security shared files.
0440	Read-only access to the file's owner and group; no access to others. Useful for shared program files or fixed data.

For the most part, files you save on a Samba server don't need execute bits, at least not from the Linux point of view. (Samba may use these bits to store the archive, system, and hidden attributes, as described in the earlier section "FAT-Style File Attributes.") Directories, however, are a special case. Because it makes no sense to execute directories, Linux uses execute permissions on directories to indicate that you can obtain information about the files in the directory. This access is a practical necessity for using a directory, so when read permissions exist on a directory, execute permissions usually exist, as well.

Samba offers a variety of options for altering the way it uses Linux file permissions. These options allow you to set up security that's more flexible than could be achieved through Linux security alone. For instance:

- You can set the permissions assigned to files a user creates, on a share-by-share basis. For instance, you might set files in a user's home directory to have very restrictive permissions (such as 0600), whereas files in a shared directory might have more permissive permissions (such as 0664 or even 0666).

- You can set the permissions assigned to directories a user creates, much as you can set the permissions for files. (Because the execute bit on directories is so important, 0644 becomes 0755, for example.)

- You can change the effective username by which a share is accessed. You could, for example, set the same username for all access to a common share in order to avoid having several owners of files in that share. When you set the username in this way, an individual logs on with his or her normal username. Once logged on, Samba creates files with the effective username, and gives access using the access rights assigned to the effective username.

- You can specify a list of users who may or may not access a share, or who may or may not write to a share. This specification is independent of the Linux ownership and permissions restrictions.

- You can specify a list of computers that may or may not access or write to a share. This restriction works much like the username-based restrictions.

Chapters 5 and 14 cover these security and permissions features in detail.

Windows NT/2000 File Security and Samba

Between basic Linux file permissions and Samba's share-by-share enhancements, you can tailor a security scheme to meet most needs. These schemes do not, however, integrate well with the security features available in Windows NT (including Windows 2000). The Windows systems include concepts of ownership and of groups that are similar to those of Linux. Rather than a file permissions string, however, these OSs use an *access control list (ACL)*.

An ACL is a list of users or groups who may or may not access a specific file. Because an ACL is a *list,* it can contain more than one entry. This characteristic allows ACLs to provide a finer-grained security model than is available in Linux. You can provide similar functionality on a directory basis through Samba's controls, but you can't easily modify these permissions directly from Windows. To address this problem, Samba implements limited ACL support, and that support is still evolving. As of Samba 2.0.7, you can convert between Linux and Windows users and groups, and set the Linux permissions via Windows ACL controls.

Partitions, Mount Points, and Shares

Most experienced Linux system administrators install Linux on multiple partitions. For instance, /usr/local, /home, and /var might each have their own partitions, in addition to the root (/) partition. Samba is completely oblivious to these issues, except for their impact upon Linux's file handling. (For instance, if you unmount a partition, it becomes unavailable to Samba.)

Samba allows you to share any directories you want to share from your Linux computer. You can create multiple shares from the same computer. Each share appears as a separate item to clients. You can even export shares from nested directory trees. For instance, you can share /winprogs and /winprogs/utils separately. The former share will include the utils directory as a directory available from its root. Exporting /winprogs/utils separately doesn't affect its availability from another share.

> **TIP** You can use the ability to export nested shares to fine-tune access control. Suppose most of the files in /winprogs require only read access. You can export that directory with read-only permissions. For those occasions when write access is required to the /winprogs/utils directory, you can export it with read/write permissions. Accessing it from the first share most of the time provides just read-only access, which might be desirable as a means of avoiding accidental file deletions or modifications, even when read/write access is available from another share. Similarly, you can restrict access to the /winprogs/utils directory to certain users, while making read-only access to /winprogs available to all.

In the DOS, Windows, and OS/2 worlds, each partition or removable disk device is assigned a unique *drive letter,* starting with C:. (A: and B: are reserved for the first and, if present, second floppy disks.) Depending upon the OS and the options you use to access your Samba shares, you may or may not mount a share on a drive letter. In Windows, there are two ways to access a share: by mounting and by browsing.

When mounting a share, you tie a share to a drive letter by right-clicking a share and selecting Map Network Drive from the resulting pop-up menu. You can then access the drive as if it were a local hard disk. Alternatively, you can use the NET USE command to accomplish the same goal.

With the browsing method, you can locate a share in Network Neighborhood (Computers Near Me in Windows 2000) and access the files on that share without mounting the share. You may also be able to access files by directly specifying their names in the form *HOST**SHARE**PATH**FILE*, where *HOST* is the computer's NetBIOS name, *SHARE* is the name of the share, and *PATH**FILE* is the path to the file relative to the share's root.

> **TIP** If you mount a share, give it a drive letter that's much later in the alphabet than any drives currently on your computer. For instance, on a computer that has drives C: through E:, give a share a drive letter such as M:. This practice ensures that you won't need to change your share's drive letter should you add or delete local drives. It can also be helpful in standardizing mount points across a network, on which client configurations may not be uniform. Note, however, that Windows uses Z: internally, so don't use Z: as a mount point.

Mounting a share sometimes makes it a bit easier to access files, because you'll do less rummaging about in deeply nested folders. Some older programs—particularly DOS programs—may also require a drive letter, so you may have to mount a share. Nevertheless, browsing can be a convenient and quick way to access a share, particularly if you don't use the share regularly.

Summary

Samba serves as a bridge between the Linux and Windows worlds, which have differences in networking and filesystem features that Samba must overcome. Some of this work has been done by the integration of SMB/CIFS networking into TCP/IP standards. This step allows Linux computers to use SMB/CIFS without NetBEUI.

Samba's work, however, is still substantial. Its two daemons (more in Samba TNG) must present the illusion of a filesystem that lacks certain features, such as filename sensitivity and Unix-style permissions, while possessing features that in fact it lacks (such as hidden and system attribute bits). In the end, Samba does a remarkably good job of these tasks, and even allows you to use Linux's security features and Samba's security extensions for very flexible control of access to shares.

Part 2

Essential Configuration

Featuring:

- Obtaining Samba
- Installing Binary and Source Packages
- Installed File Locations
- Running Samba
- Configuring Samba Using GUI Utilities
- Editing the `smb.conf` File
- Basic Configuration Options
- Setting Up File Shares
- Handling Ownership and Permissions
- File-Sharing Scenarios
- Creating Print Queues and Printer Shares
- Controlling Printer Access
- Printer-Sharing Scenarios
- Using `smbclient`
- Using `smbmount`
- Using `smbprint`

3

Installing Samba

The first step to using Samba is to install the software on your computer. Fortunately, this step is usually easy because Samba comes with all major Linux distributions. Nonetheless, there are situations in which you may need to take action to install Samba.

For one thing, although Samba *comes with* all major Linux distributions, the package may not be installed on any given system. Furthermore, Samba is constantly being improved. If a newer version adds important features or fixes bugs, you may need to update. If you want "bleeding edge" Samba (that is, the very latest version), you must normally obtain source code and compile it yourself. (Note that these development releases are potentially dangerous, however; hence the designation "bleeding edge.")

This chapter discusses your options in obtaining and installing Samba. These options range from pulling Samba off your Linux installation CD, to obtaining and compiling the source code. Also described here are some of the key Samba configuration files, as well as methods of running Samba once it's installed.

Obtaining Samba

Samba is a very easy package to obtain. It almost certainly came with your Linux distribution, but you may want to look for a more recent version of the package. As a general rule, I recommend using a version of Samba distributed by your Linux distribution's maintainer. Such packages often include startup scripts customized for the distribution, and you're less likely to run into problems such as incompatible support libraries when you stick with a binary created for your distribution.

Alternatively, you can compile Samba yourself. This approach can be beneficial when you need to customize the program in some way, such as adding NetBEUI support (`http://www.procom.com`), or when you want to add or remove unusual Samba compile-time options.

Samba with Your Linux Distribution

Every major Linux distribution comes with one or more Samba package files. Table 3.1 summarizes the names used by many popular distributions. You can check to see if these packages are installed on your system, as described shortly. If not, you can pull out your installation CD-ROM and install the relevant package.

Table 3.1   Samba Package Names in Popular Distributions

Distribution	Samba Packages
Caldera eDesktop 2.4	`samba-2.0.6-2.i386.rpm`
	`samba-doc-2.0.6-2.i386.rpm`
Corel Linux 1.2	`samba-common_2.0.7-2-cl-1.1_i386.deb`
	`samba_2.0.7-2-cl-1.1_i386.deb`
	`samba-doc_2.0.7-2-cl-1.1_all.deb`
Debian GNU/Linux 2.2	`samba-common_2.0.7-3.deb`
	`samba-doc_2.0.7-3.deb`
	`samba_2.0.7-3.deb`
Linux Mandrake 7.1	`samba-2.0.6-4mdk.i586.rpm`
	`samba-client-2.0.6-4mdk.i586.rpm`
	`samba-common-2.0.6-4mdk.i586.rpm`
LinuxPPC 2000	`samba-2.0.6-12.ppc.rpm`
	`samba-client-2.0.6-12.ppc.rpm`
	`samba-common-2.0.6-12.ppc.rpm`
Red Hat Linux 7.0	`samba-2.0.7-21ssl.i386.rpm`
	`samba-client-2.0.7-21ssl.i386.rpm`
	`samba-common-2.0.7-21ssl.i386.rpm`
Slackware Linux 7.1	`samba.tgz` (Samba 2.0.7)

Table 3.1   Samba Package Names in Popular Distributions *(continued)*

Distribution	Samba Packages
Storm Linux 2000	gnosamba_0.3.3-0.slink.0_i386.deb samba-doc_2.0.5a-1_all.deb samba-common_2.0.5a-1_i386.deb samba_2.0.5a-1_i386.deb
SuSE Linux 6.4	ksamba-0.3.4-90.i386.rpm samba-2.0.6-80.i386.rpm
TurboLinux 4.0	gtksamba-0.3.2pl1-2.i386.rpm samba-2.0.6-20000313.i386.rpm samba-nsswitch-2.0.6-20000313.i386.rpm
Yellow Dog Linux 1.2	samba-2.0.6-8.ppc.rpm samba-client-2.0.6-8.ppc.rpm samba-common-2.0.6-8.ppc.rpm

Most of these distributions use fairly standardized Linux package naming conventions. Specifically, the package names contain the following elements, usually separated by dashes (-), underscores (_), or periods (.):

- The package name, such as samba or samba-client.

- A version number: 2.0.6 in most of the distributions in Table 3.1.

- A build number, which represents minor revisions that are unique to any given distribution. The build number might be incremented, for instance, when there's a change in placement of the distribution's documentation files, or when a bug in the startup script has been fixed.

- A code for the distribution, such as mdk for Mandrake. Not all distributions use distribution codes.

- An architecture code, such as i386 for Intel 80386 or later CPUs, or ppc for PowerPC CPUs.

- The file type: rpm for a *Red Hat Package Manager (RPM)* file, deb for a Debian package, or tgz for a gzipped tar file (also known as a *tarball*).

As you can see, the distributions split Samba up in various ways. Red Hat and most of its derivatives, for instance, create three packages: samba, samba-client, and samba-common. You should install all three of these packages. (If you don't intend to use client

Essential Configuration

PART 2

functions, you can omit the `samba-client` package, however.) Debian-based distributions split off `samba`, `samba-common`, and `samba-doc` packages. Here again, I recommend installing all three packages. Some distributions, including SuSE Linux 6.4 and Storm Linux 2000, include additional packages that provide Samba-related functionality, such as GUI Samba configuration tools. Such packages are unlikely to cause problems, and they aren't discussed in any depth in this book.

If you have a distribution that's more recent than the ones listed in Table 3.1, chances are that the distribution's base name is the same, but the version or build number is higher. If you have a distribution of Linux that's not listed at all in Table 3.1, chances are it has Samba packages named in a way that's similar to those of one or more distributions listed in Table 3.1. You can probably find your Samba package by mounting your Linux installation CD-ROM and searching it with the `find` command:

```
$ mount /dev/cdrom /mnt/cdrom
$ find /mnt/cdrom -name "*amba*"
```

(You may want to alter the mount point in these commands to match the configuration of your system.)

WARNING If you have Windows 2000 clients on your network, I strongly recommend that you install Samba version 2.0.7 or later. Samba versions prior to 2.0.5a had serious difficulties with Windows 2000 clients, and even version 2.0.6 isn't perfect in this respect.

Updates from Your Linux Distributor

Even when Samba comes with your Linux distribution, you may want to obtain an updated version of the program. If so, the simplest way is usually to find one from your Linux distributor. Typically there's an updates section on your distribution's Web or FTP site. Updated packages may include bug fixes, improved functionality, better setup routines, and other enhancements.

Should you automatically apply an update if one is available? This is a tough question, for which there are two competing arguments:

- "If it ain't broke, don't fix it." This saying is often applicable to software updates. If your current Samba installation works to your satisfaction, why update? An update always carries the risk of creating new problems.

- "Bug fixes can be important." Updated versions of Samba frequently include bug fixes. Some of these fix serious problems—most notably security weaknesses. It's best to be up-to-date on these bug fixes, to head off problems.

At a minimum, I recommend frequently checking the update Web pages for Samba and your particular distribution to watch for security issues that are identified. If a security problem or some other serious bug exists, update. If no such problems are fixed in versions more recent than yours, then an update isn't critical. Decide whether to update based on the description of changes between the versions.

Getting the Most Up-to-Date Samba

Frequently, a distribution maintainer doesn't have the latest version of Samba available in a distribution or as an update. There's often a lag between the release of a new version and the time when it is compiled for a distribution. Consequently, if you need the latest version of Samba, you may need to look somewhere other than on the Linux vendor's Web site.

> **TIP** As mentioned earlier in this chapter, Samba packages compiled for a specific distribution typically include features to help Samba work properly with that distribution—specifically, startup and shutdown scripts that are tailored for a particular distribution. If you use a recent Samba package that wasn't built with your distribution in mind, start by installing a package that *was* built for your distribution. You can then save the startup and shutdown scripts (described later in this chapter, in "Common Distribution Startup Scripts") and remove the package. When you install the updated Samba, use the startup and shutdown scripts taken from the distribution-specific Samba package. (This procedure may not work with Samba TNG, because it uses more daemons than Samba 2.0.*x*.)

Following are some sources for updated Samba packages:

RPMFind The RPMFind Web site, `http://rufus.w3.org/linux/RPM/`, is an excellent resource for locating software packages in RPM format. Most of the RPMs available through this site are designed for specific Linux distributions, but some are more general in nature. You might discover a more up-to-date Samba package designed for a distribution other than the one you use, or a more general-purpose Samba RPM.

The Debian Package Site Debian maintains a database of packages at `http://www.debian.org/distrib/packages`. These are primarily from the current stable and beta-test Debian releases. In most cases, Debian packages work on other Debian-derived distributions, such as Corel Linux or Storm Linux, without modification.

Other Distribution Maintainers You can check the Web sites devoted to other Linux distribution maintainers that use the same package format as your distribution. For instance, Red Hat users can check Mandrake's Web site. In most cases, the

RPMFind site is a more efficient way to locate such packages for RPM-based distributions.

Freshmeat   The Freshmeat Web site (`http://freshmeat.net`) is a good spot to locate recent software releases in a variety of formats.

The Samba Site   Ultimately, the single best resource for Samba is the Samba Web site, `http://www.samba.org`. (This site actually presents a list of mirror sites around the world; pick the one closest to you.) You can obtain source code or precompiled binaries for any of several popular Linux distributions. The very latest versions—and particularly development packages—may be available only in source code form.

No matter what the source, you ultimately have to choose the form of your package. The easiest packages to install are binaries compiled for your Linux distribution (or at least for the correct architecture, such as Intel *x*86 or PowerPC). Most precompiled binaries come in RPM or Debian packages, but you can also get Samba as a tarball. Alternatively, you can obtain Samba as source code—again, as either a package file or a tarball. Descriptions of all these options are coming up.

Installing a Binary Package

Installation procedures for Samba vary substantially from one Linux distribution to another. Most distributions today use RPM files or Debian packages, but Slackware uses tarballs. A few others, such as Stampede Linux, use their own proprietary formats. As a general rule, if you get a binary package, get one that uses the package format favored by your distribution. If necessary, you can often convert from one format to another with the `alien` program, or you can install a tarball. (All Linux distributions can read tarballs.) It's always cleanest to start with the correct package format.

Installing an RPM

Most modern Linux distributions use the RPM format, although Debian packages are becoming more popular. Fortunately, installing RPMs is a simple process.

WARNING   Upgrading an RPM package sometimes wipes out your configuration files. Back up your `smb.conf` and `smbpasswd` files (generally located in `/etc` or `/etc/samba.d`) *before* upgrading a working Samba installation. If you're upgrading to a version of Samba that wasn't designed for your distribution, you should also back up your Samba startup scripts, which are described later in this chapter in the section "Common Distribution Startup Scripts."

Using Text-Based Tools

To install or upgrade Samba at the shell prompt, issue a command such as the following:

```
# rpm -Uvh samba-2.0.6-9.i386.rpm
```

Either issue the rpm command once for each package you're upgrading, or list multiple packages, separated by spaces, on the command line. The rpm program should respond by displaying a series of hash marks (#) to represent the command's progress; then the job is done.

The -U parameter to rpm specifies a package upgrade, which causes rpm to automatically remove the old package before installing the new one. If you're replacing a set of packages from one distribution with their equivalents from another, manually remove the old packages before installing the new ones. This reduces the likelihood that you'll run into conflicts because of differing package names and contents. Here are typical commands for this situation:

```
# rpm -e samba
```

```
# rpm -Uvh samba-2.0.6-9.i386.rpm
```

When the rpm -U command encounters no existing package, it installs the package without complaint. You could also use **rpm -ivh** in place of **rpm -Uvh** in this situation.

Verify that the package is installed by entering the **rpm -qi** command, which displays information such as when and on what computer the binary package was built. Listing 3.1 demonstrates this command.

Listing 3.1 RPM Query Output

```
$ rpm -qi samba
Name        : samba                    Vendor: Caldera Systems, Inc.
Version     : 2.0.6              Distribution: OpenLinux 2.4
Release     : 2                    Build Host: bm.calderalabs.com
Install Date: 2000-04-01T19:54:26Z   Build Date: 2000-02-17T22:50:49Z
Size        : 3763927              Source RPM: samba-2.0.6-2.src.rpm
Group       : Server/Network
Copyright   : Andrew Tridgell, John H Terpstra; GPL.
Packager    : Klaus Singvogel <klaus@caldera.de>
URL         : http://samba.org/samba
Summary     : SMB client and server.
```

This command also displays an extended plain-English summary of what Samba is, which has been omitted from Listing 3.1.

Using GUI Tools

Many Linux distributions include GUI tools to help you install, remove, update, and query RPM packages. Red Hat and Mandrake, for instance, come with Gnome RPM (Figure 3.1). To add a package using Gnome RPM, follow these steps:

Figure 3.1   Gnome RPM is one of several GUI tools used for manipulating packages installed on an RPM-based Linux computer.

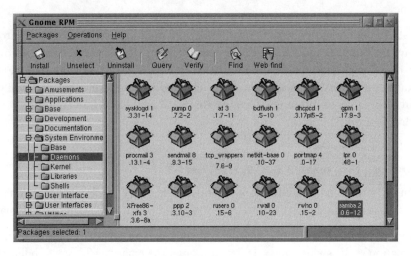

1. As root, start Gnome RPM by typing **gnorpm** in an xterm window.

2. In the main Gnome RPM window, click the Install button. Gnome RPM displays an Install dialog box in which you can select RPMs.

3. Click the Add button in the Install dialog box. In the file selection dialog box that appears, locate and select the RPM files you want to install. Note that you can select multiple files. When you've selected all your files, click Cancel.

4. Make sure that the check boxes next to all of the packages you want to install are checked in the Install dialog box, and then click the Install button. Gnome RPM installs the packages.

You can use Gnome RPM in a similar manner to update, delete, or query RPM packages. GUI configuration utilities in other distributions, such as Caldera and SuSE, differ in details but have similar functionality.

Installing a Debian Package

Debian packages are incompatible with RPM packages, but the basic principles of operation are the same across both package types. You use the dpkg command to install a Debian package, as in

```
# dpkg -i samba_2.0.6-cl-1.1_i386.deb
```

This command installs the samba_2.0.6-cl-1.1_i386.deb package.

Before you run this command, you may need to remove an old package. To do this, use the -r option to dpkg, as in

```
# dpkg -r samba
```

Some Debian-based Linux distributions, such as Corel Linux, include GUI front-ends to dpkg similar to the Gnome RPM program for RPM-based systems. If you're more comfortable with GUI tools than with command-line tools, you can use these front ends in a similar way to ease administration.

Installing a Tarball

If you have Slackware Linux or another distribution that uses tarballs for distribution, you can install Samba by using the standard Linux tar utility. You can also use this method if you want to install a tarball on a Linux distribution that ordinarily uses a package management tool. I recommend using an RPM or Debian package if your distribution supports one of these file formats, however.

> **WARNING**   When installing a new version of Samba over an older one on Slackware Linux, the new files will most likely overwrite the old ones. If you install a tarball on a system that normally uses packages, however, or if you install a tarball that was created using a different directory structure than what your current system uses, you may end up with duplicate Samba files. This can cause substantial confusion, because you might end up continuing to use the old binaries even after installing the new ones. You should therefore remove the old package as well as you can, before installing a Samba binary via a tarball. Check the directory structure contained within a tarball first, by using the tar command, as in **tar tvfz samba.tgz**. This command displays all the files in the tarball, including their complete paths.

Tarball installation is a fairly straightforward matter. As the `root` user, you issue commands similar to the following. These commands install the files from the `samba.tgz` file located in the `/root` directory:

```
# cd /
# tar xvfz /root/samba.tgz
```

Note that the first command (**cd /**) is critically important; without it, you'll install the files under whatever directory you're currently in, not in the usual directory tree. (It is possible, however, that the tarball you obtain might have to be installed under some directory other than /, in which case you should follow the directions that come with the package to install it.)

Compiling the Source Code

In some cases, a binary installation isn't adequate. For instance:

- If you need to modify the source code in any way—including applying unusual compilation options—you must compile the source code yourself unless you can locate a binary that includes those exact modifications.

- You may also need to install from source code if you've installed updated libraries that are incompatible with the default binaries. (Such a situation is unlikely, however, for two reasons: because such updated libraries would most likely break packages other than Samba, and because you can install multiple versions of most support libraries.)

- Finally, if you're running Linux on an unusual CPU architecture, you won't be able to use the Intel $x86$ binaries that are most common. You may be able to find precompiled binaries for your computer's architecture, but if not, you can compile the source code yourself.

There are two primary ways to compile Samba from source: Use source code packaged as an RPM source package, or obtain the source code in a tarball. When you compile from a packaged form, making changes to the source code is comparatively difficult, so I don't recommend this approach if you need to alter the source code. Compiling the source code "manually" from a tarball allows you to make customizations.

Compiling a Source RPM

If you want to compile your own copy of Samba because you've replaced standard libraries or are running on an unusual architecture for which you can find no binary packages, one of the easiest ways to install Samba on an RPM-based distribution is to use a *source RPM*. This contains the original source code, patches, and installation scripts in a single file. It can be distinguished from a binary RPM in that the source RPM contains `src` rather than `i386`, `ppc`, or some other architecture code as part of the filename.

To create a binary RPM from a source RPM, you issue a command similar to the following:

```
# rpm --rebuild samba-2.0.6-9.src.rpm
```

This command builds a binary package from *samba-2.0.6-9.src.rpm.* The resulting binary package will have a similar filename, but with an architecture code in place of `src` near the end of the filename. The binary package appears somewhere in the `/usr/src` directory tree, usually in a directory named after the distribution. For instance, in Caldera eDesktop 2.4, the binary appears in the `/usr/src/OpenLinux/RPMS/i386` directory. (Caldera's distributions were known previously by the OpenLinux name.) You can then change to that directory or move the file to another directory and install it as you would any other binary RPM.

> **NOTE** Building a binary RPM from a source RPM is not a foolproof process. If you're missing a critical development tool, the build process will fail. Something about a computer's architecture, libraries, or environment may occasionally cause a build to fail. Fortunately, Samba is well tested on a wide variety of Linux and non-Linux computers, so you're unlikely to run into problems caused by your host's environment.

Compiling Source from a Tarball

If you need to modify the Samba source code for any reason, or use uncommon compilation options that aren't set by default in a source RPM, then your best bet is to compile Samba directly from a source tarball. I recommend you download the tarball from the Samba Web site or from a site that houses source code for your particular Linux distribution.

> **NOTE** You *can* modify the source code in a source RPM, but the process for doing so is a bit tedious. For a single Samba server, modifying a source RPM is probably not worth the effort. If you want more information on this topic, consult the RPM HOWTO document that comes with all major Linux distributions.

The procedure for compiling Samba from source code is as follows:

1. Obtain the source tarball from your site of choice.
2. Change to the `/usr/src` directory, or some other convenient location.

3. Extract the files from the tarball, with a command such as

    # **tar xvfz** ~*/samba-2.0.7.tar.gz*

    This command creates a new directory in which the Samba source code resides.

4. Move into the Samba source code directory.

5. Examine the README file in the source code directory. This file may contain important information on the particular version of Samba you've obtained.

6. The actual source code is in a subdirectory called source under the main Samba directory. Move into this directory.

7. Type **./configure** to configure the Makefile and other critical configuration files for your system. (The many configuration options you can specify with the ./configure command are described following this procedure.)

8. Type **make** to build the Samba distribution.

9. Type **make install** to install Samba.

NOTE Depending upon permissions in the /usr/src directory, you may be able to perform steps 1–8 as an ordinary user. You *must* perform step 9 as root, however.

Configuration options for Samba are appended to the configure command in step 7 of the foregoing procedure. For instance, **./configure --with-pam** includes support for the *Pluggable Authentication Module (PAM),* an authentication library that's used on most Linux distributions. Most configuration options come in two forms: one to enable the feature and the other to disable it. These generally have the same name, but using with or without as a prefix, as in --with-pam and --without-pam. Following are the most important options, specified in their *default* states:

--without-smbwrapper   The smbwrapper package is used to mount SMB/CIFS shares. Linux can use the kernel-based smbfs instead, and smbwrapper has some incompatibilities with glibc, so it's best to leave this option disabled.

--without-afs   The *Andrew File System (AFS)* is a network filesystem from Carnegie-Mellon University. You can leave this option disabled unless you plan to share AFS mounts via Samba.

--without-dfs   DFS is an updated version of AFS. You can probably leave this option disabled. Note that this DFS is *not* the same as Microsoft's Dfs (Distributed File System).

--without-msdfs   You can add support for Microsoft's Dfs by changing this option. Chances are you don't need it; you probably know if you do.

--**without-krb5**   These options disable Kerberos 4 and 5
(Kerberos is a network authentication and security protocol.)
these options, you must specify the Kerberos base directory on
ith-krb5=/*path/to/directory*. Unless you use Kerberos on
safely ignore these options. Learn more about Kerberos at
/kerberos/www.

Automount support lets a computer automatically mount
s. Linux distributions increasingly use automounters, so you
is feature.

smbmount is the program that Linux uses to mount SMB/
end you enable this feature.

entioned earlier, PAM is an authentication method used by
ns. You should enable this option.

Lightweight Directory Access Protocol (LDAP) is a means
such as user preferences across a network. This support is
I recommend leaving it disabled unless you want to exper-

Windows 2000 (originally known as Windows NT 5)
, but Microsoft has implemented the protocol in its own
enables Samba to support Microsoft's version of LDAP. As
pport, it's best to leave this disabled unless you want to

ork Information System (NIS) is a method of distributing
twork. If your network uses NIS, you should enable this

NIS+ is a successor protocol to NIS. Change this option to
network uses NIS+.

me   NIS+ includes a feature that allows a system to locate a
a distributed network of Unix systems. If you change this
ature, Samba can automatically mount the correct home
ch a network.

Sockets Layer (SSL) is a method of encrypting network
is option allows Samba to use SSL. Such configurations are
, "Samba Security Considerations."

rmally, Samba creates its own log files. If you enable this
ba configuration options to send logging information to the
system log daemon, **syslogd**, instead of or in addition to Samba's own log files.

Essential
Configuration

PART 2

--without-netatalk   *Netatalk* is a separate package for serving files to Macintoshes using the AppleTalk protocol. If you enable this option, Samba incorporates experimental support for AppleTalk. I recommend running Netatalk separately from Samba, however.

--without-quotas   Changing this option to **--with-quotas** allows Samba to better support user disk quotas.

--prefix=/usr/local/samba   The directory in which architecture-independent files reside.

--eprefix=/usr/local/samba   The directory in which architecture-dependent files reside.

--bindir=*eprefix*/bin   The location of user-executable binary files.

--sbindir=*eprefix*/bin   The location of administrator-executable binary files.

--libexecdir=*eprefix*/libexec   The location of program executables.

--datadir=*prefix*/share   The location of architecture-independent, read-only data files.

--libdir=*eprefix*/lib   The location of program libraries.

--includedir=*prefix*/include   The location of Samba-related include files.

--infodir=*prefix*/info   The location of additional information files.

--mandir=*prefix*/man   The location of Samba's man pages.

--with-sambaconfdir=*prefix*/lib   The location of Samba's configuration file, smb.conf.

--with-privatedir=*prefix*/private   The location of the sensitive encrypted password file (smbpasswd).

--with-lockdir=*prefix*/var/locks   The location of Samba's lock files, used to implement some file access control features.

--with-swatdir=*prefix*/swat   The location of the Samba Web Administration Tool (SWAT) daemon, used for administering Samba through a Web browser.

TIP   You may want to load the configure script into a text editor to look for new Samba configuration options that may have been added since these descriptions were written.

By default, Samba installs itself entirely under the /usr/local/samba directory. This is the accepted location for packages you build on your own system (that is, locally). It's probably best to leave most or all of these options at their default values. If you're an experienced administrator who has a good reason to move files elsewhere, you may adjust these locations as you see fit.

> **NOTE** Most Linux distributions compile Samba with nonstandard options, in order to match the distribution's available features and common network configurations. For instance, if a distribution uses PAM, its Samba package includes PAM support. Most distributions also change the location for Samba files, from the default /usr/local/samba, typically to /usr. Further adjustments are usually made to other file locations, such as placing configuration files under /etc, /etc/samba.d, or a similar location.

Locating Important Files

If you compile Samba from source code, you can control where Samba installs itself by issuing appropriate configure options. If you're using a binary distribution, however, file locations are largely out of your control. It's therefore important that you know where to look for critical files—particularly the smb.conf configuration file, which controls most of Samba's features.

Common Installation Directories

Samba's default installation directory is /usr/local/samba. If compiled directly from source code without changes, Samba installs itself to this directory and creates a variety of subdirectories for storing its files. By default, Samba's binary files go in /usr/local/samba/bin. To run the Samba binaries, you must do one of three things:

- Add the Samba binary directory to your path.
- Create links to the Samba binaries in a directory that's already on your path, such as /usr/bin or /usr/local/bin.
- Include the complete pathname in every reference to a Samba binary, as in startup scripts.

Most Linux distributions don't use the default Samba installation directory. Instead, the Samba binaries and other files are placed directly in conventional directories for daemons, libraries, and so on. If you need to locate your Samba binary files for some reason, there are several ways to do so:

Use the whereis command. You can type **whereis** *progname* to find the location of the program called *progname*. This command may also return the location of the program's man pages and, if present on your computer, source files. The whereis command only works if the program for which you're looking is in a relevant path.

Use the **find** command.   You can locate a program anywhere on the computer by using the find command. For instance, **find / -name *progname*** will find the file called *progname* anywhere on the entire hard disk, even in an unusual location. This differs from whereis, which doesn't search every directory. The downside is that find takes much more time to return results than does whereis. Read the find man pages for more details.

Consult the package listing.   You can use the package database maintained by rpm or dpkg to locate your files. On an RPM-based distribution, if you know the package name, you can issue a command such as **rpm -ql *packagename*** to obtain a listing of the files in the *packagename* package. If necessary, you can pipe these results through grep to reduce the clutter, as in **rpm -ql samba | grep smbd** to locate just the smbd file. On a system that uses Debian packages, the command **dpkg-deb -c *package.deb*** lists the contents of the package file *package.deb*.

NOTE   Most Linux distributions have documentation files for various packages in the /usr/doc directory. Each package typically has its own subdirectory under /usr/doc, as in /usr/doc/samba. You can find Samba's own documentation in this directory tree, as well as on the Samba Web site, http://www.samba.org.

When installed as it is on most Linux distributions, Samba's files are scattered about many directories, such as /usr/bin, /usr/doc/samba, and /usr/man. It can therefore be tedious to track down these files individually to update or remove them—but that's what package managers such as RPM are designed to do.

Configuration Files

Samba relies on a handful of critical configuration files. On most Linux distributions, these files reside in /etc, /etc/samba.d, or a similar subdirectory of /etc. If you compile Samba yourself and don't change the default location for these files, Samba will look for them in the /usr/local/samba/lib directory. These critical configuration files include the following:

smb.conf   This file is the single most important Samba configuration file. You set almost all of Samba's options here—options used by both the nmbd and smbd daemons. Much of the rest of this book is devoted to describing the contents of this file.

smbpasswd   Samba doesn't always use this file, but when it does, the file is critically important. It contains encrypted passwords for user accounts. In some ways, this file is equivalent to the standard Linux passwd or shadow files, but the usernames and passwords in smbpasswd are used only by Samba. Samba only uses this file if you configure it to use encrypted passwords.

smbusers This is another optional file. If present, and if you configure Samba to use it, this file contains a mapping of Windows network accounts to Linux accounts. For instance, you can configure Samba to allow the user with the Windows network name TechnoM to access the Linux account galen. Chapter 15, "Managing Accounts," describes Samba's username mapping options in more detail.

lmhosts Similar in concept to the standard Linux /etc/hosts file, lmhosts provides a mapping of NetBIOS names to IP addresses. Options in the smb.conf file can enable or disable use of the lmhosts file.

In addition to these Samba configuration files, you can add your own custom configuration files. It's possible to include one configuration file inside another. You can, for instance, create custom configuration files for each user—or for specific users—and include those files in the main smb.conf file only for those specific users.

If your Samba binary is built to expect its configuration files in some location that you don't like, you can use the -s option to force the Samba daemons to look elsewhere for the smb.conf file. You can then use additional options inside smb.conf to force Samba to look in your preferred location for additional configuration files. Suppose you want Samba to look in /etc/samba-configs for configuration files. You could launch the Samba daemons with commands similar to the following:

```
# nmbd -s /etc/samba-config/smb.conf -D
# smbd -s /etc/samba-config/smb.conf -D
```

You would ordinarily include these commands in a startup script. Because most Linux distributions come with Samba startup scripts, you'd likely modify the default Samba startup script to achieve the desired effect.

Running Samba

Before you can use Samba, you have to start it. There are several ways to do this. The best way may depend upon your distribution, because most distributions include Samba startup scripts of one sort or another. As a general rule, I recommend using these startup scripts. On occasion, however, you might want to bypass the usual script, either to start Samba manually with unusual parameters for testing purposes, or to run it through inetd or a similar superserver for security or resource conservation reasons.

Running Samba Manually

To run Samba manually, start the Samba daemons from a shell prompt as root. Here are the most basic forms of the startup commands:

```
# nmbd -D
```

```
# smbd -D
```

Startup Parameters for *nmbd*

Each of the two 2.0.*x* Samba daemons supports several parameters. For nmbd, these parameters include the following:

-D Runs the program in daemon mode. This is the usual way in which to run Samba, but it's not the default.

-a When a new connection is made, appends log messages to the Samba log file for that connection. This is the default behavior.

-o Overwrites the log file for each new connection. This behavior is the opposite of the -a behavior and is not the default.

-h Displays help information for the daemon.

-v Displays the program's version number.

-H *filename* Uses *filename* as the lmhosts file.

-d *debuglevel* Sets the debug level to *debuglevel*, which must be an integer from 0 to 10. Increasing the value of *debuglevel* will increase the number of log entries. Useful values for end-users are 0–3; values above 3 are used mainly by Samba developers. I recommend using a value of 1 for day-to-day operation of Samba. The default value is 0.

-l *logfile* Sets the log file to *logfile*. In practice, Samba appends .nmb to the *logfile* name you specify. The default value depends on Samba compile-time options. Common values are

```
/var/log/samba.d/smb.nmb
```

```
/usr/samba/var/log.nmb
```

```
/var/log/log.nmb
```

-n *name* Sets the computer's NetBIOS name to *name*. This option overrides the netbios name option in the smb.conf file.

-p *port* Sets the UDP port number to which nmbd listens. The default value is 137, and unless you have some specific reason for doing so, you should not change this value.

-s *filename* Sets the configuration filename to use. This value defaults to smb.conf in a directory specified at compile time, as described in "Compiling Source from a Tarball."

-i *scope* Sets the NetBIOS scope used by nmbd. NetBIOS scopes are very rarely used, so you shouldn't have any need to change this parameter.

In most cases, you can run nmbd with only the -D option, but in a few cases you may want to add additional options. The -s option can be particularly useful if you want to experiment with a variety of different Samba configurations.

Startup Parameters for *smbd*

The second Samba daemon, smbd, sports a variety of startup parameters, most of which are identical to those of nmbd. In particular, -D, -a, -o, -h, -v, -d, -l, -p, -s, and -i have identical meanings for both nmbd and smbd (except that the default log file name uses a .smb suffix for smbd, rather than the .nmb used for nmbd). In addition, smbd supports the following options:

-P This option enables *passive mode,* in which Samba doesn't send any network traffic. Note: This feature is designed for use only by the Samba developers, and should not be confused with the -p (lowercase) option.

-O *socket options* Socket options affect the details of Samba's operation. Setting specific socket options can sometimes improve—or degrade—Samba's performance; the optimal settings vary from one network to another. You can set these options from the smb.conf file by using the socket options settings, as described in Chapter 12, "Tuning Samba for Optimum Performance;" or you can set them on the command line. Be sure not to confuse -O with -o; the two options differ only in case and meaning.

As with nmbd, you can normally run smbd using only the -D parameter. Other parameters, such as -s and -O, can be useful when you're experimenting with your Samba configuration.

Samba TNG Daemons

The latest development versions of Samba are known as The Next Generation (TNG), and the Samba TNG package includes several additional daemons. These daemons take over some of the functionality of the nmbd and smbd packages in 2.0.*x* versions of Samba, and add features needed for support of Windows NT domains. If you want to run Samba TNG or a release derived from Samba TNG, you may need to start these daemons. The daemons accept startup parameters similar to those of nmbd and smbd. Because Samba TNG is, at this writing, under active development, I recommend you run each daemon with the -h parameter to discover the options accepted by the version you have. The section "Samba TNG" in Chapter 2 tells you more about Samba TNG's features.

Essential
Configuration

PART 2

NOTE Aside from the fact that Samba TNG uses several additional daemons, its startup operation and configuration details are the same as for the 2.0.x version of Samba. You can use the same smb.conf file in Samba TNG that you use in Samba 2.0.x. Future versions of Samba may add a few additional smb.conf parameters, but old configuration files should still work.

Stopping Samba

You can stop Samba using the kill command, just as you can stop any other program. There are two ways to do this:

- Type **killall nmbd; killall smbd** to kill all instances of both nmbd and smbd, or
- Type **ps ax | grep mbd** to find all running instances of nmbd and smbd, and then issue individual **kill** commands on each instance by process ID number.

WARNING On Linux, the killall command kills all running instances of the named program. On some Unix systems, it may have other meanings. Read the killall man page before using the program, particularly on non-Linux systems.

It's best to stop the Samba daemons by sending them SIGTERM (15) signals (as in **kill -15 *idnum***), rather than SIGKILL (9) messages. The latter may leave shared memory in an inconsistent state. If you want to force the server to load new configuration settings from smb.conf, you can do so by sending the server a SIGHUP (1). Doing so protects any connected sessions from disconnection. Existing sessions maintain their current settings, but new sessions use the settings in the newly edited smb.conf file.

If your distribution uses a Samba startup script, as described in the following section, you should stop Samba by using the startup script and passing it the stop parameter. For instance:

```
# /etc/rc.d/init.d/samba stop
```

The exact location and name of the Samba start/stop script varies from one distribution to another, as you'll see next.

Common Distribution Startup Scripts

Most Linux distributions place startup scripts for daemons and other programs to be run at boot time in the /etc/rc.d directory tree. On most distributions, this directory contains a series of subdirectories called /etc/rc.d/rc1.d, /etc/rc.d/rc2.d, and so on through /etc/rc.d/rc6.d. Each subdirectory contains service start/stop scripts corresponding to specific *runlevels*. Each runlevel corresponds to a specific set of running services. For example, in Red Hat Linux (as well as many other distributions), runlevel 3 is a text-mode, multiuser boot, whereas runlevel 5 is a multiuser boot that presents an X-based graphical logon prompt.

The runlevel in which a computer runs is specified in the /etc/inittab file. This file contains a line like the following:

```
id:5:initdefault:
```

The number (5 in this case) is the runlevel of the computer. Whenever a Linux system enters a given runlevel, it runs the startup scripts in the corresponding runlevel directory under /etc/rc.d. Whenever a computer shuts down or shifts to a lower runlevel through the init command, the computer runs the scripts in the higher runlevels to shut down services that are available in higher runlevels but not in lower ones.

Startup Control

In most Linux distributions, the contents of the /etc/rc.d/rc?.d directories are actually symbolic links to scripts located elsewhere, such as in /etc/rc.d or /etc/rc.d/init.d. You can control the startup of Samba in three ways:

Editing the Startup Script   You can edit the startup script in /etc/rc.d, /etc/rc.d/init.d, or wherever it happens to be located. For instance, if you want to add specific startup parameters, as described earlier in "Running Samba Manually," you can add them to this startup script. The startup script is likely to be called samba or smb.

Creating or Deleting Links   If you want to prevent Samba from starting up, you can remove its link in the appropriate /etc/rc.d/rc?.d directory. This link is likely to have a name of the form S??samba or S??smb, where *??* is a number. The shutdown script has the same form but begins with K rather than S. Likewise, if you want to make Samba start when it doesn't do so, you can create an appropriate symbolic link.

WARNING   Be careful in numbering the Samba startup script; the numbers following the S determine the startup order. Be sure Samba starts *after* your network is brought up.

Editing a Control Script   On occasion, an additional script controls which startup scripts execute. In SuSE Linux, for example, the /etc/rc.config file contains variable assignments such as START_SMB="yes" that determine which startup scripts run when the system starts. You can edit this control script directly or leave it to GUI configuration tools such as SuSE's YaST.

Essential Configuration

PART 2

> **TIP**   If you use a Samba package designed for a distribution other than the one you're using, the Samba package's startup script may not be appropriate for your distribution. You can probably use a startup script from an earlier version of Samba for your distribution; or take a startup script designed for another daemon and modify it to run Samba on your system.

Most Samba startup scripts start both the nmbd and smbd daemons. If and when the multidaemon structure of Samba TNG makes its way into release versions of Samba, the scripts will almost certainly start all the necessary daemons.

You can use the start/stop scripts to start and stop Samba manually, by passing the script the parameters start and stop, respectively. Some scripts accept additional parameters, such as restart, which stops and then starts the daemon. If your distribution includes this feature, I recommend using these scripts rather than starting or killing Samba directly. These scripts sometimes perform small but helpful tasks in addition to starting Samba, or may pass useful parameters to the Samba daemons.

A few Linux distributions, such as Slackware, use an entirely different method of starting daemons. Rather than individual startup scripts in the /etc/rc.d directory tree, these distributions rely upon one or two monolithic startup scripts. In Slackware, the /etc/rc.d/ rc.inet1 and /etc/rc.d/rc.inet2 scripts contain commands to start daemons such as Samba. Other distributions, including those that normally use individualized daemon-starting scripts, also include general-purpose startup scripts (generally called rc.local or boot.local) somewhere in the /etc/rc.d directory tree. You might want to use such a script if you have problems with the individualized Samba startup script—say, if you've compiled Samba TNG yourself and don't want to try to modify the startup scripts to handle this version of Samba. In any event, you can add daemon startup commands similar to those described earlier in this chapter, in "Running Samba Manually."

Controlling Scripts with GUI Tools

Most Linux distributions include GUI configuration tools to help control what daemons start and stop with the system. For instance, Figure 3.2 shows the linuxconf tool that ships with Red Hat, Mandrake, and some other Linux distributions. In linuxconf, you can configure Samba to start automatically by following these steps:

1. In the left pane of the configuration window, expand Control, then Control Panel, then Control Service Activity.
2. Double-click the smb item in the list in the right pane of the window. The result is the display shown in Figure 3.2.

3. Check the Automatic box next to Startup.

4. Click Start if you want to start Samba immediately, in addition to when you reboot the computer.

5. Click Accept to implement your changes.

WARNING   Linux GUI configuration tools are sometimes quite finicky about the form of their configuration files. It's not uncommon for linuxconf to crash if you select an option that reads a configuration file you've configured by hand. When you intend to use a GUI tool, it's best if you use *only* that tool for system configuration, to avoid such problems.

Figure 3.2   linuxconf and other GUI configuration tools allow you to configure daemons to start and stop without knowing precisely where the startup files are.

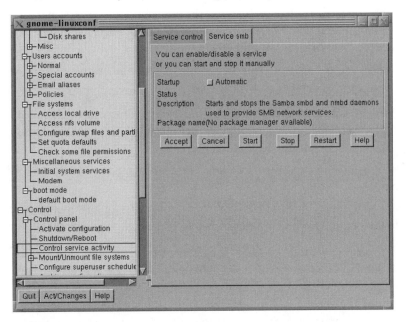

The operating details of GUI configuration tools such as linuxconf vary from one tool to another. The steps you take with another tool, such as SuSE's YaST or Caldera's COAS, will differ from those described here. In all cases, though, these utilities configure the system by editing the startup files described in this section or by creating and deleting appropriate links.

NOTE Some GUI configuration tools, including linuxconf, can run using text-mode menus in a non-GUI environment, such as a text-mode logon.

Running Samba from *inetd*

It's possible to run Samba from the inetd superserver. The advantages of running Samba through inetd or a similar package include the following:

- The server's security is improved. Particularly if you use TCP Wrappers or a more-secure inetd replacement, you can improve security for your Samba server by restricting initial connections to the server. Samba includes many security features, however, so this advantage is comparatively small if you take care in establishing your Samba configuration. Chapter 14 covers this topic in detail.

- Resources are efficiently utilized. If your Samba server is used infrequently, running Samba through inetd can minimize the impact on the server's memory. This advantage disappears, however, if it's common for one or more individuals to be connected to the Samba server at all times.

- You get central control. You may prefer, for administrative reasons, to use /etc/inetd.conf to control all your servers.

There are also substantial disadvantages to running Samba through inetd:

- You get slower response. When run through inetd, it takes time for Samba to start up whenever a request is made of it. This fact can cause annoyance on the part of users, who may expect instantaneous or near-instantaneous access to their Samba shares.

- Browsing can be unreliable. Samba servers sometimes fail to appear or respond slowly or strangely in browsing when Samba is run through inetd.

On the whole, I recommend you *not* run Samba through inetd. If the memory impact of running Samba is so substantial that you're tempted to use inetd to reduce that impact, it would probably be better to upgrade your system's RAM. The security advantages of Samba from inetd are fairly minor, and you can otherwise improve system security by using ipchains or an external firewall computer. If you try running Samba from inetd but encounter unreliable operation, try running Samba directly instead. You may find that your problems disappear.

If you must run Samba from `inetd` despite the disadvantages of doing so, follow these steps:

1. Disable any Samba startup scripts, such as those in `/etc/rc.d/rc?.d`. Kill any running Samba processes.

2. Ensure that the `/etc/services` file contains appropriate entries for all the SMB/CIFS TCP/IP ports. (Most Linux distributions ship with appropriate entries.) Specifically, the file should contain the following entries:

   ```
   netbios-ns      137/tcp    # NETBIOS Name Service
   netbios-ns      137/udp
   netbios-dgm     138/tcp    # NETBIOS Datagram Service
   netbios-dgm     138/udp
   netbios-ssn     139/tcp    # NETBIOS session service
   netbios-ssn     139/udp
   ```

3. Edit `/etc/inetd.conf` to include lines to start Samba. These lines will look something like the following:

   ```
   netbios-ssn  stream  tcp  nowait  root  /usr/sbin/tcpd smbd
   netbios-ns   dgram   udp  wait    root  /usr/sbin/tcpd nmbd
   ```

   This example shows Samba called through `tcpd`, the TCP Wrappers daemon. Some systems call `smbd` and `nmbd` directly, however. On the whole, using TCP Wrappers is usually better because it can improve security. If necessary, adjust the path to the `tcpd` or Samba daemon to match your system's configuration.

4. Find the process ID of the current instance of `inetd` by typing **ps ax | grep inetd**.

5. Send `inetd` a SIGHUP to get it to reload its configuration file. You can do this with a command such as

   ```
   # kill -SIGHUP pid
   ```

   where *pid* is the process ID revealed in step 4.

You can perform similar steps to run Samba from `inetd` replacements, such as `xinetd` (`http://synack.net/xinetd/`). The details of configuring the `inetd` replacement differ from one package to another, however.

WARNING   nmbd doesn't run well from xinetd, although smbd runs from it acceptably, and nmbd runs fine from inetd. This problem may be fixed with a future version of xinetd or Samba. In the meantime, if you want to run Samba from xinetd, you must run nmbd independently or run it from inetd, while running smbd from xinetd.

Summary

For most Linux systems, Samba installation is easy because it's done automatically during Linux installation. If you need to install Samba after the fact, you can do so most easily by using your distribution's package manager. In a few cases, however, you may want to install Samba by compiling it from source code for your own system. Doing this isn't any more complex than compiling and installing most other source code packages, but it's important that you know about critical compile-time options relating to features such as PAM support.

Running Samba is also easy to do if you stick closely to your distribution's default configuration. Many distributions give you the option of whether or not to run Samba at installation time. For others, you can set this option by editing configuration files or by using GUI configuration utilities.

4

GUI Configuration
Tools and the
smb.conf File

Τhis chapter covers the basics of Samba configuration. Samba is configured in a single file named `smb.conf` that typically resides in the `/etc`, `/etc/samba.d`, or `/usr/local/samba/lib` directory, although it might exist elsewhere on some systems.

The chapter begins with a description of configuration by direct editing of `smb.conf`. This is the most flexible means of configuring Samba, but it's also the most error prone. Next are two easier—but less flexible—methods of Samba configuration through GUI configuration tools, `linuxconf` and the *Samba Web Administration Tool (SWAT)*. Finally, a few of the key general-purpose configuration options are described. These options don't relate to specific file or printer shares but are important for the server as a whole.

Editing *smb.conf* to Configure Samba

The `smb.conf` file lies at the core of Samba configuration. It's therefore critically important that you understand how to manipulate this file to achieve the configuration you desire. If you're new to Samba and are more comfortable with GUI configuration tools, you may not want to edit `smb.conf` directly but instead use a tool such as `linuxconf` or

SWAT. I recommend you learn at least the basics of `smb.conf` configuration, though, because doing so can help you understand what the GUI tools do.

In most of this book, configuration options are described in terms of `smb.conf` features. SWAT uses the same terms, and `linuxconf` generally uses similar terms, so you should have no problem locating an option in a GUI tool based on the descriptions in this book—if the option exists in the GUI tool. Bear in mind that `linuxconf`, in particular, lacks many features available by direct editing of `smb.conf`.

Structure of the *smb.conf* File

A very minimal `smb.conf` file looks like Listing 4.1. This basic file is perfectly functional and produces a usable Samba server, at least on some networks—indeed, it's *more* than what's needed for minimal functionality. It demonstrates some key features of `smb.conf`.

Listing 4.1   A Simple `smb.conf` File

```
[global]
        workgroup = RINGWORLD
        hosts allow = 192.168.1. 192.168.2.23


[homes]
        comment = Home Directories
        writeable = Yes
        browseable = No
```

Each share begins with the share name (for example, `[global]` in Listing 4.1) and ends with the beginning of the next share name (`[homes]` in Listing 4.1) or the end of the file, whichever comes first. As you'll see, Samba is quite liberal in its handling of the `smb.conf` file's format. It doesn't care about case, and it's quite tolerant of whitespace—blank lines, spaces, and tabs. Most people (and most GUI tools for Samba configuration) format shares as it's done in Listing 4.1, with parameters indented for ease of reading.

Types of *smb.conf* Entries

The three main types of entries in the `smb.conf` file are share names, parameters, and comments.

Share Names   The names in brackets—`[global]` and `[homes]` in Listing 4.1—are *share names*. These names mark the beginnings of *share definitions,* each of which sets up a configuration for a single shared resource such as a directory or printer accessible through Samba. The [global] share is special because it sets defaults for all shares, and establishes global configuration options that apply to the server as a whole.

Parameters   Each Samba *parameter* is a variable name, such as workgroup or writeable in Listing 4.1. The parameter can be assigned a value, such as RINGWORLD or Yes. Parameters and their values

- Can contain spaces; the parameter is separated from its value by an equals sign (=).
- Are case-insensitive; workgroup is equivalent to WORKGROUP. There is an exception to this rule: Some values may be case-sensitive because the value refers to something that is itself case-sensitive. For instance, if the parameter is a pathname or filename on the Linux server, that parameter is case-sensitive because Linux treats filenames in a case-sensitive way.

Comments   Comments begin with pound signs (#) or semicolons (;). Any text on a line after one of these characters is ignored by Samba. Comments allow you to document your intent in creating a share or setting an option, particularly if you try something that's subtle and might be misinterpreted later.

You can also use comments to temporarily remove shares or parameters from the smb.conf file. When you comment out a share, you must add a comment character to the beginning of *every* line of the share—the share name and *all* its parameters. If you miss a parameter, it will become part of the previous share's definition.

NOTE   There's also a comment parameter, which sets text that can be associated with a share and viewed from client computers.

TIP   A simpler way to disable a share is to use the available = No parameter. Doing this makes the share disappear from browse lists and disables access to the share.

Parameter Values

Although the basic format of the smb.conf file appears fairly simple, you can create very complex configurations with this file. This is in part because the smb.conf file supports a large number of parameters. (The most important parameters are covered in detail throughout the rest of the book, and they're summarized in Appendix A, "Configuration

Reference Guide.") The values you assign to parameters can themselves add to the complexity of the file, however. These parameters and their values can take several forms, as explained in the following sections.

Strings   A *string* is a set of characters—generally numbers and letters, and sometimes punctuation, spaces, and so on. (You don't need to do anything special to include spaces in a value, but if you like, you can enclose the entire string in quotation marks.) In some sense, all values are strings; but some values are interpreted in special ways.

Some characters carry special meaning, such as quotation marks surrounding a string (which are ignored by Samba) or comment characters, which cause Samba to ignore the rest of the line. The backslash character (\ ) also merits mention; it allows you to continue a string on the next line. You might use this if you want to include a long list of options, such as computer names, and you want to keep the lines in the file shorter than 80 columns.

Lists   A *list* is a set of several values, separated by commas or spaces. In Listing 4.1, the hosts allow parameter is assigned a list of two values: 192.168.1. and 192.168.2.23. As described in Chapter 14, "Samba Security Considerations," this hosts allow option tells Samba to accept connections only from computers on the 192.168.1.0 network and from 192.168.2.23. The trailing period in 192.168.1. is vital for specifying the entire 192.168.1.0 network, but it's not required to separate items in the list. In some cases (explained within the parameter discussions in the relevant chapters of this book), you may use only a comma or only a space, but not either, to separate values in a list.

Booleans   A *boolean* value can accept either of two values. These can be specified as Yes, True, or 1 for the positive condition; or No, False, or 0 for the negative. The writeable and browseable parameters in Listing 4.1 are both booleans.

Variables   Samba supports variables in parameter values. Variables can be used to adjust configuration details on a share-by-share or user-by-user basis. In Samba, variables are preceded by percent signs (%). Table 4.1 summarizes the variables that Samba supports.

Table 4.1   Variables Recognized by Samba

Variable	Meaning
%a	Client's operating system (architecture); can be OS2 (OS/2), Samba, UNKNOWN, WfWg (Windows for Workgroups or DOS), Win2K (Windows 2000), Win95 (Windows 95 or 98), or WinNT (Windows NT).
%d	Server's process ID

Table 4.1   Variables Recognized by Samba *(continued)*

Variable	Meaning
%g	Primary group of %u
%G	Primary group of %U
%h	Server's DNS name
%H	Home directory of %u
%I	Client's IP address
%L	Server's NetBIOS name
%m	Client's NetBIOS name
%M	Client's DNS name
%N	NIS home directory server
%p	Path to the share's root directory, if automounted
%P	Path to the share's root directory
%R	Negotiated SMB protocol level; can be CORE, COREPLUS, LANMAN1, LANMAN2, or NT1
%S	Share name
%T	Current date and time
%u	Effective Linux username
%U	Requested username (might not be the same as %u)
%v	Samba version

Some of these variables are undefined at particular points in time. For instance, until you've accessed a share, %u is undefined. That's because this value can be set by, say, a force user parameter. %U, by contrast, is the username sent when negotiating the session, and so is available before accessing particular shares, but not before logging onto the server. You can use variables to achieve many interesting effects. For instance:

- Create separate log files for each client by using the `log file` parameter, as in `log file = /var/log/samba/log.smb.%m`.

- Create share options that are customized for specific users, machines, or client OSs by using the `include` parameter, as in `include = /etc/samba.d/smb.conf.%a`.

- Create shares that are customized for specific users, machines, or groups, by using the `path` parameter, as in `path = /home/samba/%G` to create a share for particular groups. (Note that this particular example would not work with the lowercase `%g` option, because that value is undefined until after the share is accessed.)

NOTE   Certain special shares perform such substitutions automatically, as described just below in "Privileged Shares."

- Display information on the current host in a share's comment or elsewhere, as in `server string = Samba server on %h`.

Privileged Shares

Samba recognizes a few share names as having privileged status.

[global]   This share, as mentioned earlier in "Types of `smb.conf` Entries," isn't a share in the same sense as most others. Rather, it's a placeholder for default and global configuration options. Some parameters can be used in the [global] share and nowhere else.

[homes]   This share maps to each user's home directory. By default, when viewing a Samba server, a user sees his or her own home directory and no others. (Users can still access other users' home directories, within the limits of permissions and Samba settings, by directly entering the share name rather than browsing to the share.) File shares are discussed in Chapter 5, "Configuring File Sharing."

[printers]   This share name expands into one entry for each printer defined in the server's /etc/printcap file. Printer shares are discussed in Chapter 6, "Configuring Printer Sharing."

[netlogon]   Windows computers try to access this share when logging onto a Samba server. If the share is present and properly configured, the client tries to run the batch file specified by the `logon script` parameter. This procedure allows you to create some uniform set of options for all your systems, or run logon scripts that are unique for each user (say, by specifying `logon script = %U.bat`). The available possibilities are discussed in Chapter 8, "Automation."

All other shares are ordinary file or printer shares. Unless you use variables to restrict access to some users, all users see the same files in these shares, or can access a printer share in identical ways.

Keeping Your Configuration File Readable

The `smb.conf` file can easily become unreadable, particularly if you rely upon Samba's willingness to parse files without respect to whitespace, and if you take advantage of the option to use multiple synonyms for many parameters. Here are a few simple steps you can take to help keep your `smb.conf` file uncluttered and understandable:

Be consistent. No matter how you decide to format your file, apply your formatting consistently. Inconsistent formatting can make the file difficult to parse.

Indent parameters. Follow the usual convention of indenting parameters, but do not indent share names. This practice makes it easy to locate shares when examining the configuration file.

Use comments. Although most Samba parameters are designed to be self-documenting, you can use comments to describe who *should* be able to access a share, what a variable means, and so on. It's easy to mistakenly create a share that's accessible by the wrong collection of users or that otherwise doesn't work in quite the way you intended. If you document your intent, it becomes easier to identify errors later.

> **WARNING**   The SWAT GUI configuration tool, described later in this chapter, obliterates any comments you place in the `smb.conf` file.

Use consistent parameter names. Many parameters have synonyms, and some have antonyms (mostly booleans that can be expressed one way with one parameter and the other way with another). Use just one name. Doing otherwise can cause confusion in the future, because it's easy to forget that the two names are synonymous.

Testing Your Configuration File

If you build your `smb.conf` file by hand, it's easy to make a mistake that renders the file unusable. You can use the `testparm` program to check that the file is logically correct, as in this example:

```
# testparm /etc/smb.conf
```

Essential Configuration

PART 2

If the file is logically correct, `testparm` responds by displaying output similar to the following:

```
Load smb config files from /etc/smb.conf

Processing section "[homes]"

Processing section "[printers]"

Loaded services file OK.

Press enter to see a dump of your service definitions
```

The `testparm` program identifies each of the shares in the `smb.conf` file, and you can verify that it's identified all the shares that you think it should. Press the Enter key to see your share definitions (what `testparm` calls *service definitions*), stripped of comments and unnecessary formatting details.

If there's a problem, however, `testparm` will identify it, thus:

```
Load smb config files from smb.conf

Unknown parameter encountered: "netbos name"

Ignoring unknown parameter "netbos name"

Processing section "[homes]"

Processing section "[printers]"

Loaded services file OK.

Press enter to see a dump of your service definitions
```

This output tells you that the `smb.conf` file included a misspelling: `netbos name` instead of `netbios name`. The `testparm` program has identified this misspelling as an "unknown parameter" and has further informed you that it's ignoring the parameter. Of course, you should correct the matter before using the defective file.

Using Red Hat's *linuxconf* to Configure Samba

Red Hat Linux is one of the most popular and influential Linux distributions. In addition to widespread use in its "pure" form, Red Hat Linux has spawned an assortment of spin-off distributions, including Linux Mandrake (http://www.mandrake.com), LinuxPPC (http://www.linuxppc.com), and Yellow Dog Linux (http://www.yellowdoglinux .com/ydl_home.html). All of these distributions ship with a GUI configuration tool called `linuxconf`. Operation details differ somewhat from one distribution to another, but the core of `linuxconf` remains the same. It allows you to administer your Linux computer using a text-based menu-driven tool, an X-based tool, or via a Web browser (even from a non-Linux computer). Figure 4.1 shows the main linuxconf configuration options for Samba, as displayed from Netscape Communicator in Windows 2000.

Figure 4.1   You can administer a linuxconf-equipped computer from any computer that hosts a Web browser.

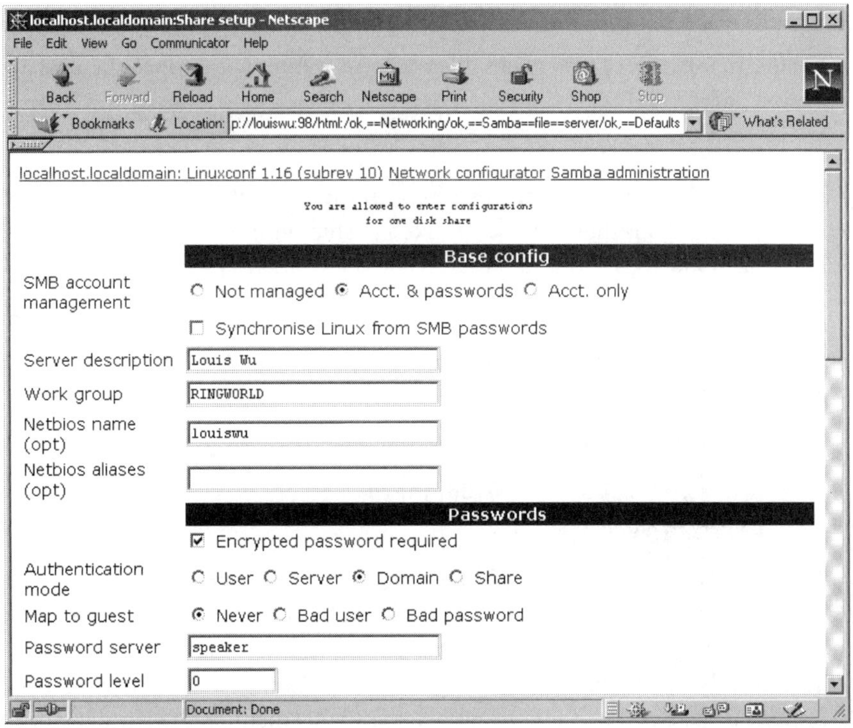

NOTE   Through version 6.2, Red Hat included a linuxconf module for Samba. This module has been dropped with Red Hat 7.0, however. The instructions in this chapter still apply to other distributions that use linuxconf, including LinuxPPC and Linux Mandrake.

Using *linuxconf* Locally or Remotely

If you're already familiar with linuxconf configuration for your system, you may want to try using it for Samba configuration. To use linuxconf locally, type **linuxconf** at a shell prompt. If you do this while Linux is running in text mode, you'll get linuxconf's text-mode interface; if you're running X and you type the command in an xterm or other command-prompt window, you'll get the main GUI version of the utility. You shouldn't need to issue any special configuration commands to make linuxconf accessible in either of these ways.

To access linuxconf from a networked computer, first configure the linuxconf server to accept remote access. To do so, follow these steps:

1. Ensure that the /etc/services file contains a line that defines the port used by linuxconf:

    ```
    linuxconf 98/tcp
    ```

2. Likewise, a linuxconf entry must exist in the computer's /etc/inetd.conf file. Most distributions that include linuxconf ship with the appropriate entry enabled, but you should verify that it's there. The relevant entry is

    ```
    linuxconf stream tcp wait root /bin/linuxconf linuxconf --http
    ```

3. If you need to add the linuxconf entry to /etc/inetd.conf, restart the inetd daemon. For instance:

    ```
    # ps ax | grep inetd
      379 ?         S       0:00 inetd
    # kill -SIGHUP 379
    ```

4. At this point, linuxconf should be running, and in such a way that it accepts network connections but promptly drops them. In order for this arrangement to be useful, you must add some extra options. The easiest way to do this is to use linuxconf itself locally. First, start linuxconf, and select Config ➢ Networking ➢ Misc ➢ Linuxconf Network Access from the expandable menu in the left pane in Figure 4.2.

NOTE   Not all linuxconf utilities look precisely like the one shown in Figure 4.2. Linux Mandrake, in particular, uses a graphical menu system rather than the expandable lists shown here in the left pane. The program's functionality is the same, however.

Figure 4.2   You can enable remote `linuxconf` access through `linuxconf` itself.

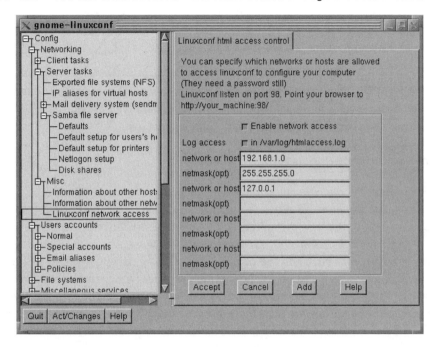

5. Click the Enable network access button in the right-hand pane. Then make the following entries, as shown in Figure 4.2:

   A. In the first Network or Host field in the right pane, enter the IP address of the *network* to which you want to grant `linuxconf` access. Note that this is a *network* address; it ends in `.0`.

   B. In the first Netmask (opt) field, enter the network mask of the network to which you want to grant `linuxconf` access.

   C. In the next Network or Host field, enter **127.0.0.1** (the `localhost` loopback address). This step grants you access from your own computer, independent of your main network connections.

6. Click Accept in the right-hand panel.

7. Click Quit in the `linuxconf` window. The program responds by informing you that the system state doesn't match what you've configured.

8. Click the Activate the Changes button to make your changes current. After a brief pause, `linuxconf` disappears.

Instead of entering a network address (steps 5a and 5b just above), you can enter the IP addresses of specific computers that are to have linuxconf access. Do this in the same manner as you entered the 127.0.0.1 address in step 5c. As a general rule, the fewer computers to which you grant access, the better.

> **WARNING**   linuxconf is itself a network server. When accessed from a remote Web browser, it requires that you send an administrative password in cleartext across the network. I therefore recommend against using linuxconf remotely except when absolutely necessary. Ideally, you should do so only from the local network on which the server itself resides.

Once linuxconf is running and configured to accept remote access, you can use it by typing **http://*servername*:98** into a remote browser's URL entry field, where *servername* is the hostname of the server. You'll first see a general introductory page with a Start button. When you click this button, linuxconf asks for your username and password. Normally, you can enter **root** and the root password, respectively, for these options. If you've configured your system to allow other users access to linuxconf, you can type those usernames and passwords instead. At this point, you can browse the linuxconf menu structure by clicking on links in the browser until you find a configuration page (see Figure 4.1).

A Tour of *linuxconf* Samba Options

The main Samba configuration options are listed under Config ➤ Networking ➤ Server Tasks ➤ Samba File Server. There are five sets of linuxconf Samba configuration options: Defaults, Default Setup for Users' Home, Default Setup for Printers, Netlogon Setup, and Disk Shares. They're described briefly in the following paragraphs, but for details you should consult the appropriate chapters of this book.

Defaults

Figure 4.1 shows the Defaults options, as seen through a Web-based linuxconf interface. These options relate to the settings in the [global] area of the smb.conf file. Following are descriptions of some critical options. (Others, which govern comparatively advanced features, are described in various chapters throughout the book.)

Server Description   This sets a comment parameter for the [global] share. Unfortunately, the parameter doesn't do much. That's because for servers, it's the server string parameter that must be set to adjust the Comment field as seen from a Windows client. This bug may be fixed in a future version of linuxconf.

Work Group   This field sets the workgroup parameter. As described later in the section "Server Identification," this parameter is critically important if your computers are to see one another properly.

NetBIOS Name and NetBIOS Aliases   These fields set the primary NetBIOS name and aliases for the computer. By default, Samba takes these values from the computer's hostname, but you can set them here explicitly.

Encrypted Password Required   Check this box if you want to use encrypted passwords on your network. Encrypted passwords are described later in the section "Password Encryption."

Authentication Mode   As a general rule, User is the best authentication mode to employ for a Samba server. If your network uses a domain rather than a workgroup as described in Chapter 1, then you may want to use the Server or Domain Authentication modes. You must then enter the NetBIOS name of the primary domain controller in the Password Server field. If you want Samba to emulate Windows 9*x*'s share-by-share access controls, you can use the Share authentication method, but this generally creates a lot of administrative headaches. These options are discussed in Chapter 14.

Allow Hosts and Deny Hosts   In these fields, discussed in Chapter 14, you can enter the names or IP addresses of hosts to be explicitly allowed and denied.

Show All Available Printers   If you enable this option, Samba creates shares for all the printers listed in your /etc/printcap file. Otherwise, you must create printer shares individually for each printer.

Default Setup for Users' Home

Figure 4.3 shows the linuxconf configuration panel that is used to configure the [homes] share. As mentioned earlier, the [homes] share defines a file share that changes dynamically for each user. Specifically, it allows each user access to his or her own home directory. Details you can configure through linuxconf include the following:

Comment/Description   The string you enter here appears as a comment field when you browse the share in Windows.

This Share Is Enabled   Check this box if you want to enable access to home directories. To disable these shares, leave the box unmarked.

Browsable   Unlike most shares, the [homes] share does *not* need to be browseable. You should therefore leave this item disabled. If you turn it on, users will see two identical shares, one called homes and one with the user's username.

Access Options   In this tab you can apply allow hosts and deny hosts rules to individual shares, just as you can to Samba as a whole.

Users Click the Users tab to set options relating to individual users. You can set lists of read-only and read/write users, lists of users who may or may not connect to the share, and the maximum number of simultaneous connections Samba accepts to the share.

Scripts You can configure scripts that Samba runs when a user first connects, and when the user disconnects. These options are described in Chapter 8.

Figure 4.3   linuxconf provides the means to edit users' home shares.

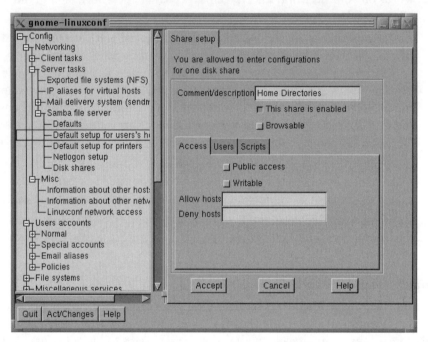

As a general rule, leaving the home accounts' configuration options set at their defaults yields a usable set of shares, one for each user. You may want to edit these options if you need to restrict access to user shares, perform some username or scripting magic, or disable user account access entirely.

Default Setup for Printers

The printer setup options are quite simple, containing only three editable options.

Comment/Description As with home directories, you can enter a string to describe the printer in greater detail. Because this is the default printer setup, which exports all printers in your /etc/printcap file, this field isn't terribly useful for distinguishing one printer from another.

This Share Is Enabled   Check this box if you want to share all the printers in your /etc/printcap file. To share some, but not all, of your printers, you must create a separate share for each printer you want to share.

Public Access   Enable this option if you want to allow anybody to print to your shared printers, without requiring a password.

The default options used by linuxconf set up sharing for all your printers. There are a variety of additional options you can use with printer shares, but linuxconf doesn't give you access to these options. If you want to configure your printer shares more extensively, you must use SWAT (described shortly) or do manual configuration. Advanced printer configuration options are discussed in Chapter 6.

Netlogon Setup

If you want to create a [netlogon] share, linuxconf can create one for you. Figure 4.4 shows the relevant linuxconf module. Here are brief descriptions of the options you can set; see Chapters 8 and 10 for details on these features.

Netlogon Share Title   The default name for the share is netlogon, but you can change it by specifying another value here.

This Share Is Enabled   Check this box to enable the share.

Directory to Export   Enter the directory you want to use as the netlogon directory. This can be any directory on the computer.

Workgroup Logon Server   This option enables the domain logons parameter, which lets Samba function as a domain controller. To fully activate this functionality, though, you need to specify additional parameters as described in Chapter 10, "Configuring Domains."

Logon Script   You can specify the name of a script for the client to run when it accesses the netlogon share.

Logon Path   You can specify the directory in which Linux stores Windows profiles, which are critical Windows configuration files.

Logon Drive   This is the Windows drive letter (for instance, M:) to which the logon home directory is mapped. This option affects *only* Windows NT clients.

Logon Home   This is the Windows network path to the user's home directory.

Essential Configuration

PART 2

Figure 4.4 Creating basic [netlogon] share information in linuxconf is easy.

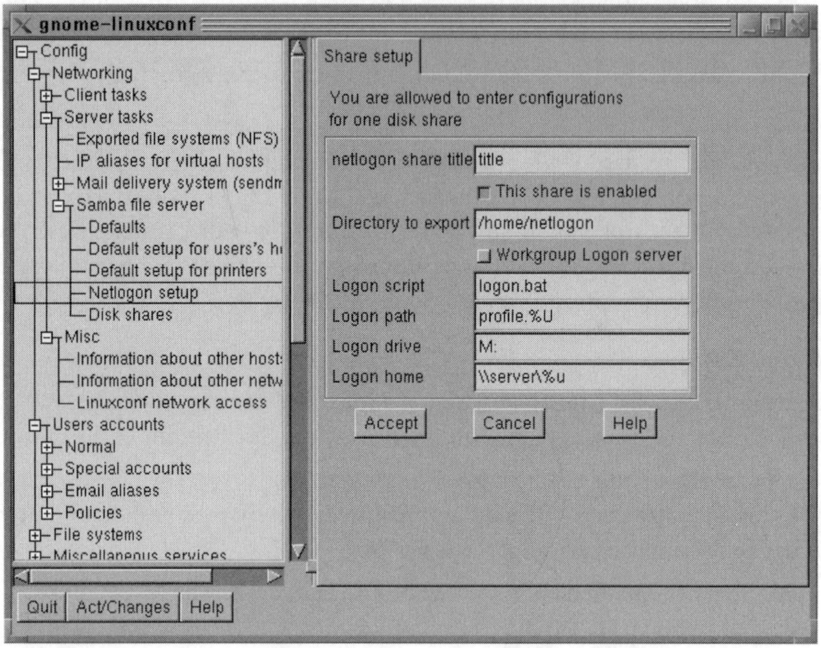

Disk Shares

The Disk Shares configuration screen presents a list of the defined disk shares, excluding the [homes] definition. You can double-click an existing definition to edit it, or click Add to create a new one. When you do so, linuxconf presents the options shown in Figure 4.5, and you can then enter the definition for a disk share. Normally, you use this panel to create a share for housing the program or data files that will be accessible to a group of people on your network.

Figure 4.5   More options are available for individual shares than for home shares (compare Figure 4.3).

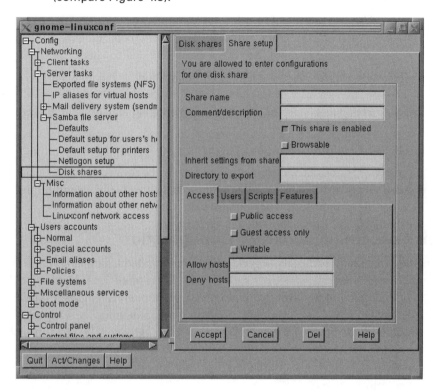

Options in the Disk Shares configuration screen include the following:

Share Name   This is the name used to identify the share.

Comment/Description   This is the comment field visible from Windows when browsing a computer's shares.

This Share Is Enabled   Check this box to make the share usable.

Browsable   If you leave this option turned off, users won't see the share in the list of shares for the computer, although they can still access the share by entering its name directly in the Address field of a Windows file browser.

Inherit Settings from Share   This setting uses the `copy` parameter to copy parameters from an existing share. You can then modify or add parameters as required to achieve the desired effect.

Directory to Export   Enter the name of the directory that will serve as the root of the exported share.

Access   Use this tab to define which computers can access the share. You can restrict access machine by machine with the Allow Hosts and Deny Hosts fields, and set options relating to public and guest access. Be sure to check the Writable option if you want users to be able to write to the share.

Users   Set user-by-user access control options on this tab, including a list of the users granted access and the per-user restrictions on read and write access.

Scripts   Use this tab to set scripts that Samba runs when the share is accessed and when the share is closed by the client.

Features   Options here include the ability to force connection as a particular Linux user or group, a per-share guest account specification, and a limit on the allowed number of simultaneous connections to the share.

Tips Concerning *linuxconf* Configuration

Using the `linuxconf` package is a good way to set up a basic Samba server, but it has its limits. Most importantly, it doesn't provide full access to all Samba options. Therefore, you may find that you have to use another tool, such as SWAT or text-based editing, to create the configuration that's precisely correct for your situation. The `linuxconf` printer-share handling is particularly deficient: You cannot use `linuxconf` to create printer-by-printer customizations to printer shares; and you don't get access to important printer options such as `postscript`, which can help solve problems created by some Windows PostScript printer drivers.

The `linuxconf` program doesn't understand all the synonyms and antonyms provided by Samba. For instance, `read only` is an antonym for `writable`; you can specify that a share be read-only by using either `read only = Yes` or `writable = No`. (Samba also accepts `writeable` as a synonym for `writable`.) If you create a share by hand and use `read only = Yes` or `writeable = No`, however, `linuxconf` doesn't pick up this option. Instead, it preserves any parameters it doesn't understand, which means you can safely use the utility to adjust the features it *does* understand—even on shares that use advanced features. The drawback is that you cannot eliminate a feature that `linuxconf` does understand if you created it using a form that `linuxconf` *doesn't* understand. You can't remove the `read only = Yes` parameter, for instance. You can, however, select the appropriate option to add a `writable = Yes` parameter, which `linuxconf` inserts after the existing `read only = Yes` parameter. Samba generally uses the last such parameter, so the effect is the same—

but the result can be confusing should you later read the smb.conf file in its raw form. As a result of its preserving options it doesn't understand, linuxconf also preserves any comments you may have inserted into the smb.conf file.

Most linuxconf installations do not, by default, accept remote logons via a Web browser, and I recommend that you do not change this to enable remote access. Indeed, you may want to tighten security further by commenting out the linuxconf line in /etc/inetd.conf and restarting inetd. Doing this will prevent crackers from exploiting any network access bugs that might be discovered in linuxconf in the future. The section "Limiting SWAT Access" later in this chapter includes information on tightening security around SWAT. Most of these techniques can be applied equally well to networked linuxconf access.

WARNING Lest you think nobody would bother trying to break into a system through linuxconf, consider this: My firewall software has recorded multiple attempts to access my Linux computer through linuxconf. Because that particular system doesn't run linuxconf at all, these access attempts have been unsuccessful.

Unfortunately, linuxconf sometimes crashes when it encounters errors in the configuration files it's designed to manipulate. Occasionally it crashes even on valid configuration files. For instance, while writing this chapter, I discovered that linuxconf on one of my systems (a Macintosh running LinuxPPC 2000 with Samba 2.0.7) crashed whenever I tried to access the Samba Defaults configuration module—no matter how simple the smb.conf file. Another computer (an $x86$ machine running Mandrake 7.0 with Samba 2.0.6) handled this same situation just fine. So if linuxconf crashes mysteriously, configure Samba manually or use another tool, such as SWAT.

Using SWAT to Configure Samba

The *Samba Web Administration Tool (SWAT)* is a standard part of Samba, although it's not required for normal Samba operation. If you require remote Samba administration but don't need remote access to other Linux configuration options, management with SWAT is less of a threat to the security of your system than with linuxconf because SWAT provides direct administrative access to fewer Linux features.

SWAT is a very network-centric configuration tool. In addition, it gives you comprehensive access to Samba features and is less finicky about the state of the smb.conf file. When used as a network administration tool, though, SWAT does allow a possible way in for would-be crackers. There are ways to restrict access to a particular group of machines, however. SWAT also requires an administrative password (such as root's) to function.

Initial SWAT Configuration

Configuring SWAT is similar to configuring linuxconf for network access. First, check /etc/inetd.conf. It should contain a line similar to the following:

```
swat  stream  tcp  nowait.400  root  /usr/sbin/swat swat
```

If this line isn't present or is commented out, add it or uncomment it.

Also ensure that the following line is present in the /etc/services file on the server:

```
swat              901/tcp
```

Once both these files are configured correctly, restart inetd using the process ID based upon the output of the ps command, as follows:

```
# ps ax | grep inetd
  379 ?         S        0:00 inetd
# kill -SIGHUP 379
```

When this is done, SWAT will be running on your computer and will be accessible from any system that can access port 901 on the server.

To use SWAT, open a Web browser and enter **http://*servername*:901** into the browser's URL field (*servername* is the DNS name or IP address of the Samba server). If all works well, SWAT asks you for a password, as shown here:

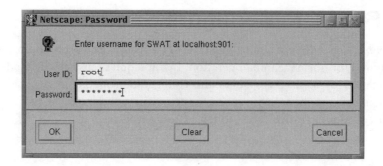

Enter a correct administrative username and password to get SWAT to display its main page (Figure 4.6). From here you can access all the SWAT configuration options, which are described shortly. As with remote access to linuxconf, you can access SWAT from any OS that supports a Web browser—Linux, Windows, MacOS, BeOS, and even DOS.

Figure 4.6   SWAT configuration options are divided into several groups similar to those used by linuxconf.

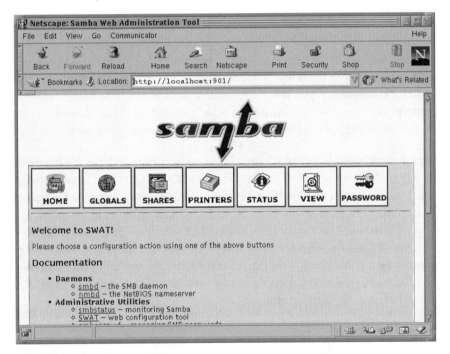

Limiting SWAT Access

I strongly recommend that you take steps to limit access to SWAT. There are several ways to do this, some of which are described in the following sections. As a general rule, TCP Wrappers can be a good starting point for limiting access to SWAT. If your Samba server is accessible from the Internet as a whole, you may do well to add an external firewall to your network; or at least use ipchains to block access to the SWAT port (901) from outside your local network. The more barriers you can put up, the better, even if they're redundant—a bug in one security tool can be blocked by another tool that serves a similar function.

Passwords

You must have a Linux password to gain access to SWAT. Normally, you must enter a user ID of root and the root password; however, if permissions on the smb.conf file allow other users to write to that file, these users can use SWAT to modify Samba's configuration. Users without write access to smb.conf can use SWAT to check the server's status, examine the smb.conf file (if it's readable to the user), and change passwords. Take care to protect the root password, or any other password that can be used to modify the Samba configuration.

> **WARNING** SWAT accepts passwords transmitted in cleartext, so depending upon your network configuration, your passwords may be "sniffed" by users of your local network. If you use SWAT from a remote location, packet sniffers on intervening computers might also be able to snatch your password. I therefore recommend *strongly* against using SWAT from remote computers.

You might be tempted to create a special Samba account, and change the ownership of smb.conf to that account. You could then use SWAT to edit smb.conf without sending the root password in cleartext. On the surface, this would seem to increase system security. Given the power of Samba, however, this practice isn't much of an improvement over passing the root password in cleartext. A cracker who gains access to the smb.conf file can quickly acquire root access by exporting the /etc directory with root privileges, thus allowing a miscreant to edit the sensitive /etc/passwd and /etc/shadow files. The Samba daemons themselves must be run as root to function fully, so using a non-root user to edit smb.conf affords little protection.

External Firewalls

If your local network has a firewall computer, configure it to block access to port 901. Doing so prevents outsiders from accessing SWAT.

Local `ipchains`

`ipchains` is Linux's packet filter tool. Use it to block access to port 901 on the local server computer, except from approved locations. Suppose you want to administer Samba from the server itself (`localhost`, or `127.0.0.1`) and from another computer with an IP address of `192.168.3.23`. The following `ipchains` commands will allow that configuration:

```
# ipchains -A input -p tcp -s 127.0.0.1 901 -j ACCEPT
# ipchains -A input -p tcp -s 192.168.3.23 901 -j ACCEPT
# ipchains -A input -p tcp -s 0/0 901 -j DENY
```

> **NOTE** For more information on ipchains, read the Linux ipchains HOWTO document. Work is underway on the Linux 2.3.x kernels to update Linux's packet filters. For the 2.3.x and later kernels, a new tool known as iptables will replace ipchains. If you're using one of these later kernels, you may need to adjust the preceding commands to match the needs of iptables.

TCP Wrappers

You can run SWAT through TCP Wrappers by replacing the call to /usr/sbin/swat in the /etc/inetd.conf file with a call to /usr/sbin/tcpd. Then use the usual TCP Wrappers controls in /etc/hosts.deny and /etc/hosts.allow to restrict access to SWAT. Using the same example as for ipchains just above, to restrict access to SWAT to localhost and 192.168.3.23 you'd create an /etc/hosts.deny file that contains the following entry:

```
swat: ALL EXCEPT 192.168.3.23 127.0.0.1
```

Additional Controls

Other network security tools can be useful in restricting access to SWAT. For instance, xinetd, a replacement for the inetd/TCP Wrappers combination, can restrict access based on the Ethernet card on which a request arrives. TCP Wrappers and xinetd both offer advanced options that can be used to allow only particular users access to servers running on the computer.

Logging Out

SWAT contains no explicit means to log out of the tool. It's therefore important that you exit from your Web browser when you've finished using SWAT. If you fail to do this and then leave your computer unattended, another individual can use your Web browser to reconfigure Samba.

A Tour of SWAT Options

SWAT options are arranged in seven groups: Home, Globals, Shares, Printers, Status, View, and Password (see Figure 4.6). Some of these groups control features similar to those controlled by the linuxconf Samba groups, but SWAT goes beyond linuxconf. You'll find descriptions of the additional options later in this section and throughout the rest of the book.

In all the SWAT configuration pages that allow you to change options, there's a button called Commit Changes. You must click this button to have SWAT write your changes to the smb.conf file.

Home

The Home configuration group (shown in Figure 4.6) is the first view you get through SWAT after entering a username and password. From this page you can jump to Samba documentation, including the Samba man pages and miscellaneous additional files. You can also select any of the six other configuration groups.

Globals

The Globals group allows you to set configuration options that go in the [global] section of the smb.conf file. Figure 4.7 shows the Globals configuration page.

Figure 4.7 In SWAT you use HTML features such as buttons and text entry fields to enter configuration options.

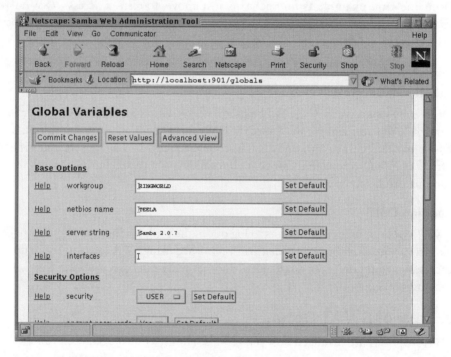

The primary Globals options are the same as those you can set from the Defaults configuration page in linuxconf: Samba's NetBIOS name, workgroup, security mode, and so on. Other [global] options are described later in the section "Important General Configuration Options," and in later chapters, particularly in Part 3, "Advanced Configurations."

> **TIP** By default, SWAT shows only the most commonly used Samba configuration options. On the Globals, Shares, and Printers pages, you can click the Advanced View button to see the more esoteric options.

The Globals page isn't available when you access SWAT as an ordinary user.

Shares

You define file shares from the Shares page. SWAT shows only a handful of options when you first open this page. You must do one of two things to see additional share options:

- Type a share name into the text entry field and click Create Share. This creates a new share with the name you've specified, and allows you to edit that share.
- Select an existing share from the list box and click Choose Share to display the share's present configuration and to edit that configuration.

> **NOTE** When using the first method, do *not* enclose the share name in square brackets ([]) as you do when editing the smb.conf file in a text editor. SWAT will add the brackets itself.

linuxconf uses one configuration panel to set up the [homes] share and a different panel for all other file shares. SWAT, by contrast, uses the same Shares page to configure both. The options you can set for file shares are similar to those available in linuxconf, but they're arranged differently. Chapter 5 covers most of these options in greater detail, and some are discussed in other chapters later in the book.

The Shares page isn't available when you access SWAT as an ordinary user.

Printers

SWAT provides much finer control over printer shares than does linuxconf. In SWAT you can adjust settings of individual printers, not just control all printer shares as a monolithic set. SWAT also gives you access to all of Samba's printer configuration parameters. These allow you to restrict access to printer shares, adjust the commands Samba uses to spool print jobs, and so on. Printer configuration options are discussed in Chapter 6.

The Printers page isn't available when you access SWAT as an ordinary user.

Essential Configuration

PART 2

Status

The Status page allows you to view and adjust the status of the Samba server. Some key features of this page include the following:

Stop, Start, and Restart Daemons   Depending upon the current status of the Samba daemons, you can stop, start, or restart the daemons (see Figure 4.8). SWAT provides this functionality separately for each daemon.

Kill Individual Connections   You can terminate individual connections from the Active Connections table at the bottom of Figure 4.8. This feature is useful when you need to terminate a connection in order to unmount a filesystem.

Active Shares   The Active Shares area (not visible in Figure 4.8) shows the connections to the server. You can also see this information in the Active Connections table, but with less information than in the Active Shares table.

Open Files   Also at the bottom of the Status page (again, not seen in Figure 4.8) is a list of open files. This information is helpful when you need to locate the user of an open file, perhaps in order to close the file or terminate the connection because you need to unmount a filesystem. To do so, check the PID column in this table, locate that PID in the Active Connections table, and kill that connection.

Figure 4.8   You can control the Samba daemons and connections from the Status page of SWAT.

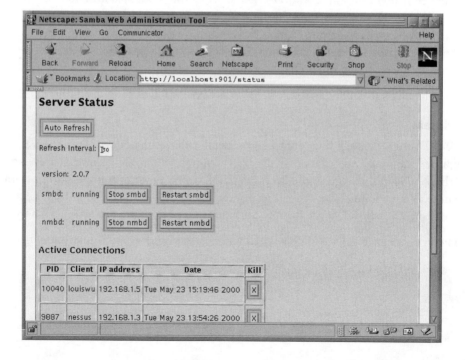

When you access SWAT as an ordinary user, you can view all the information presented on this page, but you cannot change any of it; SWAT doesn't give you the necessary buttons to effect changes.

View

The View page displays the smb.conf file's contents as text. Normally, SWAT shows you an edited version of the file; it's missing the commands that are unset—that is, those that rely upon their default values. You can click the Full View button near the top of the page to display the entire file, including all default values. You cannot use this page to modify the smb.conf file, however; if you want to tweak the configuration by hand, you must use a text editor to do the job.

You can use the View page as either an ordinary user or as an administrative user. (You must have read access to the smb.conf file, however.)

Password

Use the Password page (Figure 4.9) to change your Samba password. When you access SWAT as root, you can also add, delete, enable, and disable users by clicking the appropriate buttons. Essentially, this page is an interface to the smbpasswd program.

Figure 4.9   The Password page allows easy access to Samba's encrypted password file.

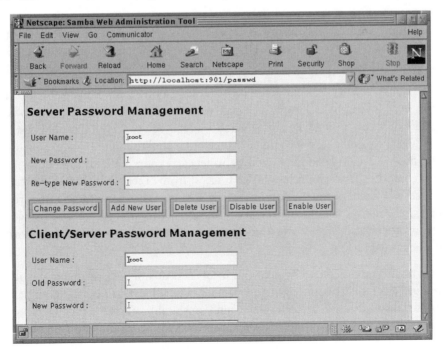

Essential
Configuration

PART 2

WARNING   The SWAT Password page does not change Linux's regular passwords. If your network is configured to use cleartext passwords for Samba access, the Password page will be useless to you, but SWAT still displays it.

To adjust an account, enter the account name in the User Name field. If you want to change the account's password, enter the password in the New Password field and again in Re-type New Password, then click Change Password. Watch for a notice that the password was changed. If you access SWAT as an ordinary user, enter your old password in the Old Password field, which isn't shown in Figure 4.9.

To add a user, type the desired username and password (twice), and then click Add New User. To delete, disable, or enable a user, you need not type the password.

The section called Client/Server Password Management allows you to run SWAT on one computer to adjust the user information on another server. This other server can be another Samba server (in which case only the Samba server's encrypted password is changed) or a Windows NT or 2000 computer (in which case the Windows computer's login password is changed).

Recommendations for Working with SWAT

SWAT can be an excellent tool for Samba configuration, particularly when you're new to Samba administration and unsure of the names of options. To get the most out of SWAT, however, you'll need to understand the fine points of Samba configuration, such as what variables represent.

SWAT's inherent network nature makes it at least potentially dangerous. As described earlier in "Limiting SWAT Access," I urge you to protect your SWAT server by disallowing outside access as much as is practical. Ideally, if you run SWAT at all, you should use TCP Wrappers, xinetd, ipchains, or some other tool to limit access to only the localhost (127.0.0.1) address. Doing this lets you use SWAT locally but not from any other computer. If you must have SWAT access from other computers, restrict it to a limited set of computers on your local network. If you need to configure Samba from a computer that's not on your local network, edit smb.conf with a text editor using a secure login protocol such as SSH (*not* Telnet, which passes all data—including passwords—in an unencrypted form).

If you run a Samba server to which your local users do not have regular logon access, you can use SWAT's Password page to allow your network users to change their Samba passwords. This feature can be convenient, but you should measure this convenience against its potential for danger should a miscreant set up a password sniffer on the local network.

Another option is to run an SSH server and configure Samba users' shells to call the smbpasswd program. Users can then use SSH to set their Samba passwords. (Note that employing Telnet in this capacity is no more secure than using SWAT; it's SSH's encryption that's a bonus in this situation.) Chapter 15, "Managing Accounts," describes password and account management issues in greater detail.

Whether or not you use SWAT for day-to-day Samba configuration, it's a good idea to learn something about "manual" configuration of smb.conf. Fortunately, SWAT uses the same terms to describe configuration options as are used in smb.conf, so learning one method of administration helps you with the other. When SWAT reads in an smb.conf file, SWAT interprets parameter synonyms and antonyms correctly and may write a changed file using different parameter names. Say the original smb.conf file includes a share parameter read only = No; SWAT correctly displays the Writeable value as Yes in the Web form. If you don't change this value before you commit your changes, SWAT will write an smb.conf file without a read only parameter, but with a writeable = Yes parameter. This has the same effect as the original read only = No.

> **WARNING**   Unfortunately, one effect of SWAT's processing of the smb.conf file is that SWAT strips away all comments. Therefore, you should *not* use SWAT if your configuration file includes important comments.

One feature that SWAT *does not* handle correctly is the use of variables within include parameters. The include parameter allows you to include one configuration file within another. In Samba you can put variables in this parameter's value to customize Samba's configuration for individual users, clients, and so on. Unfortunately, SWAT corrupts these include directives so that they're useless. You can correct them manually if you only use one or two of them, but if you rely on this feature heavily, you'll probably find it easier to edit your smb.conf file manually at all times.

Important General Configuration Options

By now, you have some idea of what sorts of options are in the smb.conf file. Most of the rest of this book—beginning with this section—is devoted to the file's specific parameters and how to make the most of them. We begin with some of the core parameters that go in the [global] section of the smb.conf file.

Server Identification

As described in Chapter 1, computers on a Windows network are identified by a NetBIOS name. These computers also belong to a workgroup or domain, which in essence is a

Essential Configuration

PART 2

name shared by several computers on a network. If given no other instructions in the matter, Samba uses the computer's TCP/IP hostname (minus the domain name) as the computer's NetBIOS name. For instance, if a computer is properly configured as gingko.pangaea.edu, then Samba uses GINGKO as the NetBIOS name. Samba doesn't know what to use as the workgroup or domain name, however, so you must explicitly configure that. (If you fail to do so, Samba will use a default based on compile-time options, but it's usually WORKGROUP.)

You can also override the use of the TCP/IP name, and set a few other name-related options.

workgroup   Use this option to set the computer's workgroup or domain name. The choice depends on the configuration of the network as a whole, although there are some Samba options that influence Linux's recognition of the network. These options are explained in Chapter 10.

netbios name   Set or override the computer's NetBIOS name with this parameter. I recommend that you set this option even if you use the same name for both TCP/IP and NetBIOS names, for completeness and to avoid problems should your system's TCP/IP name become misconfigured.

netbios aliases   You can designate two or more names for your Samba server by using the netbios aliases parameter. List all the names *other than* the main netbios name. Setting this parameter isn't typically necessary, but you might use it if, for instance, you consolidate two or more servers into one. The default value is a null string—no aliases are defined.

NOTE   The %L variable takes on the aliased name for most operations, although not if used as part of the server string. In that case, %L uses netbios name.

server string   The server string parameter sets a short identifying string that appears in the Comment field of a Windows network browser when you enable a detailed view and open a window displaying the servers in a workgroup. This string does not otherwise affect the function of Samba. The default is normally Samba %v (%v being the variable for the Samba version number). I recommend you change this string to remove the version number as a security measure. In Figure 4.10 you can see the effect of the server string parameter, which was set to Samba server on %L for the TEELA server. This server also has netbios alias = TEELAALIAS, so it appears twice in the browse list.

Figure 4.10   The server string parameter sets the text that appears in the Comment field in Windows network browse lists.

time server   This boolean option enables Samba to announce itself as a time server on the SMB/CIFS network. You can then use the NET TIME command on a Windows client to retrieve the time as maintained by the Samba server. The default value is No.

include   The include parameter, when used in conjunction with the netbios alias parameter, customizes an smb.conf file for each of two or more aliases. Specifically, you can use the %L variable in an include parameter to load customized configuration files for each alias. The statement include = smb.conf.%L, for instance, loads configuration files that can include shares for each alias, such as smb.conf.gingko and smb.conf.biloba.

When using an include parameter, be careful to place it so that it accomplishes what you want. Essentially, the contents of the specified file will replace the include directive. Thus, if the included file contains share definitions, you should place the include statement *after* the end of the [global] section in the main file. Neither SWAT nor linuxconf handles the include parameter well, so if you want to use this feature, edit smb.conf and the included files by hand.

> **NOTE**   Samba translates the NetBIOS name to lowercase when used in this fashion, so if you specify netbios name = GINGKO and use the include parameter specified earlier as an example, you should create a configuration file called smb.conf.gingko to match the netbios name.

As an example, consider the following [global] section of an smb.conf file:

```
[global]
          workgroup = ARBORETUM
          netbios name = GINGKO
          netbios aliases = BILOBA
          server string = Stinky tree
          time server = Yes


     include = smb.conf.%L
```

This definition makes the server appear under two names on the Windows network: GINGKO and BILOBA. Both these apparent computers are part of the ARBORETUM workgroup or domain. Viewed in the Details view from a Windows browser, both apparent computers bear a comment of "Stinky tree." The server provides time services to the network. Depending upon the contents of the smb.conf.gingko and smb.conf.biloba files, and the remaining contents of smb.conf, this computer may have entirely different shares under its two aliases.

Logging Options

If something about your Samba setup doesn't work, one of your best bets for correcting the problem lies with Samba's logging facilities. Ordinarily, Samba sends reports of important system events to log files. The default location of these log files depends on compile-time options but is normally in either the /var/log or /var/log/samba directory. Several log files may be used by Samba:

log.nmb or nmbd These are common default names used by the nmbd daemon. You can change the log name by using the -l run-time parameter to nmbd. When you do so, nmbd appends .nmb to the filename you provide.

log.smb or smbd These are common default names used by the smbd daemon. You can change this name by using the -l run-time parameter to smbd. Unlike nmbd, smbd does *not* in any way modify the filename you pass through -l. This file stores general information on smbd's operation, such as when it starts and stops.

log.smb.* Most Samba configurations create an entire set of log files, one for each client computer, using the client computer's NetBIOS name as the final part of the log filename. These files store information on connections from particular clients. You can set the name used to create the log files in the smb.conf file, as described shortly.

The logging options in the smb.conf file mostly affect all three of the preceding types of log files, although the log file parameter affects only the last of these file types. The smb.conf parameters are as follows:

log file   Specify the name of the log file with this option. It's not uncommon to see the %m (client NetBIOS name) variable included in a log file parameter. The effect of using %m is to create a different log file for each client, which can help when you're debugging connection problems for particular clients.

debug level   The *debug level* or *log level* is a number from 0 to 10 representing the amount of information that's written to the log file. A value of 0 means no information; 1 is the default; 3 is as much as you're likely to ever need as an administrator; and 10 is an extremely detailed log that's useful only to a Samba programmer. The default level of 1 is adequate for most purposes. A synonym for this parameter is log level.

max log size   If the log file exceeds the max log size value (in kilobytes), Samba renames the old file with a .old extension and opens a new log file. This option can keep Samba's log files from overflowing a hard disk's capacity. The default value is 5000—about 5MB.

debug timestamp   Ordinarily, Samba writes in the log file the times at which operations occur. If you set this parameter to No, however, Samba omits the time stamp, which can reduce the size of a log file.

debug pid   Ordinarily, Samba doesn't include the smbd process ID (PID) in the log file. If you use a single log file for all connections, however, including this information can be helpful in tracking which daemon (and hence which connection) belongs to each log entry. Adding debug pid = Yes enables this behavior.

debug uid   If you've configured Samba to run under multiple user IDs (UIDs), you may want to include this information in the log files. Adding debug uid = Yes to smb.conf accomplishes this goal.

syslog   Samba normally logs data itself; however, you can configure it to use Linux's syslog daemon instead of or in addition to its own logging. When you do so, the syslog parameter specifies the log levels sent through the daemon, much as debug level controls logging through Samba's own log files. To use the syslog parameter, you must adjust several other system configuration options:

> **Compilation Options**   Compile Samba with the --with-syslog compile-time option, as described in Chapter 3. Any given Samba binary might or might not have been compiled with this option.

Essential Configuration

PART 2

Syslog Configuration   Linux's syslog daemon must be configured to accept logging from other daemons. To do so, add the following line to the `/etc/syslog.conf` file, making an appropriate adjustment to indicate the file you want to receive daemon-generated messages:

```
daemon.*        /var/log/messages
```

syslog only   If you want to send logging information through the system logger *only*, set this option to Yes. When you leave this option set to its default value of No, Samba logs information to its own log file, whether or not you use the `syslog` parameter.

status   Samba maintains a status file that contains information on active connections. You can read this file using the `smbstatus` command. If you set `status = No` from its default of Yes, Samba won't be able to report what connections are active. You should therefore not change this parameter.

For most configurations, the default logging options are acceptable. Be careful, however, to specify log file locations that really exist. This is particularly true when using a Samba binary intended for one distribution on another distribution, or when copying an `smb.conf` file from one computer to another. One binary might be compiled with options to use `/var/log/samba` as the log file location, for instance, but the target distribution might not have this directory; instead, it might use `/var/log/samba.d` as the log file location. Correct such mismatches by using the `-l` run-time parameter and the `log file` configuration file parameter.

An Overview of Security Issues

Samba includes a plethora of security options, discussed thoroughly in Chapter 14. A few security issues are of critical importance from the start, however.

Samba Security Models

Windows OSs use one of two security models: In DOS, OS/2, and Windows *9x*, the server requires no username but needs a separate password for access to each resource. In Windows NT and 2000, the server requires a username/password pair that grants access to all of the computer's shares, with share-by-share control implemented using the OS's internal security model. Samba supports a variety of security options to emulate both of these security arrangements. The second model is more natural for a Samba server running on Linux, because it closely matches Linux's native security features. Two additional arrangements are extensions of the second model and are used in Windows domains. All four security arrangements are set up with the security parameter. Its allowable values are as follows:

Share   This security option attempts to emulate the Windows 9x security model. Samba tries to validate the password against a list of users provided with the username parameter, as well as against a username provided by the client, if the client sent one.

User   User-level security fits closely with Linux's native security model and is therefore the preferred security option for use with Samba. It's also the default in Samba 2.0 and later. In this model, Samba requires both a username and password. If the password matches the one stored for the user, Samba grants access to all the computer's shares, provided other security measures don't block access in some way.

Server   Server-level security works exactly like User-level security, except that Samba uses another SMB/CIFS server to authenticate users. When using the security = Server option, you must also set the name of the password server using the password server parameter.

WARNING   Never set password server to point to the computer you're configuring. Doing so sets up an infinite loop, which can cause serious problems.

Domain   Domain-level security works much like Server-level security, except that the password server is a primary domain controller (PDC), and the Samba server must log onto the domain maintained by the PDC. When using Domain-level security, you can set password server = * to have Samba locate the PDC automatically.

NOTE   When using Server- or Domain-level security, the authenticated user must still have an account on the host Linux server. For instance, if the user lorax is approved by the password server but has no account on the Samba server, then lorax won't be able to access resources except as a guest user.

Using Server- or Domain-level security can be convenient, but it slows down authentication slightly. It also poses a security risk. A troublemaker with physical access to your network may be able to remove the password server, set up another computer on that address, and gain full access to any computer that uses the password server for authentication. So if you only have one or two Samba servers, I recommend User-level security.

Password Encryption

Password encryption is the source of what may be the single most common problem encountered by new Samba administrators. Windows for Workgroups 3.1, Windows 95 prior to OEM Service Release 2 (OSR2), and Windows NT prior to version 4, Service Pack 3, all sent unencrypted (or *cleartext*) passwords. Windows 95 OSR2, Windows 98, Windows NT 4 Service Pack 3 and later, and Windows 2000 all send passwords in encrypted form. Samba has difficulty with this difference for two reasons:

- By default, Samba accepts only cleartext passwords. You have to set the `encrypt passwords = Yes` parameter to have Samba accept encrypted passwords.

- When set to use cleartext passwords, Samba uses Linux's normal authentication procedures, so the system is automatically configured to accept SMB/CIFS connections from valid Linux users. When set to use encrypted passwords, however, Samba requires a separate password database, which you must create and maintain.

In the long run, it's easier and safer to configure Samba to use encrypted passwords on a network that has a large number of machines that default to encrypted passwords. Chapter 14 has complete coverage of this configuration. For now, here's a brief explanation of how to use this method:

1. Add the `encrypt passwords = Yes` parameter to your `smb.conf` file.

2. Create an `smbpasswd` file, which normally resides in the same directory as `smb.conf`. Samba comes with a script called `mksmbpasswd.sh` to create such a file from an `/etc/passwd` file, although all the passwords are invalid, so you must then set them in some way. Alternatively, you can add users one at a time by issuing the **smbpasswd -a *username*** command. If you issue this command before creating an `smbpasswd` file, the command creates the file and adds the user to the new file.

TIP If you have a large existing user base, you can use the update encrypted parameter to automatically update smbpasswd entries. See Chapter 14.

If instead you want to use cleartext passwords, you must reconfigure recent versions of Windows to send passwords without encryption. Samba comes with several files that can help accomplish this. They're normally in a Samba documentation directory such as `/usr/doc/samba-2.0.7/docs`, and are named `WinVer_PlainPassword.reg`, where `WinVer` is a Windows version, such as `Win95`. Copy these files to a FAT floppy disk, then move the floppy to a target Windows computer. Open the floppy disk and double-click on the appropriate file. When you reboot the computer, it sends cleartext passwords.

Summary

Samba configuration is both easy and difficult. Many Linux distributions ship with an `smb.conf` file that allows the system to function in a minimal way with only minor modifications, such as setting the workgroup appropriately. If you use a GUI configuration tool such as `linuxconf` or SWAT, you can probably configure your Samba server in a variety of useful ways without too much difficulty, once you understand the basic principles outlined in this chapter. In fact, you can perform most tasks in SWAT that you can perform by changing `smb.conf` in a text editor.

The rest of this book covers the finer points of Samba configuration, focusing upon manual `smb.conf` editing.

Essential
Configuration

PART 2

Configuring File Sharing

For most installations, the single most important use of Samba is as a file server. It's therefore important that you understand how Samba shares files—how you can specify what directories to share, what permissions to give to Samba users, how Samba handles filenames and FAT-style file attributes, and so on. This chapter introduces the fundamentals of file sharing with Samba. Assorted later chapters cover related material, such as automation related to file sharing (Chapter 8, "Automation"), performance tuning (Chapter 12, "Tuning Samba for Optimum Performance"), and using Samba with non-Microsoft clients (Appendix B, "OS-Specific Issues").

First you'll see some examples of file shares, and the smb.conf parameters to set them up. Following that is a discussion of the critical interaction of Linux-style security with Samba file shares. Finally, you'll examine a number of scenarios that illustrate the use of Samba in specific situations. You may be able to use one of these scenarios as a model for your own Samba configuration.

Configuring File Shares

Basic file sharing is easy to configure with Samba. You normally create a [global] section in the smb.conf file even for a simple one-share server. Once you've configured a rudimentary [global] section, as described in Chapter 4, it takes just a few more lines to create a share—even including options to make the share more useful. Let's begin with a simple example and then modify and expand it to demonstrate options.

A Basic File Share Example

The simplest possible file share consists of a single line—a share name in brackets, like this:

```
[test]
```

This definition creates a share that provides read-only access to the Linux /tmp directory (the default values). This sort of access is, of course, of limited utility.

To make this share useful, you add a few additional lines to define the parameters you want. For instance:

```
[test]
        comment = Test share on %L
        volume name = TEST
        path = /home/samba/test
        writeable = Yes
```

Each of these parameters adds something to the share, although only the path option is really critical.

comment The comment parameter isn't critical to Samba operation, but it can help users locate their shares. This parameter adds a comment that's visible when the Details view is used in a Windows file browser, as shown in Figure 5.1. You can include variables in a comment's value, but some won't be usable because they aren't defined until after the share is accessed. (See Table 4.1 in Chapter 4 for a list of variables.)

Figure 5.1 The Comment field is visible only if you use Details view in Windows.

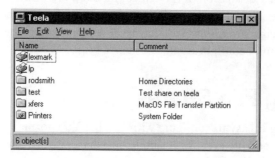

volume name   This parameter, like the `comment` parameter, is largely cosmetic. If you map a Samba share to a drive letter, the `volume name` parameter sets the DOS/Windows name used by that volume. This name is unimportant except in rare situations. For instance, if you export a CD-ROM that contains a software installation utility, that utility may work only if the volume name is set correctly.

path   The `path` parameter specifies what directory tree is to be shared. (A synonym for `path` is `directory`.) In principle, you can share any directory that exists on your Linux computer, but some directories aren't good choices for sharing. For example, Windows clients aren't likely to need access to your /usr directory tree. It's common to create one or more subdirectories under /home/samba for Samba shares, but you can also share /mnt (to provide access to removable media), /tmp, or any other directory. If you don't specify a `path`, Samba shares /tmp.

You can use variables in a `path` statement, which can be useful if you want to create shares with specific contents for specific users. For instance, `path = /home/samba/%g` creates a share that accesses a directory named after the user's primary Linux group. This might be useful when creating shares for distinct sets of users. In a university setting, you could create `faculty`, `staff`, `grad`, and `undergrad` groups, each with an associated Samba share.

writeable   This parameter controls whether Samba allows users to write to a share. The default value is `No`, which ensures that users can't damage an exported filesystem. You might want to leave this parameter at its default value for shared program directories or the like, but many shares will require write access. Synonyms of `writeable` are `writable` and `write ok`; `read only` is an antonym. The Samba Web Administration Tool (SWAT, described in Chapter 4) uses `writeable`, so I recommend you do the same to avoid confusion.

You can begin to create useful file shares using only the preceding information, particularly if you use variables as part of the `path`'s value. In fact, you may recognize that you can use a username variable (`%U` or `%u`) in the `path` value to create a share that's unique for each individual. Samba's programmers, however, are one step ahead of you. A special share—[homes]—exists to do just that.

Home Directory Shares

As mentioned in Chapter 4, Samba includes support for a share known as the [homes] share. This share is defined roughly similar to the following:

```
[%U]
        volume name = %U
        path = %H
```

As explained in Table 4.1 in Chapter 4, %U is a variable for the username of the user who requests the service, and %H is the user's home directory. Therefore, this share definition appears in a network browser under the user's username, has that same username as the volume name, and has the user's home directory as the share's root directory. [homes] is a shorthand way of creating this definition, without having to remember the meanings of the variables.

There are a few differences between the foregoing example of a share and a genuine [homes] share, however. These differences include browsing options, naming conventions, and accessibility to other users. As described in the next section, "Browsing Options," the browseable parameter has special meaning in the [homes] share. This parameter has its usual meaning in the [%U] share definition.

A [homes] share is actually accessible under two names: HOMES and the user's username. Suppose the user susani wants to access her home share on the server WARLOCK. She can access it as either \\WARLOCK\SUSANI or \\WARLOCK\HOMES. If marcusc accesses \\WARLOCK\HOMES, he doesn't find susani's files; he finds his own files. If one user enters the share name of another user's [homes] share, access is granted, with restrictions based on additional Samba parameters and Linux permissions. The sample [%U] share, however, is accessible only to the share's owner.

Samba shows the name of only one [homes] share when an individual browses a Samba server from Windows. To access another [homes] share, a user must enter the complete path to that share in an Address field or something similar. For instance, in Figure 5.2, the user is about to access halr's [homes] share, although it's not visible among the shares on the server.

Figure 5.2 Windows 9*x* allows you to enter a path to a share that's not displayed in the browse list provided by Samba.

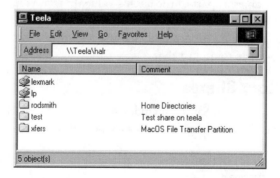

Browsing Options

Windows networking is very browser oriented. That is, users frequently locate network resources through the Network Neighborhood icon on their desktops, which works much like a file manager for local hard disks. Samba includes options that influence the way it interacts with browsers. Some of these options influence "behind-the-scenes" operation of the browser and are discussed in Chapter 11, "Local and Routed Browsing." Others are important when you configure individual shares. These parameters include the following:

hosts allow and hosts deny   These are security options that you can apply to an entire server (by placing them in the [global] section of smb.conf) or to individual shares. Use these parameters to specify lists of hosts or networks to which you want to grant or deny access, respectively. For instance, if a given share holds sensitive data that should only be accessible to a handful of computers, you can list those computers in the hosts allow parameter, and no other computers will be allowed access. These parameters do not make a share disappear from unapproved computers' browse lists, however; any attempt to access the shares is simply unsuccessful. As such, hosts allow and hosts deny can prevent browsing past the list of available shares. Synonyms for these options are allow hosts and deny hosts, respectively.

valid users and invalid users   These parameters work much like the hosts allow and hosts deny parameters, but on usernames rather than computers. You can often use Linux's own permissions settings to achieve similar results, but these parameters are easier to configure when you want to deny share access to a random group of users. For example, if you want to keep taliaw out of a share, you can use invalid users = taliaw.

browseable   This boolean option determines whether a share appears in browse lists. Its default value is Yes and you normally want to leave it as Yes, so that the share appears in browse lists. Set it to No to hide a share without making it unavailable. Even when a share is set to browseable = No, you can access the share by name. One unusual case is the [homes] shares. When present, a [homes] share is always browseable under its owners' usernames. The browseable option controls whether the share is visible under the name HOMES. To avoid confusion, it's customary to set browseable = No on [homes] shares. A synonym for browseable is browsable.

available   This parameter's default value is Yes. If you set it to No, the share effectively disappears from the server. Use this option if you want to temporarily remove a share more completely than you can with browseable = No.

You can use these browsing options as part of a security plan for your Samba server—especially hosts allow, hosts deny, valid users, and invalid users. The browseable option, aside from its common use in the [homes] share, is helpful mostly for reducing clutter. If you have a server with a large number of shares, many of which are seldom used, and then only by people who know the shares' names, then you can set browseable = No in most shares to eliminate potentially confusing shares from the browse list. Similarly, if your clients are all configured to mount a share onto a drive letter at boot time, the share can be configured browseable = No to reduce clutter in the server browse list.

Filename Options

One of the challenges faced by Samba's developers is the fact that Linux (or Unix generally) handles filenames differently from DOS, Windows, and OS/2 (the most common Samba clients). In order to operate effectively as a server for these clients, Samba includes options to present its files as expected by the clients. For many of these options, however, there is no single best way to handle the translation. Furthermore, some of these translation features slow Samba down, so if you don't need the option in question, you might prefer to disable it. Samba provides many smb.conf parameters that you can use to enable or disable these features as you see fit.

The smb.conf filename parameters all fit into one of three categories: filename case options, filename length options, and hidden filename options, all described in the following sections. Most of these options are share-level, so you can set them on a share-by-share basis; or they can go in the [global] section to apply them to all shares.

NOTE If you use SWAT for Samba configuration, most of these filename options are visible only after you select the Advanced View button.

TIP Because many of these options are best set to different values in a mixed-OS environment, you may want to consider using the include parameter with the %a (client OS) variable to set options uniquely for each client OS. A configuration file for a Samba client might set case sensitive = Yes and hide dot files = No. You might simultaneously set up a mangled map (described shortly) to convert *.html files to *.htm for a DOS client. Chapter 4 covers the include parameter.

Handling Case Differences

As explained in Chapter 2, Linux systems use case-sensitive filesystems, in which the case of letters is significant. Windows is a case-retentive operating system, in which the case of letters is preserved but is unimportant. To further complicate matters, DOS computers use case-*in*sensitive filesystems, in which filenames are all stored in one case (uppercase for DOS using its normal FAT filesystem). By default, Samba emulates the Windows case-retentive filesystem features. Because this setting works well in most environments with both Windows and OS/2 clients, you can probably leave all the filename options at their defaults. If you want to adjust Samba's handling of these issues, however, you can set several options.

preserve case By default, this option is set to Yes, which tells Samba to honor the case of files created by a Samba client. For instance, if the client creates a file called MiXEd.uP, Samba stores that file precisely that way. If preserve case is set to No, Samba converts the file's case to all uppercase or all lowercase, depending upon the setting of the default case option.

short preserve case This option works much like the preserve case parameter, but short preserve case applies only to filenames that are limited to DOS's eight-character-with-three-character extension *(8.3 filename)* format. The default value is Yes.

default case This parameter specifies the case to which Samba converts files when preserve case or short preserve case is set to No. When default case is set at the default value of Lower, it causes MiXEd.uP to be stored as mixed.up; when set to Upper, the file is stored as MIXED.UP. This option doesn't normally affect your ability to access files, though; its role is mostly to tidy up the appearance of file listings and simplify access from Linux.

case sensitive This parameter, which defaults to No, controls whether Samba treats filenames in a case-sensitive way. Suppose the server hosts a file called MiXEd.uP. When case sensitive = No, clients can use precisely that name, or they can use MIXED.UP, mixed.up, miXEd.UP, or any other name that varies only in case. When case sensitive = Yes, clients trying to access the file must pass the name in precisely the same case as is used on the server. You might use case sensitive = Yes if the share is to be accessed mostly or entirely from Linux or some other case-sensitive OS. If DOS, Windows, or OS/2 clients are involved, I recommend you leave this parameter set at the default No. Unfortunately, the default value slows Samba down slightly. A synonym for this parameter is casesignnames.

As a general rule, the case sensitive parameter is the most important of the case options. The other three may be important only for the cosmetic aspect of whether the

Essential Configuration

PART 2

server preserves the case it's given. Only `case sensitive` can make a file inaccessible to a client if an application's code changes case between reading a filename from the server and issuing a File Open command. This behavior is much more common in DOS programs than in Windows programs.

Handling Length Differences

Windows *9x* can store files of up to 128 characters in length on a local hard disk, but Linux can store files with names twice that long on its ext2 filesystem. More importantly, DOS can only cope with 8.3 filenames. If you use a Samba server only from DOS clients, this fact doesn't pose a problem. (All the files on the server's shares will have 8.3 file–names, having been created by DOS.) On the other hand, if you use multiple client OSs or if you run DOS programs (which expect 8.3 filenames) in Windows (which can create long filenames), then Samba has a larger task. It must be able to convert filenames between their true long forms and shorter forms—so-called *mangled* or *munged* file–names. Samba includes several parameters that influence how and when Samba does this filename mangling.

mangled names   If set at its default value of Yes, this parameter causes Samba to convert long filenames to unique short (8.3) filenames when communicating with DOS and other OSs that request short filenames. For instance, `longfilename.txt` might appear to a DOS client as `LONGF~A7.TXT`. If you set this value to No, the file with a long name appears with either a truncated filename (such as `LONGFILE.TXT`) or not at all, depending upon the client OS.

mangling char   This parameter sets the character used for separating the five-char-acter base of a mangled filename from the two-character code at its end. The default is a tilde (~).

mangle case   This option's default value is No, which tells Samba to preserve the case of short filenames when reporting them to clients. If set to Yes, then Samba mangles short filenames that don't conform entirely to the specified `default case` value. Consider `MiXEd.uP` again: When `mangle case = No`, Samba reports this file's name to DOS clients as `MiXEd.uP`. When `mangle case = Yes`, Samba reports the file's name as `MIXED~F3.UP`. As a general rule, you should leave this parameter at its default value.

mangled stack   When a DOS client accesses a file with a long filename on Linux, the DOS client is unaware of the file's true long filename. Therefore, the client may load the file, save it, and load it again, all using the same mangled filename. To speed up such accesses, Samba maintains a list *(stack)* of recently mangled 8.3 filenames. The `mangled stack` parameter sets the size of this stack, which defaults to 50. If your network hosts a large number of DOS clients, you may want to increase this value.

Otherwise, leave it alone or perhaps even reduce it. Increasing the size of the mangled stack can speed up file accesses using mangled filenames, but doing so increases Samba's memory requirements and slows other file accesses. Unlike the other filename parameters, this one is global in scope; it appears in the [global] section of smb.conf.

TIP   DOS and older 16-bit Windows programs use 8.3 filenames, even when running from Windows 9x, NT, or 2000. You may therefore use the mangling stack even from these OSs. Consider this fact before adjusting the size of this stack.

mangled map   You can specify additional mangling rules with this parameter, which takes the form of a series of filename pattern pairs in parentheses. Samba replaces any filename that matches the first portion of a pair with the equivalent specified by the second pair. Consider the following:

```
mangled map = (*.html *.htm) (*.jpeg *.jpg)
```

This causes Samba to replace any .html extension with .htm, and any .jpeg extension with .jpg. Note that these mangling rules apply to *all* filenames, whether or not they would normally be mangled. For instance, if you apply the preceding mangling map, you'll see all .html files as .htm files, even from Windows or Linux clients.

Filename-mangling options can be vitally important if you use DOS clients. The default parameters will work reasonably well with DOS clients, although it's possible some programs will work better if you set mangle case = Yes. You might also want to apply some special rules via the mangled map parameter, if your server contains files that might benefit from this treatment. If you use Windows clients, name mangling is less important unless you use a large number of 16-bit programs from Windows.

Handling Hidden Files

Linux shells normally hide files that begin with a dot (.)—that is, *dot files*. These files are still accessible to the user, but they don't clutter most directory listings. In most SMB/CIFS client OSs, the same effect is achieved through a *hidden bit,* which is a flag associated with filenames. Samba includes several options that affect its handling of both Linux dot files and the hidden bit that's supported by SMB/CIFS. In addition, Samba includes options that let you make certain files completely invisible to the client, beyond what a hidden bit can achieve.

hide dot files   By default, Samba sets the SMB/CIFS hidden bit on all the dot files in a share. This behavior is generally desirable, because Windows clients don't normally need to see dot files, particularly in home shares. If you use hide dot files = No, however, Samba doesn't set the hidden bit on dot files, so they appear in Windows directory listings. You might want to use this option in nonhome shares, particularly if it's important to allow clients to keep dot file clutter from accumulating in a share. You might also set it to No if you have a Windows program that creates dot files but doesn't expect them to be hidden.

hide files This parameter specifies a list of files that are to be hidden by Samba. You can use wildcards (* and ?) to specify filenames, as well as spaces—and that means you must separate filenames with something other than a space; Samba uses a slash (/) for this function. For example, you might use hide files = Mail/News/ *.rpm to hide the Mail and News directories and all Linux .rpm files from the client. Samba matches files consistent with the case sensitive parameter when applying this option. The default is a null string; no files are hidden (aside from dot files, depending upon the setting of hide dot files.)

veto files This parameter works exactly like the hide files parameter, except that vetoed files cannot be accessed at all from the client; it's as if they don't exist on the server. The default is a null string; no files are vetoed. If you set veto files = *.txt, no attempt to access files that end in .txt will succeed, even if you type a filename directly into a File Open dialog box or at a command prompt on the client.

delete veto files When you remove a directory that contains vetoed files, Samba ordinarily does *not* remove those vetoed files and therefore cannot remove the entire directory. From Windows, it appears that the directory is empty but cannot be deleted. If you set delete veto files = Yes, however, Samba removes vetoed files when a client deletes a directory containing those files.

File Locking

All multitasking OSs face a potential conflict: Two or more programs may attempt to access a file at the same time. In some cases, this doesn't cause a problem because the accesses are read-only. When two programs write to a file, however, or when one writes a file while another reads it, errors can occur. The programs may write incompatible changes to the file, or a program reading the file may be unaware of the changes written by another program. To prevent these problems, OSs implement various types of *file locking,* in which one program can "lock" all or part of a file to prevent it from being changed by another program.

Like filenames, the file-locking mechanisms for Windows and Linux are subtly different, so a number of Samba configuration parameters are devoted to bridging this gap.

share modes This option enables Microsoft-style whole-file locking. When enabled, a client program can request a lock on an entire file. The default value is Yes, and it's generally best to leave it set that way.

locking   This option enables Microsoft-style partial-file (or *byte-range*) locking. When enabled, a client program can request a lock on only part of the file. The default value is Yes, and it's generally best not to change this setting.

strict locking   This option defaults to No, which causes Samba to perform lock checks only when clients request them. Most client programs submit such requests when needed, so the default configuration works well. Some client programs, though, don't submit requests for lock checks when they should, which can result in file corruption. When set to Yes, this parameter causes lock checks prior to any operation, which reduces corruption caused by ill-behaved programs. Setting this parameter to Yes slows Samba down, however.

blocking locks   If a client tries to open a file but fails because of a lock, the client may begin *polling*—checking back frequently to try to open the file. A *blocking lock* is a way to avoid this costly practice. When support for blocking locks exists, the client can tell the server how long the client is willing to wait for a file to become available. The server then keeps the request open and, if the file becomes available in the specified time, tells the client. The default value for this option is Yes, but you can disable it if that's necessary. Normally, you should leave this setting alone.

oplocks   An *opportunistic lock* (or *oplock* for short) is a mechanism that enables a client to locally cache changes it makes to a file. This feature can improve performance, because the client need not send as many packets back to the server as a file is updated. When an oplock is granted, the server can demand an update from the client at any time, and this feature can be used to force an update should another client try to read the file. Samba enables oplock support by default; you can disable it by setting oplocks = No. When so configured, Samba refuses any request to obtain an oplock on a file. This degrades system performance, but may be safer if your users regularly access files through Samba as well as from Linux programs, or through some other server.

level2 oplocks   In a traditional oplock, the first client loses the oplock when a second client accesses the file. When level2 oplocks = Yes, the oplock is merely downgraded from a read/write oplock to a read-only oplock. This means additional clients can cache their read-only access to the file. If the first client writes changes, all other clients are notified of this change. Employing level2 oplocks can improve performance on some types of files, such as program files, so you may want to enable it. This support is new, and it defaults to No in Samba 2.0.7, but it may default to Yes in future versions of Samba.

kernel oplocks   Oplocks can be useful to keep a Windows client from stepping on other Windows clients' files, but as of the 2.2.*x* kernel series Linux doesn't support oplocks. As a result, Linux programs don't know about oplocks granted on files served by Samba. If and when kernel oplock support materializes in Linux, you can set kernel oplocks = Yes to enable this support. Until then, set this value to No.

Essential Configuration

PART 2

> **WARNING**   Without kernel oplock support, it's possible for a Linux program to wreak havoc if it opens a file on which Samba has granted an oplock. You may want to set `oplocks = No` to avoid this problem, or use the `veto oplock files` parameter (described in this section) to deny oplocks only on specific files.

fake oplocks   Early versions of Samba did not support oplocks. Instead, they supported the `fake oplock` option, which caused Samba to claim that oplocks were available, when in fact they were not. *Do not set the* `fake oplocks` *option to* Yes *on Samba versions later than 2.0.0.* This option is unnecessary on modern versions of Samba and may cause file corruption.

veto oplock files   With this option you can specify a list of files that are never granted oplocks. Identify the files with filenames (including wildcards, if desired) separated by slashes (/) just as you do with the `hide files` or `veto files` parameters, described in "Handling Hidden Files." If only a few files are likely to be accessed from Linux or some other server at the same time they're accessed through Samba, this option is preferable to setting `oplocks = No`.

lock directory   Samba stores a variety of housekeeping files related to locking in this directory, as well as some other functions such as `browse lists`. The default is a compile-time option, probably something like `/var/lock/samba` or `/usr/local/samba/locks`. You can override the default setting using this parameter.

In most cases, the default locking parameters work well. You may need to adjust these values—particularly those related to oplocks—if you need simultaneous access to files from both Linux and Windows clients. Most of these parameters can be applied either globally or share by share. The `kernel oplocks` and `lock directory` parameters, however, are global options and so must appear in the `[global]` section of `smb.conf`.

Setting Ownership and Permissions

One of the trickier aspects of Samba configuration for many sites—particularly large sites with many users and complex security needs—is integrating Unix-style and Microsoft-style file security models through Samba. As outlined in "Unix-Style Ownership and Permissions" in Chapter 2, Linux's security model is different from that of Windows. Compared to Windows 9*x*, Linux's security model is quite sophisticated, so you can do more with a Samba server than you can with a Windows 9*x* server. Windows NT and 2000, however, support *access control lists (ACLs),* which offer an alternative to Linux-style security that's different from Linux's security model and is, in some ways, more flexible. So if you're an experienced Windows NT administrator, Linux's security features may take some getting used to. If you're already experienced with Linux or Unix file permissions, you should have no trouble getting your Linux server to do what you want in this respect.

Samba adds to the Linux file permissions repertoire in important ways, some of which I've outlined earlier in this chapter, particularly in "Browsing Options." Specifically, the hosts allow, hosts deny, valid users, and invalid users parameters offer a way to fine-tune access to specific shares that is beyond the control afforded through Linux ownership and permissions. You can, for instance, deny share access to a particular user or to anybody from a particular computer. These issues are covered in greater detail in Chapter 14, "Samba Security Considerations."

Samba Ownership and Permission Options

Samba provides several options that affect the way Linux filenames and permissions are used by the server. You can use these options to help create a security configuration that works in your network environment.

Controlling Ownership

On a Linux server, every file has an *owner* and a *group*. Every user has rights to read and write files based on the user's ID and the groups to which the user belongs. You can adjust the owner and group associated with accesses to a share using a pair of smb.conf parameters:

force user Normally, when you connect to a Samba server, you send your username and password and can then access and create files using the permissions associated with that username. For instance, if you connect as susani, any files you create will be owned by the Linux user susani, and you can read existing files that can be read by susani. The force user parameter changes this. It makes Samba behave as if you logged on using what may be a different username. For instance, if a share includes the force user = marcusc parameter, then any accesses within that share occur as if marcusc originated the access, even if susani connected with her username and password. The share may be accessed by any authorized user who supplies a valid username and password.

TIP The force user parameter is often used to create a share that's accessible to—and writeable by—a group of users. You can create a share under one user's name and then use force user to allow all users to create files in the share, without worrying about the ownership of the created files. I recommend you use a "dummy" account that has little access to the system outside of the target directory when you use this parameter. This reduces the risk of abuse or mistakes that might lead to trouble.

force group   This option works much like `force user`, but it sets the group for files created when the share is accessed. It also determines what files can be read and written based on group ownership and permissions. You can use `force user` and `force group` together to create some unusual effects. For instance, even if the user susani does not belong to the group ranger, you can use `force user = susani` and `force group = ranger` to give users connecting to a share the permissions equivalent to susani *and* group ranger.

WARNING   A bug in Samba prior to version 2.0.5 set the group of files created when `force user` was in effect to the group of the individual who accessed the share. Later versions of Samba set the group to match that of the user whose identity is forced by `force user`. To be absolutely certain of the group used in a share, use `force group`.

WARNING   The `force user` and `force group` parameters are not set by default. These features are very powerful and thus potentially dangerous. Here's an example of a very poor configuration that can cause problems: Consider a directory that's world-writeable on Linux but exported with `force user = root`. If a user logs on through a valid shell account and creates a symbolic link from the share to /etc, then anybody who uses that share can edit the sensitive configuration files in /etc—at least, if Samba allows links to be followed outside of a share (that is, `wide links = Yes`, which is the default). Even if you specify some other username besides root, damage can occur because a miscreant might be able to damage other users' files.

Controlling Permissions (Modes)

As described in "Using Linux File Security with Samba" in Chapter 2, any individual user's access to a file is determined in part by the file's permissions (also referred to as the file's *mode*). The mode is represented by a three- or four-digit octal number such as 644 or 0750. Samba can use the execute bits of the file mode to store DOS- and Windows-style file attributes. This is also described in Chapter 2, and discussed again in "Storing FAT-Style File Attributes" later in this chapter. Several parameters influence the way Samba treats file permissions:

create mask   You can use the `create mask` parameter to limit the range of permissible modes. This mask is a three- or four-digit number representing the bits that *may* be set in a created file. Any bit that's *not* present in the `create mask` value is stripped from the permissions on any file created by Samba in the share. The default create mask is 0744, which allows for read-only access by nonowners of all files. This mask also allows Samba to store the archive bit in the file, but not the hidden or system bits. (See "Storing FAT-Style File Attributes" later in this chapter.) The downside, at least if the files are to be read from Linux, is that all newly created files will appear to be executable to the owner. If this fact is a drawback and the presence of the archive bit from Windows clients is unimportant, you can set create mask = 0644 (or something more restrictive) to eliminate the executable bit. A synonym for create mask is create mode.

directory mask   This option works like create mask, but it applies to directories rather than regular files. In Linux, directories normally have their execute permissions set, so the default directory mask value is 0755. A synonym for this parameter is directory mode.

Essential
Configuration

PART 2

NOTE   Both create mask and directory mask set the *maximum permissions* for a file or directory. For instance, consider create mask = 0644, applied to a file that would otherwise have the admittedly odd 0606 permissions. The owner's permissions (the first 6) are unchanged, because the mask contains all the bits in the owner's permission. The group permissions are unchanged from the original 0 because the mask can only unset bits, and 0 has none set. The world permissions are stripped from 6 (rw-) to 4 (r--) because the mask lacks the write bit. The result is therefore 0604.

force create mode   This parameter is similar to create mask, but instead of specifying bits that *may* be present in the final permissions, force create mode specifies bits that *must* be present. In an extreme case, if you set force create mode = 0777, then all files would have 0777 permissions, even if the client tried to create a read-only file. This parameter defaults to 0000. If force create mode specifies greater permissions than does create mask, force create mode's settings take precedence.

TIP   If your users regularly exchange files in a shared directory but you've configured the system to retain users' correct usernames rather than employing force user, you may want to set force create mode = 0660. This configuration ensures that members of the same group can all write to files created by any member of the group.

force directory mode   This parameter is similar to force create mode, but it applies to directories. The default value is 0000.

security mask This parameter controls what Linux security bits can be manipulated by users through Windows NT security controls, as discussed in Chapter 14. If not set explicitly, this value defaults to the same value as the `create mask` parameter.

directory security mask This parameter is the equivalent of `security mask`, but it applies to directories rather than files.

force security mode This parameter forces Linux security bits on when a user manipulates security options through Windows NT security controls. It defaults to the same value as the `force create mode` option.

force directory security mode This parameter is the equivalent of `force security mode`, but it applies to directories rather than files.

inherit permissions Ordinarily, file and directory permissions are set by options such as `force create mode` and `create mask`. The `inherit permissions` parameter overrides these settings, however, and causes permissions to be inherited from the parent directory. For instance, if a directory has permissions of 0750, then any subdirectory created in that directory has the same permissions. For files, permissions are taken from the parent directory, except that execute permissions are set by Samba's mapping of DOS-style hidden, system, and archive bits. The Linux *set user ID (suid)* bit cannot be inherited.

Examples of Usage

You can do some very unusual things with the ownership and permission options. For instance, suppose you want to give one user (say, a supervisor) full read/write access to all users' home shares, and read-only access to other members of the user's group. You could create a share definition like the following:

```
[homes]
        comment = Home Directories
        include = /etc/samba/smb.conf.%U
        create mask = 0640
        writeable = Yes
        browseable = No
```

Then you'd create an auxiliary configuration file called /etc/samba/smb.conf.*superv* (where *superv* is the username of the supervisor). This file would contain a single line:

```
        force user = %S
```

The %U variable in the `include` line in the main `smb.conf` file causes Samba to search for a file that ends in the username provided by the user of the share. If that file isn't found, Samba ignores the `include` directive. If the file is present, Samba reads it and includes its contents at that point in the file. When *superv* connects to a user's share, Samba reads the `smb.conf.superv` file, and the `force user` line it contains makes Samba treat the connection as if it were coming from %S. In the case of the [`homes`] share, the share name (%S) is the same as the share owner's username. Thus Samba grants *superv* the same permission as the owner of the share.

The `create mask` parameter causes all files to be created with 0640 permissions (except when the client program specifies read-only permissions), so the files are readable from but not writeable by other members of the group. The end result is that *superv* and the share's owner both have full read/write access to the share, while other group members have read-only access to its files. (The home directories must have appropriate permissions themselves, such as 0750.)

WARNING   Tricky configurations such as the one I've just outlined can be convenient, but they're not without their pitfalls. For instance, if ordinary users are allowed to create new files in the `/etc/samba` directory, they could create files to give themselves enhanced privileges, or even superuser access! Also, as configured in this example, *superv* can add or delete files, and those changes will look just like those made by the share's normal user—which isn't necessarily desirable from a security point of view.

Interactions with Other Services

When you set (or fail to set) file ownership and permissions through Samba, these options sometimes have effects on other Linux services. For instance, if users can use Telnet or secure shell (SSH) to access a Samba server, they can adjust their files' permissions through normal Linux shell commands, such as `chmod`. Should you configure `force user` to set a shared resource to use a specific user's ID, then that user can access files in that shared directory. This may not be a problem if the shared directory has full write permissions from Samba, but if you use `writeable = No` in Samba, the user will nonetheless have full write access from a Linux shell, where the same user has read-only access from Samba. Similarly, you might use `valid users` or `invalid users` to restrict access to a share, but if the Linux permissions for that share are set permissively, disallowed users may nonetheless be able to access the share from a Linux shell. For these reasons, I suggest you set restrictive Linux ownership and permissions on sensitive data directories. If those directories are to be accessible to a variety of users, you can use `force user` and `valid users` or `invalid users` to open access to those allowed in through Samba.

Similar considerations exist if you use the Samba server in conjunction with other network servers, such as NFS and Netatalk for Unix and Macintosh connectivity, respectively. In these cases, it's generally best to rely primarily on Linux's own security features, rather than Samba's, to control share access. If you can generate a set of Linux users, groups, and permissions that together produce the desired security effects, that set of rules can work with Samba, NFS, Netatalk, and other network servers. The `inherit permissions` parameter can be particularly useful in this situation, because non-Samba servers generally create permissions in a manner that's similar to Samba's behavior when `inherit permissions = Yes`.

Storing FAT-Style File Attributes

As described in Chapter 2, Samba can store DOS-style file attributes using Linux's execute permission bits. (Windows and OS/2 use these same DOS-style attributes.) This feature is controlled through three `smb.conf` parameters:

map archive   If map archive = Yes (the default), Linux sets the user execute bit when a client sets the DOS archive bit. Normally, the archive bit is set when a file has not been backed up, so this bit is set when a file is created and removed when a backup program backs up the system.

map system   If `map system` = Yes, Linux sets the group execute bit when a client sets the DOS system bit. Microsoft OSs use the system bit to identify a handful of files that are particularly important to the OS. This parameter defaults to No.

map hidden   If `map hidden` = Yes, Linux sets the world execute bit when a client sets the DOS hidden bit. When the hidden bit is set, most programs don't display the file as being present, although users can still read the file from certain programs. The default value is No.

WARNING   If you export a directory that contains executable Linux programs, such as programs compiled from source code or shell scripts, Samba clients may see these files as being hidden, as system files, or as having their archive bits set. If a client program then modifies those bits (when you use a DOS backup utility on the share, for example), the changes may make the file nonexecutable from Linux. You can easily correct this problem, but it's a nuisance and can in some cases cause other difficult-to-trace errors.

The default values for these file attribute parameters are useful on many configurations but may not always be ideal. It's unlikely that clients will need to store files with their system bits set. The hidden bit is also seldom used. Although the archive bit is commonly used, it's most important when you use Windows-based backup software. Chances are you'll be backing up the Samba server using Linux software, and so won't need the archive bit.

The create mask parameter can (and, by default, does) remove some or all of these bits. The default create mask value of 0744, specifically, is redundant with the default values for these map parameters, because it removes the group execute and world execute bits while leaving the user execute bit. If you set create mask = 0644, Samba can't set the archive bit, even if map archive = Yes. Likewise, force create mode can override the map settings. A value of force create mode = 0755 sets the archive, system, and hidden bits on all files, even if you've set their parameters to No.

Essential
Configuration

PART 2

> **NOTE** It's rare in Linux to see files with an execute bit set but not the corresponding read bit. You might have need to create such files in Samba, however, if you want to store a system or hidden bit but yet deny read access to users other than the owner or members of the file's group. Say you want to store the hidden, archive, and system bits but deny all access to users who don't belong to the file's group; you could use create mask = 0751. If you then set the hidden and archive bits in a client, but not the system bit, the file will take on permissions of -rwxr----x (that is, 0741).

Windows NT and Windows 2000 support ACLs, which provide additional security features. You can create shares with ACL-like security restrictions using the valid users and invalid users parameters, described earlier in "Browsing Options." Windows NT clients can be granted access to Linux's security options by setting nt acl support = Yes (which is the default). These clients can then access Linux permission information through the File Permissions dialog box shown in Figure 5.3. You can't do everything with this access that you can do with native ACLs, but you can control the read and write bits for the owner, group, and all other users of the file. Chapter 14 covers Samba's ACL-related features in greater detail.

Figure 5.3   Samba can present Linux permissions to Windows NT clients as if they were "special-access" ACLs.

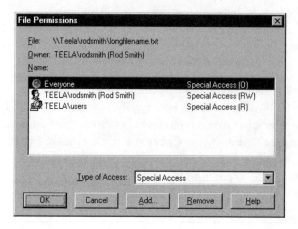

A Network Security Preview

Samba includes numerous security features that are examined in greater detail in Chapter 14, but there are a few broad issues and some specific smb.conf parameters that you should consider from the start. One of these is the mechanism for controlling one user's access to another user's files. If your system has few users who need relatively unfettered access to one another's files, you might use create mask, force create mode, and their equivalent directory parameters to set up a fairly open environment in which all users can read and write each others' files. In a high-security environment, on the other hand, you might want to use strict default security options, such as create mask = 0600, to limit access to the files in users' home directories.

Symbolic Links

One network security issue that arises on Samba servers but not on Windows servers has to do with *links,* particularly *symbolic links.* These special files allow one file to act as a stand-in for another file. Let's say you have a file called report.wpd located in your papers directory. If you want to be able to access this file from the important directory, you can create a link so that important/report.wpd accesses papers/report.wpd. In Linux, you use the ln command to create links (ln -s creates *symbolic links,* the type of interest to the current discussion). The ln command works much like cp, used for copying files. This command, for instance, creates a symbolic link:

```
$ ln -s papers/report.wpd important/report.wpd
```

You cannot create Linux links from a client computer through Samba.

> **NOTE** Windows includes a linklike feature known as *shortcuts*. Because Windows implements shortcuts as ordinary files, you can create shortcuts from Windows clients on Samba servers. These shortcuts can refer to files on the same server, files on the client, or files on other servers. Likewise, shortcuts on a client can refer to files on a Samba server.

Samba's treatment of links is affected by two parameters:

follow symlinks This boolean parameter controls whether Samba follows symbolic links. If set to No, any attempt to access a symbollic link fails. This is a useful security precaution to prevent users from setting symbolic links in shared directories to sensitive data in other users' directories or in system directories. Tight security on the Linux computer can also prevent such abuses, but you may want to deploy this option as an added precaution—particularly on shares in which you've set the force user parameter. follow symlinks does *not* affect Samba's handling of *hard links* (those created without the -s parameter to ln.)

wide links This parameter affects links to *directories* that fall outside the export's normal range. Specifically, if wide links = No, Samba won't follow links to directories that lead outside of a share's normal tree, but the links within that tree will still work. If you share the Linux directory /usr/samba/share, for example, then a link from within that share to the /usr/local directory will fail, but a link to /usr/samba/share/somedir/anotherdir will succeed. This parameter does *not* affect Samba's handling of symbolic links to *files* that fall outside of the share's directory tree, nor does it apply to hard links.

Both the follow symlinks = No and wide links = No parameters slow file accesses, so you must balance their potential security benefits against their cost in performance. These parameters are share-level and so can be set differently for individual shares.

User-by-User Access Control

You've already examined several parameters that determine who is allowed to access a share. In addition to the valid users and invalid users parameters, as well as hosts allow and hosts deny, following are a few more that deserve mention.

admin users You can specify one or more usernames in this parameter. These users attain what amounts to root privileges when accessing the share. In most cases, this option isn't needed; you can grant specific users greater-than-normal levels of access through other means, such as the write list parameter. I recommend you use admin users sparingly, if at all, because of its power and, therefore, potential for problems if misconfigured.

write list When the writeable parameter is set to No, users can't write to a share. You may nonetheless want to grant write permission to one or more users, and you can do so with the write list parameter. For instance, write list = susani grants susani write access to a share that's otherwise marked read-only. In this scenario, however, susani can't overcome her own Linux-based permissions. Without permission to create files in a share (say, because the directory is owned by somebody else and has 0750 permissions), susani's presence in the write list doesn't enable her to write in the directory.

read list The read list parameter is the opposite of write list; it specifies users who are to have *reduced* privileges in a share, with respect to creating or modifying files. To users on the read list, the share is effectively the same as one created with writeable = No. Like write list, this parameter does *not* override Linux's normal rules for file permissions.

username This share-level parameter specifies a list of usernames against which the supplied password is tested. You might use this option when the client computer doesn't send usernames, or sends incorrect usernames. Setting username slows down authentication, however, and increases the security risk. You can specify groups of users rather than individual users in one of three ways:

- If the username is preceded by an @ sign (as in @users), then the name is expanded to all users in the Linux group (in /etc/group) or NIS netgroup.

- If the username is preceded by a plus sign (as in +users), then the name is expanded to all users in the Linux group of that name.

- An ampersand preceding the name (as in &users) indicates that the name is to be expanded to the corresponding NIS group.

For instance, username = susani, @rangers tests passwords against susani and all members of the group rangers. This parameter is generally used with security = Share. Synonyms of this parameter are user and users.

WARNING The user list in /etc/group must be stated explicitly. Samba does not automatically add users whose /etc/passwd entries indicate that they're members of a group if they aren't listed in that group's /etc/group line.

Guest Access

SMB/CIFS networking includes the concept of a *guest user*—one who does not have a password, but to whom you may want to grant access to the system. Naturally, it's best to avoid such configurations, but that isn't always possible. In addition, you might want to configure guest access to some low-security shares, such as shared printers on a network that's not connected to the Internet. Having guest access can make life easier for your users, because they won't need to remember passwords for these shares. Here are the parameters that control guest access:

map to guest   This global parameter controls the circumstances in which Samba invokes the guest account access. Options are as follows:

- When `map to guest` = `Never`, Samba rejects all accesses to shares when invalid usernames or passwords are provided. This is the default. It makes guest access effectively impossible, even if you enable other guest access options.

- The `Bad User` setting means Samba rejects the access attempt if an invalid password is presented with a valid username. If an invalid username is presented, Samba maps the access onto the guest user.

- With `map to guest` = `Bad Password`, if Samba receives an invalid password, it maps the access onto the guest account whether or not the username is valid. This arrangement can be annoying to users who type their correct usernames but mistype their passwords.

guest account   This share-level parameter specifies the name of the Linux account that's used for guest access. In some cases, `nobody` is a good choice for this account, and in fact `nobody` is the default guest account. In other cases you may want to create a "dummy" account that has more access than `nobody`. In the event you need the guest user to have permission to read a particular group's files, for example, you can create a special guest account that belongs to that group.

guest ok   This share-level parameter, when set to `Yes`, allows guest access to the share. The default value is `No`, so even if you set `map to guest` to `Bad User` or `Bad Password`, guest access won't work. You *must* also set `guest ok` = `Yes` to allow guest access to a share. A synonym for `guest ok` is `public`.

guest only   When `guest only` = `Yes` for a share, all accesses to that share are treated as guest accesses. This option requires that `guest ok` = `Yes`. If you access the share with a valid username, the access is accepted or rejected depending on the accuracy of the password entered and the setting of the global `map to guest` parameter. If you use an invalid username, access is accepted, assuming that `map to guest` is not set to `Never`.

Depending upon your client OS, you may still be asked for a username and password when you try to access a guest share; but depending upon how you've set the preceding parameters, you'll be granted access no matter what you type. With the exception of the global `map to guest` parameter, all of these parameters are share-level, and so can be set on a share-by-share basis.

Essential Configuration

PART 2

Consider a share that contains data files that you want to make accessible to all users of your network, even if these individuals don't have accounts on the Samba server. You could set `map to guest = Bad User` and then create a share like the following:

```
[guest]
        comment = All Users Welcome
        path = /home/samba/guest
        guest account = nemo
        writeable = No
        write list = marcusc, susani
        guest ok = Yes
        guest only = Yes
```

This definition allows everybody equal but limited (read-only) access to the share. All the files in the directory must be readable by the user `nemo` in order for this definition to be useful. Note also that `marcusc` and `susani` are on the `write list`, so they have read/write access to the share (provided that `nemo`, the guest user, has write access to the `/home/samba/guest` directory). These two users can therefore maintain the files in this shared directory. Because of the `guest only = Yes` line, all other users have read-only access with the permissions granted `nemo` on the computer. Because the `[global]` section includes `map to guest = Bad User`, individuals who have accounts on the system must present valid passwords when using their normal usernames. (If this is the only guest share on the computer, `map to guest = Bad Password` might be a better choice because it will prevent guest users from being rejected if they happen to try a username that's used by a valid user.)

Some Common File-Sharing Scenarios

To illustrate many of the parameters described in this chapter, let's examine them in action. This section is devoted to some file-sharing scenarios you may encounter in real life. Each one includes a small but complete `smb.conf` file that can be used in the stated situation, with descriptions of its effects and consequences.

Shared Program and File Server

Many networks place common programs such as word processors, archiving tools, and graphics utilities on a central server for all to use, while simultaneously allowing users to store their personal files on the server. Though convenient, this configuration is slow compared to an arrangement where program files are stored on individual workstations. You must also be cautious not to violate your programs' license agreements, which may limit the number of computers on which you may use the software.

One particularly onerous problem with this sort of setup is that many Windows programs store program files both in a directory dedicated to the program, and in the WINDOWS directory. The result is that you may need to reinstall such programs on every client, despite the fact that the program is stored on the Samba server. These problems can make the configuration awkward, but still be useful for programs that are seldom used and don't insist on installing parts of themselves in the WINDOWS directory.

The sample smb.conf file for this type of configuration is shown in Listing 5.1.

Listing 5.1 An smb.conf File for Sharing Files and Programs

```
[global]
        workgroup = EF
        netbios name = WARLOCK
        server string = Samba server on %L
        encrypt passwords = Yes
        log file = /var/log/samba/log.%m
[homes]
        comment = Home Directories
        writeable = Yes
        browseable = No
        create mask = 0664
        directory mask = 0775
[winprogs]
        comment = Windows Programs
        path = /home/samba/winprogs
        force user = winuser
        write list = susani
        read only = Yes
        create mask = 0600
        directory mask = 0700
```

The definition in Listing 5.1 is fairly straightforward. Note the following:

- The [global] section sets assorted configuration options described in Chapter 4. The computer's NetBIOS name is WARLOCK, even if the machine's TCP/IP name is something else. Samba creates a different log file for each client that connects to the computer.

- Users' home directories are explicitly set to be writeable but not browseable. This combination lets users write to their home directories, and prevents a share called HOME from showing up in Windows clients when browsing the computer. Samba automatically presents a home share named after the user, however, even with browseable = No.

- The create mask and directory mask parameters in the [homes] share set very liberal access policies. This arrangement is suitable for an environment in which users must be able to easily collaborate by reading and writing one another's files. You can create separate Linux groups for each collaborating group. Members can thus read and write files owned by the group's members, but they can only read files from other groups' directories.

- The winprogs share relies upon a user known as winuser. The /etc/passwd file on the Linux server must be configured with a user of this name, but the user need not have—and indeed, *should not* have—any login capabilities. Set the user's shell to something like /dev/null so that nobody can log in with that username, and disable the user's password.

- susani has write privileges in the winprogs share, but for everybody else, it's a read-only share. The create mask and directory mask parameters ensure that the files susani creates are readable only by winuser, which is fine for this share because it's accessed using winuser's permissions only. If you want users to be able to get to these files from Linux shell accounts, you must modify this aspect of the configuration.

On the whole, the preceding arrangement is a good starting point for many Samba configurations. You can, of course, customize it in various ways to attain the security and other options you require.

User Files on a High-Security Central Server

Some installations require substantial security for user files. Samba's default settings are relatively lax in this respect, and they can be made even *less* strict (as in the preceding example, by specifying create mask = 0664 in the [homes] share). To tighten security for user shares, you can use an smb.conf file similar the one shown in Listing 5.2.

Listing 5.2 A High-Security Server Configuration for User File Storage

```
[global]
        workgroup = EF
        netbios name = WARLOCK
        server string = Magic Group File Sever
        encrypt passwords = Yes
        log file = /var/log/samba/log.%m
        hosts allow = 192.168.3. 10.45.23.5 10.48.98.10
[homes]
        comment = Home Directories
        writeable = Yes
        browseable = No
        valid users = %U
        create mask = 0600
        directory mask = 0700
        follow symlinks = No
```

This definition isn't much different from the one in Listing 5.1 in terms of the contents of the [global] and [homes] sections. Here are some key points to note about this configuration:

- The server string parameter removes mention of this being a Samba server. There's no point in advertising your server, and hence its vulnerabilities, to would-be crackers.

- This server uses encrypted passwords. So did the definition in Listing 5.1, but encrypted passwords are more critical in a high-security environment.

- This definition uses a global hosts allow parameter to restrict access to the 192.168.3.0/24 network, and to two computers outside of that network. In a real configuration, you should also use measures such as a firewall to deny access to the Samba server.

- The [homes] share uses valid users = %U to restrict logins to only the share's owner. Without this parameter, other users could log onto the share, although they'd not be able to read its files because of other aspects of the definition.

- The [homes] share sets the masks on files and directories to 0600 and 0700, respectively. This feature prevents other users from reading files created through this share, even using a shell login instead of Samba.

- The follow symlinks = No parameter slows access, but it ensures that users can't follow symbolic links out of their assigned directories.

Security doesn't stop with the Samba configuration. On a high-security server, you should disable all unnecessary services; use ownership and permissions to prevent snooping from shell logins; use protocols like SSH rather than Telnet for shell access; enforce password-change rules; and deploy other security measures as appropriate. Some of these issues are explored in Chapter 14, but overall server security is well beyond the scope of this book.

Serving Files to Legacy DOS Systems

A network with a number of DOS computers has file-sharing needs that are different from those of a network of Windows or OS/2 computers. DOS doesn't need long filename support, for instance, and some of Samba's default values work best with computers that understand long filenames. A simple server for individuals' files using older DOS computers might have an smb.conf file similar to the one shown in Listing 5.3.

Listing 5.3 An smb.conf File for a DOS Network Server

```
[global]
        workgroup = EF
        netbios name = WARLOCK
        server string = Samba server on %L
        encrypt passwords = No
        security = Share
        log file = /var/log/samba/log.%m
[%m]
        comment = Home Directories
        path = /home/samba/%m
        username = susani, @lurker
        writeable = Yes
        short preserve case = No
        default case = Upper
        create mask = 0775
        directory mask = 0775
```

This definition is substantially different from the preceding ones in some important ways:

- `encrypt passwords` is set to No, because DOS SMB/CIFS clients don't use encrypted passwords by default. One potentially undesirable consequence of this setting is that recent Windows clients won't be able to access the server unless you disable their encrypted password settings, as described in "Password Encryption" in Chapter 4.

- `security` is set to Share, because some particularly old clients don't send usernames. If you're dealing with a newer SMB/CIFS implementation for DOS, you can use `security = User` and a more conventional [homes] share.

- Rather than a [homes] share, this definition uses a share called [%m], which creates a unique share for each client computer. It's an effective approach if there's a one-to-one correspondence between client computers and their users, but it's not without its drawbacks. For instance, you cannot access one computer's share from another computer, short of installing symbolic links within the shares. Even specifying the share by name (as opposed to browsing to it) won't work.

- The `username` parameter specifies the users who may access the pseudo-home share. The value of this parameter (`susani`, `@lurker`) grants access to the user `susani` and all users in the `lurker` group. When the user enters a password on the client system, it's checked against the passwords of each specified user.

- The `short preserve case = No` and `default case = Upper` parameters force Samba to store short (8.3) filenames using all-uppercase characters. These options help the Samba server's files blend into a DOS environment more consistently than the defaults would do. In most cases, though, these parameters aren't strictly necessary. If the files are to be accessed from Linux as well as from DOS, you might want to omit the `default case` parameter, which defaults to Lower. This makes the case consistent, but files will have lowercase filenames (more typical in Linux than all-uppercase filenames).

- The `create mask` parameter's value of 0775 allows the DOS clients to set the archive, hidden, and system bits on all files. This option probably isn't required, and there's no reason to think it's more likely to be required for DOS than for Windows clients. You may find a need for it in some cases, though, and it makes a good example.

On the whole, a configuration like that in Listing 5.3 is quite extreme. Many DOS systems work well with a conventional Samba [homes] share, although you might want to use the case options from Listing 5.3. You could use a [%m] share similar to this one in other circumstances, though. For instance, to create shares that map to specific computers (say, to store computer-specific drivers), a [%m] share may fit the bill.

Sharing Files Using Multiple Protocols

One of Linux's strengths as a server platform is that it supports so many protocols. Samba enables Linux to serve files on an SMB/CIFS network, Netatalk supports AppleTalk computers, NFS serves Unix systems, and mars_nwe and lwared support NetWare protocols. To use Samba in such a multiprotocol environment, however, you must ensure that your security measures and file-sharing defaults are appropriate for *all* the servers. For instance, suppose you create a common directory for file exchange among users. Under Samba, using the force user parameter to force access to that share under a specific username simplifies configuration; you need not ensure that all users have full read/write access to the directory, nor that they all create files that can be read, written, and deleted by other users. Unfortunately, other file-sharing protocols may not support this option, so in the end you'll need to employ Linux's ownership and permissions to open up access to this directory. You can still use force user on the Samba definition, but you must guarantee that the designated username won't cause problems to the other servers. You may also want to ensure that Windows NT clients can change the permissions on the files through the security mask parameter, so that NT users can correct any problems that arise with security on specific files.

Another challenge that can emerge in a multiprotocol network involves filenames. This problem can be particularly irksome when dealing with Macintosh clients and filenames that contain non-Roman characters, which are common in many European languages. Macintosh users also sometimes include unusual characters, such as bullets (•), in their filenames. Linux servers have various methods for encoding these filenames. Typically, the unusual filenames look fine on the client that created them, but they are ugly or unintelligible on other clients. The best way to handle this is usually to avoid these non-Roman characters in filenames.

Further, filenames longer than what a client can understand often disappear. The most limiting client in this respect is usually the Macintosh, which supports only 31 characters in its filenames—enough for most purposes, but users may accidentally create overlong filenames. One solution is to reduce the number of servers in use. For instance, you can use DAVE from Thursby Software Systems (http://www.thursby.com) to allow Macintoshes to access a Linux Samba server.

Clients and servers occasionally create system-specific files. OS/2 clients, for instance, often create files called WP DATA. SF. Netatalk creates directories called .AppleDouble and Network Trash Folder. You can use Samba's hide files or veto files parameters to hide or remove such files from view. (The WP DATA. SF file will be hidden if you enable the map hidden parameter and set the create mask appropriately, but these settings aren't the defaults. The .AppleDouble directory will be hidden by default but will re-appear if you set hide dot files to No.)

It's possible to use a Linux computer as an intermediary between otherwise incompatible network servers. For instance, suppose you've got a Windows-dominated network with a small number of Macintoshes. If you want your Macintosh users to have access to shares exported by the Windows computers, you can use the Linux computer as a sort of translator. Use the smbmount utility (see Chapter 7, "Using Linux as an SMB/CIFS Client") to mount the Windows computers' shares, and then use Netatalk to export them to the Macintoshes. It's a useful trick for limited use. Unfortunately, you can't presently do the opposite, because the existing Linux client for AppleTalk file shares is extremely primitive. A better solution on the whole is to create a direct connection between client and server, perhaps by using DAVE to enable the Macintosh computers to use SMB/CIFS directly. Using Linux as a bridge between two otherwise incompatible network protocols results in greater network traffic and more potential for problems than does direct access.

One particularly common cross-platform issue is that of end-of-line characters in text files. DOS, Windows, and OS/2 all use one system—a combination of a carriage return and a line feed (or CR/LF for short). Linux and Unix, by contrast, use only a LF; Macintoshes use only a CR. Short utility programs—dos2unix, unix2dos, mac2unix, and unix2mac—come with many Linux distributions and will handle the appropriate conversions to work around these differences. Also, many editors will convert from non-native end-of-line conventions to the native format for the platform on which the editor runs.

A final issue is file locking. Samba takes great pains to implement SMB/CIFS-style file-locking mechanisms, using Linux's underlying file-locking support along with Samba-specific features to fill in the gaps. When you use Samba with one or more other file servers, however, the other servers can't use Samba's add-on file-locking support for features such as oplocks. You can therefore run into problems with file corruption if users try to write the same files from two different platforms. This likely won't be a problem if you use file sharing mainly to export platform-specific files, or even users' home directories. If you export shared directories for user-to-user file exchange, however, problems may arise. It's possible that using oplocks = No in Samba will reduce or eliminate these difficulties. Another option is to tell users about the possibility of such issues and suggest that whenever possible they write new files only, rather than overwriting existing files. Of course, this last solution is awkward at best.

Chapter 13, "Integrating Samba into a Broader Network," further discusses issues of running Samba and other network servers—including several specific file-sharing servers.

Essential Configuration

PART 2

Summary

File sharing is Samba's primary raison d'être. Samba can also be used for printer sharing, as described in Chapter 6—but in most cases, a Samba server serves files. Fortunately, configuring Samba to serve files is fairly easy, at least if your needs are close to typical.

This chapter covers the fundamentals of Samba file-sharing configuration, as well as some midlevel topics such as file locking and filename handling. Using the options described in this chapter, you can fine-tune the behavior of your Samba server to best suit your clients' needs. In fact, Samba's plethora of options allow you to configure it in ways that aren't possible with Windows servers. This flexibility is one of Samba's appeals.

6

Configuring Printer Sharing

Although file sharing (described in Chapter 5) is the most commonly used networking feature of Samba, printer sharing is also quite important. In fact, it's possible to employ Samba exclusively as a print server, without configuring a single file share. Both types of sharing are similar in many respects. In both cases, files are transferred among computers, and Samba does this through named shares.

Printer sharing is simpler than file sharing in some respects, because printer sharing doesn't involve issues relating to file-naming conventions, file locking, and so on. Printer sharing is also a largely one-way process: Clients pass files to be printed to the server, but the server doesn't pass files back to the client, as is common when sharing files. On the other hand, printer sharing does involve configuration issues not found in file sharing. These include the details of sending the files through the Linux print queue, configuring that queue, and selecting Windows printer drivers. Samba's printer sharing therefore involves several parameters in addition to those used to configure file sharing.

> **TIP**   An unused computer (even an old 80486 or 80386) makes an excellent print server, particularly if outfitted with a couple of extra parallel-port cards, serial cards for serial printers, or a USB card for USB printers. A Samba print server can do other duty as a file server, DHCP server, and so on—although some of these roles may stretch the capacity of old hardware. If you *only* need print server functions, you might want to look into dedicated hardware print servers. These devices have an Ethernet port and one or more parallel ports, and typically understand several network printing protocols. They're usually smaller and easier to maintain than a dedicated Linux computer.

This chapter begins with a review of Linux print queue configuration. With few exceptions, if you can't use a printer natively from Linux, you can't serve it to Windows computers. Next is a discussion of setting up a Samba print queue based upon your existing Linux print queues, and then descriptions of important printer security options. The chapter concludes with some examples of printer-sharing configurations.

Creating Print Queues

Samba operates by accepting a file from the client computer and sending that file through Linux's normal print queue system. It's therefore vital that you have a print queue configured on the Linux system for every printer you intend to share. For most printers, there are two possible types of queues: PostScript queues that print through Ghostscript, and "raw" queues that feed data directly to the printer without processing. (These two types are essentially the same if the printer's native language is PostScript.) Each print queue has its advantages and drawbacks.

You can also configure Samba as a fax server, in which the "printer" is a fax modem. An office that sends a lot of faxes of electronically generated documents can thereby devote a single telephone line to computer-generated faxes; Linux queues these just like any other print job.

Ghostscript and PostScript Printing

Traditionally, Unix computers have used PostScript printers. Instead of using a printing API, as is common in Windows, Unix programs generate PostScript code, which the Unix print queue passes on to the printer in a relatively unprocessed form. If a print job requires processing, it is passed through a program called a *filter* that is associated with the print queue.

As a Unix clone that runs many Unix programs, Linux follows this model; but many Linux users don't have PostScript printers. Therefore, all major Linux distributions ship with a program called *Ghostscript,* which is a PostScript interpreter that runs on the host computer rather than the printer. Ghostscript takes the PostScript that's generated by Linux programs and turns it into a bitmap, along with whatever control codes a specific printer model requires to print that bitmap. The Linux print queue processes the print job through Ghostscript using a *smart filter* that calls Ghostscript only when it's needed.

The result of this processing is that any printer—be it a top-of-the-line PostScript model or a $100 ink-jet—can be treated as a PostScript printer in Linux. Because Samba is a Linux program, this rule extends to Samba and Samba's clients. So if you like, you can use PostScript drivers on Windows or other Samba clients to drive even most non-PostScript printers connected to a Samba print server. You don't *have* to share all printers as if they were PostScript printers, though; the alternative (a "raw" printer share) is described shortly, in the section "Raw Queues." The Windows driver configuration issues are covered later in this chapter, in "Windows Printer Driver Installation." For now, though, let's look at Linux print queue configuration.

Before you can configure a non-PostScript printer in Linux, you must know certain things about it. Most importantly, you must know what type of hardware interface it uses and what printer command language it emulates—that is, what Ghostscript driver it uses. For information on Ghostscript drivers for printers, consult the Linux Printing Support Database (`http://www.linuxprinting.org/printer_list.cgi`).

Essential Configuration

PART 2

Aladdin vs. GNU Ghostscript

Ghostscript is available in two forms: *Aladdin Ghostscript* and *GNU Ghostscript.* The former is the cutting-edge release of the program, available from `http://www.cs.wisc.edu/~ghost/`. It's distributed under a license that allows for completely free redistribution, but anyone who charges for a package containing Aladdin Ghostscript must obtain permission. Therefore, Linux distributions do not ship with Aladdin Ghostscript; they ship with GNU Ghostscript, which uses the popular GNU's Not Unix (GNU) General Public License (GPL).

After a given version of Aladdin Ghostscript has been available for a while, Aladdin changes its license terms, and that version becomes the new GNU Ghostscript. The replacement Aladdin Ghostscript adds new features. If you're using a particularly new printer, you may need to obtain Aladdin Ghostscript to get it to work properly. If you use an older printer, or one that uses a well-established printer language such as Hewlett Packard's PCL, GNU Ghostscript should be adequate.

Using a GUI Printer Configuration Tool

The easiest way to configure a printer in Linux is to use a GUI printer configuration tool. Most Linux distributions ship with such a program, but the details differ. Caldera eDesktop uses a COAS module to configure printers, but SuSE uses options in its YaST tool. Several distributions (including Debian, Red Hat, and Red Hat derivatives such as Mandrake and LinuxPPC) use a utility called `printtool` to configure printers. Figure 6.1 shows the main `printtool` window, which you can obtain by typing **printtool** in a shell prompt window such as an xterm.

Figure 6.1   The main `printtool` window helps you create, delete, and edit print queues and perform tests on existing queues.

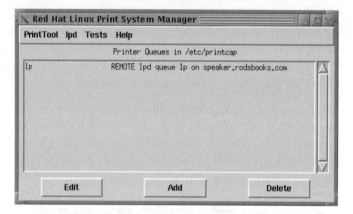

To create a print queue using `printtool`, follow these steps:

1. Start `printtool`.

2. Click the Add button in the main window.

3. `printtool` displays a dialog box that asks you to specify the type of queue to be created—a local printer, remote Unix queue, etc. Because you're presumably configuring a print server, select the first option, Local Printer. (If you want to use Samba to share a printer that exists on another server, you can do so, however.) When you've selected the appropriate option, click OK.

4. The program will probably display a brief message box showing the printer ports it has found on the system. If your printer is a USB or RS-232 serial printer, you can disregard this notice. In my experience, `printtool` isn't very good even at detecting parallel-port printers, so don't be alarmed if it doesn't detect all your ports. You'll get to specify the correct device in the next step. Click OK to continue.

TIP Linux's support for USB printers is essentially nonexistent in the 2.2.*x* kernel series. The new 2.4.*x* kernels, however, include support for USB printers. To serve USB printers, therefore, you may need to upgrade your kernel, if you're not already using a 2.4.*x* kernel.

5. Next you'll see a display similar to the one just below, in which you'll complete several fields. You can often leave the default values as is for these fields, but at least check that they're reasonable for your configuration:

    A. Name your print queue by entering the queue name in the Names text-entry field. (You can use a different name when exporting the printer under Samba, if you like.)

    B. You can adjust the name of the spool directory, which I recommend you name after the print queue's name.

    C. You must set the printer device, which is the Linux device file to which the printer is attached—/dev/lp0 for the first parallel port, /dev/ttyS1 for the second serial port, and so on.

    D. If you want identifying headers to print along with every print job, uncheck the Suppress Headers check box. *Do not* click OK yet!

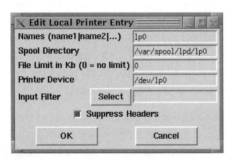

6. Click the Select button to choose your printer type. printtool displays the Configure Filter dialog box shown in Figure 6.2.

    A. The most important feature of this dialog box is the Printer Type list on the left, in which you'll select your printer. This list does not include entries for the vast majority of printers on the market today; instead, it relies on you to know which major printer yours emulates. For instance, many laser printers today emulate the Hewlett-Packard LaserJet 4/5/6–series printers, so you would select this entry for any of these laser printers—even models that aren't manufactured by Hewlett-Packard. (These printers use Hewlett-Packard's *Printer Command Language [PCL]*, version 5e or above.)

Figure 6.2   Select the Ghostscript driver and options in the Configure Filter dialog box.

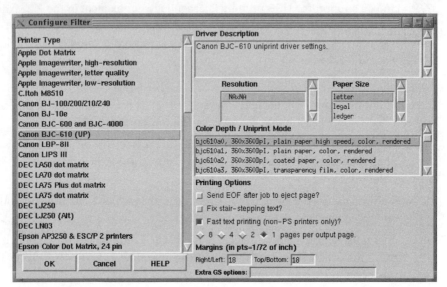

NOTE There is a single entry for all PostScript printers in the Printer Type list. The standard Linux printer system doesn't know anything about the specific features of individual PostScript printers, so one entry suffices. Some Linux programs, however, know about specific printer features. Windows PostScript drivers also provide access to these features.

B. Once you select a printer type, the right side of the dialog box will adapt. Some models allow you to select a resolution or paper size, but others don't support these options. Other printers provide various options in the Color Depth/ Uniprint Mode area. Select the configuration you want.

C. Check the options you need in the Printing Options area. You can fix problems such as printers that don't eject their last pages, "stair-stepped" text (illustrated in Figure 6.3), and so on. The Fast Text Printing option sends raw text files to the printer as text, rather than converting them to PostScript. This option can speed up printing of text files on non-PostScript printers, but there's a good chance it will have no effect for printing text from Windows clients.

D. When you've set all your options, click the OK button to close the Configure Filter dialog box.

Figure 6.3   *Stair-stepping* is an effect caused by printers that expect DOS-style end-of-line characters consisting of a carriage return/line feed pair, when they are sent only the Unix-style end-of-line characters.

```
Line 1
        Line 2
                Line 3
                        Line 4
```

7. You should see the Edit Local Printer Entry dialog box again, this time with a Ghost-script driver name listed in the Input Filter field. Click OK to save this queue definition.

8. Next you should see your new queue in the main `printtool` list; Figure 6.1 shows one queue defined, for example. Choose lpd ➤ Restart lpd to restart the lpd printer daemon.

9. Select the queue you've just defined.

10. The Tests menu item contains three options: Print ASCII Test Page, Print PostScript Test Page, and Print ASCII Directly to Port. You can use these options to test your new print queue definition. Be sure to turn on your printer, then try the tests.

   A. The Print ASCII Test Page option produces a page filled with ASCII text, including centered text, vertically aligned exclamation marks, and tips concerning features to enable if particular options didn't work. This test attempts to print the file through the normal Linux print queue as an ASCII file (normally, Ghostscript is *not* involved).

   B. If Print ASCII Test Page produces a blinking light on a laser printer but no output, try hitting the Page Eject button on your printer. If you then get the test page, go back to step 6C and enable the option called Send EOF After Job to Eject Page.

   C. If Print ASCII Test Page produces no output—not even a blinking light on the printer—then try Print ASCII Directly to Port. If this test works, something is causing your print queue to fail. Such problems are rare. If the test fails, you may need to change the port you selected in step 5C, or you may need to add a printer driver to your system.

   D. The Print PostScript Test Page option works much like Print ASCII Test Page, except that the program prints a full-page PostScript test page. This page includes color samples so you can check that you're getting at least minimal color functionality out of a color printer. If this test fails, you may need to select another printer (or at least printer options) in step 6. It's also possible that you need to upgrade to a newer version of Ghostscript.

11. When you're satisfied that your printer is working correctly, choose PrintTool ➢ Quit to exit from the program.

In some cases, you may want to create two or more print queues for a single printer. Perhaps you want to create one queue to print to an ink-jet printer at low resolution and another at a higher resolution. If so, create two or more queues, each with its own name but sending output to the same printer device.

Configuring a Print Queue Manually

If your distribution doesn't include a GUI printer configuration tool, or if you need to modify the configuration produced by such a tool, you must edit your printer configuration manually. The key file in printer configuration on most Linux systems is /etc/ printcap. This file lists all the print queues defined on a computer. Listing 6.1 contains an example /etc/printcap queue definition.

Listing 6.1 Basic /etc/printcap Queue Definition

```
lp|hp4000:\
        :sd=/var/spool/lpd/lp:\
        :mx#0:\
        :sh:\
        :sf:\
        :lp=/dev/lp0:\
        :if=/var/spool/lpd/lp/filter:
```

NOTE The sort of print queue definition shown in Listing 6.1 is used on BSD-style systems and printer systems modeled after the BSD printing system. Such queues are the most common type on Linux computers. A few Linux systems use other printing systems, however, which involve different print queue definition files and file contents.

Technically, each /etc/printcap entry is a single line; the backslash characters (\ ) at the ends of most lines are *line continuation characters* that tell the system to treat consecutive lines as if they were one line. Entries are separated by colons (:). Each entry is either a single code or a code assigned a value by an equal sign (=) or pound sign (#). You can find what all the possible options mean by reading the printcap man page, but here are the key items:

lp|hp4000   This string identifies the queue. You can specify multiple names for a single queue, separated by vertical bars (|). In the example in Listing 6.1, the queue can be called using either the lp or the hp4000 names.

sd   This option sets the *spool directory*, where the system stores files that are to be printed.

mx   This option specifies the maximum file size, in kilobytes. If it's set to 0, there's no maximum file size. You can use this setting as protection against huge files overrunning your server's disk capacity.

sh   This is the *suppress header* option. Remove it if you want Linux to print a header page identifying the user who starts each print job.

sf   This is the *suppress form feed* option. It prevents Linux from ejecting the last page of a text-only print job. You may need to include this parameter if you define a raw queue for use by Samba, or else Linux may eject a blank sheet at the end of each print job.

lp   This option specifies the device file for the printer device. In the case of printing to a remote Unix queue, there is no lp option; instead, the definition uses the rm and rp options, described next.

rm   This option, which doesn't appear in Listing 6.1, specifies the name of a remote Unix print server. If you're configuring a Linux print server, chances are you won't set this option, but you might if the Linux server is just an intermediary way-station. If you use this option, you must also use the rp option.

rp   If you use rm to specify a remote print server, you must also use rp, which specifies the remote queue's name.

if   This option sets the *input filter*—the program through which the system passes a print job before sending the job on to the printer device. If all your print jobs were PostScript jobs, you could use a script that calls Ghostscript with the appropriate parameters for your printer as the input filter. Most Linux distributions, though, ship with at least one *smart filter*. These filters try to determine the type of the file and process it appropriately for the printer type. The GUI printer configuration (step 6 in the preceding section) sets up the smart filter used by Red Hat and similar distributions. If you want to use a smart filter other than what came with your distribution, you should consult the filter's documentation for configuration details. These specifics differ substantially from one filter to another.

Other Configuration Issues   Once you've configured /etc/printcap, your printer should work—if there are no filter-related issues that need adjustment. You may find that you need to change settings related to your print filter. If you're tweaking a queue that you originally configured using a GUI utility, check the file pointed to by the if line in /etc/printcap. This file is probably a script that calls other scripts or loads other files for their parameters. Sooner or later in this chain, you'll find parameters that get passed to Ghostscript. These parameters control most of the interesting aspects of printing, such as the

Essential Configuration

PART 2

Ghostscript driver used by the queue. For instance, in a Red Hat system, these features are controlled by the file /var/spool/lpd/*queuename*/postscript.cfg. It contains lines such as these:

```
GSDEVICE=laserjet
RESOLUTION=300x300
COLOR=
PAPERSIZE=letter
EXTRA_GS_OPTIONS=""
```

You can adjust these values as you see fit. For example, installing a new version of Ghostscript to obtain a very recent driver may require configuring a queue using an incorrect Ghostscript device, and then editing the GSDEVICE line to specify the new Ghostscript device driver. You can also use the EXTRA_GS_OPTIONS line to include unusual Ghostscript parameters. (You can also enter these values in the Configure Filter dialog box of printtool shown earlier in Figure 6.2.)

Raw Queues

To share your printers as PostScript devices, you should create a conventional PostScript queue, as just described. You can also share non-PostScript printers "raw," however. When you do this, you configure your Samba clients to print to the printer model you have, not to a PostScript printer. The client then sends a file that contains printer codes appropriate for that model of printer, and Linux passes this file on to the printer without attempting to use Ghostscript or any other program to process it.

Raw queues have several advantages and disadvantages compared to Ghostscript-driven queues. In terms of speed, raw queues sometimes print more quickly than PostScript queues. This is because native Windows drivers frequently make use of features (such as built-in printer fonts) that can reduce the size of printer files, hence reducing parallel-port transmission times. For some printer and file types, though, the speed equation favors PostScript queues when PostScript can more efficiently describe a page than can the native printer language. This is sometimes true of complex graphics, particularly when Ghostscript's driver for the printer is unusually efficient.

All other things being equal, you want to reduce the load on your network. PostScript files are generally quite space-efficient and thus reduce network load. This is particularly true when the printers are low-end devices with few built-in fonts, but it may not be true of sophisticated PCL laser printers.

Using a raw queue almost invariably reduces the amount of CPU time the server must devote to processing the file. This may be a factor if your server handles several printers, or if it's an old computer with limited CPU power. On the other hand, raw queues reduce the CPU load on the server largely by shifting the CPU work to the clients.

Ghostscript support for most printers is good but not universal. Some printers for which no Ghostscript support is available can be shared with Windows clients using a raw queue. The Windows client then needs to have appropriate driver support. This rule isn't universal, however. If the Windows printer driver requires bi-directional communication (as is true of some low-end laser printers), the printer can't be shared from a Linux computer.

In sum, the best queue type for you—raw or PostScript—depends on your network, your printers, and the types of files you print. You may want to try both queue types to see which works best for you.

NOTE Raw and PostScript queues are virtually identical when the printer is a PostScript printer. In this case, the input filter on a PostScript queue should identify PostScript files and pass them to the printer unmodified. Some Windows PostScript drivers, however, include extraneous information that can confuse a Linux print filter. One way around this problem is to use a raw queue for true PostScript printers that are to be served through Samba.

Configuring a raw queue is just like configuring a PostScript queue. The only difference is that you must *omit* the filter definition. If you use a GUI configuration tool like `printtool`, you skip the filter definition step (step 6 in "Using a GUI Printer Configuration Tool"). When creating the definition by hand, omit the `if` line in `/etc/printcap`.

Fax Queues

Theoretically, using Samba to create a "printer" definition that really works as a fax queue is simple: You define a print queue that pipes its input through a fax modem by using a package such as mgetty+sendfax (included with most Linux distributions) as the print queue's input filter. In fact, matters are more complex than this for two reasons:

- The system needs to know the destination telephone number. The system might be able to extract this information from the transmitted file, if it's a letter with the fax number in some obvious location. In practice, however, it's better to enable an interactive configuration that acquires the fax number from the user's entry in a dialog box.

- Linux fax configuration is not as simple as it might be. Most Linux fax packages are tedious to set up and debug.

Some Linux fax packages, such as HylaFAX (`http://www.hylafax.org/index.html`), include direct support for a client/server fax architecture. If you use such a package, there's no need to involve Samba in the equation. Employing Samba as a fax server can be fairly simple, though, if you obtain one additional package to incorporate with the Samba fax server. A very useful such package is Respond (`http://www.boerde.de/~horstf/`), which works through either mgetty+sendfax or HylaFAX.

You should download at least three programs from the main Respond Web page:

Respond   The main package is available in 16- or 32-bit versions for Windows. Use InfoZip, PKZip, or a similar utility to unzip the program, and place the `RESPOND.EXE` program in the client's Windows Start-up Items folder.

`printfax.pl`   This file is a Perl script that controls the fax process from Linux. Download it and place it in `/usr/local/bin` or another convenient binary location.

`readme.txt`   This is the Respond documentation, where you'll find more detail concerning Respond configuration than is given here.

When you've downloaded and installed these files, create a special entry in `smb.conf` for the fax queue (this entry is shown in Listing 6.2). It uses some special features described in "Samba Options for Printer Shares" later in this chapter.

Listing 6.2   Sample Respond-Based Samba Fax Queue

```
[fax]
        comment = Fax
        postscript = Yes
        print command = ( /usr/local/bin/printfax.pl %I %s %U %m; ↵
           rm %s ) &
        printable = Yes
        path = /var/spool/samba
```

You may need to edit the `path` parameter to match your Samba print spool directory, as described shortly. You may also need to adjust the location of the `printfax.pl` program in the `print command` parameter, if you place it somewhere other than `/usr/local/bin`. Finally, you can add security features, change the fax queue name, and so on. Remember to restart the Samba daemon so that it makes the `[fax]` share available to clients.

NOTE   In theory, you could create a Linux print queue that runs the `printfax.pl` script as an input filter. The configuration I've just described bypasses the Linux print queue system entirely, however, and it works well.

In order to use this configuration, set up and configure either mgetty+sendfax or HylaFAX. Briefly, here are the steps to configure mgetty+sendfax:

1. *Install the package.* Locate and install mgetty+sendfax. The package is usually called `mgetty+sendfax`, `mgetty-sendfax`, or `mgetty`, depending on your Linux distribution. If you can't find it on your distribution, check `http://alpha.greenie.net/mgetty/`, the package's home page.

2. *Configure mgetty+sendfax.* Most distributions place mgetty+sendfax's configuration files in `/etc/mgetty+sendfax`. You should adjust at least four files:

   - `fax.allow` contains a list of users who are allowed to send faxes. Place one username per line in this file.

   - `faxheader` contains the header information for outgoing faxes. You should adjust it to list your fax number.

   - `sendfax.config` contains miscellaneous fax configuration information. Most of the items in this file are well commented. Change the `fax-id` item to your fax number. The `fax-devices` item is also critically important. It should list your fax device filename (without the leading `/dev/`), as in `ttyS1` or `modem`.

   - `faxrunq.config` contains additional, miscellaneous fax configuration information. At a minimum, you should set the `fax-devices` item to point to your fax device filename, as you did on the same line in `sendfax.config`.

3. *Launch* `faxrunqd`. This is a daemon that watches for faxes to appear in the fax queue directory. Installing the mgetty+sendfax package normally creates this directory, usually at `/var/spool/fax`. To use your system as a fax server on a regular basis, you should configure it to run `faxrunqd` at system start-up, say by adding it to `/etc/rc.d/rc.local` or a similar start-up file. When you do, be sure to include an ampersand (&) on the start-up line, because `faxrunqd` does not normally start up in the background.

At this point, the server is configured to accept fax jobs and send them on their way. You must configure the client to print to the [fax] share as if it were a PostScript printer. "Windows Printer Driver Installation" describes this process later in this chapter.

When you print to the resulting queue from Windows, Windows displays the Respond Query dialog box (Figure 6.4). Enter the destination fax number, the recipient's name, and the sender's Linux username and real name. Next to the Fax-Number(s) field is an icon of a Rolodex, which you can click to maintain a fax address book on the Windows client. You can add recipients to the address book, or select a number for entry in the Fax-Number(s) field from the address book. After you click OK, there may be a delay of up to a minute before `faxrunq` notices the fax, after which mgetty+sendfax sends the fax. This delay doesn't affect the client, however.

Figure 6.4 The Respond program prompts a Windows user for a fax number, and passes that information back to the Linux server.

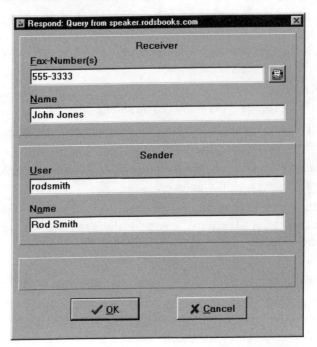

Configuring Printer Shares

Printer shares work very much like file shares. In particular, they begin with a share definition, such as [inkjet], and continue with a series of parameters. Many of the parameters used in file sharing (described in Chapter 5) apply to printer shares as well. In particular, options relating to access control (valid users, hosts allow, and so on) apply to both file and printer shares. File sharing options relating to factors such as filenames and file ownership either don't apply to printer shares or aren't terribly useful when they are applied. Because of the similarities, I recommend you read Chapter 5, even if you want to configure a Samba server to function only as a print server.

A Basic Printer-Sharing Example

Listing 6.3 is a basic example of a printer sharing definition.

Listing 6.3 Minimal Printer Share Definition

```
[inkjet]
        comment = Inkjet Printer
        path = /var/spool/samba
        printable = Yes
```

In fact, this definition is quite verbose—the comment and path parameters are both optional. The key aspect of the printer definition is the printable = Yes parameter. This parameter defines the share as a printer share. (A synonym for this option is print ok.) There are two special considerations of which you should be aware.

First, the path parameter specifies the location of Samba's print spool directory. Samba stores print spool jobs in this directory before handing those jobs off to Linux's print queue. If you don't specify a path, Samba uses /tmp for this task.

> **WARNING** The printer path directory should have the sticky bit (t) set, to pre-vent one user from deleting another's files. You can set this bit by issuing a com-mand like **chmod 1777** */var/spool/samba* or **chmod o+t** */var/spool/samba*. The printer path directory must also be writeable by all users who might use the exported share. When you use **ls -l** to view the permissions on the directory, they should resemble drwxrwxrwt, although the group and world write permis-sions are optional, depending on who is allowed to use the printer share.

In addition, the name of the share ([inkjet] in Listing 6.3) should match the name of the Linux print queue to which it's linked. You can get around this requirement, as described shortly, but the simplest configuration uses the same name for the Linux and Samba print queues.

Once you've defined a basic printer share, you can browse to it from Windows, as shown here:

PART 2

Essential Configuration

The printer appears in the same browse list as file shares, but Windows uses a different icon to identify the printer share. You cannot make good use of the printer share directly from the Windows browser; first, you must link the share to a local Windows print queue, a process described later in the "Windows Printer Driver Installation" section.

NOTE Sometimes (particularly on Windows NT clients), Windows displays a Printers folder among the Samba server's shares, but this folder is empty. Printers appear on the same level with file shares in all Windows browsers.

Sharing All or Some Printers

In some cases, a Linux computer is the server for several printers. For example, the server might have Linux queues for two parallel-port printers, a USB printer, and an AppleTalk printer. You might also create multiple print queues for a single printer, such as when an ink-jet printer supports multiple resolutions. If you create PostScript queues for non-PostScript printers, you need a separate queue for each resolution you intend to use. You might also want to create both PostScript-driven and raw queues for a single printer. With all of these factors, it's not uncommon to see a Linux computer that has half a dozen or more separate print queues. You must decide whether you want to share all of these queues or just some of them.

One easy way to share all the queues is to create a single smb.conf print queue entry under the special name [printers]. This special share name creates as many queues as you have entries in /etc/printcap and exports them under the first name of each printer in /etc/printcap. You must also ensure that load printers is set to Yes, which is its default. Setting load printers = No prevents the [printers] share from reading the /etc/printcap file. In some ways, the [printers] share is similar to the [homes] share for sharing home directories: [homes] allows each user to see one home share bearing the user's login name, whereas [printers] produces as many visible printer shares as the system has /etc/printcap entries.

Although the [printers] share can be convenient, it does have its drawbacks.

All shares use identical parameters.   You can't fine-tune each printer's parameters with a single [printers] share. You can, however, create a [printers] share with the parameters used on most printers, then create separate shares for every printer that requires customization. For instance, a system that has six print queues but only needs unusual parameters on the okidata queue could have one [printers] share followed by an [okidata] share. The clients will see six printer shares; the [okidata] share will be derived from the unique [okidata] definition rather than from the generic [printers] definition, even though the /etc/printcap file defines an okidata queue. A specific share definition takes precedence over a like-named queue created by the [printers] share.

All printers are available.   You can't easily omit printers included in your /etc/printcap file when you use the [printers] definition. If you want to export only some of your printers, you must create separate definitions for each printer. Alternatively, you can create an edited version of /etc/printcap under another name, and use the Samba printcap name parameter to use the edited file rather than the genuine one.

Printer names are immutable.   The [printers] definition uses the first printer name to appear in the /etc/printcap file for each print queue. On many systems, this name is short and potentially confusing, such as lp. If you define your queues separately, you can adjust the name of the share, as described shortly. You may be able to achieve similar effects by rearranging the order of names in each print queue's definition in /etc/printcap. For example, if a queue lists its names as lp|lexmark|lexmark-optra-45, you can reverse that order (lexmark-optra-45|lexmark|lp) to share the queue in Samba as lexmark-optra-45, while maintaining use of the other two names from Linux.

If you prefer, you can export all your printers individually. You can even create more than one Samba printer share for a single Linux print queue. This is done to export a share using multiple sets of options. One reason this is useful is that some smart filters, which automatically handle PostScript files as well as files in a printer's native language, become confused by some Windows PostScript drivers. The Samba parameter postscript = Yes helps in such situations. You might therefore want to create two queues, one that includes this parameter and one that does not, in order to use either PostScript or the printer's native drivers from Windows.

You can also export just some of your printer's queues under Samba. As mentioned, you might create multiple queues for an ink-jet printer to allow Linux users to print using a variety of resolutions. (Under Linux, resolution setting on most ink-jet printers is handled by parameters sent to Ghostscript, and these parameters are coded into the print queue definition, immutable by most applications.) Under Windows, however, it's probably simpler to print using the printer's native drivers and a Linux raw queue, so there's no need to export all the queues for that printer if you intend to use only the printer's native drivers.

If you use linuxconf to configure Samba, you can *only* configure a single [printers] share. SWAT, by contrast, allows you to create a [printers] share, individualized shares, or both. linuxconf is also extremely limited in the printer parameters it supports.

If you want to use a GUI configuration tool for printer configuration, SWAT is far superior to linuxconf. Both these tools are explored in Chapter 4.

Samba Options for Printer Shares

As mentioned earlier in "Configuring Printer Shares," Samba recognizes many of the same options for both file and printer shares, such as the path parameter and assorted security options. There are also printer-specific parameters to adjust the way Samba treats printer shares. These options include the following:

load printers   This is a boolean global parameter that defaults to a value of Yes. When configured in this way, Samba loads the printers found in /etc/printcap for use by a [printers] parameter, if present.

print ok   This parameter, which also goes by the name printable, identifies a share as a printer share. It's required on all printer shares.

printcap name   This parameter specifies the name of the printer definition file. On most Samba installations, it defaults to /etc/printcap, but it doesn't hurt to set it to make sure it's configured correctly.

printer name   Use this parameter to specify the name of a print queue. For instance, if your Linux server's printer is a Hewlett-Packard 4050 known locally as lp, you might create a share called [hp4050] and use printer name = lp to map the share to the correct Linux print queue, while providing a more descriptive name to client computers. A synonym for this parameter is printer. By default, Samba tries to use a Linux print queue with the same name as the share definition, except for the special case of the [printers] share.

min print space   Samba can refuse a print job if the server is running low on disk space. You can use the min print space parameter to set the amount of disk space in kilobytes required to accept a print job. For example, if you set min print space = 2000 and a client tries to print a job when the server has only 1,000KB left on the Samba spool partition, then Samba refuses to accept the print job. The default value is 0, which means that Samba doesn't apply this test.

postscript   Many Windows PostScript drivers place a Ctrl+D character at the front of each print job. This practice can confuse Linux print filters into thinking that the print job is ASCII text. The result is a printout of PostScript code rather than the page described by that code. You can correct this problem by setting postscript = Yes, which causes Samba to insert a PostScript comment (%!) at the start of the file.

printing   This parameter specifies the name of the printing system used on your Linux server. Adjusting the parameter affects the default values of several others; if printing is set incorrectly, you may find that printing won't work because Samba issues incorrect print commands. This parameter's default can be set as a compile-time option, and the Samba package included with a given Linux distribution should set it appropriately for that distribution. Therefore, you shouldn't need to adjust `printing` unless you replace your distribution's default printing system, or replace your distribution's Samba package with one intended for a distribution that uses a different system. Values accepted by this parameter are `Bsd`, `Aix`, `Lprng`, `Plp`, `Sysv`, `Hpux`, `Qnx`, `Softq`, and `Cups`. More options may be added in the future.

TIP   To find what `printing` values a future version of Samba will accept, try using SWAT. Select a print queue, enable the Advanced View, and locate the `printing` parameter. SWAT includes all the possible values in a selectable list. Of course, your version of SWAT must match the version of the Samba daemons you're using.

print command   The `print command` parameter specifies the command used to send a print job to the printer. The default depends on the `printing` parameter, but it is usually based on `lpr` because most Linux systems use BSD or LPRng printing. You can adjust this parameter to achieve special printing effects. Read the man pages associated with your printing software to determine what types of effects are possible. You can also use this parameter to use an entirely different program to process print files. The fax queue presented in Listing 6.2 uses this feature to pass the print job through a Perl script that uses Ghostscript and calls mgetty+sendfax to send the result to a remote fax machine. You can use assorted variables in this command, the most important of which is `%s`, the file to be printed.

lpq command   On a properly functioning Samba server, a client can request information about jobs in the print queue. Samba uses the Linux `lpq` command to locate this information, but you are allowed to adjust this command and its options to suit your printing system. The default of the `lpq command` parameter therefore depends on the `printing` parameter. Also, Samba's interpretation of the output depends on the `printing` parameter. If included in the command, `%p` refers to the printer name.

lprm command   This parameter specifies the command Samba issues when a client requests that a job be deleted. You can use `%p` and `%j` to refer to the printer name and job number, respectively. The default value depends on the `printing` parameter.

lppause command   Windows clients can pause a printing job. On Linux, this is often achieved by setting the job to a very low priority, but details differ from one printing system to another. The default value of this parameter is usually null (no command is specified), but `Sysv`, `Hpux`, and `Softq` printing types include appropriate commands. `%p` and `%j` refer to the printer name and job number, respectively.

lpresume command This parameter specifies the command used to resume printing of a specified print job; it is essentially the opposite of the lppause command.

queuepause command In addition to pausing individual jobs, Windows clients can request that an entire queue be paused. This parameter specifies the command that Samba uses to pause a queue. The default value of this parameter depends on the printing parameter's value. A %p in the value refers to the print queue name.

queueresume command This parameter specifies the command Samba uses to resume printing on the queue specified by the %p variable. It is essentially the opposite of the queuepause command.

On the whole, the default parameters work well for most installations, although you *must* include a print ok = Yes parameter to turn a share into a printer share. You may need to adjust additional parameters on some installations, particularly if the Samba package doesn't match the rest of your Linux printing system. The postscript parameter is also particularly helpful if you have a PostScript or Ghostscript-driven printer and your Windows printer drivers insert Ctrl-D characters at the start of print jobs.

Linux Printing Systems

Most Linux distributions today ship with BSD-style printing systems, featuring a print command called lpr. This printing system is functional and familiar to most Linux and Unix system administrators. A few Linux installations use printing configurations based on System V (or SysV) protocols, which have a somewhat different stable of commands, such as lp to print a file. SysV printing is familiar to many Unix administrators but is less common on Linux.

Unfortunately, both systems are showing their age, in terms of inflexible design and a great potential for security problems. For this reason, many alternatives to these systems have emerged over the last few years. Some, such as LPRng, are designed to be familiar to users of old systems. LPRng ships with Caldera and a few other Linux distributions. It emulates BSD's utilities in many respects, but with some options removed and others added. CUPS is a new system that's designed to provide more in the way of interactive features to Linux programs—that is, CUPS provides information about printers' capabilities to programs, much the way Windows printer drivers do.

Because of the Samba printer options, you can use just about any Linux printing system with Samba. If you choose a particularly exotic system, however, you may need to learn enough about it to specify a print command, lpq command, and so on.

Windows Printer Driver Installation

Before you can print from Windows, you must install a Windows printer driver and create a local queue on the Windows client. The same is true of printing from DOS, OS/2, or Linux clients—although DOS printer drivers normally reside in individual application programs, and Linux clients can be configured to print as to a PostScript printer if the server exports the share as a PostScript device.

The details of Windows printer driver installation vary from one driver to another, but there are basically two ways to install a driver: manually or automatically. Manual configuration requires that you have a printer driver available at each client computer. (You can put the drivers on a Samba file share, if you like.) For automatic configuration, you automate the driver configuration process by setting up Samba to provide driver files for the Windows clients. Before you can set up an automatic share, you must install the driver manually on at least one client.

Manual Driver Installation

There are three major sources for Windows printer drivers: Microsoft, the printer manufacturer, and third-party suppliers. The Microsoft Windows installation CD-ROM includes a wide selection of printer drivers. These drivers usually don't have as many features as some others, but they're generally adequate. The Microsoft-supplied drivers for the Apple LaserWriter series, in particular, work well with Ghostscript-driven printers. Most printers come with Windows drivers on a CD-ROM or, for older printers, floppy disks. You can also download updates from most manufacturers' Web sites, and occasionally find drivers from third parties. This is particularly true for PostScript printers, because Adobe (`http://www.adobe.com/`) offers a generic PostScript driver that works with any PostScript printer. Adobe's driver uses *printer page description (PPD)* files to customize its features for each printer.

> **WARNING**   The Adobe PostScript driver is licensed for use with printers that include PostScript interpreters written by Adobe. You will be in violation of Adobe's license if you use the driver with Ghostscript-driven printers or with printers that use PostScript clones.

In the case of manufacturer-supplied or third-party drivers, you should consult the driver's documentation to learn how to install the software. The procedures used may resemble those I'm about to describe, but these drivers sometimes use custom installation routines.

> ***TIP*** Sometimes installation routines for manufacturer-supplied drivers don't provide a means to link a printer to a networked print server. If you encounter this problem, tell the installation routine that the printer is connected locally. You can correct the problem later by adjusting the destination of the installed print queue.

To install a Microsoft-supplied driver, follow these steps in Windows 98 (the procedure is similar for Windows NT):

1. Open the Printers folder in the Windows Control Panel.

2. Double-click the Add Printer icon to start the Add Printer Wizard.

3. Click the Next button. The display changes to allow you to choose between installing a local or a network printer. Select the second option.

4. Click Next again. You can now enter the path to the network printer, as shown in Figure 6.5. This path consists of the NetBIOS name of the Samba server and the share name. If you're uncertain of the path, you can click Browse to open a browser to locate the share. If you print from DOS programs, be sure to select Yes to the question, "Do you print from MS-DOS-based programs?" Checking the Yes option automatically maps the drive to a virtual printer port for the benefit of DOS programs.

Figure 6.5 When you add a network printer, you must specify its host and share name.

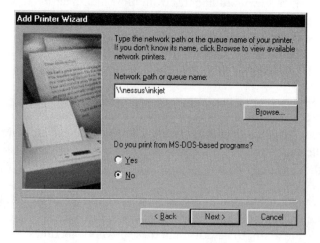

5. Click Next again. The wizard now displays a list of manufacturers and printers (Figure 6.6). Choose your printer's manufacturer and the exact model printer. If you're printing to a Ghostscript-driven printer, Apple LaserWriter drivers generally work well. You can install some manufacturer-provided and third-party drivers by clicking the Have Disk button at this point. The installer then prompts you for the location of the new files and, when you provide this information, replaces the main list with a list of drivers available in the location you've specified.

Figure 6.6   Microsoft provides drivers for a wide selection of printers, or you can install some manufacturer-supplied drivers by clicking Have Disk.

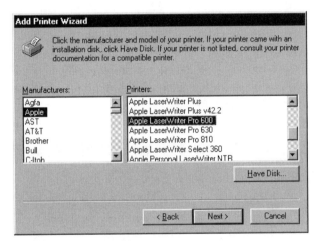

6. Click Next again. Windows asks you to name the printer. This name need not bear any resemblance to the printer driver name or the Samba print queue name. Windows users see this name as the name of the local print queue, so it's best if it's descriptive, such as "Inkjet in Room 220." You can also choose whether to set this as the default printer.

TIP If you install drivers on a large number of Windows clients, you may want to use the same name for client queues that print to the same Samba queue. Consistent naming can help you track down problems when they occur.

7. Click Next again. Windows gives you the opportunity to print a test page; I recommend you do so. At this point, Windows may ask for its installation CD-ROM. Insert it; Windows installs the driver and, if you asked for a test page, prints it.

Essential
Configuration

PART 2

8. Windows asks if the page printed correctly. If you respond in the affirmative, Windows ceases printer setup activities. If you respond that the test page did not print, Windows launches a troubleshooting routine, which may or may not help you track down the problem. In case of problems, you'll find Chapter 17, "Troubleshooting," helpful.

Changing the Ctrl-D Configuration As I've mentioned before, some Windows PostScript drivers send a Ctrl+D at the start of each print job. You can change this configuration as follows:

1. Right-click the newly installed printer icon in the Printers window and select Properties from the pop-up menu. This action opens a Properties dialog box.

2. Click the PostScript tab in the Properties dialog box.

3. Click the Advanced button near the bottom of the dialog box. This produces the Advanced PostScript Options dialog box, Figure 6.7.

Figure 6.7 The Send CTRL+D Before Job option, if enabled, can cause problems for Samba print queues.

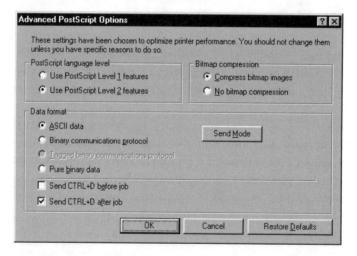

4. If it's checked, uncheck the Send CTRL+D Before Job option near the bottom of the dialog box. The option to send a Ctrl-D after the print job is usually not harmful. (It can sometimes cause spurious output at the end of a print job sent to a Ghostscript-driven queue.)

5. Click OK in the Advanced PostScript Options dialog box, then in the main Properties dialog box.

> **NOTE** Non-Microsoft PostScript drivers may present dialog boxes that look different from the Microsoft drivers described here. You may need to browse through the options to find the one related to sending Ctrl-D to the printer.

In many cases, it's simpler to add a `postscript` = Yes parameter to your Samba printer shares than to reconfigure potentially dozens or even hundreds of Windows clients. Reconfiguring the clients may make more sense if you want to use a single Samba printer share for both PostScript and the printer's native language drivers, however. In this case, it's vital that your smart filter be able to detect both the printer's native language and PostScript, and process each appropriately.

Automatic Driver Installation

To configure Samba for automatic driver installation, you must first manually install a driver on one client computer. You can then create special shares, as described shortly, and adjust the definition to allow for automatic driver installation on additional clients.

> **WARNING** As of Samba 2.0.7, automatic printer driver installation works only for Windows 9*x* clients. If you use Windows NT or 2000 clients, you *must* use manual installation methods. Attempting to use the automatic methods described here won't work and could crash the client computer.

To create a printer share that supports automatic driver installation, follow these steps:

1. Create a Samba printer share. The share need not have precisely the features you expect it to ultimately support, but it should link to the correct printer and in the appropriate way—if you expect to ultimately use Ghostscript, for example, your initial share should use Ghostscript.

2. Install a printer driver on a single Windows 9*x* client system and link it to the share created in step 1. Test this setup to be sure it works correctly.

3. Set up a Samba file share called [printer$]. Note that this share *must* have this name, including the dollar sign ($). This share should look something like the following, although the path can point to any convenient directory (preferably an empty one):

```
[printer$]
            path = /home/samba/printer-files
            public = Yes
            writeable = No
            browseable = Yes
```

4. Locate the Windows .INF files, which include descriptions of your printer driver. For Microsoft drivers, these filenames usually take the form MSPRINT*.INF and usually appear in the C:\WINDOWS\INF directory. The equivalent descriptions for other manufacturers' files may appear in other .INF files in this directory. These files may be called OEM*.INF or may be named after the printer manufacturer, as in HP45.INF.

TIP If the client is configured to share its C: drive, you can mount that drive in Linux using smbmount, as described in Chapter 7, "Using Linux as an SMB/CIFS Client." You can then use Linux tools such as grep to locate the driver files by searching for an appropriate string. For example, to install a Brother printer, you can cd to the appropriate directory and then issue the command **grep Brother** *.INF *.inf to locate any .INF files that contain the string *Brother*. (Note that you need to specify both cases of .INF in this command because Linux is case-sensitive, although Windows is not.)

---

5. Once you have located the appropriate .INF file, copy it to the directory you specified in the [printer$] definition.

6. Search through the .INF file and write down the *exact* name of the printer driver you want to use. This name appears in quotes on the left of a line, followed by an equals sign (=) and a list of files. MSPRINT.INF contains names such as Apple LaserWriter Pro 600 and Lexmark Optra E+. Note that case, spacing, and similar minutiae are extremely important, so you may want to use cut-and-paste to move the name into a spare text file.

7. Issue the following command, making appropriate substitutions for *MSPRINT.INF* and *Printer Name*:

```
# make_printerdef MSPRINT.INF "Printer Name" >> printers.def
```

TIP If you can't find an appropriate .INF file for your printer, you can request a test printout from an installed driver. This printout contains the names of the files used by the driver. You can then run `make_printerdef` using a randomly selected printer name and modify the resulting entry to refer to the files listed on the test printout page.

---

8. When you execute the `make_printerdef` command, it displays a list of files required by the driver. Locate these files on the Windows client on which you've installed the driver and copy them to the [`printer$`] share. These files should all reside in the `C:\WINDOWS\SYSTEM` directory.

NOTE Although Windows is not case-sensitive, Linux is. In most cases, Windows asks for files using lowercase names, even when the filenames in `printers.def` are in uppercase. If in doubt, you can use links to allow access to the files using both upper- and lowercase names.

---

9. Add the following item to your `smb.conf` [`globals`] section (if it's not already present), making appropriate adjustments to the path, if necessary:

   `printer driver file = /home/samba/printer-files/printers.def`

10. Add the following lines to the printer share that uses the drivers you're configuring, making appropriate adjustments for your printer:

    `printer driver = `*`Printer Name`*

    `printer driver location = \\%h\printer$`

11. Restart Samba.

Repeat the preceding steps for additional printer shares and printer drivers. I recommend testing each one as you create it. As you add printer definitions, your `printers.def` file grows in size; this file is essentially Samba's equivalent to the Microsoft .INF files containing printer driver file information. You should also take care that users who connect to the [`printer$`] share can read the files it contains. Setting permissions on all files to 0644, and on the directory to 0755, should guarantee this is the case.

To install a printer driver using this automatic printer share, follow these steps:

1. Log on to a Windows client on which you have not configured the printer in question.

2. Use Network Neighborhood to browse to the printer you want to install.

3. Double-click the printer icon. Windows responds by displaying a dialog box asking if you want to set up the printer.

4. Click Yes. The Add Printer Wizard asks whether you print from MS-DOS programs. Respond Yes or No, as appropriate.

5. Click Next. Windows responds by asking you for a printer name. You can call the printer anything you like—preferably something descriptive such as "Inkjet in Room 220." You can also elect to make this the client's default printer. As with manual configuration, I recommend you name the print queue consistently across clients to avoid ambiguity when troubleshooting problems in the future.

6. Click Next. You now have the opportunity to print a test page. Select Yes or No, as you see fit (but I recommend you do print a test page, at least for the first time or two you install a printer in this way).

7. Click Next. Windows may ask for the Windows installation CD, although it should not do so for any of the files listed in your `printers.def` file. When the process is finished, Windows asks if the test page printed correctly. If you respond in the negative, Windows opens a troubleshooting Wizard that may or may not help you diagnose the problem.

If your network contains a large number of Windows *9x* clients, the automatic printer installation procedure can save a considerable amount of time. Not only does installation become easier, but it's more foolproof—a user is less likely to mistakenly install an incorrect driver when you use this procedure. Although Linux printing is largely bound to PostScript devices (or devices that can be made to act like PostScript printers via Ghostscript), you can install any sort of printer drivers you like in this way. Of course, the type of Linux queue you use should match the type of printer driver you configure the queue to distribute.

NOTE   Automatic driver installation does *not* allow you to automatically update the printer drivers on all clients by replacing files on the server. Each client copies relevant printer driver files to its own boot partition, so if you need to update printer drivers, you must still rerun the installation process on each client.

Controlling Access to Printers

Samba printer access control is essentially identical to file-sharing access control, at least in terms of Samba's configuration options. Normally, though, you don't use Linux file permissions to control access to printer shares, as you can with file shares. Linux printer daemons frequently include access control methods that may interact with Samba's options, so you should understand these interactions when you set up a printer share.

Why would you *want* to control printer access, though? After all, an intruder can't read critical files from a printer, so it might seem unreasonable to take strong measures to protect a printer share or even a server that functions exclusively as a print server. There are three good reasons to protect your print server.

By protecting your print server, you can conserve supplies. In a worst-case scenario, you may have a printer that has a large input tray and expensive media, ink, or toner. A dye-sublimation printer with a large input tray loaded with expensive letterhead or overhead projector transparencies is just such a printer. Dye-sublimation technology is expensive on a per-page basis, so if some troublemaker sends a job to this printer that produces completely dark pages, you may end up paying hundreds, and perhaps thousands, of dollars for this illicit print job. Even on a lower-end ink-jet or laser printer, the results could be costly. Although toner and ink typically produce print costs of less than $0.05 per page, completely black pages can cost ten times that much.

You also protect yourself against potential server bugs. If you run the latest version of Samba, chances are there are no *known* bugs that can cause security breaches through a printer share. Note, however, that I said *if* you run the latest version, and I emphasized the word *known*. It's conceivable that somebody will discover a bug in Samba that can be exploited to give the intruder full access to the server computer through an unsecured printer share. You don't want to be the first victim of this discovery.

Finally, you'll have a way to enforce access policies. Even on a network that's completely disconnected from the Internet, you may have internal policies regarding who may use which printers. For instance, you might want to restrict access to certain printers that have high per-page costs to the individuals who truly need the use of those printers.

For these reasons, I recommend you take at least minimal steps to secure even a seemingly low-security system like a dedicated print server. You can read more about security in Chapter 14, "Samba Security Considerations," and Chapter 5 introduced many of the concepts described here in Chapter 6.

Security Options and Printer Shares

Normal Samba share-level access control parameters apply to printer shares. In particular, you can use the following parameters to limit access to your printer shares.

Guest Services   The parameters that control access to guest services—guest ok, guest account, guest only, and the global map to guest—can be applied to printer shares. (See the "Guest Access" section of Chapter 5.) In brief, if you set map to guest = Bad User or map to guest = Bad Password, then you can set guest ok = Yes in the printer share to give access to individuals who don't have passwords for the Samba server. You may also need to set the guest account parameter to a valid user, as in guest account = waltert. Setting the guest options in this way opens your Samba server to potential abuse, but on some networks this potential danger is small, and the gain from not having to maintain accounts for printer access is substantial.

hosts allow and hosts deny   These security parameters allow you to list computers and networks that are or are not, respectively, allowed to access the server or share. For instance, hosts allow = .threeroomco.com lets any computer in the threeroomco.com domain have access to the system. Chapter 14 describes these parameters in greater detail.

valid users and invalid users   These parameters work much like hosts allow and hosts deny, but operate on the level of individual users. When only a few users should have access to a server, you might use valid users = emilyk, @paper to restrict access to the user emilyk and all the users in the paper group.

The valid users and invalid users parameters can accomplish a great deal when it comes to restricting printer access. These options, as well as hosts allow and hosts deny, can be applied to a server as a whole or to individual shares. One server can therefore host both an open printer that's available to many individuals (perhaps even including guest users) and a restricted printer that's available to only a handful of users.

Interaction of Samba Options with *lpd* Options

Linux's printing system includes its own set of tools for restricting access. For instance, the default printing system on most distributions is BSD-style printing, and this system supports an /etc/printcap parameter called rg. This parameter restricts access to the printer to a particular group of users, as in rg = paper which creates a print queue that's accessible only to members of the paper group. This parameter is similar to the Samba valid users parameter when used with a single group as the value. When Samba submits a print job for a client, it does so using the permissions associated with the user who connected to the share—unless you use the force user or force group parameter, in which case Samba uses the username or group specified. It's generally best to leave the user identification alone when printing via Samba, but if you really need to circumvent restrictions imposed by the underlying printing system, you can often do so by using these options.

You can think of the security features of both Samba and of lpd (or of whatever printing engine your system uses) as being successive filters. You can use Samba's security features to filter out certain types of undesirable accesses, and features of the underlying printing system to do the same—and to do so for accesses by local users and perhaps other network users, as well. Any access must pass *both* the Samba and 1pd security checks.

Some Common Printer-Sharing Scenarios

It may help your understanding of these topics to examine some specific examples of smb.conf files for particular printer-sharing tasks. Use the examples in this section for informational purposes or as templates for your own configurations.

Sharing All Local Printers with Variations

Suppose you have three printers connected to your Linux computer: a PostScript dye-sublimation printer, a PostScript laser printer, and an ink-jet printer that uses a PCL variant. To use each of these printers with its native Windows drivers—PostScript for the first two and PCL for the third—you must configure three "raw" Linux queues. Each of these should pass the output directly to the printer without processing. The queues are called dyesub, laser, and inkjet. This configuration makes the ink-jet printer nearly useless from Linux programs, but in this example, the computer functions only as a print and file server, so it's not a concern. (If it is for you, you can add a fourth queue to process PostScript through Ghostscript and pass the result on to the ink-jet printer.)

Because of the cost of dye-sublimation printouts, you want to restrict access to this printer to a few specific users authorized to produce the high-quality color output this device offers. You want all users to be able to obtain black-and-white output from the laser printer or lower-quality color output from the ink-jet.

A simple smb.conf file to achieve these results appears in Listing 6.4.

Listing 6.4 smb.conf Settings for Sharing All Printers

```
[global]
        workgroup = PAPER
        server string = %h server
        encrypt passwords = Yes
        load printers = Yes


[printers]
        comment = All Printers
        path = /var/spool/samba
        print ok = Yes
         browseable = No
```

```
[dyesub]
        comment = Dye Sublimation Printer
        path = /var/spool/samba
        valid users = charlesk, emilyk, jedl
        print ok = Yes
        browseable = Yes
```

The result of this configuration is that each of the three printers connected to the server is available from the network, under the same names used on the server's internal queue—dyesub, laser, and inkjet. The [dyesub] share overrides the settings specified in [printers], but only for the [dyesub] share. Therefore, this printer is accessible only by charlesk, emilyk, and jedl.

> **NOTE** The browseable parameter has slightly different meanings for the [printers] share than it does for the [dyesub] share. In the [printers] share, setting browseable = Yes would produce a useless printer share called printers on client systems, so this parameter is set to No. It's necessary to set browseable = Yes on individual printer shares, however, if you want the share to be browseable.

The shares in this configuration don't use the postscript parameter. You *cannot* add this parameter to the [printers] share, because it would break access to the ink-jet printer. Because the underlying Linux print queues are raw queues, there should be no need for Samba to adjust the output destined for PostScript printers. If you use queues that incorporate smart filters, and as a result need to add the postscript = Yes parameter to the PostScript devices, you could remove the [printers] share and create two individualized shares in its place. One of these would be a [laser] share with postscript = Yes, and one would be an [inkjet] share without that parameter.

Re-Exporting a Remote Printer

It's possible to use a Samba server as a bridge between otherwise incompatible networks—either as a literal network bridge or as a virtual bridge between incompatible protocols on a single set of network hardware. For instance, suppose your network includes Macintoshes running MacOS and using AppleTalk, and *x*86 computers running Windows. If you've invested in AppleTalk printers, you may want to provide your Windows computer access to those printers. When expanding in the future, you might choose to add printers to your Samba server, which can double as an AppleTalk print server by using Netatalk. You can also provide access to printers hosted on Unix computers on which Samba is not installed.

To be concrete, let's suppose that your network has three printers:

- A PostScript laser printer that communicates via AppleTalk
- A color PostScript laser printer connected to a Unix host, shared via lpd
- A PCL laser printer connected directly to the Linux computer

The smb.conf file shown in Listing 6.5 allows you to share all three printers through Samba.

Listing 6.5   An smb.conf File for Sharing Remote Printers via Samba

```
[global]
        workgroup = PAPER
        server string = %h server
        encrypt passwords = Yes


[apple-laser]
        comment = AppleTalk-shared laser printer
        print command = pap -p lw630 %s; rm %s
        postscript = Yes
        path = /var/spool/samba
        print ok = Yes
        browseable = Yes


[color-ps]
        comment = Color PostScript printer
        path = /var/spool/samba
        postscript = Yes
        print ok = Yes
        browseable = Yes


[pcl-laser]
        comment = PCL laser printer
         path = /var/spool/samba
        print ok = Yes
        browseable = Yes
```

Because each of these shares requires unique parameters, each merits its own definition; there is no [printers] share. Of most interest in terms of Samba configuration is the [apple-laser] share, which passes data from the Windows clients to a printer shared using AppleTalk. This share uses the print command parameter to pass the file to the lw630 AppleTalk printer using the pap command, which is part of the Netatalk package. When using the print command parameter, be sure to remember the %s variable, which signifies the file to be printed. Many printing packages, including pap, don't remove the files they've just printed, so it's necessary to include rm %s as part of the print command.

The [color-ps] share exports the file to a queue hosted on another Unix computer. This share doesn't use a print command parameter, however. That's because the usual configuration in this situation is to create a local Linux queue, but to configure /etc/printcap with rm and rp to specify the remote machine and remote print queue rather than lp to specify a local printer port. (You could configure an AppleTalk printer in the same way, which would provide access to the AppleTalk printer to all Linux programs through a normal Linux print queue.)

NOTE In the case of both the [apple-laser] and [color-ps] printer shares, using the shares may increase the traffic on your network. The print job must travel from the client to the Linux server, and then from the Linux server to the printer or ultimate print server. If the Linux server acts as a bridge between physically separate networks, with printer and Samba clients on opposite sides of the bridge, this configuration won't increase network traffic. But if all the devices are on one network segment, this configuration does increase traffic on that segment. It might be better to configure the ultimate destination systems to accept SMB/CIFS print jobs directly, or to configure the clients to send print jobs in the form expected by the ultimate print server.

The [pcl-laser] queue is distinguished from the preceding two in that it doesn't have a postscript = Yes parameter. The PCL printer must use either a raw queue or a queue that uses a smart print filter that can distinguish PCL from other output and pass the PCL to the printer without processing it.

Using Samba as a PostScript Processor

One of the advantages of using Linux as a print server is that you can easily create two or more Samba queues to process data destined for a single printer in two or more ways. An example is exporting a non-PostScript printer using one queue that accepts the printer's native language and one that passes the results through Ghostscript. You can treat the latter queue as a PostScript printer from Windows.

There are advantages to exporting a printer both as a raw queue and as a virtual Post-Script printer:

- As described earlier in "Raw Queues," the client, network, and server resource use varies substantially depending on the type of file you're printing, whether you use PostScript or printer-specific drivers, and what type of printer you use. Once you have some experience with these matters on your network, you can minimize resource use by choosing an appropriate print queue for each print job.

- You also optimize quality. In most cases, color bitmap graphics print better when you use a printer's native drivers. Text, however, often prints equally well with either driver, or sometimes better when you use PostScript.

- Sometimes you simply must print PostScript. Say you use a desktop publishing program and import Encapsulated PostScript (EPS) files; you may need to print to a PostScript (or Ghostscript-driven) printer. You might also find a PostScript file that you want to print on a Web site. You can also use a low-cost printer and Linux server as an inexpensive way to produce page proofs for documents you intend to send to a service bureau for high-volume printing.

All of these factors vary substantially from one printer and network to another, so having both types of queue available can be a great boon. The tight integration of Ghostscript into Linux's print queue makes this configuration a simple matter. Listing 6.6 is an example of an `smb.conf` file that exports the same printer in three different ways—raw, as a PostScript printer at low resolution, and as a PostScript printer at high resolution.

Listing 6.6 Samba Configuration to Share a Printer in Three Ways

```
[global]
        workgroup = PAPER
        server string = %h server
        encrypt passwords = Yes
        load printers = Yes


[printers]
        comment = PostScript exports
        path = /var/spool/samba
        print ok = Yes
        browseable = No
        postscript = Yes
```

Essential Configuration

PART 2

```
[inkjet-raw]
        comment = Raw (non-PostScript) export
        path = /var/spool/samba
        print ok = Yes
        browseable = Yes
```

This configuration is a variant of the one in Listing 6.4. It relies upon the presence of three Linux lpd print queues on the host computer: two with names of your choosing (say, inkjet360 and inkjet720 for the 360dpi and 720dpi Ghostscript-driven queues) and one called inkjet-raw that uses no input filter. Using this configuration file results in three queues as seen from Windows: inkjet360, inkjet720, and inkjet-raw.

Windows clients should use the printer drivers supplied by Microsoft or the printer manufacturer to send data to the inkjet-raw device. You can use any of a wide variety of PostScript drivers for the inkjet360 and inkjet720 queues. Apple LaserWriter drivers tend to work well. Because these Windows drivers are written for printers other than the ones you're actually using, though, the match to your printer is imperfect.

Fortunately, the printer resolution as set in Windows isn't as important for PostScript printers as it is for most non-PostScript printers (although it can be important when printing some types of bitmapped graphics). Instead, you determine the resolution of the output by printing to specific Samba queues. Likewise, even PostScript drivers for black-and-white printers usually pass color information through untouched, although this might not always be the case. Page margin information, however, is often incorrect when you use a PostScript driver for some arbitrary printer. The result is that you may be allowed to set your margins too close to the edge of the paper—or you might not be able to set margins as close to the edge as you'd like—when you use a PostScript driver for a Ghostscript-driven printer. It's also possible that the driver you use supports fonts that aren't installed in Ghostscript, in which case selecting those fonts will result in another font appearing—usually Courier. You can add fonts to Ghostscript, if you can find appropriate matching ones. Consult the Ghostscript documentation for details.

Windows applications often make subtle adjustments to their margins, font sizes, and so on depending on the printer you select. Therefore, you may find that the number of pages and appearance of your printouts varies if you switch back and forth between a raw and Ghostscript-driven printer definition. On the other hand, if your network includes a wide variety of many printers, you can make your documents print with more consistent layout across printers by using Ghostscript and a common PostScript driver for all your printers.

Summary

Linux makes an excellent print server. You can configure even an old 80486 computer to serve several printers using Samba, thus freeing up resources that might be better used elsewhere. With its fine control over share access, Samba allows you to fine-tune who may use a printer.

Linux's native printing mechanisms are not entirely uniform; many systems use BSD-style printing, but a few distributions now ship with LPRng or other variants. Therefore, the exact commands that underlie your configuration vary. Fortunately, Samba can adjust itself for these changes almost automatically; although if you want to do anything complex, you need to know the capabilities of your printing system.

Essential
Configuration

PART 2

7

Using Linux as an SMB/CIFS Client

Most of this book focuses on using a Linux computer as a server on a network of clients that use SMB/CIFS—probably Windows computers. Occasionally, however, you might want to use a Linux computer as a client on an SMB/CIFS-dominated network. Fortunately, Linux and the Samba package include features that allow your Linux computer to function as an SMB/CIFS client. Although these features aren't as polished as Samba's server features, they are functional and reliable.

When using your Linux computer as an SMB/CIFS client, the associated servers may host any OS that can function as an SMB/CIFS server—Windows, OS/2, Linux, or various others. Therefore, you *can* use Samba as a Linux-to-Linux networking protocol. For most functions, however, other protocols work better. The *Network File System (NFS),* for instance, supports Linux filesystem features far better than does SMB/CIFS, so NFS is usually a better choice for Linux-to-Linux file sharing. If you need Samba support on both client and server for other systems, you might consider using Samba for Linux-to-Linux printer sharing, although Linux's usual `lpd` includes this capability by default. (There are some security plusses and minuses to both `lpd`-style and SMB/CIFS printer sharing, some of which are discussed later in the chapter.)

This chapter begins with an overview of the reasons for using Samba as a client package, including some possible alternatives. Then it moves on to explain two methods of accessing files using Samba as a client: via the smbclient and smbmount programs. Finally, the chapter describes the process of printing to remote SMB/CIFS printers from Samba.

When to Use Samba as a Client

It's useful to understand some of what you can accomplish when using Samba's client features. With this knowledge at hand, you can better see how to apply the options available in the specific client programs. In reading this section, you may also discover possible uses for Samba as a client that you had not previously considered.

Accessing Resources on a Windows Network

One of the most obvious and general of Samba's client roles is to provide access to Windows network resources. Specifically, you can give Linux clients access to network file and printer shares. SMB/CIFS also provides some underlying support and minor services, such as time servers, user authentication, and browsing. Most of these are not used by Samba, however; for instance, Samba doesn't provide access to Windows time servers. Other minor services are used somewhat transparently by another service, as in the case of configuring a Samba server to use a network logon server, described briefly in Chapter 4.

For the most part, the two types of SMB/CIFS service you're likely to access in Linux are file shares and printer shares. Both types of access are discussed in detail later in this chapter. Note that the other uses of Samba as a client described here all fall into one or both of these two categories. Most generally, though, you can consider file shares and printer shares to be a means for Linux users to directly access resources that exist on Windows computers. Some specific examples of direct end-user access to resources include the following:

Linux as a Client in a Client/Server Network   Your network may have an SMB/CIFS server on which users' files are stored. If one or more of your client computers is configured to dual-boot between Windows and Linux, or runs Linux at all times, it may be convenient to use Samba to allow those computers' users to access the remote server's files.

Linux as a Peer in a Peer-to-Peer Network   You may run a small network and find that you occasionally need to read files from a Windows machine that's ordinarily a client, or a peer in a peer-to-peer configuration. It's easy to configure such a system to provide SMB/CIFS services. Once that's done, you can use Linux to access those files. The alternative would be to go to the target computer and transfer files from that system, which may be much less convenient.

Linux-to-Linux File Sharing I've already stated that using Samba for Linux-to-Linux file sharing is generally a less than ideal solution. There are a few cases, however, in which this method is desirable. Suppose you want to use passwords as part of your file-sharing authentication. (NFS uses a trusted hosts model, in which the IP address of the client is the primary means of authentication.) In such a case, SMB/CIFS's lack of Unix-style permissions and ownership may be less important than the authentication features Samba does support.

Accessing Shared Printers If your network already includes printers shared by SMB/CIFS, Samba's client printer tools help you access those printers as easily as you can local printers or network printers shared through Unix-style lpd protocols. As it does for file sharing, SMB/CIFS printer sharing normally requires password authentication, so you may prefer this method even in a Linux- or Unix-dominated network.

As a general rule, Samba as a client is best used on networks that are dominated by Windows computers, either in a peer-to-peer configuration or in a client/server configuration in which the server is a Windows computer. You might want to use Samba as a client to a Samba server, however—to reduce the use of unnecessary protocols and hence disable NFS, for example. There may be security reasons for this Samba-client-to-Samba-server arrangement, or you may prefer to use passwords as part of the system authentication.

File shares can be accessed using either an FTP-like client program known as smbclient, or mounted much like local disk shares using a program known as smbmount. The latter option provides seamless access to the SMB/CIFS shares, within limits imposed by the SMB/CIFS protocols. For printer shares, you can either print directly using smbclient, or use a tool called smbprint with your Linux printer queue so that printing is seamless. Most Linux distributions include tools to help automate this task, and we'll get to those later.

Linux as a Translator

One unusual role for Samba is as a "translator" between otherwise incompatible network protocols. Consider the network outlined in Figure 7.1, where a Linux computer serves as a bridge between two networks: a Macintosh (AppleTalk-based) network and a Windows (SMB/CIFS-based) network. Each network includes several computers and a printer. Because AppleTalk and SMB/CIFS are entirely different and incompatible protocols, neither set of computers can directly use the other's resources, even if the two networks use the same set of network cables.

Figure 7.1   Windows and Macintosh network protocols are different, but a Linux computer can help bridge the gap.

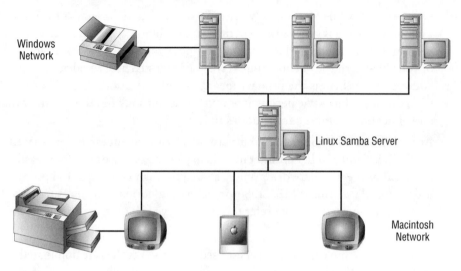

NOTE   Figure 7.1 shows the two networks as separate, but with the Linux computer connected to both. Such a situation requires two network cards in the Linux computer. The networks could also use the same set of cabling, in which case the machines could directly intercommunicate if outfitted with appropriate client and server packages. Linux can still function as a bridge for the SMB/CIFS and Apple-Talk *protocols* in this situation, however.

Samba can be useful in a client when you are bridging networks, because you can use Samba to mount resources from the Windows network. You can then re-export these resources using another network package, such as Netatalk for Macintosh networks. The Macs in Figure 7.1, for example, would see shares exported from the Windows machines as if they were local to the Linux Samba server. Similarly, if Netatalk is configured to export printer shares, Macintosh clients can print to the printer on the Windows network.

As described in Chapter 6, you can also run this process in reverse for printer shares—that is, the Windows computers in Figure 7.1 can access the printer on the Macintosh network. Because Linux client support for AppleTalk file sharing is still embryonic, however, file sharing can't work in this way, at least not for AppleTalk networks. Were the Macintosh network a Novell or Unix network, file shares could be exported to the Windows network—but that uses Samba as a server, not as a client.

NOTE Figure 7.1 shows a Macintosh network, but the same principles apply to other network types, such as networks of Unix systems. For this trick to work, Linux must include servers for the non-Windows network.

Re-exporting shares as described here does have its drawbacks. Primarily, it reduces efficiency, because two network accesses are involved for every file access. In Figure 7.1, these accesses occur on physically separate networks, so although this process may take some time, it doesn't clog the networks with large amounts of unnecessary traffic. On the other hand, if the two types of machines share network cables, the result can be two transfers on a single cable for every one access. That consumes an excessive amount of network bandwidth.

Whenever possible, it's better to use Linux as a server for both networks than to use it as a bridge. Rather than re-exporting shares from Windows computers, you might place those files on the Linux machine and export the files' directory to both networks. Similarly, if you can connect the printers directly to the Linux computer, you can reduce network traffic for print jobs.

Despite these recommendations, it may not always be convenient or even necessary to re-export a Windows share by mounting it using Samba and exporting it with another protocol. If you find yourself relying on this technique, though, you may want to consider redesigning your network's architecture.

Using Linux Programs on Windows Files

One reason for mounting Windows shares in Linux is to accommodate an individual using a Linux computer and wanting access to those files. A twist on this idea is that a user may need to use a Linux program to process data that's ordinarily stored on a Windows computer. The individual's OS preference in this case is irrelevant; it's a matter of using the right tool for a job.

As an example, consider a user who has acquired or produced a PostScript file, but wants to create an Adobe *Portable Document Format* file (*PDF,* also known as Acrobat Reader file) from that PostScript file. One way to accomplish this goal is to use Ghostscript (http://www.cs.wisc.edu/~ghost/) to convert from PostScript to PDF. If you're familiar with Linux or have read Chapter 6, you know that all major Linux distributions ship with Ghostscript. Therefore, instead of installing Ghostscript on the client computer merely to perform a single conversion, the user can convert the file using Linux as follows:

1. Configure the Windows computer to export the drive on which the PostScript file resides.

Essential Configuration

PART 2

2. Log on to the Linux computer.

3. Mount the Windows computer's drive using the Linux `smbmount` command, as in

   ```
   $ smbmount //northquad/severance psych
   ```

4. Use Ghostscript to convert the file. The following command converts the file on the shared partition:

   ```
   $ ps2pdf psych/james.ps
   ```

5. Unmount the shared partition, using a command such as **smbumount psych**.

> **NOTE**   As described in Chapter 8, "Automation," it's also possible to create special Samba shares that run scripts for common tasks. Chapter 8 includes an example configuration of a printer share that converts PostScript to PDF.

Putting Samba in the role of client in this way can be a convenient means of sharing the power of Linux while allowing users to maintain their files on their local computers. If you use it a lot, however, it might be simpler to increase the disk space on the Linux computer and allow users to store their files directly under Linux.

Linux as a Backup Server

One potentially compelling use for Samba as a client is to use a Linux computer as a backup server. In this sense, the terms *client* and *server* are used in somewhat unusual ways. A *backup server* is a computer that backs up other computers. The backup server may use software that is technically either client or server to accomplish the backup task. In the case of using Samba for this role, the most convenient way is often to use Samba as a client. You configure each computer on the network to share its important partitions. You can then create a Linux `cron` job or scripts that you run manually to mount the client filesystems and back them up using Linux backup tools. Depending on the size of your network, the speed of your network hardware, and the speed of your backup hardware, you may be able to perform complete backups of all your Windows computers in a single night or spread out over several nights—all through a single backup server.

> **NOTE**   Using Samba as part of a backup strategy is an important topic, to which Chapter 16, "Backups," is devoted.

Using *smbclient* to Access Remote Files

One of the crudest of Samba's client programs is known as `smbclient`. In fact, this program is at the core of several others, but it can be used directly by end-users, and it's useful for "quick and dirty" file transfers on SMB/CIFS networks.

TIP   `smbclient` operates very similarly to the standard text-mode Linux `ftp` program. If you know how to use `ftp`, you'll have little trouble with `smbclient`. In fact, if your current network uses both SMB/CIFS and FTP protocols, you might consider dropping the latter and using `smbclient` in its place. Reducing the number of protocols your computers support can improve security and reduce your required administrative efforts.

Essential
Configuration

PART 2

Accessing Remote Computers

The first step in using `smbclient` is to launch the program. Here is the command to run `smbclient` in its most basic form:

```
$ smbclient //server/share
```

NOTE   Windows uses backslashes (\) in server identification, but Linux uses slashes (/). Alternatively, you can use backslashes, but you must then use twice as many as you would slashes, as in **smbclient \\\\server\\share**. Normally, backslashes have special meaning to Linux shells, but doubling them up in this way disables the special meaning, allowing `smbclient` to process the backslashes as it does forward slashes.

In this example, *server* is the NetBIOS name of the server, and *share* is the name of the share to which you want to connect. Note that *server* is the NetBIOS name of the computer, which may not be the same as the TCP/IP machine name. Also, *share* is the name of the share—like the share name (without brackets) listed in a Samba `smb.conf` file, or the entry in the Share Name field in the Sharing tab of the Windows Properties dialog box (Figure 7.2). The share name need bear no relationship to the Windows drive letter or volume label, or to the Linux directory in which the share resides.

Figure 7.2 In Windows you specify a share name using the Properties dialog box for a drive.

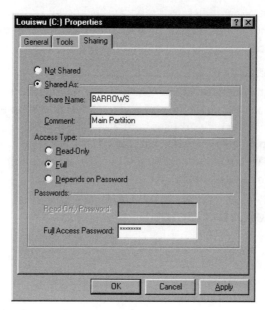

There are several parameters available for modifying how smbclient performs its job.

password If you pass the password to the program immediately after the server and service names, smbclient uses that password. For instance, if you type **smbclient //northquad/barrows mypass**, then smbclient sends mypass as the password. If you omit the password, smbclient prompts you for one.

-s *smb.conf* With this parameter, you can pass the complete path to the smb.conf file you want to use.

-O *socket options* This parameter passes socket options to smbclient. These options are the same as those described in Chapter 12, "Tuning Samba for Optimum Performance."

-R *name resolve order* You can tell smbclient to resolve NetBIOS names using lmhosts, host, wins, and bcast, in whatever order you specify. This parameter overrides the setting of the name resolve order parameter in the smb.conf file.

-M *servername* This parameter lets you send a *WinPopup message,* which appears in a small window on any Windows computer running the WINPOPUP program, as illustrated in Figure 7.3. You can omit the usual share name, and you specify the server name following the -M parameter; for instance, launch the program in Linux by typing **smbclient -M northquad**. After you start smbclient, you can type your message, followed by Ctrl+D. If the recipient is running WINPOPUP, the message appears in the WINPOPUP window.

Figure 7.3 WinPopup can be a convenient way to send short messages to others on a network.

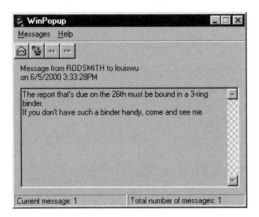

Essential Configuration

PART 2

> **WARNING** Don't use a WinPopup message for critical information, because there's no guarantee that the recipient will see the message. If the recipient computer isn't running WINPOPUP, the system quietly drops the message, so the sender has no way of knowing it didn't get through.

-N This parameter suppresses the usual password request. You should only use it if you know that the server doesn't require a password.

-n *name* Normally, smbclient sends the computer's TCP/IP hostname as the NetBIOS name. You can override this behavior by using the -n *name* parameter, which sends *name* as the NetBIOS name.

-d *debuglevel* *debuglevel* is an integer from 0 to 10 which represents the debug level. Useful values range from 0 (no debugging) to 3. Values above 3 are useful mainly to Samba developers.

-p *port* This parameter specifies the TCP port number to which smbclient tries to connect. The default is 139.

-l *logfilename* You can specify a custom log filename with this parameter. The default is a compile-time option, but the file usually appears in /var/log, /var/log/ samba, or a similar directory.

-h This paramenter causes smbclient to print a brief list of its options.

-I *IP address* You can specify the IP address of a server using this parameter. Ordinarily, smbclient uses normal NetBIOS name resolution to locate the server. You might use the -I parameter to specify a server that's located off your local network. Specify the IP address in dotted quad notation, as in **192.168.4.43**.

-U *username* By default, smbclient uses your Linux username as the username with which it connects to a remote share. You can override this default with the -U parameter, however.

TIP You can append a percent sign (%) and password after the username, if you like. The command **smbclient //wilder/cox -U nancyd%mypass** connects user nancyd with password mypass.

WARNING Including a password on a command line makes it visible to anybody who may be peering over your shoulder, or who can view your shell's command history. If you use this form in a shell script, the password is also potentially at risk. You should therefore be cautious about these uses.

-L Use this parameter to find the shares on a computer. When doing so, you can omit the leading double slashes (//) and share name. For instance, smbclient -L northquad displays the shares available on the computer NORTHQUAD.

TIP You can usually obtain a list of shares without sending a password. Samba servers occasionally refuse share list requests if you send a password—even a correct one. Therefore, using -N in conjunction with -L is usually a good idea.

-t *terminal code* This is a comparatively untested option that affects how smbclient interprets filenames. It is intended mainly for use in Asia. Possible values include sjis, euc, jis7, jis8, junet, hex, and cap.

-b *buffersize* This parameter controls the size of transmit buffers. The default value is 65520, but setting it lower (to around 1200) improves file transfer speed with some clients, including many Windows 9x systems.

-W *workgroup* smbclient normally takes the workgroup name from the workgroup parameter in smb.conf, but this parameter allows you to override that setting.

-T *tar options* You can use smbclient to transfer files to/from a tar file on the Linux system. When you do so, you can specify tar options using this parameter.

-D *directory*   Changes to *directory* on the Linux computer before beginning operations.

-c *command string*   *command string* is a semicolon-separated list of commands that smbclient executes instead of taking input from the user. You can use this feature to use smbclient in scripts.

You can use these parameters to fine-tune smbclient's operation and to connect to precisely the computer you want to use. The -U, -I, and -W parameters are particularly useful if you want to connect to a computer that's not on your local subnet, or if you use different usernames on your Linux client and the Windows server. When a command-line parameter sets options that can also be specified in smb.conf, the command-line parameter takes precedence.

Transferring Files

Once you're connected to a remote host, you can use commands similar to those available in Linux's basic ftp program to transfer and manipulate files. The most critical commands for navigating the server's filesystem and transferring files are listed here.

Command	Description
help or ?	Displays a list of the commands that smbclient accepts. You can follow either of these commands with the name of another command, to obtain a brief description of that command. Typing **help help**, for example, yields [command] give help on a command.
dir or ls	Displays a listing of the files available on the remote host.
du	Displays the space consumed by all files on the current share of the server, as well as available disk space.
cd *directory*	Changes to a new directory on the server.
lcd *directory*	Changes to a new directory on the client.
pwd	Displays the current directory path, including the server's NetBIOS name.
get *filename*	Gets a single file from the server.
mget *files*	Gets multiple files from the server. You can either list the files individually, as in **mget file1 file2 file3**, or use wildcards, as in **mget file***.
put *filename*	Sends a single file to the server.
mput *files*	Sends multiple files to the server. As with **mget**, you can list files individually or use wildcards.

Essential
Configuration

PART 2

Command	Description
prompt	Normally, smbclient prompts you for each file to be transferred via mget or mput. The prompt command toggles this prompting off or on again.
more	Displays a file using the Linux more pager.
lowercase	By default, smbclient transfers files using the case you type. If you type the lowercase command, however, the program converts the file's case to lowercase. It's a convenient option if you want to transfer files that appear in uppercase on the server.
tar *commands tarfile*	Transfers files from the remote host into a tar file on the client, or from a tar file on the client to the server.
print *filename*	Prints a file from the client to the server's printer. (You must connect to a printer share to use this command.)
translate	Toggles end-of-line translation for printing text files with Linux end-of-line characters on DOS or Windows printers.
exit or quit or q	Exits from smbclient.

In Listing 7.1, the directory listing obtained by the dir command provides useful information, including the files' attributes (D for directory, A for archive, H for hidden, S for system, and R for read-only). It also shows the files' sizes in bytes, and their creation dates and times. The file transfer doesn't provide any indication of its progress, so you may think the transfer has hung if you're transferring a large file or if your network is slow. In this example, I transferred a single file by using the get command, and I copied the entire contents of the directory using tar. The result of the latter command is a file called files.tar on the client, which contains the entire \files\ directory from the server.

Listing 7.1   Sample Run of smbclient

```
$ smbclient //northquad/east
Password:
smb: \> cd files
smb: \files\> dir
  .                                   D        0  Tue Jun  6 12:15:↵
18 2000
```

```
   ..                                  D        0  Tue Jun  6 12:15:↵
18 2000
   icewm-1.0.3-1.i386.rpm             A   295554  Tue Jun  6 12:15:↵
40 2000
   icewm-switch.txt                   A     1162  Tue Jun  6 12:15:↵
42 2000
   samba-2.0.7-20000425.i386.rpm      A  5924630  Tue Jun  6 12:16:↵
28 2000
   samba-2.0.7-20000425.src.rpm       A  4228351  Tue Jun  6 12:16:↵
36 2000
   samba-tng-alpha.2.5.3.tar.bz2      A  3036450  Tue Jun  6 12:16:↵
40 2000
               38668 blocks of size 65536. 19653 blocks available
smb: \files\> get samba-2.0.7-20000425.src.rpm
smb: \files\> tar c files.tar *
   295554  (  882.7 kb/s) \files\icewm-1.0.3-1.i386.rpm
     1162  (  283.7 kb/s) \files\icewm-switch.txt
  5924630  (  940.2 kb/s) \files\samba-2.0.7-20000425.i386.rpm
  4228351  (  920.9 kb/s) \files\samba-2.0.7-20000425.src.rpm
  3036450  (  915.5 kb/s) \files\samba-tng-alpha.2.5.3.tar.bz2
tar: dumped 5 files and directories
Total bytes written: 13487616
smb: \files\> exit
```

Manipulating Remote Files

In addition to transferring files, you can perform a number of manipulations on files on the server. File manipulation commands include the following:

Command	Description
rename *oldname newname*	Renames a file from *oldname* to *newname*.
del *files* or rm *files*	Deletes a file or files from the server.
md *dirname* or mkdir *dirname*	Creates a new directory on the server.
rd *dirname* or rmdir *dirname*	Deletes an empty directory from the server.
setmode *filename permission*	Sets the specified permissions on the remote file. This command is roughly equivalent to the DOS or Windows ATTRIB command. Permissions are one or more of a, h, s, or r, preceded by a plus (+) or minus (-) sign. The command **setmode file1 +sr** sets the system and read-only bits on file1.

| queue | Displays the contents of the remote print queue. (This command works only on printer queues.) |
| cancel *jobid* | Removes the specified print job from the print queue. (This command works only on printer queues.) You can find a job's ID by using the queue command. |

These commands help you perform routine file maintenance on an SMB/CIFS server from a Linux computer. You can also use these commands to clear up enough space to transfer files, if necessary. Unfortunately, smbclient doesn't contain any tools to let you alter the local filesystem, so if you find you need to create a local directory or otherwise manipulate local files, you must do so with other Linux tools.

TIP   smbclient responds to the customary Unix and Linux convention of Ctrl+Z to suspend the foreground program. Therefore, you can press Ctrl+Z to temporarily place smbclient in the background and return to your regular shell. When you're done making your local changes, type **fg** to return to smbclient.

Mounting Remote Filesystems

Although smbclient is a convenient tool for performing a quick file transfer, it's not the ideal way to access a remote filesystem when you want to use files directly in Linux programs. Suppose you want to use WordPerfect on Linux to edit a file that's stored on a Windows server. To accomplish this goal with smbclient, you must transfer the file to the Linux client, edit it, and then transfer it back with smbclient. To simplify this task—particularly if you want to access several files—you can use smbmount to mount the remote filesystem. This utility lets you mount the SMB/CIFS share as if it were a local disk partition or an NFS export. The fine points differ from a normal mount operation, though, so this section presents a detailed description of the smbmount utility. In addition, the latest versions of Samba allow you to use the Linux mount command instead of smbmount to mount SMB/CIFS shares.

> **NOTE** Although most of this book's contents apply quite well to Samba run on non-Linux Unix platforms, smbmount is a tool that's unique to Linux. It relies upon the SMB/CIFS support in the Linux kernel. Non-Linux systems can use a tool called smbwrapper, which accomplishes much the same goal in a different way. There are efforts underway to port smbmount to at least some other platforms, such as FreeBSD.

The Evolution of *smbmount*

One of the problems with smbmount is that it's changed substantially over the various 2.0.*x* releases of Samba. The syntax that works with earlier versions of smbmount doesn't work with newer versions, and vice-versa. This chapter focuses on the syntax of the 2.0.7 release of Samba, but you may need to use another smbmount syntax if you have an earlier version of Samba. It's possible that the syntax will change again in the future, so be prepared to check the documentation if your version of Samba doesn't work as described here.

> **WARNING** The man pages accompanying some versions of Samba did not describe smbmount correctly; they described how to use an earlier version of the program. Be aware that this could happen again.

Versions 2.0.0–2.0.3

These versions of Samba include smbmount support that requires fairly complex syntax, which is

```
smbmount //server/share -c 'mount /mountpoint'
```

You can include assorted options inside the single quotes and after the mount point specification to assign ownership and permissions on the mounted filesystem. For instance, -u and -g set the user and group IDs, and -f sets the permissions (in octal form). You can also set the username for accessing the server by passing a -U parameter outside of the single quotes.

Note that the preceding syntax assumes a 2.2.*x*-series or later kernel. For a 2.0.*x*-series kernel, these versions of smbmount use a syntax that more closely resembles that of later versions of smbmount.

NOTE Samba packages numbered 2.0.4 are extremely rare; all major Linux distributions skipped from 2.0.3 to 2.0.5 or 2.0.5a.

Versions 2.0.5 and 2.0.5a

These versions of Samba's smbmount use a simplified syntax. The syntax for mounting a remote share is

```
smbmount //server/share /mountpoint
```

Unfortunately, this version does *not* provide options for specifying ownership and permissions on the mounted filesystem. The owner is the person who issues the command. You can, however, use a -U parameter to specify the username for accessing the server.

Most 2.0.5a installations include incorrect man pages that describe previous versions of smbmount.

Versions 2.0.6–2.0.7

These versions of smbmount use a syntax similar to previous ones:

```
smbmount //server/share /mountpoint
```

In addition, you can enter parameters to alter the ownership and permissions on files, as described shortly. Some 2.0.6 installations include incorrect man pages.

These versions of smbmount can also be accessed through the ordinary Linux mount command, using a filesystem type of smbfs, as in **mount -t smbfs //server/share /mountpoint**. In practice, however, you may need to include the password on the command line (as discussed shortly).

All Versions

In all cases, smbmount requires that you have SMB/CIFS support compiled into your kernel. This support is present in the default kernels of all major distributions. If you want to recompile your kernel, be sure you include this support. The relevant option is located under Network File Systems ➢ SMB Filesystem Support or File Systems ➢ Network File Systems ➢ SMB Filesystem Support in the kernel configuration menu, depending upon your kernel version. You can compile this option either as a module or directly into the kernel file. If you recompile Samba, you must also use the --with-smbmount configure option to include smbmount, as shown here:

```
# ./configure --with-smbmount
```

NOTE   Chances are you'll want to include other compilation parameters, too. Consult Chapter 3 for details.

Technically, smbmount wasn't an official part of Samba prior to Samba 2.0.6. The status of this tool changed with Samba 2.0.6, however, which is part of the reason for the changes in the preceding versions; work was underway to bring smbmount into the official Samba fold. Despite the unofficial status of smbmount, the tool was included in all major Linux Samba packages.

Mounting Remote Shares

In the 2.0.6 and later releases of Samba, you can mount shares with either the smbmount or mount programs. The syntax of smbmount is

```
smbmount //server/share /mountpoint [-o options]
```

The equivalent syntax for mount is

```
mount -t smbfs //server/share /mountpoint [-o options]
```

NOTE   The smbmount and mount commands accomplish much the same results, but in subtly different ways. If you use one tool to mount a filesystem, you must use its equivalent unmount command (smbumount or umount, respectively) to unmount the filesystem. You cannot mix smbmount with umount or mount with smbumount.

For both smbmount and mount, *server* and *share* are the NetBIOS names of the server and the share, respectively; *mountpoint* is the directory you want to use as a mount point. smbmount is a bit finicky about the ownership of the mount point; the user who issues the smbmount command must own the mount point. This is true even if you create an /etc/fstab entry to allow users to mount shares.

TIP   If you intend to keep an SMB/CIFS share permanently mounted, you can create an /etc/fstab entry to do so, as described shortly. For the purpose of allowing individual users to mount remote shares, in my experience smbmount works better than does mount.

Essential Configuration

PART 2

The *options* available for `smbmount` or `mount -t smbfs` are as follows:

username=*name* This option specifies the username to be used on the server. If the user's Linux username is `jennie`, but the username on the server is `jennie1`, the user could add `-o username=jennie1` to the `smbmount` command line. If the username is unspecified, `smbmount` uses the setting of the environment variable USER, which is normally the user's Linux username. You can also add a NetBIOS workgroup preceded by a slash (/), a password preceded by a percent sign (%), or both to reduce the overall number of parameters passed to `smbmount`. For instance, `-o username=jennie/work%passwd` connects to the machine on workgroup WORK and using the password passwd.

password=*pass* If you don't include this option with `smbmount`, the program prompts you for the password. If you omit it when you use `mount`, however, the program may not prompt for the password but will report back that the password was invalid. This bug may be fixed in future releases of Samba.

WARNING Including the password on the command line can be convenient, but it also makes your password visible to anybody who can see your system, as well as in your shell's command history. Similarly, although including the password in this way allows you to write scripts that mount SMB/CIFS shares, keep in mind that your password becomes compromised if those scripts are ever read by others.

---

netbiosname=*name* This option sets the name by which the client goes when it connects to the server. It defaults to your system's TCP/IP host name.

uid=*id* This option sets the apparent owner of the files on the mounted filesystem. You can use either a numeric ID or a username as *id*. If you set `uid=jim`, for example, all the files will appear to be owned by the user `jim`.

NOTE The username option sets the username that `smbmount` sends to the server in order to gain access to files. The `uid` option, by contrast, sets the Linux user who owns the files, for purposes of Linux's filesystem housekeeping.

---

gid=*id* To set the apparent group of the files on the mounted filesystem, you can use either a numeric group ID or a group name as *id*.

port=*portnum* This option sets the networking port number to which `smbmount` tries to connect. The default is 139, and you probably will never have to change this.

fmask=*mask*   The fmask option sets the permissions used for remote files once the remote share is mounted. A setting of fmask=640 assigns permissions of 640 (-rw-r-----) to files on the remote filesystem. The server can remove write permissions, however, by setting the read-only bit. If the server is a Linux or Unix computer running Samba, the fmask permissions might bear no resemblance to those on the server.

> **WARNING**   Suppose a Samba server exports a share with permissions granted only to a single user, jennie. If Jennie mounts this share on a remote system and specifies a permissive fmask, such as 666, then this carefully restricted share may be accessed by any user on the client.

dmask=*mask*   Sets the permissions used for remote directories once the share is mounted. This option works just like fmask, except that it applies to directories rather than files.

> **WARNING**   The *mask* value in the fmask and dmask options is interpreted differently from the create mask and directory mask parameters in the smb.conf file, and from the umask option that's used with the mount command for many filesystems. fmask and dmask specify bits that are *set* on the mounted filesystem, but create mask, directory mask, and umask specify bits that are *removed* from the permissions.

debug=*level*   This option sets the debugging level for smbmount-driven file accesses.

ip=*dest*   This option sets the numeric IP address or host name of the server. You can use this option to connect with a computer that's not on your local network.

workgroup=*group*   This option sets the NetBIOS workgroup to which the server belongs.

sockopt=*options*   This option sets the socket options for this session. Socket options are discussed in Chapter 12.

guest   This option tells smbmount not to ask you for a password; smbmount attempts a guest login to the server.

ro   With this option, you specify that the remote filesystem is to be mounted read-only, even if it's available for read/write access.

rw   This option specifies that the remote filesystem is to be mounted for read/write access, if possible. This is the default.

Essential Configuration

PART 2

In addition to these options, you can use `mount -t smbfs` to accept normal mount options such as `user` and `auto`. These options are most useful if you create an /etc/fstab file entry for a share (as explained shortly).

If you want to use multiple options, separate them with commas. Here's a command that provides universal local read/write access to a share:

```
$ smbmount //wilder/mudd /mnt/mudd -o fmask=666,dmask=777
```

This command sets the file mask at 666, so all users have full read/write access, and the directory mask at 777, providing full read/write access plus execute permissions (required for normal directory access).

By default, many Samba installations give the `smbmnt` and `smbumount` programs conventional execute permissions (`smbmnt` is a helper program to `smbmount`). If ordinary users must be able to use these programs, however, these programs must be set user ID (suid) root. To do so, you can issue a command such as

```
$ chmod a+s /usr/bin/smbmnt /usr/bin/smbumount
```

You may need to adjust the path to the executables for your system. If you expect only root to run `smbmount`, you can leave the files as ordinary executables, which is safer from a security point of view.

You can add an entry in /etc/fstab for any remote filesystem you want to have mounted at system startup. Such an entry looks something like this:

```
//wilder/mudd /mnt/mudd smbfs ⏎
username=kevin,password=dollar,fmask=666,dmask=777   0 0
```

WARNING An /etc/fstab entry for auto-mounted filesystems may not work correctly if Linux tries to mount the filesystem before networking support is up and running. You may be able to work around this problem by adding the `noauto` option to the list of mount options and then adding an explicit mount command to an appropriate startup script. Some versions of Samba (including 2.0.5 and 2.0.7, but not 2.0.6) may cause the computer to hang on reboot if mounted SMB/CIFS filesystems are not first unmounted, so I advise caution when configuring always-mounted filesystems.

Access Quirks of a Mounted Share

Once you've mounted a share, you can use it much as you do a local filesystem—with some important limits. As a first approximation, you can think of an SMB/CIFS share as if it were a VFAT partition you've mounted using the Linux filesystem type vfat, but with some specific limitations and quirks:

Filenames   You're restricted to Windows-style file naming rules. Most importantly, you ordinarily aren't allowed to create two files that differ only in case in the same directory. If a directory contains file.txt, you cannot create File.txt, File.TXT, file.TXT, or any other variant. The case restriction may not apply, however, if the server is a Linux or Unix computer running Samba with the case sensitive = Yes parameter set in smb.conf. Also, SMB/CIFS filenames are limited to 128 characters in length.

Ownership and Permissions   These characteristics are set by the uid, gid, fmask, and dmask options to smbmount, not by the remote filesystem. One exception is the write bit, which can be removed by setting the read-only bit on the remote filesystem. You cannot adjust these characteristics on a file-by-file basis. If you need to adjust them for all files, you must unmount the filesystem and remount it using different options.

Special File Features   You cannot create the various special file types supported by Linux on an SMB/CIFS share. For instance, you cannot create links (hard or symbolic) or device files on an SMB/CIFS share.

Filesystem Updates   If a user of the server, or another client that has mounted the same share on the server, adds files or directories on the server, those changes may not show up in Linux for several minutes. You may be able to force an update by creating a new file yourself.

Most of these restrictions aren't major concerns when dealing with SMB/CIFS shares. It makes little sense to create Linux device files on a network filesystem, for example. Most such shares are intended to be accessed without using client-based security features. If necessary, you can mount the same share two or more times using different ownership in order to provide access to several users—but it's often possible to obtain the desired result by setting local ownership and permissions appropriately using a single mount.

GUI Browsers

If you like to use GUI-based tools for network access, there are several such tools available for use with Linux and SMB/CIFS network access. In some cases these browsers attempt to emulate the Windows Network Neighborhood behavior, although to do so they use smbmount or similar tools to accomplish their goals. A GUI utility might mount a share at some point in the user's home directory and then open a file browser on that directory. As a user, you could instead use smbmount at the command line or configure your window manager to do so for you, and then use your file manager much as does the GUI network browser. A GUI network browser can be friendlier for new users, however.

Here are some common GUI network browsers for Linux:

LinNeighborhood This browser is a general-purpose browser that can be configured to work with a wide variety of file managers. Its home page is `http://www.bnro.de/~schmidjo/`.

Kruiser This browser is designed to be used with the popular KDE system. It's headquartered at `http://devel-home.kde.org/~kruiser/`.

xSMBrowser This program is another general-purpose browser, similar to LinNeighborhood in concept and basic functionality. Its home page is `http://www.public.iastate.edu/~chadspen/`.

LinNeighborhood Example

If your users are new to Linux, you might want to install one of these browsers and configure users' accounts so that the tool is easily accessible from their desktops. As an example, consider LinNeighborhood. When it's configured and working correctly, LinNeighborhood's main window resembles that shown in Figure 7.4. This display shows all the servers on your local network, each of which can be expanded to show the available shares. You can double-click on a share to open a file manager window on that share.

Figure 7.4 LinNeighborhood provides an easy-to-use GUI interface on a Windows network from within Linux.

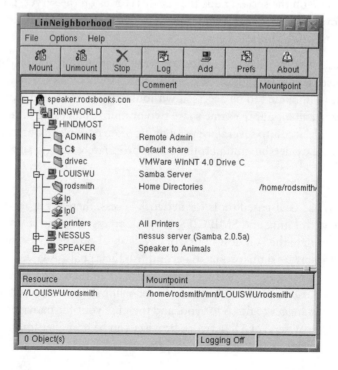

Before you can use LinNeighborhood in this way, you must configure it. To do so, click the Prefs button in the main window or select Options ➤ Preferences. In the Preferences dialog box that appears (Figure 7.5), you can set options on four tabs.

Figure 7.5   You must configure LinNeighborhood with information specific to your network before you can use it.

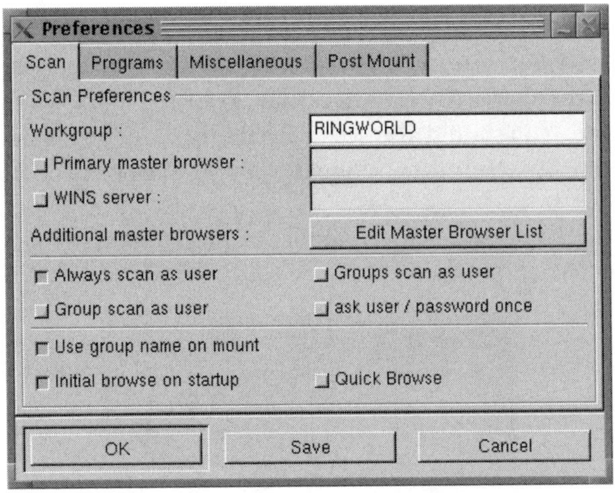

Scan   The Scan tab displays information on how LinNeighborhood performs network scans. For instance, you can configure the default workgroup name, set the primary master browser and WINS server, and tell the program when and how to use usernames. Some information, such as the master browser, should be obtainable from the network itself; the values in LinNeighborhood can be used to optimize performance or debug network trouble.

Programs   In this tab you tell LinNeighborhood what programs to use for mounting shares, scanning the network, and so on. You can also specify what version of Samba you're running, so the browser knows how to pass parameters to smbmount.

Miscellaneous   Here you tell LinNeighborhood where to mount shares. You can also configure the browser to automatically mount previously mounted shares at start-up.

Post Mount   In order to integrate with multiple file managers, LinNeighborhood has to know how to launch a file manager. You can configure this characteristic from the Post Mount tab. Select your type of file manager and click the arrow button to move the command into the edit field. You can then edit the command to customize it for your system, if you like. If your file manager isn't one of the supported types, you can edit the command to launch your preferred file manager.

Essential Configuration

PART 2

When you've configured the program, click the Save button to save your changes, and then OK to dismiss the dialog box. If the main LinNeighborhood window doesn't show the machines available on your network, select Options ➢ Browse Entire Network to see the available machines. Enter your network username and password if LinNeighborhood asks for them. If all goes well, the result should resemble Figure 7.4. (At first the individual machines won't be expanded to show all their available shares.)

To access a file share, double-click it. LinNeighborhood responds by displaying the Mount dialog box (Figure 7.6). You can enter or edit assorted options; then click the Mount button to mount the share. After a brief delay, your file manager should open, showing the mounted share. You should also see the share listed in the listing at the bottom of the main LinNeighborhood window. (Figure 7.4 shows one share open in this window.)

Figure 7.6   LinNeighborhood lets you enter assorted options associated with the smbmount command.

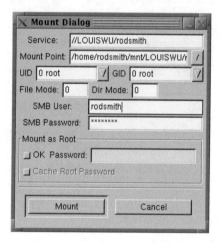

After you're done using a share, you can unmount it from within LinNeighborhood. Either select the share and click the Unmount button, or right-click the share and select Unmount from the resulting pop-up menu. If a file on the share is still in use on the client, LinNeighborhood displays a small dialog box informing you that the device or resource is busy. Note that unmounting the share does *not* close the file manager window that's open on the share; you must do that yourself.

Printing Files on Remote Printers

Samba includes a client program called smbprint to print files on remote printer shares. This program is actually a shell script that calls smbclient with appropriate options to send a file to the printer. The smbprint script is intended to be used as an input filter to a Linux printer queue, or by smart filters called from the input filter. Most Linux distributions include options to configure SMB/CIFS printers in their printer configuration routines, as described shortly.

Printing a File Using *smbclient*

If you don't want to bother configuring an SMB/CIFS printer share on the client computer, but instead want to print a single file to a remote printer, you can accomplish the task with smbclient. To do so, follow these steps:

1. Launch smbclient, giving it the name of the printer share on the server. For instance, you might type **smbclient //tappan/lexmark** to connect to the printer called LEXMARK attached to the computer called TAPPAN. Depending on the configurations, you may need to include additional parameters to set your username, and you may be prompted for your password.

2. If the file you want to print is a text file, type **translate** to turn on end-of-line translation. Otherwise you'll get "stair-stepped" text on some printers.

3. Issue the print command to print a file. To print the file gazebo.txt, you'd type **print gazebo.txt**.

4. If you want to monitor the progress of the print job, you can type **queue** to see what jobs are queued ahead of yours. You can also use the **cancel** command to abort a print job, if necessary.

Note that smbclient sends files directly to the remote printer as is; with the exception of optional end-of-line translations, smbclient doesn't process files in any way. Therefore, you may need to process files before sending them through smbclient. Say the remote printer uses Hewlett Packard's Printer Command Language (PCL) and you want to print a PostScript file to this printer. You must first use Ghostscript to convert the file to PCL, thus:

```
$ gs -dNOPAUSE -r300 -dBATCH -sDEVICE=laserjet -sOutputFile=file.pcl ↵
file.ps
```

Depending upon the exact model printer you have, you might want to use a different device instead of laserjet, and perhaps a resolution higher than 300. Once you're done, you can send the file using smbclient's print command, and it should appear on the server's printer.

Essential
Configuration

PART 2

Configuring a Linux Printer Queue to Use *smbprint*

If you want to print to an SMB/CIFS server more than occasionally, you should probably create a Linux print queue that processes its input through `smbprint`. This works just like an ordinary Linux print queue, but instead of sending output to a local printer or to a printer that's shared through the `lpd` protocols, the printout appears on an SMB/CIFS shared printer.

Chapter 6 includes a description of how to set up a Linux print queue, including configuration by both the GUI `printtool` utility (included with Debian, Red Hat, and Red Hat derivative distributions) and by editing the `/etc/printcap` file directly. (See the section "Creating Print Queues.") If you're using `printtool` or a similar GUI printer configuration utility, you can set up an SMB/CIFS printer queue just as you can configure a local printer queue, with only these differences:

- When `printtool` asks what type of print queue you want to define, select SMB/ Windows 95/NT Printer rather than Local Printer.

- When you select an SMB/CIFS printer type, `printtool` displays warning information concerning password security. This issue is discussed in the upcoming section.

- The list of options available for SMB/CIFS printers includes a few options unique to this printer type, as shown in Figure 7.7. Specifically, you must enter the names of the print server and the print share, a username and password for accessing the print share, and the name of the server's workgroup. You may also enter the server's IP address, but this option isn't usually needed; it's most helpful when you're trying to print using a server that's not on your local network.

Figure 7.7   Enter SMB/CIFS identification and security information to print to an SMB/CIFS printer.

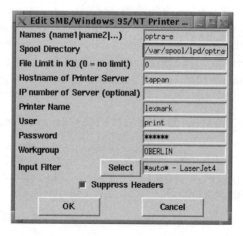

When you've entered this information and finished configuring the printer, `printtool` creates an appropriate entry in the Linux `/etc/printcap` file. Listing 7.2 shows a typical entry.

Listing 7.2 Sample */etc/printcap* Entry for Printing to an SMB/CIFS Shared Printer

```
optra-e:\
        :sd=/var/spool/lpd/optra-e:\
        :mx#0:\
        :sh:\
        :if=/var/spool/lpd/optra-e/filter:\
        :af=/var/spool/lpd/optra-e/acct:\
        :lp=/dev/null:
```

This queue includes several normal-looking options, including the `sd`, `mx`, `sh`, and `if` entries. The `lp` entry is unusual; instead of pointing to a regular printer device, it points to `/dev/null`. The printer daemon never sends the file to a conventional device; instead, `smbprint` uses `smbclient` to send the file to the server. This entry also includes an `af` entry, which specifies an accounting file. This file's name and location aren't important, so long as it doesn't overwrite an existing file.

Note that most of the information you tell `printtool` to help it locate and use the printer doesn't appear in the `/etc/printcap` entry. Instead, this information appears in `/var/spool/lpd/`*queuename*`/.config`. This filename is hard-coded into the `smbprint` script. Listing 7.3 shows a file consistent with the information shown in the dialog box in Figure 7.7.

Listing 7.3 Sample *smbprint* Configuration File

```
share='\\tappan\lexmark'
hostip=
user='print'
password='passwd'
workgroup='OBERLIN'
```

The standard print queue's smart filter knows to use `smbprint` to process these jobs. In the case of Red Hat and similar distributions, the filter knows this because of the following entry in the `general.cfg` file in the printer queue directory:

```
export PRINTER_TYPE=SMB
```

This entry flags the queue as an SMB/CIFS queue. Other distributions generally use similar mechanisms, but the details differ.

Essential Configuration

PART 2

If you're not using a printer configuration tool like `printtool`, you can still use `smbprint` to process your print jobs. To do so, follow these steps:

1. Create a printer queue entry using whatever method you prefer. Remember to create the spool directory.

2. Create a file called `.config` in the printer's spool directory (typically `/var/spool/lpd/`*queuename*). This entry should resemble the one shown in Listing 7.2, but with appropriate entries for your network.

NOTE   The details of what variables in the `.config` file are called have changed in the past, and may change again in the future. If you run into problems, browse the `smbprint` script to see what it expects.

---

3. Set the `lp` entry in `/etc/printcap` to point to `/dev/null`, as shown in Listing 7.2.

4. Set the `if` entry in `/etc/printcap` to point to the `smbprint` script. You may need to use `whereis` to locate this script on your system.

5. Create an `af` entry in `/etc/printcap`. This file's name is unimportant, so long as it doesn't overwrite any existing files.

6. Restart the printer queue.

These instructions create a simplified printer queue that works well when the remote printer is a PostScript printer and you print only PostScript files. If you need to process your files through Ghostscript, you'll need to replace the call to `smbprint` in step 4. Use an appropriate smart filter, or at least a simple script that passes the PostScript input through Ghostscript and then calls `smbprint`. If you use a smart filter, consult your filter's documentation to see how it interacts with `smbprint`.

Security Implications of *smbprint*

SMB/CIFS printing works using a different security model than does the standard Linux and Unix `lpd` printing. In `lpd` printing, the system works on a trusted hosts model, in which the server grants access to any client based on its IP address. SMB/CIFS, by contrast, works on a username/password model. (If you use a Samba server, however, you can adjust this model in a variety of ways, as described in Chapters 6 and 14.)

In one sense, the username/password model of SMB/CIFS printing is more secure because it imposes a higher standard for authentication—as opposed to `lpd`-style trusted host security, which can be easily circumvented by IP spoofing. This analysis omits the client's side of the equation, however. To a client, and particularly to a Linux client, it may be very convenient to store a password—often in plain text—on the client's hard disk. In the case of `smbprint`, the password goes in the `.config` file, which must be readable by any user who prints. Thus all users of that system have access to at least one password on the server, resulting in a potentially major threat to security.

When you print to a Windows 9*x* computer, the server normally operates in share-level security, which means each share has its own password. Therefore, the password stored on the Linux client need not be a major security risk; you must simply ensure that the server uses the printer password *only* for the printer and not for any regular file shares. At worst, an individual could steal this password and use it to print from otherwise unauthorized hosts.

If the print server is a Windows NT, Windows 2000, or Samba system, however, the default mode of operation is one of user-level security (or another security mode that operates similarly). In this case, several users can access the same resource (such as a printer), each using his or her own username and password. You must specify *one* of these usernames and passwords in the Linux .config file. To reduce the risk of a security breach, you should create a special user on the server. Give this user extremely limited login rights and a home directory that's unreadable (permissions of 000, if the server runs Linux). You can then use this username and password for printer access.

Figure 7.7 illustrates this approach; this figure shows a username of print, which is a limited-access account on the server. If somebody steals the printer access password, the risk of a break-in is greatly reduced. Alternatively, you can create the share with full guest access, and provide a completely invalid username and password on the client system. This approach completely eliminates the threat of a password stolen from a client, but it also increases the risk of problems caused by a direct attack on the printer share itself (for instance, an outside troublemaker's printing a ream of completely black pages).

> **WARNING**   The worst possible way to configure an SMB/CIFS printer share on a Linux client is to specify a normal user's username and password in the .config file. This allows any user of the client computer to grab the .config file and access the compromised user's files on the server.

Note that these issues don't normally apply in quite the same way to Windows clients, because those clients store individual users' network passwords in encrypted form. Once a user is logged on to a Windows system, Windows passes that same logon password to all servers, so there's no need to store a password associated with an individual printer share. The storage of passwords on local systems is nevertheless a security issue, and it's discussed in Chapter 14.

In the end, you'll need to balance the risks of storing printer passwords on clients against those of allowing guest access to printers—and then against the dangers of using another network printing technology, such as lpd with its trusted-host security model. No one solution is uniformly superior from a security point of view. The benefits and risks vary with factors such as the server's availability to the outside world, and how much you trust those with access to the clients on which the passwords are stored.

Summary

Although primarily a server tool, Samba includes support for client access to Windows networks. You can use these tools to give Linux users full access to a peer-to-peer network. You can also arrange to use Linux as a client on an SMB/CIFS client/server network. In addition, you can set up a Linux server to occasionally access its clients' drives, as in a network backup server scenario. These tools—smbclient, smbmount, the ordinary mount command, and smbprint—are best used in a mixed Linux/Windows network, but you might occasionally want to use Samba as a client to access a Samba server. This is particularly true of printer shares, should you prefer a username/password-driven security model to a trusted-hosts security model for this service.

Part 3

Advanced Configurations

Featuring:

- Uses for Automation
- Server-Side and Client-Side Automation
- The Function of NBNS
- Configuring Samba as an NBNS Server
- NBNS Peculiarities of Various OSs
- The Structure of Domains
- Controlling Windows Domains
- Understanding Browsing
- Samba Configuration Options for Browsing
- Browsing Examples
- Testing Your Network's Performance
- Finding Bottlenecks
- Samba Performance-Tuning Options
- Windows Performance-Tuning Options
- Samba and NFS or `lpd`
- Samba and Netatalk
- Samba and Miscellaneous Network Protocols

8

Automation

Computers are very good at performing repetitive tasks. For this reason, it simply makes sense to use network servers such as Samba to help ease the burden of performing routine networking tasks. When you start up a computer, you shouldn't need to perform the same half-dozen or more actions before you can begin doing productive work. Linux users have long been able to use logon shell scripts to help automate their logons—to start a core set of programs, set useful environment variables, and so on. Samba and SMB/CIFS networking include similar features to help you perform routine tasks with less fuss.

There are two main types of automation you can configure with Samba: *server-side* and *client-side*. In server-side automation, you configure some set of commands to be run on the server when specific events occur, such as when a user logs on to a share. In client-side automation, you configure a network logon script similar to a DOS or Windows 9*x* AUTOEXEC.BAT script. You can use this script to provide a common configuration for all clients or for all users. Similarly, you can configure Windows clients to store some of their configuration information on a Samba server, thus allowing an individual to use those customizations at any of several computers on a network. Between these two types of automation, you can configure your network to be a very friendly and consistent environment for your users.

This chapter begins with an overview of what you can accomplish with automation. It moves on to the process of configuring server-side automation, and then proceeds to describe client-side automation.

Uses for Automation

You can use automation in several ways, some of which are fairly simple, but many of which you might not think of in conjunction with a file and print server. In fact, Samba's automation features allow you to integrate Linux and Windows in ways that may obviate the need for conventional Linux logon access on some networks.

Dynamically Configuring Samba

One of the more conventional uses of server-side automation is to dynamically configure Samba or the Samba environment. Suppose you've configured a Samba server to access removable media such as floppies and Zip disks. In order to make this access comparatively automatic, you can use a `preexec` script to mount a disk when a user connects to a share, and a `postexec` script to unmount a disk when a user disconnects. The result is that a user can insert a disk in the server, log on to a share, and access the disk's files. When finished with the share, the user can close the connection and remove the disk. This procedure isn't without its drawbacks, but it may be useful in some situations.

Although it's not technically "automation," you can also use variables in ordinary share definitions to create customized configurations. This method is particularly flexible when used with the `include` parameter, which includes another file into the main `smb.conf` file. To include customized parameters on a per-user basis, you'd use this parameter:

```
include = smb.conf.%U
```

You could then create specialized configuration files for specific users, such as `smb.conf.susanc`. If such a file doesn't exist for a particular user, Samba ignores the `include` parameter.

Dynamically Configuring Windows

Windows machines feature the capability to obtain some of their configuration information from a network server. Specifically, they can run network logon scripts and can obtain network user profiles from a server. Samba can work with these capabilities to help you configure your Windows computers in useful ways. For instance, you can provide unique logon scripts for individual computers or computer types (say, one script for Windows 9*x* computers and another for Windows NT systems). As with included files, you can perform these customizations by using Samba variables when specifying the relevant scripts. This type of customization is described in more detail in the section "Client Network Scripts."

Performing Linux Tasks from Windows

One of the most exotic classes of automation tasks involves having Samba execute Linux programs on cue from a Windows client. This task can be performed using the same preexec and postexec parameters that can be included with any share. In most cases, though, these tasks are performed through a custom print command in a printer share.

When you use a print command parameter, you can send a file to the Samba server, which can then perform some set of operations either on that file or independent of it. The server could process a PostScript file through Ghostscript and leave the output in another share as an Adobe *Portable Document Format* (PDF, aka Acrobat) file; or you could send a file containing data to be added to a database, and the server could do the updating.

You can do almost anything with these commands that you can do by executing a Linux program or script on a single file. In fact, you're not even limited to a single file, because you can send a file package (such as a .ZIP file) to the server, and its server-side script could unpack this file and work on its contents. In sum, you're limited only by your imagination when it comes to linking Linux tasks to Windows clients.

Server-Side Automation

The most complex types of automation fall into the server-side category. In these tasks, you specify a command that Linux is to execute in the Samba smb.conf file. This command can be a simple command, a complex compound command, or a script that performs still more complex commands. In the case of the magic script parameter, the client sends a script that's to be executed by the server.

> ***WARNING*** Because the client sends the script in the case of the magic script command, you should be particularly security conscious when using this feature. For example, although force user = root is seldom a good idea, it's a *particularly bad* idea when you specify a magic script for a share, because this effectively gives root privileges to anybody who can access the share.

A Review of Variables

Chapter 4 introduced the use of variables in smb.conf. This topic is important enough to server-side automation to deserve a brief review here. Table 8.1 presents all the variables that are understood by Samba.

You can include a variable in the variable portion of a parameter. Some variables don't have meaning in conjunction with some shares or parameters, however . %s is useful only with printer shares. %u is useful only after a user has logged onto a share; it's undefined in, for instance, the comment parameter. %U, though, is defined before a user has accessed a share, and so can be used in the comment parameter. As a general rule, %a, %h, %H, %I, %m, %M, %s, %S, %T, %u, and %U are the most useful variables in Samba server-side automation.

Table 8.1   Variables Recognized by Samba

Variable	Meaning
%a	Client's operating system (architecture): can be OS2 (OS/2), Samba, UNKNOWN, WfWg (Windows for Workgroups), Win2K (Windows 2000), Win95 (Windows 95 or 98), or WinNT (Windows NT)
%d	Server's process ID
%g	Primary group of %u
%G	Primary group of %U
%h	Server's DNS name
%H	Home directory of %u
%I	Client's IP address
%j	Print job number
%L	Server's NetBIOS name
%m	Client's NetBIOS name
%M	Client's DNS name
%N	NIS home directory server
%p	Path to the share's root directory, if automounted
%P	Path to the share's root directory
%R	Negotiated SMB protocol level; can be CORE, COREPLUS, LANMAN1, LANMAN2, or NT1
%s	The filename passed to a print share

Table 8.1   Variables Recognized by Samba *(continued)*

Variable	Meaning
%S	Share name
%T	Current date and time
%u	Effective Linux username
%U	Requested username (might not be the same as %u)
%v	Samba version

Using *preexec* and *postexec*

The preexec and postexec parameters specify commands that Samba runs when a user connects to and disconnects from a share, respectively. Both of these parameters can be paired with the root keyword to designate commands that Samba runs using root privileges. (Without the root keyword, the script executes with the ownership associated with that share.) Samba runs these commands in the following order:

1. root preexec
2. preexec
3. postexec
4. root postexec

Between numbers 2 and 3 lie all the accesses a user performs with this share, such as copying or deleting files. This order applies even if you list the parameters in another order in a share's smb.conf definition.

One important additional parameter is preexec close. This is a boolean parameter that controls whether a nonzero return value from a preexec command (that is, an error) closes the share. This parameter defaults to a value of No, but if you set preexec close = Yes, an error occurring while executing the script will close the connection. You might use this feature if it's critically important that the preexec script run correctly before a share can be used.

Advanced Configurations

PART 3

NOTE As a general rule, you should avoid the use of root `preexec` and root `postexec` whenever possible, because these parameters are potential security risks. This is particularly true when you specify complex commands or shell scripts to be run in this way.

Just what might you want to do with these commands? Some possibilities include the following:

Logging   You can set up scripts that use `cat` to write logging information to a specified file, perhaps for debugging or accounting purposes. You can use these logs instead of or in addition to Samba's normal logging information.

Linux File Protection   Uninformed users sometimes delete Linux dot files from Samba shares. As protection against this, you can include `preexec` and `postexec` scripts that back up and restore these dot files. There's one possible negative consequence of doing so, however—if a user logs into a shell account and then logs out while connected using Samba, any changes the user *intends* to make to the dot files may be lost. Your `postexec` restore script could be written to restore files only if the original file has been deleted to overcome this problem.

Device Mounting   If your Samba server serves removable-media devices, you can have the `preexec` script mount a device and the `postexec` script unmount it. There are two major drawbacks to such an arrangement:

- Most clients don't detach from a share in a timely fashion. The device is likely to remain mounted for some time after the user is finished with it. This can be particularly awkward for floppy disks, which can be ejected from the drive when the filesystem is in an inconsistent state.

- If two people try to access the same device, the `preexec` and `postexec` commands can trample on each other. When one user disconnects, the other user may find that the device suddenly has no files. Writing scripts that keep track of the number of connections can eliminate this problem. Another way around it is to use the `max connections = 1` parameter, which limits the number of connections to a share to 1.

Share Preparation   You might want to prepare a share in other ways than I've already described, such as removing temporary files or forcing file ownership or permissions to specific values.

File Processing   You can create a share that allows you to copy files to the share, and then process those files when you're done using the share. You might use this technique to create an image file for burning a CD recordable (CD-R) disc, or to compress data in a seldom-used share.

An example use of these scripts is the share definition shown in Listing 8.1. Users of a Windows network can use this share definition to create an image file for burning files to a CD-R. The resulting image file supports both Windows-style Joliet long filenames and Linux/Unix-style Rock Ridge long filenames. The image file appears in the user's home directory after the user logs off the share.

Listing 8.1 A Share to Create a CD-R Image File from Files Saved on a Samba Server

```
[cd-create]
        path = /home/samba/cd-create
        writeable = Yes
        create mask = 0666
        directory mask = 0777
        max connections = 1
        short preserve case = No
        hide dot files = No
        preexec = rm -r /home/samba/cd-create/*
        postexec = mkisofs -a -J -r -log-file %H/log-%d.txt↵
          -o %H/image-%d.iso /home/samba/cd-create/
```

Key points to consider about this share include the following:

- When a user accesses the [cd-create] share, the preexec parameter causes Samba to delete all the files in the share.

- Because old files are deleted with the preexec parameter, the files that go on a CD-R remain on the server until the next person creates a CD-R. This can be a disadvantage if a CD-R contains sensitive files or if the server is short on disk space—but it's an advantage if you want to check the contents of the CD-R from a Linux shell account after creating the image. You can modify the definition to remove the original files after creating the CD-R, and remove the preexec parameter, if you prefer. To do so, move the rm command after the mkisofs command in the postexec parameter, separating the two with a semicolon (;).

- The max connections = 1 parameter ensures that only one user can be connected to the share at a time, thus preventing one user's CD-creation attempt from trampling another's.

- The short preserve case = No parameter causes short filenames to be converted to lowercase, for the convenience of Unix and Linux users of the resulting CD-R.

- The hide dot files = No parameter allows Windows users to see any dot files on the share, so they aren't accidentally included on the resulting CD-R.

Advanced Configurations

PART 3

- The create mask = 0666 and directory mask = 0777 parameters ensure that all users can delete others' files from this share, including subdirectories. You must be sure that the main share directory has 0777 permissions, as well.

- When a user disconnects from a share, Samba runs the mkisofs command specified in the postexec parameter. This command creates a CD image file called image-*procid*.iso in the user's home directory, with a log of mkisofs's output going in log-*procid*.txt. In both cases, *procid* is the process ID, which should differ for two share accesses, ensuring that a user doesn't accidentally overwrite an image file.

There's one caveat about the configuration arranged in Listing 8.1: The CD image won't be created until the user has disconnected, which may be some time after the user closes all windows on the share. A user can force a disconnect by rebooting the client computer. Another client-side strategy is to explicitly mount a share to a drive letter and then unmount it, rather than opening the share via Network Neighborhood. This definition could be easily expanded to burn a CD-R from the resulting image file, to include better security features or to incorporate other useful tasks.

Using Pseudo-Printers

Pseudo-printer is a term that may be applied to a Samba printer share using the print command parameter to set up a "printer" share that doesn't send output to a printer. For instance, Chapter 6 included a printer share definition that caused output to be faxed via a fax modem connected to the Linux computer. This share qualifies as a pseudo-printer and an example of automation.

In many respects, a pseudo-printer share resembles a file share with a preexec parameter set. The print command, however, is executed whenever a client sends a print job to the server, rather than at the time of connection to the share. In principle, a client might connect to a pseudo-printer once and submit several print jobs before disconnecting. Each job submission results in a fresh execution of the print command.

Another important difference between the print command parameter and the preexec parameter is that a server sends a single file (which can be referenced with the %s variable) with the former, whereas any number of files may be transferred or changed with a conventional file share. A pseudo-printer share, therefore, works well when a user can send a single file to the server and expect the server to process it in some way.

An Example: Creating a CD-R

There is considerable overlap in the potential applications of pseudo-printers and shares that use extensive `preexec` and `postexec` scripts. The CD-creation task outlined earlier can be handled with a pseudo-printer that takes a `.ZIP` file as input, as shown in Listing 8.2.

Listing 8.2 Samba Share to Convert a `.ZIP` File into a CD-R Image File

```
[cd-print]
        comment = Create a CD
        path = /var/spool/samba
        printable = Yes
        print command = /usr/local/bin/cdprint %P %d %s %H
```

This share accepts as input a single `.ZIP` file from the client and processes it through the cdprint script, which is located in `/usr/local/bin`. In order to process the script correctly, the `print command` also passes several Samba variables to the script. The cdprint script appears in Listing 8.3.

Listing 8.3 Shell Script Used in Conjunction with Listing 8.2's Share Definition

```
#!/bin/sh
# $1 = Path to share (%P)
# $2 = Process ID (%d)
# $3 = Filename (%s)
# $4 = User's home directory (%H)
mkdir $1/$2
cd $1/$2
unzip ../$3
rm ../$3
mkisofs -a -J -r -log-file $4/log-$2.txt -o $4/image-$2.iso ./
cd ..
rm -r $2
```

> **NOTE** Linux shell scripts may include variables passed from the calling program. These variables are identified by a dollar sign ($) followed by a number that refers to the order in which the parameter was passed to the script. Thus, $1 in the cdprint script refers to the first parameter passed to it by Samba; $2 is the second parameter; and so on.

Advanced
Configurations

PART 3

The cdprint script makes a subdirectory in the share's root directory, changes into that directory, unzips the file that's been passed, removes the .ZIP file, runs the mkisofs command, and removes the temporary directory that held the .ZIP file's contents. The result is much the same as in the preceding CD-creation share, with some subtle differences: If you create the .ZIP file on a Linux or Unix host, the resulting CD-R image file maintains execute permissions in its Rock Ridge extensions. Similarly, file case is maintained for files with short filenames.

To use this CD-creation "printer" share, you must copy the file to the share *without processing it in any way.* Most Windows printer drivers will attempt to process the file, so you must pass it to the share in some way other than through a normal printer driver. One way to accomplish this task is to use the following command at a command prompt:

```
C:> COPY FILE.ZIP \\SERVERNAME\CD-PRINT
```

As a general rule, the most convenient way to use a configuration like this is to create a DOS/Windows batch file that takes any file you send it and passes the file to the pseudo-printer unchanged, using a command like the preceding one. Here's a batch file called CDPRINT.BAT that accomplishes this goal for the [cd-print] queue on the USRMM server:

```
COPY %1 \\USRMM\CD-PRINT
```

If you like, you can then create a desktop icon that's a shortcut to this batch file. Thereafter, if you drag a .ZIP file onto the desktop icon, an image file appears in your home directory on the Samba server, ready to be burned to CD.

Configuring a Queue for Input through a Printer Driver

In some cases, it may be desirable to receive input directly from a Windows program, such as a text editor. When this is so, you may want to select a generic text printer, which sends output to the pseudo-printer queue as ASCII text (albeit with extraneous carriage returns and spaces to position text) in what Windows believes to be a sensible manner. If your Linux-side processing scripts can cope with the extraneous carriage returns, you should have no problems. Should the input file take some other form, you may be able to use another printer driver. For example, you can create a Samba share that accepts PostScript input just like many other Samba printer shares, but creates a PDF file from the input. A share like this can be used with a normal Windows printer driver—although you may need to configure it to omit a Ctrl+D at the start or end of a print job, as described in Chapter 6. An example of such a share is shown in Listing 8.4.

Listing 8.4 Share to Create a PDF File from a Windows Print Job

```
[pdf-create]
        comment = Create a PDF file
        path = /var/spool/samba
        printable = Yes
        print command = gs -dNOPAUSE -sDEVICE=pdfwrite -q -dBATCH↵
           -sOutputFile=%H/%s.pdf %s; rm %s
```

You can use an ordinary Windows PostScript driver with this queue (Apple LaserWriter drivers tend to work well for this purpose). When you "print" to this queue, Samba passes the results through Ghostscript and sends the output to a file named after the Windows printer queue filename, but with .pdf appended. Such a queue can be a convenient alternative to using a commercial PDF-creation tool, although it's not as flexible because Ghostscript's PDF output options are still fairly primitive. You could use a similar share, but with different Ghostscript options, to create output in a bitmap file format such as TIFF or JPEG.

Important Information Concerning Pseudo-Printers

One important point to note concerning the previous definitions, and pseudo-printers in general, is that you must normally include an explicit command to remove the file passed from the client (%s). If you fail to do this, these files usually build up until you run out of disk space. Some commands you perform may remove these files automatically, but most don't.

It's important to understand the security implications of pseudo-printers—or of server-side scripts generally. Both of the preceding examples place files in the user's home directory and create temporary files in the printer share directory. You could easily create a pseudo-printer that would allow a malicious individual to wreak havoc, particularly if the script can be broken by feeding it bad input. For example, the [cd-print] share creates files that might have the set user ID (suid) bit set, if that bit is set on the files in the .ZIP file. As described, this share runs with the privileges of the user who connects to it, but adding a force user parameter could make it a potentially *very* dangerous share, should a malicious individual use an suid file from the relevant directory while mkisofs is processing that directory.

In sum, when you want a Linux server to automatically process information provided by Windows clients, a pseudo-printer can be an excellent way to accomplish this goal, especially if you're willing to write a couple of simple scripts.

Advanced Configurations

PART 3

Using Magic Scripts

A *magic script* is a type of server-side automation that involves the execution of a script provided by the client. In the `smb.conf` file, you specify the name of a script to be executed by the server when that file is written by the client. You can then send a script to the server and have it run immediately, provided you give it the "magic" name. After running the script, Samba deletes it from the share, provided the share's permissions allow this action. Magic scripts are a fairly recent addition to Samba, so they're relatively untested as compared with `preexec` and `postexec` scripts or pseudo-printers. On some networks, they may not work at all.

To use a magic script, you must include two special parameters in your `smb.conf` file:

magic script = *filename*   This parameter specifies the name of the magic script file. If you include `magic script = myscript` in a share's definition, the server executes the file called `myscript` when the user writes and closes the file.

magic output = *filename*   If the magic script produces output, Samba redirects that output into the file specified by this parameter. It allows you to check the output of the process. The *filename* defaults to the name of the magic script file, with `.out` appended.

The great advantage—and danger—of magic scripts is that the share's users can affect what the scripts do. A user can create dozens or hundreds of Linux scripts to perform assorted tasks, then copy the scripts to an appropriate magic share directory to run them. Magic scripts are thus much more flexible than the administrator-defined automation tasks of `preexec`, `postexec`, and pseudo-printers. This sort of flexibility can be very useful in some environments. On the other hand, if you want to operate a fairly closed server in which users don't have normal shell account privileges, magic scripts can be undesirable.

WARNING   The Samba documentation warns against relying upon magic scripts because of their unreliability and potential security problems. In fact, they're very difficult to get working correctly. Magic scripts usually fail on Samba versions past 2.0.5.

Client Network Scripts

If your Linux Samba server functions as a domain controller for Windows 9*x* clients, you can provide a special Windows batch file to control the configuration of your Windows clients. In fact, using Samba's variables (see Table 8.1), you can fine-tune the *logon script* (as this batch file is called) for each client, user, or other characteristics. This feature can be quite powerful if used appropriately. Suppose you want to customize the environment given to each user; you can do so, in part, by using customized logon scripts. You can achieve similar effects, as well as many others, by configuring your Samba server to host *roaming profiles*. These allow individual users to store preferences on a server for use on the client computer.

Both network logon scripts and roaming profiles require that the Samba server be configured as a network logon server—a topic covered in greater detail in Chapter 10, "Configuring Domains." Therefore, only the briefest description of domain controller configuration is presented here. Be sure to read Chapter 10 if you intend to use this feature in anything other than a trivial fashion.

Basic Domain Controller Configuration

A domain controller allows one computer to authenticate logon attempts to other computers across the network. Configured properly, this setup improves network security by making it more difficult to gain unauthorized access to a client system. It also greatly reduces administrative headaches, both because it centralizes passwords in one location and because it allows you to configure and, when necessary, modify logon scripts.

A basic Samba domain controller configuration looks something like this:

```
[global]
        workgroup = ISAAC
        netbios name = USRMM
        security = User
        domain logons = Yes
        domain master = Yes
        wins support = Yes
```

Following are the key points of this configuration:

security parameter is *not* Share Share-level security doesn't authenticate users and so cannot be used. Normally, you'll set security = User, but you can use Server or Domain if you want to authenticate against yet another domain controller.

domain logons = Yes This setting configures Samba to accept domain logons. It's required for any Samba domain controller.

Advanced Configurations

PART 3

domain master = Yes   Like domain logons = Yes, the domain master parameter must be Yes for Samba domain controllers.

wins support = Yes   This parameter provides support for NetBIOS Name Service (NBNS). Windows systems normally expect a primary domain controller (PDC) to provide NBNS support.

You can read more about domain controller configuration, including configuring Windows clients to use domain logons, in Chapter 10. The rest of this chapter assumes that you have configured at least some of your Windows clients to use domain logons.

Creating a Logon Script

A logon script is a DOS/Windows batch file. You must therefore be familiar with the DOS/Windows batch-file language to create such a script. This script can perform useful tasks such as mounting remote shares (even shares that don't reside on the Samba server you're configuring), setting environment variables, and so on. As an example, here's a simple logon script that configures the system to mount the user's home share on M: and open a Windows Explorer window on that share:

```
NET USE M: \\USRMM\HOMES /YES
EXPLORER M:
```

> **NOTE**   Because the logon script is a *Windows* script, it uses Windows commands and must conform to Windows conventions. In this example, note the backslashes (\ ) in the network name, and the slash (/) as an identifier for a switch to the NET USE command. Also, these logon scripts *must* use Windows-style end-of-line characters—carriage return/line feed pairs. If you create such a script on Linux, you must be careful to convert the file using a utility like unix2dos, or manually add Ctrl+M characters to the ends of all lines in the file if your editor allows you to do so. It's generally easier to use Windows to create such files.

Once you've created a logon script, you can place it in a special share called [netlogon]. This share definition should resemble the one shown in Listing 8.5. It's a fairly ordinary share, using the writeable = No and guest ok = No parameters as security measures but using write list = susanc to allow susanc to modify logon scripts.

Listing 8.5 Share Definition for Storing Network Logon Scripts

```
[netlogon]
        comment = Network Logon Service
        path = /home/samba/netlogon
        guest ok = No
        writeable = No
        write list = susanc
```

A Windows logon script might go under the filename /home/samba/netlogon/logon.bat. You must then modify the [global] portion of smb.conf to include a reference to the logon script file:

```
        logon script = logon.bat
```

Now, whenever a client logs on to the network by using the Samba domain controller, it runs the logon.bat file. By itself, this isn't terribly exciting—after all, you can often achieve similar results by using the Windows AUTOEXEC.BAT file or the Windows StartUp folder. A Samba-served logon script is potentially much more interesting, however, because you can use Samba's variables in the script's filename. For instance, if you specify the script's filename as %U.bat, then Samba passes a different file to the server depending upon the user's logon name—susanc.bat for susanc, gregp.bat for gregp, and so on. Similarly, you can use client NetBIOS names, user groups, OS codes, and so on, or even combinations of these variables. A network logon script also has the advantage of being centrally administered, so you can modify the script used by potentially hundreds of clients just by editing a single file.

> **NOTE** You can include variables as part of the logon script's name, but not as part of any parameters you pass to the script.

As mentioned earlier, it's generally a good security precaution to make the [netlogon] share read-only—but this can be inconvenient if you want to let users modify their own logon scripts. You may therefore want to make the share writeable, or at least use the write list parameter to make it writeable for some users. If you do so, however, be sure that you do *not* use the force user parameter; and set permissions such that users can't overwrite others' files.

Setting Up Roaming Profiles

Although logon scripts can be useful for setting up some configurations, they can't do everything you might like in the way of system customization. Much of the Windows GUI environment is configured through a *profile*—a set of information relating to icon placement, desktop background preferences, and so on. Even when settings can be adjusted through a batch file, this can be awkward, because most users don't know how to manipulate batch files and because doing so requires editing the text files. Profiles, by contrast, are handled more-or-less transparently by Windows—a user need only change that background bitmap image, and Windows will remember it.

NOTE   Many Linux systems allow the user to create a file called ~/.profile, which contains account configuration information. Although the purpose of a Windows profile and a Linux ~/.profile are similar, their implementations are completely different.

If your users routinely use the same computer at all times, there's no problem with employing profiles because they are normally stored locally. In some environments, however, users move frequently from one computer to another—in academic computer labs, for example. In such situations, you may want to configure Samba to support roaming profiles. To do so, you must add a new Samba share, which can look something like the one shown in Listing 8.6.

Listing 8.6   Samba Share for Storing Users' Roaming Profiles

```
[profile]
        path = /home/samba/profile
        read only = No
        create mode = 0600
        directory mode = 0770
        browseable = No
        guest ok = No
```

You must also put a special entry in the [global] section of smb.conf to tell Samba (and Windows clients) about the availability of the [profile] share. In Samba versions up to and including 2.0.5a, use the following:

```
        logon path = \\%L\PROFILE\%U
```

In Samba versions 2.0.6 and later, however, logon path doesn't work; instead, you should use logon home, as in

```
        logon home = \\%L\PROFILE\%U
```

Here are some key points about the preceding definitions:

Backslashes in logon path and logon home   The logon path and logon home parameters' values require the use of Windows-style backslashes (\ ) rather than Linux-style slashes (/). Be sure to get this right!

%U Subdirectory Name   The %U variable specifies a subdirectory named after the user and residing in the [profile] share. This format allows each user to maintain his or her own profile. You could also create profiles by group or in some other way, but such configurations are usually less functional.

Automatic Directory Creation   You don't need to create the subdirectories in which the profiles are stored; Samba does this automatically. (You *do*, however, need to create the directory pointed to by the path parameter in the [profile] share. It should be owned by root and have 777 permissions.)

Using Roaming Profiles from Windows Clients

When roaming profiles are configured correctly, you must activate profiles on the Windows clients. To do so, follow these steps:

1. Double-click the Passwords item in the Control Panel. This opens the Passwords Properties dialog box.

2. Click to open the User Profiles tab, shown in Figure 8.1.

Figure 8.1   By default, Windows displays the same desktop to all users, but you can change this behavior.

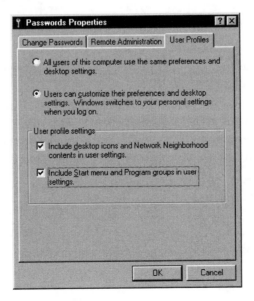

3. Select the second radio button option (Users can customize...).

> **NOTE** When the computer is *not* configured for domain logons, Windows stores profiles locally. When the computer *is* configured for domain logons, however, the computer tries to store profiles both locally and on the domain logon server and then uses whichever set of profiles is newer when you log on again.

4. In the User Profile Settings area, select one or both of the check boxes, as you see fit.
5. Click OK. Windows informs you that it must reboot to activate the changes.
6. When Windows starts up again and you log on, it presents the following dialog box. Choose Yes to store your profile remotely as well as locally.

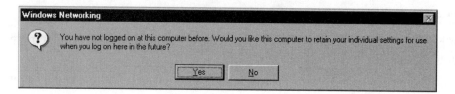

In this arrangement, Windows now stores profiles locally and on the server as well. If you use these steps to set up another computer in this way, you can share configuration settings across those two machines, provided you use the same username on both machines.

Caveats about Logon Scripts and User Profiles

Logon scripts and user profiles can be very useful tools in many network environments. You can use these features to provide configurations that are consistent across machines when individuals use more than one computer. There are, however, some things to be aware of when you do this.

Inconsistent Hardware When two computers use dissimilar hardware, you might not get good results if any of your configuration features rely upon the hardware. For instance, a configuration that relies upon a high screen resolution may not work well on, or may be "downgraded" by, a computer that uses a lower resolution.

Incompatible Shortcuts If a desktop configuration includes shortcuts to program objects or data files that are local to a specific computer, those links won't work well with a roaming profile unless all the client systems place equivalent files in the same location. It's therefore important that you install software in consistent locations when you install it locally.

Simultaneous Profile Use Anomalies   If a user logs on to the network from two Windows clients simultaneously, changes that affect the profile may overwrite one another. As a general rule, the saved profile matches that of the last client to log out.

Time Peculiarities   If two clients' clocks are set to different times, you may experience peculiar behavior as a result. Specifically, you might find that changes made on the clock that's set to the earlier time are never saved, if the time difference is great enough.

TIP   You can fix this problem by including the command `NET TIME \\SERVER /SET /YES` in the network logon script to set all the clients' clocks to the time maintained by `SERVER`. If your Samba server's `smb.conf` file includes the `time server = Yes` parameter, it can function as a time server for the network.

Summary

Automation can greatly expand your network's capabilities. You can use `preexec` and `postexec` to perform routine tasks associated with share access or to convert an otherwise ordinary share into a data-processing tool. You can use `print command` to mildly or radically alter the function of a Samba printer share. In principle, `magic script` can be used to provide extremely flexible script-handling features, but in practice this parameter often doesn't work. On the client side, one or more network logon scripts and roaming profiles can be configured to help provide customized configurations based on computers, OSs, groups, usernames, or other factors. Although not always necessary—or even desirable— these features can help immensely in certain situations.

Advanced Configurations

PART 3

9

Samba as an NBNS Server

One of the core features of a TCP/IP-based Windows network is the *NetBIOS Name Service (NBNS),* which Microsoft calls the *Windows Internet Name Service (WINS).* As described in Chapter 1, NBNS/WINS is a means of converting NetBIOS names into TCP/IP IP addresses. As such, NBNS bears a superficial similarity to the *Domain Name Service (DNS)* of the Internet. In fact, it's possible to link the two in various ways, and both Samba and some versions of Windows can use DNS as a stand-in for NBNS.

> **NOTE** NBNS is a core feature of *TCP/IP-based* Windows networks. Windows networks that rely exclusively upon NetBEUI don't use NBNS.

This chapter serves as an introduction to NBNS—precisely what NBNS does, when you should use it, and how to configure a Samba server to function as an NBNS server. The first part of the chapter is devoted to NBNS theory and the relationship between various computer-naming technologies. Following that is a discussion of practical NBNS configuration issues, on Samba and on client OSs.

Understanding NBNS

To have Samba function as an NBNS server, you must understand what such a server does and why it is desirable. It's also helpful to know how NBNS is similar to, is dissimilar from, and interacts with some common alternatives. Once you understand this material, you'll be better able to configure Samba as an NBNS server or client.

The Function of NBNS

Windows networking protocols were built in part around a *broadcast* name-resolution system. Configured in this way, whenever one computer wants to communicate with another, it sends out a broadcast transmission that can be received by any computer on the network, asking for the IP address of a target computer. Suppose the computer KITHRUP wants to communicate with the computer JIJO. KITHRUP can send a broadcast message asking for JIJO's address. This broadcast, however, is also received by other computers on the network, as shown in Figure 9.1. Such a configuration is wasteful of network resources and can be slow. It is, however, easy to configure, because you need not assign any computer to be a central name server.

Figure 9.1 Broadcast name resolution requires attention by many computers and can cause a great deal of network "chatter."

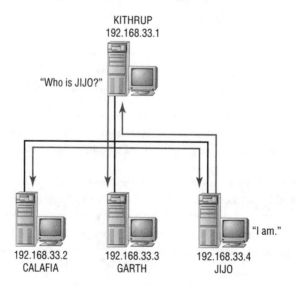

A more efficient arrangement in terms of network resources is to use an NBNS server, as shown in Figure 9.2. In this arrangement, the client knows the IP address of the NBNS server and queries that computer to find the IP address of *any* computer. Conceptually, this arrangement is quite similar to that of the Internet's DNS, although the two protocols are incompatible.

Figure 9.2   NBNS name resolution results in less network traffic than does broadcast name resolution.

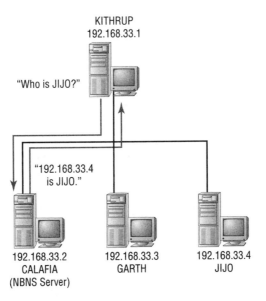

In addition to these differences at the time of name resolution, broadcast and NBNS networks differ when a computer comes online. In a broadcast network, a machine broadcasts the name it wants to use in an effort to *register* that name. If no other computer claims the name, the newly booted computer begins responding to that name. If two computers try to use the same name, they must "fight" over the right to do so, which sometimes results in difficulty reaching either computer. In an NBNS network, by contrast, individual computers register their names with the NBNS server, which arbitrates any disputes over name registration.

On the whole, NBNS offers several advantages over broadcast name resolution:

Reduced Network Traffic   NBNS involves point-to-point network traffic instead of broadcasts. Particularly if your network uses a switch rather than a hub or coaxial Ethernet, this fact can reduce extraneous traffic carried on the network. Point-to-point network traffic also reduces the need for computers to process name requests that aren't destined for them.

Operation across Subnetworks   If your network is composed of two or more subnetworks linked by routers or other devices that block broadcast packets, NBNS allows your Windows network to span all subnetworks. Broadcast name resolution restricts you to using two independent Windows networks, one for each of your subnetworks. (Samba provides some mechanisms that may allow you to get around this problem, but it's usually better to use NBNS.) Clients must know the IP address of the NBNS server, whereupon name resolution can proceed as if the two subnetworks were one.

Improved Reliability   If your NBNS server is itself reliable, or if your network hosts a backup NBNS server, NBNS can be more reliable than broadcasts, particularly on a busy network. Packets may be lost on a busy network, causing delays or failures in broadcast name resolution.

TIP   SMB/CIFS networks sometimes experience difficulties in which computers mysteriously disappear from the Windows Network Neighborhood, or are available from some computers but not from others. You can often fix such problems by switching the network to use NBNS rather than broadcast name resolution.

The downside to NBNS is that it requires extra effort to configure. You must set aside one computer to function as an NBNS server, and you must point your other computers to this server for NBNS operations. As described shortly, if your network uses the *Dynamic Host Configuration Protocol (DHCP)* to assign IP addresses to computers, some of this work can be done through DHCP, which can reduce the administrative effort of maintaining an NBNS-based network.

Before you try configuring Samba as an NBNS server, you should be aware that Windows NT systems tend to link NBNS, *primary domain controller (PDC)*, and *master browser* functions. (See Chapter 10, "Configuring Domains," for more on PDCs; and Chapter 11, "Local and Routed Browsing," for more on master browsers.) If your network includes Windows NT or 2000 systems, and if one serves as any of these three server types, it's best for that system to function as all three server types. Therefore, avoid configuring Samba as an NBNS server when a Windows NT system already functions as a PDC or master browser. (The PDC is the more important of these functions, in most cases; the master browser role can change fairly dynamically.) In addition, Windows NT servers can function as either *primary* or *backup* NBNS servers, but Samba can function only in the primary role. When Samba functions as the primary NBNS server, there can be no backup NBNS server. You might therefore want to give the NBNS function to a Windows NT server even if a Linux computer is your main file and print server.

Although Windows NT links these three roles, they are conceptually distinct. NBNS deals with name resolution—associating names and IP addresses. The PDC serves as a centralized authentication machine and can often host specialized shares such as roaming profiles (described in Chapter 8). The master browser maintains a list of computer names available on the network, so that users can "browse" from one computer to another in a way analogous to browsing a hard disk's directory tree. In order to access a specific computer from such a browse list, though, the browsing computer must perform name resolution.

NBNS and DNS

As stated earlier, NBNS and DNS are similar protocols, in that both provide computers with the IP addresses that are associated with specific names. The two protocols differ in important ways, however:

- DNS is a protocol used on TCP/IP networks and on the Internet at large. It's used for a wide variety of TCP/IP networking protocols. NBNS, by contrast, is used on NetBIOS over TCP/IP networks only and is used exclusively by SMB/CIFS protocols.

- DNS provides for multi-tiered hostnames, such as `garth.eclan.mway.org`. NBNS provides for only two levels of naming—the machine name and the workgroup name. The workgroup name is unimportant in determining name collisions, though. No two computers on a single network can have the same NetBIOS machine name, even if they're in different workgroups.

- DNS is centrally administered. To add a machine to a domain for which a specific DNS server is authoritative, you must manually configure that DNS server, or at least arrange for a script of some sort to do so. NBNS, by contrast, is self-regulating; an NBNS server adds and removes machine names as the individual clients make requests. You therefore don't need to adjust the NBNS server when you add a computer to a NetBIOS network.

- DNS is a massively distributed system of machine naming. Specific computers are responsible for entire branches of the name space, although they need not know every detail of the domains for which they're authoritative. DNS works because one name server can pass requests to another or can redirect the original requestor to another name server. NBNS, by contrast, is flat and not interconnected. One NBNS server knows about machines on its own network and no more. Unless you reconfigure a client to query a remote NBNS server, you can't obtain information about a nonlocal network through NBNS.

DNS and NBNS are incompatible protocols, but a given network can support both protocols. Indeed, this is usually the case when NBNS is involved in a network. If possible, you should use the same names for both DNS and NBNS identification, omitting the portions of the DNS name that don't fit in the NBNS model. For instance, the computer called garth.eclan.mway.org in DNS terminology might be GARTH in the ECLAN or MWAY workgroups in NBNS terminology.

Samba, Windows NT, and Windows 2000 all support the use of DNS instead of or in addition to NBNS, broadcasts, or lmhosts for NetBIOS name resolution. Such a configuration is nonstandard from a Windows 9x point of view, but it's sometimes quite helpful. This is especially true when DNS and NetBIOS names are identical and a network's NBNS servers are nonexistent or unreliable.

NBNS and *lmhosts*

Small NetBIOS networks may use a file called lmhosts instead of broadcasts or NBNS. The lmhosts file is almost identical in format to the Linux or Unix /etc/hosts file. Like /etc/hosts, lmhosts contains a listing of machine names and IP addresses associated with those names. Also like /etc/hosts, lmhosts is used to perform name lookups without doing network accesses, thus speeding up the process and reducing network traffic.

Upon installation, Windows systems include a file called LMHOSTS.SAM, usually in the C:\WINDOWS directory. This file includes comments describing the exact parameters accepted by the file. A simple lmhosts file resembles the following:

```
192.168.33.3     garth
192.168.33.4     jijo
192.168.33.1     kithrup
```

NOTE Windows machines can use several special qualifiers in their lmhosts files, most of which Samba doesn't recognize. A basic file such as the one above works on both systems, however.

On a Windows 9x system, you should put the file (called LMHOSTS, with no extension) in the main Windows directory (usually C:\WINDOWS). Windows then uses the file automatically. On Windows NT 4 systems, you must enable use of this file by following these steps as the Administrator:

1. Place the LMHOSTS file in the C:\WINNT\SYSTEM32\DRIVERS\ETC directory. (You may need to adjust the drive letter and WINNT directory name on some systems.)

2. Open Control Panel.

3. Double-click the Network icon. Windows opens the Network dialog box.

4. Click the Protocols tab, and select the TCP/IP Protocol line.

5. Click Properties. Windows opens the Microsoft TCP/IP Properties dialog box.

6. Click the WINS Address tab. The display should now resemble Figure 9.3.

Figure 9.3   Windows NT allows you to use LMHOSTS, DNS, or a WINS (NBNS) server for name resolution.

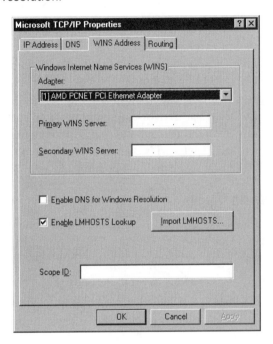

7. Make sure the Enable LMHOSTS Lookup box is checked. It should be enabled by default.

8. Click OK in the Microsoft TCP/IP Properties dialog box, then click Close in the Network dialog box.

> **NOTE** Windows 2000 enables LMHOSTS use by default. You can enable or disable it by following steps similar to those for Windows NT 4, but you must access the Advanced TCP/IP Settings dialog box from the main Internet Protocol (TCP/IP) Properties dialog box.

On Linux, you can create an lmhosts file in the main Samba configuration directory (usually /etc, /etc/samba, or something similar). Note that in Linux, the filename must be

Advanced Configurations

PART 3

all lowercase. You enable use of lmhosts in Linux by using the `name resolve order` parameter in `smb.conf`, as described shortly.

NBNS and lmhosts don't interact much. Depending on how the computer is configured, it may check the lmhosts file before performing a broadcast or NBNS query. But changes to the NBNS server don't affect the contents of client lmhosts files, and adding entries to lmhosts doesn't affect the NBNS server.

As a general rule, lmhosts can be a useful way to configure name resolution on a small network—but on such networks, broadcasts usually work acceptably, too. Another possible use for lmhosts is to add a limited number of entries for machines that reside on separate network segments from the client. Suppose your NetBIOS domain or workgroup consists of several systems on one network segment, plus two computers at a remote location. You can add those two remote machines to the lmhosts files on the main network's computers, and add the main network's computers to the two remote clients' lmhosts files. Using NBNS throughout is probably a better solution in this situation, however.

Setting the Node Type

When using NetBIOS over TCP/IP, each client must determine which name-resolution methods it uses and in which order it tries them. This characteristic is called the *node type,* of which there are four:

b-node   A b-node uses broadcasts for name registration and resolution. The DHCP code for a b-node is 1.

p-node   A p-node uses point-to-point (NBNS) registration and name resolution. The DHCP code for a p-node is 2.

m-node   An m-node first tries to use broadcasts, but if a broadcast fails, it uses NBNS resolution. The DHCP code for an m-node is 4.

h-node   Also known as *hybrid* nodes, h-nodes first try to use NBNS resolution and then fall back on broadcasts. The DHCP code for an h-node is 8.

On Windows systems, you can find the node type by typing **IPCONFIG /ALL**. The resulting output includes a line similar to the following:

```
Node Type . . . . . . . . . : Hybrid
```

If the computer is configured as an h-node, p-node, or m-node, a subsequent line should list the IP addresses of the primary and (if configured) secondary NBNS servers, thus:

```
Primary WINS Server . . . . : 192.168.34.100
Secondary WINS Server . . . : 192.168.34.200
```

The simplest way to configure a Windows computer's node type is through a DHCP server. If your network's DHCP server is the popular BIND package, you can include the following lines in /etc/dhcpd.conf to set the node type for all Windows DHCP clients:

```
option netbios-name-servers 192.168.34.100;

option netbios-node-type 8;
```

These two lines set the IP address of the NBNS server and set the node type to be used by the clients. After making these changes, any Windows 9x, NT, or 2000 computers should use these settings, provided other settings on the computer don't override them. (Some of these override settings are described in the "NBNS under Various OSs" section.)

Samba doesn't use the node type delivered by a DHCP server; instead, you set its name-resolution order with the name resolve order parameter. This parameter is described shortly, in the section "Name Resolution Order."

Samba NBNS Operations

Samba's NBNS-related parameters are fairly simple as such things go. On the server side, you can configure Samba to function as an NBNS server. You can also set a few options that adjust the way Samba runs as an NBNS server. On the client side, you can adjust the order in which Samba performs NetBIOS name lookups.

Advanced Configurations

PART 3

> **NOTE** A Samba server can still be a client for NBNS lookup purposes. Your network might have a Windows NT NBNS server, for example, in which case a Samba server could use that server for name lookups. Similarly, if you have two or more Samba servers, you should configure only one as an NBNS server.

Configuring Samba as an NBNS Server

Basic Samba NBNS configuration involves setting just one parameter in the [global] section of smb.conf:

```
wins support = Yes
```

This parameter tells Samba to operate as an NBNS server. Because NBNS is a self-maintaining protocol, you need not specify any additional configuration files or options. Once operational, the NBNS server begins collecting NetBIOS names and IP addresses, and passes that information on to clients.

WARNING   Don't use the wins server parameter (described shortly) if you set wins support = Yes. Doing so can cause Samba to behave strangely.

WARNING   Don't configure more than one computer as a primary NBNS server on any given network. Samba doesn't support secondary NBNS servers (either Windows systems or other Samba computers), so if you use Samba as an NBNS server, you should have only one NBNS server on the network. If you have two NBNS servers, name resolution may not work for some clients.

Samba supports a few global parameters that can modify the behavior of NBNS functions in potentially useful ways:

wins proxy   If set to Yes, this parameter causes Samba to respond to broadcast NetBIOS name requests for other hosts. For instance, if a client sends a broadcast to request the IP address for JIJO, and if JIJO has registered itself with Samba's NBNS server, then Samba can respond with the correct IP address for JIJO. This feature may be useful if you're transitioning a network from broadcast to NBNS-based name queries. The default for this parameter is No in Samba versions since 2.0, but it was Yes in earlier versions.

dns proxy   If set to Yes, this parameter indicates that Samba's NBNS server code should attempt a DNS lookup on the NetBIOS name, should Samba's NBNS database contain no match to the name. This feature might be useful if clients don't reliably register their names with Samba but have fixed IP addresses and correct DNS names that match their NetBIOS names. The default for this parameter is Yes.

wins hook   This parameter allows you to specify the name of an external program that Samba calls whenever Samba makes a change to its internal NBNS database. You might use this feature to have a script automatically update DNS entries, for example. The external program must accept five parameters:

Operation	The operation that's being performed. This may be add, delete, or refresh, for adding, removing, or updating entries, respectively.
Name	The NetBIOS name being added, deleted, or refreshed.

Name type	The NetBIOS name type as a two-digit hexa-decimal code.
Time-to-live	The time, in seconds, for which the new entry is valid.
IP list	The IP address or addresses associated with the name.

The `wins hook` parameter is seldom used but can be helpful in some situations. If you need more information, you can study the example script `dns_update`, which comes with the Samba source code and many Samba binary distributions in the Samba documentation examples directory. This script adds or deletes DNS entries for the names added or deleted through NBNS actions.

Name Resolution Order

Linux systems don't use the DHCP-provided node types. Instead, you configure a Linux system's NetBIOS name resolution priorities through the global `name resolve order` parameter in `smb.conf`. This parameter takes any combination of the following four options, separated by spaces:

lmhosts This option causes Samba to access the system's `lmhosts` file, if it's present.

host This option causes Samba to use the host's normal TCP/IP name-resolution features. For instance, If the computer is set to use the `/etc/hosts` file and DNS lookups, then Samba does the same. Note that this option causes Samba to use DNS hostnames as if they were NetBIOS machine names, which is not standard behavior for most Windows clients. On most networks, however, this option works well and produces less network traffic than do NetBIOS broadcasts.

wins This option causes Samba to use NBNS (WINS) lookups, much like a Windows client. Use of this option also requires either the `wins support = Yes` parameter (which causes Samba to function as an NBNS server) or the `wins server` parameter (in which you can list the IP addresses of one or more NBNS servers).

bcast This option causes Samba to use broadcast name lookups, much as a Windows client can.

The order in which these options are listed is significant; Samba tries each method in the order in which it's listed on the `name resolve order` line. By default, Samba sets these options as follows:

```
name resolve order = lmhosts host wins bcast
```

This configuration usually results in efficient NetBIOS name lookups. You can change this order for specific networks, however. Say your network's NetBIOS and DNS host-names don't match; you might want to remove the host option, or at least move it after the wins, and perhaps the bcast, options. Samba tries to resolve a machine name using one method after another until a method succeeds. For instance, if the lmhosts file contains an entry for a specific name, Samba does *not* try to use DNS, NBNS, or broadcast lookups, if the default order is used.

When a Linux computer uses an NBNS server, you must specify the IP address or DNS name of that server. As mentioned earlier, you do this with the wins server parameter. In use, this parameter looks like the following:

```
wins server = 192.168.34.100
```

If you like, you can use the DNS name of the server instead of its IP address. Note, however, that though you can use the DNS name, you cannot use a NetBIOS name. The two names may, of course, be identical, in which case the NetBIOS name will work; but if the names differ, only the DNS name works.

WARNING Do not set the wins server parameter if you use the wins support = Yes parameter. The former tells Samba to look elsewhere for an NBNS server, but the latter tells Samba that it *is* an NBNS server. Setting both options can cause Samba to fail as a server and as a client. If your Samba server is an NBNS server, you can still use wins support = Yes. In this case, Samba uses itself for NBNS lookups; there's no need to set the wins server parameter.

NBNS under Various OSs

NetBIOS name resolution rules vary under different OSs. Most Windows OSs use the node-type settings passed by a DHCP server, if the network uses DHCP for IP address assignment. This is therefore an efficient way to configure NBNS information; you can set the information once, on the DHCP server, and not touch it again. If your NBNS server changes, you can change it once rather than having to reconfigure dozens or hundreds of clients.

Occasionally, however, you may need to configure computers individually, or use non-standard options available only in specific OSs. One such unusual configuration, in the form of Samba's name resolve order parameter, is described earlier in this chapter. Windows NT and 2000, in particular, also provide for unusual name resolution options.

Windows 9x

Windows 95 and 98 offer the fewest name-resolution options of most common SMB/CIFS OSs. If your network uses fixed IP addresses or if you don't want to use DHCP to set computers' node types and NBNS server addresses, you can perform these tasks as follows:

1. Open the Windows Control Panel.

2. Double-click the Network icon to open the Network dialog box.

3. Select the TCP/IP component and click the Properties button. Windows displays the TCP/IP Properties dialog box.

4. Click the WINS Configuration tab, which produces the display shown in Figure 9.4.

Figure 9.4   In Windows 9x you can manually add an NBNS server, using the WINS Server Search Order field.

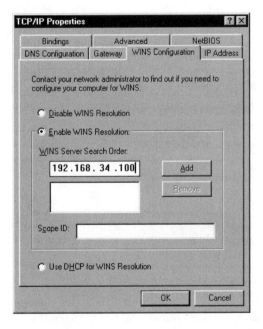

5. If you want to use the name resolution settings configured via DHCP, be sure the Use DHCP for WINS Resolution radio button is selected, then skip to step 9. (This setting is the default.)

6. If you want to configure name resolution manually, be sure the Enable WINS Resolution button is selected.

7. In the WINS Server Search Order field, enter an IP address for your primary NBNS server; then click Add.

8. Repeat step 7 for each NBNS server you maintain on the network.

9. Click OK in the TCP/IP Properties dialog box, then OK in the Network dialog box.

Windows 9*x* automatically configures itself as an h-node when you enter NBNS information as described above; otherwise it configures itself as a b-node. Unlike more advanced OSs, you can't configure Windows 9*x* to use DNS should a lookup fail. In all cases, though, Windows 9*x* will use an LMHOSTS file if one is present in the C:\WINDOWS directory (or in whatever directory you've used to store the main Windows files).

Windows NT 4

Windows NT 4 NetBIOS name resolution works similarly to Windows 9*x*'s upon first installation. Windows NT provides some additional configuration options, however. These options are in the WINS Address tab of the Microsoft TCP/IP Properties dialog box shown in Figure 9.3. To get to this dialog box, double-click the Network icon in the Control Panel, select TCP/IP Protocol on the Protocols tab, and click the Properties button.

By default, Windows NT accepts NBNS configuration options provided through DHCP, so you can use DHCP to configure basic Windows NT name resolution. In addition, the Microsoft TCP/IP Properties dialog box provides these options:

WINS Servers   You can enter the IP addresses of up to two NBNS servers in the Primary WINS Server and Secondary WINS Server fields.

DNS Resolution   As with Linux, you can configure Windows NT to use DNS as a stand-in for NetBIOS name resolution. Check the Enable DNS for Windows Resolution check box.

Enable LMHOSTS Lookup   Select this check box to use the LMHOSTS file, as described earlier. In addition, you can import the contents of another lmhosts file by clicking the Import LMHOSTS button.

Its ability to use DNS name resolution makes Windows NT more flexible than Windows 9*x*. You might want to enable DNS resolution if you find your network's NetBIOS name resolution is unreliable. Of course, you should be able to configure a Samba or Windows NT system as an NBNS server to achieve good reliability, as well.

Windows 2000

Windows 2000 continues the evolution of Windows SMB/CIFS networking away from NBNS. By default, Windows 2000 uses DNS instead of NBNS for NetBIOS name lookups. You can, however, enable an NBNS server and adjust Windows 2000's settings much as you can for Windows NT 4. The relevant dialog box is somewhat harder to find—to get to it, follow these steps as the Administrator:

1. Open the Control Panel, and from there open the Network and Dial-up Connections folder.

2. Right-click the Local Area Connection object and select Properties from the resulting pop-up menu. Windows displays the Local Area Connection Properties dialog box.

3. Select the Internet Protocol (TCP/IP) component and click the Properties button. Windows displays the Internet Protocol (TCP/IP) Properties dialog box.

4. Click the Advanced button. Windows displays the Advanced TCP/IP Settings dialog box.

5. Click the WINS tab. You'll see a dialog box resembling Figure 9.5.

Figure 9.5 Windows 2000 uses DNS instead of NBNS by default, but allows you to add NBNS (WINS) servers to the mix.

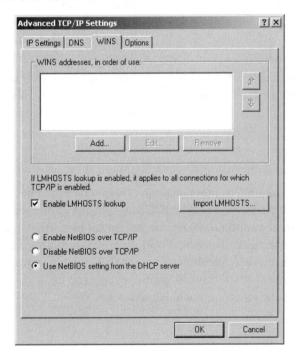

Like Windows 9*x* and Windows NT 4, Windows 2000 by default uses name-resolution options provided by DHCP, if the system is configured to use DHCP to obtain its IP address. You can adjust the NetBIOS name resolution through the options of this dialog box. Specifically:

NBNS Servers   You can manually add an NBNS server by clicking the Add button. You'll get a small dialog box in which you enter an IP address.

Enable LMHOSTS Lookup   Check the Enable LMHOSTS Lookup button (it's enabled by default).

NetBIOS Options   Windows 2000 gives you three options for the use of NetBIOS over TCP/IP, which is normally required for the use of Samba:

Enable NetBIOS over TCP/IP	Allows Windows to use NetBIOS over TCP/IP with manual configuration of name resolution.
Disable NetBIOS over TCP/IP	If you select this option, you won't be able to use Windows 2000 with Samba unless you patch your Samba and kernel with the NetBEUI support from Procom Technology (`http://www.procom.com`).
Use NetBIOS Setting from the DHCP Server	Enabled by default, this causes Windows 2000 to accept the NBNS server and node-type options from the DHCP server.

Summary

Samba can be configured to function as an NBNS server for a network of Windows computers. This configuration is the NetBIOS equivalent of a DNS server but is much simpler to set up because the configuration is largely driven by clients appearing on and disappearing from the network. You can also adjust how Samba approaches the network when it needs to locate another NetBIOS computer. The default approach uses each of four name-resolution methods in turn, so Samba is almost certain to find something, provided the named computer exists on the local network.

10

Configuring Domains

Netbios domains are confusing to many Windows networking newcomers. This is particularly true when comparing NetBIOS domains to workgroups. These two concepts are similar, and they're implemented in similar ways, but domains contain centralized administration features that are absent in workgroups. In some sense, NetBIOS domains are similar to Internet domains, but the similarity is largely superficial.

This chapter describes NetBIOS domains and explains how Samba works in a domain setting. Samba includes features that allow it to perform many of the tasks associated with domain control, so in many cases it's possible to replace a Windows NT or 2000 domain controller with a Linux computer. We'll begin with a theoretical overview of domains, describing what they are and comparing them to NetBIOS workgroups and to Internet domains. The remainder of the chapter discusses Samba domain configuration details, which are subtly different for Windows 9x and Windows NT or 2000 clients.

NOTE Some domain control features are absent in the 2.0.x Samba releases up to and including 2.0.7, but are present in the TNG (The Next Generation) release of Samba, which is experimental as of mid-2000. Sooner or later, however, these features will find their way into a mainstream Samba release. Whenever a TNG feature is described in this text, it's accompanied by a statement that the feature is experimental and presently available only in the TNG release of Samba. There are tentative plans to release a version of Samba numbered 2.2 later in 2000, and this version may include some of Samba TNG's domain controller enhancements.

Understanding Domains

If you're new to Windows networking, domains and workgroups may be alien to you, but they're relatively easy to understand. The first step in grasping these concepts is to ignore the fact that the word *domain* is also used in describing a group of Internet computers. A NetBIOS domain and an Internet domain are entirely different things, although both are means of collecting computers on a network. Before comparing NetBIOS and Internet domains, let's examine NetBIOS domains "from the ground up."

What Is a NetBIOS Domain?

A NetBIOS domain is a collection of computers that share a common domain name and one or more *domain controllers*—machines that allow users to log on to the network. Although domains are often restricted to a single network segment, this need not be the case. Similarly, two or more domains may coexist within a single network segment. Figure 10.1 illustrates a simple two-segment network that contains two domains, one of which spans both network segments. In this example, the TROUT domain is confined to the upper network segment, and the TMBG domain spans both network segments.

Figure 10.1   A domain can span two or more network segments, and a single network segment can contain two or more domains.

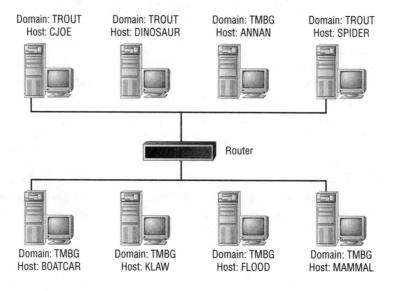

It's often convenient to create a one-to-one correspondence between domains and network segments, because this helps ensure that broadcasts for one domain reach all the relevant computers and don't interfere with the operations of another domain. You may also have security-related reasons for blocking interdomain access. For instance, if your domains correspond to functional units in your organization, it may be that members of one domain have no business using another domain's resources. Configuring a router to block all NetBIOS traffic between network segments can help reduce the chances of unauthorized use of network resources.

If your domains do span network segments, it's especially important that you configure your network appropriately. You can't, for example, rely on broadcast name resolution in a multisegment domain, and you'll need to take steps to ensure that browsing your domain proceeds smoothly. (Broadcast name resolution and domain browsing are discussed in Chapters 9 and 11, respectively.)

A key feature of a domain is the presence of one or more domain controllers. One of these, the *primary domain controller (PDC),* is officially in charge of key aspects of the domain—most importantly, password authentication. A domain may contain one or more *backup domain controllers (BDCs),* which can respond to authentication queries and perform other domain control tasks in the event of a failure of the PDC. Samba can fill many PDC functions but cannot yet serve as a BDC. Many of Samba's PDC features, particularly with respect to Windows NT domains (as opposed to Windows 9*x* domains), are experimental but improving rapidly under active development.

The phrase *logging on to a network* may seem a bit odd to those accustomed to Unix-style networking, in which one logs on to an individual computer. That computer may then provide network resources, but the basic logon is to a single machine on a network, not the network as a whole. One of the key features of NetBIOS domains is centralized authentication of users. It allows administration of users and groups on a NetBIOS network in much the same way as for an individual Unix or Linux computer—hence the phrase *log on to a network.* Any user approved by the domain controller attains at least minimal access to all the domain's servers.

In practice, Windows domain authentication works much like administering a Unix-style NIS or NIS+ authentication scheme. Of course, you can set assorted security features for individual servers on the network as you see fit, to strengthen security beyond what is provided by the domain controller. In the case of Samba, you can tell the system to use its own passwords (by setting `security = User` or `security = Share`), or to accept a domain controller's authorizations (by setting `security = Server` or `security =` `Domain`; see "Using Samba on a Domain" later in this chapter). You can also use Linux's

**Advanced
Configurations**

PART 3

file permissions and assorted security features for shares, such as `hosts allow` and `valid users`, as described in Chapters 5 and 14.

Using the Windows Network Neighborhood browser allows the easiest access to resources located on your computer's own domain (or workgroup, if the network isn't configured for domains). Accessing other domains' resources requires moving up the hierarchy, typically by double-clicking an icon labeled Entire Network. You can then see the other domains and workgroups available on the network.

Unlike the Internet's domain space, the NetBIOS naming scheme is *flat,* meaning that even the two-tiered hierarchy visible in Network Neighborhood is something of a sham. Each computer includes its domain's name as part of its own name, but the hostnames (such as `ANNAN` and `SPIDER` in Figure 10.1) can't be repeated on the same network, even on two hosts that belong to separate domains.

Domains and Workgroups

NetBIOS domains are closely related to NetBIOS workgroups. In fact, the two are essentially the same, except that domains support centralized services—most importantly, centralized logon authentication and home directories—not present on workgroups. In a workgroup, each server is responsible for deciding whether a specific client may access a given share. The client must therefore send a password (and often a username) to a server in order to gain access. This authentication process can actually consume several network transfers, particularly when encrypted passwords are used. In a domain, by contrast, the client logs on to a domain by registering with the domain controller. It returns an encrypted token with which the client can more simply gain access to servers. Figure 10.2 illustrates this difference.

Although the domain access in Figure 10.2 uses four transfers, versus two for the workgroup, domains can actually reduce network traffic. This apparent contradiction is explained by the fact that the authentication procedure actually involves multiple transfers, whereas sending a token with an initial server-access request involves fewer transfers. Therefore, the overhead of the initial domain logon is recovered by simplified individual server logons.

One key point to understand about domains and workgroups is that they are characteristics of networks as a whole, but they rely on the configuration of individual computers on the network. It's possible for a network to be configured with a PDC and other network trappings, but if half the clients are configured as for a workgroup, the network as a whole will be part workgroup and part domain.

Figure 10.2 In a workgroup (top), each server maintains its own authentication databases. These are centralized in the domain controller for a domain (bottom).

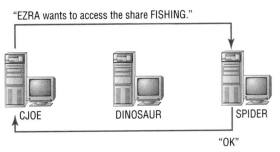

In addition to centralized logon facilities, domains offer some additional features, some of which have been described in previous chapters:

Network Logon Scripts A network logon script is a DOS/Windows batch file that a client runs whenever one of its users logs on to the network. You can use these scripts to execute a consistent set of commands on all clients automatically. Using Samba as a domain controller, you can also customize these scripts for specific clients, OSs, users, or groups. See the section "Client Network Scripts" in Chapter 8 for more on this topic.

Roaming Profiles You can set aside space on a server (which may or may not be the PDC) for storing Windows *profiles*—configuration files controlling the placement of icons on the desktop, background images, and so on. If you use roaming profiles (discussed in Chapter 9), users can obtain consistent desktops no matter what specific computers they use.

NOTE In Samba 2.0.6 and later, you also use the `logon home` parameter to set the location of roaming profiles. Windows clients discard the portion following the share's root when mounting the home directory, but they use the entire string when dealing with roaming profiles. Therefore, you can use a parameter such as `logon home = \\%L\%U\profile` to set both the /HOME directory and roaming profile storage area to reasonable values

Home Directories   Just as each user on a Linux computer has a home directory, each user on a Windows domain can have a network home directory, which is a share assigned to that user. You can set this feature using the global `logon home` parameter in Samba, as in `logon home = \\%L\%U`. You can then mount a user's home directory on a Windows client by using the command **NET USE** *X:* **/HOME**. This command maps the home directory (wherever it might be) to the *X:* drive on the client.

TIP   You can use Samba's `include` parameter in conjunction with variables (see Table 8.1 in Chapter 8) to set up users' home directories on different servers. Instead of a global `logon home` parameter, you'd use the parameter `include = smb.conf.logon.%g` to incorporate customized `logon home` parameters for each Linux group. Then you'd place unique `logon home` parameters in each `smb.conf.logon.`*groupname* file to put specific groups' home directories on specific servers. Consider the example of a school: `smb.conf.logon.faculty` might consist of `logon home = \\SPEEDY\%U\profile`, and `smb.conf.logon.students` might specify `logon home = \\SLUGGISH\%U\profile`. Members of the group `faculty` would then have home directories on the SPEEDY server, with the `students` group's home directories residing on the SLUGGISH server.

Why Use a Domain?

Windows networking is built around domains and workgroups; you *must* use one or the other, and in most respects configuring domains is identical to configuring workgroups. For instance, you set both the domain and workgroup names using the `workgroup` parameter in Samba's `smb.conf` file. The question of when to use a domain is therefore really one of when to use a domain versus a workgroup.

As with so many things in SMB/CIFS networking, it's often easier to set up a network using the simpler technology (workgroups) than the more complex one (domains).

Domains are easier to administer in the long run, however, and they offer very real advantages over workgroups, particularly in a large network. Specifically:

Centralized Password Maintenance   In a workgroup, each server must maintain its own set of SMB/CIFS passwords. When the workgroup includes many servers, this can become an administrative nightmare. Centralizing passwords on a single server saves a great deal of effort.

Elimination of Distributed Password Files   Windows 9*x* clients, especially, tend to store passwords locally in order to easily send those passwords to servers. This can present a security risk. Although switching from a workgroup to a domain network model doesn't eliminate Windows 9*x* password files, an extra configuration step *can* do so, thus improving your network's security. This extra measure is covered later in "Removing Windows .PWL Files."

Network Automation   Network logon scripts, roaming profiles, and network home directories work only in a domain configuration. If you want the benefits of these features, you must run a domain.

On the downside, domains take more administrative effort to set up initially, especially for a small network. In particular, you must configure one machine as a PDC, and in some cases you may want a BDC as well. To get the full benefit of domains, ensure that all your clients are configured for domains. If you have Windows NT or 2000 clients and Samba servers, you may need to update your version of Samba, possibly to the experimental Samba TNG. This will depend on the precise mix of domain features you require.

On the whole, workgroups are probably adequate for most small networks. For larger networks, however (say, those with more than a dozen computers or more than two or three servers), it's usually beneficial to configure a domain. The added initial effort in configuration will pay off in the long haul in terms of the centralized maintenance and improved automation features.

NetBIOS Domains and Internet Domains

I've said before that NetBIOS domains and Internet domains are largely unrelated concepts. Internet domain names are registered through authorized Internet registrars (see `http://www.internic.net/regist.html` for a listing of accredited registrars). Once you've registered a domain name, you're in charge of maintaining a DNS listing for your domain, so that other computers on the Internet may contact yours. You may also carve your domain into subdomains for easier administration. Many large organizations do just this; for example, universities often create subdomains for major academic departments, as in `physics.pangaea.edu`. The departments can then create individual computers, such as `bohr.physics.pangaea.edu` and `hawking.physics.pangaea.edu`.

Advanced Configurations

PART 3

NetBIOS domains, by contrast, are not registered with any central authority. This fact creates no chaos because NetBIOS domains are essentially local in nature; the NetBIOS domains at pangaea.edu aren't visible to an unrelated network such as that at threeroomco.com—at least, not without expending deliberate effort to bridge the gap. Therefore, both pangaea.edu and threeroomco.com can have NetBIOS domains called TROUT without creating problems.

To avoid confusion for your users, I recommend naming your NetBIOS domains (or workgroups) after your Internet domains or subdomains whenever possible. For administering the computers at pangaea.edu, you might name the NetBIOS domains PHYSICS, PSYCH, ENGLISH, and so on, after your Internet subdomain names. If pangaea.edu is particularly small, you might assign a single NetBIOS domain called PANGAEA. Using a totally unrelated name (such as TROUT) will not result in disaster, but there could be confusion, particularly if your NetBIOS domains cross your Internet domain or subdomain names. In this example, the NetBIOS domain TROUT could conceivably span both the physics.pangaea.edu and psych.pangaea.edu Internet domains, which might be perplexing to users.

Windows 9*x* and Domains

Samba's support for Windows 9*x* domains is quite good, so if your network consists mostly of Windows 9*x* clients, you should have little trouble configuring Samba to perform most domain controller tasks. Some of these tasks (namely, logon scripts and roaming profiles) are fully explained in Chapter 8. Following is a description of basic Samba domain configuration.

Configuring Samba as a Domain Controller

To configure Samba as a domain controller, set these global parameters in the smb.conf file:

security = User Setting user-level security on the Samba domain controller allows Samba to authenticate users against its own smbpasswd file.

encrypt passwords = Yes Windows domains work using encrypted passwords, so set this option to Yes.

domain logons = Yes This parameter controls whether Samba accepts domain logon requests. If you set it to No, Samba will not function as a domain controller.

The foregoing three parameters are required for a Windows 9*x* domain controller configuration. Once set, Samba is prepared to function as a domain controller for the domain specified with the workgroup parameter. (Recall that domains are essentially workgroups with a domain controller.) Of course, other parameters can influence the functioning of a domain. Some particularly important global parameters in this respect are the following:

domain master = Yes   This parameter is one of several that help Samba gain (or lose) status as the domain master browser, discussed in more detail in Chapter 11, "Local and Routed Browsing."

os level = 34   This is another parameter related to master browser status, which is determined in part by the OS used on each computer on the network. An OS level of 34 beats out most other OSs for master browser status.

wins support = Yes   Just as it's constructive to link domain controller and master browser status in a single server, it's also useful to include support for NetBIOS Name Service (NBNS; aka Windows Internet Name Service or WINS). Setting wins support = Yes tells Samba that it should function as an NBNS server. Chapter 9 covers this topic in greater detail.

WARNING   Windows NT systems often link together domain controller, master browser, and NBNS functions on a single server. Although breaking these functions up across multiple computers is technically possible, doing so often causes problems; a Windows server may try to grab one function and be unable to cope with not having the others as well. It's therefore generally a good idea to set aside one computer to serve all three functions. That computer can be a Windows NT or 2000 computer or a Linux system running Samba.

---

time server = Yes   This parameter tells Samba that it should respond to NetBIOS time server requests. You can include the command NET TIME \\SERVER /SET /YES in Windows computers' startup scripts to ensure that all the computers on a network are set to the same time. System clock settings can be important in some domain-related operations, such as roaming profiles. Clock settings also matter to some applications, as in software development make scripts.

TIP   An ideal location for the NET TIME command is in a network logon script, as described in Chapter 8. Networking isn't fully active when a Windows 9x computer's AUTOEXEC.BAT script executes, so that script isn't a good location for the NET TIME command.

Once you've set these options, restart your Samba server to put them into effect; then configure your client systems. I recommend starting with a single client—ideally an unimportant one—to test basic functionality. You can then proceed to configure or reconfigure the rest of your network to take advantage of the new domain controller.

Configuring Clients to Use the Domain

By default, Windows 9x computers don't attempt to use a domain but rather a workgroup. Even on a network that supports domain features, this behavior usually works, because a domain is essentially a workgroup with centralized password databases. When a workgroup-configured client tries to access a domain's servers, the servers authenticate the access by passing the request back to the domain controller. As a result, a client that's misconfigured to use a workgroup may not be obvious to inexperienced users.

One prime clue to this event comes soon after Windows starts up. When configured with SMB/CIFS networking features, Windows clients typically display a two-field Network Password dialog box (Figure 10.3). Users typically enter their usernames and passwords here, and Windows remembers those values when making access attempts to network resources.

Figure 10.3   When configured as part of a workgroup, Windows 9x displays this two-field logon dialog box.

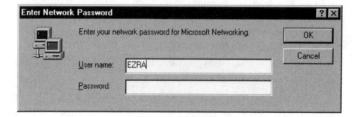

WARNING   The ordinary Windows 9x logon, unlike the ordinary Linux or Unix logon, offers *no* security! A user can click Cancel in the Enter Network Password dialog box and still gain complete access to the Windows computer. This dialog box exists primarily as a convenience, so that the computer can store users' profiles locally (if so configured) and remember passwords for access to other computers' resources.

To turn the computer into one that uses the domain's password authentication, follow these steps:

1. Open Control Panel.

2. Double-click the Network icon, bringing up the Network dialog box.

3. Select Client for Microsoft Networks and click the Properties button. Windows displays the Client for Microsoft Networks Properties dialog box (Figure 10.4).

Figure 10.4   Reconfigure Windows to use a domain logon, and specify the domain logon name.

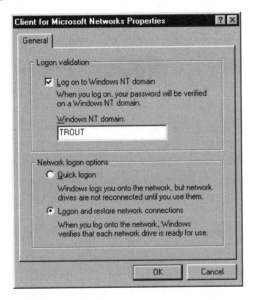

4. Check the Log On to Windows NT Domain option, and type in the domain name.

> **NOTE** Windows 9*x* and Windows NT machines can share the same domain controller and other domain resources. Windows 9*x* refers to domains as "Windows NT domains." Critical aspects of domain logon are different for Windows 9*x* and Windows NT clients, but Windows NT domain controllers can handle both types of domains, as can recent versions of Samba. (Versions of Samba prior to 2.0.5 accommodated Windows 9*x* domain logons only.)

5. Click OK in the Client for Microsoft Networks Properties dialog box, then in the Network dialog box. When prompted to reboot the computer, do so.

When the system starts up again, you'll see a new three-field logon dialog box (Figure 10.5). This dialog box looks just like the one in Figure 10.3 except that it includes a Domain field, which should be preconfigured with the default domain.

Figure 10.5 A Windows 9x computer that uses a domain has a three-field logon dialog box.

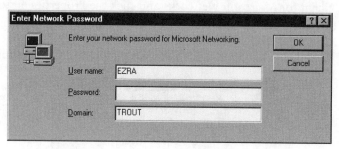

NOTE You need not tell Windows 9x the identity of the domain controller. Windows is designed to locate the domain controller automatically, although it sometimes fails to do so if the controller changes. For instance, if the PDC crashes, Windows may not update its domain controller information, and a logon can fail.

Removing Windows .*PWL* Files

If you try to log on to a Windows domain from Windows 9x but enter an incorrect username or password, Windows won't let you access the computer. This feature is valuable if you mistype a password, since the system won't try to access servers using the wrong password. It does not constitute a local security improvement over workgroup logons, however, because the Cancel button still gets you into the client. (Windows does deny your access to the domain's resources, though.)

In addition to allowing access without a password, Windows 9x stores logon passwords locally. These passwords appear in files with .PWL extensions in the C:\WINDOWS directory, even when you use a domain logon. So you may want to reconfigure your system to remove these local password files. Eliminating the local .PWL files has two principal benefits: It reduces risk of password theft and simplifies network password administration.

Although the contents of Windows .PWL files are encrypted, the encryption algorithm is exceedingly weak. If a malicious individual acquires the .PWL files from a system, all these passwords can be broken fairly easily. This can be a major problem for a network in which individuals use a wide variety of computers.

When you log on to a Windows 9x computer that's configured for domain access, the computer first verifies your password using the domain controller, and then verifies it against the locally stored password. Should you decide to change your password on either system, you have to change it on both or be presented with a second password prompt. This can be annoying, particularly if you routinely use several Windows 9x clients.

To remove the local .PWL files, follow these steps with the Windows Registry Editor:

1. Open a Windows command prompt window and type **REGEDIT** to start the Registry Editor. You'll see a window resembling the one shown in Figure 10.6, except that it won't yet show the entry you're about to edit (highlighted in the right pane in the figure).

Figure 10.6   The Registry Editor allows you to edit critical Windows configuration information.

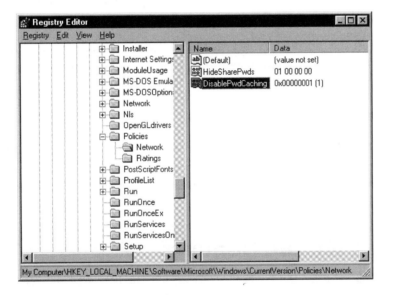

2. *Back up your registry file!* A mistake in any of the following steps can cause serious problems. Backing up the Registry allows you to recover from most of these mistakes. To back up, select Registry ➢ Export Registry File, and designate a filename under which to save the backup. If you find that networking doesn't work properly when you reboot, start REGEDIT and select Registry ➢ Import Registry File to recover.

3. Using the expandable options in the left pane of the Registry Editor, select HKEY_ LOCAL_MACHINE ➢ Software ➢ Microsoft ➢Windows ➢ CurrentVersion ➢ Policies ➢ Network.

4. In the main menu, select Edit ➢ New ➢ DWORD Value. The Registry Editor responds by creating a new item in the right pane.

5. While the new item is still selected and editable, type a new name for it: **DisablePwdCaching**. *Be sure to type this name correctly!* When you're sure, press Enter.

6. Double-click the new DisablePwdCaching item to open an editor on the item. Enter **1** in the Value data field and click OK. Your Registry Editor window should now resemble the one in Figure 10.6, including the DisablePwdCaching entry.

7. Exit from the Registry Editor by selecting Registry ➢ Exit. As it's now configured, your computer will not attempt to create or update .PWL files, but the system still contains any .PWL files that have already been created.

8. To delete the existing .PWL files, type **DEL C:\WINDOWS*.PWL** at a Windows command prompt. (If necessary, adjust the C:\WINDOWS portion of this command to suit your system.)

TIP   After you log off or restart the computer, at your next logon verify that Windows hasn't created any new .PWL files. If it has, you may have mistyped DisablePwdCaching, or placed it in the wrong location, or forgotten to change its value to 1.

Once you've performed these steps, Windows will not store .PWL files on the local hard disk or try to verify your logon against any existing .PWL files. This arrangement can enhance network security and reduce administrative headaches for the network as a whole.

Windows NT and Domains

Domain configuration for Windows NT resembles that for Windows 9*x* but isn't identical. Windows NT (and now Windows 2000) includes support for domain features that simply aren't present in Windows 9*x*. Many of these features are still being added to Samba in the 2.0.*x* series—in fact, up until version 2.0.5, Samba didn't support Windows NT systems as domain logon clients at all. As a result, if you need to use advanced domain features, you may have to use one of these solutions:

- Samba TNG: This experimental branch of Samba includes more advanced Windows NT domain support. It is, however, an *experimental* branch, so I don't recommend using it in any critical environment.

- A more recent Samba: It's possible that by the time you're reading this, more stable Samba NT domain support exists.

- A Windows NT domain controller: You can use a Windows NT computer as a domain controller, even if you want to use Samba as your main server. To see how to configure Samba to participate in a domain for which it is not the controller, refer to "Using Samba on a Domain" later in this chapter.

Windows 2000 is essentially an updated version of Windows NT and therefore uses the NT structure for domains, although 2000 introduces a few twists of its own. If you want to use Samba as a domain controller on a network with Windows 2000 clients, no version of Samba through 2.0.7 will work; you must use Samba TNG. It's possible that the anticipated 2.2 release will handle Windows 2000 domain logons.

Differences between Windows 9*x* and Windows NT Domains

Differences between Windows 9*x*'s and Windows NT's domain handling lie largely beneath the surface. To the user doing day-to-day tasks, the two OSs handle things quite similarly. Here are the differences:

Logon Authentication Methods   The two OSs use different logon authentication methods. This is why Samba versions prior to 2.0.5 didn't support Windows NT domain logons.

Trust Accounts   Windows NT domain handling includes the concept of *trust accounts*—special accounts used by computers rather than users. You must create trust accounts for individual computers on a Samba server that functions as a Windows NT domain controller.

Remote Administration   Windows NT systems can modify domain features such as network users, passwords, and allowable computers. Most of these features aren't supported by Samba 2.0.*x*, but some are supported in Samba TNG.

In addition to these client differences, there's an important server difference: Windows 9*x* computers cannot function as domain controllers, but Windows NT and 2000 computers can.

Features of Samba PDC Support

As a PDC, Samba supports basic domain logons for Windows 9*x*, Windows NT, and (with Samba TNG) Windows 2000 clients. When you use a Windows NT client, you must perform some additional configuration tasks, or you won't be able to use Samba in this role. These tasks are described in the upcoming section. Samba versions through 2.0.7 support only domain logons, however, not the more advanced Windows NT domain control features. Samba TNG adds support for some additional domain control features, including

- User Manager for Domains
- Server Manager for Domains

- Event Log
- Service Control Manager
- Registry Editor

Unfortunately, Samba TNG is presently alpha code, and may not work well with Windows *9x* clients; its utility is therefore limited. Sooner or later, however, some of these features will find their way into a mainstream Samba release—possibly in 2.2, which is rumored for a late-2000 appearance.

Configuring Samba as an NT PDC System

To configure Samba as a domain controller for Windows NT clients, follow these steps:

1. Configure Samba for Windows *9x*-style domain control by setting the smb.conf global parameters described earlier.

2. Create a trust group for your Samba trust accounts; **groupadd -r trust** will accomplish this goal. (This step isn't strictly necessary; you can use some existing group account if you like.)

3. Create a trust account for each Windows NT client on your network. This account should be named after the computer's NetBIOS name but with a dollar sign ($) appended to it, as in cjoe$ for the CJOE client. You can create this account by using a command such as

   ```
   # useradd -r -g trust -d /dev/null -s /dev/null cjoe$
   ```

   Alternatively, you can use other utilities or manual editing of system files to accomplish this task if you prefer. This account will *never* be used for logons, so it can be a system account (indicated by the -r parameter in the useradd command), although the system account configuration is not strictly required. In any event, there's no need for this account to have a Linux logon password associated with it, and in fact for security reasons it should not have a password.

4. Use smbpasswd to create a Samba encrypted password entry for each trust account. Use the -m parameter to smbpasswd to specify that this is a trust account. Then smbpasswd doesn't prompt for a password, but instead sets it to the name of the computer. You do not need to include the dollar sign as part of the name. For instance, **smbpasswd -a -m cjoe** will add an appropriate entry for the computer CJOE.

NOTE When you first configure the client to use the domain, the client changes the password automatically. Do not change the password manually.

5. Restart Samba. (This step isn't necessary if you restarted as part of step 1.) Samba is now configured for Windows NT domain logons.

When a Windows NT client joins the domain, it registers itself with the PDC using the trust account and its password. The PDC then trusts the client with authorization tokens as illustrated earlier in Figure 10.2. These tokens provide streamlined access to resources on other servers on the network.

Adding Client Computers

To configure a Windows NT client to use a domain controller, you'll perform steps analogous to those done in Windows 9x, but the details differ. Specifically:

1. Log on as the Administrator.

2. Open Control Panel and double-click the Network object. Windows displays the Network dialog box.

3. On the Identification tab, click the Change button. Windows responds by displaying the Identification Changes dialog box (Figure 10.7).

Figure 10.7   Configure Windows NT as part of a domain, using the Identification Changes dialog box.

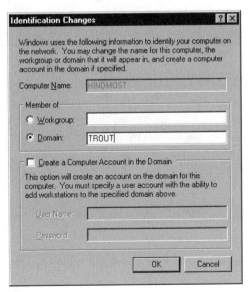

Advanced
Configurations

PART 3

4. Click the Domain item in the Member Of area, and type in the domain name.

5. Click OK. Windows attempts to communicate with the domain controller and authenticate itself. If all goes well, you'll see a message welcoming you to the domain.

6. Click the Close button in the Network dialog box. Windows informs you that you must restart the computer; do so.

When the computer starts up again, it should display a new three-field logon prompt, shown in Figure 10.8. When you log on to the domain, Windows should use your domain's passwords (maintained on the domain controller) rather than your local passwords. You can check this by changing the encrypted Samba password for a user account on that domain and attempting to log on to the Windows NT client using the old and the new password. Only the new password (changed on the Samba server) should work. Also, any network logon script you've configured will run.

Figure 10.8   The Windows NT Logon Information prompt includes a list of domains when the computer is configured for domain logons.

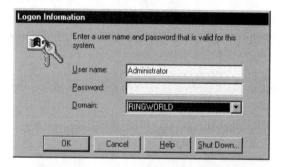

One advantage of Windows NT over Windows 9*x* is that the former provides real logon security. Although the Windows NT Logon Information prompt (Figure 10.8) includes a Cancel button, this button does *not* bypass the logon prompt, as does its counterpart in Windows 9*x*. Instead, clicking Cancel returns you to a prompt that instructs you to press Ctrl+Alt+Del to log on to the computer.

Switching between Domain and Workgroup Configurations

The Logon Information dialog box provides a drop-down list of domains. One of these isn't a domain at all; rather, it's the local machine. This feature lets you access the computer if your domain controllers fail. Unless you've created an Administrator account on your PDC, you may need to use the local machine "domain" to access the Administrator features of your Windows NT client. One further consequence of this is that if your PDC is configured to store roaming profiles, Windows NT stores profiles for domain logons on the PDC (or whatever computer the PDC specifies for such storage). Therefore, when you switch from a workgroup to a domain logon, you may find that your desktop configuration vanishes. Windows NT stores its profile information in different files than does Windows 98, so a user who switches between Windows 98 and Windows NT clients will have two roaming profiles, one for each OS.

Watch out, though: If you configure a Windows NT workstation to use a domain, then switch the workstation's configuration to a workgroup, and then switch back to a domain again, you may be unable to rejoin the domain. This happens because the Windows NT client changes the initial password set by smbpasswd for the trust account. When the client tries to rejoin the domain, it has forgotten the new password. The solution is to remove the line in the smbpasswd file for the client's trust account, and then add it again by typing **smbpasswd -a -m** *clientname* on the Samba server.

Windows 2000 Considerations

Windows 2000 is essentially the next version in the Windows NT line after Windows NT 4. It substantially alters the way it handles SMB/CIFS networking, however, and the differences are great enough in terms of domain interactions that Samba—at least as of version 2.0.7—can't cope very well with Windows 2000. If you have Windows 2000 clients, therefore, you must use the alpha-level Samba TNG or an as-yet-unreleased (as of mid-2000) production version of Samba. When you do this, Samba configuration issues are largely the same, except that the Samba TNG release has split much of its functionality off from the traditional smbd and nmbd daemons, as described in Chapter 2 under "Samba TNG."

> **TIP** If your existing network uses domains with a Samba domain controller, but you want to add a few Windows 2000 clients, you may not need to use Samba TNG. You can configure the Windows 2000 clients to treat the domain as a workgroup, and they should be able to access all the network resources. You'll give up the benefits of domains, however, including centralized administration, for the Windows 2000 systems. When Samba's Windows 2000 domain support has matured, you can upgrade Samba and convert the Windows 2000 systems to use domains. Or you can add a Windows NT or 2000 system as a domain controller, should the need arise.

If you do run Samba TNG or a newer release of Samba, you can configure Windows 2000 for use on a domain in much the way you configure a Windows NT 4 computer. There are two principal differences, however:

- Instead of using the Network dialog box (step 2 of "Adding Client Computers"), you open the System Properties dialog box by right-clicking the My Computer icon on your desktop and choosing Properties from the resulting pop-up menu. The Windows NT Identification tab is called Network Identification in Windows 2000, and you should click the Properties button to change the system's configuration.

- When you change to a domain configuration (step 5 of "Adding Client Computers"), Windows 2000 asks you for an administrative username and password. Enter an ordinary user's username and password. (Your prior Samba configuration took care of the steps for which this username and password are required.)

Subsequent logons use the domain controller for user authentication, provided you change the logon to a domain logon (from the default of a system logon). With Samba TNG, you can also view some Samba configuration settings from a Windows 2000 system. To do so, open the Control Panel and then the Administrative Tools folder, and launch the Computer Management tool. As of mid-2000, Samba TNG still supports only a few administrative actions from Windows 2000's Computer Management tool, but this situation will likely change in the future.

Using Samba on a Domain

In addition to using Samba to *control* a domain, you can configure a Samba server to be *part of* a domain. The server might be one of several Samba servers; in this situation, only one should be the domain controller. You might also want to configure a Windows NT 4 or 2000 system as the domain controller, but use Samba servers for file and print sharing.

Whatever the case, there are a few `smb.conf` parameters you need to set for such a configuration:

password server   Set this parameter to the IP address or DNS hostname of the domain controller. For example: `password server = 192.168.34.192`.

domain logons = No   This setting is the default, but it won't hurt to set it explicitly just to be sure there's no mix-up. When Samba functions as just another system on a domain, it should *not* accept domain logons.

security   You should set the `security` parameter to either `Server` or `Domain`. The former option passes every authentication request on to the system identified in the `password server` parameter. In this mode, Samba isn't truly a full part of the domain, although it does use the domain controller for authentication. When `security = Domain`, on the other hand, Samba acts like a full member of the domain; it accepts the tokens that the domain controller gives to clients for access, provided the appropriate user accounts exist on the Samba server.

For `security = Domain` to function properly, you must log the Samba server on to the domain in question, by using a command such as this:

```
# smbpasswd -j DOMAINNAME
```

In addition, it's necessary to specify the use of encrypted passwords (via the `encrypt passwords = Yes` parameter) when you use `security = Domain`. With either domain- or server-level security, if a logon attempt fails, Samba reverts to using its own logon facilities. If you've configured Samba to use encrypted passwords, this means you must have a valid `smbpasswd` file. In all cases, users must still have accounts on the Linux computer, either under the same username as on the domain or using appropriate Samba mapping options, as described in Chapter 15, "Managing Accounts."

Summary

Converting a Windows network from workgroups to domains provides several benefits in terms of administration, security, and flexibility. Domains allow you to keep a single centralized password database, eliminate the risk of Windows *9x* `.PWL` files, and use client-side automation features such as network logon scripts and roaming profiles. Configuring Samba as a primary domain controller for Windows *9x* systems is fairly simple, requiring only a few changes to `smb.conf`. Adding Windows NT support requires additional effort, and Samba as yet supports only minimal Windows NT domain features. Windows 2000 domains are not yet fully supported in stable versions of Samba, but this situation is likely to change by the end of 2000, or at latest in 2001. You can use a Samba server on a domain-based network, even when another computer functions as the domain controller.

11

Local and Routed Browsing

Most Windows users expect to locate network resources—particularly file shares—by *browsing* for them in a File Open dialog box or using windows opened from the Network Neighborhood (or, in Windows 2000, Computers Near Me) icon. Like many aspects of NetBIOS networking, browsing doesn't happen entirely automatically, although it appears automatic to the average end-user. Browsing relies on the proper functioning of one or more computers as *master browsers* for a workgroup.

When a Windows user opens the Network Neighborhood icon, the Windows computer consults the master browser to construct the display of computers in the network. If the master browser malfunctions, or if it contains incomplete or inaccurate information, the user may not be able to locate a network resource. It's therefore important that browsing functions properly on any Windows network.

> **NOTE** Browsing operates on workgroups and domains. For purposes of browsing, these two constructs are nearly identical. For brevity's sake, therefore, *workgroup* is used as shorthand for *workgroup or domain* throughout this chapter. When it's important, a workgroup is explicitly distinguished from a domain.

Samba includes the features necessary to let it function as a master browser. Samba master browser configuration can be confusing, and the results depend on the context—that is, two identically configured Samba servers may function differently in two different networks. This chapter describes the nature of NetBIOS browsing, Samba's browsing configuration options, and examples of Samba configurations that are suitable for a variety of common network configurations.

Understanding Browsing

Before you configure Samba to function as a master browser of any sort, it's useful to know something about browsing protocols.

DNS represents the closest analogy to browsing in normal TCP/IP networking. You can use a DNS utility such as nslookup to locate the names of all the computers in a specified Internet domain. There's usually little call to do this, however, so DNS is better known as a means of finding IP addresses given a hostname (or vice versa).

The equivalent role in SMB/CIFS networking is handled by the NetBIOS Name Service (NBNS, described in Chapter 9), which is actually an optional service on many networks. Most NetBIOS networks, by contrast, require a master browser. (One exception is networks of OS/2 systems, which use LAN Manager announce messages instead, as mentioned later in this chapter and in Appendix B.)

What Is Browsing?

Browsing is probably best understood visually. Figure 11.1 shows a hierarchy of NetBIOS networks and systems as displayed in Windows. (You can obtain a similar display for your network by right-clicking the Network Neighborhood icon and choosing Explore from the resulting pop-up menu.) The left pane of Figure 11.1 shows the resources, particularly network resources, available from the computer's desktop.

> **NOTE** Another way to browse the network is to double-click the Network Neighborhood icon on the desktop. This produces a window with just a single view of the network, much like the right-hand pane in the Exploring window in Figure 11.1. The Exploring window has the advantage of displaying a connection "tree" in the left pane, which reveals the organization of elements as accessed from Windows.

Figure 11.1   You can explore your computer's surroundings using the Network Neighborhood desktop icon.

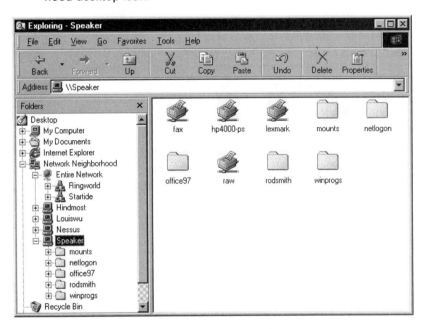

In Windows 9*x* and NT 4, the Network Neighborhood consists of two classes of objects:

Workgroup or Domain Contents   The servers on the computer's home workgroup
all appear immediately under Network Neighborhood. In Figure 11.1, these computers are HINDMOST, LOUISWU, NESSUS, and SPEAKER. You get quick and easy access
to these computers' resources.

Entire Network   The Entire Network icon provides access to all the workgroups to
which the computer has immediate access (RINGWORLD and STARTIDE in Figure 11.1).
This list includes the computer's current workgroup, so you can access the same
computers as items under both Network Neighborhood and one of the workgroups
in Entire Network.

This organization is actually somewhat deceptive. The placement of the computers in the
client's workgroup at the top of the Network Neighborhood hierarchy might lead one to
believe that these computers hold some privileged place in the network's structure, much
as medieval Europeans believed Earth was the center of the universe. This is not so; the
computers that appear immediately under Network Neighborhood are simply "close" to
the client, in the sense that they're in the same workgroup as the client.

Advanced
Configurations

PART 3

The layout of workgroups and computers in Windows 2000 is somewhat different. Instead of Network Neighborhood, Windows 2000 sports a desktop icon called My Network Places. This icon opens a window similar to the Network Neighborhood window, except that computers in the client's workgroup appear in a subgroup called Computers Near Me. The My Network Places window also hosts an Entire Network window, from which you can access other workgroups.

It's important to understand that the information shown in the Exploring - Speaker window of Figure 11.1 is maintained on a variety of computers. Specifically:

- Non-network icons in the left pane of the Exploring window, such as My Computer and Recycle Bin, refer to the local computer. These items are maintained by the local computer, but if you configure a NetBIOS domain to support roaming profiles, the local computer may store these items on another computer as well as locally. (Consult "Setting Up Roaming Profiles" in Chapter 8 for more information on this topic.)

- Workgroup and computer names shown in the left pane, such as RINGWORLD and NESSUS, are maintained by the workgroup's master browser. When you use Network Neighborhood, or a file access dialog box, or some other means to view the local network, you're really consulting the workgroup's master browser.

- Information on the shares and files available on a specific server, such as the expansion of Speaker and the contents of the right pane in Figure 11.1, are maintained on the server in question. When you browse to a specific server, therefore, you consult that computer to learn what shares it makes available and to access those shares.

Browsing is a networking activity undertaken by humans. A person who browses a network uses the Network Neighborhood and its subsidiary icons, a File Open dialog box, or similar tools to view what network resources are available, and ultimately to use one of them—say, to edit a file that resides on a server. When you browse a network, you access data maintained by several computers—the local computer, the workgroup's master browser, and ultimately a server. In some cases, two or even three of these computers may be the same; for instance, the server you access may function as the master browser. In other cases, you may access more than three computers, as when you copy a file from one computer to another, which may involve two separate servers.

Browsing is essentially a convenience. It's not strictly necessary for NetBIOS networking to operate. Indeed, if you use Linux SMB/CIFS clients such as smbclient and smbmount (described in Chapter 7), chances are you won't use the master browser. Instead, you'll type the client's name directly and from memory, as in **smbclient //speaker/winprogs**. GUI front-ends for Linux (LinNeighborhood, for example, discussed in Chapter 7) use the master browser much as Windows does.

SMB/CIFS Browsing Characteristics

Because Windows clients rely on a master browser to implement features that Windows users expect, it's useful for Samba to support master browser functionality. As described throughout the rest of this chapter, however, this functionality usually isn't vital, because even a lowly Windows 95 computer can function as a master browser. Windows networks periodically hold *elections* (described later in "Electing a Master Browser") to determine which computer functions as the master browser. As a general rule, browsing works most reliably when a reliable computer serves as the master browser. The election rules therefore favor Windows NT computers as master browsers, because these computers are usually up for longer periods than are Windows 9x computers. You can rig a browser election so that your Samba server always wins or loses the election.

NetBIOS's naming scheme is limited to two levels: computer names and workgroup names. Each computer belongs to precisely one workgroup, and there are no network structures higher than the workgroup (although Windows displays its desktop as if it were at a higher level than workgroups). This structure means that you cannot create or browse groups of workgroups, aside from the deviations from the network's true structure imposed by Network Neighborhood.

One of the problems with browsing is that Network Neighborhood's display of available computers isn't always accurate. Inaccuracies creep into the display for a number of reasons, including computers that crash (leaving invalid entries behind), delays in propagating changes to master browsers, incorrect browsing configurations relating to routers, and problems associated with a change in the master browser. On a large network, it can be difficult to predict what computers will become master browsers and to coordinate those computers. If you elect to use a Samba server as your master browser, you can explicitly specify certain configuration details to help make your network function smoothly. We'll examine these options throughout the rest of this chapter.

Windows NT and 2000 computers frequently expect to function as either a combination of the master browser, primary domain controller (PDC), the NBNS (aka WINS) server, or none of these. Attempting to wrest just one of these functions from a Windows NT or 2000 computer can cause bizarre problems. Therefore, if you need to use advanced PDC features that aren't yet implemented by Samba, you may want to configure Samba to *not* win browser elections. The linkage is particularly strong between PDC and the domain master browser (described in the following section), so you should ensure that one computer functions as *both* PDC and domain master browser whenever possible. Samba can still function as a *local* master browser on a subnet that doesn't contain the PDC.

Local versus Routed Browsing

Up to now, we've discussed *the* master browser, as if there were only one on a network. This may be true of small networks that consist of just one network segment, but when a network includes multiple segments, the situation becomes more complex.

Networks can be segmented either *physically* (by the presence of routers, bridges, and so on) or *logically* (by including machines with IP addresses from different ranges). A logical network address space is specified by the use of a network mask or *netmask*. The netmask can take one of two forms:

- A series of four 8-bit bytes, generally expressed in decimal notation, in which each bit indicates whether the corresponding bit in an IP address is on the same local network as the client or target IP address. For example, 255.255.255.0 works out to all binary 1s in the first three bytes, and all binary 0s in the final byte. This indicates that the first three bytes constitute the network segment of the address, and the final byte is an individual machine's address.

- A single decimal number, generally following a network address and separated from that address by a slash (/). This number indicates the number of bits in the address that form the network address. The address 192.168.23.0/24 indicates a 24-bit netmask—this is the same as specifying 192.168.23.0 with a 255.255.255.0 netmask.

When two IP addresses are identical in all the network bits of the address, those IP addresses reside on the same *subnet* or *network segment*. If two IP addresses differ on any of the bits that make up the network portion of the address, then those IP addresses belong to different subnets. Both these terms (*subnet* and *network segment*) are sometimes also applied to physical network divisions, such as subnets joined by a router.

TIP   When possible, configure your network so that logical and physical network segments coincide precisely. This arrangement can reduce problems with browsing and name resolution in Samba and is generally less confusing than trying to configure routers to route along lines that aren't cleanly defined in terms of netmasks.

The local network definition is extremely important to browsing, because the local master browser normally collects information only on the local network segment. This network segment is defined principally in terms of the logical (IP address–based) network segment. If routers or other network hardware break up a logical network segment into two or more physical segments, however, a local master browser may be useful only to computers on its own physically isolated network segment.

It's not always possible to configure a Windows network in such a way that it's confined to a single subnet. In such a situation, a Windows network uses two different types of master browser:

Local Master Browser   The local master browser functions as the master browser for the network segment on which it resides. Computers on a given subnet periodically hold an election to determine which computer functions as the local master browser. Therefore, the local master browser can change from moment to moment. Such changes can be disruptive, so it's to your advantage to configure your computers so that only one reliable machine is likely to win the local master browser election. A large network can have many local master browsers, each in its own network segment.

Domain Master Browser   The domain master browser is a step up from the local master browser. The domain master browser coordinates browse lists from all the local master browsers in a workgroup, no matter what their network segments. Normally you must manually configure a computer to function as a domain master browser.

NOTE   Domain master browsers are often associated with domains, and in fact a multisegment network consisting entirely of Windows computers can function as a unit only by being configured as a domain. You can configure a Samba computer as a domain master browser even when you use a workgroup network configuration, but then the domain master browser effectively doesn't function as anything more than a local master browser. A domain master browser on a single-subnet domain also doesn't coordinate browse lists, and so functions only as a local master browser.

If a workgroup spans only a single subnet, it may contain only a local master browser. You can use some of Samba's features to spread a workgroup (as distinct from a domain) across multiple subnets, as described in "Communicating with Other Master Browsers" later in this chapter. This configuration uses multiple local master browsers but no domain master browser. It is also a configuration that cannot be achieved with Windows master browsers; it relies on special features of Samba. Such a domain can contain Windows clients, however.

If a domain covers more than one subnet, then all but one will contain a local master browser. The remaining subnet will have a domain master browser, which simultaneously functions as a local master browser for its subnet. This situation is illustrated in Figure 11.2, where three subnets exist (192.168.1.0/24, 192.168.5.0/24, and 192.168.10.0/24). The first two subnets each have local master browsers, and the third hosts the domain master browser. ARTEMIS (the domain master browser) must periodically exchange browse lists with ZEUS and HADES (the local master browsers). If ZEUS and HADES both run Samba, you can configure them to communicate with each other directly, as well. When a computer wants to locate the names of resources on the network, it contacts whatever master browser is local to it—so ATHENA contacts ZEUS, and APOLLO contacts ARTEMIS. If everything is working properly, if all the computers have shared resources available, and if all the computers have been running for enough time, the result should be a browse list containing all six computers on the network.

Figure 11.2   When a domain spans multiple subnets, a domain master browser coordinates the browse lists of the local master browsers.

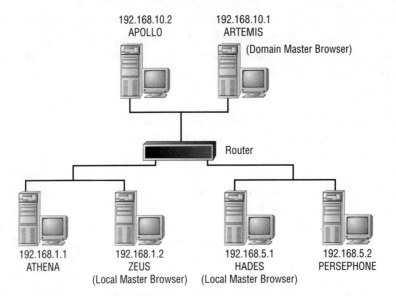

Electing a Local Master Browser

Local master browser elections are quite important. For this reason, Samba gives you control over how it presents itself to the network during browser elections. You can therefore control whether Samba is elected as a local master browser or not—provided another Samba computer isn't configured to take higher honors than your specified champion! Before you can configure Samba to win or lose a browser election, however, you must understand the election process.

In principle, any computer can call a local master browser election at any time. In practice, however, these elections aren't called very frequently. Typical circumstances in which a computer calls an election include the startup of a computer (or of Samba's nmbd daemon) when that system is configured to prefer being the master browser, and when a computer discovers that no local master browser can be found on the network. Browsing doesn't work during the election process (typically about 30 seconds), so you should try to minimize the number of elections held on your network.

When a computer calls for a local master browser election, it broadcasts a message calling for the election and putting forth its own set of *election criteria,* used to determine which machine wins the election. When a computer receives a call for an election, it compares the election criteria and, if it can meet or exceed the criteria of the original broadcast, replies with a broadcast of its own criteria. Each involved computer then listens for additional election packets and rebroadcasts its own election criteria every 200–800 milliseconds if those criteria have not been exceeded. As computers with higher election criteria broadcast their election packets, those with lower criteria cease broadcasting their credentials. Computers with losing criteria therefore typically only broadcast those criteria once or twice, if at all. After a computer broadcasts its criteria four times, it claims victory (although it may need to engage in a tie-breaking procedure, described shortly).

The criteria used in a browser election are as follows, ranked by order of importance:

1. **Election protocol version.** The computer with the highest version wins. As of mid-2000, all SMB/CIFS implementations use version 1 of the election protocol, so this criterion invariably results in a tie.

2. **OS levels.** The OS level is a one-byte code. Table 11.1 summarizes common values of the OS level code. A higher level wins the election. You can use the `os level` parameter in `smb.conf` to adjust Samba's OS level.

3. **PDC status.** The computer operating as PDC wins out over other computers having the same OS level and election protocol version.

4. **NBNS status.** If a computer is configured as an NBNS server, it wins, assuming a clear winner hasn't already emerged.

5. **Preferred master browser.** This feature is unique to elections; it has no other meaning in SMB/CIFS networking. A computer designated as the preferred master browser has an edge over other computers, but as you can tell by the position of this criterion in the election hierarchy, preferred master browsers can easily lose based on other criteria. You set this option through the `preferred master` parameter in `smb.conf`, as in `preferred master = Yes`.

6. **Running master browser.** When a computer is already running as a master browser, it wins the election if earlier criteria result in a tie.

7. **Browse list maintenance.** A computer configured to maintain a browse list wins the election if preceding factors produce a tie. This option is affirmative by default, but you can change it by editing a Windows Registry entry or by setting `browse list = No` in Samba.

8. **Running backup browser.** A computer that's currently running as a backup browser wins out over others if every other criterion results in a tie.

Table 11.1   OS Levels of Common Microsoft OSs and Samba

Operating System	OS Level
Samba 2.0.5a and earlier	0
Windows for Workgroups 3.1	1
Windows 9x	1
Windows NT Workstation 3.51 and 4.0	16
Windows 2000 Professional	16
Samba 2.0.6–2.0.7	20
Samba TNG	32
Windows NT Server 3.51 and 4.0	32
Windows 2000 Server	32

Each election criterion is sufficient to overcome all subsequent criteria. That is, if a computer is configured as the preferred master browser, no combination of subsequent criteria (running master browser, browse list maintenance, and running backup browser) can win over the preferred master browser.

These criteria are normally enough to decide the master browser election, particularly if you "stack the deck" on a Samba server by setting a very high OS level. On rare occasion, however, the browser election process may produce a tie. If that's the case, the election moves into a second tie-breaking phase, in which two additional criteria are used to decide the winner.

1. **Up time.** The computer that's been online longest wins the election. You can't adjust Samba's response to this setting, except by leaving your Samba server (and Samba daemons) running for a long time.

2. **NetBIOS name.** The name that comes first alphabetically wins; HADES wins out over PERSEPHONE.

The computer that's first runner-up in the election process may take on the role of a backup master browser. This backup maintains browse lists and will take over the role as local master browser should that machine go down. Samba doesn't support this function, however, so a Samba server will never take on the backup master browser role. For this reason, if you want a Windows computer to win the local master browser election, you may want to configure your Samba servers to ensure that they don't come in as #2. Let another computer (even a lowly Windows for Workgroups machine) take the #2 position to marginally increase the reliability of browsing on your network.

NOTE   For specific practical advice on configuring Samba to win or lose an election, see "Winning or Losing an Election" later in this chapter.

You can determine whether a specific computer is a master browser by examining the output of the Linux nmblookup -SR *name* or Windows NBTSTAT -a *NAME* commands. For example:

```
$ nmblookup -SR speaker
querying speaker on 192.168.1.255
192.168.1.1 speaker<00>
Looking up status of 192.168.1.1
received 9 names
        SPEAKER           <00> -           M <ACTIVE>
        SPEAKER           <03> -           M <ACTIVE>
        SPEAKER           <20> -           M <ACTIVE>
        .._MSBROWSE__. <01> - <GROUP> M <ACTIVE>
        RINGWORLD         <00> - <GROUP> M <ACTIVE>
        RINGWORLD         <1b> -           M <ACTIVE>
        RINGWORLD         <1c> - <GROUP> M <ACTIVE>
        RINGWORLD         <1d> -           M <ACTIVE>
        RINGWORLD         <1e> - <GROUP> M <ACTIVE>
num_good_sends=0 num_good_receives=0
```

Advanced Configurations

PART 3

There are two key lines here:

- The line that lists `.._MSBROWSE__.` indicates that `SPEAKER` is the local master browser for its network segment.
- The `RINGWORLD` line with a code type of `1b` indicates that the computer named `SPEAKER` is a domain master browser for the `RINGWORLD` domain.

This command comes in handy when you adjust your Samba configuration to acquire or lose master browser status. You can make your changes, restart Samba, and issue `nmblookup` or `NBTSTAT` commands on the Samba server and on any other computers you expect to be affected by the changes. Because a browser election can take several seconds to complete, you may need to wait half a minute or more before the command returns valid results.

The Role of NBNS in Browsing

For browsing to function properly, your network must have reliable name resolution. On a simple, single-segment domain with no routers, this isn't likely to be a problem. It could be, however, on a more complex network. For this reason, it's a *very* good idea to configure NBNS on complex networks. Without NBNS, it's possible that browsing will fail for at least some computers. Typically, such a failure manifests itself as a machine's appearing in the browse list but being inaccessible. Such problems are most likely to occur on a network composed of two or more subnets. (To learn more about NBNS, consult Chapter 9.)

Browsing reveals the computer's NetBIOS name—the name that's registered with an NBNS server if the network is configured with an NBNS server. To avoid confusion caused by one machine's using multiple names, I recommend using the same DNS and NetBIOS names for all computers whenever that's possible. Some Samba options (described shortly, in "NetBIOS Name Options") let you assign different NetBIOS and DNS names to a computer. You can do this if necessary, but I don't recommend it. It's best to avoid these options, or to use only `netbios name` to reaffirm the DNS name as the NetBIOS name.

Configuring Samba for Browsing

As described earlier in this chapter, the full browsing experience involves both the master browser and the server computer that a client wants to access. Should the user of `ATHENA` in Figure 11.2 begin browsing, the main browse list comes from `ZEUS`. If the user opens the icon for `APOLLO`, though, `ATHENA` connects directly with `APOLLO`. There are therefore two aspects to configuring Samba for browsing: configuring it to allow clients to browse its shares, and configuring it as a network master browser (either domain or local).

Allowing Clients to Browse Shares

Providing clients with access to a list of local resources is basic to Samba configuration. In fact, these options have made appearances elsewhere in this book—primarily in Chapter 5. Because of their importance to browsing, they're briefly described again here.

NetBIOS Name Options

By default, Samba uses the computer's DNS hostname (without the domain name) as the NetBIOS name. As described in Chapter 9, an individual client either uses broadcasts to announce itself and stake a claim to its name, or registers the name with an NBNS server. You can change the name of the Samba server by using either or both of two global smb.conf parameters:

netbios name   Use this parameter if you want the computer to appear in browse lists under a different name than its DNS name. If you want weakling.legend.org to appear as HERCULES in Network Neighborhood, you would use netbios name = HERCULES.

netbios aliases   Use this parameter to make the computer appear under more than one name in Network Neighborhood. For example, if the computer's main name (set either by default via its DNS name or via the netbios name parameter) is ZEUS, you could use netbios aliases = JUPITER IUPITER to list the computer under these two additional names. Do *not* list the main system name (such as ZEUS) as an alias.

TIP   You can use the %L variable in conjunction with an include parameter to create server and share customizations on a per-alias basis. For instance, include = smb.conf.%L with configuration files named smb.conf.zeus, smb.conf.jupiter, and smb.conf.iupiter together allow you to create custom settings and shares for each alias. You can use this feature to consolidate several old servers into one newer and faster server without disrupting network operations.

Samba also supports a few options that influence how it identifies itself to other computers. These options are unlikely to have a serious impact on how Samba operates in your network, but you can adjust them if you have good cause to do so.

announce as   This global parameter controls the OS type that Samba claims to be. Valid options are NT, NT Server (a synonym for NT), NT Workstation, Win95, and WfW (Windows for Workgroups). The default value is NT. Because Samba tries to emulate Windows NT as much as possible, this is the best setting in the vast majority of cases.

announce version   This global parameter sets the OS version number that Samba provides in conjunction with the announce as OS type code. The default value is 4.2, which works well on most networks.

WARNING   Don't use announce version = 5.0, even if you're using Windows 2000 (aka Windows NT 5.0) clients on your network. Samba emulates Windows NT 4.0 in most of its features, and setting announce version = 5.0 has the potential to cause problems.

NOTE   The announce version parameter is unrelated to the OS level set by Samba's os level parameter. The OS version set by announce version influences some details concerning the communication of one computer to another but doesn't influence browser elections. This parameter is also unrelated to the remote announce parameter, which makes Samba add itself to browse lists on remote subnets, as described in "Communicating with Other Master Browsers" later in the chapter.

Making Servers and Shares Visible

The NetBIOS name options can be useful for fine-tuning the names used in your network, particularly if you're forced to make a quick change or substitution without disrupting work flow. Those options cannot, however, make a server or share disappear; no matter what the name, the computer appears in Network Neighborhood. There are smb.conf parameters that can make shares disappear from browse lists, and others that can cause certain systems to not see the server. Using these parameters does *not* make the resources inaccessible, however. If a user knows that a share exists, he or she can type its name directly into the Address field of a Windows file browser, or use smbclient or smbmount to access the share from Linux.

The following parameters affect *only* the appearance of the server or share in Network Neighborhood or similar network browsers.

server string   This global parameter sets a string that can be associated with a server when Windows is set to Details view. You can use this string to describe a share more completely than is possible via the computer's name alone.

lm announce   Some computers (particularly OS/2 systems) require that servers announce their presence periodically, or those systems won't be visible in OS/2's network browser. The global Samba `lm announce` parameter controls whether Samba makes these periodic announcements (`Yes` causes Samba to make the announcements, and `No` causes Samba to not make them). This parameter also accepts a value of `Auto`, which causes Samba to make announcements only if it first detects such announcements from another computer. `Auto` is the default value and usually produces optimum performance.

`lm interval`   This global parameter controls the time, in seconds, between the announcements set by the `lm announce` parameter. The default is 60. Setting `lm interval` = 0 disables announcements, even if `lm announce` = `Yes`. Chances are you won't need to adjust this value, but if browsing seems unreliable from OS/2 clients, you can try altering this parameter.

`auto services`   This global parameter sets a list of services that will be visible in browse lists even if they would ordinarily not be visible. Suppose you want all users to have easy access to the user `homer`'s home directory. You could specify `auto services` = `homer` to accomplish this task. (Ordinarily, each user sees his or her own home share in browse lists, but not those belonging to other users.) A synonym for this parameter is `preload`.

`load printers`   This global boolean parameter tells Samba to load the names of all the printers in your `/etc/printcap` file for display in the browse list. The default is `Yes`. The setting only works, however, if you have a `[printers]` section in `smb.conf`, as described in Chapter 6.

`comment`   This share-level parameter is the share equivalent of the global `server string` parameter; it sets a short (one-line) comment that's visible when a user views a server's shares in Details view.

`browseable`   This boolean share-level parameter determines whether or not the share appears in browse lists. The default value is `Yes`. Setting this parameter to `No` does not make the share inaccessible; it's simply not visible in browse lists. A synonym for this parameter is `browsable`.

`default service`   You can specify a share that Samba will open if a user tries to access a nonexistent share. As an example, you could create a `[help]` share and then set `default service` = `help`. Some help files could then be stored in the `[help]` share. Then, if a user tries to access a share that doesn't exist on the server, Samba instead displays the `[help]` share. This option isn't strictly one that makes shares visible in a browser or not, but it can be useful if your users frequently don't use a browser to access shares. A synonym for `default service` is `default`.

You can use any of these options to influence the way your server and its shares appear on the network, whether or not the server is configured as a master browser.

Advanced Configurations

PART 3

Samba as a Local or Domain Master Browser

Samba provides you with fine control over options that influence whether it will become a master browser, as well as how it communicates with any other master browsers on the network. Because the local master browser is elected, you must change the Samba server's election credentials in order to win or lose an election, and hope that no other computer has outdone your own "candidate" in this respect. Domain master browser status is not handled through an election, but through explicit configuration. It is, however, possible to misconfigure a network with more than one domain master browser, which can lead to incomplete browse lists and other browsing problems.

NOTE   If you control all the Samba servers on your network, avoiding election troubles is largely a matter of planning a consistent set of election criteria for all Samba servers, working around the criteria (particularly the OS levels; see Table 11.1) of Windows systems. If one or more Samba servers on your network isn't under your direct control, you may need to coordinate your plans with the administrators of those Samba servers. An inexperienced Samba administrator is likely to leave election parameters at their defaults, which you can easily work around. Another administrator with a little knowledge might just decide that being a master browser is a good idea, and could damage your network's browsing capabilities.

Winning or Losing an Election

As described earlier, the most important election criterion is the version of the election protocol. This version is the same for all current SMB/CIFS clients, however, so there's no way to adjust this criterion in Samba. Of the remaining criteria, the most important is the OS level. You can therefore usually "fix" an election by specifying the desired OS level on your Samba server. Samba provides some additional election options, however, so you can allow Samba to compete against other servers in the way Microsoft intended. Following are the relevant `smb.conf` parameters:

browse list   This global parameter tells Samba to compile and maintain a browse list and make it available to other computers. The default is Yes, but if the computer does not become a master browser, the parameter's setting is meaningless. On the other hand, if set to No when the computer *is* a master browser, the workgroup will appear to be empty to anybody who browses it.

local master   This global parameter determines whether or not Samba attempts to become the local master browser. The default value (Yes) causes Samba to participate in elections but does *not* guarantee victory. This parameter doesn't even provide an edge in the elections; it just guarantees that Samba participates. If you want to ensure that a Samba server does *not* become a master browser, set `local master` = No. Samba will then lose all browser elections, no matter what values you specify for other parameters.

os level This global parameter represents the OS level of the Samba server. You set it to an integral base-10 value between 0 and 255. The default depends on the version of Samba you're running, as shown in Table 11.1. If you want Samba to win against any Windows server, set `os level` = 33 or higher—many sources recommend `os level` = 65 or higher in case a future version of Windows uses an OS level of 64. A value of 255 will win against anything except another Samba server configured in the same way. You can use Table 11.1 to select an appropriate `os level` value if you want to win against some types of Windows computers but not others. Set the `os level` value high or low enough, and no other parameter can affect Samba's winning or losing the election, because other parameters come into play only if there's a tie at the OS level portion of the election.

WARNING If you administer a Samba server but not all the computers on the network, either consult with the network's primary administrator or set `os level` = 0 to avoid conflicts with a planned master browser configuration.

preferred master This global parameter has two effects. First, it causes Samba to call an election when it starts up. If `preferred master` = No (the default), Samba will call no election when it starts. The current local master browser therefore retains that status for a time, even if Samba is configured to win elections. Second, you can set `preferred master` = Yes to set the preferred master bit in browser elections. This action gives Samba an edge in winning a master browser election, but does not guarantee a win. A synonym for this option is `prefered master`.

WARNING Ensure that each network segment contains only one preferred master browser. If you set `preferred master` = Yes (or if you set similar options in Windows) on more than one computer, the spurned computers will call frequent elections, which can cause frequent temporary failures in browsing the network. If you're in charge of just one Samba server on a network, you should set `preferred master` = No for this reason, because another system on the network is probably configured as the preferred master browser.

Advanced Configurations

PART 3

These final three parameters control how aggressively Samba will pursue the local master browser role. So if you want Samba to assume this role, you should set these options as follows:

```
local master = Yes
preferred master = Yes
os level = 65
```

On most networks, an os level of 33 will be more than sufficient. Indeed, if you only have Windows 9x clients, an os level of 1 will do the job. If you want to be as positive as you can be that Samba will win the election, set os level = 255.

WARNING   If a network segment includes a Windows NT PDC, you should let it function as the local and domain master browsers. You should therefore set local master = No on all Samba servers on such a subnet.

To confirm that your changes have had the desired effects, issue the Linux nmblookup -SR *name* or Windows NBTSTAT -a *NAME* command on the old and new master browsers, after altering your Samba configuration and restarting Samba. You should find that the new master browser's output includes a line with an entry for ..__MSBROWSE__.., whereas the old local master browser (which should have lost the election) does not. If this hasn't happened, then your changes haven't had the desired effect of shifting master browser status to the target computer. Because browser elections can take about 30 seconds to complete, you may have to wait that long before the new master browser system's status becomes apparent.

Becoming the Domain Master

The domain master browser functions much like a local master browser, except that the domain master browser coordinates the transfer of browse lists between local master browsers. Here are the smb.conf parameters relevant to the domain master browser:

Local Master Browser Options   The first step to configuring a machine as the domain master browser is to configure it to win the local master browser election for its subnet. Although not strictly necessary, such a setup simplifies your network configuration.

PDC Configuration   Windows NT systems that are domain master browsers are almost invariably also PDCs for their domains. In order to avoid problems with browsing and domain control, it's simplest to configure Samba in the same way. (Read Chapter 10 for more information on this topic.) If you already have a Windows NT PDC and don't want to shift to a Samba PDC, you should allow Windows NT to assume the domain master browser role.

NOTE You might wonder about the possibility of configuring a domain master browser when you use a workgroup rather than a domain. Such a configuration isn't normally possible with Windows networking, because the PDC and domain master browser functionality are so tightly tied together. You can configure Samba in this way, but using the cross-subnet communication parameters described in the next section, "Communicating with Other Master Browsers," is a simpler way to split a workgroup across subnets.

---

domain master The domain master = Yes parameter instructs Samba to assume the role of the domain master browser.

Communications Options On a normal Windows network, the local master browsers locate and exchange data with the PDC, which also functions as the domain master browser. You therefore don't need to specify the machines or subnets with which the domain master browser must communicate. If the local master browsers are Samba computers, however, it won't hurt to use the remote browse sync parameter (described in the following section) to facilitate this communication.

After restarting Samba, you can verify that your server has become the domain master browser by using either the Linux nmblookup -SR *name* or Windows NBTSTAT -a *NAME* command, where *name* is the name of the Samba server. (You may need to wait a few seconds after restarting Samba for this change to take effect.) Look for an output line similar to the following:

```
RINGWORLD          <1b> -           M <ACTIVE>
```

The workgroup name (RINGWORLD in this example) bears the code 1b, which identifies the domain master browser. You know the name of the machine that bears this code, because you typed it on the command line.

It may take some time—several minutes—for browse lists to propagate and stabilize once you assign a new domain master browser. Changes within each subnet can also take some time to work their way through the network. For instance, when a user turns on a computer, it may not appear in browse lists for a few minutes, particularly on computers on other subnets.

Communicating with Other Master Browsers

In order for a domain master browser to do its job, it must be able to exchange browse lists with the network's local master browsers. In a network composed only of Windows computers, this process occurs as a side effect of the PDC status of the domain master browser. Every local master browser knows the PDC's address (through the NBNS server) and so exchanges browse lists with the PDC/domain master browser. If Samba is the PDC and the domain master browser, and one or more local master browsers are Windows boxes, this same mechanism works.

For special situations, Samba offers a few additional options that can help.

remote browse sync   With this parameter you list the IP addresses of one or more remote master browsers. Say you want to synchronize browse lists between the computer you're configuring and Samba servers at 192.168.29.34 and 192.168.129.103. You can use this parameter:

```
remote browse sync = 192.168.29.34 192.168.129.103
```

If you don't know the exact IP address of the remote server, you can use a *directed broadcast,* in which you fill out binary 1s in the machine portion of the IP address, as in 192.168.29.255.

This parameter allows you to communicate *only* with other Samba servers; if the remote master browser is a Windows computer, remote browse sync won't help you synchronize browse lists. You can use this parameter to explicitly exchange browse lists between a domain master browser and a local master browser or between two local master browsers. This last possibility is what allows a Samba-mediated workgroup to span multiple subnets—an option that's not available when Windows computers function as the master browsers. ("Workgroup across Subnets," later in this chapter, describes such a configuration in detail.)

remote announce   This parameter is much more limited than remote browse sync. Instead of exchanging browse lists, remote announce allows a single Samba server to announce its presence to the master browser on a subnet other than its own. You might use this feature if you have one or two isolated Samba servers that you want to integrate into a workgroup that is otherwise restricted to a single subnet; you can use remote announce on the isolated computers to link them to the larger subnet.

As with remote browse sync, you can list the IP address of the master browser; or, if you don't know the exact IP address, you can use a directed broadcast. If the remote network uses a different workgroup name than the server's, you must specify your computer's workgroup name. The following example adds a system to the browse lists on the 192.168.29.255 and 192.168.129.255 subnets:

```
remote announce = 192.168.29.255/LEGEND 192.168.129.255/LEGEND
```

As you can with remote browse sync, you can use remote announce to communicate with either a local or a domain master browser. This parameter is not restricted to communications with Samba master browsers. "Small Network with Isolated Samba Servers," later in this chapter, provides a detailed example configuration using this parameter.

With both `remote browse sync` and `remote announce`, if you use a directed broadcast, the configuration of any router or other equipment used to connect these subnets must allow directed broadcasts. Many routers block directed broadcasts. If you have a problem because of this, consult your router's documentation; or switch to using specific IP addresses.

Although neither `remote browse sync` nor `remote announce` is strictly necessary in a domain configuration, I do recommend using `remote browse sync` when both the domain and local master browsers are Samba computers. Include appropriate parameters on both the domain and local master browsers to ensure that they exchange their browse lists regularly. Doing this provides insurance against failure of the normal Windows-style browse list exchange mechanisms. (`remote browse sync` uses a Samba-only protocol, and because you provide the IP addresses explicitly, this mechanism doesn't rely on automatic master browser location.)

Common Configuration Examples

The preceding description of browsing should help you understand the issues and the configuration options involved in browsing. Nevertheless, these descriptions are still fairly abstract; by examining some examples you'll better be able to see just how each option can and should be applied. The four examples presented in this section range from the simple to the complex. With any luck, your network's configuration will resemble one of them.

Small Network, No Routing

The simplest case is a small network in which no routing occurs, as illustrated in Figure 11.3. This configuration is simple enough that it makes little difference whether the network is structured as a workgroup or a domain. The domain configuration is used here. A workgroup configuration would be the same, but without the `domain master = Yes` parameter.

Figure 11.3   A small, nonrouted network requires only a single local master browser.

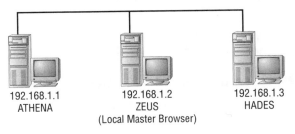

192.168.1.1
ATHENA

192.168.1.2
ZEUS
(Local Master Browser)

192.168.1.3
HADES

The small network depicted in Figure 11.3 can use an NBNS server or broadcast name resolution, and it doesn't really matter what any of the computers does. ZEUS, the local master browser, could conceivably be a client computer, although Microsoft's intent in giving its computers the OS codes listed in Table 11.1 was that servers would be more likely to gain status as local master browser. If ZEUS is a Samba server and you want to ensure that it acquires and holds local master browser status, you would include the following lines in the [global] section of ZEUS's smb.conf file:

```
os level = 65
local master = Yes
preferred master = Yes
domain master = Yes
```

The final option (domain master) is harmless in a workgroup. In a domain, however, include it only on the PDC computer, which should correspond with the domain master browser. The os level = 65 parameter will beat out any current Windows computer and probably future Windows computers, for local master browser status.

If ZEUS crashes for some reason, another computer will eventually take over as the master browser. If you want a specific Samba system to take over this task, you should configure it with the following global smb.conf parameters:

```
os level = 64
local master = Yes
preferred master = No
domain master = No
```

This configuration uses an os level one lower than that of the preferred master browser. In practice, os level = 65 will do as well, if other parameters are set appropriately; os level = 64 is simply a redundant method of ensuring that the desired computer attains master browser status. The preferred master = No and domain master = No parameters, on the other hand, are quite important. If you set these incorrectly, a network will still work—but it will almost certainly experience browsing "dropouts" in which all computers disappear for a time, and perhaps other problems as well. Because No is the default for both preferred master and domain master, you may omit these parameters if you like. Setting them explicitly does no harm and may help to document your intentions.

Small Network with Isolated Samba Servers

On occasion, you may have a small network like the one shown in Figure 11.3 and want to add one or two computers to that network from another subnet. The result resembles the network illustrated in Figure 11.4. In this configuration, the isolated computers are intended to function as members of the main workgroup. If these isolated computers are Samba servers, setting up this configuration is fairly straightforward. If they are Windows clients or servers, you may need to move on to a more complex configuration, such as a full domain, described in "Domains across Subnets."

Figure 11.4   You can use smb.conf parameters to link isolated Samba servers to a core workgroup or domain.

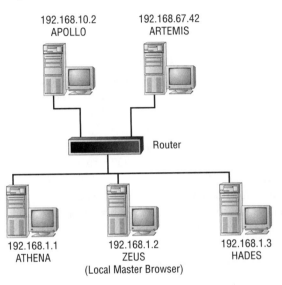

The main master browser, ZEUS, can be configured precisely as described in the "Small Network, No Routing" example. In fact, ZEUS can be a Windows computer. The critical configuration options appear in the smb.conf files of Figure 11.4's two routed computers, APOLLO and ARTEMIS. Both of these computers should have *one* of the two following lines:

```
remote announce = 192.168.1.255/LEGEND
```

or

```
remote announce = 192.168.1.2/LEGEND
```

Use the first option if you don't know the exact IP address of the master browser, or if you think the master browser might change from time to time. Use the second option if you know the exact IP address of the master browser, and if you're confident that it won't change. In the first case, your router must be configured to pass directed broadcasts, so this option might not work correctly on all networks. Both of these examples specify the workgroup name (LEGEND), but that's not strictly necessary if all the computers are configured to use the same workgroup name.

In addition to setting the `remote announce` parameter, you must configure an NBNS server on one of the computers or use `lmhosts` to provide name resolution for all the computers that might want to access the isolated systems. Without this detail, the isolated servers will appear in browse lists, but clients will be unable to browse to those servers because broadcast name resolution will fail. Consult Chapter 9 for details on configuring Samba in this role.

> **NOTE** Both APOLLO and ARTEMIS may be part of their own local subnets, and may or may not function as Samba servers on those subnets. (Restricting access to the Samba servers from the local subnets may require the use of advanced security features, described in Chapter 14, "Samba Security Considerations.") You can use the `remote announce` parameter in this way to let a single Samba server function on two separate subnets, without creating a more complex domain configuration. You might use this feature if you have two or more subnets that normally require little integration but that do need to share network printers or other resources. If APOLLO and ARTEMIS are print servers, they can announce themselves to multiple subnets using `remote announce`, thus providing printer access from all these subnets with minimal fuss.

Workgroup across Subnets

A workgroup configuration (as opposed to a domain) is normally easy to set up and configure—but only on a single, isolated network segment, as depicted in Figure 11.3. If you don't need domain functionality but do need to use multiple subnets, you're forced to configure a domain when you use Windows computers as master browsers. Samba, however, provides some useful nondomain workarounds for cross-subnet browsing.

Consider the network configuration shown in Figure 11.5. This network includes three subnets: 192.168.1.0/24, 192.168.5.0/24, and 192.168.10.0/24. Each subnet contains its own local master browser. If you configure each subnet to use a workgroup configuration, a normal configuration provides no browsing from one subnet to another, even if you use the same workgroup name in each subnet. This configuration is effectively three separate workgroups.

Figure 11.5   Multiple subnets create separate workgroups—unless you configure Samba to break that barrier.

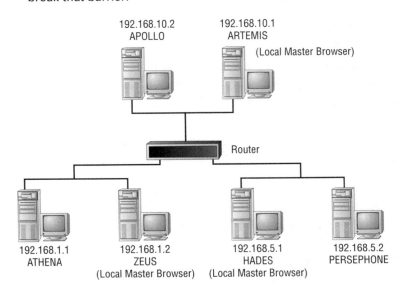

You can use Samba's `remote browse sync` parameter to knit these three separate workgroups together into one. Alternatively, each subnet can use its own workgroup name—but using `remote browse sync` lets all three workgroups appear in Network Neighborhood from any client computer. Both arrangements require that all the master browsers be Samba servers, however; if one master browser is a Windows computer, that subnet will be isolated from the others in terms of browse lists.

In addition to using `remote browse sync`, you must configure one computer as an NBNS server, as described in Chapter 9. In theory, you can use `lmhosts` entries to get around this requirement, but this is awkward at best. If all your clients are Samba, Windows NT, or Windows 2000 computers, you can rely on DNS to take the place of NBNS, but you must be sure that each client is properly configured to use DNS for SMB/CIFS name resolution.

All in all, if you configure one computer (let's say ARTEMIS from Figure 11.5) to function as both a local master browser and an NBNS server, it would include the following global `smb.conf` parameters:

```
os level = 65
local master = Yes
preferred master = Yes
```

Advanced Configurations

PART 3

```
remote browse sync = 192.168.1.2 192.168.5.255
wins support = Yes
wins proxy = Yes
dns proxy = Yes
```

These parameters accomplish the following tasks:

Local Master Browser Configuration   The os level, local master, and preferred master parameters cause the computer to become the local master browser (assuming no other computer on ARTEMIS's subnet has a higher OS level).

Browse List Exchange   The remote browse sync parameter causes ARTEMIS to exchange its browse lists with ZEUS and HADES. Note that the exact parameter used points directly to ZEUS (192.168.1.2) but not to HADES—instead, the configuration points to HADES's subnet. Therefore, if HADES isn't up but another Samba server is running as the local master browser on 192.168.5.0/24, the browse list exchange will still occur. The router must allow directed broadcasts for this exchange to work, however.

NBNS Server Configuration   The wins support parameter is the critical one to configure ARTEMIS as the network's NBNS server. The wins proxy parameter lets ARTEMIS respond to unanswered broadcast name-resolution requests, and the dns proxy parameter lets ARTEMIS use a DNS lookup as a fallback should an NBNS lookup return nothing. These two final parameters are optional, but their use is recommended to improve reliability. All are described in more detail in Chapter 9.

In addition to this configuration of ARTEMIS, it's necessary to configure ZEUS and HADES in a similar way. For these computers, though, you omit the NBNS configuration options and substitute a setting to let these computers use ARTEMIS as an NBNS server. You must also make changes to the IP addresses in the remote browse sync parameter. ZEUS's configuration should include these lines:

```
os level = 65
local master = Yes
preferred master = Yes
remote browse sync = 192.168.10.1 192.168.5.255
wins server = 192.168.10.1
```

Note that the os level and other browser parameters are identical, aside from issues of IP addresses. ZEUS and ARTEMIS both trying to attain local master browser status causes no conflict because these two computers participate in different elections—ZEUS in the 192.168.1.0/24 subnet and ARTEMIS in 192.168.10.0/24.

In a configuration like this, it's usually simplest and safest to configure one system as both a local master browser and an NBNS server. If necessary, however, you can shift the NBNS server function to another computer, such as ATHENA. If you do so, ARTEMIS's configuration would resemble that of ZEUS or HADES, and ATHENA would acquire the NBNS server parameters.

Unlike a domain master browser configuration, a distributed workgroup configuration such as this one uses no master browser that holds any special significance, aside from the fact that one of them is probably configured as an NBNS server in addition to doing duty as a master browser. Such a setup is not difficult to configure when your network is simple. In a rapidly changing network, however, it can become a nuisance to have to frequently change the configurations of all the master browsers whenever one master browser changes. Large networks also often benefit from the features of domains, so you may want to configure your network using a domain model rather than a workgroup model.

Domain across Subnets

On the surface, a domain that spans multiple subnets looks much like a workgroup that spans multiple subnets. Figure 11.5 comes close to fitting this model, except that one local master browser is also the domain master browser. Check Figure 11.2 to see the veridical domain-across-subnet configuration.

As with a workgroup split across subnets, a split domain more or less requires an NBNS server. As a domain, the network also requires a PDC. Conventionally, all three functions are handled by a single computer. Windows computers are incapable of separating the PDC function from the domain master browser function, and some clients assume that the NBNS server is also the PDC. Therefore, unless you have some very strong reason not to do so, I recommend you assign one computer for all three roles. Even if you have a compelling reason to split these roles, you should reconsider your plan and develop a backup arrangement. If necessary, you can use a Windows NT or 2000 system as the PDC/NBNS server/domain master browser system, and Linux or Windows computers as the local master browsers.

Assuming you use Linux for all these tasks, the domain master browser's configuration (ARTEMIS in Figure 11.2) would include the following global parameters:

```
os level = 65
local master = Yes
preferred master = Yes
domain master = Yes
wins support = Yes
```

```
wins proxy = Yes
dns proxy = Yes
security = User
encrypt passwords = Yes
domain logons = Yes
```

These parameters determine several aspects of Samba's behavior:

Local Master Browser   The os level, local master, and preferred master parameters ensure that Samba wins the local master browser election, unless another Samba server is configured with a higher os level.

Domain Master Browser   The domain master = Yes parameter configures Samba to function as the domain master browser.

NBNS Server   The wins support parameter allows Samba to function as an NBNS server for the domain. The wins proxy and dns proxy parameters are optional extras. Chapter 9 covers these parameters in greater detail.

Security Options   The security = User parameter configures Samba to use user-level security, which is typical for a PDC. (You can also use a remote password server, if you like, but the PDC normally does its own authentication. If you use a remote password server, you must use security = Server and set the password server parameter to point to the password server computer.) The encrypt passwords parameter sets Samba to use encrypted passwords, which are required for domains. These options also require that you have an smbpasswd file, as described in Chapter 14.

PDC Configuration   The domain logons = Yes parameter is the key to PDC configuration, although this parameter relies on the two security options described just above. Chapter 10 discusses this topic, including necessary details about account creation for handling Windows NT clients.

Configuring the local master browsers is somewhat simpler than for the domain master browser. An appropriate configuration includes the following global parameters:

```
os level = 65
local master = Yes
preferred master = Yes
wins server = 192.168.10.1
domain logons = No
```

```
security = Domain
encrypt passwords = Yes
password server = 192.168.10.1
```

The final three lines of this configuration are somewhat optional. In terms of master browser configuration, the computer will function properly even if it doesn't use domain-level security. (You can use security = Server for a very similar effect, or user- or share-level security if you have reason to keep the server aloof from the domain; see Chapter 10 for more information.)

As in the "Workgroup across Subnets" example, this configuration uses the same os level value for each of the preferred master browsers. There's no conflict because browser elections are local to each subnet.

The preceding examples omit remote browse sync parameters because they are *theoretically* unnecessary, and because they won't work if a remote master browser is a Windows computer. In practice, however, adding remote browse sync parameters to both the domain and the local master browsers will do no harm, and it may improve browsing reliability when most or all of the master browsers are Samba systems. I therefore recommend you use them, as is done in the "Workgroup across Subnets" example.

Summary

In a simple network, browsing is handled automatically. It is difficult to misconfigure because SMB/CIFS systems include protocols to assign a master browser computer to help control this small but important service. You may have cause to force a particular computer to be a master browser, however, and the configuration can be somewhat difficult to accomplish properly on a complex network that includes multiple subnets. Fortunately, Samba includes several parameters to help you force its behavior in browser elections and in handling browsing tasks such as exchanging browse lists with other Samba computers. If you understand your network's topology and plan appropriate placement of servers and clients on that network, you can produce a reliable browsing experience for all users, given a reasonable mix of Samba and Windows master browsers.

Advanced
Configurations

PART 3

## 12

Tuning Samba for Optimum Performance

Configuring Samba to perform basic file- and printer-sharing operations can be a fairly straightforward process, as described in Part 2, "Essential Configuration." Most of Samba's default options work reasonably well on most networks, so a simple file or print server needs adjustments to just a handful of smb.conf parameters in order to function. Unfortunately, some administrators find that their Samba servers don't provide the anticipated level of performance in sharing files with Windows clients. There can be many performance-robbing problems on SMB/CIFS networks, some of which can be difficult to track down. This chapter contains information and suggestions to help you locate and correct such problems.

The chapter begins with a discussion of performance testing. Before you embark on a project to improve performance, it's critical that you understand how to evaluate your network's operations. A flawed speed test can lead to a great deal of pointless debugging. Once you're using reasonable performance measures, you must be able to locate the source of a problem, be it hardware or software related. A discussion of common network bottlenecks will help you with that task. You'll also find descriptions of specific Linux, Samba, and Windows tuning options that can help to improve network performance.

Network Performance Testing

The first step in fixing network performance problems is to quantify the problem. If a user tells you "the network seems slow," that's not enough information to provide a fix, even if you're a veritable font of networking information. The usual way to obtain more information is to run one or more *benchmarks*—tests that measure the speed of a system's performance. In terms of Samba, benchmarks typically measure file transfer speed, although in a few cases you may need to measure something else, such as the time it takes a PDC to log a user onto a domain.

Once you've run a benchmark and compared the results to some baseline value, you can begin looking for a bottleneck in your network configuration. These may lie in the hardware or software. Locating bottlenecks is sometimes a matter of tweaking network configurations and running experiments, but sometimes you can use patterns of benchmark results from several systems to narrow down your search criteria. Once you've identified the source of the problem, you can adjust your configuration to work around it or correct it.

Samba includes several `smb.conf` parameters that can influence the package's performance. The default settings tend to work well on most networks, but occasionally a default may degrade performance on a specific network. It's therefore worth at least reading about these parameters (described later in "Samba Configuration Options"), even if you haven't noticed slow performance from Samba.

Network Benchmarks

There are several benchmark programs that are relevant for understanding Samba performance. Following are the two most common benchmarks for this task:

Do a Samba/FTP comparison.   You can compare the performance of Samba to that of FTP. This comparison is reasonably easy to do because it requires no special software. Because FTP is a fairly simple protocol, it usually runs about as well as can be expected from your hardware. In comparison, Samba's performance should reach approximately 70–80% that of FTP's.

Use Ziff-Davis's NetBench.   Ziff-Davis Publishing, Inc., uses a benchmark known as *NetBench* in its own magazine reviews and makes this program available for download. (Version 6.0 is available from `http://www.zdnet.com/etestinglabs/stories/benchmarks/0,8829,2326318,00.html`.) NetBench allows you to set up several clients to simultaneously access a server, thus testing its behavior under a multiuser load.

In addition to these network benchmarks, other hardware benchmarks may be important. Many hardware components play a role in Samba's performance, and you can test for degradation in various ways (see the "Hardware Bottlenecks" section). For these specific hardware components you may need to obtain and use benchmark utilities such as disk benchmarks.

Benchmark Measurements

Precisely how you run a benchmark and what data you record depend on the exact nature of the problem you're investigating. For example, if you suspect that file transfers from the server to Windows 2000 clients are slow as compared with transfers to Windows 98 clients, you should emphasize this comparison by performing controlled transfers using Windows 2000 and Windows 98 as clients. Ideally, you'd use a single client computer that dual-boots between these two OSs. If that's not possible, at least ensure that the two clients are on the same network segment. They should have hardware that's as similar as possible, especially with respect to Ethernet and disk hardware. On the other hand, if you believe that transfers *from* the server are slow as compared with those going *to* the server, you can use a single client for testing and compare transfer rates in both directions.

As a general rule, I recommend you take the following baseline measurements (in all cases, the client initiates the transfer):

- FTP transfers from the client to the server
- FTP transfers from the server to the client
- Samba transfers from the client to the server
- Samba transfers from the server to the client

As appropriate for your network, perform these tests using all client OSs available; for example, you might test from Windows 98, Windows 2000, and Linux. When you perform a Samba transfer from Windows, you'll need to use a large file (probably at least 5MB, ideally 20MB or more) and a stopwatch, because Windows doesn't provide exact file-transfer time statistics. Alternatively, you can use a script or simple program that transfers the files and measures the time it takes to do this. Many FTP clients and smbclient provide you with file transfer statistics.

WARNING   In computing circles, *b* is an abbreviation for *bit*, whereas *B* is an abbreviation for *byte*. Therefore, *Kb* stands for *kilobit* and *KB* stands for *kilobyte*. Unfortunately, smbclient doesn't follow this convention; it reports values using the abbreviation *kb*, when it means *kilobyte*. Even outside of smbclient, you must be cautious about units of measure, because various hardware and software uses an assortment of transfer rate measurement units—Kb/s, KB/s, Mb/s, MB/s, and more. If you're not careful to record and convert units appropriately, you can become hopelessly confused about your network's performance.

Advanced Configurations

PART 3

Benchmark Timing

Factors you don't want to measure in your tests, such as disk caching and brief spikes in network load, can cause deviations on single benchmark tests. It's best to run network benchmarks more than once to prevent being fooled by such factors. If all the tests return similar results, you can average them and use the average as the true measure of performance.

Local and remote filesystem caches can wreak havoc with your data. Specifically, the first time you transfer a file from a server, the server must read the data from the disk. If disk performance is poor, you may see a poor network transfer speed. If you immediately transfer the data again, some or all of the data may reside in Linux's file cache, thus improving performance and giving a truer measure of your network's performance as distinct from the server's disk performance. Similar arguments apply to transfers from a client's disk to the server. By the same token, it's possible that file compression can cause problems. If a system uses a compressed filesystem, handling the compression can reduce performance. On the other hand, if the data are highly compressible, the net effect may be a benefit to performance if the disk is slow. (These compression effects relate to filesystems that automatically compress files, not to files such as tarballs that are themselves compressed and transferred without being uncompressed.)

It's important to perform your benchmarks when your network is lightly loaded, and ideally when your tests comprise all of the network's traffic. If your tests are competing against normal network use, you may obtain spurious results as your packets collide with others, or if the server delays your transfers in favor of others.

Your benchmark results may be influenced not only by the server software you use, but by the client package. In particular, you may find that you get very different results from the same server when you use Samba's smbclient than when you use Windows. For that matter, even different versions of Windows can produce radically different results. It's therefore best, when testing, that you use the client OS you expect to employ regularly. Even if initial tests with different client OSs produce similar results, you can't be sure that this will be true after you've applied any adjustments you discover.

Evaluating Benchmark Results

Once you've performed your benchmarks, you'll need to evaluate them to know if you have a problem or want to improve performance to meet some goal. Precisely how you do this depends upon the type of benchmark and comparison you're performing. Some suggestions:

- If you want to determine if Samba is performing reasonably well given your hardware, compare your Samba performance numbers against FTP tests using the same server, or possibly against the performance of an *identically outfitted* Windows NT or 2000 system.

- When performance varies from one client or subnet to another, sample from different types of clients (OSs, critical hardware components, subnets, and so on) and compare these values. If you can spot a type of system that underperforms, you can concentrate your troubleshooting on that system type.

NOTE   Even if problems are isolated to a specific type of client, it's possible that a Samba configuration option can improve performance. The nt smb support parameter, for example, may influence performance with Windows NT computers, but not with Windows 9x clients. (Ironically, the performance impact is usually negative when nt smb support = Yes.)

- NetBench may be useful if you expect growth in your network and want to evaluate your server's capacity to handle that growth. You can configure the program to hit your server with a greater-than-normal load to see how performance degrades. Alternatively, you can try to locate existing hardware bottlenecks and evaluate their capacity to handle the increased load.

- To determine if a software configuration or hardware adjustment might improve performance, you can start with some baseline network measurements. Unless a problem area sticks out, however, you'll need to dig deeper to discover where the hardware and software bottlenecks appear on your system. These may not be obvious from a handful of broad benchmark results. You may therefore need to perform benchmarks on specific hardware components, and perhaps swap out some components for others to test the effect of upgrading hardware.

Remember when you perform these tests that you are essentially conducting a scientific experiment. You want to discover what causes performance on your network to degrade, and to do this, you must independently control several variables, with the aim of testing an hypothesis. Initially your hypotheses may be quite broad (such as "Windows 2000 performance is worse than Windows 98 performance"), but as you experiment with system settings, your hypotheses will become more refined (such as "the nt smb support parameter is degrading Windows 2000 performance").

Whenever you conduct a test to diagnose network problems, design the test so that you vary only one factor; or, if you vary more than one factor, you must test all possible combinations. For instance, you might test Windows 98 versus Windows 2000 performance. When you do so, you should ensure that your Windows 98 and Windows 2000 systems are as identical as possible. Ideally, you should use one computer that dual-boots between these OSs. If you also want to test how these OSs interact with a router that sits between them and the Samba server, you must gather data from four situations, as illustrated in Figure 12.1. In this hypothetical example, the router degrades performance for both clients, but the effect is far more pronounced for the Windows 2000 client. You might therefore want to begin investigating router configuration issues and settings in Windows 2000 that might interact with the router, such as *Maximum Transport Unit (MTU)* size and default gateway settings.

Figure 12.1   If you carefully plan the conditions you test, the test results will be much easier to interpret.

	Windows 98	Windows 2000
No Router	4.5MB/s	4.6MB/s
Router	4MB/s	1.8MB/s

Locating Bottlenecks

In most cases, data communication systems include one or more *bottlenecks*, which are components or processes that cannot handle the capacity of data produced by earlier components or processes. These bottlenecks therefore limit the rate of the information's flow, much as the physical neck of a bottle restricts the rate of a liquid's flow out of the bottle. Bottlenecks are the cause of many performance problems in computing, and Samba servers are no exception to this rule. Fixing performance problems is therefore often a task of locating bottlenecks and "widening" them. (Many people refer to "eliminating bottlenecks," but they can seldom truly be eliminated. Rather, they're made wide enough that another bottleneck becomes the limiting performance factor.)

Either hardware or software can cause bottlenecks. Hardware bottlenecks are sometimes easier to understand because they're associated with specific devices for which performance specifications are available. Say you're getting 1.2MB/s transfers through a 10Mbps Ethernet adapter; it's likely that the bottleneck lies in the Ethernet adapter. (Because 1MB = 8Mb, 1.2MB/s = 9.6Mbps—close enough to the theoretical limit of 10Mbps that the difference isn't worth mentioning.) Software bottlenecks, too, can be quite significant. Performance-tuning features in Samba, Linux, and Windows can help widen these bottlenecks, as described in "Linux Configuration Options" and "Windows Configuration Options" later in this chapter.

Hardware Bottlenecks

Hardware bottlenecks are, as you might imagine, associated with specific hardware components. In many cases, if you determine that a network performance problem is caused by a hardware component, your only choice is to replace or upgrade that component. Occasionally this necessitates further hardware upgrades—for example, if your network currently uses 10Mbps coaxial Ethernet, upgrading the Ethernet cards to 100Mbps models will also require upgrading the Ethernet cabling to Category 5 twisted-pair cabling, and adding hubs or switches. In a few cases, software solutions may exist, as for slow hard disks that might be configurable as RAID (redundant array of independent disks) devices for improved performance.

Many hardware components exist on both the client and the server. In most cases, bottlenecks occur on the server side, because the server is typically much more heavily loaded than is any one client. On occasion, however, and particularly when the clients are very old, the client hardware may be the source of the bottleneck. Some components, such as network cables, are part of neither the client nor the server.

Central Processing Unit

The CPU performs all the computations necessary for the computer. For the most part, Samba's CPU requirements are minimal, so the CPU is not likely to be the source of a bottleneck on a small or midsized network. An underpowered CPU could cause problems on a large network that sees lots of accesses, however. In addition, the CPU can become a bottleneck in print servers that share non-PostScript printers as if they were PostScript models, because the CPU also does the work of converting PostScript into a format that's usable by the non-PostScript printers (see Chapter 6).

To discover if the CPU is a bottleneck on your system, try running performance tests when the server is lightly loaded and when it is heavily loaded. You can load the CPU with a simple "do-nothing" program like the one shown in Listing 12.1.

Type this program in using your favorite text editor, save it as donothing.c, and compile it with a command such as **gcc -o donothing donothing.c**. You can then run the program in conjunction with the nice utility to specify how much CPU time Linux will give to the program. Start the program using the following command:

```
# nice -n value donothing
```

Here *value* ranges from –20 to 19, where negative values represent higher-than-normal priority, and positive values represent lower-than-normal priority. You must be running as root to use negative nice values, but any user can enter positive values.

Advanced Configurations

PART 3

Listing 12.1 C Program to Consume CPU Cycles for Test Purposes

```
#include <stdio.h>
int main(void)
{
   int i;
   long j;

   for (i = 1; i < 101; i++) {
      printf ("Pass %d\n", i);
      for (j = 0; j < 1000000000; j++)
   }
   printf ("DONE!");
   return 0;
}
```

To estimate the importance of the CPU in Samba bottlenecks, run a benchmark test without donothing running, and then another with the program running at a nice value of –20. If there's no change in the benchmark value, you can be confident that your CPU is powerful enough to handle the network load you imposed at that time, and probably substantially more. If your benchmark results dropped when you ran donothing, try using other nice values to get a feel for how much of a CPU load you can impose before performance degrades.

Memory

Memory is unlikely to be a bottleneck for small networks unless your server is seriously underpowered (less than 16MB or so for a network with a handful of light users). Large networks with many users, however, may impose enough of a memory load that the server begins excessive swapping during normal operation, which will quickly degrade performance. Realistically, most Samba servers should have at least 64MB of RAM, and often more, for optimal performance.

As a general rule of thumb, Samba's nmbd daemon consumes about 0.5MB on x86 versions of Linux; smbd consumes about 1.5MB per connection. Memory consumption on non-x86 versions of Linux may be different (usually higher on RISC CPUs). Local file caching requires memory, too, but the amount depends on the files in question. (Linux gives low priority to file caches for memory allocation, but will use memory for this purpose if it's available. Adding memory for use as a disk cache can improve Samba's performance, particularly if users regularly access the same set of files.)

You can use the `ps aux` command to monitor memory use for Samba's daemons, as demonstrated here:

```
$ ps aux | egrep "(USER|mbd)"
USER    PID %CPU %MEM  VSZ  RSS TTY STAT START TIME COMMAND
root   1939  0.0  0.1 3340  172 ?   S    Jun22 0:00 [smbd]
root   1941  0.0  0.5 1552  524 ?   S    Jun22 0:08 nmbd -D
root   1943  0.0  0.0 1468    0 ?   SW   Jun22 0:00 [nmbd]
root  12490  0.0  1.5 3704 1444 ?   S    Jun27 0:04 smbd -D
```

The RSS column lists the total *resident set size*—the amount of memory consumed by the process. Samba spawns a new process for each connection, so if a Samba server has many connected users, you'll see many instances of the Samba daemons.

You can also track overall system memory usage with the `free` command, which produces output similar to the following:

```
$ free
             total     used     free   shared  buffers   cached
Mem:         95772    91468     4304    34712     9852    44720
-/+ buffers/cache:    36896    58876
Swap:       136512    19036   117476
```

Here the `total` column lists the total amount of memory on the computer, in kilobytes—both physical RAM (on the `Mem` line) and swap space (on the `Swap` line). The `used` column indicates the amount of used space, and the `free` column lists the amount of free memory. Although this system appears to have very little physical RAM available (about 4MB), in fact a great deal of RAM is used by the disk cache. (This will be true of almost all Linux computers just minutes after booting.) The `-/+ buffers/cache` line removes this RAM from consideration, revealing a much more substantial 57MB available.

The easiest way to verify that RAM isn't a bottleneck is to use the `free` command (or other memory-checking commands, such as `vmstat`) to observe the memory load on your system when many users are connected, or when you expect the system's memory to be stressed for some other reason. If you want to anticipate future needs from Samba expansion, factor in about 1.5MB per connection—so if you expect to add ten users, each of whom will be using the system most of the time, add 15MB.

Advanced Configurations

PART 3

> **NOTE** Each *connection* consumes 1.5MB. If a user accesses two shares, that user consumes 3MB of RAM. This fact suggests a strategy to reduce memory use: Consolidate shares. If your users regularly mount multiple shares, merging some of these shares can reduce Samba's memory needs.

Motherboard Bus

The motherboard bus type (that is, whether it uses PCI, ISA, or an outdated or exotic design) can be a limiting factor in Samba's speed when the server uses very high performance components. Let's say you have multiple high-speed SCSI hard disks, an exotic high-end network adapter, enough CPU and memory power to handle it all, and appropriate network connections outside of the computer; in this environment, the motherboard's bus may become the bottleneck. Unfortunately, if you've run into this problem, there's not much you can do about it aside from splitting your one Samba server into two in order to distribute the load, or replacing the computer with one that uses a higher-performance bus.

If the computer uses the outdated ISA bus even for just one critical component, the bus limit can become a very real one. The ISA bus is capable of only 8MB/s maximum speed, which is below that of 100Mbps Ethernet. If your ISA motherboard also supports PCI, you may be able to move a component from ISA to PCI to improve matters. If not, you may need to replace the motherboard—and with it a large number of supporting devices such as RAM, the CPU, the video card, and so on. Buying a whole new computer is probably more cost-effective.

> **NOTE** The motherboard bus isn't a factor in most components that aren't directly related to Samba's operations. For example, if you have an ISA sound card, this fact won't degrade Samba's performance (unless you use the sound card in conjunction with some CPU-intensive task such as speech recognition). ISA parallel-port cards are common in Samba print servers. Because the printer port itself is slower than the ISA bus, this setup causes no problems—but the slow speed of the parallel port may become a bottleneck when printing files. This fact will affect printout time, but it won't degrade other Samba operations, such as the time it takes to accept a print job from the client.

Hard Disk Subsystem

Modern hard disks are capable of transferring at least 10 to 20MB/s in sustained throughput. This sort of performance is comparable or superior to that of 100Mbps (that is,

12.5MB/s) Ethernet hardware. Therefore, you might think that hard disk performance isn't a factor as a Samba bottleneck. Unfortunately, disk accesses usually require head movements, which do degrade disk performance. It's therefore possible that disk performance is an issue.

You can check your Linux disk's performance using the hdparm command, as in the following:

```
# hdparm -tT /dev/sda


/dev/sda:
  Timing buffer-cache reads:   128 MB in  4.36 seconds =29.36 MB/sec
  Timing buffered disk reads:  64 MB in  4.04 seconds =15.84 MB/sec
```

You may need to change the device filename (/dev/sda in this example) for your system. The first result (29.36MB/s) is for reads to and from cache memory and reflects your system's memory subsystem more than the disk subsystem. The second value (15.84MB/s) is the disk's raw performance.

If you have two or more older disks that don't perform to your satisfaction, you may be able to bind them together as a RAID package. This configuration requires some work to set up, but it can improve performance substantially. Consult the RAID HOWTO document (which comes with all Linux distributions) for more information.

Another factor besides the hard disks themselves is the hard disk interface. Most *x*86 computers sold today use *Enhanced Integrated Device Electronics (EIDE)* interfaces, but some use *Small Computer System Interface (SCSI)* interfaces. Both types are available in a wide variety of speeds, ranging from less than 5MB/s to more than 160MB/s. If your hard disk is capable of a higher speed than what your disk interface can deliver, you'll get the lower speed of the interface. Fortunately, this isn't normally a problem if your hardware is well matched in terms of purchase date, but the speed difference may be an issue if you use a newer drive with an older controller. Also, the EIDE bus is designed such that only one device at a time can transfer data. Therefore, if you have two EIDE hard disks, you should put them on separate EIDE chains whenever possible. SCSI devices don't suffer from this problem, however. Depending on the speeds of the SCSI host adapter and disks, you may be able to put two, three, or more SCSI drives on a single host adapter without difficulty.

> **WARNING**   Most hard drive manufacturers emphasize the *interface speed* of their drives, rather than the *disk speed* (also known as the *internal transfer rate*). It's the disk speed that's usually the bottleneck, assuming the drive is matched to a sufficiently speedy controller.

Some older interface boards, particularly for EIDE, required a great deal of CPU time. Indeed, even modern boards can operate in this *programmed input/output (PIO)* mode. This mode reduces performance and increases CPU load, which can itself cause problems. SCSI host adapters automatically operate in the more efficient *direct memory access (DMA)* mode whenever possible, but you may need to use the hdparm utility to force an EIDE drive into DMA mode. The command **hdparm -d1 -X34 /dev/hda** should do this for the first EIDE disk on most systems, but consult the hdparm man page for details. You must also have support compiled into your kernel for your particular variety of EIDE controller in order to use EIDE DMA mode.

> **WARNING**   On rare occasion, hdparm can crash your system if you try to use it to activate DMA mode. On some systems—particularly those with experimental EIDE DMA support—DMA mode may be unreliable. For these reasons, use caution when running DMA mode on EIDE drives for the first time.

> **TIP**   SCSI offers enough advantages, including multitasking access to multiple devices per chain and the availability of higher-performance SCSI drives, that SCSI is preferable to EIDE on most servers. Unfortunately, SCSI is also more expensive, but if your network uses a client/server architecture, this added expense can benefit a large number of clients.

Network Adapter and Cables

Ethernet is the most common type of network medium for small networks today. Until the late 1990s, 10Mbps Ethernet was the most common Ethernet variety, but 100Mbps hardware is now used for most new installations, and 1Gbps hardware is waiting in the wings. Some big servers use exotic high-capacity network interfaces, which then link up to multiple Ethernet networks via a router. This lets the server provide greater-than-100Mbps total throughput while using inexpensive 100Mbps hardware for clients. Unless you have such a high-end configuration, the network adapter and associated cables are likely to be the most important hardware bottlenecks, and the most difficult to overcome.

Linux's support for Ethernet adapters is excellent but not perfect. You're most likely to get the best possible throughput from Ethernet adapters manufactured by Intel or 3Com, or those that use the popular Tulip chipset or clones thereof. These products are all well supported by Linux, and the Linux drivers are mature and well maintained. Some cards that use less-popular chipsets cause occasional problems, produce lower throughput, or impose a higher CPU load on the host. As a general rule, PCI cards impose less CPU load than do ISA cards. (ISA cards, too, are incapable of reaching the 100Mbps speeds of modern Ethernet networks, because the ISA bus itself is more limited than this.) PC-Card (aka PCMCIA) Ethernet adapters usually can't reach full 100Mbps speeds. These devices are common on notebook computers, so you may find that such computers perform poorly as clients. For this reason (and many others, such as high cost and poor expandability), you should avoid using a notebook computer as a server.

Cables can become a speed issue if they're substandard in quality or damaged. With 10BaseT and 100BaseT Ethernet, you can easily swap out a single cable if you believe it's damaged. (This is a good thing to try early in troubleshooting if only one client appears slow.) With coaxial cabling, diagnosing and fixing problems is much more troublesome, because a single cable attaches to all the computers on the network. Still, the location of the trouble can be a clue to problems—if all the computers past a certain point on a coaxial network are slow, the cable may be the culprit.

Switches, Hubs, and Routers

10BaseT and 100BaseT Ethernet networks rely on hubs and switches to connect computers. Each computer in a physical subnet connects to one of these central devices, which allow all connected devices to communicate with one another. Hubs and switches fill virtually identical roles in a network, but they operate differently. Hubs merely echo data packets from one computer to all other computers on the network. Switches, by contrast, attempt to send only packets destined for a specific computer to that computer. Switches therefore cut down on unnecessary packet transmissions, thereby reducing the number of collisions and improving speed. Instead of 100Mbps *total* bandwidth on a 100Base-T network, a switch enables 100Mbps bandwidth between *each pair* of communicating computers. Another speed benefit of switches is that they allow *full-duplex* communication between computers, in which both computers can transmit simultaneously. With a hub, simultaneous transmissions result in a collision, which requires both transmissions to be redone. Finally, switches allow you to mix 10Mbps and 100Mbps Ethernet devices on one network without speed degradation. If you use a hub, adding a single 10Mbps device causes all the computers to operate at 10Mbps, even when the two computers involved in a transaction are capable of higher speeds. All told, a 100Mbps network can benefit substantially from using a switch rather than a hub. If you're seeing speeds of 50Mbps or lower on your hub-based network, there's a good chance that upgrading to switches will improve matters.

All switches are not created equal, however. Switches have total bandwidth values, which can become bottlenecks. For example, consider a network of 10 computers. In theory, if these computers match up as five pairs in which each computer communicates full-throttle at 100Mbps, this 10-computer network requires 1,000Mbps (1Gbps) of bandwidth. If a switch provides only 500Mbps of bandwidth, however, you'll see average maximum transfer speeds of only 50Mbps, assuming no other bottlenecks come into play. Depending on your network topology and its use, therefore, you might want to examine the quality of your switches if you're experiencing problems that appear to be linked to computers served by particular switches.

When a network comprises multiple physical subnets, chances are they're linked with one or more routers. A router links networks together and may be able to translate from one type of networking medium to another (from Ethernet to Token Ring, for instance). Compared to hubs or switches, routers process network packets at a high level, and in so doing can introduce new bottlenecks. At a minimum, you should ensure that your router is capable of handling the amount of data that passes through it. Your router may come with diagnostic tools to help you make that determination. Some routers work best with network packets of a particular size. If packets are too large, the router may split them, reducing efficiency; if they're too small, the router isn't used to its fullest ability. You can adjust Linux's MTU size, as described in "Linux TCP/IP Performance," if this appears to be a problem and you can't adjust the router's MTU size.

Network problems related to hubs, switches, and routers are almost certain to manifest themselves equally across protocols. Therefore, comparing Samba performance to FTP performance won't show a dramatic difference if the only problems are related to these devices. Problems with these devices may be localized, however, or may relate only to communications between *groups* of devices. You might have excellent performance between computers within groups on each side of a router, but when packets pass through that router, performance may degrade. For hubs and switches, you're more likely to see problems isolated to computers that are directly connected to a given hub or switch.

Software Bottlenecks

Software bottlenecks occur within a software package or in communications between packages. Most of the configuration options described in the later sections "Linux Configuration Options" and "Windows Configuration Options" are designed to fix software bottlenecks. Some bottlenecks associated with hardware may in fact be software bottlenecks of a sort. Poor drivers or firmware, for example, can produce inferior performance even when the hardware is capable of better performance.

Drivers

One common source of software bottlenecks is poor drivers. Under Linux, weak drivers are particularly likely to be associated with new hardware. For example, the 2.2.*x* kernel series includes very limited support for ATA/66 EIDE hard disk controllers. This support is vastly improved in the 2.4.*x* kernels, but not all such controllers are yet supported. If you've got an unsupported ATA/66 EIDE controller, you may not be able to use it in DMA mode, which can greatly degrade system performance. Your best bet in such a situation is to replace the hardware. Alternatively, if you're a skilled enough programmer or can hire one, you might develop your own drivers to replace the weak or nonexistent ones.

Although most hardware is well supported in Windows 9*x,* not all hardware has good support in Windows NT and 2000, or in non-Microsoft OSs like OS/2. You may therefore need to update drivers or replace hardware in these OSs to get reliable and speedy drivers. Even in Windows 9*x,* although most hardware is supported, some drivers are faster or more reliable than others. Try doing a search on Deja News (`http://www.deja.com/usenet/`) to learn about peoples' experiences with drivers for specific devices.

The most reliable way to spot driver problems is to replace the driver in question. Unfortunately, this can be a tedious process. It often requires replacing the hardware component as well as the driver, so you may not know if the problem was truly caused by the driver or by the hardware. A few devices work with multiple drivers. In Windows, the OS may come with a driver, which may be different from the driver produced by the manufacturer. It may be worth trying both. A few devices sport multiple drivers in Linux. Most notable among these are various EIDE controllers, which work with both generic EIDE drivers and DMA-enabled variants for specific chipsets. In addition, the popular Tulip Ethernet chipset and its clones work with the `de4x5` and `tulip` drivers, as well as a modified version of `tulip` for some recent clones.

Network Stacks

As described in Chapters 1 and 2, Samba typically operates over the TCP/IP networking stack. SMB/CIFS networking in general, however, can operate over the NetBEUI or IPX stacks, as well; and Procom Technology (`http://www.procom.com`) released a NetBEUI stack for Linux in 2000. Fortunately, most OSs today have mature and efficient TCP/IP stacks, so these implementations are unlikely to be the sources of important bottlenecks. Occasionally, however, TCP/IP options can cause poor network performance, as when two computers are configured to use mismatched packet sizes. Some of these issues are described in "Linux TCP/IP Performance" and "Windows TCP/IP Options" later in this chapter.

Support computers on a network can occasionally cause performance problems. This is the case when a router causes performance degradation, for example. Other possible sources of trouble include the following:

Slow DNS Servers If DNS resolution is slow, there can be delays in hostname look-ups, but subsequent operations work well. This is likely to be an issue only when Samba is configured to use DNS before other forms of name resolution (via the `name resolve order` parameter), or when similar options are used in Windows NT or 2000 clients. By default, Windows 2000 uses DNS before NBNS or broadcast name resolution. Hostname lookup delays will also manifest in non-SMB/CIFS network protocols.

Misconfigured DHCP Information If your network uses a DHCP server to config-ure other systems, a misconfiguration on this server can have profoundly negative consequences. Because you can use DHCP to configure Windows clients' NetBIOS name-resolution features, DHCP misconfiguration can cause slow name resolution. (Consult "Setting the Node Type" in Chapter 9 for more information.) An incorrect network mask, whether set manually or via DHCP, can cause delays or an inability to contact specific computers.

Overloaded PDCs, NBNS Servers, or Master Browsers The critical support com-puters in a Windows network can cause problems if they're overloaded. Fortunately, neither NBNS nor master-browser functions consume a lot of resources, so these ele-ments are unlikely to become bottlenecks. PDCs often host home shares, however, and in some cases authentication may be modestly CPU-intensive. Underpowered computers in any of these roles tend to produce delays in browsing and in connecting to computers.

Client Software

Another potential source of poor network performance is poorly written client software. Because network transfers usually take more time than local disk accesses, any program that reads files repeatedly or unnecessarily can have a negative impact. This affects the cli-ent on which the software runs, as well as other computers on the network (because the client uses bandwidth and server resources that might otherwise be devoted to other users). Most major office and productivity applications are written with network access in mind and so do not require tweaking in this respect. Nevertheless, in evaluating soft-ware you may want to consider its need for disk (and hence possibly network) access. If two packages are otherwise similar but one requires more file reading and writing, you may want to favor the one that's more frugal with disk/network access.

The popular office application Microsoft Word includes a feature called *fast save*, which reduces the time taken to save files. This feature works by appending data to an existing file rather than rewriting the entire file. You can enable or disable this feature from the Options menu shown in Figure 12.2, obtained by choosing Tools ➤ Options and clicking the Save tab. Be sure the Allow Fast Saves option is checked to enable this feature.

Figure 12.2   Microsoft Word's fast save feature influences the amount of data the program transfers when reading and writing files.

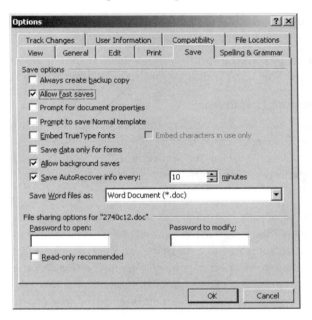

WARNING   Although the fast save feature can reduce usage of network bandwidth if substantial network traffic comes from *saving* Microsoft Word files, this option has two major disadvantages. First, the files produced are ultimately larger and thus *increase* network traffic when read back. Second, fast-saved files are much more difficult for non-Microsoft programs to read. If you are reading these files in programs such as Linux's StarOffice, Applix Words, or WordPerfect, you should turn off the fast save option.

Server Software

For the purposes of this book, "server software" is usually Samba, although in some cases you may use Linux as a client and a Windows computer as the server. The section "Samba Configuration Options" describes many of Samba's performance-affecting parameters.

Advanced Configurations

PART 3

Unfortunately, optimizing Samba for one client may have the effect of robbing performance for another.

If you're interested enough in tuning Samba performance to want to dig into the code, you're welcome to do so. You can learn how to contribute to the Samba project from the Samba Web page at `http://www.samba.org`.

Working Around Bottlenecks

On some occasions, it may not be worthwhile or possible to widen a bottleneck to your satisfaction. You may need to find a way to work around the bottleneck rather than tackle it head-on. This section offers some general approaches you might take.

Reducing Network Requirements

You can reduce the need for network resources by changing the software your clients use, or by asking your users to adjust their usage patterns. You might also be able to install popular static packages such as major program files on individual clients rather than on a server. Unfortunately, these approaches also tend to reduce the utility of a network server.

NOTE   On the whole, working around bottlenecks is usually not what you want to do. It's best to address the cause of the problem. Sometimes this isn't possible, however, and a workaround may be all you can handle. In other cases you may find that a workaround presents benefits you hadn't previously considered. You may find that switching to a PostScript printer driver yields better text quality, for example, or that rearranging your network produces less administrative effort in the long run.

Rearranging Computers

Some bottlenecks are the result of network traffic traveling great distances across a network that contains multiple subnets. Consider the network shown in Figure 12.3. If PIERCE is a heavily used server, then its location on the network is less than optimal, because traffic destined for PIERCE from some systems (namely, TYLER and POLK) must clutter all three subnets to reach PIERCE. A better location for PIERCE in this scenario is in the middle subnet, along with TAYLOR and FILLMORE. If PIERCE were used mostly by TYLER and POLK, it would be best placed in their subnet. Another option would be to eliminate one router and link all three subnets directly to one router. This way, no two-computer communication needs to involve more than two subnets. You can also reduce the impact of such cross-net traffic by using switches rather than hubs within each subnet.

Figure 12.3   Inefficient network layouts can produce poor performance.

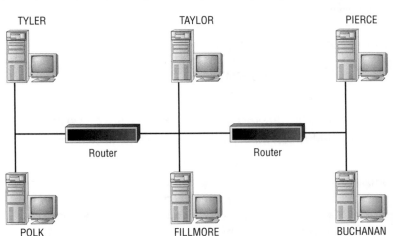

Changing Printing Protocols

Chapter 6 describes two ways to serve non-PostScript printers via Samba. You can share the printer "raw" and use a printer's native drivers on clients; or you can share it as a PostScript printer, feeding the results through Ghostscript. In most cases, the second option yields smaller print files and hence reduces network traffic. If the bottleneck is caused by low CPU power on the print server, on the other hand, switching to raw mode without Ghostscript may produce faster printing, at the expense of increased network traffic.

Avoiding the Problem Procedure

In some cases, you can avoid using a feature that's slow. This advice isn't likely to do you much good in cases of slow network file transfers. You may, however, be able to avoid slow browsing by mounting shares on drive letters in a network logon script or by creating shortcuts on the Windows desktop to specific shares. Adding an lmhosts file or configuring an NBNS server can reduce broadcast name lookup problems.

Linux Configuration Options

Optimizing Linux's performance involves three classes of configuration: Samba, general networking, and other configuration options such as hard disk optimization. I emphasize the Samba configuration options here because the other areas are quite broad and are not strictly Samba issues—this is a book on Samba, after all.

Most of these configuration options are highly context-sensitive—that is, what works well on one server or network may not work well on all of them. Fortunately, Samba's and Linux's defaults are reasonable for a majority of networks, but you may find a few areas that can stand improvement for yours.

Samba Configuration Options

Samba's performance options fall into two broad categories:

- Those designed with no other goal than to alter Samba's performance characteristics
- Those that add functionality but that have a negative impact on Samba's performance

For the most part, the options designed to tune performance come set with reasonable defaults, but you can experiment with their settings to see if some could be improved for your network. Many of the parameters that add functionality come set by default to add functionality—but they rob performance. You might try adjusting these, but be prepared to switch them back to their old values if you run into problems with client programs.

Performance-Tuning Options

Samba's performance-tuning options usually work by adjusting the low-level SMB/CIFS protocols. Some of these options add or delete features from Samba's repertoire or change the way Samba transmits data.

socket options This global parameter lets you set options that Linux uses on individual connections. You specify one or more options as the value of the parameter, as in `socket options = SO_SNDBUF=8192 TCP_NODELAY`. In the options that take values, an equals sign separates the option from the value. You must *not* include a space before or after that equals sign, although you *may* include spaces around the equals sign following the `options` parameter itself. Following are the specific options you can set:

SO_KEEPALIVE — Samba checks every four hours to see if a connected client is still active. If not, Samba terminates the connection, which can save server resources. The `keepalive` and `deadtime` parameters serve the same function, but in different ways.

SO_REUSEADDR — Enables reuse of local addresses. This option shouldn't be required (Linux should set it by default).

SO_BROADCAST	Enables use of broadcast packets. This option shouldn't be required (Linux should set it by default). Enable it if you suspect Samba isn't doing broadcast name resolution or isn't finding the master browser.
TCP_NODELAY	Causes Samba to send multiple packets on each transfer, to reduce the time spent waiting for acknowledgments. This option is the default on Samba 2.0.4 and later.
IPTOS_LOWDELAY	Another option that affects delay times between packets, but it's tuned for networks that use routers. You can use it in conjunction with TCP_NODELAY.
IPTOS_THROUGHPUT	Another option that can influence performance on networks that include routers.
SO_SNDBUF=*value*	Sets the send buffer for outgoing packets. A *value* of 8192, or occasionally even higher, can improve performance on some networks.
SO_RCVBUF=*value*	The receive buffer counterpart of SO_SNDBUF. Adjusting it to 8192 or above sometimes improves performance.

read raw and **write raw**   These global boolean parameters enable Samba to receive and send, respectively, SMB/CIFS packets of up to 64KB. When set to No, Samba is forced to use smaller packets, which degrades performance. You should leave them set to the default Yes, unless a very old client operates unreliably with Samba.

max xmit   This global parameter sets the maximum packet size, in bytes, that Samba will negotiate with a client. The default is 65535, which produces optimal performance on most networks. On rare occasion, a smaller value will deliver better performance, but values below 2048 are likely to cause problems.

nt smb support   This global parameter determines whether Samba uses Windows NT-specific SMB/CIFS commands. In theory, these commands should improve or have no effect on performance, but as of Samba 2.0.7, the opposite is sometimes true. Set this option to No if you experience performance problems with Windows NT or 2000 clients.

change notify timeout One Windows NT-specific SMB/CIFS command is the ChangeNotify command, which a client can issue to have a server respond only when a directory's contents have changed. The change notify timeout parameter lets you set the interval, in seconds, at which Samba checks for such changes. Increasing this value improves performance, but at the cost of less timely notification. The default value is 60.

deadtime This global parameter sets the amount of time, in minutes, that Samba waits before disconnecting an inactive client. Setting this parameter to a small number can free resources and improve performance, but it also introduces minor delays if a client needs to auto-reconnect to a service after being disconnected. The default is 0, which disables the auto-disconnect feature.

keepalive This global parameter sets the number of seconds between keep-alive packets sent to clients to determine if they're still up. This parameter is similar to the socket options = SO_KEEPALIVE parameter. Like the deadtime parameter, keepalive can help free resources on the server if clients regularly come and go from the network. The default value is 0, which disables keep-alive packet use.

oplocks Opportunistic locks (oplocks) are a way for clients to cache network file accesses, thus improving performance by as much as 30 percent. Setting this feature requires coordination on the server, to prevent one client from stepping on another's changes. The default setting for this share-level parameter is therefore Yes, but there are cases in which you may want to disable oplocks. Examples include most database files, and files that are likely to be changed by both Samba clients and in other ways (locally or through a non-Samba file server such as NFS or Netatalk). You can either use oplocks = No to disable oplocks on a share, or veto oplock files to disable oplocks on specific files in a share. Chapter 5 describes these and related options in greater detail.

strict locking This share-level parameter defaults to No, which causes Samba to perform file-locking checks only when asked to by the client. Some buggy clients work better with strict locking = Yes, but accesses will slow down.

blocking locks If a client tries to open a file but fails because of a lock, the client may try *polling* the server to access the file—that is, repeatedly trying to open the file. A *blocking lock* is a way to prevent this performance-robbing practice, by letting the server contact the client if and when the file becomes available. The share-level blocking locks parameter therefore defaults to Yes, which can improve performance in some situations.

strict sync   This share-level parameter, when set to No (the default), causes Samba to ignore clients' disk sync requests. Many Windows programs, including the Windows 98 file browser, issue these requests much more frequently than is necessary, thus severely degrading performance if strict sync = Yes. The downside to setting this option to No is that data may be lost if the server crashes. On most networks and with reliable Linux systems, No is the appropriate choice, but you might want to set it to Yes if data safety is more important than speed.

sync always   If you set strict sync = Yes, you can take the approach one step further by setting sync always = Yes, which causes a sync to disk on *every* disk access, whether the client requested it or not. Using this option *severely* degrades Samba's performance, so you shouldn't use it unless your Samba server is quite unreliable. If that's so, however, you have major problems that you should address through other means, such as upgrading unreliable hardware or tracking down a buggy kernel module.

getwd cache   This global parameter causes Samba to remember the path to the current directory. Setting it to Yes can therefore improve performance slightly, although the default value is No.

read size   If Samba reads data from a disk and then transmits it over the network, there will be a delay between beginning the read and sending the data. Accumulated over several packets, this can cause some reduction in throughput. The global read size parameter can minimize this reduction by causing network transmissions to start before the disk read has completed; instead, the network transmission begins when the specified number of bytes have been read from disk. For instance, at the default value of 16384, if Samba must transmit 64KB of data, it begins that transmission after reading just 16KB from the disk. Values of read size ranging from 1024 to 65536 are possible, and the optimum value depends highly on the speed of your server's disk and the network.

lpq cache time   This global parameter defaults to 10, which causes Samba to cache the results of the print command (set via the print command parameter) for 10 seconds. If your print command takes a long time to execute, you may want to increase this parameter to keep Samba from calling the command multiple times.

shared mem size   This global parameter isn't strictly a performance parameter, but it does affect memory consumption and reliability. By default, Samba requests 1MB of RAM to be shared by all smbd processes. On very large servers, this amount may be inadequate, so you can increase it by using the shared mem size parameter. A value of shared mem size = 2097152 sets the value to 2MB.

Advanced Configurations

PART 3

If you're experiencing Samba performance problems, you can try adjusting any of these parameters that seems likely to be the source of the difficulty. It's best to adjust them one at a time, though, so you can determine which parameters are most important on your network. You might want to pay particular attention to the socket options, nt smb support, oplocks, and read size parameters, since these are the most likely to cause trouble. Particularly in the case of the read size parameter, an optimal setting on one server may not be optimal on another. These performance-tuning options are not the only ones that can influence performance, however; others are designed to add important functionality but can degrade performance in some situations. We'll examine these next.

Convenience Features That Affect Performance

Samba includes some options that add features at the cost of performance. If you want a blazing-fast server, you can change the settings of these options—but you may find that some clients or client applications no longer function well, or at all. Many of these options are discussed elsewhere in this book, but their influence on Samba's performance is the subject here.

log level   Samba supports log levels ranging from 0 (no logging) to 10. Because logging involves writing data to disk, increasing the log level, and hence the number of disk accesses per transaction, reduces performance. Increasing the log level from 0 to 3 is likely to reduce Samba's performance by roughly 5 percent, and higher log levels can have even more dramatic speed consequences. A synonym for this global parameter is debug level.

hide files   This share-level parameter causes Samba to set the hidden bit on files that match a specified parameter. For instance, hide files = Mail/News/*.rpm causes Samba to hide files or directories called Mail or News, as well as files that end in .rpm. This parameter slows down file listings.

veto files   Another share-level parameter, this works much like hide files, but instead of setting the hidden bit, it doesn't let the client see the files at all. Like hide files, veto files slows file listings.

case sensitive   This share-level parameter defaults to No, which causes Samba to match filenames without regard to case. Because Linux uses case-sensitive filenames, however, this option exacts a performance hit when opening files. You might therefore want to try setting case sensitive = Yes, but be aware that doing so may prevent some programs from opening some files.

TIP You can put the `case sensitive = Yes` parameter into a supplementary configuration file and then call it using the `include` parameter with an appropriate variable. For example, call the file `smb.conf.samba` and use `include = smb.conf.%a` to use that file only for Samba clients. Such a configuration allows you to optimize Samba's performance for some clients even when the option is detrimental to others.

wide links This share-level parameter determines whether Samba follows links that lead outside a share's normal area. Consider a share that's rooted at `/home/samba/shared-stuff` and that contains a link to `/etc`. With `wide links = Yes` (the default), the user can use that link to access files in `/etc`. Setting `wide links = No` blocks such access, improving security but perhaps causing some inconvenience. Setting `wide links = No` also degrades performance, because Samba must check each link to see if it's allowable.

follow symlinks Like `wide links`, `follow symlinks` affects Samba's treatment of links. `follow symlinks`, however, allows or blocks *any* symbolic link, not just those leading outside of a share's normal range. This share-level parameter defaults to Yes, and setting it to No degrades performance slightly.

username level and **password level** SMB/CIFS uses case-insensitive usernames and passwords, but Linux uses case-sensitive usernames and passwords. It's therefore sometimes necessary for Samba to adjust usernames and passwords when logging a user onto the server. Both of these parameters set the maximum number of characters that Samba tries to switch to uppercase in doing these adjustments. (In the case of `password level`, Samba first tries the password as it's been given and then converted to all-lowercase. For usernames, Samba tries the username set to all-lowercase and with the first letter capitalized.) For example, if `password level = 1` and the user enters the password GDA11AS, Samba first tries GDA11AS, then gda11as, and then all variants in which one character is uppercase, such as Gda11as, gDa11as, and so on.

These parameters are occasionally required because some clients convert usernames or passwords to all-uppercase or all-lowercase form. Unfortunately, when enabled they can slow down logon attempts. They also reduce security; if they're set high enough, a would-be cracker need not know the case of a username or password. Both `username level` and `password level` default to 0, and I recommend you leave them so unless you find you must change them.

You'll have to decide for yourself whether a feature is worth its cost in performance. You may want to run some experiments to determine what you can gain with certain settings for Samba's parameters. Be sure to perform your tests on real-world shares, or shares that closely resemble real-world shares. Features such as `case sensitive` may have different performance impacts on shares with few files as opposed to many files.

Linux TCP/IP Performance

Unless you use the Procom NetBEUI stack for Linux, Samba relies on Linux's TCP/IP stack for low-level network access. For the most part, Linux sets default TCP/IP parameters that optimize performance, but if you encounter poor network performance generally in Linux, you may want to examine the TCP/IP network stack settings. These settings include:

MTU Size   The *Maximum Transfer Unit (MTU)* size is the number of bytes packaged into an individual data packet that's sent over the network wire. For Ethernet, the MTU size is generally 1,500 bytes, but this may be different on other media. You can determine your MTU size by typing **ifconfig *eth0*** (adjusting *eth0*, if necessary, for your interface). One of the output lines lists the MTU value. To adjust the MTU, issue the `ifconfig` command along with its `mtu` *value* parameter. In the command **ifconfig eth0 mtu 1400**, the MTU on eth0 is reset to 1400. Many routers use an MTU size of 576, so if you're having performance problems that appear to be router-related, setting the MTU size to 576 may improve matters. For optimum performance, the Samba `max xmit` parameter should specify a size that's larger than the MTU size. (The default `max xmit` value is 65535.)

Window Size   The *window size* is the amount of data that one computer can send to another before the sender checks that the data has arrived safely. In Linux, the default window size is 32KB, but some older Ethernet cards don't handle large window sizes well. You can adjust this parameter when you issue the `route` command to link a network interface to a specific network. Normally, this command resembles `route add 192.168.23.0`, but you can add `window` *value* to set the window to the specified *value* in bytes. (On most Linux distributions, the relevant `route` command appears in a network startup script.) You normally use the `window` parameter only on the `route` command for your local network segment, not for the one defining the gateway system or any others. I don't recommend using this option unless **ifconfig eth*n*** reveals a large proportion of dropped or overrun packets.

Duplex Operation   If your network uses Ethernet and a switch or a crossover cable between two computers, you can configure both systems to use *full-duplex* operation, in which two computers can simultaneously transmit and receive data. Ethernet networks using hubs or coaxial cables, on the other hand, *must* use *half-duplex* mode, in which only one computer can transmit data at a time. (In half-duplex mode, a collision occurs if two computers try to transmit simultaneously, and both systems must pause for a random period of time and retransmit.) Full-duplex mode is faster than half-duplex, but only if full-duplex is supported by the hardware. As a general rule, Linux negotiates full-duplex mode when the network, card, and driver all support it. If you believe Linux is *not* setting full-duplex mode when it's possible, you can add the `full_duplex=1` parameter to the `insmod` command that's used to load a driver module, as in **insmod 3c59x.o full_duplex=1**.

WARNING If you try to set full-duplex operation inappropriately, you'll get, at best, absolutely miserable network performance. At worst, networking won't function at all. Before you try setting this option, be sure your computer doesn't rely on any network connections for basic operation (such as NFS-mounted home directories or a remote font server if the system boots straight into X).

Of course, a wide variety of problems can cause poor network performance in Linux, ranging from faulty hardware to misconfigured default routes. If Linux is misconfigured in such a way, Samba will almost certainly perform poorly as well. Before you blame Linux, however, you may want to check the configuration on whatever system you're using to test Linux's performance. If you only use one other system to check Linux's speed, it's possible that the other system is the source of networking problems.

Additional Linux Options

A wide variety of Linux configuration options can influence Samba and general networking performance, aside from the network-specific options. You may want to investigate one or more of the following if you're having problems, or if you want to tune your Linux Samba server to its best level of performance:

Hard Disk Performance   As described earlier, in "Hard Disk Subsystem," Samba is heavily reliant on the hard disk and its host adapter or controller. If these components are not working well, Samba won't perform well, either. You can use the **hdparm -tT /dev/*hda*** command to test the performance of /dev/*hda*. If the **buffered disk reads** output line shows performance that's less than about 75 percent of what the disk manufacturer claims, you may need to adjust the DMA mode or other disk options, many of which are highly dependant on your specific host adapter or disk controller.

Swap Space   Linux, like all modern OSs, can use swap space to stand in for RAM. In some cases, swap space can degrade performance. In others, it can increase performance by giving more RAM to processes that are using it heavily, at the expense of dormant processes. As a general rule of thumb, you should have one-and-a-half to two times your available RAM in swap space, although you might relax this rule if your server is unusually RAM-heavy.

TIP You can temporarily (or permanently) add swap space by creating an empty file (let's call it swapfile), running mkswap on it, and then using **swapon swapfile** to add it to the available swap space.

Filesystem Choice In mid-2000, the most popular native Linux filesystem by far is ext2fs. This filesystem generally produces the best performance under Linux. In some cases, you might be tempted to use another filesystem on a Linux Samba server. For example, if you're converting a system from use under Windows to use under Linux, you might think of leaving a data partition set as FAT, because Linux can read and write FAT partitions. Such a choice is likely to result in degraded performance, however. In the case of FAT, writes are fairly speedy, but read operations are unusually slow. In the future, new filesystems such as ext3fs, Reiserfs, and XFS are likely to become popular on Linux. Chances are these filesystems will perform about as well as ext2fs and should reduce filesystem check time if the system crashes. Some newer non-native filesystems, including Windows NT's NTFS, are now or will be supported, but their performance in Linux is uncertain at best. Research this matter carefully or perform some experiments before relying on such a filesystem.

WARNING Linux's NTFS driver includes read/write support in both the 2.2.*x* and 2.4.*x* Linux kernels, but the write support is officially experimental. I therefore don't recommend writing to NTFS from Linux. If you must dual-boot a server between Linux and Windows NT or 2000, and you wish to share the same files from both OSs, use a FAT partition for the shared files. These cautions don't apply to using Linux as a client to a Windows NT server that runs NTFS; in this case, it's Windows NT that's doing the writing to NTFS.

Disk Partitions A careful layout of partitions on your disks can improve performance. As a general rule, try to gather frequently accessed partitions together, to reduce head seek times. If you have two or more disks, put the frequently accessed partitions on separate disks, to spread the load around and reduce the head movements of reading from different partitions. If you're up for the challenge, you can configure your system for RAID.

Compiler Optimizations You can often improve the performance of Linux programs by recompiling them for your specific architecture—Pentium-level CPUs versus 386-level CPUs, for instance. This is particularly true of the Linux kernel. I therefore recommend you recompile your kernel and specify the correct CPU type, as well as any other optimizations that seem appropriate for your network. Some Linux distributions, such as Mandrake and Stampede, optimize most or all of their packages for Pentium-level CPUs. Most other *x*86 Linux distributions use 386 optimizations. You might see a modest performance boost in Samba if you recompile Samba and specify appropriate compiler switches for your CPU, or use an experimental Pentium-optimized compiler such as PGCC (`http://www.acnatsci.org/ ~gnielsen/pgcc/`). Performance gains from compiling Samba in this way are likely to be quite modest, though, so I recommend doing this only if you're eager to eke out the last bit of speed from your server.

Most Linux distributions use reasonable defaults for matters such as disk performance optimization and filesystem use, but it doesn't hurt to check. Because the optimum DMA settings vary from one EIDE controller to another, it's particularly worth your time to inspect these details if your server uses EIDE disks.

Windows Configuration Options

Just like Linux, Windows includes several configuration options that can influence the performance of Windows clients or servers. In fact, many of these options are the same as some of the Linux and Samba options, but they're accessed in different ways—usually through configuration dialog boxes.

> **WARNING** Various Web sites offer tips on optimizing Windows systems for use with dial-up PPP connections. Many of these optimizations are actually detrimental to use on a local area network.

Windows 9*x* TCP/IP Options

Few options are available for Windows 9*x* network performance-tuning. The most accessible options can be manipulated from the dialog box for your network adapter, which you can locate as follows:

1. Open the Control Panel window.

2. Double-click the Network icon. Windows responds by displaying the Network dialog box.

Advanced Configurations

PART 3

3. Select your network adapter in the Network dialog box and click Properties. Windows displays the dialog box for that adapter.

4. Any advanced tuning options are on the Advanced tab, which is shown in Figure 12.4 for a Linksys EtherFast 10/100 card.

Figure 12.4 The available tuning options vary from one network adapter to another.

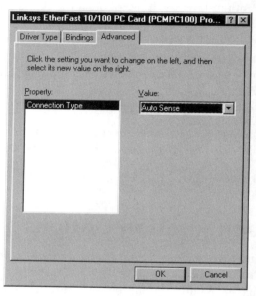

In the case of the Linksys EtherFast 10/100 card in Figure 12.4, only one advanced property can be adjusted: the connection type. By default, this value is set to Auto Sense, but you can change it to 10 or 100Mbps, full- or half-duplex. Other network cards may support other options, which may or may not help or hinder performance.

You can adjust the size of the Windows MTU, if necessary. Windows defaults to an MTU of 1500, which is appropriate for most local networks, but your router may expect a smaller MTU. To adjust it downward, create a file called MTUADJ.REG containing the following text:

```
REGEDIT4


[HKEY_LOCAL_MACHINE\System\CurrentControlSet\Services\Class\⤶
NetTrans\0000]

"MaxMTU"="576"
```

> **WARNING** The line beginning "[HKEY_LOCAL_MACHINE" and ending in "0000]" is split across two lines above, but it must be entered on one line in the file you create.

You may need to adjust two items in this listing:

- The 0000 at the end of the next-to-last line assumes that the computer has just one network interface. If the computer has two or more (including a PPP interface), you may have to adjust this value to 0001 or above. Use the REGEDIT program to examine this path and make the changes manually, if necessary.

- The MaxMTU value may need adjustment to some value other than what I've specified here (576). Consult your router's documentation to see what MTU value it uses.

Once you've created this file, double-click it to make the appropriate changes to your Registry. Reboot to implement the changes.

> **WARNING** The MTUADJ.REG file described here gives Windows instructions to edit its Registry file. This is a potentially very dangerous procedure, so be 100 percent positive that you've typed the information correctly before you double-click on the file you create. If you're in doubt about this procedure, don't perform it.

A change to one other option may improve Windows 9*x* networking performance slightly, and that is to set the receive window size (described earlier, in "Linux TCP/IP Performance") to 32KB. To set this value, start your favorite text editor and enter the following text *exactly* as it appears here:

```
REGEDIT4

[HKEY_LOCAL_MACHINE\System\CurrentControlSet\Services\VxD\MSTCP]
"DefaultRcvWindow"="32767"
```

When you're done, save the file under the name TCPRW32K.REG. You can then double-click on this file to change the default receive window size to 32KB and reboot to implement the change.

As with the MTU edit, making this change to the Registry is potentially quite dangerous, so I recommend you proceed only if you're confident that you're making the change correctly.

Windows NT TCP/IP Options

Windows NT and 2000 support a few TCP/IP tweaks similar to those available to Windows 9x. To access these tweaks, follow these steps in Windows NT 4.0:

1. Log on as the Administrator.
2. Open Control Panel.
3. Double-click the Network icon. Windows displays the Network dialog box.
4. Click the Adapters tab, select your network adapter, and click Properties. Windows displays a dialog box in which you can adjust properties:

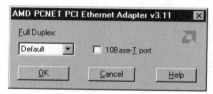

In Windows 2000, the steps for TCP/IP tweaks are somewhat different:

1. Log on as the Administrator.
2. Open Control Panel.
3. Double-click the Network and Dial-up Connections icon. Windows opens the Network and Dial-up Connections window.
4. Right-click the Local Area Connection icon and choose Properties from the pop-up menu. Windows displays the Local Area Connection Properties dialog box.
5. Make sure the correct network adapter is listed in the Connect Using field, and click Configure. Windows displays a dialog box for configuring this device.
6. Click the Advanced tab, which offers properties similar to those in Windows 98's network adapter configuration tab (Figure 12.4). You can adjust any properties that are available for this device.

Chances are you'll only see a handful of choices when you configure advanced network card options for Windows NT or 2000. You may be able to set duplex or speed options, for example. Consult the documentation that came with the TCP/IP adapter for more information.

You can adjust the Windows NT or 2000 MTU size by editing the Registry, much as you can edit the Windows 9*x* Registry to change its MTU size. To do this, create a text file called MTUADJ.REG that contains the following text:

```
REGEDIT4


[HKEY_LOCAL_MACHINE\SYSTEM\CurrentControlSet\Services\↵
Tcpip\Parameters]
"MaxMTU"="576"
```

> **WARNING** The line beginning "[HKEY_LOCAL_MACHINE" and ending in "Parameters]" is split in the above listing, but it must be entered as one line in your text editor.

Once you've created this file (or one like it but with a different MaxMTU value), you can double-click it as Administrator to set the new MTU value.

> **WARNING** As it is for the Windows 9*x* Registry, editing the Windows NT/2000 Registry is potentially dangerous. I recommend you triple-check your typing before proceeding. If you have any doubts, don't attempt this modification.

You can set the TCP/IP receive window size by editing the Windows NT/2000 Registry file, just as you can for Windows 9*x*. To create a file to do this, type the following into a text file called NTTCP32K.REG:

```
REGEDIT4


[HKEY_LOCAL_MACHINE\SYSTEM\CurrentControlSet\Services\↵
Tcpip\Parameters]
"TcpWindowSize"=dword:00007fff
```

> **WARNING** Once again, the line beginning "[HKEY_LOCAL_MACHINE" is split across two lines in the above listing, but be sure you enter it on one line when you create the file.

Double-click this file as the Administrator to set the window size to 32,767 (0x7fff) bytes. Once again, this procedure is potentially risky, so do it only if you're positive you've entered the information correctly.

PART 3

Advanced Configurations

Summary

Samba usually performs reasonably well when first installed, but a little experimentation can often produce modest performance improvements. In rarer circumstances, Samba behaves very poorly in its default configuration. Often such serious problems are the result of misconfigured network hardware, suboptimal drivers, or poor non-networking hardware configurations, such as EIDE hard disks running in slow PIO modes. Performing benchmarks on network and even non-network hardware and configurations will help you track down such problems. In some cases, you can improve Samba's performance by tuning its clients; and adjustments in Windows network card drivers and TCP/IP parameters can help Windows work well with Linux and Samba.

Integrating Samba into a Broader Network

Linux is a very flexible network operating system. You can run Samba on Linux in order to serve files and printers to Windows computers and others that use the SMB/CIFS protocols. You can also run a wide variety of other network servers on Linux—and you can do so on the *same computer* that runs Samba. Indeed, in some networks, this flexibility is vitally important. You might need to make the same files available to both Windows and Macintosh or Unix users; or you might want to use Samba as a means of letting Web designers upload new Web pages to a Web server. Whatever the reason, it's often necessary to make Samba coexist not just with Windows client systems, but with other server programs running on the same server computer.

Samba can sometimes cause problems for other servers that must use the same files, because Samba provides so many options to get around Linux/Windows differences and to provide features that are useful in a Samba/Windows environment. Likewise, other protocols can sometimes create holes in a carefully designed Samba security scheme. This chapter addresses these issues, to help you avoid unpleasant surprises or problems when configuring a server to be more than a Samba server.

The chapter begins with a discussion of three popular file and print server packages: the Unix NFS and lpd programs, and the Netatalk package for Macintosh file sharing. Then we'll look at other protocols that are less tightly bound into the network-share-as-disk model; these include FTP, Web, mail, and remote logon protocols. Whether you want to integrate Samba and one or more of these other protocols to provide benefits to your users, or you simply want a single computer to function as a central, well-endowed server for multiple protocols, it's important to understand how Samba integrates (or doesn't) with these protocols.

Samba Interactions with NFS and *lpd*

It's quite common to see a network with a mixture of client systems—Windows, OS/2, Macintosh, Unix, and so on. Samba can function as a server for many of these systems, but some work better with other protocols. One such OS is Unix, or Unix variants such as Linux and FreeBSD. These usually work best with NFS, designed by Sun for its own versions of Unix and now universally supported on Unix-like OSs including Linux. Similarly, Unix printer-sharing protocols, which are built around the traditional lpd daemon, typically work quite well with Unix and Linux clients. There are some cases, though, when you might want to use Samba for printer sharing even between Unix OSs (as described later in the section "Printer Sharing Trade-Offs").

When you configure a Linux file server with both Samba and NFS, be careful to design the Samba and NFS configurations so that they don't cause problems for each other. As a first approximation, think of NFS client systems as extensions of the Linux system—these computers see the permissions and ownership used by Samba just as a local user would. Samba and NFS file-locking mechanisms are different, too, so you may run into difficulty with file locking if you're not careful. You can also use a Linux Samba server as a bridge between SMB/CIFS and NFS protocols, but this tends to be inefficient.

The following sections describe some NFS configuration options; for more details, consult a book devoted to NFS, such as Erez Zadok's *Linux NFS and AMD Administration* (Sybex, 2001).

Controlling Ownership, Permissions, and Filenames

When you export a Linux directory via NFS, Linux shares the ownership and permission information with the clients. If a file has, say, 0640 permissions on Linux, then the client as well sees the file as having 0640 permissions. There are a few caveats to this equivalence, however:

- Ownership is shared via user ID numbers, not usernames. You must therefore be cautious about matching user IDs on both client and server. If a given user has one user ID on one system but a different user ID on another, you'll have to take precautions to ensure that the user has ownership over the correct files. This is an NFS-specific consideration and so is not covered in this book.

- If you export a filesystem as read-only, write permissions on the individual files are meaningless. Even if the client tries to mount the filesystem for read/write access, writing to the export won't be possible.

- By default, NFS servers *squash* access from root—that is, they treat accesses from the client's root user as if they came from the user nobody on the server. This is a handy security precaution, to limit damage should the client computer be compromised.

- If a file is marked as executable on Linux, it will be seen that way on the client, although most clients support options to disable execution of executable files on servers. Should the client use a different architecture or OS than the server, however, binary executable files probably won't run. Executable scripts may work across platforms, though.

By themselves, these factors have little impact if you share a directory using both Samba and NFS. Keep in mind, however, the effects of the Samba share on ownership and permissions, and the impact of normal Linux-style access on Samba's security precautions. These options can interact in ways that cause problems. For example:

- If you use force user and force group in Samba to create consistent usernames and groups for files created in Samba, you may nonetheless find a wide array of ownership on files created via NFS. You may be able to use NFS's username mapping options to create an effect similar to Samba's force user and force group parameters.

- Because SMB/CIFS has no conception of executable bits, Samba uses these bits in different ways than does NFS. Specifically, Samba may use these bits to store the FAT-style hidden, system, and archive bits. By default, only the last of these is supported, and in its default configuration Samba creates files that appear to be executable to NFS clients because of the presence of the archive bit. You can adjust Samba's options by setting the map archive = No parameter, or you can live with spurious executable bits on the NFS clients.

  Conversely, if an NFS client creates a file with executable bits set, it may appear as a system or hidden file if you use map system = Yes or map hidden = Yes on Samba. You should leave these parameters at their default value of No, or instruct your NFS client users not to create executable files on NFS shares that are also Samba shares.

- NFS clients are free to create files with any permissions they want. An NFS client user can use a command such as **chmod 0600 somefile.txt** to restrict access to somefile.txt. This might cause trouble under Samba, if users other than the one who issues this command can access the share. You might prefer that the file be left with 0640 or some other permissions for just such sharing purposes. Precisely what permission changes might be problematic will depend on your precise configuration and use patterns. Your main defense against trouble is user education.

As a general rule, I recommend sticking to fairly simple configurations when you plan to share a directory by both NFS and Samba. Playing elaborate games with Samba parameters such as `force user` and `create mode` tends to disrupt NFS. If you can design a security scheme of users and groups that works in NFS, chances are that same scheme will work fine in Samba as well, if you allow Samba to give each user default ownership and permissions.

In addition to ownership and permissions, another more subtle difference between Samba and NFS is in the treatment of filenames. By default, Samba handles filenames in a case-retentive way, so that `somefile.txt`, `Somefile.TXT`, `SOMEFILE.TXT`, and other variants all refer to the same file. NFS doesn't operate in this way; to NFS clients, each of these files is unique, and all of them can exist in a single directory. When an NFS client creates two or more files that differ only in case, Samba clients will be able to access only one of these files. A Windows client may see both filenames, but they both point to the same file. You can change Samba's operation to match NFS's by using the `case sensitive = Yes` parameter, but this option may break some applications that rely on the case-insensitivity of filenames.

When dealing with some clients, including DOS, Samba *mangles* (or *munges*) filenames so that clients can access files with long names. Depending on the setting of options such as `short preserve case`, you may see strange results if an NFS client creates a short filename on a Samba share. For example, even a short name such as `short.txt` may be mangled to something else, if its case doesn't match the default case and if `mangle case = Yes`. Chapter 5 describes these options and their consequences in greater detail.

Working with File Contents

Unix and Linux systems use one line feed (LF) character to represent the end of a line of text. Windows systems and most other SMB/CIFS clients use a carriage return/line feed (CR/LF) pair instead. This difference can cause a great deal of frustration when simple text files are being exchanged between systems. Fortunately, many editors can automatically convert from one format to the other, and the Linux `dos2unix` and `unix2dos` programs can convert back and forth between these two formats.

Many applications use proprietary file formats, so files can be shared only if the applications are available on both clients, or at least if both clients have applications that can read the relevant file formats. Cross-platform programs such as WordPerfect and StarOffice are very useful tools in such an environment, as are file formats such as JPEG that are handled the same on all OSs.

Creating Workable File-Locking with NFS

One of the most troublesome aspects of NFS/Samba integration is file locking. As described in Chapter 5, Samba includes a variety of options to implement advanced SMB/CIFS file-locking mechanisms, particularly opportunistic locks (oplocks). These tools allow an SMB/CIFS client to *lock* a file, which permits the client to cache file accesses locally, thus improving performance. Unfortunately, Samba's oplock mechanisms don't integrate well into the Linux filesystem structure. Therefore, a local program—or an NFS client—may make changes to an oplocked file, which can result in file corruption or, at least, inaccurate file contents shown on the client.

For best reliability, you should set oplocks = No to disable oplocks in any share that corresponds to an NFS export. This will, however, exact a hit on performance (perhaps as much as 30 percent) for the SMB/CIFS clients. If this level of performance degradation is unacceptable, you may want to isolate in a specific directory the files that must be accessible via both protocols, and then share that as a separate Samba share. You might also be able to use the veto oplock files parameter to specify disabled oplocks for certain files.

In the future, Linux may support oplocks in its kernel. If and when this happens, the Samba kernel oplocks parameter may be useful. On systems that support it, kernel oplocks = Yes allows Samba to use the kernel's oplock support to implement oplocks, so they're effectively shared between Samba and Linux.

Re-Exporting Shares

On occasion, you may want to use Samba to make one computer's shares available to another computer that doesn't understand the first one's file-sharing protocols. With respect to Samba and NFS, there are two specific possibilities:

- Your network includes an NFS server that's not equipped with Samba, but you need to make the NFS server's shares available to DOS, Windows, or OS/2 clients. You can mount the NFS export on the Linux computer and make that directory available via a Samba share.

- Your network includes a computer capable of exporting shares via SMB/CIFS but not NFS (such as a Windows or OS/2 computer with no NFS server installed), and you want to make that computer's shares available to a Linux or Unix computer on which Samba is not installed. You can use smbmount to mount the SMB/CIFS shares, then export that directory via NFS (by adding it to the /etc/exports file).

> **NOTE** For purposes of this discussion, the Linux "translator" computer is the *intermediary,* and the terms *client* and *server* are used only in reference to the computers to which the intermediary acts as server and client, respectively.

Using a Linux computer as an intermediary is occasionally convenient, but it's almost always more efficient to install appropriate client or server software (such as Samba) on the client or server computer. If the client, intermediary, and server computers are on the same network segment, then using an intermediary arrangement results in twice as much network traffic and a substantial speed penalty. If the intermediary lives on two networks, with the client on one of these and the server on the other, the penalty for configuring matters in this way may be smaller—but there will still be some speed hit (assuming the two subnets are linked in more conventional ways, and Linux can function as a conventional router between such subnets, if necessary).

Unless it's planned carefully, an intermediary system can easily insert an undesirable wedge into the server's security. A flaw in the intermediary's configuration can result in a security breach on the server. This is particularly true because features such as Samba's force user parameter can work around a carefully designed server security structure. At the very least, you should consult with the administrator of the server before configuring Linux as an intermediary system.

When you link a client and a server using an intermediary, you introduce increased possibility for confusion because of "translations" of filenames, permissions, and so on. In the case of NFS and SMB/CIFS, these issues are largely the same as for Samba as a simple server or client; Samba parameters such as force user and case sensitive have the same effect on the server's disk as they do when Samba serves local shares. Likewise, smbmount options to set ownership, permissions, and the like will show up on NFS exports just as they do on the intermediary system.

A Linux computer can be used as an intermediary print server as well as an intermediary file server. To do this, you must normally create an /etc/printcap entry for the server's printer and then export this entry using smb.conf or the /etc/hosts.lpd files (for lpd clients). Because print sharing involves little in the way of file-attribute and name complications, such a setup tends to be fairly simple and easy to configure and maintain. It does, however, create twice the network traffic, just as does file sharing via an intermediary.

When should you consider using an intermediary? The preceding description implies that this configuration should be avoided, and for the most part it should be. Because Samba runs on all major Unix and Unix-like OSs (that is, almost anything for which NFS is the native file-sharing protocol), it's almost always more logical to install Samba on the NFS server and serve the same files directly via both protocols. There are some exceptions, though, as follows:

Buggy Samba or No Samba   You might be running some particularly exotic form of Unix, or even a non-Unix OS for which Samba is either unavailable or unreliable. This might also apply to non-Linux versions of Samba, which use `smbwrapper` rather than `smbmount` for client operations. In such a situation, you might prefer to take a performance hit to gain reliable file sharing.

Linux as Router   If the Linux computer straddles two networks, it may be simpler to configure an intermediary setup than to extend an SMB workgroup or domain across two networks. Such intermediary configurations usually involve using an NBNS server (Chapter 9), paying greater attention to browsing (Chapter 11), and possibly setting up a domain rather than a workgroup (Chapter 10). An intermediary setup may therefore be simpler to configure initially, but installing Samba on the Unix server or client is probably still the better solution.

Minimizing Configuration Effort   If you have a Unix-centric network with one or two Windows servers, installing Samba on all the Unix clients can be a major hassle. Setting up a single Linux box as an intermediary to grant all the Unix computers access to SMB/CIFS resources may take less effort administratively, at least in the short term. You might therefore consider this as a stopgap measure. Nevertheless, work toward installing Samba on the Unix clients as time permits, to reduce network load and avoid problems. Alternatively, you could install NFS or `lpd` servers on the Windows computers.

Convenient Placement of Ghostscript   If you have a Windows print server providing access to non-PostScript printers, you might prefer to have a Linux intermediary run Ghostscript to process PostScript files from Unix clients, rather than running Ghostscript on the Unix clients themselves. This might be appropriate if the Linux intermediary is particularly fast or if you don't want to devote CPU time to PostScript processing on the clients.

WARNING The preceding list of exceptions does *not* include getting around security policies on the server. Although you *can* use one server to broaden the number of computers that have access to another server, such practices are potentially dangerous. If a server has tight security restrictions, chances are they exist for a reason. Working around those security policies invites disaster. Some employers even consider such an action to be grounds for termination.

Advanced Configurations

PART 3

If you decide to share an export from another system, be prepared for poor performance using the double-transfer configuration this entails. I recommend you try to make this linkage in a more direct way.

Printer Sharing Trade-Offs

Sharing a printer through both SMB/CIFS and `lpd` is unlikely to create any difficulty, except for the fact that the two protocols increase security risks on the print server. In a normal configuration, both types of printer sharing require that the printer have an `/etc/printcap` (or equivalent configuration file) entry.

You might want to use Samba for printer sharing even from Unix or Linux clients. As described in Chapter 6, Samba's usual share-access options apply to printer shares. It's therefore possible to control printer access via a username/password pair rather than via the trusted-hosts method used by `lpd`. This configuration may be desirable if you want to protect against IP address spoofing. In practice, however, using Samba as a print server for Unix or Linux systems has a serious drawback: Storing the password in an unencrypted form on the client is a practical necessity. This fact creates a potentially major security hole, should the client system be compromised.

Samba Interactions with Netatalk

Netatalk enables a Linux computer to function as an AppleTalk file server for Macintosh networks. In essence, Netatalk is to Macintoshes as Samba is to Windows computers—but Netatalk is not as polished as Samba. This section does not describe Netatalk configuration. If you need more information, you can check these Netatalk Web sites:

> `http://www.umich.edu/~rsug/netatalk/`
>
> `http://thehamptons.com/anders/netatalk/`

or my book, *Linux: Networking for Your Office* (Sams, 2000).

NOTE   An alternative to running both Samba and Netatalk on a Linux computer is to equip your Macintoshes with DAVE, an SMB/CIFS client and server for Macintosh machines. More information is available at the Web page for DAVE's publisher, Thursby Software Systems, `http://www.thursby.com`. (See Appendix B for a brief description of DAVE.)

Many of the issues described in this section are very similar to those for sharing files using both Samba and NFS, so be sure you read "Samba Interactions with NFS and 1pd" earlier in this chapter.

Controlling Filenames, Ownership, and Permissions

MacOS supports filenames of up to 31 characters in length and no longer. Rather than perform Samba-like filename mangling, Netatalk ignores files with names longer than 31 characters. Therefore, if you expect to exchange files between Windows and Macintosh users, you'll need to educate your Windows users to create files with names that don't exceed 31 characters.

Samba and Netatalk use the same encoding scheme on the server for filenames that consist of only Roman alphabet characters, numbers, and ordinary symbols like - and $; but the two differ in their encoding of more exotic characters, including some common to many European countries. Even U.S. Macintosh users sometimes insert peculiar characters in their filenames, such as bullets or copyright symbols. These filenames may be translated to very strange and ugly things on the Windows side.

The simplest solution is often to avoid such strange filenames, but this isn't a practical solution in some cases. If you run into this problem, you may want to try experimenting with the `client code page` Samba parameter, which lets you specify a *code page* to use for encoding filenames. A code page specifies a standard encoding of symbols for various groups of languages. The default is 850, which works well for English and most other European languages, but Samba also accepts the values listed in Table 13.1.

Table 13.1   Code Pages Usable in Samba

Code Page	Use
437	Latin U.S.
737	Greek
850	Latin 1
852	Latin 2
861	Icelandic
866	Cyrillic
932	Japanese SJIS

Advanced Configurations

PART 3

Table 13.1   Code Pages Usable in Samba *(continued)*

Code Page	Use
936	Simplified Chinese
949	Korean Hangul
950	Traditional Chinese

Netatalk's default handling of ownership and permissions is quite similar to that of Samba: Netatalk assigns ownership of a file to the user who has connected using Netatalk, and the server uses Linux permissions to determine whether a user should be able to read or write a file. Netatalk ignores the Linux executable bits and hides Linux dot files from the Macintosh user. Unfortunately, Netatalk contains very little in the way of permission and ownership adjustment features comparable to Samba's create mask or force user commands, among others. This fact means that you must rely on Linux's underlying security features to create directories that can be shared appropriately between Samba and Netatalk users.

Left to their defaults, both Samba and Netatalk tend to create files with 0644 or 0744 permissions (but the details differ from one Linux distribution to another); in either case, only the creator of the file can modify it. In Samba, if you want all users to be able to modify files, you might use force user to make Samba "convert" all users to one specified user. Because Netatalk lacks this feature, however, when using both servers you must instead rely on a Linux solution, such as setting the ownership of all files to 0664 or higher. You can do this in Samba with the create mask and force create mode parameters, but again, Netatalk lacks these features. Instead, it uses the permissions on the parent directory to determine the permissions on files and directories created inside that directory. So if you want to have Netatalk create 0664 files in a share, ensure that the share's main directory and any existing subdirectories in the share all have 0775 permissions. (The execute bit is a practical necessity on directories to allow access to its contents, but Netatalk strips the execute bit away when creating ordinary files, thereby changing 0775 to 0664.)

> **NOTE**   The default configurations for both Samba and Netatalk do not conflict when sharing files in a user's home directory. You can therefore leave the default parameters alone on home directory shares. You may need to adjust settings for shares that must be accessible to many users, however.

Because Netatalk ignores the execute bit on files and does not create files that contain execute bits, all Netatalk-created files will appear under Samba to *not* have their archive, system, or hidden attributes set. If you enable appropriate Samba options, you can manipulate these bits; Netatalk will not be adversely affected, but neither will it use these bits. A hidden file in Samba will *not* be hidden in Netatalk. (If you hide a file by turning it into a Linux dot file, however, Netatalk will not reveal the file to its clients.)

Netatalk creates a few special directories on all of its shares. Two of these, `.AppleDouble` and `.AppleDesktop`, are dot files and hence are absent from a client's file listing in a normal Samba configuration. A third, `Network Trash Folder`, does appear to Windows clients. To hide this directory, use the `hide files` parameter, as in `hide files = /.AppleD*/Network Trash Folder/`. (You can also use this method to hide `.AppleDouble` and `.AppleDesktop` if you set `hide dot files = No`.) If you prefer, you can use the `veto files` parameter in much the same way. `veto files` doesn't just set the hidden bits on these directories; it makes them completely inaccessible to Windows clients. This can be a useful precaution, particularly for the `.AppleDouble` and `.AppleDesktop` directories, which contain critical Macintosh-specific information as described later in "Coping with Netatalk Resource Forks."

Working with File Contents

Windows computers use CR/LF pairs to signal the ends of lines in text files; Linux and Unix use a lone LF. MacOS, by contrast, uses a single CR. If you mix Windows and Macintosh clients, therefore, you may have difficulties with line termination characters on shared text files. Fortunately, many text editors, particularly on the Macintosh, can cope with either text-file format. Some experimentation should help you find suitable cross-platform text editors.

Netatalk includes a configuration option that you can set in the `AppleVolumes.default` configuration file: `crlf`, which converts Mac-style to Unix-style end-of-line characters for text files. This option occasionally causes problems, however, when it doesn't identify a file type correctly. Furthermore, from a Windows point of view the option doesn't improve matters, because the Mac-style and Unix-style end-of-line characters are equally foreign to Windows programs.

As with file formats shared between Windows clients and Unix or Linux clients, a variety of file formats are common to both Windows and Macintosh. Microsoft's popular Office package, for example, is available on both platforms, so you can readily exchange Microsoft Office documents using a Samba/Netatalk server. Many "generic" document formats, such as JPEG graphics files, are also usable on both platforms.

Creating Workable File-Locking with Netatalk

File-locking issues between Samba and Netatalk are almost identical to those (described earlier) of Samba and NFS. In brief, you can't count on Samba's oplock features to work correctly across these two servers. The safest course of action is to disable Samba's oplocks by including the `oplocks = No` parameter on any Samba share that corresponds to a Netatalk share. If you need protection on only a few files or file types, you can use the `veto oplock files` parameter to stop Samba from granting oplocks on specific files.

Re-Exporting Shares

Netatalk is a file server but does not include a client package. Therefore, although you can use a Linux computer as a link between a Macintosh client and a Windows server, Linux cannot serve as a link in the opposite direction—at least, not when using the AppleTalk and SMB/CIFS protocols.

Most of the issues involved in using Linux as an intermediary system in a Windows/Macintosh link are the same as those in a Windows/Unix link. For instance, both situations involve a reduction in speed and the potential for increased security risks. The best solution when you need to directly link Windows and Macintosh computers is to install DAVE on the Macintosh systems. DAVE works better than the AppleTalk support available for Windows NT and 2000.

In one situation, Linux as an intermediary can be beneficial—when the Linux computer serves as a link between a TCP/IP network on which SMB/CIFS clients and servers reside, and a LocalTalk network on which Macintoshes reside. *LocalTalk* is the name given to Apple's original networking hardware. It's now largely obsolete, but a substantial installed base of LocalTalk hardware still exists. Linux can use a few LocalTalk boards designed for *x*86 computers, so Linux can serve as a bridge between these two networks. Also, LocalTalk-to-Ethernet adapters can link the two networks. A LocalTalk network might not use TCP/IP, so providing access to one network's resources from the other can be a tricky problem, one that Linux running both Samba and Netatalk can help to solve.

Although Netatalk includes no file-sharing client, the package does include a printer-sharing client. The core of this support is the `pap` program, which queues a print job on an AppleTalk printer much as `lpd` queues a print job locally. "Re-Exporting a Remote Printer" in Chapter 6 describes the use of `pap` in an `smb.conf` file to provide access to AppleTalk printers from Windows clients. In brief, you must include an explicit `print command` parameter in `smb.conf`, as in

```
print command = pap -p lw630 %s
```

This prints a file to the printer called `lw630`. It's a very convenient solution if you have a printer that understands AppleTalk network protocols, but not SMB/CIFS or `lpd` protocols.

Coping with Netatalk Resource Forks

MacOS relies heavily on an unusual filesystem feature known as *forks*. Every file has two forks: a *data fork* and a *resource fork*. The data fork contains ordinary file data, such as plain text, spreadsheet data, or image data. The resource fork contains specialized information, including icon images and binary data for executable programs.

Because the resource fork is vital for many Macintosh files, Netatalk stores resource forks in a subdirectory called `.AppleDouble`. Suppose a Macintosh user creates a file called `MacFile` on a Netatalk server. `MacFile` will contain the data fork, and the server will silently create a file called `.AppleDouble/MacFile` that holds the resource fork. Because the `.AppleDouble` directory names begin with dots, they aren't visible to normal Linux file listings and Samba normally hides them. Nonetheless, for added safety, you may want to use Samba's `veto files` parameter to guarantee that Windows users don't mistakenly delete this important directory.

Resource forks are most important for Macintosh program files. Most files that Macintosh and Windows users are likely to want to share either won't have resource forks, or the resource forks will be largely unimportant to the Macintosh programs that use the files. You can change the associated data forks with impunity from Windows. For example, you need not be concerned about users losing resource fork information by editing Microsoft Word files from Windows when those files were created on a Macintosh. Don't assume that the resource fork data are unimportant, however—they are critical for files such as program files and font files. Netatalk also stores file association data in the `.AppleDouble` directory. MacOS uses this information to link data files to the programs that created those files.

Netatalk uses another dot file directory, `.AppleDesktop`, to store information on the locations of icons in the root directory of a share's window. Although it's not as critical as the resource fork data, this information should be protected if you want to present a consistent view of data in shares' root windows.

Using a Samba Server to Serve Additional Protocols

In addition to integrating Samba with other file-sharing servers such as NFS and Netatalk, you can run Samba on a computer that serves other network protocols. On occasion, these servers may interact, usually indirectly through files that they both access.

In such situations, it may be important to ensure that both servers are configured in a way that allows each server appropriate access to files the other creates.

For this discussion, the non-Samba protocols are divided into groups of file serving protocols (those that exist to explicitly send or receive files); protocols that may alter files; and protocols that mostly don't affect files but may interact with Samba in one way or another. Each of these groups is described in turn, followed by a discussion of the merits of running the servers on one computer versus running multiple server computers, each with a different server or set of servers.

Integration with File-Serving Protocols

This discussion makes a somewhat subtle distinction between two types of file-transfer protocols:

File-Sharing Protocols These protocols, of which SMB/CIFS is one example, present the user with an interface similar to that of a local disk. Users can transfer files back and forth between the server and client, of course; in addition, they can open remote files for modification, using software on the client system to directly modify files on the server.

File-Exchange Protocols These protocols resemble file-sharing protocols in some ways, but they're simpler. The file-exchange protocols allow for the transfer of files between client and server (sometimes in only one direction, sometimes in both directions). A user can't open a remote file using an arbitrary application on a client, however; to modify a file, a user must transfer the file in one direction, modify it, and then send it back.

The distinction here is somewhat arbitrary, because the differences between file-sharing and file-exchange protocols are minor on the level of the protocol definition. The differences are more significant in terms of the way client software is written, and therefore the way users use the software.

NOTE Samba's smbclient program handles SMB/CIFS shares in a way that's consistent with the definition of a file-exchange protocol. Most other SMB/CIFS clients, however, including Samba's smbmount, present a file-sharing interface to the protocol.

FTP

The *File Transfer Protocol (FTP)* is one of the Internet's oldest file-exchange protocols. FTP client programs range from simple text-mode utilities to user-friendly GUI tools such as the xmftp program shown in Figure 13.1. No matter how you use FTP, the protocol was designed for transmitting complete files from one system to another. Although it can resume an interrupted transfer, FTP wasn't designed for full random access to the server's files. Some FTP clients try to present a filesystem-like view of FTP servers, but you can't normally access files directly from client applications.

Figure 13.1 GUI FTP programs resemble file managers but don't provide direct application access to FTP servers.

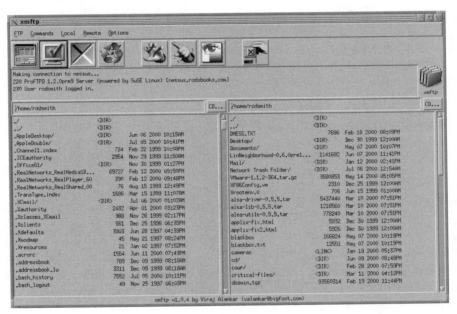

Linux supports several FTP servers. Two of the most popular are the Washington University FTP (WU-FTP at http://www.wu-ftpd.org) and ProFTP (http://www .proftpd.net). Most Linux distributions ship with one or both of these servers. Depending on your distribution and the installation options you selected, the FTP server may or may not be installed by default. Most Linux distributions launch the FTP server through inetd, so you can check to see if it's configured to run by examining the /etc/ inetd.conf file. Look for a line like this:

```
ftp     stream tcp     nowait root    /usr/sbin/tcpd proftpd
```

The server name may be different, of course, depending on the server you use. If this line is commented out by a pound sign (#) at the start of the line, Linux is configured to *not* run the FTP server. Some distributions ship with inetd.conf files that contain two or more FTP lines, one for each possible FTP server or configuration, so don't stop looking if you see one entry that's been disabled; there may be another FTP server entry.

Users may log on to an FTP server using either of two security modes:

Username and Password   The default method of FTP access is to use a normal username and password pair. This method grants the user full access to the server, employing the user's normal permissions. The user can read and write the same files that would be allowed at a shell prompt, and files the user uploads to the server are owned by the user who's logged in.

Anonymous Access   An FTP administrator can configure the server to accept *anonymous* logons, in which the user enters the username anonymous and any string as the password. Typically, anonymous logons provide very restricted access to the server—users normally can't upload files, and can only read files available to a low-security user. Most FTP servers come configured to *not* allow anonymous logons by default, because they're a potential security risk.

The trick to ensuring a happy relationship between Samba and an FTP server is to guarantee that neither server creates files that the other can't access or manipulate, assuming the user *should* have this ability. If you use Samba features such as force user and create mode to configure a share to use a restricted range of file ownership and permissions, you should set up some file access restrictions. Ensure that either FTP access to that share is impossible (say, because the permissions don't let any real users into the share) or that any access that is possible won't disrupt your Samba security scheme. To accomplish this latter, you might provide read-only access to the share, or perhaps set the user mask on the FTP process so that all Samba users can overwrite or remove files created via FTP.

To control the permissions given to FTP-created files, edit the FTP server's configuration files. In WU-FTP, the configuration file is normally called /etc/ftpaccess, and you use the defumask *umaskval* parameter to set this option. For ProFTP, the equivalent can be done by editing the /etc/proftpd.conf file and setting the Umask *umaskval* parameter. In both cases, *umaskval* is the user mask value. Bits set in the *umaskval* are removed from the 0777 (for directories) or 0666 (for files) permissions of any file created by the FTP daemon. If *umaskval* is 027, for example, files will have permissions of 0640 and directories will have permissions of 0750. You may want to configure this value to ensure that files created by FTP users can be read and, if appropriate, deleted by Samba users.

Unfortunately, although Samba allows fine control of security options on a share-by-share basis, FTP servers do not. An FTP user has access to the entire Linux directory tree, assuming the user's permissions allow this level of access. This fact can create security and access-control headaches. Your best defense is often to use Samba's force user parameter and permissions on Samba share directories to block access to FTP users, at least for shares that are accessible to many users. FTP users normally have full access to their home directories, and this access doesn't normally create problems for Samba because both servers create files with similar permissions.

As with integrating Samba with NFS or Netatalk, using Samba and FTP together can pose a problem because of Samba's support for oplocks. If you anticipate the need for overlapping FTP and Samba access to the same files, you should set oplocks = No on the relevant Samba shares, or at least use veto oplock files to block oplocks on files that are likely to be accessed from both servers simultaneously.

If you're running Samba on a system, one question you should ask is whether you *need* FTP access to that same system. Very often, the answer is no. SMB/CIFS is typically a more convenient protocol for Windows clients, so providing FTP access merely adds a potential security problem. In some cases, you may want to provide FTP access for non-Windows users who don't need or have access to other file-sharing protocols, or for off-site users who don't have easy access via SMB/CIFS.

> **TIP** Even an off-site user can often gain access to a server via SMB/CIFS. In Windows, a user can create an entry in the C:\WINDOWS\LMHOSTS file for a remote server. Suppose that the user of tampa.threeroomco.com wants to access seattle.pangaea.edu (IP address 172.29.34.122), on a network across the continent. Adding an entry such as 172.29.34.122 seattle to the C:\WINDOWS\ LMHOSTS file on TAMPA lets TAMPA's user access SEATTLE. Once this is done, TAMPA's user can type something like NET USE L: \\SEATTLE\BIGSHARE to access BIGSHARE on SEATTLE. This assumes that firewalls between the two systems don't block the SMB/CIFS traffic. If the client passes encrypted passwords (as is done by default in Windows 95 OSR2, Windows NT 4.0 SP 3, Windows 98, and Windows 2000), this practice can actually be more secure than FTP, because FTP uses unencrypted passwords.

HTTP

The *HyperText Transfer Protocol (HTTP)* is the protocol used by World Wide Web servers. As such, it's largely a one-way protocol, at least as far as most file transfers are concerned. A user connects to a Web server using a Web browser such as Netscape Navigator or Internet Explorer, requests some files, and the server passes those files back to the browser. Although Web servers can be configured to require usernames and passwords, these servers are normally set up as public servers, available to anybody without authorization.

In Linux, the program most often used as a Web server is Apache. This server comes with all major Linux distributions, and it's installed by default on many of them. Apache can be run through inetd, and hence may have an entry in /etc/inetd.conf similar to the following:

```
http            stream tcp    nowait nobody /usr/sbin/tcpd httpd
```

If a line like this one is commented out of your /etc/inetd.conf file, it does *not* mean that Apache is not running on your system. Apache is often run as a stand-alone server separate from inetd, much like Samba. To check for this configuration, type **ps ax | grep httpd**. If your system responds with one or more lines listing httpd processes, Apache is running on your system. If not, and if there's no /etc/inetd entry, chances are Apache isn't running. You can also try accessing the system from another one using a Web browser to find out if Apache is running.

Most Apache installations by default serve files from subdirectories in the /home/httpd directory. /home/httpd/html is frequently the site's home directory, accessed by typing **http://*servername*** at another computer's Web browser. You can adjust these locations using Apache's configuration files, of course, and you can create links to other locations that may contain Web server files.

In a normal configuration, Apache doesn't provide the sort of complete access to a server that FTP allows, although Apache can be misconfigured to do so. Getting Samba and Apache to coexist peacefully is therefore a matter of ensuring that their directories don't overlap or, if they do, making sure that Samba creates files that Apache can serve.

One possible use for running both Apache and Samba on the same computer is to allow Windows users to update files on the Web server. To do this, create a Samba share similar to the following:

```
[apache]
        path = /home/httpd
        writeable = Yes
        force user = apache
        valid users = scott, emily
        create mask = 0644
        directory mask = 0755
        hide dot files = No
```

Here are some key points to consider about this share:

- The share's root directory is /home/httpd. The main HTML files go in the html directory of that share, and users can modify other Web server files, such as Perl scripts, from other subdirectories. If you want to grant access to modify *only* HTML files, you could use path = /home/httpd/html instead. You might also adjust the root directory if you use something other than the default Apache configuration.

- The share uses force user = apache to set all users connecting to the share to the user apache, which you must create on the server. You must then ensure that this user has full read/write permissions in the /home/httpd directory tree. A default Apache installation on most systems allows only root write access to this tree.

- As a security measure, the valid users = scott, emily parameter prevents users except for scott and emily from connecting to the share. You can use other access-restriction parameters as well; see Chapter 14, "Samba Security Considerations."

- The create mask and directory mask parameters configure the share so that all files can be read by all users. This is necessary because Apache normally spawns sub-processes as nobody, a very low-security user, in order to reduce the risk of serious compromise in case of a security bug in the program. As a result, all users must be able to read files in an Apache directory.

If you use Samba as a tool for transferring Web pages to a Web server, make sure users who transfer Web pages by some other means (such as FTP or Netatalk) don't create files that the Samba users can't modify or delete. You may therefore need to coordinate your configuration across multiple servers.

WARNING   Apache, like Linux, treats filenames in a case-sensitive manner. Most Samba clients, though, are case-retentive or case-insensitive. A user might therefore create and test Web pages that reference each other using case-insensitive filenames. For instance, the main page (index.html) might call a subpage (somepage.html). But if that file is stored on the Apache server as SomePage.html, Apache won't find it when a client tries to access it. It's important for anybody creating a Web page on a Windows system to understand this, and to test all links on a page *after* uploading the page to the Web server.

Protocols That May Affect Shared Files

All network protocols are designed to transfer data from one system to another, but not all protocols transfer files *per se*. Nonetheless, some of these protocols can affect files on a Samba share, so you should understand the implications of running these protocols on a Samba server.

Mail Protocols

Many Linux systems run e-mail servers. There are two types of e-mail protocols: *push* and *pull*. Push protocols allow a sender to initiate a network connection in order to send mail, whereas pull protocols require that the recipient initiate the connection in order to receive mail. Most servers on the Internet use a push protocol known as the *Simple Mail Transfer Protocol (SMTP)*, which is implemented in servers such as sendmail (`http://www.sendmail.org`) and Postfix (`http://www.postfix.org`). Typically, one SMTP server talks to another, but e-mail readers such as `pine` and Netscape Messenger can also initiate SMTP connections to send mail.

Pull protocols include the *Post Office Protocol (POP)* and the *Internet Message Access Protocol (IMAP)*, both of which are implemented in a variety of servers, such as Qpopper (`http://www.eudora.com/qpopper/`) and `imap`. These servers respond to pull mail requests but do not place such requests themselves. End-user mail clients such as `pine` and Netscape Messenger can initiate pull mail connections to retrieve e-mail. The Linux fetch-mail program (`http://www.tuxedo.org/~esr/fetchmail/`) can initiate pull mail sessions and inject the retrieved mail into the Linux computer's local mail queue.

No matter how mail reaches its destination, it's ultimately stored in files, and these files are potentially accessible to Samba. Most Linux systems come with sendmail by default. Sendmail stores incoming mail in a *mail queue*—a file that stores one or more mail messages. The mail queues normally go in the `/var/spool/mail` directory and are named after their owners. Most other push mail servers store mail in a similar manner. These files are unlikely to be affected by Samba, because you're not likely to want to export the mail queue directory (though it's possible to do so). In most cases, it makes more sense to set up a POP or IMAP server on the Linux computer. These servers can read the mail queues and serve them to client computers using pull mail protocols.

A few push mail servers, including qmail (`http://www.qmail.org`), store their mail queues in users' home directories. The same is true of most end-user programs that can initiate pull mail sessions and of programs that retrieve mail from the local mail queue. Once you read a message on a Linux system, it can remain in the mail queue, be deleted, or be moved to a *mail folder,* which is a file in your home directory, typically in a directory called `Mail`, `mail`, or `mbox`.

If your users see unexpected files or directories on their Samba shares, they may try to delete these files. It's therefore possible that your users might mistakenly delete their mail folders. You can protect against this possibility by using the Samba `hide files` or `veto files` parameters, to set the hidden bit or make unavailable mail files and folders. Include these parameters in the server's [homes] share, or any other share through which users can access their home directories. For instance, veto files = \Mail\mbox\ makes the Mail folder and mbox file in a user's home directory disappear from Samba's view.

On the other hand, you may want to provide shared access to mail files. If a user regularly uses both Linux and Windows for mail access, and if the tools on both platforms use identical mailbox formats, you may be able to configure the systems so that both systems access the same files. This is easiest to do if the user has the same program on both platforms. Netscape Messenger can be used in this way. The trick in the case of Netscape is to point both Linux and Windows versions of the program at the same mailbox files. In Linux, these files by default go in a subdirectory of the ~/.netscape directory. In Windows, you can specify where Netscape stores this information by using the User Profile Manager utility, which is installed with Netscape. When you create a user profile, this utility gives you the chance to designate the location where Netscape stores its profile information, as shown in Figure 13.2. Specify the user's home share .netscape directory, and both versions of Netscape will use it.

Figure 13.2   A user's profile can specify that different versions of Netscape will use the same directory.

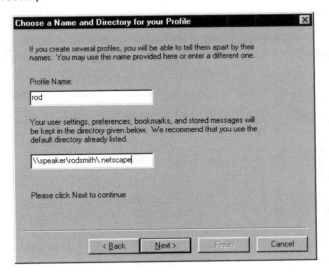

TIP Netscape for Windows stores bookmarks in a file called bookmark.htm, whereas Netscape for Linux uses the filename bookmarks.html. You can use a link from one to the other to share bookmarks between both versions of Netscape.

It's often easier to use an IMAP server to share e-mail messages between OSs. IMAP includes methods that are designed to keep e-mail messages on the e-mail server, so two or more clients can access the same messages more or less seamlessly. This is usually a safer solution than attempting to share e-mail files via Samba.

Logon Protocols

Logon protocols allow you to access one computer from another computer on the network. You can then run programs from the remote computer as if you were sitting at its console. The two most common logon protocols in use today are Telnet and Secure Shell (SSH). Telnet clients are extremely common; they come with most major OSs, including Windows and Linux. SSH clients are somewhat less prevalent but are still readily available, often as add-on modules to Telnet packages such as Zap-O-Com (http://www.emtec.com/zoc/).

On the server side, all major Linux distributions ship with a Telnet server. This program is normally launched through inetd. Check your /etc/inetd.conf file for a line resembling the following:

```
telnet  stream  tcp     nowait  root    /usr/sbin/tcpd in.telnetd
```

If this line is commented out, you can uncomment it and restart inetd to enable Telnet logons to your system.

SSH doesn't ship with most Linux distributions in 2000 for legal reasons; some of the algorithms used in the program have been patented in the United States until September of 2000. Some countries also restrict the use or export of cryptographic software, and SSH qualifies for these restrictions. Assuming the software is legal in your country, you can obtain both client and server packages for Linux at http://www.openssh.com/. SSH encrypts passwords and all data it sends, so it's much safer to use than Telnet, which sends all data, including passwords, in an unencrypted form.

Telnet and SSH are both text-based protocols, but it's also possible to use X programs remotely. X is inherently a networking GUI environment, so if appropriate software exists on both sides, you can launch X programs after doing a Telnet or SSH logon. You may also be able to use strictly X-based logon protocols.

No matter how you log on remotely, such a logon opens a figurative can of worms as far as Samba goes. A user who has full logon privileges can issue commands such as chown and chmod to change the ownership or permissions on files. Depending on the security of the system as a whole, the user may be able to create files in odd locations. These Abilities can wreak havoc with a carefully designed Samba security system. If you use Samba's force user and valid users parameters to set permissions on files, an ordinary user may be able to use a remote logon to circumvent these security controls, depending on the users and permissions involved. For this reason, if you use force user, I also recommend you use force create mode = 0600 and set the share's directory permissions to 0700, to prevent most users from accessing the share from a remote logon.

If the computer is intended to be used only as a Samba server, I recommend you either completely disable remote logon protocols, or set all but a handful of users' shells to something useless such as /dev/null, to prevent them from doing remote logons and causing problems. At the very least, you should consider what actions an ordinary user can take using a shell account, and what consequences these actions might have on the shares you create. Will Samba share users be able to read, write, and delete files an ordinary user creates? Will the shell user be able to read, write, and delete files created by Samba users? Any of these possibilities could be desirable or undesirable, depending on your needs and policies.

Additional Protocols

Most additional servers have little or no impact on Samba. A few servers, however, don't normally transfer or create files but can interact with Samba in one way or another. In some cases, these servers need not run on the Samba server computer itself to interact with it, although they *can* do so. These servers include DNS, DHCP, and time servers.

> **NOTE** Most servers use configuration files. If Samba exports these files, it may be possible to damage a server's configuration by editing a configuration file from a Samba client. There's seldom a reason to export the relevant directories, however. (Most server configuration files reside in the /etc directory.)

DNS Servers

As described in Chapter 9, Samba can be configured to use the Domain Name System (DNS) to resolve NetBIOS names. In fact, the default configuration is to use DNS *before* the NetBIOS Name Service (NBNS) or broadcast name resolution. If your network's machine names are registered with a DNS server apart from your Samba server, you don't really need to be concerned with this issue, except when you want to optimize the name resolve order parameter, as described in Chapter 9.

In some cases you might need to configure your own DNS server, possibly on a Samba server. These situations usually involve small private networks that either are not connected to the Internet as a whole, or reside behind a very tight firewall or IP masquerading router so outside computers can't see the bulk of the computers on the network. In these networks, an outside DNS server has no reason to list the computers.

Configuring a DNS server is well beyond the scope of this book, but you can run both DNS and Samba servers on one computer, if necessary. You can consult a DNS book such as Craig Hunt's *Linux DNS Server Administration* (Sybex, 2000) for more information. Whether or not the DNS server runs on the Samba system, you can use the `wins hook` Samba parameter to perform actions whenever a Samba NBNS server updates its records. If you pass to this parameter the `dns_update` script that comes with Samba's source code and some binary distributions, you can have Samba update your network's DNS server whenever the NBNS server registers a machine starting up or shutting down on the network. (You must edit the `dns_update` script to reflect your domain name and set it to be executable. Read the `README` file that comes with the script for more information.)

DHCP Servers

You can use the Dynamic Host Configuration Protocol (DHCP) to configure basic TCP/IP options on both Linux and Windows clients. DHCP supports passing basic TCP/IP information to clients, but it also supports sending a few pieces of SMB/CIFS information, such as the network's NBNS server and NetBIOS node type. (Chapter 9 covers these topics.) The standard set of Samba documentation also includes a file called `DHCP-Server-Configuration.txt`, which covers DHCP server setup more generally. As with DNS configuration, this topic is quite broad and well beyond the scope of this book. Consult a DHCP book, such as Droms and Lemon's *The DHCP Handbook* (Macmillan, 1999), for more information.

Samba doesn't use the SMB/CIFS-specific information from a DHCP server, nor are any Linux DHCP servers designed to take node type or NBNS server location from Samba running on the same system. Therefore, you must configure this information independently in Samba (for the local server) and in DHCP (for your Windows systems). Of course, if your network doesn't use DHCP, all of this is moot; you enter the relevant information manually on each computer.

Time Servers

Broadly speaking, a *time server* implements a protocol for transmitting the current time over a network. The most widely used Internet time-server protocol is the *Network Time Protocol (NTP)*. Several computers around the world use atomic clocks and NTP servers to provide other systems with access to a veridical time source. The computers that talk directly to atomic clocks are known as *stratum 1* time servers. Computers that synchronize themselves to the stratum 1 time servers are known as *stratum 2* time servers if they allow others to synchronize to them, and so on. Each stratum's time is slightly less accurate than the one above it, but the error is usually small—generally under a second for several stratas' depth.

The NTP Web site is http://www.eecis.udel.edu/~ntp/, where you can obtain further information and time server packages for a variety of OSs. Most Linux distributions ship with a time server called xntpd. When properly configured, xntpd synchronizes the Linux server's clock with a time server on the Internet at large and allows other computers to synchronize their clocks with the Linux computer's clock. This package therefore functions as both a client and a server.

> **WARNING** The NTP Web site includes a list of publicly accessible time servers. To avoid overloading the stratum 1 servers, *do not* synchronize directly to one of them unless your time server in turn serves a large number of additional servers, or if you have some extraordinary reason for having an accurate system clock (as in scientific research that requires knowing the exact time). Many stratum 2 and stratum 3 servers accept anonymous clients, so you can synchronize from one of them and still have a very accurate time set on your system.

> **TIP** Many large organizations such as universities, corporations, and even ISPs run time servers internally. These servers may not appear on the list maintained on the NTP Web site, but using such a server may result in time readings more accurate than those obtained from outside servers because of reduced network latencies. Check to see if your organization or ISP runs a time server you can use, before linking to an outside time server.

It's often helpful to have all your SMB/CIFS clients and servers synchronized. One way to do this is to run an NTP client package on each Windows computer, as well as on every Samba system. You can set up a Samba server with xntpd and then point all your other systems to this server to set accurate times on all. A simpler option for the Windows systems is to use the time protocol that's built into SMB/CIFS. Add the line time server = Yes to the global section of a Samba server's smb.conf file, and Samba will advertise itself as an SMB/CIFS time server and will provide those services.

You can set the time on a Windows client by issuing the command **NET TIME \\\\SERVER /SET /YES**. This command sets the client's clock to the time maintained by *SERVER* and doesn't require that the client be running NTP software. You can create a batch file that includes this command and place it in the Windows StartUp folder to have it run when the system starts. Alternatively, if you use a domain configuration, you can include the command in a network logon script. *Do not* use the command in the Windows 9*x* AUTOEXEC.BAT file, however. Windows's networking features are inactive when AUTOEXEC .BAT executes, so trying to use SMB/CIFS time services from AUTOEXEC.BAT won't do any good.

Once you've set a Windows system's clock, that clock will begin to drift. Because most Windows 9*x* systems are rebooted frequently, this isn't a major problem. If you have Windows NT or 2000 servers that remain up for long periods, however, you may want to install an NTP package on these servers. (NTP programs typically check the time periodically and record information on a system clock's drift, to allow for automatic correction even if the time server becomes inaccessible.)

Although Samba supports operating as an SMB/CIFS time *server,* it doesn't support functioning as an SMB/CIFS time *client.* Therefore, if you want to set a Samba server's time by an outside clock, you must use xntpd or some more exotic solution.

Multiple Dedicated Servers vs. Single-Server Networks

It's often tempting to run a large number of servers on a single computer. Certainly Linux is capable of running dozens of servers at once. As this chapter describes, however, running too many servers on a single computer is often problematic because these servers may treat files differently and end up in conflict. There are also security and performance implications of running multiple servers on a single computer.

Certainly if you need to serve the same files to a diverse assortment of computers, running multiple file-sharing servers on a single system can be convenient and even necessary. When you do so, you should be careful when you design your permissions system, to prevent problems in which files created via one server can't be read through another.

If a computer has enough network bandwidth and processing power left over after running Samba and any other file-sharing servers you want to run, you may want to feed the computer some other task, such as handling a small local DNS or DHCP server. On a small network, such duties can help save you from having to buy and maintain additional computers. On a large network, however, you might do well to relegate additional tasks to other computers, for two principal reasons:

Performance   You want to get the best possible performance out of a large network's file servers. Running unnecessary services on an expensive server will degrade that server's performance. You can probably locate a small computer that can run these secondary services quite handily, without cutting into your file server's finely tuned performance and limited network bandwidth.

Security Bugs are being found all the time in a wide variety of servers. Every server you run on a system is one more chance for a cracker to break into the sensitive files on that system. Chances are that the files on a Samba server don't need to be accessible to the outside world, so the best location for a Samba server in a network topology is protected behind a firewall. Many network services, including mail servers, Web servers, and often DNS servers, must run on publicly accessible computers, thus exposing the server to the Internet as a whole. Even if these servers are only needed on an internal network, it's possible that a disgruntled employee might abuse the system and break in through such a server.

Of course, sometimes *Samba* is the secondary server. You might install Samba on a Web server in order to allow internal users to upload Web pages to the server. Even here, however, the security issue applies somewhat—an external cracker might be able to exploit a bug or configuration error in Samba to break into the Web server computer. On the other hand, you need *some* mechanism to get Web pages onto a Web server, and Samba is certainly more convenient than hand-coding every Web page at the console of the Web server itself!

On the whole, if a computer is designed primarily as a Samba server, you're probably best off running as few other services on that computer as possible. Certainly shell accounts and remote logon access can be a real headache in such a situation, although possibly a necessary one. If the computer functions primarily as some other type of server, you shouldn't run Samba on it unless you need access to that system's files through an independent protocol (as may be true of a Web server).

Summary

Many networks use a wide variety of OSs, which in turn use a wide array of file-sharing protocols. Linux can be an excellent way to integrate these diverse networks because it supports so many file-sharing protocols. Samba is part of this diversity, but you should be aware of how Samba interacts with other servers before you try to configure such a system. File ownership and permissions are particularly likely to produce difficulties, especially when you're configuring shares that must be both readable and writeable by all users. File locking is another potential stumbling block.

Outside of file sharing, Samba may interact with other servers in a variety of ways. File server protocols such as FTP and HTTP impose file-ownership and permissions challenges similar to those of file-sharing protocols. Samba sometimes interacts with more diverse protocols such as DNS, DHCP, and time server protocols. In most of these cases, you can coordinate the protocols in one way or another to ease Samba or Windows configuration and improve the overall functioning of your network. Although running multiple protocols on a single server can be convenient at times, doing so poses security risks and may degrade performance. It's generally best to run Samba separately from protocols that don't need access to the same data.

Part 4

Maintaining a Healthy System

Featuring:

- Encrypted and Cleartext Passwords
- File Ownership and Permissions
- Samba and SSL
- Additional Tools to Improve Security
- Synchronizing Passwords
- Controlling Non-Samba Access to Linux
- Backup Options
- Local Backup of a Samba Server
- Remote Backup of a Samba Server
- Using Samba to Back Up Clients
- Domain Control Problems
- Browsing Problems
- Share Access Problems
- File Access Problems

14

Samba Security Considerations

Samba is an extremely powerful server and can therefore be an extremely useful network tool. Unfortunately, Samba's power also makes it a potentially dangerous tool, particularly if an unwanted outsider (or even an unauthorized *insider*) gains access to the server. A miscreant who breaks into a computer through a Samba logon may be able to do anywhere from no damage to substantial damage, depending upon Samba's configuration and the configuration of other servers on the computer. This chapter describes Samba's security features and presents information to help you design a Samba security system that can help keep out those who should remain out.

We begin with an overview of Samba's first lines of defense: by-system access control, passwords, and password encryption. The chapter then proceeds to describe Samba's interactions with Linux's file security features—ownership and permissions. In particularly high security environments, you may want to use the *Secure Sockets Layer (SSL)* to encrypt all the data passing between the Samba server and its clients, so we'll discuss this option. Finally, the chapter covers an assortment of Samba characteristics and methods you can use to help secure Samba by using other programs and network features.

Controlling Initial Access to Samba

Samba provides a wide range of access control options. You can configure a Samba server with extremely lax security, so that anybody can access the server without even sending a password; or you can configure Samba to be very fussy about the systems and individuals it allows to connect. There are two main types of access control: restrictions based on the client computer, and those based on usernames and passwords sent by the calling system. Microsoft Windows employs the latter method, and it's the method that's been referred to most frequently in earlier chapters of this book. The by-system access methods can be extremely powerful and useful, however, and if you want to run a secure server, it's generally a good idea to set up by-system access controls in addition to password-based access controls.

No matter what security methods you opt for, they'll have implications and uses that are both more and less appropriate for particular situations. It's important that you understand these access restrictions and how they interact, so that you can design an appropriate security system for your network.

Binding Samba to Specific Network Interfaces

Some servers host more than one network interface—one that links to a network from which Samba must be accessible, and another that doesn't. This might be the case if your Samba server runs on a network of Windows computers as well as a network of Unix or Macintosh systems. You can run appropriate servers for both networks, serving the same files to a wide variety of computers. In such situations, it's ideal to bind servers only to the interfaces that require them. Fortunately, Samba includes two global parameters to allow just such a configuration:

interfaces   This parameter allows you to specify interfaces to which Samba will bind itself. Remember that it's important to add the local host address (127.0.0.1) to this line, if you use it. Failure to do so may cause SWAT and smbpasswd to work improperly, because they use this interface internally. You can list interfaces in any of several formats:

- An interface name, such as eth0. You can also use wildcards, as in eth*, to bind to all Ethernet interfaces.

- The IP address by which the server is known on a network, as in 192.168.56.9. Samba then locates the interface associated with that address.

- The network address with netmask, as in 192.168.56.0/24 or 192.168.56.0/ 255.255.255.0.

bind interfaces only   By itself, the interfaces parameter has little effect. You must also set bind interfaces only = Yes to limit access to the server. This parameter has a slightly different effect on the nmbd name server daemon than on the smbd file server daemon. To be precise, nmbd uses the interface information to reject accesses from clients based on their claimed IP addresses, whereas smbd rejects accesses based on the network interface. This fact means that nmbd may be susceptible to IP spoofing attacks even when bind interfaces only = Yes is in use; smbd, on the other hand, is only vulnerable to such attacks if the real and spoofed addresses both arrive over the same physical interface.

If you want to provide Samba services to only one physical interface, using the interfaces and bind interfaces only parameters is a very good idea. When Samba isn't listening to packets coming from a less-trusted network, no amount of password theft or similar actions will gain an intruder access to your system.

There are other ways to erect similar barriers, using external utilities such as ipchains and xinetd. As a general rule, I recommend using several layers of defense; if one fails, another may succeed in keeping intruders out. A few external tools that can help secure Samba are mentioned later in this chapter, in "Samba in the Broader Security World."

Restricting Access by Computer

Whenever a client connects to a Samba server, the client must provide a way for the server to return information, such as files to be read. When using TCP/IP networking, as is normally the case with Samba, this return information comes in the form of an IP address. This fact provides an opportunity for restricting access to the server: The server can be programmed to ignore access attempts from unauthorized IP addresses.

Access restrictions based on IP addresses can take one of two forms: absolute restrictions, which replace the more traditional SMB/CIFS usernames and passwords; or initial screens, which block access from unauthorized sources but that leave the username/password requirements intact. When you configure Samba to use absolute restrictions, the system operates much like an NFS server; Samba effectively passes all responsibility for authentication to the client. An initial screen configuration is usually more secure, because any would-be client must pass multiple tests before gaining access.

Samba options for per-computer accesses include the following:

allow trusted domains This global parameter works only with Server or Domain security (described shortly, in "Authenticating Users by Username and Password"). When set to Yes (the default), Samba accepts logons from clients in all the domains that are trusted by the domain controller. When set to No, Samba accepts logons only from computers belonging to its own domain.

hosts equiv If you want Samba to trust certain computers or users without asking for passwords, you can list the names of those computers and users in a file, and pass the name of the file with the global `hosts equiv` parameter. The file format used is the same as in the /etc/hosts.equiv file, if it's present on your computer. Specifically, each line of the file contains an optional plus sign (+) to allow access, or a minus sign (-) to deny access, followed by a hostname and optional username. (The username is ineffective with most Samba clients.) Activating this option can create a major gap in security.

use rhosts If you set `use rhosts = Yes`, individual users can create files called .rhosts in their home directories, and Samba allows connections from any computer listed in these files without further authentication. These .rhosts files are the same as those used for `rlogin` and similar protocols, and they take the same form as the file used by `hosts equiv`. Just like `rlogin` and the `hosts equiv` parameter, the global `use rhosts` is potentially very dangerous, so it defaults to `No`.

NOTE The `hosts equiv` parameter can point to a file other than /etc/hosts .equiv, so you don't need to activate host equivalency in other utilities that use this file, such as `rlogin` and rsh. The `use rhosts` parameter, by contrast, uses the ~/.rhosts file and no other. Therefore, any utility that looks for this file is affected if you set `use rhosts = Yes` and your users create ~/.rhosts files for Samba use only.

---

hosts allow This parameter can be used either globally or on individual shares. You can specify one or more computers or networks with this parameter. Samba allows access from computers listed on the `hosts allow` line, but disallows access from all others. The default is to allow access to all computers. This parameter does *not* bypass Samba's normal password authentication features. Even if you list computers, 127.0.0.1 (the local computer) is given access, unless explicitly denied via the `hosts deny` parameter. A synonym for this parameter is `allow hosts`.

hosts deny This parameter is the opposite of `hosts allow`—it specifies a "blacklist" of computers that aren't allowed access to the server. The default value is a null string—no computers are denied access to the server. A synonym for this parameter is `deny hosts`.

The `hosts allow` and `hosts deny` parameters can both take fairly complex lists of hosts. You can specify individual computers, networks, and exceptions. You can also use either IP addresses or DNS hostnames. The rules Samba allows are very similar to those used by the /etc/hosts.allow and /etc/hosts.deny configuration files of TCP Wrappers. Specifically, you can designate the following:

- An individual computer by IP address, as in `hosts deny = 192.168.66.6`.

- An individual computer by its DNS name, as in hosts allow = dreyfus.panther .edu. You can omit the network name if the Samba server is in the same network.

- A network of computers by IP address, by listing only the numbers for the network address, followed by a period; hosts allow = 192.168.65. is an example of this usage.

- A network of computers by IP address, by using an IP address/netmask pair, as in hosts allow = 192.168.65.0/255.255.255.0.

- A network of computers by its DNS name, preceded by a period, as in hosts deny = .panther.edu. This example matches dreyfus.panther.edu, clouseau.panther.edu, olga.diamond.panther.edu, and so on.

- A network of computers by its NIS name, preceded by an ampersand, as in hosts deny = @panther. For this option to work, your computer must have access to an NIS server.

- Any combination of options, separated by spaces. For instance, hosts allow = clouseau.panther.edu 192.168.34. allows access to all computers on the 192.168.34.0/24 network and the computer clouseau.panther.edu.

- An exception, which can be any pattern preceded by the keyword EXCEPT. In hosts deny = 10.34. EXCEPT .diamond.panther.edu, access is denied to all computers in the 10.34.0.0/16 network, except for computers in the diamond.panther.edu subdomain.

TIP As a general rule, I recommend you set hosts allow to a value that grants access only to computers in your network. This greatly reduces the risk of your Samba server's being accessed and damaged by someone outside your environment.

You can use hosts allow and hosts deny together, or in conjunction with other security-related parameters. If a computer is listed on both the hosts allow and hosts deny lists, hosts allow takes precedence. Therefore, if you want to grant access to all but a few computers on a network, use the EXCEPT clause to hosts allow to block the exception computers; do *not* rely on hosts deny to override hosts allow!

Authenticating Users by Username and Password

The usual method of authentication for Samba is to accept a username and password from the client, and to authenticate the user based on this information. Samba includes several parameters that influence the way it goes about this task. It's important that you understand these parameters, so that you can design an authentication system that's appropriate for your network.

NOTE One set of user authentication features—the use or nonuse of encrypted passwords—is of critical practical importance. Details about this essential feature are provided later in this chapter, in "Encrypted versus Cleartext Passwords."

The Security Model

The security global parameter determines the *security model* used by the server. There are two basic security models: *share* and *user*. In share-level security, Samba attempts to protect each share independently of the others, and Samba doesn't explicitly require a username before it allows a connection. In user-level security, Samba uses a more traditional username/password pair to grant users entry to all shares. Samba supports three variants of user-level security: one for local authentication, and two that defer to a domain controller for authentication. Altogether, then, the security parameter has four possible values: Share, User, Server, and Domain.

NOTE Samba's security model does *not* affect SWAT. To use SWAT, you must enter a valid Linux username and password, and SWAT authentication is never passed on to a domain controller.

Share-Level Security When security = Share, Samba attempts to validate users much as a Windows 9*x* computer does. By default, Windows 9*x* associates a password with each share, and allows a client access to those shares if the client sends the correct password. Windows 9*x* does not, by default, use usernames, and each share can have a different password. Adapting this security model to Samba is tricky, because in Linux every action by a server program such as Samba must be associated with a user. It's therefore not possible to create a password that's directly linked to a share. Rather, Samba tries to associate the password against several different usernames. It works like this:

1. If the share specifies guest only = Yes, then Samba tries to match the password against the username specified by the guest account parameter. If this test fails, then Samba rejects the authentication request.

2. If the client sent a username along with the password, then Samba tries to authenticate the password against that username.

3. If the client has successfully logged on to another share, then Samba tries authenticating the current password against the username that worked on the previous share.

4. Samba tries using the share name as a username. For example, if the share is [bigdrive], then Samba tries authenticating against the user bigdrive.

5. Samba tries the client's NetBIOS name as the username.

6. If a share specifies an explicit username parameter, then Samba uses the usernames listed on that parameter.

To best mimic the security operation of a Windows 9x computer, you should set the guest only = Yes parameter for each share, and set the guest account parameter to a "dummy" account (possibly a different account for each share). Samba then skips the subsequent authentication steps. (No other steps bypass subsequent attempts.)

It's seldom advantageous to use security = Share authentication. Unless you set guest only = Yes, share-level security opens several opportunities for matching passwords, which creates greater exposure to security risks than are present with other security models. The other three security models (user, server, and domain) are much closer matches to Linux's native security model, and all modern SMB/CIFS clients work quite happily with these more Linux-friendly security arrangements. Share-level security only makes sense are when you must replace an existing Windows 9x server with minimal disruption to users, or if you're using very old clients that don't pass usernames to the server.

User-Level Security   When you set security = User, Samba requires that the client send a username along with a password. Without the username, the user cannot gain access to the computer. (Guest access is an exception to this rule, as described in Chapter 5.) Unless the share includes a force user parameter, Samba uses the username passed with the password (or a derivative based on the username map parameter, described in "Other Authentication Parameters") to determine the user's permissions. If jacques connects to a share to which he has read-only permissions based on the Linux permissions on the server, then jacques cannot create or modify files on the share, even if the share is read/write for other users.

One implication of user-level security is that every Samba user must have an account on the server, unless you enable guest access. With share-level security, a user can potentially access the server even without a Linux account. Depending on the password encryption options, Samba run with user-level security may use the user's normal logon password or a special Samba-only encrypted password to determine whether or not to allow access to the server.

Server-Level Security   If security = Server, Samba operates much as it does in user-level security, except that Samba passes authentication requests along to the domain controller. You must specify the domain controller in the password server parameter, which

Maintaining a Healthy System

PART 4

takes a NetBIOS name or IP address as its value (for example, `password server = DREYFUS`). The password server computer can be another Samba computer that's configured to accept such requests via the `domain logons = Yes` parameter. Alternatively, the password server can be a Windows NT or 2000 domain controller.

> **WARNING**   No matter what you use as the password server, be sure that system can be trusted! If your chosen password server has been compromised, then the individual who's broken into the password server can gain access to any user's shares. Also, be sure you *do not* set `password server` to point to the Samba server you're configuring. You can set this value to point to *another* Samba server, but if it points to itself, the result is an endless loop of password lookups that causes nothing but problems and possibly even a server crash.

Using `security = Server` does not by itself obviate the need for local accounts associated with each user. Your Samba server must still have these accounts—it's just that, for purposes of Samba access, another computer handles the authentication. You can use the `add user script` parameter in conjunction with `security = Server`, however, to bypass the need to maintain user accounts. Give the complete path to a script that accepts as its only parameter a username. This script should add a Linux user to the system. If Samba doesn't find a user of a given name, but the password server does authenticate the username and password, Samba calls the script indicated by `add user script`.

> **TIP**   The `add user script` parameter is a convenient way to add user accounts to a Linux computer that's been added to an existing network of Windows computers.

> **WARNING**   When you create a user-adding script, be sure it doesn't set the password on new accounts to anything constant or obvious. Ideally, the account should be disabled for Linux shell access. If you want to automatically provide Linux log on access, be sure the script generates random passwords and delivers them to the user in some secure way.

If you use a Windows NT system as the password server, the Samba server must have a trust account on that system. This is not a requirement, however, if you use a Samba server as the password server.

Domain-Level Security   Server-level security can be a useful way to centralize authentication. Instead of having to store and, potentially, change passwords on several servers, one domain controller handles the task. A Samba system running with server-level security does not, however, participate fully in the domain. As described in Chapter 10, a NetBIOS domain is a workgroup that includes several special features. One of these features is that the password server issues *tokens* to clients. These tokens help provide speedy logons to all the servers in the domain. When you set `security = Domain`, Samba participates more fully in the domain than when you set `security = Server`. In both server- and domain-level security, you must specify the domain controller with the `password server` parameter. Domain-level security also requires that you use encrypted passwords, which is not a requirement for server-level security.

When a server uses domain-level security, it must have a trust account on the domain controller. Chapter 10 describes setting up such an account when a Samba server functions as the domain controller. The Samba server must also join the domain. You can accomplish this with the `smbpasswd` command, as in

> `# smbpasswd -j PANTHER -r DREYFUS`

This command joins the Samba server to the `PANTHER` domain, using the domain controller `DREYFUS`. The domain controller listed in this command is normally the same one you list with the `password server` parameter in `smb.conf`, although you can mix and match if your domain uses both primary and secondary domain controllers.

In the end, domain- and server-level security operate very similarly as far as a Samba server is concerned. Both of these, in turn, look the same as user-level security from the client's point of view. Which model you use therefore depends on whether or not you want to centralize your authentication.

At present, the extent of Samba's participation in a domain is limited, even with domain-level security specified. The experimental Samba TNG branch of Samba development includes additional domain support. Future versions of Samba will no doubt further Samba's domain participation, to allow remote administration of Samba servers from Windows systems using Windows tools, rather than only local administration or administration through Samba-specific tools such as SWAT, which work equally well no matter what security model you use.

Other Authentication Parameters

In addition to the `security` parameter, Samba includes a number of other parameters that affect how it performs authentication.

> **`min password length`**   This parameter sets the minimum number of characters Samba accepts in a cleartext password. The default value is 5. There is no way to set a minimum number of characters for an encrypted password.

null passwords   This parameter defaults to No, which disallows access to accounts that have no set passwords. When it's set to Yes, users can log on to Samba using no password when an account has no password set—a potentially huge hole in security.

password level   SMB/CIFS uses case-insensitive passwords, so m1nkey and M1NKEY are equivalent. Linux, on the other hand, uses case-sensitive passwords—and Samba uses the password level parameter to bridge the gap. No matter how this parameter is set, Samba first tries to use the password as it's sent by the client, and then converted to all lowercase. If password level is set to a value higher than the default 0, Samba then tries all possible passwords with some characters converted to uppercase (from 1 to the value of password level). For example, if the client sent m1nkey as the password and if password level = 2, Samba tries M1nkey, m1Nkey, and so on through m1nkeY, then M1Nkey, M1nKey, and so on through m1nkEY.

The password level parameter is critical when your users have mixed-case passwords and a client converts passwords to all uppercase or all lowercase before sending them. This sometimes happens with Windows for Workgroups. The parameter is only useful when Samba uses unencrypted passwords; encrypted passwords aren't afflicted by the password case differences between Samba and Linux.

username level   This parameter works much like password level, but applied to usernames rather than passwords. Initially, Samba tries the username as sent but converted to all lowercase, then with the first letter capitalized. For example, if the client sends JACQUES as the username, Samba tries jacques and then Jacques. When username level is set higher than the default 0, Samba tries converting some letters to uppercase, as described for password level.

The username level parameter is particularly likely to be useful with DOS clients, which convert usernames to uppercase. Unlike password level, this parameter works with both encrypted and unencrypted passwords.

restrict anonymous   If set to Yes, this parameter causes Samba to refuse all anonymous connections to the server. Normally, some clients (such as Windows NT 4.0) rely upon anonymous access for some tasks—renewing browse lists, for example. The default value is therefore No, because Yes can cause browsing problems, particularly after a user has logged off a Windows NT client.

revalidate   This parameter works only when security = User. Normally, revalidate is set to No, which allows a client to connect to new shares on a server without going through the authentication procedure a second time. Setting the parameter to Yes can improve security by a small amount, but at the cost of marginally increased network traffic. Also, if the client doesn't cache passwords, users may have to enter passwords several times.

All of these parameters are global and affect access to the server. Samba also includes many additional parameters that affect access within specific shares, many of which are described in "File Ownership and Permissions" later in this chapter. Others appear in the discussions of file sharing in Chapter 5.

Encrypted versus Cleartext Passwords

One point mentioned repeatedly earlier in this chapter is the distinction between *cleartext* and *encrypted* passwords. This is a critically important aspect of Samba's password handling, and in fact is perhaps the most common challenge for new Samba administrators. That's because Samba's default encryption policies don't work with the most recent versions of Windows, as described shortly, in "Default Encryption for Versions of Windows."

When something is transmitted as ordinary text, it's said to be sent as *cleartext*. A *cleartext password* is therefore a password that's sent as plain (ASCII) text. If a client sends m1nkey as a cleartext password, the string m1nkey appears somewhere in the packets that travel from the client to the server.

Encrypted information, on the other hand, is scrambled in some way. The goal of a typical encryption algorithm is to allow only the desired recipient to use the encrypted information. Typically, two *keys* are used—one to encode the text and another to decode it. In transferring a password, the server can send an encryption key to the client, and retain a matched decryption key locally or store pre-encrypted passwords locally. When the client sends the password using the encryption key, nobody else can decode the password, because only the server has the matching decryption key. When the client sends the password m1nkey in an encrypted form, that string doesn't appear in any packet; instead, it traverses the wire as something completely different.

Advantages and Drawbacks of Encrypted and Cleartext Passwords

Both cleartext and encrypted passwords have their advantages and disadvantages. Before reviewing these, you should understand that TCP/IP networking is inherently insecure. Consider the network depicted in Figure 14.1. If CLOUSEAU is a server, and DALA connects to CLOUSEAU, several different types of computer may be able to inspect every packet that travels between the two computers, including packets containing sensitive passwords. Specifically:

- LITTON, on DALA's home network, can inspect all traffic from and to DALA if the local network uses coaxial Ethernet, twisted-pair Ethernet with a hub, or various other types of networking hardware. Chances are a switch will keep LITTON from examining DALA's traffic, though.

- DREYFUS, on CLOUSEAU's home network, can inspect all traffic from and to CLOUSEAU, under the same circumstances applying on the other side of the connection.

- Figure 14.1 depicts the Internet as a blob. In fact, the Internet is a mass of computers. Although the vast majority of these computers cannot inspect packets that pass between systems, many can. In particular, routers that lie between the two end-point networks, and possibly other computers on these routers' local networks, can inspect packets that traverse the network.

Figure 14.1   Network traffic from one computer to another passes through a potentially large number of intermediary computers.

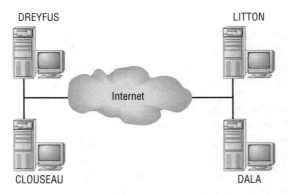

The key point to remember is that, on most network accesses that involve routing from one network to another, a large number of computers over which you have no control may be able to access your data, including passwords. Even on local networks, passwords can often be "sniffed" from computers on those local networks. If one of your network's computers has been compromised by an outsider, that outsider may be able to obtain passwords by using a packet sniffer utility on your own computer.

Considering Samba specifically, password encryption has several advantages and disadvantages. On the plus side, encryption provides these important benefits:

Improved Security   When you use encrypted passwords, you make it harder for an outsider to sniff passwords. This benefit is particularly important if you must allow access to Samba from outside your local network.

No password level Hassles   The password level parameter, described in "Other Authentication Parameters," applies to unencrypted passwords, not encrypted passwords. This fact makes the handling of encrypted Samba passwords simpler in some ways than the handling of unencrypted passwords, because you need not be concerned with configuring Samba to try matching variants of the password provided by the client.

Separate Linux and Samba Passwords   When you use encrypted passwords, you maintain separate Linux and Samba passwords. Your users can therefore use different passwords for shell access and Samba access. Alternatively, you can disable password-based access to Linux except through Samba, if you want users to be able to use a server *only* through Samba.

Defaults for Recent Versions of Windows   As described in greater detail in "Default Encryption for Versions of Windows," all currently available versions of Windows use encrypted passwords by default. If you do not enable encrypted password use in Samba, these clients *will not* be able to access shares on a Samba server, at least not without being modified themselves to send cleartext passwords.

Required for Domains   Domains function on encrypted passwords. This is a rule that cannot be broken; so if you use a domain, you *must* use encrypted passwords.

The advantages of encrypted passwords create a very powerful argument in their favor. There are, however, drawbacks to their use, including

Separate Linux and Samba Passwords   This feature is both an advantage and a disadvantage to encrypted passwords. Maintaining a separate encrypted password database for Samba requires extra administrative work on your part. Fortunately, Samba includes some tools that can help you keep your Linux and Samba password databases synchronized, if that is your desire. Unfortunately, setting up encrypted passwords initially, particularly if your server hosts many users, can be a major nuisance.

Older Client Expectations   Older clients use cleartext passwords. Although Samba can fall back on cleartext passwords when it's configured for encrypted passwords, doing so can result in verification of cleartext passwords against Linux's normal password database, and of encrypted passwords against Samba's encrypted password database. This can cause user confusion if the two don't match.

Maintaining a
Healthy System

PART 4

NOTE   Linux's passwords, stored in `/etc/passwd` or `/etc/shadow`, are encrypted. Linux uses a different encryption scheme for its own passwords than what NetBIOS uses for its passwords, and the two can't be converted from one to another. When it receives a cleartext password (whether from Samba or for any other purpose), Linux encrypts the password and checks the result against the encrypted form stored in its database.

On the whole, the advantages of encrypted passwords outweigh the advantages of cleartext passwords for most networks. If you have an isolated network that's already configured to use cleartext passwords, however, converting it to encrypted passwords may be more trouble than it's worth. You may be planning to add new Windows 98, Windows Me, or Windows 2000 computers, and so can prepare to convert to encrypted passwords. You should also give serious consideration to doing so if your network is accessible from the Internet at large. If a cracker breaks into one of your computers (even a client system), cleartext passwords can often be easily sniffed, opening a door into your Samba server.

Default Encryption for Versions of Windows

As installed, the versions of Windows use different default encryption policies:

- Cleartext is used by Windows for Workgroups, Windows 95, and Windows NT 3.1–4.0.

- Encryption is used by Windows 95 OEM Service Release 2 (OSR2), Windows 98, Windows Me, Windows NT 4.0 Service Pack 3, and Windows 2000.

It's virtually certain that future versions of Windows will use encrypted passwords by default. Samba's default encryption policy is to expect cleartext passwords. When configured to send encrypted passwords, Windows computers don't fall back to using cleartext passwords. Therefore, if both Samba and Windows clients are set for their defaults, Samba cannot authenticate recent versions of Windows clients. You must change either Samba's configuration or the Windows configuration to use Samba with recent Windows clients. The next two sections describe how to do this.

Using Samba's Encryption Policy

Samba includes a large number of features that control its handling of password encryption. Many of these are parameters in the smb.conf file. Others are support programs that allow you to change encrypted passwords or prepare the system to use encrypted passwords.

Encryption Parameters in *smb.conf*

A handful of global smb.conf parameters control Samba's password encryption policies.

encrypt passwords   This boolean parameter defaults to No, which causes Samba to use normal Linux authentication methods and cleartext passwords. If you change it to Yes, Samba uses encrypted passwords stored in the smbpasswd file or an external password server in lieu of Linux's normal authentication methods. The security parameter controls whether Samba uses an smbpasswd file or an external password server.

smb passwd file   This parameter sets the name of the smbpasswd file, including a complete path. The default value is a compile-time option, but it's normally a file called smbpasswd located in the same directory as the smb.conf file, or in a subdirectory with tighter security settings.

WARNING   The smbpasswd file is extremely sensitive. Although the passwords stored in smbpasswd are encrypted, crackers can attack the encryption of these passwords in various ways (such as by encrypting every word in a dictionary and comparing the results against smbpasswd's contents, to locate weak passwords). You should therefore ensure that smbpasswd has very restrictive permissions— 0600 with root ownership works well in most cases. You may also want to store the file in a directory with 0700 permissions and root ownership, to prevent ordinary users from even finding the file.

update encrypted   This parameter is intended as a tool when migrating a network from cleartext to encrypted passwords. It defaults to No; but when set to Yes, Samba runs smbpasswd to update the Samba encrypted password file whenever a user logs on using a cleartext password. The idea behind use of this parameter is that you create an encrypted password file with null passwords for all users, and then set update encrypted = Yes and leave encrypt passwords = No for a time. Users can then use the server normally and, after a few days, most or all of the encrypted passwords will be set to the same values as the normal Linux passwords. You can then set update encrypted = No and encrypt passwords = Yes and add clients that require encrypted passwords, or convert clients to use encrypted passwords. The transition is smooth from your users' point of view. The alternative is to require all users to run smbpasswd from a Linux shell prompt, or you can assign passwords randomly and require users to use these assigned passwords. "Samba's Password Support Programs" describes migrating from cleartext to encrypted passwords in more detail.

unix password sync   This parameter controls whether Samba tries to change the Linux password for a user whenever the Samba encrypted password is changed. The default value is No, which leaves the user or administrator to synchronize passwords manually, if desired.

passwd program   This parameter specifies the complete path to the program that Linux uses to change users' passwords. On most systems, this value defaults to /bin/passwd, but you can change it if necessary. Samba uses this value only when changing the encrypted password and if unix password sync = Yes.

passwd chat   A typical Linux passwd program displays information, accepts a response, displays more information, and so on until the password is changed.

Samba uses the `passwd chat` parameter to control its responses to the `passwd` program's output, in order to change the password. The default value of this parameter varies from one installation to another, but probably resembles the following:

```
*new*password* %n\n *new*password* %n\n *changed*
```

Components of this parameter include the following:

Asterisks (*)	These represent any received character or set of characters.
Ordinary text	Plain text represents itself. It's most likely to be used in the expect portion of the string—that is, what Samba expects to see from the `passwd` program.
Variables (%o and %n)	These may be used in the send string to represent the old and new passwords. Depending on how the program is called, however, Samba may not know the old password. Specifically, if you call the `smbpassword` program as `root`, `smbpassword` doesn't ask for the old password, and because the encryption used to store the password isn't reversible, Samba can't provide the old password in this situation.
Escape characters	You can use the standard two-character escape sequences for carriage return, line feed, tab, or space: \r, \n, \t, or \s, respectively.
Double quotes (")	Use double quotes to enclose strings that contain spaces, to ensure that they're interpreted correctly.
Full stops (.)	In the `passwd chat` parameter, full stops (aka periods) are interpreted as meaning no input or no output.

Many Linux distributions come with `smb.conf` files set with `passwd chat` and related parameters that are appropriate for the distribution's version of the `passwd` program. If this isn't the case and you want to use automatic password updates, try using the default values; just set `unix password sync = Yes` to enable password synchronization. When you change a Samba password, as described in "Samba's Password Support Programs," check to see if the matching Linux password also changed. If it didn't, try using `passwd` directly and compare its output and what it expects against the default `passwd chat` parameter's contents, and adjust it as necessary. Attention to detail is critical when setting this feature, because chat scripts like this are notoriously picky about things that humans easily overlook, such as the case of strings and the presence or absence of spaces or tabs.

One critical point to consider when you create a password change script is that Samba runs `passwd` *as root*. When run in this way, `passwd` doesn't normally ask for the original password.

Samba's Password Support Programs

Samba includes several support programs that allow you to create and maintain an encrypted password file. The `smbpasswd` program is the most important of these in day-to-day use, but additional tools are critical when it comes to setting up your server or migrating it from using cleartext to encrypted passwords.

Using *smbpasswd*

The most important password support tool is `smbpasswd`, and it's the Samba equivalent of the `passwd` program—it lets you change encrypted Samba passwords. The `smbpasswd` program uses the following syntax:

```
smbpasswd [-a] [-d] [-e] [-D debuglevel] [-n] [-r machinename] [-U ↵
username] [-h] [-s] [username]
```

> **NOTE** Don't confuse the `smbpasswd` *program* with the `smbpasswd` *file*. Both bear the same name, but they're very different things. Because they're so different, you'll be able to see from context which one is meant in any given discussion in this book. When necessary, the words *program* or *file* are used to distinguish the two.

The various optional parameters to `smbpasswd` include the following:

-a   This parameter adds a user to the `smbpasswd` file. This option is only honored when `root` runs `smbpasswd`.

-d   This parameter disables the specified username. Subsequent attempts to log on using the specified username fail. Only `root` can use this option.

-e   The opposite of `-d`, this parameter enables the specified username. Only `root` can use this option.

-D *debuglevel*   This parameter sets the debug level to a value between 0 and 10 (the default is 0). Higher values write additional information to the Samba log files.

Try -D 1 if you have a problem. Levels above 3 are likely to be useful only to Samba developers.

-n Only available to root, this parameter sets a null password for the specified user. If you use null passwords = Yes, as described in "Other Authentication Parameters," anybody is allowed to log on to the share. Otherwise, the result is effectively the same as disabling the username with -d.

-r *machinename* This parameter lets you adjust the password on a remote computer, which can be either another Samba server or a Windows NT or 2000 system.

-U *username* Use this parameter in conjunction with the -r parameter to specify the user whose password you want to change.

-h Use this parameter to display a summary of options available from smbpasswd.

-s This parameter causes smbpasswd to use standard input and output, rather than /dev/tty. If you want to write a script that calls smbpasswd, this option may be necessary. You can use it along with redirection operators (such as < and >) to get smbpasswd to accept input from and send output to files or other programs.

username When root runs smbpasswd, you have to specify the user whose password should be changed.

The two most common uses of smbpasswd are by a user who changes his or her own password, and by the administrator to change a user's password. In the first case, the exchange resembles the following:

```
$ smbpasswd
Old SMB password:
New SMB password:
Retype new SMB password:
Password changed for user jacques
```

When run in this way, smbpasswd doesn't require that a username be specified, but the program does need the user's old password. Neither the old nor the new password echoes to the screen, as a security measure.

When root runs smbpasswd, the behavior is slightly different:

```
# smbpasswd jacques
New SMB password:
Retype new SMB password:
Password changed for user jacques.
```

In this case, `root` must specify the username, but does not need to provide the old password.

Setting Up Encrypted Passwords

When you first configure a Samba server to use encrypted passwords, you must do several things:

1. Create an `smbpasswd` file. There are a couple of options for doing this, as described shortly.

2. Populate the `smbpasswd` file with valid passwords. You can do this in a couple of different ways, as described shortly.

3. Reconfigure Samba to use `smbpasswd`. This is a matter of setting `encrypt passwords = Yes` in `smb.conf`.

4. Add clients that use encrypted passwords to your network, or convert existing clients to use encrypted passwords.

One way of creating an `smbpasswd` file is to run `smbpasswd` as `root` with the `-a` parameter. Although `smbpasswd` complains about not being able to open a file, it creates a new one and adds the user you specify. You can then rerun `smbpasswd -a` to add more users to its list. This procedure may be useful if you have few users or want to assign passwords, rather than let users choose their own. If you have many users, however, creating them all in this way can be awkward. Although you can automate the process by using a script, the issue of password assignment can impose difficulties.

Another way to create an `smbpasswd` file is to run the helper program `mksmbpasswd`—a script that comes with most Linux Samba distributions. (On some distributions, it's called `mksmbpasswd.sh`.) This program accepts as input the `/etc/passwd` file and creates as output a model `smbpasswd` file with null passwords. You can use it as follows:

```
# cat /etc/passwd | mksmbpasswd > smbpasswd
```

Once you've created the `smbpasswd` file, you should edit it to remove users who have no need to access Samba. Chances are the file created by `mksmbpasswd` will have several such users at the top—these are users that Linux uses internally, such as `ftp` and `daemon`. Be sure to remove `root` from this list, as well. When you're done editing the file, move it to `/etc`, `/etc/samba.d`, or wherever Samba expects to find the `smbpasswd` file. You then have three choices for how to proceed.

You can use `smbpasswd` as `root` to assign passwords to all users. If you intend to do this, though, there's no reason to use `mksmbpasswd`; you could simply call `smbpasswd` with the `-a` parameter to do the job in one step.

Maintaining a
Healthy System

PART 4

Another option is to have users set their Samba passwords. There are several ways this could be accomplished, including the following:

- Have users log on using shell accounts and issue the smbpasswd command. This may be a viable option if users have shell access.

- Setting smbpasswd to be the users' logon shells. When users use Telnet or SSH to try to log on, they get the smbpasswd program and can set their passwords, then the system ends the connection. This can be a good option if users don't have or need shell access to the server. It can also be useful for future Samba password changes.

- Using SWAT (described in Chapter 4) to enable users to change their passwords.

- Having users approach you individually to run smbpasswd. This approach allows you to supervise the process, but may be very time-consuming if you have many users.

The third choice is to set the update encrypted = Yes parameter in smb.conf, which lets Samba automatically update the encrypted passwords based on the cleartext passwords used by Linux. This option is useful if your network currently uses cleartext passwords but you want to migrate over to encrypted passwords. It's not useful if your network already uses encrypted passwords. This option is described earlier, in "Encryption Parameters in smb.conf." After running for a time with this option set, most or all of the users' smbpasswd entries will be set to match their Linux passwords.

As you can see, setting up encrypted passwords on a new server can involve a substantial amount of work, particularly if you're trying to migrate an existing large user-base from another platform. By planning carefully, though, you can minimize your troubles by letting your users do the bulk of the work of entering passwords, either through smbpasswd or the update encrypted parameter. Another option is to use an existing password server. If your network already contains such a server, it's likely to be much easier to set up Samba to use that server than to duplicate its user and password list locally.

Setting the Windows Encryption Policy

As described in "Default Encryption for Versions of Windows," Microsoft in the late 1990s shifted its default encryption policy for Windows from using cleartext passwords by default to using encrypted passwords. If you're running an older network that still employs cleartext passwords, it's often easier to reconfigure new clients to use cleartext passwords than it is to enable encrypted passwords on your Samba server—at least in the short term.

To continue to use cleartext passwords, you can enable them on Windows clients by following these steps:

1. On the Samba server, locate the *WinVer*_PlainPassword.reg files (where *WinVer* is a version of Windows, such as Win98). These files should be in your Samba documentation directory, such as /usr/doc/samba-2.0.7 or /usr/doc/packages/samba.

2. Copy the *WinVer*_PlainPassword.reg files to a floppy disk that uses the FAT file-system. You only need to copy the files that correspond to the clients you have on your network.

3. Remove the floppy disk you created in step 2 from the Linux server and insert it in the floppy drive of a client that you want to reconfigure to use cleartext passwords.

4. On the client, open the floppy disk and double-click the appropriate *WinVer*_PlainPassword.reg file. This action creates a new Windows Registry entry that disables the use of encrypted passwords. (On Windows NT and 2000 clients, you must perform this step as the Administrator.)

5. Reboot the client computer. It should now use cleartext passwords.

NOTE You can use a method other than a floppy disk to transport these files, if you like—FTP, for instance. You can't use Samba, however, at least not directly, because Windows clients configured to use encrypted passwords can't access a cleartext-only Samba server.

To reverse this process, you'll have to edit the *WinVer*_PlainPassword.reg file. This file should have a line that reads

```
"EnablePlainTextPassword"=dword:00000001
```

Change this line so that it reads

```
"EnablePlainTextPassword"=dword:00000000
```

You can then perform steps 2 through 5 with the modified file to re-enable encrypted passwords.

File Ownership and Permissions

One important aspect of security on a Samba server is in configuring ownership and permissions on individual shares and files. Samba includes a number of parameters, including force user, create mask, and directory mask, that affect who can access a share, what Linux permissions Samba gives to files it creates, and so on. Chapter 5 describes many of these parameters, so I recommend you read that chapter if you're not already familiar with these features. This section describes some of the consequences of using these file-sharing parameters in greater detail.

Evaluating Per-Share Ownership and Permissions

Each share has associated with it certain security characteristics. For example, you can make a share read-only or read/write (via the writeable parameter); you can set the permissions Samba uses to create files in a share (via `create mask`, `force create mode`, and similar parameters); and you can set the ownership of files created in a share (via `force user`).

Chapter 5 covers these parameters in detail, including their security implications. It's worth reiterating, however, that you should give considerable thought to the security consequences of any configuration you might produce. Here are some questions to ask yourself:

- When a user accesses the computer from a shell prompt, does that user have any sort of special access to a share? Can the user create links that lead outside the share from a shell prompt? Can the user create or delete files in a read-only share from a shell prompt? Can the user change permissions in ways that might cause problems?

- When a user accesses a share using Samba, what privileges are granted? If a link exists in a share pointing to an area outside the share, can a user do any damage using that link? Can a user overwrite other users' files? If so, is this desirable?

- If you use `force user`, with what Linux privileges will Samba users be accessing the computer? Does that account have unusual rights? Does it correspond with a real user (which is usually not a good idea)? Do you use the same "dummy" account for multiple shares? (Again, this may be a step toward problems in some cases.)

- Do you rely on specific ownership or permissions in a share? If so, is there any way, short of intervention from `root`, that files with differing ownership or permissions might appear in the share? This might happen because of users with shell access or other servers, for example, and might cause files to be undeletable or inaccessible from Samba.

The answers to many of these questions can be good, bad, or indifferent, depending on your uses for the shares and your server's configuration. For example, the ability of users to create files with assorted ownership within a share can cause problems in some cases, but this ability may be desirable or even necessary in others. You should therefore think about the answers to these questions with respect to *your environment's specific* requirements.

If you carefully consider the security consequences of share-level access controls when you configure your Samba server, you should have no problems as a result of these features. Failure to consider the consequences of a configuration, however, may entangle your server in a web of file-access difficulties. When you first deal with a Samba server, it's probably best to stick to simple configurations, if at all possible. Providing access to users' home shares and perhaps one or two read-only shared areas is usually not too demanding. On the other hand, juggling multiple groups of users with complex needs for cross-group sharing and security can turn into a brain-teasing logical puzzle.

Evaluating Per-User Access Controls

Many of Samba's access control mechanisms operate on the level of individual users. These parameters are normally share parameters, so you can set one share's security features to be quite different from another share on the same server. Chapter 5 covers these parameters in some detail, but following is a brief rundown:

read list   With this parameter you can specify a list of users who are to be given read-only access to an otherwise read/write share. For example, read list = jacques, simone prevents these two users from writing to a share.

write list   This parameter functions as the opposite of read list; users included on the write list can write to a share that is read-only to other users. If a share includes both a read list and a write list and a user appears on both lists, the write list entry takes precedence.

valid users   When you want to restrict access to a share to just a few users, this parameter lets you do so. For example, valid users = jacques, simone configures Samba to allow only jacques and simone to access a share. Other users can see the share in browse lists, but they aren't allowed in.

invalid users   This parameter is the opposite of valid users; users listed in this parameter are *not* allowed access to the share, whereas other users can access it. If a share has both valid users and invalid users lists and a user appears on both lists, then invalid users takes precedence; the user is not granted access.

Per-user access controls can be extremely useful in tightening security on a Samba server. Considered only within the Samba security model, these parameters give you fine and arbitrary control over user access to shares. You can restrict access such that simone, for instance, cannot read a share, or can read it but not write to it, even when simone belongs to all the same Linux groups as other users who can access the share. This arbitrary control can be extremely useful if you want to restrict access. It can also be employed when you want to *loosen* restrictions for some reason. For example, you might have a read-only share that contains program files. In the event you need to update those files, however, it's necessary that somebody have write access to the share. Using write list provides a wedge into the share; you can use one account as a designated maintenance account for otherwise read-only shares.

Be aware that the utility of these per-user access parameters is reduced when you add Linux shell account access to the mix. When a user has access to a directory from a shell account, Samba access restrictions suddenly become meaningless—at least, if serious security is your goal. If you only want to protect against accidents, the Samba-only features may be adequate. When your users have Linux shell accounts, you must consider how permissions on the directories in question interact with standard Linux security to bypass Samba's features.

Integrating ACLs with Samba

Windows NT and 2000 support a security model built around access control lists (ACLs). ACLs use users, groups, and both read and write permissions to files, just as does Linux's native security model. ACLs go further, however, in that they use *lists* of users and groups to control access. You can therefore specify an arbitrary list of users or groups who have particular types of access to a file or directory. Although it's often possible to mimic the effects of ACLs in Linux by using a large number of groups, one for each arbitrary group of users, this practice can be tedious to implement.

Because ACLs are more flexible than Linux's native file ownership and security model, Samba doesn't completely implement ACLs. Samba does, however, provide Windows NT and 2000 clients with access to Linux file security options through Windows's ACL mechanisms. Samba includes several parameters that influence ACL support:

> **nt acl support**   This global parameter determines whether Samba gives Windows NT clients access to Linux security information. The default value is Yes.
>
> **security mask**   This parameter sets the permission bits that a Windows NT client may access. The default value is the same as the create mask parameter. To give Windows NT clients full access to Linux permission bits, set security mask = 0777.
>
> **directory security mask**   This parameter works much like the security mask parameter, but it applies to directories rather than files. The default value is the same as the directory mask parameter.
>
> **force security mode**   The security mask option sets permission bits that a Windows NT client *may* set. The force security mode parameter, in contrast, sets the permission bits that will automatically be set when clients try to change permissions. It defaults to the value of the force create mode parameter, which has a default of 0000.
>
> **force directory security mode**   This parameter works like force security mode, but it applies to directories rather than files. It defaults to the value of the force directory mode parameter.

NOTE   Windows NT's permission controls provide access to the Linux execute bit. Samba uses this bit to double for the FAT-style archive, system, and hidden bits. Therefore, if you change the execute bits on any file, you'll also find that the file's archive, system, or hidden status changes. This mapping is described in more detail in Chapter 5.

On most networks, the default values for these ACL-integration parameters produce reasonable results. Windows NT clients can adjust permissions on files and directories on the Linux server up to the limits imposed by the create mask and directory mask parameters.

From Windows NT 4.0, you can access the Linux permission information as follows:

1. Open a window on the directory that contains a file or directory you want to modify.

2. Right-click on the file or directory you want to modify. In the pop-up menu, select Properties. Windows displays a Properties dialog box.

3. In the Properties dialog box, click the Security tab. The Properties dialog box should now resemble the one shown in Figure 14.2. Windows provides three security features: Permissions, Auditing, and Ownership. Auditing does not work with a Samba server. Ownership allows you to see who the owner of the file is, but the Take Ownership button in the Owner dialog box doesn't work. Permissions works within the limits of the Linux permissions model, as described in the next steps.

Figure 14.2   Of the three security features, only Permissions can be changed on files stored on a Samba server.

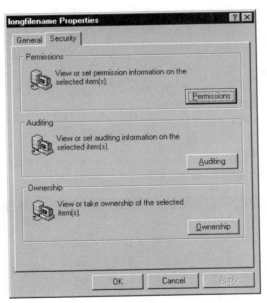

4. Click the Permissions button. Windows displays the File Permissions dialog box shown in Figure 14.3. There are three access groups in this case: Everyone (Linux's world permissions), the owner (rodsmith), and the group (users).

Figure 14.3 Files stored on a Samba server always have three sets of permissions: Everyone, the owner, and the group.

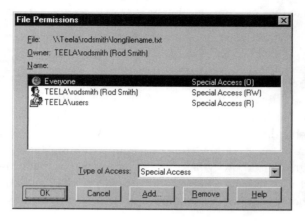

5. Click one of the three permissions groups, and then click Special Access... in the Type of Access field. Windows displays the Special Access dialog box shown in Figure 14.4.

NOTE Windows displays two entries called Special Access in the Type of Access field. One is followed by an ellipsis (...), and the other isn't. Select the one that includes the ellipsis. The one without the ellipsis doesn't allow you to modify the settings.

Figure 14.4 You can set Linux permission bits in the Special Access dialog box, but not all of the box's features are useful.

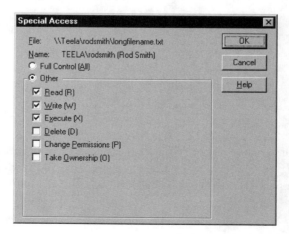

6. In the Special Access dialog box, you can check Read (R), Write (W), or Execute (X) to set the appropriate bits on the Samba server, assuming the `security mask` or `directory security mask` parameters allow you to do so. If you enable other options, or options that are disallowed by your `smb.conf` configuration, Samba ignores them.

7. Click OK in the Special Access dialog box. Windows shows your changed permissions in parentheses following the words "Special Access" in the File Permissions dialog box (Figure 14.3). If you've removed all permissions, Windows displays an "O" in parentheses (you can see this in the Everyone line in Figure 14.3). At this point, Windows displays your changed permissions as you've entered them, even if you've selected options that Samba doesn't support or allow.

8. Click OK in the File Permissions dialog box, and again in the Properties dialog box.

The result of all this activity is a change in permissions on the Samba server. Because Samba maps Linux user, group, and world permissions onto constructs that Windows can deal with, access to those permissions from Windows is fairly straightforward.

As an alternative to steps 5–7 just above, you might try selecting a preconfigured set of permissions from the Type of Access list. Samba will accept such a selection, but if the option you choose includes permissions that are meaningless under Linux, Samba ignores these meaningless settings just as if you selected them from the Special Access dialog box (Figure 14.4).

Setting permissions in Windows 2000 is somewhat easier than in Windows NT 4.0. In Windows 2000, you have direct control over the permissions from the Security tab of the Properties dialog box (Figure 14.5). There's no need to click a Permissions button in the Properties dialog box or open a Special Access dialog box to change permissions.

> **NOTE** If the server runs Samba 2.0.6 or earlier, Windows 2000 doesn't display the owner or group name correctly; instead, it displays a long numeric code. With Samba 2.0.7 and later versions, Windows 2000 displays the file's owner and group names accurately.

When you manipulate files on an NTFS partition on a Windows computer, you can use the Add button in the File Permissions dialog box (shown earlier in Figure 14.3) to add permissions for an arbitrary number of users or groups. You cannot do this with files stored on a Samba server. If you try, you'll get an error message, either when you select the group or when you click the OK button in the Add Users and Groups dialog box.

Figure 14.5 Windows 2000 provides more-direct access to Linux permissions than does Windows NT 4.0.

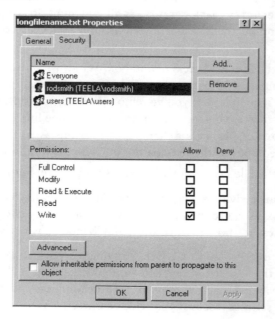

Samba over SSL

SMB/CIFS was designed at a time when network security concerns were, by today's standards, simple. Aside from encrypted passwords, SMB/CIFS doesn't encrypt any other data passing over the network. As a result, all the files you transfer with SMB/CIFS might be read by somebody using a packet sniffer on the source, destination, or an intervening network. This fact can be a major drawback to the protocol in certain situations—for example, if you want to pass data across the Internet, or if you're using SMB/CIFS in a *very* high-security environment that requires encryption even on your local network connections. In these cases, it's useful to be able to add another package to encrypt SMB/CIFS connections. Samba includes support for one such protocol, the *Secure Sockets Layer (SSL),* which is also used on many secure Web sites. Unfortunately, configuring Samba and its clients to use SSL is a bit tedious, but it can be done, and it greatly enhances security if you need to use clients and servers that are separated by networks you don't trust.

> **NOTE**   Another option is to use Samba in conjunction with the *Secure Shell (SSH),* which is most commonly used as a replacement for Telnet. Like SSL, SSH can be used to encrypt data from a wide variety of programs. Samba includes no explicit support for SSH, however.

The type of security addressed by SSL and SSH is that of the readability of the *files* you transfer. An SSL link also automatically encrypts your passwords, but if you're only concerned with password security, `encrypt passwords = Yes` is a much simpler (although also somewhat less effective) option than SSL. You should consider SSL only if your shared files contain extremely sensitive data, such as trade secrets or confidential medical information.

> **WARNING**   Before proceeding further, check to be sure that running SSL in your environment is legal. Russia and some other countries restrict the use of cryptographic software such as SSL and SSH. In the past, the United States restricted the export of cryptographic software, even when it was readily available outside of the U.S. For these reasons, SSL hasn't been integrated more closely into Samba or Linux. The U.S. has loosened its export restrictions, however, leading to easier availability of SSL and similar packages.

Configuring SSL

The first step to using SSL with Samba is to install and configure an SSL package. This process can be intimidating if you're not used to dealing with cryptographic software, certificates, and so on, but it's not too difficult if you follow the steps described here.

Installing SSL on Linux

There are two major SSL implementations available for Linux:

- SSLeay (http://www2.psy.uq.edu.au/~ftp/Crypto/ssleay/)
- OpenSSL (http://www.openssl.org/)

In addition, you can find links to many mirror sites that host OpenSSL RPMs at http://www.openssh.com/portable.html, and the Debian Web site (http://www.debian.org/) lists SSL packages for Debian-based distributions.

> **NOTE**   Red Hat 7.0 ships with both OpenSSL and an SSL-enabled version of Samba. Future versions of other distributions may follow suit. Chances are you won't need to install SSL on such a system, but you will still need to create SSL certifcates.

The following sections discuss the configuration of OpenSSL, but the configuration of SSLeay is quite similar; only the locations of a few configuration files differ.

Assuming you have an RPM-based Linux distribution, you can install the OpenSSL RPMs just as you would any other RPM files, like this:

```
# rpm -Uvh openssl-0.9.5a-1.i386.rpm⏎
openssl-devel-0.9.5a-1.i386.rpm
```

If you need to compile SSL from source, follow the instructions that come with the package. Typically, you must run a `configure` script, and then run `make` and `make install`.

TIP In preparing this chapter, I ran across an SSLeay binary package that didn't work well with Samba. During the Samba configuration phase, the `configure` script complained that it could not create a summary. Replacing this binary with an OpenSSL binary or a version of SSLeay compiled from source code on the same system solved this problem. If you encounter difficulties compiling Samba with SSL, try replacing the SSL package with another one.

Basic SSL Configuration

Basic SSL configuration involves telling SSL where it will find certain key files, and setting the program up so that it can be easily run. Perform the following configuration steps as `root`:

1. Set up the SSL binary so that it's accessible on your path. If you installed the program from an RPM or Debian package, this has probably already been done. If you compiled the program yourself, you may need to add the SSL binary path to your `PATH` environment variable. You can adjust this variable systemwide by editing it in `/etc/profile`. Alternatively, you can create a link called `ssleay` in a directory that's on your path (such as `/usr/local/bin`), to the SSL binary (`ssleay` or `openssh`) in its particular directory.

2. SSL relies upon random numbers for part of its security. To prime SSL's random number generator, you'll need to create a file with random characters. To do so, enter the command

   ```
   # cat > /tmp/private.txt
   ```

   and then type characters randomly for a minute or more. When you're done, press Ctrl+D to stop input. The result will be a file called `/tmp/private.txt` that contains gibberish.

3. Convert the `/tmp/private.txt` file you just created into a form that's usable by SSL. To do this, enter the command

   ```
   # ssleay genrsa -rand /tmp/private.txt > /dev/null
   ```

The result is a 1024-byte file called /root/.rnd based on /tmp/private.txt. You can and should then delete /tmp/private.txt.

4. Create a directory in which SSL will store certificates. A good choice for this duty is /etc/certificates. Be sure to use chmod to restrict access to this directory once you've created it, as in **chmod 0700 /etc/certificates**.

5. Edit the /var/ssl/misc/CA.sh file (which may reside in some other directory if you built SSH yourself or used SSLeay rather than OpenSSH). Locate the line that defines CATOP; it probably reads CATOP=./demoCA. Change this line to read CATOP=/etc/certificates.

6. Edit the /var/ssl/openssl.cnf file. This file may reside elsewhere if you built SSL yourself, and it's called ssleay.cnf in SSLeay. Find the entry that reads dir = ./demoCA and change it to read dir = /etc/certificates.

These steps lay the groundwork for creating certificates, as described next. These certificates help to authenticate one computer to another, but they don't replace the usual SMB/CIFS password mechanisms.

Creating Certificates

Ordinarily, SSL is used in conjunction with a *certificate* issued by a *certification authority (CA)*. The CA's "stamp of approval" guarantees that a Web-based retailer, for example, is the organization it claims to be and not an imposter. In most Samba SSL configurations, you don't need an external CA to provide this sort of guarantee; you can generate your own certificates, thus serving as your own CA. This arrangement is certainly good enough for in-house use of Samba and SSL. If you run a secure Web site, however, you'll probably want to register with a CA. You can use these registrations with Samba over SSL.

Web servers typically don't require certificates on their clients, because the primary concern in Web commerce is that the server be trustworthy. In file sharing, however, the identity of the client is at least as important as the identity of the server; you don't want unauthorized computers accessing your server. Generating certificates for your clients can help verify that your clients are who they claim to be.

Creating a CA Configuration

The first step to creating a certificate is to run the certificate authority setup script, CA.sh. If you installed SSL from the OpenSSL RPM files, this script is in the /var/ssl/misc directory. Listing 14.1 shows the results of running this script. You'll be asked to enter information identifying yourself and your organization. The pass phrase you enter early on is like a password but should be substantially longer than a typical password. The script doesn't echo the pass phrase you type, for security reasons.

Maintaining a Healthy System

PART 4

Listing 14.1   Results of Running the Certificate Authority Setup Script

```
# /var/ssl/misc/CA.sh -newca
mkdir: cannot make directory `/etc/certificates': File exists
CA certificate filename (or enter to create)

Making CA certificate ...
Using configuration from /var/ssl/openssl.cnf
Generating a 1024 bit RSA private key
........................................++++++
........++++++
writing new private key to '/etc/certificates/private/./cakey.pem'
Enter PEM pass phrase:
Verifying password - Enter PEM pass phrase:
-----
You are about to be asked to enter information that will be incorporated
into your certificate request.
What you are about to enter is what is called a Distinguished Name or a DN.
There are quite a few fields but you can leave some blank
For some fields there will be a default value,
If you enter '.', the field will be left blank.
-----
Country Name (2 letter code) [AU]:US
State or Province Name (full name) [Some-State]:Massachusetts
Locality Name (eg, city) []:Malden
Organization Name (eg, company) [Internet Widgits Pty Ltd]:The Panther School
Organizational Unit Name (eg, section) []:None
Common Name (eg, YOUR name) []:clouseau.panther.edu
Email Address []:jacques@panther.edu
```

Most of the details you enter, such as the organization's name, are unimportant. By default, however, the client and server must contain the same information for the country code, state, and organization name. (The upcoming section, "Creating Client Certificates," describes entry of this information for the client certificates.)

As indicated early in the CA.sh output, the script creates a file called /etc/certificates/private/cakey.pem. This is a highly sensitive key file, so do *not* copy it onto other systems.

Creating Client Certificates

The next step is to create certificate files for use by clients. You can skip this step if you don't intend to use client certificates. Nevertheless, because client certificates can provide an added component of security, I recommend you use them. Suppose the client you want to link to the server using SSL is called SIMONE. To avoid confusion, you can create certificates whose filenames are based on the client's name. First, you create a file called simone.key, by using the ssleay program, thus:

```
# ssleay genrsa -des3 1024 >simone.key
Generating RSA private key, 1024 bit long modulus
...............++++++
...................++++++
e is 65537 (0x10001)
Enter PEM pass phrase:
Verifying password - Enter PEM pass phrase:
```

Note that creating the simone.key file requires that you enter a pass phrase, just as you did when creating the cakey.pem file. This pass phrase should not be the same as the pass phrase used for the server.

You must now create a temporary client file, thus:

```
# ssleay req -new -key simone.key -out simone-csr
Using configuration from /var/ssl/openssl.cnf
Enter PEM pass phrase:
```

The pass phrase you enter here is the one for the client, not for the server. You only need to enter it once, because it's being used for authentication purposes, not to change or create the pass phrase to begin with. At this point, you must enter the organization information from Listing 14.1 again, but this time, you should respond in a way that's appropriate for the client.

You must now use your CA configuration to "sign" the client's certificate. This will allow the server to verify that the client has been approved to connect to the server. To do this, you use ssleay again:

```
# ssleay ca -days 1000 -infiles simone-csr >simone.pem
Using configuration from /var/ssl/openssl.cnf
Enter PEM pass phrase:
Check that the request matches the signature
Signature ok
```

To sign the client certificate, you enter the pass phrase *for the server*. As with other pass phrase entries, this information is not echoed to the screen. The program proceeds to display the information you've entered about the client's certificate. If all goes well, the program asks if you want to sign the certificate. Respond by typing **y**. Before committing changes to the server's certificate database (in /etc/certificates), the program asks once more for confirmation. Again, respond **y**. The program finishes by confirming that it's written the changes.

If, rather than asking for these confirmations, the program complains that data did not match (for instance, if the states for the client and server don't match), then you should check your client and server configurations and make changes as appropriate.

> **NOTE** You specify the number of days for which a certificate is valid when you create it. This is the -days 1000 parameter in the preceding example. At the end of this time, you'll need to generate a new certificate.

The result of this certification creation process is as follows:

- An entry is made in the SSL certificates database on the server, in the /etc/certificates directory. You don't need to concern yourself with the details of this entry, except to be sure it's protected from harm, tampering, or unauthorized access.

- Two files (simone.key and simone.pem in the examples) are created that you will ultimately transport to the client. These files are very sensitive; with them and the client pass phrase, an unscrupulous individual could gain access to your server. You should therefore transport these files in the most secure manner possible—hand-delivered by floppy disk, for example.

I recommend that you generate client certificates for the server. This will allow you to test the server configuration using smbclient to connect to the local computer.

With these certifications in hand, you'll now configure Samba to use SSL, and set up SSL on your client system.

Configuring Samba to Use SSL

Before you can use SSL with Samba, you must compile an SSL-enabled version of the server. Unfortunately, Samba servers in most Linux distributions do not come with SSL support enabled. (Red Hat 7.0 is an exception to this rule, and there may be more exceptions in the future.) Once you've recompiled Samba with SSL support (and installed an SSL package), basic SSL functionality is a matter of setting a few parameters in smb.conf. You can then test for basic functionality by using smbclient to connect the server to itself.

Creating an SSL-Enabled Samba

Chances are good that you'll need to compile a copy of Samba with SSL support enabled. If you're uncertain about this requirement, skip ahead to "Setting Samba's

SSL Parameters." Create an `smb.conf` file that contains SSL support, and then type **testparm**. If `testparm` complains that it doesn't recognize the SSL parameters, you need to remove your current Samba installation and create a new one with SSL support.

Read Chapter 3 to learn how to compile Samba from source code. Of critical importance is the `--with-ssl` parameter to `configure`. You *must* include this parameter to compile Samba with SSL support. In order for this option to work, SSL *and* the SSL development libraries must be installed on your system. These libraries often come in a separate package from the main SSL package, with a name similar to `openssl-devel-0.9.5a-1.i386.rpm`.

Note that Samba's SSL support assumes that certain SSL development files, most importantly `ssl.h`, are in typical locations. This arrangement isn't true of some SSL packages, including OpenSSL. In theory, using the `--with-sslinc=`*/path/to/ssl/libraries* parameter should fix this problem. In practice, you may need to create a symbolic link from a directory on your include path to the `ssl.h` file, wherever it might be. Alternatively, try creating a directory called `/usr/local/ssl`; then create in that directory a symbolic link called `include` to wherever your SSL include files are; and *do not* use the `--with-sslinc` parameter to `configure`.

Setting Samba's SSL Parameters

Samba includes a fairly large number of global SSL-related parameters. You can configure a basic SSL-enabled Samba server with just a handful of these parameters, including the following:

ssl   This boolean parameter enables or disables SSL support. The default value is `No`, so you must set this parameter to `Yes` to allow SSL connections.

ssl server cert   This parameter accepts the full path to the SSL server certification file. If you've used `/etc/certificates` as the SSL certificates directory, you should use `ssl server cert = /etc/certificates/cacert.pem`. There is no default value.

ssl server key   You designate the location of the server's own key file in this parameter. If you've configured your server as specified in this chapter, then an appropriate setting is `ssl server key = /etc/certificates/private/cakey.pem`. This parameter has no default value.

The foregoing three parameters are enough to enable a basic SSL server configuration, but this configuration supports only encryption and *not* certificates. To use certificates, you must set the following additional options:

ssl ca certfile   This parameter specifies the location of the certificates of all the trusted CAs. On a small server, this file may contain information on just one CA. To use certificates, you *must* use either this parameter or the `ssl ca certdir` parameter (but not both). If you've configured SSL as described earlier in "Basic SSL Configuration," you should point this parameter to /etc/certificates/cacert.pem. There is no default value.

ssl ca certdir This parameter specifies the location of the SSL CA certificates directory. The directory works like an SSL certification file, but each CA has its own file in the directory. This configuration, although it involves more work to set up if you have just a few CAs, may be preferable if you use a large number of CAs. There is no default value.

ssl client cert This parameter specifies an SSL client certificate file's location, such as the simone.pem file described earlier in "Creating Client Certificates." smbclient uses this client file when connecting to an SSL-enabled server. This file must be located in a directory that's readable by anybody who uses smbclient. If you want to use certificates as a client, you must set this option.

> **WARNING** Even though the SSL client certification file must be readable by anyone using an SSL-enabled connection, the file is still sensitive, so you should protect it as best you can given its required availability. You may want to create an SSL user group that can read the file, while restricting access to other users.

ssl client key This parameter specifies the location of an SSL client key file, such as simone.key, described in "Creating Client Certificates." This option is required if you want to use the computer as a client with a certificate. This key should be protected by placing it in a directory that's readable only by root.

ssl require clientcert This boolean parameter determines whether Samba as a server will accept a connection from a client that lacks a certificate. The default value is No, which means that the server does not require a client certificate. Such connections are encrypted, but there's still a chance that one will come from an unauthorized source.

ssl require servercert This boolean parameter determines whether smbclient will connect to a server that has no certification. As with ssl require clientcert, the default value is No, which enables encryption of connections but does little to guarantee the identity of the server.

Samba supports a number of additional SSL features, some of which require configuration options. You may want to use one or more of the following options to expand or fine-tune your configuration:

ssl hosts This parameter allows you to specify clients that *must* use SSL to connect to the server. It takes a list of computer names or IP addresses as a value, using the same syntax as the `hosts allow` and `hosts deny` parameters, described in "Restricting Access by Computer" at the beginning of in this chapter. If neither this parameter nor the `ssl hosts resign` parameter is used, and if `ssl = Yes`, Samba requires *all* connections to be made through SSL.

`ssl hosts resign`   This parameter is the opposite of `ssl hosts`; it specifies a list of clients that need not use SSL to connect to an SSL-enabled server. You might set up this parameter if you require only connections that arrive through routers to be SSL-enabled. You can specify your local network's IP addresses on `ssl hosts resign`, to exempt them from using SSL.

`ssl ciphers`   You can specify which *ciphers* (that is, encryption schemes) Samba will use when negotiating a connection. Possible values are `DEFAULT`, `DES-CFB-M1`, `NULL-MD5`, `RC4-MD5`, `EXP-RC4-MD5`, `RC2-CBC-MD5`, `EXP-RC2-CBC-MD5`, `IDEA-CBC-MD5`, `DES-CBC-MD5`, `DES-CBC-SHA`, `DES-CBC3-MD5`, `DES-CBC3-SHA`, `RC4-64-MD5`, and `NULL`. Unless you're an SSL expert, I recommend you not adjust this parameter.

`ssl version`   This parameter specifies which versions of the SSL protocol Samba will attempt to use. The default value is `ssl2or3`, which indicates that versions 2 and 3 will both be accepted. If necessary, you can set this parameter to `tls1`, `ssl2`, or `ssl3`.

`ssl compatibility`   This parameter configures Samba to use some older SSL implementations. The default value is `No`, and chances are you won't need to change this.

If your server accepts both SSL-encrypted and unencrypted connections, you may need to use the `ssl hosts` or `ssl hosts resign` parameters. The latter is generally more secure because it sets up an exception to the SSL requirement rather than requiring SSL for only some connections. The rest of these parameters are advanced features that you probably won't need to adjust.

Testing Samba's SSL Functionality

The easiest way to test Samba's SSL functionality is to configure SSL with the three necessary SSL parameters (described in "Setting Samba's SSL Parameters") plus any certificate parameters necessary for your SSL configuration. You must then restart the Samba daemons. When you start `smbd`, you must enter your server's pass phrase. If you're not asked for a pass phrase, you're *not* using an SSL-enabled version of Samba with SSL features turned on.

Once Samba is running, use the `smbclient` program from the SSL-enabled Samba package to connect to the local computer. For example, if Samba is running on `clouseau`, you might type **`smbclient //clouseau/shares`**. If all goes well, `smbclient` prompts you for the client's pass phrase. After that, `smbclient` prompts for the normal Samba password for your user. During this process, the SSL component reports what SSL encryption method (or *cipher*) has been negotiated, such as `DES-CBC3-SHA`.

> **WARNING** If SSL reports that it's using NULL for a cipher, it means your data are *not* being encrypted. You should review your settings, particularly the ssl ciphers parameter.

If SSL reports an error, such as unknown error 18, check your certification settings. Although you can connect without certification and ignore this error message, any attempt to use either client or server certificates with incorrect certification parameters will cause the system to fail.

Configuring a Client to Use SSL

Some of the Samba configuration options discussed in "Setting Samba's SSL Parameters" govern client configuration. You can use these options to configure smbclient as an SSL-enabled client. As of Samba 2.0.7, smbmount does not support SSL functionality, but you can use smbmount through an SSL proxy. Windows doesn't natively support SSL. Therefore, the only way to use Windows systems as SSL-enabled Samba clients is to use them through a proxy. There are two ways to do this: by running a separate proxy server computer or by running an SSL proxy on the client itself. Both options are explained in the next two sections.

Using an SSL Proxy Server Computer

If you're using Windows clients, SSL functionality is much more difficult to implement than it is when using smbclient. The usual way to use SSL with Windows clients is to use an SSL *proxy server*. This is a computer that stands in for another one. In the case of an SSL connection to a Samba server, it works as shown in Figure 14.6. The client computer connects to the proxy server, which then encrypts the communications that pass over an untrusted network to reach the server.

Figure 14.6 An SSL proxy server uses unencrypted communication with the client, but encrypted communication with the server.

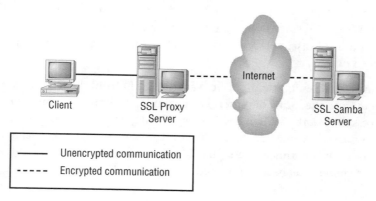

Several SSL proxy servers support SMB/CIFS networking. Two popular choices are SSL Proxy (http://obdev.at/Products/sslproxy.html) and Stunnel (http://www.stunnel.org/). Both of these packages are available for both Windows and Unix. For Linux, you can compile the Unix source code. You'll need the same SSL libraries that are required to compile an SSL-enabled version of Samba.

> **WARNING**   The Windows binary versions of SSL Proxy available from the SSL Proxy Web site include separate .EXE and .DLL files. Unfortunately, Netscape for Windows corrupts .DLL files when downloading them. You can download the files with Internet Explorer or the Linux version of Netscape to work around this problem.

As an example, let's consider SSL Proxy. Once you have a binary version and client certificate files, you can run it as follows:

```
# sslproxy -l 139 -R server -r 139 -n -c certif.pem -k certif.key
```

You can run the program in precisely the same way on either a Windows or Linux proxy server. The program asks for the client pass phrase. It should then display the following information:

```
SSL: No verify locations, trying default
proxy ready, listening for connections
```

The first line is merely information to the effect that the program is reading some information from default files. The second line indicates that the program is running correctly. You can then try using an unencrypted connection from a client on the proxy server's local network to the proxy server. The proxy server should allow connections to shares on the SSL-enabled Samba server.

One drawback to using SSL Proxy as just described is that the program only forwards TCP port traffic. This means the proxy server (and hence the remote system) won't show up in Network Neighborhood. You can, however, directly address the server by entering the proxy server's name in a Windows file browser's Address field, as in \\PROXY. This should produce a list of the shares available through the proxy server. If the proxy server is a Linux system, you can run nmbd *without* smbd on the proxy server to work around the problem.

Using a Proxy Server Directly on a Client

As I've just described it, the proxy server usurps TCP port 139, which is normally used by smbd or the Windows implementation of SMB/CIFS. This fact means you can't use normal SMB/CIFS tools on the proxy server. If you must run Samba on a Linux SSL proxy, you can use the -p option to the Samba daemons to bind them to nonstandard ports—but it will mean that only clients supporting similar options, such as smbclient, can use the Samba server. On either Linux or Windows, one alternative is to bind the proxy server only to the localhost (127.0.0.1) address. You can accomplish this task by using a command like the following:

```
# sslproxy -L 127.0.0.1 -l 139 -R server -r 139 -n -c certif.pem ⤸
-k certif.key
```

When you use this technique, it helps to add an entry to the lmhosts file (this is C:\WINDOWS\LMHOSTS on Windows 9x, C:\WINNT\SYSTEM32\DRIVERS\ETC\LMHOSTS on Windows NT, or lmhosts in your Samba configuration directory on Linux). The entry in lmhosts should link the 127.0.0.1 IP address to some useful name, like localhost. Such an entry looks like this:

```
127.0.0.1   localhost
```

When you run SSL Proxy in this way, you can access the SSL-enabled Samba server by connecting to the computer called LOCALHOST. For instance, you can mount a share in Windows with this command:

```
C:> NET USE G: \\LOCALHOST\JACQUES
```

If the server you specified in the sslproxy command hosts the JACQUES share, this command mounts that share as G:. From the point of view of Windows's SMB/CIFS networking, Windows is making an unencrypted connection to itself. Because this connection is entirely internal, no unencrypted data leaks onto the network. SSL Proxy encrypts the data and sends it out over the network. This sort of configuration can be extremely useful if you want the highest level of security even on your local network wires.

Windows normally binds its SMB/CIFS servers only to real network interfaces, not the localhost interface. Samba, however, binds to the localhost interface as well as others. You can use the interfaces and bind interfaces only parameters, described earlier in "Binding Samba to Specific Network Interfaces," to keep Samba from using these interfaces so that SSL Proxy can use them. Unfortunately, this causes SWAT and smbpasswd to malfunction because they use the localhost interface internally.

Samba in the Broader Security World

As discussed in this chapter, Samba includes many features that can enhance your server's security. The capability of blocking accesses based on port or IP address can present a high initial hurdle to troublemakers. Appropriate use of password policies and password encryption can help more. Encrypting entire sessions with SSL contributes still more.

All of these features are built into Samba, however, or they at least use Samba in conjunction with SSL or another tool. In principle, a critical flaw at a low enough level of Samba could make many of these security features moot. It's therefore wise to use external mechanisms to block access to Samba from at least some potentially undesirable sources. This section covers a few such tools: external firewalls, the Linux `ipchains` program, and `xinetd`.

Ports Used by SMB/CIFS

External security tools usually work by blocking access to specific *ports* on a computer. In this context, a port is a means of reaching a particular program that's running on the server. A port is analogous to a telephone number. When a client contacts a server, it does so by contacting the port number associated with the server, just as you can contact a person by dialing that individual's telephone number. In some cases, including Windows SMB/CIFS clients, the client calls from a fixed port number itself; but in most cases, including Samba clients, the client's originating port number is variable.

The TCP/IP stack supports several different types of ports. The two that are important for this discussion are the *User Datagram Protocol (UDP)* and *Transmission Control Protocol (TCP)*. UDP ports are used for quick and possibly unreliable transmissions, whereas TCP is used for extended and reliable connections. A specific port number may be used by one protocol for UDP and another for TCP, although in most cases a single protocol claims both UDP and TCP ports, even if it doesn't use both.

SMB/CIFS uses port numbers 137 and 138 as UDP ports, and 139 as a TCP port, but the entire range 137–139 is reserved for SMB/CIFS on both UDP and TCP. You can use this arrangement to block access to Samba from clients that should not be accessing the server—you need only block both TCP and UDP ports from 137–139.

Using *ipchains* or a Firewall to Block Samba Access

A *firewall* is a computer that sits between a protected network of computers and an untrusted network (such as the Internet), to block undesirable access from the outside, and sometimes to block unauthorized access to the outside from the inside. Figure 14.7 illustrates this arrangement. As illustrated in this figure, the only way for traffic to pass between the internal network and the Internet is for it to pass through the firewall computer.

Maintaining a
Healthy System

PART 4

Figure 14.7 A firewall computer, like a physical firewall in a car or building, serves as a barrier to prevent undesirable things from happening to a protected region.

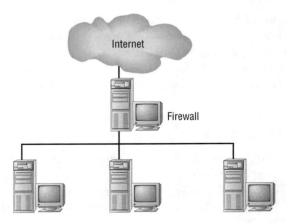

Firewalls can be specialized pieces of equipment, or ordinary computers running an ordinary OS but configured with minimal but specialized tools. If you have a stand-alone firewall, you should consult its documentation to learn how to block ports 137–139. Assuming the firewall works properly, this configuration will protect your network from attack via SMB/CIFS.

Linux computers can function as firewalls. At the core of Linux's firewall capabilities is the ipchains tool. With ipchains, you can configure Linux to accept or reject packets based on characteristics such as the network interface, the source address, the destination address, the source port, and the destination port. You can use ipchains either to create a simple stand-alone firewall, similar to the one in Figure 14.7, or to protect a single computer. Although the details of ipchains configuration are well beyond the scope of this book, an example set of ipchains rules that can run on a Samba server is shown in Listing 14.2.

Listing 14.2 ipchains Rules to Protect Samba

```
ipchains -A input -p tcp -s 192.168.34.0/24 137 -j ACCEPT
ipchains -A input -p udp -s 192.168.34.0/24 137 -j ACCEPT
ipchains -A input -p tcp -s 192.168.34.0/24 138 -j ACCEPT
ipchains -A input -p udp -s 192.168.34.0/24 138 -j ACCEPT
ipchains -A input -p tcp -s 192.168.34.0/24 139 -j ACCEPT
ipchains -A input -p udp -s 192.168.34.0/24 139 -j ACCEPT
ipchains -A input -p tcp -s 0/0 137 -l -j DENY
ipchains -A input -p udp -s 0/0 137 -l -j DENY
```

```
ipchains -A input -p tcp -s 0/0 138 -l -j DENY
ipchains -A input -p udp -s 0/0 138 -l -j DENY
ipchains -A input -p tcp -s 0/0 139 -l -j DENY
ipchains -A input -p udp -s 0/0 139 -l -j DENY
ipchains -A output -p tcp -d 192.168.34.0/24 137 -j ACCEPT
ipchains -A output -p udp -d 192.168.34.0/24 137 -j ACCEPT
ipchains -A output -p tcp -d 192.168.34.0/24 138 -j ACCEPT
ipchains -A output -p udp -d 192.168.34.0/24 138 -j ACCEPT
ipchains -A output -p tcp -d 192.168.34.0/24 139 -j ACCEPT
ipchains -A output -p udp -d 192.168.34.0/24 139 -j ACCEPT
ipchains -A output -p tcp -d 0/0 137 -l -j DENY
ipchains -A output -p udp -d 0/0 137 -l -j DENY
ipchains -A output -p tcp -d 0/0 138 -l -j DENY
ipchains -A output -p udp -d 0/0 138 -l -j DENY
ipchains -A output -p tcp -d 0/0 139 -l -j DENY
ipchains -A output -p udp -d 0/0 139 -l -j DENY
```

Although it contains 24 lines and 24 rules, Listing 14.2 is actually fairly simple. It's constructed of four sections, each of which has six variant commands, one for each of the three UDP ports and three TCP ports. The four major sections control the following accesses:

- Input to the Samba ports from the 192.168.34.0/24 network is explicitly allowed. This set of rules allows computers on the local network to use the server. (Naturally, you must change this address to fit your network.)

- Input to the Samba ports from all other IP addresses is explicitly denied. Foreign computers therefore can't use the server.

- Output directed at the SMB/CIFS ports on the 192.168.34.0/24 network is explicitly allowed. This set of rules allows Samba to reply to requests that originate from the SMB/CIFS ports, which is how most Windows systems operate. It also lets the computer run as a client.

- Output directed at the SMB/CIFS ports on all other IP addresses is explicitly denied. This set of rules blocks output directed at foreign SMB/CIFS servers, or replies to foreign Windows SMB/CIFS clients. These rules can prevent local users from abusing others' computers.

Although ipchains is often thought of as a firewall tool, it can be very useful for restricting access to server programs on individual server computers. In fact, the rules in Listing 14.2 are designed for such a configuration. If Listing 14.2 were used as the basis for a Samba policy on a stand-alone firewall, you'd need to add options to restrict the rules' application to particular network interfaces.

NOTE ipchains is the tool used for packet filtering on the 2.2.*x* kernel series. The older 2.0.*x* kernels used a similar tool called ipfwadm, and the newer 2.4.*x* kernels (not yet released at this writing) will use a newer utility called iptables. Configuration details for these packages differ, but the basics as I've described them here are the same: You can block access to Samba's ports based on IP addresses, network interface, and so on.

Whether you use a stand-alone firewall computer or a set of ipchains rules on your Samba servers, blocking access to Samba with something other than Samba is a good idea. In fact, it wouldn't hurt to use *both* an external firewall *and* a set of ipchains rules on your Samba servers.

Running Samba through TCP Wrappers or *xinetd*

Most serious Samba servers run the Samba daemons directly. It is possible, however, to run Samba through inetd, the so-called *super server*. Doing this can result in a reduced memory load on the server, but at the cost of slowed responses to access attempts and seriously hindered capacity as a domain controller, NBNS server, or master browser. These drawbacks make running Samba through inetd a poor choice for most servers. You might want to consider using this option if your server is seldom used (for instance, if your computer is principally a client to which others connect only rarely).

If the drawbacks of running Samba through inetd aren't overwhelming, you can use assorted access control features to help improve Samba's security. One of these is to use TCP Wrappers to block access to Samba based on the client's IP address or assorted other features. This functionality is similar to that provided by the Samba hosts allow and hosts deny parameters. Because it's implemented in a separate program, however, there may be some modest security benefits should a flaw be discovered in Samba's implementation of these features. Chapter 3 explains Samba running through inetd, including TCP Wrappers used as part of the configuration.

One alternative to inetd and TCP Wrappers is a package called xinetd (http://www .xinetd.org). This program improves on inetd with TCP Wrappers because xinetd allows you to bind a server to a specific network interface. This fact can reduce the susceptibility of the servers to IP spoofing attacks. Unfortunately, Samba's nmbd doesn't run properly from xinetd, although smbd does. If your Samba server has two or more network interfaces and you don't need access to Samba from all of them, you might want to consider running nmbd separately and running smbd via xinetd.

Non-Samba Servers

As a general rule, you should run as few servers as possible on any one computer. Many Linux distributions ship with a distressingly large number of servers active by default. This fact leaves the system vulnerable to outside attack. Bugs or misconfiguration of any of these servers could allow outsiders access to the server, or make it possible for a malicious local user to abuse the system. Ideally, a Samba server should run *only* Samba. In practice this is often impossible; you may require SSH or Telnet to gain access to the system to administer it, or you may need to run NFS, Netatalk, or some other file server to make the system a useful cross-platform server. Nevertheless, it's wise to examine your server's configuration for opportunities to remove unnecessary servers.

The /etc/inetd.conf file is a good place to start tracking down unnecessary servers. In this file, a typical Linux computer includes many lines like the following:

```
ftp     stream  tcp  nowait  root  /usr/sbin/tcpd  proftpd
telnet  stream  tcp  nowait  root  /usr/sbin/tcpd  in.telnetd
# nntp  stream  tcp  nowait  news  /usr/sbin/tcpd  /usr/sbin/leafnode
pop3    stream  tcp  nowait  root  /usr/sbin/tcpd  /usr/sbin/popper -s
```

These four lines enable three servers—FTP, Telnet, and POP3. The NNTP server line is commented out and thus disabled.

> **TIP**   As a general rule, if you don't know what a server does, you should disable it. A better policy is to learn what a server does, and disable it once you've determined you don't need it. Adding a pound sign (#) to the start of the server's line in /etc/inetd.conf disables it.

Some servers run apart from inetd. Typically, these servers are started through startup scripts located in the /etc/rc.d directory tree. You can disable these servers by moving their startup scripts from /etc/rc.d or /etc/rc.d/init.d to some other directory. "Running Samba" in Chapter 3 discusses various options for running Samba, including startup scripts. These same options apply to most other servers.

For added safety, you should remove unused servers entirely from your system. If you're using an RPM- or Debian-based Linux distribution, you can accomplish this removal quite easily using the rpm or dpkg tools. For example, **rpm -e proftpd** removes the proftpd FTP server package.

Once you've removed unnecessary servers from your system, Samba will be more secure because it's that much more protected from compromise via an intermediary network server.

Summary

By default, Samba provides a modest level of security based on password authentication. Most configurations require alterations because new Windows clients use encrypted passwords, which involve setting Samba options and preparing a special password file. If you're security conscious, Samba offers a large number of options that can improve the server's level of security. These range from blocks based on client IP addresses, to tightened security on files within shares, to encryption of all data that passes over your network wires. You can also employ non-Samba security measures such as external firewalls, `ipchains`, and `xinetd` to protect Samba from harm.

How far you take these measures depends on the level of security you require. Because they're so easy to configure and provide substantial potential benefit, most sites would do well to use the `hosts allow` parameter and external `ipchains` tool to block access to all but a narrow range of approved host computers. You should also review your server's internal security model and verify that it's not running unnecessary non-Samba servers. Additional measures may be necessary in some environments, as when sensitive data pass over the network or when you use SMB/CIFS networking across the Internet.

## 15

Managing Accounts

Unless you use share-level security (described in "The Security Model" in Chapter 14) or make extensive use of guest accounts (described in "Managing Guest Access" here in this chapter), Samba users must have regular Linux accounts. This is true even when you use another system as the password server for Samba. In most configurations, Samba works well with normal Linux account setups, at least when used to provide access to individual users' files. In some cases, you may need to use specialized Samba features to work around differences between the Linux and Windows ways of handling accounts and passwords. Many of these options are described in Chapter 14, particularly in "Encrypted versus Cleartext Passwords." This chapter is devoted to the additional account-management features of Samba, and to a discussion of Samba's interaction with normal Linux account handling.

We begin with a look at usernames and groups in both Linux and Windows, including the translations necessary when the two don't match. We'll also examine guest accounts. Passwords, including synchronizing Windows, Samba, and Linux passwords and strategies for changing passwords, are the topics in the second half of the chapter.

Using Linux Usernames and Groups

Linux employs usernames as the most basic form of user identification. Each username has an associated account, and the account has specific permissions. These permissions apply largely to the ability to read, write, and execute files and directories. Because Linux uses files to provide many other system features (such as device files in the /dev directory, which provide access to hardware such as disk drives and serial ports), usernames and their associated accounts are extremely important in Linux.

Linux also uses groups to assign permissions. Each file, in addition to user permissions, has an associated group and group permissions. You can create arbitrary groups of users, as described in "Creating Groups to Emulate ACLs," and you can create appropriate permissions on files to accommodate group members' access to those files.

Matching Windows and Linux Usernames

One of the challenges of integrating Windows and Linux lies in the fact that it's not always possible to use the same usernames on Linux that you work with on a Windows network. If you're setting up a new network, this isn't normally a problem, because you can be careful to use the same usernames for both Linux and Windows networking. If you're faced with the task of adding a Samba server to an existing Windows network, however, you may run up against the fact that NetBIOS provides greater flexibility in usernames than does Linux. NetBIOS usernames can contain spaces and can be longer than what Linux allows, for instance. Your existing Windows network might include usernames like Marie Curie and Neils Bohr. Because Linux doesn't cope well with these usernames, you may need to use substitutes such as mcurie and nbohr. The challenge, then, is to map the Linux usernames onto the NetBIOS usernames.

The Username Map File

Samba's global parameter username map provides the means to map from Windows to Linux usernames. You use this parameter to point to a text file containing the mappings you want to maintain. You might specify username map = /etc/samba/usermap.conf, for instance. You could then create a usermap.conf file similar to the one shown in Listing 15.1.

Listing 15.1 Sample Username Mapping File Demonstrating Critical Features

```
# Username map file
!nbohr = "Neils Bohr"
!curie = "Pierre Curie"
!mcurie = "Marie Curie" curie
!nobel = @prize
!mplanck = Planck
amateur = *
```

A username map file contains a series of lines, each of which consists of a Linux username followed by an equals sign and one or more Windows usernames or Linux username groups. Following are the details of the file shown in Listing 15.1:

- Lines that begin with pound signs (#) or semicolons (;) are comment lines; Samba ignores them.

- When a Windows username includes one or more spaces, it must be enclosed in quotation marks ("), like the usernames `Neils Bohr` and `Marie Curie` in the example.

- You can map two or more Windows usernames onto a single Linux username by listing all the Windows usernames after the equals sign. This was done with the Linux user `mcurie` in the example.

- You can map all the members of an NIS network group or a Linux group onto a single Linux user by preceding the group name with a @ character, as is done in the example with the Linux user `nobel`, who matches all members of the group `prize`.

- If a line starts with an exclamation point (!), Samba stops trying to match when that line results in a match. This feature is most useful if you intend to use a wildcard to match unknown users to a specific Linux username, as is the case in Listing 15.1. You might also want to use this character if your Windows and Linux systems include the same username but assigned to different people. For example, consider the Linux users `curie` and `mcurie` in the example. The username `curie` under Linux refers to Pierre Curie; but the same username (`curie`) refers to Marie Curie under Windows. If the exclamation marks were removed from the `curie` line, Linux would map `Pierre Curie` onto `curie`, then proceed to map `curie` onto `mcurie`. As a result, when Pierre logged on he'd be unable to access his account because Samba would be expecting Marie's password.

- You can include an asterisk (*) as a wildcard that matches any username (but see the Warning that follows). For example, the last line of Listing 15.1 matches all usernames to the Linux user `amateur`. If you do use a wildcard, put exclamation points on preceding lines to halt processing, as does the example file; otherwise, all users will end up mapped to the wildcard username.

WARNING As of Samba 2.0.7, the handling of wildcards is buggy. Specifically, if a wildcard is present, Samba expects the wildcard user's password for all access attempts, even if earlier lines are preceded by exclamation marks as in Listing 15.1. If a user enters the wildcard user's password, that user is let in with the wildcard user's permissions, but using the named user's home directory (if applicable). Because of this bug, I recommend you *not* use wildcards in your username map. Try using a guest account instead (which requires no password), or the `force user` parameter (which requires a valid username and password).

In addition to the username map, Samba 2.0.7 and later supports a similar map file for mapping Linux groups to Windows NT groups. The parameter that points to this file is called map groupname, and the file format is similar to that of a username map file.

The Mapping Process

When a user tries to log on to the Samba server using a Windows username included in the map file, Samba tries to authenticate the user as if the matching Linux username had been given. In the case of Listing 15.1, if a user enters Marie Curie as the username, Samba tries to authenticate against the password stored for mcurie. If this user tries to access her home directory, Linux displays the contents of mcurie's home directory (probably /home/mcurie).

The presence of a username map file does not normally prevent application of normal Linux usernames. In the Listing 15.1 example, a user could enter usernames Marie Curie, curie, or mcurie to gain access. Pierre Curie isn't so lucky, however; his "legitimate" username of curie is usurped by Marie's Windows username. Users who are not listed in the username map file can also access the system with their normal usernames. For instance, if the entry for nbohr were not included in Listing 15.1, that user could still enter nbohr as a username to access the server.

The mapping provided by username map is one-way; Samba interprets the Windows username as if it were the matching Linux username, but Samba *doesn't* map the Linux username to a matching Windows username. For the most part, this creates no problems. Should you create a [homes] share, though, users will see their home directories under their Linux usernames rather than their Windows usernames. Also, Windows clients might refuse to allow users to delete their own print jobs, because from the point of view of the Windows clients, the jobs aren't owned by the correct users.

Security Issues

The username map parameter, particularly in conjunction with a wildcard, might appear at first glance to be a potentially major security hole, but in fact it's not. Unlike the force user parameter, username map doesn't allow one user to access another user's files without having the target user's password. In Listing 15.1, for example, although a wildcard maps all unknown usernames onto the user amateur, Samba still requires amateur's password before granting access to that account. Thus, a user could type in the Windows username Velikovsky, but unless the amateur password is entered as well, Samba doesn't let the user in. This user could as easily type amateur as the username, so the only security risk comes from the fact that every username is effectively a valid one, albeit one that leads to a specific account. Even this modest risk is reduced to nearly nothing if there's no wildcard in the username map file.

The `username map` parameter appears superficially similar to `force user`, but the two are very different. Setting up a username map essentially allows Samba to accept one or more alternative usernames as synonyms for a Linux username. The target Linux password is still required for access. By contrast, `force user` forces Samba to give one Linux user the access privileges of another, effectively making two or more Linux users indistinguishable once they've logged on to the Samba server. The difference between the two parameters is illustrated in Figure 15.1.

Figure 15.1   The `username map` parameter juggles usernames *before* a password is entered, whereas `force user` does so *after* authentication.

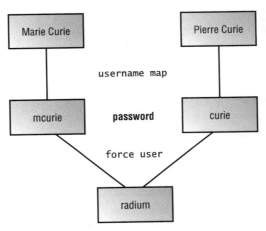

Managing Guest Access

Sometimes you'll want to grant limited or even complete access to one or more Samba shares without bothering with accounts and passwords. You might do this, for example, when setting up a computer that functions only as a print server on a trusted internal network. Assuming that all the users of that internal network should indeed have access to the printer, heavy security for the printer shares probably isn't needed. Similarly, you might want to use guest accounts on a file server for files to which all your users have access—particularly read-only access, for which you need no username-based accounting.

> **WARNING** Although there's no need to protect some shares against unautho-
> rized local users when all local users are authorized, it may still be necessary to
> protect against unauthorized *remote* users. You don't want to leave a print server
> vulnerable to a miscreant halfway around the globe who decides to print a ream
> of completely black pages on an expensive dye-sublimation printer, for instance.
> At the very least, consider using the Samba hosts allow parameter to block
> access except from authorized hosts. You might also want to use a firewall or
> ipchains rules for similar reasons.

Chapter 5 discusses the options available for guest access, in the section "Guest Access."
As a brief summary, here are the four guest access parameters offered by Samba:

map to guest This global parameter determines when Samba invokes guest
access. The default value is Never, in which case Samba disallows all guest access.
Other options are Bad User (Samba allows guest access only when Samba is given
a username it doesn't recognize) and Bad Password (Samba allows guest access
whenever it's given a username *or* password it doesn't recognize).

guest account You specify the Linux username that's associated with guest access
using this share-level parameter. This should normally be a low-privilege account,
because guest access allows anybody into the system.

guest ok This boolean share-level parameter determines whether Samba permits
guest access to a share. The default value is No. A synonym for this parameter is
public.

guest only When set to Yes, this parameter specifies that *all* accesses to a share be
treated as guest accesses, even if the user enters a valid username and password. The
default value is No. A synonym for this parameter is only guest.

Guest access can be very convenient when you don't want to maintain an extensive list of
usernames and passwords on a server, and you need little or nothing in the way of security. One of the most important issues surrounding guest access is the username under
which that access is granted—that is, the value of the map to guest parameter. One common option for this parameter's value is nobody, which is an extremely low-privilege user
on most Linux installations. With map to guest = nobody, any unwanted access via a
guest share is likely to cause minimal problems, because the user nobody has little power
to affect other users' files. Another option is to create a special guest user account. Typically, this account has its own associated group, so it doesn't have group-level access to
anyone else's files. If guest users need such access, though, you may want to make the
guest account part of the target group.

Unlike Windows, Samba supports multiple guest accounts. One share can set the guest account to one user; another can set it to another user. This is a feature you won't notice from Windows clients, but you can use it on a server to slightly enhance security, even while providing guest access. Use one guest account for a printer share, another for a read-only file share, and a third for a read/write file share. Each of these guest accounts can have slightly different minimum permissions. For example, the read-only share's guest account might require the ability to read files belonging to a certain group, but the others might not. Using multiple guest accounts therefore lets you add an extra layer of security, in case a misconfiguration or Samba bug allows, say, a break-in through the printer share. When the printer share's underlying account has limited rights, you reduce the damage possible from that share, even if an uncompromised guest share uses an account with higher privileges.

Creating Groups to Emulate ACLs

Many experienced Windows NT administrators find Linux's permission scheme to be limiting. Certainly Windows NT's access control lists (ACLs) are flexible, but Windows NT administrators often underestimate the flexibility of Linux's own groups. It's often possible to use Linux groups to achieve effects similar to ACLs, although the process can be tedious.

Linux maintains a list of user groups in the /etc/group file. This file consists of multiple lines, each of which is a colon-delimited list of four components:

- The group name.
- An encrypted group password. In most cases, this is x, indicating that the system uses shadow passwords. Samba doesn't use group passwords.
- A numeric ID for the group. Most Linux systems use numbers of 100 and up for user groups.
- A comma-delimited list of users who are members of the group.

Here's an example of a line from /etc/group:

```
physics:x:102:mcurie,nbohr,mplanck
```

This line adds the users mcurie, nbohr, and mplanck to the physics group. If a file is associated with this group, then these users can read, write, or execute that file based on the file's group permissions. (If the user owns the file, or if the file's configuration oddly allows greater permission to all users than to the group, then the user may have greater permissions with respect to that file.)

The key to emulating ACL flexibility lies in creating *multiple overlapping* groups. To handle the three users in our example, you could create eight groups: one with all three users, three that omit one user each, three that contain but one user, and one with none of the users. Of course, creating one group for every possible combination of users becomes impractical as the number of users grows. A more practical approach is to create groups based on utility. You can add or delete users from groups as the need arises, and if you need a new group, you can create one from scratch, populating it with users who are members of no existing group, one group, or more.

Once you've created some groups, you can set the group to which files belong based on which collection of users you want to have access to the files; then set group permissions appropriately. The drawback to this approach is that it may require a phenomenal number of groups if you need substantial flexibility in individuals' access to files. You can't change a file's group ownership from Windows, so making an individual file accessible to other users from a Windows client is impossible.

Despite these drawbacks, limited utilization of customized groups can be a good approach to controlling file access. Let's say you've got half a dozen working groups, and some individuals belong to multiple groups. You'd create Linux groups, each of which contains appropriate group members, and then use those groups when you create Samba shares for the groups. You can't adjust access on a file-by-file basis from Windows clients, but you *can* adjust access to shares in this way—and even fine-tune access within shares by setting group ownership as root from a shell prompt.

Using *valid users* and *invalid users* to Create Pseudo-Groups

Another approach to handling groups of users is to use the Samba valid users and invalid users parameters described in Chapter 5. These parameters allow you to give an arbitrary set of users access to a share. For example, suppose you've got two Linux groups as follows:

```
physics:
    nbohr, mcurie, mplanck
biology:
    cdarwin, dfossey, gmendel
```

You can provide access to specific shares to subgroups, or to collections that span multiple groups, as illustrated by Listing 15.2. In this listing's definition, the share [subgroup] can be accessed by only part of the Linux physics group, whereas the [crossgroup] share can be accessed by one or more members of both Linux groups.

Listing 15.2   Example of `valid users` as a Means of Restricting Share Access

```
[subgroup]
        valid users = nbohr, mcurie
        path = /home/samba/subgroup

[crossgroup]
        valid users = mcurie, dfossey, gmendel
        path = /home/samba/crossgroup
```

> **NOTE**   In practice, Listing 15.2 may be inadequate. Especially if you need to create read/write shares, you may need to use parameters such as `force user` or `create mask` to allow users from disparate groups to modify each others' files cleanly.

Using `valid users` and `invalid users` to create pseudo-groups is not without its drawbacks, however. These include the following:

- Adding or removing pseudo-group members requires editing `smb.conf`—a tedious process if your groups change frequently.
- These pseudo-groups are only effective in Samba. If users have shell accounts on the server, they may be able to access shares to which they should not have access. You can use dummy accounts, include `force user` in `smb.conf`, and set up restrictive permissions to block unauthorized shell access, but these measures will also block access from authorized users.
- Pseudo-groups can be used to control access only to shares, not individual files within shares.

On the whole, when you need to restrict access to some arbitrary group of users, putting the `valid users` parameter to work can be a quick and easy way to achieve the goal. You can also combine this parameter with others, such as `read users` and `write users`, to fine-tune the type of access granted. For finer control of access to individual files, though, Linux groups are probably a better solution.

Managing Passwords

One critical aspect of account management is password management. On a network with many servers, one user might conceivably have several different passwords—or one password duplicated in the password databases of many servers. Chapter 14, and particularly the section "Encrypted versus Cleartext Passwords," covers many of the issues involved

Maintaining a
Healthy System

PART 4

in managing users' passwords. Some of these same issues deserve elaboration here, as part of the discussion of user accounts. In particular, it's important to understand how to use a single domain controller or password server to reduce administrative headaches; how users can change passwords on such a server; and how to set a policy concerning password changes.

Passwords in Workgroups and Domains

One of the principal differences between a workgroup and a domain (see Chapter 10) is the fact that each server in a workgroup is essentially an island, providing its own authentication mechanisms. In a domain, on the other hand, all servers defer to a domain controller for the task of authenticating users. This fact makes domains much easier to administer than workgroups when the same set of users must have access to multiple servers. If you have five servers, it's much easier to administer a single set of passwords on a domain controller than it is to administer five independent sets of passwords.

Samba can blur the lines between workgroups and domains with respect to password authentication. Even in a workgroup, you can set `security = Server` and set `password server` appropriately to have Samba defer to a password server computer. This option may be preferable to using a full domain configuration if you don't need other domain features, such as network logon scripts, because it's slightly easier to configure than a full-fledged domain.

Although using a centralized password server can help reduce some administrative headaches, it doesn't eliminate the need to maintain user accounts on all servers. For example, if `mcurie` and `nbohr` must both have access to five systems, it's still necessary to create ordinary user accounts for both users on all five computers. Employing a centralized password server lets these users change their Samba passwords for all five systems in one operation, but you as network administrator must still add or remove accounts individually. If all your servers have the same list of users, you can use a network account management system such as NIS (Network Information Service) or NIS+. These tools allow you to maintain a centralized database of user accounts. If you use unencrypted passwords, Samba can use NIS or NIS+ for authentication, as well; this configuration is just like using local passwords. Encrypted passwords must rely upon either a local password database or an SMB/CIFS password server, however. The NIS or NIS+ server can double as an SMB/CIFS password server.

Normally, Windows 9*x* computers store copies of their passwords locally, in files that end in `.PWL`. These files can be security risks, because a would-be cracker with access to these files can run password-cracking programs on these files to discover poorly chosen passwords. It's therefore wise to remove these files if possible. Chapter 10 discusses this issue, in "Removing Windows `.PWL` Files." It's most practical to remove `.PWL` files from Windows clients if you've configured your network as a domain.

Changing Passwords

Password maintenance is a task that's done largely by your users. Nonetheless, you should know about the ways this task can be accomplished, so that you may configure your Samba server appropriately, and instruct your users how to do it. There are two sides to the password-changing coin: changing the Samba or Linux password and changing the Windows password. If you use a domain configuration, the latter task may not be necessary, because Windows uses the domain password locally.

Changing Samba Passwords

At the core, there are two ways to change passwords used by Samba:

passwd   The `passwd` command is the normal Linux password-changing command. If Samba is configured to use cleartext passwords, `passwd` changes the password that Samba uses, because Samba uses the normal Linux password in this case.

smbpasswd   This command works much like `passwd`, but it changes users' encrypted Samba passwords.

If your users have shell accounts on the Linux server, they may use these programs to change their Samba passwords. As stated in several other chapters, however, shell accounts can cause problems for Samba, because these accounts give users a level of access to the server that can undermine Samba-specific security measures. You might therefore want to avoid giving users full shell access to the server. In such cases, there are other ways to let users change their passwords:

Using passwd or smbpasswd as logon shell   In this method, you configure users' accounts so that their logon shells point to the `passwd` or `smbpasswd` programs, as appropriate for the server's Samba encryption option. You can adjust the logon shell for a user by editing the `/etc/passwd` file. Each line of this file corresponds to one user, identified by username. Each line consists of several colon-delimited fields, the last of which is the logon shell—normally a common shell such as `/bin/bash` or `/bin/tcsh`. Modify this entry to point to the `passwd` or `smbpasswd` program. Thereafter, the user sees the password-changing program at every log on using the console, Telnet, SSH, or a similar means. Once the password is changed, the logon prompt reappears or the connection is closed.

Changing the password from another Linux system   If your users have shell access to just one computer that runs Samba, they can use the `smbpasswd` program with its `-r` *machinename* parameter to change the password on a remote computer (called *machinename*). This option only works with encrypted passwords.

Changing the password from a Windows 9x system You can use Windows's password-changing features to change the password on a domain controller, including a Samba server that functions as domain controller. In Control Panel, double-click the Passwords icon and then click the Change Other Passwords button. Select Microsoft Networking in the resulting Select Password dialog box (Figure 15.2) and click Change. Windows displays a password-change dialog box, allowing you to change the password on the domain controller.

Figure 15.2 The Microsoft Networking item represents a domain controller when changing passwords in Windows 9x.

Changing the password from a Windows NT system Windows NT's password-changing procedure is different from that of Windows 9x systems. You type Ctrl+Alt+Del, which produces a dialog box with half a dozen buttons, one of which is Change Password. Click this button to display a Change Password dialog. You should then select the domain and username whose password you want to change, and enter the old and new passwords in the appropriate fields. Click OK to execute the change.

Using SWAT for password changes SWAT, the GUI Samba Web Administration Tool (described in Chapter 4), can be used to change encrypted passwords. As normally configured, ordinary users can access SWAT, but they can't change most features. They do, however, have access to the personal password-changing options shown in Figure 15.3. Samba users can therefore change their passwords from any computer with a Web browser by typing **http://*servername*:901** into the browser's address field, where *servername* is the browser's DNS name or IP address. SWAT allows you to change the password on the server where it runs (using the Server Password Management area), or on another server (using the Client/Server Password Management area).

Figure 15.3 SWAT allows you to change either local or remote passwords.

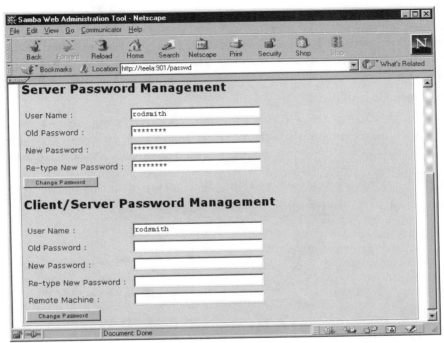

WARNING Most of these password-changing schemes have the drawback that they pass an unencrypted password across the network. They should therefore *never* be used when the data traverses an untrusted network. Indeed, even on an internal network, sending unencrypted passwords over the network is risky if one system has been compromised. I therefore recommend that you allow password changes only from the console of the Samba server or through an encrypted connection, such as an SSH logon using smbpasswd as a logon shell. Of course, if your network uses unencrypted passwords, there's little additional risk to passing unencrypted passwords at password change time.

If you use a single password server (either as part of a domain or as part of a workgroup with security = Server), your users need only change their passwords on the password server computer. You don't have to configure password-changing mechanisms on any other servers.

Changing Windows Passwords

If you use a workgroup configuration or don't eliminate .PWL files, your users will almost certainly want to change their *local* Windows passwords as well as their Samba passwords. Failing to do this will result in annoying requests to enter the new password when accessing network resources. In Windows 9*x*, you change a local password by following these steps:

1. Open Control Panel.

2. Double-click the Users icon. If your system is already configured for multiple users, you'll see a dialog box similar to that in Figure 15.4. Otherwise, you'll be guided through an account-creation process, and then forced to log off and start again.

Figure 15.4   Windows 9*x* provides a simple GUI tool for administering local users.

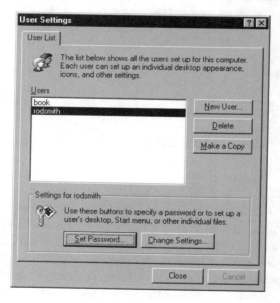

3. Click the name of the user whose password you want to change.

4. Click the Set Password button. Windows displays the Change Windows Password dialog box.

5. Enter the old and new password (twice for the new one), then click OK in the Change Windows Password dialog box. Windows displays a message that the password has been changed.

6. Close the User Settings dialog box.

> **NOTE** To change the domain password, you can also use a procedure similar to that described earlier, in "Changing Samba Passwords." Instead of clicking Change Other Passwords in the Passwords Properties dialog box, though, you click Change Windows Password. This procedure allows users to change only the password with which they access the computer. The somewhat less simple procedure involving the Users object in the Control Panel allows you to change *any* user's password.

Changing the local password isn't necessary if you use a domain and configure Windows not to store passwords in local .PWL files. On Windows NT clients, the procedure is similar to that for changing passwords for domains, except that you select the computer's name rather than the domain in the Domain field of the Change Password dialog box.

Password Change Strategies

As a system administrator, you must set policies regarding password changes. Ideally, all users should change their passwords periodically. Unfortunately, Samba provides no tools to help enforce such a policy with encrypted passwords. If you use cleartext passwords, Linux's shadow password suite (used by most Linux distributions, Corel Linux being a notable exception) includes the capacity to specify when a password is to expire, thus enforcing a password change. If a user never uses a logon shell, however, there may not be advance notice of password expiration; it will simply stop working one day.

One possible solution, requiring some intervention from you, is to announce to all users the requirement to periodically change passwords. To enforce a monthly password change, for instance, you could tell all users that they *must* change their passwords on the first of each month. You can then back up the smbpasswd file prior to this date and, on the second of each month, use diff to compare the old file to the new one. You can then track down any users who have *not* changed their passwords.

In addition to enforcing periodic password changes, educate your users about what constitutes a good password. The ideal password is a random collection of letters, numbers, and symbols. Unfortunately, most humans find such random passwords difficult to remember and so choose easy-to-remember but poor passwords. Particularly poor passwords include the following:

Any real word in any language Unmodified real words are very poor choices for passwords because dictionary-based password attacks are common. If an intruder can acquire a password file (such as smbpasswd or a Windows .PWL file), the intruder can try encoding every word in a dictionary and see if any word matches what's in the password file.

The user's username   This is one of the first passwords many crackers try, and it succeeds far more often than it should.

Proper names   Names of family members, friends, pets, hometowns, and so on can be used in a dictionary-style attack.

Personally relevant information   Birthdays, Social Security numbers, street addresses, and so on can easily be discovered and used by a cracker who wants to break into a particular individual's account.

Minor variations on any of the above   Mixing case is particularly ineffective for encrypted passwords, because Windows *9x* sends encrypted passwords in a case-insensitive form. Tossing a letter or two into a common word seldom does much good, because crackers can do the same thing randomly. Spelling a word backwards is also quite ineffective.

Here's how to create a good and easily remembered password:

1. Begin with a base that consists of a pair of *unrelated* short words, such as *bun* and *pen*. Alternatively, use an acronym that has meaning only to you, such as *yiwttd,* for *yesterday I went to the dentist.*

2. If the base words are long, it may be necessary to shorten them, because normal Linux passwords are limited to eight characters in length with most distributions. Samba encrypted passwords can be longer, but if you want to use the same passwords for Samba and Linux as a whole, your Samba passwords must then also be no longer than eight characters.

3. Add random digits or symbols to the base. For instance, the base *bunpen* might become *bu3np&en.*

You might want to perform some additional steps, such as reversing the order of one or more words in the base, mixing upper- and lowercase characters, using base words from two different languages, and so on. (Mixing upper- and lowercase characters helps little for Samba encrypted passwords, but it may be useful for Linux passwords.) The goal is to build a password that's both easy to remember and not easily guessed from a dictionary attack.

Some Linux password-changing tools can be configured to require that passwords meet certain criteria, such as being greater than a certain number of characters or containing a minimum number of digits. If you use `unix password sync` and related `smb.conf` parameters, as described in "Encryption Parameters in `smb.conf`" in Chapter 14, these criteria are effectively imposed on `smbpasswd`. This is because `smbpasswd` doesn't change the Samba encrypted password until the `passwd chat` script executes successfully.

Summary

Most Samba servers have several users, and some host hundreds or more. Because Samba relies upon Linux's underlying user accounts, you must normally create and maintain these accounts on a Samba server just as you would on a system that's used for Linux shell access. Samba provides its own unique account management features and challenges, however. Integration of Samba with Windows accounts is one of these challenges, albeit one that's easily handled through the use of a username map file. You can set up guest accounts to provide users with anonymous access to your Samba server. Linux groups, as well as some of Samba's share-level parameters, let you approach the utility of Windows NT's ACLs in some ways.

Managing accounts is also an ongoing task, since users should periodically update their passwords. Samba password changes are done with either the `passwd` or the `smbpasswd` program (depending on whether Samba uses cleartext or encrypted passwords, respectively). You can use these programs in various ways or through proxies such as SWAT, to allow users to change their passwords even from their normal client computers. However you set it up, you should encourage your users to change their passwords on a regular basis to reduce the risk of passwords being stolen and falling into the wrong hands.

Maintaining a
Healthy System

PART 4

16

Backups

Your network presumably includes a large amount of data. Some of this information may be irreplaceable—it's documents generated over months or years, containing information that's vitally important to you, your business, or your organization. You may have selected Linux as a server OS because of Linux's reputation for reliability, in order to protect your precious data. Even Linux cannot protect against some disasters, however. Users may inadvertently delete vital files or overwrite them with useless information. Hard disks can fail. Entire computers can be stolen. To protect against such eventualities, it's vital that you have a good backup strategy. With regular backups, none of these misfortunes need be a disaster.

Two aspects of backup are important in the context of Samba. First is backing up the Samba server. Ideally, you can back up the server using a backup device that's attached directly to the server. If necessary, though, you can use network backup options to do the job. The second Samba-related backup task is to back up client computers. Samba helps you do this job, using a single centralized computer to back up an entire network. Once everything is in place, when disaster strikes you'll be ready. You can replace hardware if necessary, pull out your backup, and restore the lost data.

This chapter begins with a discussion of what's involved in performing backups, including hardware and software issues, scheduling, and backup storage. The next topic is Samba server backup, both using local hardware and over a network. This chapter's final topic is backing up clients using Samba.

An Overview of Backup Options

If you're adding a Samba server to an existing network, chances are you've already got some sort of backup system in place. Your task, then, is to integrate your Samba server into your existing configuration. If you're building a new network, however, you may need to design your backup system from scratch. In either case, there are many possible backup configurations, in terms of both hardware and software.

When it comes to network backups, you must decide between client-initiated backups and server-initiated backups. You must also decide on a backup schedule, and where to store backup media.

Backup Hardware Options

Several different types of backup hardware are available. Each has its own unique advantages and drawbacks. On some networks, it may be beneficial to use two or more different backup media, in order to get the best each medium has to offer.

Tapes

Perhaps the most traditional computer backup medium is *magnetic tape*. These are quite similar to cassettes or videotapes in principle, although the actual cartridges are seldom compatible across tasks. Following are the relevant characteristics of magnetic tapes:

Cost	Magnetic tapes are quite inexpensive on a per-gigabyte basis. In mid-2000, prices are typically in the neighborhood of $1–$4 per gigabyte, but this varies considerably. Tape drives cost from little more than $100 to several thousand dollars; for network backup needs you'll be better served with a more expensive, high-capacity unit.
Reliability	Magnetic tapes are not the most reliable backup medium available, although higher-priced professional tape types such as DLT are reasonably reliable. Lower-end media such as Travan are more likely to give problems.
Sequential access	Tapes are sequential-access devices (it's necessary to read over some or all of the data between the start of the tape and your target data before reading the target data). This is not a problem when creating a fresh backup on a tape, but it can be a nuisance if you only need to restore a few files.

Speed   Tapes are reasonably speedy but not as fast as most hard disks. Typical speeds are in the 100 to 900MB/minute range. (Expressed in these units, 100Mbps Ethernet is theoretically capable of 750MB/minute.)

Capacity   Modern tapes range from 4GB to over 100GB, uncompressed. (Compression typically doubles capacity.)

Tapes are a desirable backup medium because they achieve reasonable speed, have high capacity, and maintain low cost per megabyte. Less-than-perfect reliability and the sequential-access nature of tapes are their main drawbacks. The potentially high cost of the tape drives (as opposed to their media) can also be a drawback, but if you equip one computer and use it to back up the entire network, this cost is effectively distributed over the entire network.

Some tape drives feature built-in compression. These drives automatically apply compression algorithms, and so can squeeze more data onto a tape (typically about twice what the tapes can hold uncompressed). Most backup programs support software compression features, so hardware compression isn't strictly necessary. It can be useful for reducing CPU load on the backup server, however. Hardware compression is also a big advantage if you use `tar` as a backup program, because using `tar` in conjunction with `gzip` as a compression program results in archives that are very error-sensitive. If a single error occurs while reading a `gzipped` `tar` archive, the remainder of the archive becomes inaccessible. Given the less-than-perfect reliability of tape for backup purposes, this fact makes hardware compression highly desirable in any tape drive you intend to use with `tar`.

There are several different types of tape in common use today. These formats are mutually incompatible—like 8-track and cassette tapes for audio recording, or Beta and VHS formats for videotapes. Unlike the audio and videotape formats, however, all the data tape formats are currently available.

Travan   The Travan format is a creation of Imation (`http://www.imation.com`), the leading supplier of Travan tapes. These tapes are an evolution of the now rare *Quarter-Inch Cartridge (QIC)* format. Travan devices mostly populate the low end of the tape spectrum; they're popular as personal backup devices for desktop systems. A few Travan *changers* are available, however. These devices use several tapes to achieve higher capacity. In their single-tape incarnations, Travan drives are inexpensive, but the tapes are costly compared to some other formats. Capacities range from 400MB for the obsolete TR-1 subvariant to 10GB for TR-5 and NS-20 drives (the latter include built-in compression and so can store 20GB of typical data on a TR-5/NS-20 cartridge).

DAT   *Digital Audio Tape (DAT)* was developed as an audio recording medium but has been adapted as a data backup format. Subvariants, labeled DDS-1 through DDS-4, increase in capacity and speed from 2GB through 20GB uncompressed. DAT devices tend to be slightly more reliable than their Travan counterparts. The drives are more expensive than Travan drives, but DAT tapes are less costly. Most DAT drives support hardware compression features, and DAT changers are available for larger networks.

DLT   The *Digital Linear Tape (DLT)* format is used on some midrange and high-end tape backup systems. This technology has a reputation for being fairly reliable and high in capacity; 20–35GB tapes are common. DLT drives tend to be fairly expensive, often exceeding $3,000 for a single-tape unit.

8mm   A few tape-backup drives exist that are built around the 8mm format used in some video camcorders. The tapes require slightly different formulation than a standard camcorder tape, though. These drives are typically sold to the small server market, as are DLT and high-end DAT drives. Exabyte (`http://www.exabyte.com`) is the only major 8mm supplier today.

ADR   One of the newest tape formats available is called *Advanced Digital Recording (ADR)*. It features uncompressed capacities in the 15 to 25GB range, with hardware data compression doubling those values. Early indications are that ADR drives are more reliable than most tapes, but the technology is still new enough that long-term reliability is unknown. ADR drives are less expensive than similar DAT drives, with comparable media costs.

Others   A wide variety of oddball formats exist, some aimed at desktop systems and others at servers.

For a network server, you should probably look at a high-end DAT, DLT, 8mm, or ADR drive, or possibly a more obscure format. Travan drives tend to be too slow and too low in capacity for network backups, although if your network is small or you use the tape only to back up the server, a high-end Travan drive might suffice.

Independent of the choice of tape medium is the selection of interface. Parallel-port, USB, ATAPI, and SCSI devices all exist. For a network backup device, SCSI is the best choice because it gives the best performance. An ATAPI backup device may be acceptable on a small network. Most high-end backup devices are available only in SCSI format, although ADR drives are available in ATAPI and USB (which is slower than ATAPI) interfaces. In the past, many low-end tape drives (including some Travan models) interfaced through the floppy port. These floppy-interfaced drives tend to be slow and unreliable, so they're unsuitable for use by a network backup server.

Optical Media

Optical backup devices include *CD Recordable (CD-R)* and *CD Rewriteable (CD-RW)* drives. These devices allow you to record data on discs the size and shape of ordinary CD-ROMs. Most CD-ROM drives can read CD-R discs, and many newer models can also read CD-RW discs. This fact provides one great advantage for optical media: They can be read back on almost any computer equipped with a CD-ROM drive. This fact can greatly simplify recovery of client systems.

Optical storage based on the newer *Digital Versatile Disc (DVD)* format is becoming increasingly available. These recordable DVD technologies may be enticing for small networks, but the technology is still new and is changing rapidly.

Following are the characteristics of optical storage media:

Cost	The cost of CD-R media currently hovers at about $1/GB, roughly the same as the less-expensive magnetic tape formats. CD-R are not reusable, however. CD-RW media cost slightly more and are reusable. DVD-based media are much more expensive, but their cost is likely to drop rapidly in 2000 and beyond.
Reliability	Optical media are extremely reliable. Current estimates suggest that these media may last 50–100 years if stored properly. This makes optical storage the ideal solution for long-term archival backups.
Random access	Unlike tapes, CD-R are random-access media, meaning that the computer can seek directly to any randomly selected part of the disc without reading intervening data. This means quick restoration of arbitrary files.
Speed	Compared to other backup media, optical media are slow. CD-R and CD-RW drives available in 2000 typically record at 8x speed, meaning 8 times the speed of a 150KB/second CD-ROM drive (or 70MB/minute expressed in terms typically used by tape drive manufacturers). This places optical media at the very low end of the range of speeds for tape drives, at best.
Capacity	Capacity is the Achilles' heel of CD-R and CD-RW media, both of which are limited to 650MB on standard discs. (Some discs stretch that to about 700MB.) DVD-based media have several times this capacity, but still nothing approaching the 100+GB available on high-end tape drives.

Maintaining a Healthy System

PART 4

Unless your backup needs are very modest, optical media don't have the necessary capacity for making regular and complete backups of a server. These devices can be very useful, however, in backing up clients that have comparatively low capacity and are slow to change. For example, if your network includes many clients with little in the way of installed software and data files, you may be able to squeeze an entire backup of such a client onto a single standard CD-R disc, which can store as much as 1,300MB when compressed. If the client's hard disk crashes or the OS becomes corrupt, you can then insert the backup CD-R directly into the client and restore it, without invoking network accesses.

Removable Disks

A variety of removable-disk devices exist, ranging from 100MB Iomega Zip drives (http://www.iomega.com) to 2.2GB Castlewood Orb drives (http://www.castlewood .com), and similar devices with still higher capacities. These disks typically use technologies comparable to those of floppy disks or hard disks, although some use magneto-optical technologies or other variants. In any event, these drives can be a convenient way to back up or transport data, from a few tens of megabytes to a few gigabytes.

Various types of transportable hard disks are available, as well, ranging from EIDE drives in special removable mountings to external SCSI drives. You can use these devices to make complete backups of your normal hard disks, and then remove them from the premises for safe storage.

Following are the characteristics of removable disks:

Cost — Most disk-based solutions are quite expensive, costing $10–$50 per gigabyte. The cost of some solutions, particularly those based on regular hard disks, may be appealing at first because they cost little up front for a separate drive, unlike tape drives or CD-RW devices. Because this class of removable drive uses a unitary drive and medium, however, the cost of buying multiple media is quite high.

Reliability — Removable-disk devices are typically very reliable—certainly more so than tapes. They're often more sensitive to shocks than are tapes, however, so take care how you transport them.

Random access — Like optical drives, removable-disk drives are random-access devices, making for quick restoration of arbitrary files.

Speed	Removable-disk devices vary substantially in speed, ranging from a leisurely 0.8MB/second (48MB/minute) for low-end Zip drives to 30MB/second (1800MB/minute) or more for removable hard disks.
Capacity	Capacity of removable disks varies widely, ranging from 100MB for Zip drives to tens of gigabytes for removable hard disks.

On the whole, disk-based devices make poor choices for network backup devices. Most of these devices have capacities and speeds so low that they're useless for complete backups. Others, particularly those based on hard disks, may have adequate capacity but their costs are prohibitive—particularly if you want to keep multiple backups of each system, as is a wise precaution in the event a backup fails. Nonetheless, disk-based devices can play an important role in performing backups. Because they're random-access and read/write in nature, they make for quick backup and restoration of individuals' current projects. They are a good way to move files from machines at work to those at home. Used in these ways, these drives are best placed on client computers, but you can use a Samba server to serve removable-media devices, if you like. You have to create a share corresponding to a drive's mount point, and provide some way for users to mount the devices.

Removable-media drives can also play an important role in disaster recovery plans. You can place stripped-down Linux or Windows installations on these drives, providing a minimal but working environment to use in restoring the original system. These options are described later in the chapter in "Preparing for Disaster: Developing a Recovery Plan" and "Emergency Recovery Options."

Server- vs. Client-Initiated Backups

When backing up any computer through the network, you must decide what computer initiates the backup—the one whose files are being backed up (the client) or the one possessing the backup device (the server). This choice determines what software you can use and how you can perform the backup. For example, if you want to use a server-initiated backup, your backup client computers must be configured as file-sharing servers, so that the backup server can access the backup client's shares. On the other hand, if the backup client initiates the process, the backup clients need not be configured as file servers; however, there must be some method of sharing the backup hardware on the backup server.

Maintaining a Healthy System

PART 4

NOTE This chapter slightly twists the usual definitions of *client* and *server*. Here the term *backup server* refers to the computer that hosts the backup hardware. The *backup client,* by contrast, is the computer that's being backed up. As explained just above, this means the backup client may require configuration as a file server, and the backup server may function as a file-sharing client. This usage, although odd with respect to the typical meanings of *client* and *server,* best describes the actual *functions* of the systems involved.

As a general rule, using Samba as a server-initiated backup server makes sense on networks that you want to back up automatically. You can configure Linux to run a backup script at a regular interval, and then ensure that your backup device is loaded with an appropriate medium whenever that script is scheduled to run. If all the clients are up and running at the appointed time, the backup should proceed smoothly. You can use this arrangement to back up an entire network (or a reasonably sized part of one) nightly, weekly, or monthly.

Client-initiated backups, on the other hand, work better with small networks when the individuals responsible for particular client computers can decide when best to perform a backup. Automatic backups don't work as well with such a system because one client's backup attempt may cause problems for another client. You can still schedule automatic backups if you can stagger your backups—for example, on a small network with fewer than five clients, you could configure each client to perform an automatic backup on a different night of each week.

Client- and server-initiated backups have software differences in addition to scheduling differences. With a Samba system working as the backup server, you can use tools that ship with Samba if you use a server-initiated backup strategy (see "Using Samba to Back Up Client Computers"). Although client-initiated backup packages are available to help you back up Windows systems using a Linux backup server, these packages aren't part of Samba, and therefore aren't described in this book. ARKEIA (http://www.arkeia .com/) is one such package.

Backup Software Choices

A wide variety of backup software exists for Linux, much of which is compatible with Samba. Samba itself also ships with software specialized for backing up Windows computers. Here are some of the more popular choices of Linux backup programs:

tar   The tar program is a flexible Linux archiving utility. Although it's often not the best choice for backups because of an error-intolerant compression system and assorted additional shortcomings, it's available on all but the tiniest Linux computers, and it's well understood by Linux administrators. I therefore use tar as a sample program throughout the rest of this chapter.

smbtar   This program is part of the Samba package. It's a modified version of tar, which uses smbclient to access a backup client's shares. Because smbtar uses smbclient rather than a mounted SMB/CIFS filesystem, smbtar can access and use SMB/CIFS backup features—most notably the *archive bits* that SMB/CIFS provides to indicate whether a file has been modified since it was last backed up. This feature lets smbtar easily perform incremental backups (described shortly, in "Backup Schedules"). On the whole, smbtar is a very useful backup utility for Samba networks.

dump   The dump program is another fairly standard Linux backup utility. It's used to create a basic copy of a filesystem onto tape and is preferred by many administrators for tape backup purposes. Restoring backups created with dump requires the use of another program, restore.

cpio   Like tar, cpio is an archive creation program, but many administrators prefer it because it can be more robust against errors than tar.

AMANDA   The *Advanced Maryland Automatic Network Disk Archiver (AMANDA)* is a set of tools that help automate a network backup via tar or dump. The program includes support for NFS backups of Unix and Linux clients, as well as Samba backups of Windows clients. See http://www.cs.umd.edu/projects/amanda/ for more information.

CD-R Utilities   If you use a CD-R or CD-RW drive for backup purposes, you will need to employ CD-R utilities for backup. At a minimum, you'll need to use cdrecord or something similar to write data to a CD-R drive. You may also want to use mkisofs to create an ISO-9660 filesystem image from the files you want to back up. mkisofs, however, discards some critical types of information (for instance, it makes all files read-only); so for full system backups, you should use a utility like tar instead of or in addition to mkisofs. A typical CD-R backup session therefore involves three utilities: tar (or some other archiving tool), mkisofs, and cdrecord, in that order. Most examples in this chapter assume you'll be backing up to tape, so you'll need to adjust the procedures appropriately if you use an optical medium.

BRU   EST's *Backup and Recovery Utility* (BRU, at http://www.estinc.com) is a commercial backup program that features a good GUI control system. The personal version ships with some boxed Linux distributions, but in order to back up a network you need the more expensive commercial edition. BRU contains no explicit support for Windows clients, but it *can* back up smbmounted shares.

ARKEIA   ARKEIA (http://www.arkeia.com) is a commercial backup package similar in many ways to BRU. This package, however, includes explicit support for backing up Windows clients without using Samba.

The backup software you use is largely a matter of personal preferences and your specific network needs. smbtar can do a very good job backing up Samba clients, so its use is emphasized in this chapter. tar, as well, is used as an example, mainly because it's commonly available and well understood. You should have little trouble adapting the tar examples to another package, should you prefer something else.

Maintaining a
Healthy System

PART 4

Timing Backups

The timing of backups is important to any backup plan. There are two aspects to this issue: determining the frequency of backing up specific systems or files on specific systems, and scheduling backups to run automatically. Both issues are critical for any major installation—if you forget or mis-schedule an important backup, you'll pay the price when you need to restore data.

Backup Schedules

One of the most important aspects of configuring a computer or network for backups is the question of a schedule. Ideally, you should perform backups regularly, and at intervals just short enough that a catastrophic failure of a hard disk won't wipe out too much of the data you've created in the meantime. Just how much is "too much" is a subjective matter that you must determine based on your own and your coworkers' needs. In some environments, one day's data lost may be too much. In others, systems may change slowly enough that monthly or even yearly backups are acceptable. In fact, on a single network you may have an assortment of needs for various computers. One common situation is on a network with highly centralized data storage. This network's server may require very frequent backups, but the client systems may change very slowly and so require backups only once a month or less.

Even when a system's data needs regular backup, it's not always necessary to back up every file. Most OS and program files don't change very often, but many data files do. You might therefore want to break down your backups into multiple types of files, and back up the frequently changed files more often than the others. On Linux systems, one easy way to make this distinction is by filesystem branches. Typically, the /home and /var directory trees contain the frequently changed files, whereas /usr, /opt, and most other trees contain the less-active files. You might therefore try backing up the /home and /var directories daily, but perform a full system backup only once a month. Such an approach minimizes wear and tear on your backup hardware and reduces the time the system spends performing backups. It can also reduce the capacity required of your backup media, although you do still need to have enough capacity to handle the periodic full system backups.

Another way to make the most efficient use of your time and backup hardware is to let the computer determine precisely which files have changed since the last backup, and back up only the changed files. Considered in these terms, there are two principal types of backup:

> **Full Backup**   A full backup includes all the files on the computer or network, whether or not they've changed since the last backup. Full backups are convenient

when you need to restore an entire system from a backup—say, because your hard drive has failed. Full backups take the most time, however. If your backup medium isn't large enough to handle a full backup, you must split it across media, which increases the effort involved and the chance of problems.

Incremental Backup   An incremental backup saves only files that are new or have changed since the last backup. There are two main variants on this theme: One backs up all files that have changed since the last full backup; the other backs up all files that have changed since the last full or incremental backup. The first variant guarantees that a full restore will require restoring no more than two tapes; however, as time passes since the last full backup, the size of the incremental backups increases. The second variant may require half a dozen or more tapes to completely restore a system, depending upon the backup schedule, but each incremental backup is roughly the same size.

One of the features of the filesystems used by Microsoft OSs is that they include an *archive bit* to help in the performance of incremental backups. This bit is set when a file is created or modified, and unset when a backup program backs up the file. As a result, incremental backups can be performed merely by backing up files that have their archive bits set. SMB/CIFS also supports the archive bit. Linux filesystems don't support an archive bit, however, so most Linux backup programs can't use it; to perform incremental backups, they must maintain a list of files that they've backed up. The Samba `smbtar` program is an exception to this rule; it understands the archive bit and can use it to perform incremental backups without maintaining a list of previously backed-up files.

> **NOTE**   As described in Chapter 5, Samba supports emulating the archive bit on its shared filesystems. This is normally of interest only if you plan to back up Samba shares using Windows network backup software. In most cases, using Linux backup software is a better idea. Linux backup software saves the execute bits used by Samba to emulate Windows filesystem features, and it can back up the Linux server software itself, in addition to the shares. You cannot reliably and directly back up the Samba server itself via SMB/CIFS, so you must use Linux tools to do that job, or leave the OS itself unprotected.

When backing up a large network, you may run into problems relating to network or backup medium capacity. For example, consider a 40-computer network on which each computer holds 20GB of data. The total required backup capacity for this network is 800GB, which exceeds that of all but the highest-capacity tape backup units. Furthermore, assuming a 100Mbps network operating at its theoretical maximum speed (an unrealistic assumption), backing up 800GB of data takes over 18 hours. In practice, then, backing up such a network would monopolize the network's capacity for a full day. You might be able to get away with this by running backups on weekends, but even this might be disruptive if your site operates seven days a week. Another option is to stagger the backup over several days. Instead of backing up all 40 computers at once, you can back up eight computers a night for each of five weeknights. The result is a more manageable 160GB per night requiring a bit under four hours to complete, assuming near-optimal conditions. (In practice, this backup will probably take twice that time, given typical bottlenecks.)

You may need to design still more complex backup schedules, in order to accommodate peculiarities of your site. If you have several servers, for example, you may need to back up each one separately on one night of the week, and back up clients on a more complex schedule, say once a month, several clients per night.

Using *cron*

One common backup strategy is to schedule backups to run automatically late at night or during other off-hours. Many commercial packages include utilities to help you schedule backups, so if you're using a commercial backup program, consult its documentation to determine how to schedule automatic backups.

If you use a tool such as tar or smbtar to perform backups, chances are you'll want to use Linux's cron facility to schedule the backups to run automatically. cron is a tool that runs specified scripts at scheduled times. You can therefore create a cron job consisting of a backup script that runs at some convenient time, such as midnight on weekdays. There are two ways to set up a cron job to run at regular intervals:

- Place a script in the /etc/cron.*interval* directory, where *interval* is hourly, daily, weekly, or monthly. Linux runs these scripts with the designated frequency, although at different times for the various distributions. Daily scripts may run at anywhere from midnight to 5:00 A.M., for instance.

- Create a custom cron job to run at any arbitrary interval.

The first option is simple to implement, but the second requires some elaboration.

Creating *cron* Jobs   In order to create a cron job, you create a special file (often called a crontab file) that specifies what you want to happen and when. This crontab file contains three types of lines: comments (which start with #), environment variable settings, and cron commands.

Environment variable settings take this form:

```
VARIABLE = value
```

You can set some common variables to help the system locate programs, like this:

```
SHELL=/bin/bash
PATH=/sbin:/bin:/usr/sbin:/usr/bin
```

The cron commands take this form:

```
minute hour day-of-month month day-of-week command
```

The first five fields of the cron command specify the time at which the command listed in the final field is to run. Each of these fields accepts specific values as follows:

minute   Acceptable values are 0–59.

hour   Acceptable values are 0–23.

day-of-month   Acceptable values are 0–31.

month   Acceptable values are 0–12 or the first three letters of the month's name.

day-of-week   Acceptable values are 0–7 or the first three letters of the day's name (0 and 7 both refer to Sunday).

You can specify multiple values in any field, in any of several ways:

- An asterisk (*) indicates any possible value.
- To list specific allowable values, separate them with commas, as in 1,8,15,22,29.
- To indicate a range, use a hyphen (-), as in Mon-Fri, which specifies a run on every weekday if used in the *day-of-week* field.
- To specify skipped values, use a slash (/) character and a number after a range. For instance, */10 indicates that a run occurs on every tenth number (10, 20, and so on); and Jan-Dec/2 specifies that the job runs every other month.

The *command* field itself can be any command or script you care to specify. For a backup job, chances are you'll create a special backup script. This script can include backup commands like those described throughout this chapter.

A *crontab* File   As an example of a complete crontab file, consider Listing 16.1. This simple file runs a weekly backup on Tuesdays (day 2) at 3:15 A.M., and a daily backup every other weekday at 3:15 A.M. Both backups are performed by scripts stored in the /root/backup-scripts directory.

Listing 16.1   Sample crontab File

```
SHELL=/bin/bash
#
15 3 * * 2      /root/backup-scripts/weekly-backup
15 3 * * 1,3-5  /root/backup-scripts/daily-backup
```

Once you've created a `crontab` file, you must tell Linux's `cron` daemon about it. You do this by issuing the `crontab` command:

 # crontab -u root *crontab-file*

You can specify this command without the `-u root` component if you're running as `root`, or you can specify another user (or run as the target user) if you want the job to run with another user's permissions. Chances are you'll want a backup to run with `root` privileges, though.

> **WARNING**   Before specifying that a job run as a `cron` job, be absolutely positive that the scripts it contains won't cause problems. Try running the scripts yourself, and try creating a `cron` job that runs the scripts while you're around. Do this *before* you run the job at a time when you won't be present to kill it and clean up any mess it creates. Also, check the job's handling of error conditions. One such error you might encounter in doing a network backup is that the backup client computer may not be turned on. Ideally, your backup script should notify you of a problem (say, by e-mail), so that you don't incorrectly believe that a backup has worked.

Backup Storage

It's tempting to think that once you've created a backup you're safe. This isn't always the case, however. If your office is burglarized, or damaged in an event such as a fire or earthquake, your backup data could be lost along with the original data. It's therefore important to arrange for off-site storage of your backup data. Here are some possibilities:

- Storing backup media in a bank's safety deposit box
- Exchanging backup media with another office of your organization, in another building
- Taking backup media home with you (or to work, if you're backing up a home network)
- Giving backup media to a friend or neighbor

Of course, if your data are unusually sensitive, some of these options may be unacceptable; you may need to arrange for secure offsite storage, or use backup software that supports data encryption.

One common method of offsite storage is to rotate through multiple sets of backups. The most recent one stays on site in case you need to recover data quickly. You can then put an older backup in off-site storage. When the time comes to perform another backup, you retrieve the off-site backup, overwrite it with a new backup, and send the old on-site backup to the off-site location.

When storing backups locally, it's a good idea to store them in a fireproof safe. This protects the backup media from damage in case of fire *and* keeps them locked away from prying eyes.

> **WARNING**   Backup tapes often contain sensitive data such as password files, and so can be of interest to would-be crackers. Unless they're encrypted, these tapes offer no protection against unauthorized access should they fall into the wrong hands. The same is true of original hard disks.

Backing Up a Samba Server Locally

On a small network or a network that has several high-capacity servers, you may want to attach a backup device directly to the server. Backing up the server is therefore an entirely local operation that need not affect network performance greatly, unless disk access speed is an important bottleneck. Local backups are also often faster than are network backups, so backing up locally can save time.

An Example Using *tar*

The details of backing up a server will differ from one program to another, so be sure to consult your favored program's documentation. The example in this section employs tar to back up a server to tape. You can use it as a baseline for subsequent discussions of network tape backups.

> **NOTE**   Backing up to optical devices is typically more complex than described here, because you must create temporary tar files and then write them to disk using cdrecord, or pipe the results of tar directly to cdrecord. You may also want to invoke mkisofs to store the tar files on a conventional ISO-9660 CD-ROM filesystem.

The *tar* Utility and Its Options

To use tar, you must combine precisely one command with one or more qualifiers. Table 16.1 lists the available tar commands, and Table 16.2 summarizes the more common qualifiers. For details, consult the tar man page.

Table 16.1 tar Commands

Command	Abbreviation	Purpose
--create	c	Creates an archive
--concatenate	A	Appends tar files to an archive
--append	r	Appends files to an archive
--update	u	Appends files that are newer than those in an archive
--diff or --compare	d	Compares an archive to files on disk
--list	t	Lists archive contents
--extract or --get	x	Extracts files from an archive

Table 16.2 tar Qualifiers

Qualifier	Abbreviation	Purpose
--directory *dir*	C	Changes to directory *dir* before performing operations
--file [*host*:]*file*	f	Uses file called *file* on computer called *host* as the archive file
--listed-incremental *file*	g	Performs incremental backup or restore, using *file* as a list of previously archived files

Table 16.2 tar Qualifiers *(continued)*

Qualifier	Abbreviation	Purpose
--one-file-system	l	Backs up or restores only one filesystem (partition)
--multi-volume	M	Creates or extracts a multi-tape archive
--tape-length *N*	L	Changes tapes after *N* kilobytes
--same-permissions	p	Preserves all protection information
--absolute-paths	P	Retains the leading / on filenames
--verbose	v	Lists all files read or extracted
--verify	W	Verifies the archive after writing it
--exclude *file*	(none)	Excludes *file* from the archive
--exclude-from *file*	X	Excludes files listed in *file* from the archive
--gzip or --ungzip	z	Processes archive through gzip or gunzip

Of the commands listed in Table 16.1, the most commonly used are --create, --extract, and --list. The most useful qualifiers from Table 16.2 are --file, --listed-incremental, --one-file-system, --same-permissions, --gzip, and --verbose.

Maintaining a
Healthy System

PART 4

> **WARNING** The `tar --one-file-system` option is critically important to back-ups. Ordinarily, `tar` backs up everything under the directory it's been given as input. Although this works fine if you feed `tar` the name of a directory that has nothing mounted on it, it can cause problems for certain types of mounts. For example, if you tell `tar` to back up the root directory (that is, `/`), the program backs up everything mounted on that directory or any subdirectory, including NFS or Samba shares served by other machines. Worse, `tar` also backs up the Linux `/proc` filesystem, which is a virtual filesystem that represents the computer's sta-tus, including all its memory. At restoration time, `tar` tries to overwrite the `/proc` filesystem's contents, which is likely to cause serious problems, possibly even including a system crash. For this reason, it's best to always use `--one-file-system` and feed `tar` the names of each partition you want to back up.

The `tar` command backs up files to or from *files*. Because Linux treats hardware devices as if they were files, you can tell `tar` to back up to or from an appropriate hardware device file, in order to use that device directly. (This approach works best for tape devices. For CD-R and CD-RW drives, it's necessary to pipe `tar`'s output through CD-R control soft-ware like `cdrecord`. For disk devices, it's best to store the archive as a regular file on a file-system, although you *can* store the archive "raw" to the device.)

> **NOTE** Backups on tapes are logically equivalent to the tarballs often used to distribute software, as described in Chapter 3. You can think of the tape device as being a `.tar` or `.tgz` file.

Linux Tape Device Files

Table 16.3 summarizes the filenames of several common Linux tape devices. You can access specific tape drives by using one of these device filenames. One important differ-ence is between *rewinding* and *nonrewinding* devices—the former rewind after every operation, but the latter do not, allowing you to fit more than one backup on a tape. Typ-ically, each physical tape drive supports one rewinding and one nonrewinding tape device file. You can use the `mt` utility to access multiple `tar` archives on a single tape; consult the `mt` man page for details.

Table 16.3   Common Linux Tape Device Filenames

Device Filename	Rewinding	Hardware Type
/dev/st*n*	Yes	SCSI tape #*n* (0–7)
/dev/nst*n*	No	SCSI tape #*n* (0–7)
/dev/ht*n*	Yes	EIDE tape #*n* (0–4)
/dev/nht*n*	No	EIDE tape #*n* (0–4)

> **NOTE**   USB support is new in Linux, added only with the 2.3.*x* development kernels. If you're using a USB tape-backup device, you need a recent 2.3.*x* or 2.4.*x* kernel, or at least a 2.2.*x* kernel with USB support patched into it. When properly configured, these devices use SCSI device identifiers.

Sample Commands

Putting all this together, then, a typical `tar` command to back up a computer looks like this:

```
tar --create --verbose --gzip --one-file-system --same-permissions ↵
    --file /dev/st0 / /home /usr/local
```

This command can be expressed somewhat more succinctly using command abbreviations:

```
tar cvzlpf /dev/st0 / /home /usr/local
```

In either form, this `tar` command backs up the root (/), /home, and /usr/local filesystems to /dev/st0 (the first SCSI tape device). The assumption here is that the computer has three Linux partitions, corresponding to the three specified directories. A system with different partitions would need to specify the appropriate local partitions.

To do an incremental backup, you could add the `--listed-incremental` parameter, as in

```
tar cvzlpf /dev/st0 --listed-incremental /root/increments / /home ↵
    /usr/local
```

This command stores information on the incremental backup in the /root/increments file, and uses the contents of that file to designate which files are to be backed up.

Preparing for Disaster: Developing a Recovery Plan

One of the most difficult aspects of planning a backup strategy is in developing a plan to recover the entire server in case of a major disaster, such as a complete failure of all your hard disks. (Even if you use a RAID configuration, this event can occur because of a failure of the server's power supply, theft, and so on.) The challenge in case of a disaster is to create a working system identical to the one you had prior to the disaster, in as little time and with as little effort as possible. Typically, you want to avoid having to reinstall Linux from an installation CD-ROM and then reconfigure it. Ideally, you should be able to boot from an emergency recovery medium, insert your backup medium, and restore the system to its original working state by issuing a handful of commands. Thankfully, this ideal is achievable, although it takes some planning to achieve.

Your Emergency Linux System

As a first stage in a recovery effort, you should create an emergency Linux system. This can be something as simple as a floppy disk with a micro-Linux distribution, or as complex as a small hard disk that's been set aside with a complete Linux distribution installed on it. Some possibilities you might consider in creating such a setup include the following:

Floppy-Based Linux Micro-Distributions   Many Linux distributions come with emergency recovery disks of one type or another. Typically, there are one to three floppy disks that you can boot to acquire a minimal working Linux system. You can then use text-based tools to partition a new hard disk, create filesystems on it, and restore data from your backup medium. The trick with these tools is to ensure that they can actually perform each of the required steps, especially the recovery of data from your backup medium. If the micro-distribution lacks drivers for your tape device, it is useless in this emergency role. In addition to checking whatever comes with your regular distribution, you may want to investigate muLinux (`http://sunsite.auc.dk/mulinux/`) and ThinLinux (`http://www.ThinLinux.org`) as possible bases for a floppy-based micro-Linux configuration.

Mini-Installation on High-Capacity Removable Media   A second option is to create a small Linux installation on a removable-media device such as an Iomega Zip drive or LS-120 disk. Each of these can store about 100MB and have sufficient capacity to host regular installations of at least some Linux distributions. In fact, Slackware Linux includes a variant called *ZipSlack* designed for just such a purpose. I've found Debian to be a useful distribution in this role, as well. If you plan carefully, you may even be able to include XFree86 and GUI tools in such a system. Some high-capacity removable-media disks are bootable by the BIOS, so you can treat them just like normal Linux partitions. Others aren't bootable by the BIOS and so may need the help of a DOS boot floppy with LOADLIN.EXE, similar to the emergency boot system described shortly.

CD-ROM with a "Live" Linux System A few Linux distributions (including Slackware) ship with a "live" Linux filesystem on CD-ROM. This means that the CD-ROM is bootable and will boot to a working Linux system, much of which exists on the CD-ROM. These systems can be very complete, including XFree86 and a wide assortment of tools. Finnix (`http://www.finnix.org`) is a specialized CD-ROM–based Linux distribution.

Whatever recovery system you use, it is *imperative* that you thoroughly test its ability to recover a system. Ideally, you should use it to "restore" a working Linux system on a spare computer. Failing that, at least test that you can restore a small test backup to the main server using this system. If you want to use the recovery system on multiple computers, verify that it works on all the potential target systems.

Booting a Recovered Computer

In addition to restoring data, one critical hurdle comes in booting a recovered computer for the first time. Typically, a Linux server relies upon the Linux Loader (LILO) to boot. All major Linux distributions install LILO at system installation time, but an installed copy of LILO isn't an ordinary file. It therefore cannot be restored by `tar` or other backup programs. You can re-install LILO by typing **lilo** once you've booted Linux.

One of the simplest ways around this catch-22 is to use an alternate method of booting your restored system the first time you boot it. Together, a DOS boot floppy, the `LOADLIN.EXE` program included with all major Linux distributions, and a copy of your Linux kernel constitute such a solution. To prepare this solution, follow these steps:

1. Create a DOS boot floppy. If you don't have a convenient copy of DOS, use FreeDOS (`http://www.freedos.org`).

2. Copy `LOADLIN.EXE` from your Linux installation CD-ROM to the DOS boot floppy.

3. Copy your Linux kernel from your Linux system to the DOS boot floppy.

> **TIP** Both LOADLIN.EXE and your Linux kernel files must reside on the same floppy. If you can't fit them both on the DOS boot floppy, try removing unnecessary files from the DOS boot floppy, or use a second floppy for LOADLIN.EXE and the Linux kernel.

4. *Test the emergency floppy!* Shut down the server, then boot the DOS boot floppy. You should be able to boot the server with a command like **LOADLIN *ZIMAGE* root=/dev/*sda2* ro**. You may need to adjust the names of the kernel file (*ZIMAGE* in this example) and the Linux root partition (/dev/*sda2* in this example) to match your system.

5. If in the future you recompile your kernel, copy it to the emergency floppy and retest it.

To summarize, you'll create and test *two* emergency recovery disks: one to restore files to the server, and one to boot the server after restoring the files. Both disks are critical to restoring a working system. After you've booted a restored system with the emergency boot disk, you can type `lilo` to restore your LILO configuration. If you've changed your partitioning scheme, though, you may need to edit your `/etc/lilo.conf` file to reflect those changes.

Backing Up a Samba Server Remotely

Some networks host several Samba servers but use a single centralized backup server to perform all network backups. On such networks, it's necessary to back up the Samba servers using network connections. As with ordinary clients, there are two ways to initiate such a backup: from the backup clients (that is, the Samba servers) or from the backup server.

When backing up a Windows client system, Samba serves as a good network protocol. This is not the case when backing up Samba servers, however. Samba lacks the necessary support for Linux filesystem features such as ownership, permissions, and special files such as device files. Therefore, other protocols are generally used for this task. When using the backup server to initiate the backup, the most common method is to use the Network Filesystem (NFS) to mount the Samba server's filesystems on the backup server, which can then copy all the files to disk. When using the Samba server to initiate backups, the usual method is to directly access the backup server's tape device from the network. It is possible, however, to force a client-initiated backup through Samba, by using Samba to receive a tar file prepared by the backup client.

Using NFS to Back Up a Server

NFS was designed as a Unix network file-sharing solution. It therefore includes support for the most important Linux filesystem features, such as ownership, permissions, and special file types. Although it's simpler than Samba configuration, NFS configuration still involves many subtleties that are well beyond the scope of this book. This section presents merely a brief overview—enough to let you back up your Linux Samba server using NFS.

Configuring a File Server for NFS File Sharing

NFS server configuration is a matter of adding directories you want to share to the `/etc/exports` file. Each line in this file specifies a single directory to be exported. The format is as follows:

```
directory client(options) [client(options)[...]]
```

NFS supports quite a few options. Following are the most important of these for the present discussion:

ro   This parameter exports the directory read-only. Clients will be unable to write to the system. This is adequate for NFS-based backups, but if you need to restore data, you'll need read/write access.

rw   This parameter exports the directory read/write. Assuming users have adequate permissions, they can write to the exported filesystem.

noaccess   Use this parameter to block access to this directory tree, even when a higher-level directory is exported. This is useful to block access to the Samba server's /proc filesystem.

root_squash   This parameter treats accesses from the client system's root user as if they came from the local nobody account. This is the default, but it's undesirable for accesses from a backup server, because it prevents a complete backup of the system.

no_root_squash   Turns off the root_squash function; root on the client can access all files, just as can root on the server. Though this option is a practical necessity for the backup server, setting it is a potentially major security problem, should an undesirable system successfully masquerade as the backup server.

Listing 16.2 shows a typical /etc/exports entry on a Samba server that's to be backed up by another server. This listing explicitly exports both the root (/) and /usr filesystems, and explicitly denies access to /proc. These filesystems are exported read-only, in order to reduce the risk posed by the no_root_squash option.

Listing 16.2   Sample /etc/exports File

```
/ backup(ro,no_root_squash)
/usr backup(ro,no_root_squash)
/proc backup(noaccess)
```

An important consideration when exporting filesystems is the kernel configuration option called Emulate SUN NSF Server (shown in the Network File Systems kernel configuration screen in Figure 16.1). When set to y, this option causes a server to automatically export all filesystems mounted under one that's exported. For example, if /usr is a separate partition, exporting / automatically exports /usr as well. When Emulate SUN NFS Server is set to n, on the other hand, each filesystem must be exported separately; hence /usr must be explicitly exported—and mounted—even if / is exported.

Listing 16.2 is peculiar in that it straddles both worlds. If Emulate SUN NFS Server is set to y, then the /usr export isn't necessary; its contents can be reached from the root

export. If Emulate SUN NFS Server is set to n, then the /proc noaccess export is unnecessary, because /proc as a separate filesystem won't be exported. Check your kernel configuration or examine an export to see how your system is configured.

Figure 16.1   The Linux kernel includes separate client (filesystem) and server support
options for NFS.

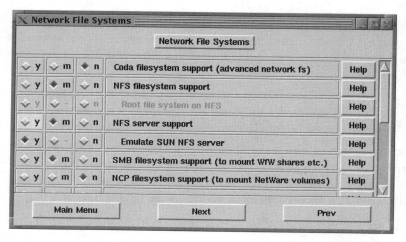

Once you've configured the /etc/exports file, you must ensure that your NFS server is
running. Several NFS server packages are available for Linux. These are typically called
nfsd, knfsd, nfsserver, or something similar. Be sure the server is installed and running.
Recent servers rely upon support in the kernel to operate, but some older servers do not.

NOTE   The Emulate SUN NFS Server kernel option is only relevant when the
NFS server uses the kernel's NFS support option. Older NFS servers don't use this
feature and so can work without kernel NFS server support.

Configuring a Backup Server to Mount NFS Exports

Mounting an NFS share is a matter of using the ordinary mount command, but specifying
an NFS server and export rather than a device file. For example:

```
# mount buclient:/ /buclient
```

```
# mount buclient:/home /buclient/home
```

These two commands mount the backup client's root and /home directories at /buclient
and /buclient/home, respectively. If you have several servers to back up, you may want

to include commands like these in a backup script. You can then use matching `umount` commands to unmount the backup client's filesystems after you've backed them up.

You may also want to add the backup client's filesystems to the backup server's `/etc/fstab` file, in order to mount the filesystems when the backup server boots, or to allow ordinary users to mount these filesystems. Chances are this isn't necessary for a backup server, but if you want to do it, here are the appropriate `/etc/fstab` entries:

```
buclient:/        /buclient       nfs   user,noauto  0 0
buclient:/home  /buclient/home  nfs   user,noauto  0 0
```

You can use an assortment of options in place of the `user,noauto` options (which allow ordinary users to mount the filesystem, and block automatic mounting at bootup). Consult the `mount` man pages for more information on available options.

Performing a Backup

Once you've mounted an NFS export, you can back it up just as you would an ordinary filesystem. For example:

```
# tar cvplf /dev/st0 /buclient /buclient/home
```

This command backs up the `/buclient` and `/buclient/home` exports.

As presented, the command includes the `buclient` prefix on all files—for example, the `/etc/fstab` file on the backup client is stored as `buclient/etc/fstab`. This fact means that you *must* restore files when the client's filesystem is mounted at the same mount point as when the files were backed up—which may be inconvenient for some restoration schemes. You may therefore want to use the `--directory` option to `tar`, or change to the target directory before performing a backup, as in

```
# tar cvplf /dev/st0 --directory /buclient ./ ./home
```

If you do this, you must remember to use equivalent options when it comes time to restore data from the backup.

WARNING If your backup client uses Sun-style NFS exports, in which all mounted subdirectories are automatically exported, and if that system hasn't explicitly blocked export of the /proc filesystem, you should use the `--exclude` option to `tar` to block backup of the /proc filesystem. If you fail to do this, serious problems may occur when you restore the backup, because the restoration damages critical configuration items in /proc.

Restoring Data

Restoring data works just like backing it up, except for some key concerns:

- During backup, the backup client can be configured to export filesystems read-only. During restore, this cannot be the case. You may need to temporarily reconfigure the backup client in order to restore files.

- In case of an emergency restoration, you may need to have an emergency boot system, similar to the one described in "Preparing for Disaster: Developing a Recovery Plan," prepared for the backup client. This emergency boot system must be capable of serving NFS exports.

Performing a Client-Initiated Backup

It's possible to initiate a backup operation from one Linux box using another as a backup server. Doing this shifts the responsibility for managing the tape unit from the backup server to the backup clients, which can lead to chaos when there are more than a handful of backup clients. Nonetheless, you might have reasons to do something like this, particularly on a small network. One advantage of initiating backup from a client is more security; you need not expose all the files on a Samba server to scrutiny by the backup server, and thus possibly to crackers who can masquerade as the backup server. Of course, the flip side is that the backup server may be more vulnerable to abuse.

There are two primary approaches to performing a client-initiated network backup. One is to more-or-less directly access the backup server's tape drive. Essentially, this technique works by copying a tar file from the backup client to the tape device file on the backup server. The second approach is to copy files to the backup server's hard disk, and then let some process on the backup server back up these files to tape or other medium and remove them. One example of each approach is presented in the following pages—but these are only examples. For instance, you could use the scp tool from the SSH package to send a tar file to a remote tape drive, or use NFS and a cron job to process files in a way comparable to the Samba [backup] share I describe.

Directly Accessing a Remote Tape Drive

The simplest way to remotely access a tape drive using tar is to include the backup server's server name as part of the tar command. In "An Example Using tar," we used this tar command:

```
# tar cvzlpf /dev/st0 / /home /usr/local
```

This command backs up the /, /home, and /usr/local directories to the /dev/st0 device.

Almost the same command works when the tape drive rests on another computer:

```
# tar cvzlpf buserver:/dev/st0 / /home /usr/local
```

This command, instead of sending data to the /dev/st0 device file on the local computer, sends it to the /dev/st0 device file on the computer called buserver.

Unfortunately, there are several caveats to the arrangement for directly accessing a remote tape drive:

- The backup server must be running the rshd server (often called in.rshd). Unfortunately, this server is a notorious security hole, because it relies exclusively on the client's IP address for authentication. It's therefore fairly easy to break into such a system.

- In order to perform an adequate backup of the client, tar must normally be run as root. By default, however, rshd refuses connections from root, as a security precaution. You can work around the problem by running rshd with the -h parameter, but this increases the security risk inherent in running rshd.

- If you run the backup as a non-root user, the backup server may refuse access to the backup device file, which often has 0700 permissions. You may need to loosen permissions on that file if you want non-root users to have access to it. Once again, this can pose a security risk.

On the whole, the security problems inherent in running a backup server so that its tape drive can be accessed directly by a client are formidable. I only recommend running a system in this way if it's well protected behind a firewall and has itself been thoroughly stripped of tools that might be useful to crackers, such as compilers, telnet, and other network utilities.

Using a Samba Share as an Intermediary

If your backup server has a large hard disk, you can use a Samba share as a data "weigh station" between the backup client and the tape or other medium. The key to this type of intermediary configuration lies in Samba's automation features, described in Chapter 8. In fact, Chapter 8 presented examples of using Samba shares as a means of creating CD-R image files. These examples can be modified to create a full-fledged backup technique.

Listing 16.3 presents a basic Samba backup share. This share appears to clients much as does any other share. Clients can mount the share, copy files to it, and so on. The key to this share lies in its postexec parameter, which copies the backup.tar file stored in the share to the tape device, then wipes the share clean of all files, so they don't clutter the hard disk.

Listing 16.3   A Samba Tape Backup Share

```
[backup]
        path = /home/samba/backup
        writeable = Yes
        create mask = 0666
        directory mask = 0777
        max connections = 1
        postexec = cp /home/samba/backup/backup.tar /dev/st0; ↵
        rm -r /home/samba/backup/*
```

To use this share from Linux, you can issue commands similar to the following:

```
# smbmount //buserver/backup /mnt/buserver
```

```
# tar cvplf /mnt/buserver/backup.tar / /home /usr/local
```

```
# smbumount /mnt/buserver
```

These commands create a backup of the client, stored in a file called backup.tar on the backup server. The [backup] share's postexec parameter causes Samba on the backup server to copy that file to the tape device, once the share is unmounted. The result is the same as if tar had written the file directly to the tape drive, as described in the preceding section, "Directly Accessing a Remote Tape Drive."

Like direct access, access through an intermediary share has several caveats:

- As presented in Listing 16.3, the /dev/st0 device must be accessible to all users. You could use the force user parameter to ensure that Samba runs the postexec command using only one user's permissions, and configure /dev/st0 to be accessible to this user. Alternatively, you could use root postexec instead of postexec, to run the command as root.

- The backup server must have enough disk space to temporarily hold all the files from the largest server on the network.

- If the backup user writes the file to the wrong filename, it won't be backed up.

- Attempts to access the share twice in quick succession could create problems, as the system tries to back up one file before the first has been cleared away.

Using a backup share similar to Listing 16.3's offers advantages as well as limitations. For one thing, it's much safer, from a network security point of view, than allowing direct access to the tape device through rshd. It's also possible to use the share to perform client-initiated backups of Windows systems, using a version of tar for Windows or a simple rewrite of the command. You can create a much more elaborate script to perform additional checks on the data, to back up to a CD-R or CD-RW drive, to collect backup data from multiple clients on one tape, or to perform other tasks.

On the whole, using a Samba backup share similar to that in Listing 16.3 is safer than using direct access to the tape devices through rshd. The disk space requirements may be prohibitive, though. I recommend you use Listing 16.3 only as a starting point for your configuration. Evaluate it with respect to your backup server's security needs, and perhaps create a system-specific script to handle the transfer to tape more intelligently than does Listing 16.3.

Using Samba to Back Up Client Computers

Routinely backing up your Samba servers is a very good practice, but Samba can play a more active role in backup than most of the preceding examples suggest. Specifically, Samba can be used at the core of a backup strategy for your SMB/CIFS client computers, and even for Windows NT or 2000 servers.

In order to use your network in this way, you'll employ Linux as the SMB/CIFS *client* rather than as the server (although when performing backups in this way, the Linux system is still the backup server). You can use the special smbtar program to do a backup fairly directly, or you can use other backup programs after mounting the backup clients' filesystems with smbmount. This section offers procedures for both these techniques.

Preparing Windows Clients

In order to use Linux and Samba as a backup server for Windows clients, you must first prepare those clients. Specifically, you must install and configure file-sharing *server* software on the backup clients. Chapter 2 provides a brief description of installing file sharing *client* software in Windows. The process of installing server software is quite similar. In Windows 9*x*, follow these steps:

1. In Control Panel, double-click the Network item. Windows displays the Network dialog box (Figure 16.2). If the File and Printer Sharing for Microsoft Networks item is present, you don't need to install the server software because it's already installed. Skip ahead to step 5. If the server software is not installed, proceed with step 2.

Figure 16.2 To configure a Windows system as a backup client using a Samba backup server, you need the File and Printer Sharing for Microsoft Networks item installed.

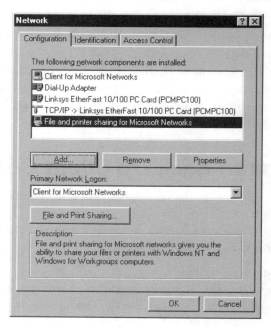

2. Click the Add button. Windows displays a dialog box entitled Select Network Component Type.

3. Choose Service in the Select Network Component Type dialog box, and click Add. Next up is the Select Network Service dialog box (Figure 16.3).

Figure 16.3 If it's not present, install File and Printer Sharing for Microsoft Networks.

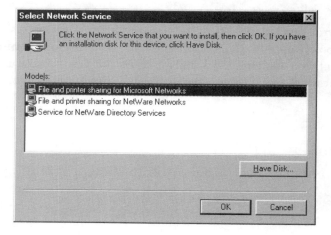

4. Select File and Printer Sharing for Microsoft Networks and click OK. Windows may ask for your installation CD. When it's done installing the server software, you may need to reboot your computer.

5. When the system has rebooted, open the My Computer window.

6. Right-click on an icon belonging to a drive you want to back up.

7. Select the Sharing item from the resulting pop-up menu. Windows displays the Properties dialog box, with the Sharing tab selected, as shown in Figure 16.4.

Figure 16.4   You'll use the Share Name to mount a share in Linux to back up a drive.

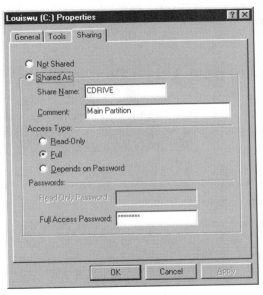

8. Click the Shared As radio button near the top of the Properties dialog box.

9. Enter a name for the share in the Share Name field and, if you like, a comment in the Comment field.

10. Windows allows you to control whether it grants read-only or read/write access based on the access password for a share. You can select a type of access to grant using the Access Type radio buttons. Depending on which option you select, you must then enter a Read-Only Password, Full Access Password, or both.

11. Click OK in the Properties dialog box.

12. If the computer has more than one *local* drive you want to back up, repeat steps 6 through 11 for each of these drives. Do not export drives that are shares mounted from other computers, however; you can access these shares directly from the backup server.

At this point, the Windows client is ready to be backed up. You can test this from another Windows client by trying to access the first computer as if it were a server. Alternatively, try using smbclient from Linux to access the share. Chapter 7 covers smbclient in more detail.

TIP   Although read-only access is adequate for performing regular full backups, you may be better off providing full read/write access if you intend to use smbtar and perform incremental backups. smbtar can use the SMB/CIFS archive bit to help it perform incremental backups, but this requires that smbtar have full read/write access to the share. If you don't intend to do incremental backups, providing read-only access is adequate for backup purposes, until it comes time to restore files.

Using *smbtar* to Back Up a Client

The smbtar program ships with Samba and functions as a utility that merges the features of smbclient and tar. (In fact, smbtar is a shell script that calls both these other programs.) Once you've configured backup clients as SMB/CIFS servers, you can use smbtar to back up directly from the client to a tape backup device or tar file. smbtar supports a number of options, including the following:

-s *SERVER*   This option specifies the name of the NetBIOS server to which smbtar should connect, such as BUCLIENT.

-x *SERVICE*   Name the service you want to back up with this parameter. This is the name you specified in step 9 of the "Preparing Windows Clients" procedure. If you omit this parameter, smbtar tries to use a share called BACKUP.

-X   Use this option to run smbtar in exclude mode. Filenames listed on the command line after other parameters will *not* be backed up. Ordinarily, such filenames are the ones that *will* be backed up.

-d *directory*   Use this parameter to change to the named directory on the backup client before transferring files.

-v   This parameter activates verbose mode, which lists files as they're backed up or restored.

-u *user*   Use this parameter to designate the username to use when accessing the share. You can omit this parameter when backing up Windows 9*x* clients.

-p *password*   This parameter specifies the password to use to access the share.

-t *device*   This parameter gives the filename of the tape device, such as /dev/st0.

-N *filename*   Include this parameter to back up files only newer than *filename*. You can use this option to implement incremental backups.

-i   This parameter activates incremental mode, which backs up only those files with set archive bits. This bit is unset when smbtar reads the file.

-r   This parameter activates restore mode. smbtar copies files from the local archive to the remote system, rather than in the opposite direction (the default).

-l *loglevel*   Use this parameter to set the smbclient log level (equivalent to the -d parameter of smbclient).

The following command backs up an entire Windows system, exported as CDRIVE:

```
# smbtar -s BUCLIENT -x CDRIVE -p password -v -t /dev/st0
```

This smbtar command displays a running list of the files being backed up, so you can watch its progress. When it's done, the result is an ordinary tar archive on the tape, so you can read it back with tar. (It's best to restore archives created with smbtar using the same tool, though, in order to most easily match smbtar's specific tar options.)

WARNING   If you use smbtar (or smbmount or other programs that require passwords) in scripts or cron jobs, remember that the password appears in plain text in the script. Security on the backup server is therefore critically important. Ordinary users should not have access to the backup server, and this system should not run unnecessary servers. If at all possible, you should ensure that any file or script that contains a password be owned by root and have 0600 or 0700 permissions.

Using *smbmount* to Back Up a Client

Using smbtar is not always the best choice to back up a client. Here are some reasons to use something else:

- You may want to create a single archive that contains several shares. smbtar backs up a single share to a single tar file or archive. On the other hand, if you mount several shares and back them up in another way, you can fit several shares into a single backup. (You can place several smbtar archives on a single tape by using a non-rewinding tape device, however.)

- You may need to include some specific tar options that aren't supported by smbtar, such as tar's multivolume features or gzip compression.

- You may prefer to use a backup utility other than tar, such as cpio or BRU.

Fortunately, backing up a client can be a fairly straightforward combination of mounting a share with smbmount and backing it up with tar, cpio, BRU, or any other backup program. The procedure is essentially the same as that described earlier, in "Configuring a Backup Server to Mount NFS Exports," except that the mounted shares are Samba shares rather than NFS exports.

As an example, consider the following commands:

```
# smbmount //BUCLIENT/CDRIVE /mnt/buclient/cdrive
# smbmount //BUCLIENT/DDRIVE /mnt/buclient/ddrive
# cd /mnt/buclient
# tar cvlpf /dev/st0 ./cdrive ./ddrive
# smbumount /mnt/buclient/cdrive
# smbumount /mnt/buclient/ddrive
```

This string of commands mounts two shares (CDRIVE and DDRIVE) from a Windows client called BUCLIENT, backs them up, and unmounts the shares. The result is an archive with two main directories, called cdrive and ddrive, corresponding to the two mount points. At restoration, it's important that the to-be-restored shares are mounted under the same names.

> **NOTE** Some commercial backup programs are sold in several versions, and some of these versions are incapable of performing network backups. This is an arbitrary crippling of the program in order to segment the marketplace. If you encounter problems doing an smbmount backup like this using a commercial program, but you have no problems backing up local data, check the program's documentation to see if the software is so restricted. If it is, updating to a network-enabled version of the program should correct the problem.

One disadvantage to performing backups using smbmount is that the backup can only store file attributes that smbmount maps to Linux attributes. In particular, you're likely to lose hidden and system attributes. Fortunately, these attributes aren't critically important for most files, and those for which they are important will be replaced after a full restore (see "Emergency Recovery Options" at the end of the chapter).

Cautions Concerning Remote Backups

Using Linux to back up Windows systems usually works quite well, but problems occasionally occur. Some specific issues to consider are the preservation of three Windows elements: short filenames, the Windows Registry, and special filesystem features.

Preservation of Short Filenames

Windows systems store short filenames along with long filenames. In some cases Windows relies upon the short filenames rather than the long filenames. This is particularly true of some Registry entries, which sometimes use short rather than long filenames. When you back up Windows using Linux, Linux does *not* store the short filename. Chances are these short filenames will be duplicated correctly when you restore files. For example, `longfilename.txt`'s original matched short filename may originally have been `LONGFI~1.TXT`, and it will be again upon restoration. On occasion, however, the original short filename won't be restored correctly. If some program or database relies upon the short name rather than the long one, that program or database will not work correctly. Because the Windows Registry file sometimes uses short filenames, you may wind up with serious and difficult-to-trace problems.

The best way to preserve short filenames is to use a Windows backup program that's designed for the job. Unfortunately, this can create a logistical nightmare in scheduling access to the Linux backup server. Cross-platform network backup tools such as ARKEIA sometimes work around these problems. Even then, restoration can be difficult. Some people find that braving the difficulties of short-filename preservation is preferable to using Windows native tools for backup; others think the opposite. You may want to try both paths and decide for yourself.

There are some steps you can take to reduce the likelihood of trouble caused by Linux's inability to store Windows short filenames.

Give files short names.   If you assign short names to files and directories on clients, there's no need to store a separate long filename and thus there's no conflict. This is a particularly constructive solution for directories holding many files and subdirectories. I usually create a directory called APPS in which I store programs, rather than using the Windows default of `Program Files`. Because a mix-up in short filenames seldom causes problems for data files, there's little need to take precautions with them; at worst, you'll lose a few links from the Documents item in the Windows Start menu. Because long filenames are most useful for data files, restricting the lengths of just a handful of program directory names can go a long way towards keeping your clients functional after restoring data.

Store files on a Linux server.   Samba uses an algorithm to generate short filenames, so its short filenames aren't any more likely to change after a restore than before one.

Avoid long filenames that are similar.   Windows uses the first six characters of a file's name as the base for its short filenames—LONGFI from `longfilename.txt`, for example. The first long filename takes on a ~1 as the seventh and eighth characters, the second (`longfilecabinet.txt`, say) acquires ~2, and so on. If you keep your long filenames and directory names unique in their first six characters, you'll avoid creating many ~2 filenames, and hence the possibility of confusion on restoration. Using different extensions can have similar benefits; there's no conflict between the short filenames created for `longfilename.txt` and `longfilename.exe`, for example. Unfortunately, arbitrary filename extensions can cause errors in associating files to their parent programs, so changing an extension isn't usually a useful ploy.

Use long filenames in filename lists. If your files are stored using long filenames (or long directory names), use those names rather than their short equivalents whenever you're asked to store filenames in some way. For example, enter long filenames in the PATH statement in AUTOEXEC.BAT, or in file-locating dialog boxes like the one in Figure 16.5, from Microsoft Word 2000.

Figure 16.5 Specifying long filenames rather than short filename equivalents can head off trouble after a restoration.

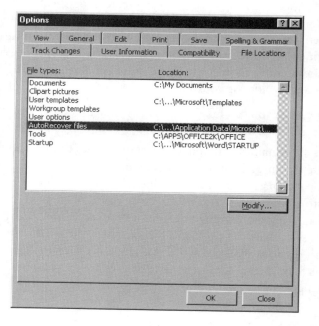

Back up and restore using the same tool. Linux and Windows have slightly different means of handling FAT partitions. It's therefore best to restore files backed up from Windows using Windows. Although you *can* run Linux on the client to restore files, doing so slightly increases the chance of problems matching short filenames. This is particularly true if you use the `nonumtail` mount option, which alters the way Linux creates short filenames when storing files on FAT partitions.

If you follow these suggestions and if your clients hold few files, chances are you won't need to worry about preserving short filenames. Should you encounter peculiar behavior on a client after restoring files, you may have little choice but to re-install whatever program is afflicted.

Preservation of the Registry

Windows relies upon its Registry file for many functions, including storing information on drivers, desktop settings, and so on. It's therefore critically important that the Registry file be backed up and restored correctly. Unfortunately, because Windows continually uses the Registry file, it's possible that it won't be backed up correctly when Windows is running—the file may be unavailable when your backup software tries to read it. The Registry is usually backed up correctly, but it's wise to take some precautions concerning this critical file.

Quite a few Windows programs are designed to help handle the Registry. In fact, Windows ships with one, called REGEDIT.EXE. A wide assortment of third-party utilities, including Registry Configurator Pro (http://www.triadnet.net/products.shtml) and RegMedic (http://www.easydesksoftware.com), improve on REGEDIT's features. They offer improved backup options, Registry repair facilities, and more. You can use such a tool to create backups of Registry files before backing up clients. Unfortunately, these tools require operation from the client systems themselves, which might be a problem if you've got many clients to back up on a regular basis. If your system behaves strangely or won't boot completely after a restore, consult the Registry backup software's documentation for advice on how to recover a backed-up Registry file.

> **NOTE**   Registry backups are ordinary files on the Windows filesystem; there's no need for the Registry backup program to interact with Samba or the Linux server. Upon restoration of the client system, the Registry backup file is also restored and so can be accessed by the Registry software.

One way to avoid problems with the Registry is to perform backups when the backup client is *not* running its normal Windows OS. If the computer dual-boots between Linux and Windows, you can back up the client when it's running Linux. To perform separate Linux and Windows backups, you can do the Windows backup using a Samba server running on the backup client. Another choice is to use an NFS server, as described earlier in "Using NFS to Back Up a Server." Even if the computer doesn't normally run Linux, you can use a small Linux distribution for this purpose; this option was discussed in "Preparing for Disaster: Developing a Recovery Plan." Finally, you can use a secondary or Zip-disk-based Windows installation; this alternative is described shortly, in "Using Windows for a Complete Restore."

Preservation of Filesystem Features

Some filesystems include features that aren't supported by Linux. In fact, the storage of short filenames by FAT and NTFS partitions is one such feature, important enough to have earned its own heading in this discussion. Other features are more subtle, but some are crucial, including the following:

System, Hidden, and Archive Bits   The system and hidden bits are doomed to extinction when you use Linux-based backup software. Fortunately, losing these bits is unlikely to cause any serious difficulties. `smbtar` can use the archive bit to control incremental backups, but other Linux backup software can't use this information.

NTFS Ownership and ACLs   Although SMB/CIFS supports NTFS-style ownership and access control lists (ACLs), neither `smbmount` nor `smbtar` preserves this information. Therefore, if you use Samba to back up a Windows NT or 2000 system that uses NTFS, you will lose this information in the backup process. A system recovered from such a backup can still be made to boot, but these NTFS security features will have to be manually re-created after the restoration.

OS/2 EAs   OS/2 uses *Extended Attributes (EAs)* to store information such as program icons and WorkPlace Shell (WPS) objects. EAs are therefore critically important for OS/2 systems, but they can't be directly backed up through Samba. You have two choices for backing up OS/2 systems:

- Run a client-initiated backup, using a tool such as `tar` on OS/2 and a remotely accessible tape unit or a Samba backup share. (Both of these options are explained earlier, in "Performing a Client-Initiated Backup.") OS/2 backup packages, including a port of `tar` (available in an open source package called GTAK) understand EAs and back them up correctly.

- Run the `EABACKUP` utility program on OS/2 clients prior to backing them up. This utility, available from major OS/2 archive sites, backs up EAs into a regular file. After restoring files, you run the companion restore utility to reattach EAs to their files.

Macintosh Resource Forks   If you use a Macintosh with the DAVE server (`http://www.thursby.com`), you can use Samba to back up the Macintosh. This backup may be incomplete, however, because of the Macintosh's unique resource forks. A better choice is to run a client-initiated backup using a client/server backup package or a Samba backup share, as described in "Using a Samba Share as an Intermediary." Because this method uses Macintosh native backup software, you can be sure that the Macintosh filesystem will be backed up completely and correctly.

Unix Backup Clients   SMB/CIFS doesn't support all the features of Unix filesystems and is therefore unsuitable as a means of mounting those filesystems for direct backup. The exception is when you use the client to package files and send the package to the server (see "Using a Samba Share as an Intermediary" earlier in this chapter).

As a general rule, Samba backs up the most important information from the filesystems with which it can communicate. If you have doubts, perform a test backup and complete restore to a fresh hard disk. For any problems that occur, research your client OS and filesystem. Find out what features it doesn't support.

TIP   One way to preserve all important filesystem information is to use a "raw," low-level disk backup utility such as Linux's dd, or a commercial tool such as PowerQuest's (http://www.powerquest.com) Drive Image or Symantec's (http://www.symantec.com) Ghost. These tools create image copies of the partition, including all filesystem information. The less-sophisticated of these (including Linux's dd) only allow restoration to a partition of precisely the same size as the original. Others are more flexible and may be your best bet for backing up and restoring NTFS partitions.

Emergency Recovery Options

A backup is useless if you can't recover its data. Your preparation of recovery options is critical, both for routine restoration of a handful of files and for complete recovery in the wake of a disk failure or other event requiring a full restore. For a complete restore, some additional steps are necessary to make a Windows computer bootable once again. As with recovering your files, you should be prepared to take these steps when it becomes necessary to restore a system to full health.

Partial Restores

In some cases, you don't need to do a complete restore; you may just need to restore a few files or directories. When this is true, you can reverse the backup process. This goes most smoothly when you use the backup server as a client to mount shares exported by the backup client. Mount the exported shares again and use your backup software to do a selective restore.

For example, using smbtar, you'd issue this command on the backup server:

```
# smbtar -s BUCLIENT -x CDRIVE -p password -v -t /dev/st0 ⏎
-r SomeDir/SomeSubDir
```

This command restores the contents of SomeDir/SomSubDir from tape to its original resting place on BUCLIENT's CDRIVE. Similarly, you can mount a share and use ordinary tar or another backup program to restore files. If your backup client normally exports its shares read-only, you must temporarily change that configuration to allow a restore to work.

Partial restores are more complex if you used an intermediary file-storage stage, such as the [backup] share presented in "Using a Samba Share as an Intermediary." If the backup configuration stored files in a conventional form on a backup medium, it may be possible to restore them using smbtar or an smbmount of the remote filesystem, even if the backup was initially created in a different way. The alternative is to restore the entire backup file from tape and then access that file from the client, in a reverse of the process used to create it. Such a two-tiered restore procedure can be cumbersome.

Using Windows for a Complete Restore

The worst-case restore scenario is when a system's hard disk is completely lost through theft, malfunction, or some other misfortune. Particularly in the case of a network restore, this situation poses something of a chicken-and-egg scenario—you can't access the backup medium without installing the OS, but you can't recover the OS without accessing the backup medium. When performing a network-based restore, there are several possible solutions to this conundrum. The next two sections, "Using Linux for a Complete Restore" and "Using Direct Access to Backup Media," describe two of these solutions.

Another option is to use Windows itself, in one form or another, to access the network backup media. There are two specific routes for this type of access.

Performing a Partial Install for Recovery   Starting with a blank hard disk, you can install Windows in a minimal way—just enough to make the target system's hard disk accessible to the backup server. You can then restore the entire system using the reverse of whatever process you used to back it up, such as smbtar. The difficulty with this procedure is that the partial installation may interfere with the restoration, because the files to be restored must overwrite the partial installation's files. If you must take this route, I recommend you install Windows on a small primary partition, and restore the old system to another primary partition. You can then boot the restored system and wipe out the temporary partial installation (or leave it in place in case you need it in the future).

Using an Emergency Boot Disk   If your clients are DOS or OS/2 systems, you may be able to create boot floppies with the necessary network tools to make the damaged system accessible from the backup server, and hence restore it. This approach won't work with Windows, but there is a tool for Iomega Zip disks that accomplishes much the same purpose. It is called Norton Zip Rescue (NZR), available from both Iomega (http://www.iomega.com/software/featured/nzr.html) and Norton (as part of its Norton Utilities package). NZR produces a Zip disk and floppy disk pair that contain a complete bootable Windows 9x system, from which you can export a freshly formatted hard disk for restoration from the backup server. If necessary, you can also install backup client software on the disk, providing the package is small enough to fit. Unfortunately, this package doesn't work with Windows NT or 2000.

TIP Even if you don't normally use Zip disks, you may want to purchase one or two parallel-port Zip drives in order to use NZR software. You can easily move one of these drives to a system that needs recovery, and then remove it when you've restored a working OS.

Using Windows as the restoration OS has certain advantages. Specifically, if you use Windows for both backup and restore, you need not be concerned that your filenames will be subtly altered by the Windows-versus-Linux handling of FAT partitions. A partial install may also be the only practical way to recover a Windows NT or 2000 system, particularly if that OS was installed on an NTFS partition. Configuring and testing an emergency restore system can take a lot of effort, however. Furthermore, if you have an office full of clients, you may need to create a *unique* restoration system for each computer, unless the computers are nearly identical in their hardware configurations. Windows is very finicky about its hardware—if even one card is different, an emergency recovery system for one computer may not work at all on another.

Using Linux for a Complete Restore

Linux is worth consideration as a temporary client for an emergency restoration. You can create a minimal Linux recovery floppy, or a Linux system on a Zip or other removable disk, as described in "Preparing for Disaster: Developing a Recovery Plan." This system can then be used on what are ordinarily Windows clients in order to restore those systems. Under this plan, the emergency recovery system normally includes at least a minimal Samba setup (although you may be able to restore via NFS rather than Samba if you didn't use smbtar to back up). After preparing a hard disk by creating a FAT filesystem, you can mount that filesystem as type vfat, export it under an appropriate name, and restore data from the backup server.

Using Linux in this capacity has several advantages:

Single Restore Configuration   In principle, you can use a single emergency restore setup for both Windows and Linux systems. This can greatly reduce the amount of time and effort invested in preparing for disaster. Unlike an NZR setup, a single emergency Linux restore disk can usually function on a wide range of hardware.

Greater Media Options   Although NZR is a very useful tool, its utility is limited to Iomega Zip disks. You can't use this tool with LS-120 disks, magneto-optical disks, or similar media. Linux is not so constrained; you can create an emergency Linux restore system on any sufficiently large media—even on floppy disks.

Flexible Configuration Options   You can configure a Linux emergency restore system with all the Samba options described in this book. These options might be useful—say, to set the `netbios name` to something other than the name provided by DHCP.

Despite the flexibility provided by a Linux emergency restore disk, this approach also has its drawbacks:

Poor Windows NT or 2000 Restore Capability   Chances are you won't be able to restore a Windows NT or 2000 system. Linux does include NTFS support, but it's very weak. With a tool such as Partition Magic, you might be able to restore a Windows NT system to FAT and then convert the FAT partition to NTFS. Such an approach is not guaranteed to work, though.

Small File-Naming Differences   Windows treats short filenames as if they were all uppercase (as in `README.TXT`), but Linux treats these filenames as all lowercase (as in `readme.txt`). This difference creates discrepancies when you're using one OS to restore files backed up from another. A backup created under Windows will have all-uppercase short filenames, but when Linux restores them, it will create a matching long filename to preserve the case. For most files, this conversion does no damage, but it does mean you'll see some subtle differences when you reboot in Windows. For instance, Windows converts short filenames without matching long filenames to appear with a leading capital when displayed in a file manager window (for instance, `Readme.txt`). After restoration via a Linux system, these filenames may appear in all uppercase. There may also be subtle differences in the short filenames assigned to long filenames, which can be a more serious issue, as described earlier in "Short Filename Preservation."

Utility Differences   Linux doesn't include the same low-level disk utilities that Windows has (such as `FDISK`, `CHKDSK`, and `FORMAT`). Linux does include its own versions of many of these (such as `fdisk` and `mkdosfs`), but they aren't exactly equivalent. Partitions created with Linux tools occasionally cause problems in Windows. As a workaround, I suggest you use a Windows emergency disk to create and format Windows partitions, then use Linux tools to restore files to these Windows-created partitions.

On the whole, using Linux to restore Windows systems works best on large networks with a wide variety of client hardware. On such networks, the flexibility of a text-mode Linux emergency boot disk outweighs the drawback of the differences between Linux's and Windows's handling of filesystems.

If you have Windows NT or 2000 clients, I recommend you not rely on a Linux emergency recovery disk. Painful as it may be, such systems are most reliably restored by doing a minimal OS installation on a small emergency partition and then restoring the old OS to the main partition. If you have only a few Windows 9x clients or if your clients all use identical hardware, these systems are best restored by using an NZR disk.

Using Direct Access to the Backup Media

One final method of restoration is to provide direct access to the backup media. In truth, this approach can be used in conjunction with either a Windows or a Linux emergency boot medium. The difference in comparison to the network approaches lies in the fact that the backup medium is directly accessible to the client, instead of being accessible only from the network. Such an approach can simplify the emergency restore disk's configuration.

There are several specific approaches you can take to connect the backup medium directly to the target restoration disk:

Installing the Target Disk in the Backup Server   One radical approach is to install an empty hard disk in the backup server. You can then partition it and use Linux tools on the backup server to restore client files to the target disk. Afterward, you can remove the target disk from the backup server and install it in the client computer. This technique has the benefit of requiring very little in the way of special restore configuration. You need only the existing backup server configuration and an emergency Windows floppy to make the disk bootable, as described shortly in "Making Windows Bootable Again." It's inconvenient, however, because it requires temporarily attaching a hard disk to the backup server—which means shutting down the backup server twice and probably opening its case. Avoid this approach unless you're caught unprepared by a system crash.

Moving the Backup Drive to the Client   With an external tape backup unit, you may be able to temporarily attach it to the client computer and then access its media directly. Chances are this approach will work best if you use Linux as the restoration OS, because the tapes were originally written by Linux using a utility such as tar. You have the advantage of direct access to the backup medium, and if your clients are equipped to handle the backup's interface (probably SCSI), it may be a reasonably convenient solution. Unless you have a spare backup drive, though, you'll have to shut down the backup server, which may be undesirable.

Using CD-R or CD-RW Media   If you use CD-R or CD-RW as backup media, you can insert the backup media in the standard CD-ROM drive on the client and read the media directly, without moving any drives from one system to another. (To read CD-RW media, you'll need a fairly recent CD-ROM drive.) This approach can be extremely convenient if a backup will fit on just one or two CD-R discs.

In most situations, the only worthwhile direct-access arrangement is direct access to CD-R media. This approach can be extremely convenient because it requires no network access for a restoration. If your client computers' files can fit on one or two CD-R discs, you may want to plan your client restores around this approach. The other methods usually entail moving hardware from one computer to another, which is inconvenient and always carries the risk of damaging the hardware involved.

Making Windows Bootable Again

Once you've restored all the files to a computer, you may believe that your work is done. Flip the power switch now, however, and chances are you'll be greeted by a message that the computer is unable to boot. Although you've restored all the files to their proper places, there are two aspects of booting that should be done from a Windows emergency boot floppy:

- Setting the appropriate partition as the *active* or *bootable* one
- Configuring boot files on the Windows boot partition

Windows 9x   To perform both these tasks on a Windows 9x system, you must first have a Windows emergency boot floppy. It doesn't have to be an elaborate disk with network tools or backup utilities. You can create this simple disk from a working Windows setup by following these steps:

1. Open Control Panel and double-click the Add/Remove Programs icon. Windows displays the Add/Remove Programs dialog box.

2. Click the Startup Disk tab in the Add/Remove Programs dialog box. You'll see a display similar to that in Figure 16.6.

3. Click the Create Disk button. Windows may ask for its CD-ROM. If so, insert the disk and click OK. A progress indicator bar appears as Windows gathers files to write to the floppy disk.

4. When you're prompted for a floppy disk, insert a blank floppy and click OK in the Insert Disk dialog box. The progress bar in the Add/Remove Programs dialog box continues to advance, while your floppy disk indicator shows floppy disk activity.

Figure 16.6 You can create a text-mode Windows boot floppy from the Add/Remove Programs dialog box.

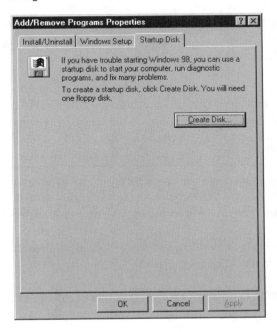

5. When Windows has created the boot floppy, click OK or Cancel to dismiss the Add/Remove Programs dialog box.

Once you've created the Windows boot floppy, you can boot it. The system you get in response is *not* a full-fledged Windows system with GUI; it's really nothing more than DOS, but the version of DOS that underlies Windows. To ensure that the Windows boot partition is active, follow these steps:

1. Type **FDISK** to start the FDISK program, which allows you to modify partitions. (You can use this tool to create partitions, if you haven't already done so.)

2. Type **2** (Set Active Partition). FDISK responds by displaying a list of primary partitions.

3. Type the number associated with the Windows partition. In the event there's only one primary partition, Windows should make it active at this point.

4. Press Esc until you've exited from FDISK.

TIP   You can use a Windows 9x boot floppy to set the active partition even on a DOS, Windows NT, or OS/2 system. OS/2 emergency floppies should include OS/2's version of FDISK, which can achieve the same results, although OS/2's FDISK works quite differently from Windows's.

Finally, it's necessary to ensure that the boot sector on the Windows partition points to the required Windows boot files. To do this, type **SYS C:**. After briefly accessing the floppy and hard disks, the result should be the message System transferred. Now you can boot the computer from the hard disk.

WARNING   Although the Windows 9x emergency floppy is essentially a version of DOS, do *not* use a DOS boot floppy's SYS command on a Windows 9x system. The system files that this command copies from the floppy must match the version of the OS installed on the hard disk. Likewise, don't use a Windows 95 emergency floppy on a Windows 98 system, or vice-versa. Do not try this procedure on a Windows NT or OS/2 system.

DOS, Windows NT, OS/2, and Others   If you're recovering a DOS, Windows NT, or OS/2 system, the steps you follow are similar, but not always identical, to those for Windows 9x. Specifically:

- You restore a DOS system to bootability as explained just above, but you must use an emergency DOS boot floppy to issue the SYS command.

- Create a Windows NT or 2000 emergency disk as described for a Windows 9x disk, but the NT/2000 disk is *not* bootable. Instead, you use this disk in conjunction with the NT/2000 installation floppies to automatically check and recover a damaged disk. After restoring an NT/2000 system, this process should restore it to working order.

- OS/2 includes a facility to create a set of emergency disks. These are bootable disks, and they include the OS/2 FDISK utility. After restoring an HPFS partition, the system should be bootable. If you restore an OS/2 system to FAT, you may need to run OS/2's equivalent of SYS, which is called SYSINSTX. This utility is present on the OS/2 installation CD-ROM, in the OS2IMAGE/DISK_0 directory.

If you've performed an image backup using a utility such as dd, Drive Image, or Ghost, there should be no need to run SYS or a similar utility. You may still need to set the active partition, however.

Summary

Backup is a critically important aspect of running a network. On highly centralized client/server networks, backing up the servers is the most important backup task, so you should be familiar with Linux's native backup techniques. On less-centralized networks, or when clients host significant customizations or other data, you should back up the clients as well. Fortunately, Samba includes features that can make this task fairly painless. Restoring data in small quantities is usually not difficult, either, but it can be tedious when a system requires a complete restoration because of a failed hard disk or other disaster. In most cases, such restorations are simpler than complete re-installations of the OS, making backups a worthwhile precaution even for many client systems.

**Maintaining a
Healthy System**

PART 4

17

Troubleshooting

Samba is a robust package that can perform reliably for months on end with little supervision. At the same time, Samba is a finicky set of programs that can result in hairpulling sessions as you try to discover why it won't work. This seeming contradiction is the result of flexibility—both of Samba and of SMB/CIFS. As demonstrated by the many configuration options described in this book, both Samba and an SMB/CIFS network can be set up in a number of ways. Many of these configuration options can backfire if used incorrectly, producing a network that operates slowly, sporadically, or not at all. This book's chapters include various admonitions against configuring Samba in certain ways, or warnings about possible negative consequences of specific configurations or actions. You should therefore read relevant sections of this book if you're having trouble with a particular feature. If your print server isn't working correctly, for instance, you can turn to Chapter 6, "Configuring Printer Sharing." Here in Chapter 17 you'll find additional troubleshooting information to help you out. It includes tips aimed at specific tasks as well as general-purpose problems and solutions.

The chapter begins with some overall problem-solving techniques for use with Samba. Then it moves on to specific issues. One set of problems often encountered by new Samba administrators is in obtaining initial access to the Samba server. Sometimes these obstacles are a result of domain configurations; other times they're not. These initial-access problems are covered in the second and third sections of the chapter. Once you've located a Samba share from a client, other irregularities can crop up when you try to access a specific share. Finally, you may run into difficulty accessing specific files or sending print jobs to a printer share. The chapter covers both these topics, as well.

General-Purpose Troubleshooting

There are several troubleshooting techniques that are useful when investigating a wide range of Samba problems—and many non-Samba problems, as well. You should be familiar with these techniques and use them to run some preliminary tests on your network's functionality in general, before proceeding with in-depth Samba troubleshooting.

Testing Basic Networking

Samba can't work if the underlying TCP/IP networking doesn't function. New administrators sometimes leap to the conclusion that Samba isn't operating correctly, when in fact it's the basic network functions that are at fault. Although configuring these basic functions is beyond the scope of this book, this section offers a few tests you can run to see if the basic features are working correctly on a Linux server. If they aren't, consult the Linux Networking HOWTO (http://www.linuxdoc.org/HOWTO/Net-HOWTO/). You can also try a general-purpose Linux networking book, such as Craig Hunt's *Linux Network Servers 24seven* (Sybex, 1999) or my *Linux: Networking for Your Office* (Sams, 2000). In addition, the man pages for the utilities described in this chapter may be useful, because you can use these tools to set networking options as well as check them.

Checking the Network Interface and Routing Table

You can verify that your system's network interface is working correctly by typing **/sbin/ifconfig**. This command produces output that includes something like Listing 17.1.

Listing 17.1   Output of the Linux ifconfig Command

```
eth0      Link encap:Ethernet  HWaddr 00:A0:CC:24:BA:02
          inet addr:192.168.1.3  Bcast:192.168.1.255  Mask:255.255.255.0
          UP BROADCAST RUNNING MULTICAST  MTU:1500  Metric:1
          RX packets:2018995 errors:11 dropped:0 overruns:0 frame:11
          TX packets:1936143 errors:0 dropped:0 overruns:0 carrier:0
          collisions:2410 txqueuelen:100
          Interrupt:10 Base address:0xbc00
```

The output of ifconfig should also include a similar listing for an interface called lo, which you can ignore, and possibly others. eth0 is the interface for the first Ethernet adapter; it may be called something else on your system if your network isn't Ethernet-based. The following critical information is displayed in Listing 17.1:

    Hardware Address   The field labeled HWaddr gives you the hardware address of the Ethernet adapter. You may be able to check this against an address printed on a sticker on the board. Occasionally, bugs in Ethernet boards or drivers cause all boards of a given type to take on the same hardware address, which causes the network to malfunction. An updated driver or setting special driver parameters may fix this problem.

TCP/IP Addresses   The computer's TCP/IP address, as assigned by you or by DHCP, is listed in the `inet addr` field. The associated broadcast address and network mask are shown in the remaining fields of that line. Verify that these addresses are correct.

Miscellaneous Settings   The line that begins UP BROADCAST presents miscellaneous networking settings. It's possible you'll spot a problem setting on this line, but most likely it won't display any suspicious information.

Errors   The lines beginning RX packets and TX packets show statistics on received and transmitted network packets, respectively. The next line gives information on collisions. It's normal to have a small number of errors and collisions, as demonstrated by Listing 17.1. If you see more than a few percent collisions or errors, though, there's something seriously wrong with your network configuration—perhaps a bad cable or an inappropriate duplex or speed setting. A large number of collisions may simply mean that your network is overloaded; replacing hubs with switches or breaking your network into multiple segments may speed things up.

Hardware Settings   The final line in Listing 17.1 shows the network adapter hardware settings. These should not conflict with settings of other hardware components, such as sound cards or SCSI host adapters. Such conflicts can produce system failures and system crashes. (PCI devices can share interrupts, but ISA devices cannot. Shared interrupts can slow the system even when both devices are PCI cards.)

If your network interface appears to be working correctly, check your system's *routing table* next. A routing table controls how Linux directs outgoing packets. TCP/IP protocols let Linux automatically find the hardware address associated with local IP addresses, so Linux can send those packets directly to the correct computer. More-distant IP addresses must be handled through a *router* (aka a *gateway*). To check your routing table, type **/sbin/route -n**. The result resembles Listing 17.2.

Listing 17.2   Typical Output of the Linux route -n Command

```
Kernel IP routing table
Destination   Gateway       Genmask          Flags Metric Ref    Use Iface
192.168.1.0   0.0.0.0       255.255.255.0    U     0      0        0 eth0
127.0.0.0     0.0.0.0       255.0.0.0        U     0      0        0 lo
0.0.0.0       192.168.1.1   0.0.0.0          UG    0      0        0 eth0
```

Maintaining a
Healthy System

PART 4

The Destination and Genmask columns in Listing 17.2 determine a destination address range, such as 192.168.1.0 and 255.255.255.0, which collectively specify the 192.168.1.0/24 network. In Listing 17.2's routing table, all traffic destined for that network is sent over the eth0 interface (specified in the final column). The 0.0.0.0 destination (which may appear as default if you omit the -n parameter) indicates any address that's not matched by prior entries. The fact that this row includes an entry under the Gateway column indicates that it's a gateway address—packets are directed at the specified gateway computer, which then routes the packets elsewhere. Computers with multiple network adapters can have more complex routing tables, directing packets for one network (say, 192.168.1.0/24) to one interface, and another's packets (say, 10.0.0.0/8) to another interface.

At a minimum, your routing table should include your local network's IP address range. A gateway system associated with a default destination is necessary for any system connected to the Internet, or even a smaller network using routers. If these features aren't present, look into using the route command to fix your network configuration, or consult your distribution's network configuration tools to fix matters more permanently.

NOTE   Windows, too, has a ROUTE command, but it works somewhat differently from Linux's route. Typing **ROUTE PRINT** in Windows produces results similar to those of **route -n** in Linux, but the details differ. Nonetheless, you may want to study the routing table on Windows clients on your network if those clients are misbehaving.

Using *ping* to Test Basic Connectivity

The ping command is extremely useful when testing basic network connectivity. The basic syntax is:

```
ping address
```

where the *address* can be either a numerical IP address or a TCP/IP hostname. If it's the latter, though, your network's name resolution must be functioning correctly. For the most basic tests, therefore, you should use numerical IP addresses. Here are some addresses you should try:

127.0.0.1   This is the *loopback* or *localhost* address, which corresponds to the lo interface (see Listing 17.2). Pinging this address should work on all systems.

Your IP Address   You should try pinging the IP address associated with your computer's main network interface, such as 192.168.1.3 for the computer represented in Listings 17.1 and 17.2.

Your Gateway   Try pinging the IP address associated with your gateway computer, such as 192.168.1.1, revealed by **route -n**, as shown in Listing 17.2.

External Network Addresses   If you know the IP addresses of some convenient external system, ping one or two of them to be sure the gateway system is functioning as you expect. (If you specify the wrong gateway address in your routing table, you may be able to use local networking but not access remote systems.) Some systems are programmed not to respond to external pings or may themselves be offline. So if an external ping test fails, try another external site.

Named Systems   You can perform any of the preceding tests using names rather than IP addresses. If the IP addresses work but the names don't, it means your DNS configuration is not working.

A basic ping test looks like this:

```
$ ping 192.168.1.1
PING 192.168.1.1 (192.168.1.1): 56 data bytes
64 bytes from 192.168.1.1: icmp_seq=0 ttl=255 time=0.298 ms
64 bytes from 192.168.1.1: icmp_seq=1 ttl=255 time=0.470 ms
64 bytes from 192.168.1.1: icmp_seq=2 ttl=255 time=0.424 ms
64 bytes from 192.168.1.1: icmp_seq=3 ttl=255 time=0.448 ms
--- 192.168.1.1 ping statistics ---
4 packets transmitted, 4 packets received, 0% packet loss
round-trip min/avg/max = 0.298/0.410/0.470 ms
```

This command sends repeated simple packets to the destination, which should respond. The local ping program can then check the transit time and spot lost packets. Your local network connections should have low ping times (10ms or less) and few or no lost packets. If this is not the case, look for hardware flaws such as defective cables or switches. It's also possible that network overload will cause problems; you may want to consider upgrading to faster network hardware.

Linux's version of ping keeps sending ping packets until you stop it by typing Ctrl+C. Windows, too, includes a PING command, but it sends four packets and then stops by default.

Testing Complex Connectivity

If your basic tests, including ping, reveal connectivity between two clients but Samba doesn't work, you may want to test using some non-Samba network protocol. Possibilities include FTP, HTTP (Web server/browser), SMTP (e-mail), POP (e-mail), Telnet, and

Maintaining a Healthy System

PART 4

many others. Most Linux distributions ship with servers for at least some of these protocols operating by default. Although you probably don't want all of these running on a production Samba server, using one for testing purposes on a malfunctioning system is a good idea. Telnet is particularly easy to configure and so makes a good example. To test using Telnet, follow these steps:

1. On the server, ensure that the Telnet server package is installed. It may be called `netkit-telnet`, `nkitb`, `telnet`, or something else. The relevant server file is usually `/usr/sbin/in.telnetd`.

2. On the server, verify that the Telnet server package is enabled in `/etc/inetd.conf` or in `/etc/xinetd.conf`. The relevant line begins with `telnet` and should *not* be commented out—that is, it should not be preceded by a pound sign (#).

3. If you modified `/etc/inetd.conf`, restart the `inetd` daemon.

4. Verify that the Telnet server is running by using the client to connect to the local server, as in **telnet 127.0.0.1**. This command should produce a Linux `login:` prompt.

5. Try using the Linux `telnet` command from another computer to access the server, as in **telnet chica** to test the server `chica`. Most OSs, including Windows, sport `telnet` clients, so you can do this using any client OS you like.

If the preceding steps produce a Linux `login:` prompt in the Telnet client program, then your network is functioning correctly and you can move on to more Samba-specific troubleshooting. If you can't establish a Telnet connection, though, you should investigate further. Whatever is causing Telnet problems may be causing Samba problems, as well. Fortunately, this sort of trouble is quite rare when basic ping tests succeed.

Checking Log Files

As described in Chapter 4, "GUI Configuration Tools and the `smb.conf` File," Samba stores certain types of information in *log files*. You can specify the level of detail stored in log files by using the `debug level` parameter in `smb.conf`. This parameter's value ranges from 0 (no logging) to 10 (a level of logging far beyond what a system administrator is likely to need). On most functioning Samba servers, `debug level = 1` is an appropriate setting. If you're encountering problems, though, you might want to set this value as high as 3. You can then examine the log files for clues. Setting the debug level higher than 3 is usually not helpful, however, particularly on a working system. That level of detail is far too high to be useful except to Samba programmers; also, increasing the debugging levels slows down Samba and requires more disk space for the log files.

Even at a level of 1, log files contain valuable information such as logon attempts and failures. If you're having trouble logging onto the server, a log file may reveal that Samba is— or is not—receiving those logon attempts, and perhaps give a clue as to why they're failing.

Using Samba Utilities

Samba ships with a number of utilities that can help in debugging. The most important of these are nmblookup and smbclient. Chapter 7 describes smbclient in some detail. Several earlier chapters refer to nmblookup, but not in detail. This program is used as follows:

nmblookup [*parameters*] *name*

where *name* is the NetBIOS name of the target system, such as chica. Possible parameters include the following:

-M   This parameter, which searches for a master browser, is normally used with a *name* of -, signifying that the system is to search the network for the master browser rather than query a specific computer.

-R   Use this parameter to perform a recursive search. This search uses an NBNS server to look up information, when possible, rather than query a system directly.

-S   With this parameter, nmblookup performs a node status query, which returns the names of all the shares associated with a server.

-r   With this parameter, nmblookup attempts to send queries using port 137. This is a workaround for a bug in Windows 95, which often ignores nmblookup requests from ports other than 137. You must be root to use this parameter.

-A   This parameter tells nmblookup to interpret *name* as an IP address, rather than a NetBIOS name.

-B *broadcast address*   Tells nmblookup to query the specified broadcast address. The default behavior is to send queries using the primary broadcast address of the computer. You can use this parameter to query a secondary network card's network.

-d *debuglevel*   This parameter sets the debug level of the utility. Like most Samba programs, nmblookup logs its activities according to its debug level. You can set this value to an appropriate level to help spot problems that might not be obvious from the program's standard output alone.

-s *smb.conf*   nmblookup uses some smb.conf parameters to control details of its operation. You can use this parameter to tell it what smb.conf file to use.

The nmblookup command is very useful at helping to diagnose browsing and name resolution problems; you can use this utility to report on the shares advertised by servers, to see what systems respond to what names, and so on. The smbclient program is useful for checking out share functions. You can perform tests on a share from the server itself, or from another Linux computer. Because both commands send information to log files, you can check these files for information that's simply not available when running SMB/CIFS clients on Windows.

Problems with Domain Controllers

One broad class of potential Samba misbehavior occurs because of its coexistence with computers on a Windows domain. As described in Chapter 10, a domain is a group of Windows computers that share an authentication mechanism, provided by a computer known as a *domain controller*. When a person logs on to a client computer on a domain, that client passes the user's username and password to the domain controller, which either approves or disallows network access for that user. Subsequent accesses to servers don't require additional authentication, provided the servers are all configured to participate in the same domain.

Unfortunately, domain configurations don't always work the way they're supposed to. Individual clients and servers may be misconfigured, and it's easy to misconfigure a Samba server in such a way that it disrupts the normal functioning of a domain. If you add a Samba server and find that your existing domain isn't working, or if you're trying to use Samba as a domain controller but aren't getting anywhere, you should read this section and Chapter 10.

Conflicts with Windows Computers

One class of problem you may encounter is in conflicts between Samba and Windows computers. These conflicts come in two basic types: Samba can interfere with the operation of a domain controller, or Samba as a domain controller may not understand a client's requests. The first is likely to cause network-wide difficulties, whereas the second event affects only specific types of clients, such as Windows 2000 computers.

Usurping the Rightful Domain Controller

Samba includes several global `smb.conf` parameters that affect whether or not it attempts to become the domain controller or to take on any other tasks that a Windows NT or 2000 domain controller normally expects to perform. Following are the relevant parameters:

domain logons If set to Yes, Samba announces itself as a domain controller. *This parameter should be set to No if Samba is not the rightful domain controller!*

domain master This option controls whether Samba attempts to become the domain master browser. Although the domain master browser and domain controller can be different computers, Windows NT systems normally expect both tasks to be handled by the same computer. You should therefore set `domain master = No` if another system is the domain controller.

local master This option controls whether Samba attempts to become the *local master browser*. If the domain controller resides on the same subnet as the Samba computer, you should set this option to No because the domain controller will expect to be the local master browser.

wins support   Large networks often host an NBNS server, also known as a WINS server. NBNS functions much like DNS for TCP/IP networks and is described in more detail in Chapter 9. As with master browser functions, domain controllers often expect to be the NBNS server, so you should set `wins support = No` on all other computers.

If you inappropriately set any of these `smb.conf` options to `Yes`, you may see peculiar behavior, ranging from gaps in browse lists to a complete inability to log on to your domain. Sometimes these events won't occur, or they'll occur only sporadically because of interactions with other parameters. Setting all these options to `No` should head off difficulties—unless, of course, you want the Samba system to function as the domain controller, in which case the parameters should normally all be set to `Yes`.

Samba as a Domain Controller for Windows

If you want Samba to function as a domain controller on a Windows network, read Chapter 10. You should be particularly aware of the fact that domains operate differently for specific versions of Windows.

Windows 9x   Samba's domain support for Windows 9x is the best, largely because these clients expect the least of a domain. To use Windows 9x clients in a Samba-controlled domain, you need only set a handful of `smb.conf` parameters and configure the clients to operate as part of a domain.

Windows NT 4.0   To use Windows NT 4.0 systems as clients on a Samba-controlled domain, you must use Samba 2.0.5 or later. (Earlier versions lacked NT domain control support.) You also have to create special *trust accounts* on the Samba server to support NT domain clients.

Windows 2000   Much like Windows NT 4.0 domain clients, Windows 2000 clients rely upon trust accounts. Samba versions through 2.0.7 do not support Windows 2000 domain clients, but the experimental Samba TNG release does. This support will likely be added to a 2.2 or 3.0 Samba release, or possibly a post-2.0.7 2.0.x version of Samba.

If your Windows 9x clients can use your Samba-controlled domain but your Windows NT or 2000 systems can't, you may need to add trust accounts or update your version of Samba. Chapter 10 discusses these issues in detail.

One problem frequently reported by those trying to configure Samba as a domain controller is that clients claim they aren't able to locate a domain controller. With Windows NT or 2000 clients, the cause is often a missing or misconfigured trust account. You can check whether Samba is advertising itself as a domain controller by issuing the Linux **nmblookup -SR** *NAME* or the Windows **NBTSTAT -a** *NAME* commands, where *NAME* is the NetBIOS name of the domain controller. These commands produce output similar to the following:

```
$ nmblookup -SR sultan
querying sultan on 192.168.1.255
192.168.1.1 sultan<00>
Looking up status of 192.168.1.1
received 9 names
        SULTAN          <00> -          M <ACTIVE>
        SULTAN          <03> -          M <ACTIVE>
        SULTAN          <20> -          M <ACTIVE>
        .._MSBROWSE__. <01> - <GROUP> M <ACTIVE>
        GESTALT         <00> - <GROUP> M <ACTIVE>
        GESTALT         <1b> -          M <ACTIVE>
        GESTALT         <1c> - <GROUP> M <ACTIVE>
        GESTALT         <1d> -          M <ACTIVE>
        GESTALT         <1e> - <GROUP> M <ACTIVE>
num_good_sends=0 num_good_receives=0
```

The critical line for determining domain controller status is the line with the <1b> code. This code advertises the computer as the domain controller for the GESTALT domain, and as the domain master browser. If that line is missing, review your domain controller configuration options, and be sure you restart the Samba daemons. If the line is present, check that no other computer on your network sports the same <1b> code—two battling domain controllers can wreak havoc on a network.

Rejected Passwords

Domains operate with encrypted passwords. You must therefore include the encrypt passwords = Yes parameter in your domain controller's smb.conf file, and in every Samba server that operates on a domain. In addition, you must create and use an appropriate encrypted password file (usually called smbpasswd). Chapter 14 discusses encrypted passwords, including configuring these options appropriately on a Samba server.

If your Samba server is rejecting passwords but is supposed to be part of a domain, look to see whether the server is set to use server- or domain-level security (that is, security = Server or security = Domain). If the security parameter is set incorrectly, Samba will try to authenticate usernames and passwords locally, bypassing the domain controller's security. Even when your `security` parameter is set correctly, you must create accounts on the Linux computer corresponding to the users who are trying to access the computer. If your users' usernames are different in Windows than in Linux, you must use the `username map` parameter to point Samba to a map file, which ties Windows usernames to corresponding Linux usernames. Chapter 15 describes the `username map` parameter and map files in detail.

If you're using domain-level security, you must tell Samba to join the domain. To do this, create an appropriate trust account on the domain controller, and issue the **smbpasswd -j** *DOMAIN* command on the Samba server to join the domain called *DOMAIN*. (You need only issue this command once.) Chapter 10, particularly the section entitled "Using Samba on a Domain," contains more information.

Problems Locating a Samba Server

Even when your network functions as a workgroup rather than a domain, you may encounter odd network access problems. Your clients might not see a computer in Network Neighborhood, or they might see the computer but be unable to access it. In most cases, this behavior is related to one of three issues: binding SMB/CIFS to TCP/IP, network browsing, or name resolution.

Checking SMB/CIFS Binding to TCP/IP

Chapters 1 and 2 describe the assorted network stacks in common use today. A network stack is a set of interlocking protocols that control networking at different layers of abstraction, ranging from drivers for network cards to high-level tools for transferring files and other data from one system to another. Traditionally, Windows networks have used the NetBEUI stack, but Linux doesn't support NetBEUI unless you add an open-source but third-party NetBEUI stack from Procom Technologies (`http://www.procom.com`). Fortunately, Microsoft has been moving away from NetBEUI for years, in favor of the more prevalent TCP/IP, upon which the Internet is based. All but the oldest SMB/CIFS implementations can work through TCP/IP, and this is the only mode that Samba supports unless patched with Procom's NetBEUI stack.

On some networks, however, NetBEUI is still in use. If you've tried to use a Samba server on an existing NetBEUI-based network, you might experience delays or some clients may not be able to use the Samba server. The section "Binding SMB/CIFS to TCP/IP in Windows" in Chapter 2 describes how to ensure that your Windows systems use TCP/IP networking rather than NetBEUI.

Browsing Problems

As described in Chapters 1 and 11, browsing is the process of examining the computers and shares on a network in order to locate needed information. In Windows, browsing is done through the Network Neighborhood icon (or My Network Places in Windows 2000). This icon creates a window similar to the one shown in Figure 17.1, which shows all the computers that are readily accessible on a NetBIOS network.

Figure 17.1 Windows provides a graphical face for the list of computers and shares available on a network.

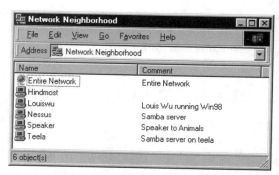

Browsing involves a delicate interplay of operations, so it's easy to disrupt. Browsing irregularities can be quite peculiar—one client might show different computers available than another, for example. When diagnosing browsing problems, it's sometimes helpful to turn off as many computers as possible in order to simplify your network configuration. You should read Chapter 11, which describes how to configure Samba systems to function as master browsers—or to *not* take on those duties, which can be just as important to overall network functioning.

Preliminary Diagnostics

When diagnosing any browsing problem, it's useful to gather some critical information. Sometimes you'll discover the cause of trouble in the course of collecting this information. Other times, you need the information to track down the real source of the problem. In any event, you should take these steps to collect the needed data:

Identify the local master browser. You can use the Linux `nmblookup` utility to locate the local master browser. Use the following command to accomplish this task:

```
$ nmblookup -M -
```

The output is the IP address of the local master browser, such as `192.168.89.202`. You may want to run this test repeatedly over a period of time. If the local master browser changes over time, the result can be disruptions in browsing when one of those changes occurs. Chapter 11 describes how to ensure that a specific Samba server is always the local master browser.

Identify the domain master browser.   On a network that spans multiple subnets, one computer functions as the domain master browser, which coordinates browse lists across the subnets. This computer is normally the primary domain controller (PDC), but you should ensure that you haven't misconfigured a non-PDC Samba server to function as the domain master browser. Use `nmblookup` to check this, by typing **`nmblookup -SR`** *`hostname`* to check the computer called *hostname*. If the output includes a line with a <1b> code, then the system is configured as a domain master browser.

Identify the NBNS server.   NBNS isn't a necessary feature of all networks, nor is it necessary for a browse list to appear on a client. If NBNS functions are misconfigured, however, you may not be able to browse *into* computers that appear in Network Neighborhood.

Take notes on the problem.   If some computers don't appear on browse lists, which ones are missing? Are missing computers missing from all clients' Network Neighborhoods, or are the gaps random? Are there any correlations to server OSs, client OSs, or network topologies? Noting a regularity in the problem may help point you toward a solution.

In checking these issues, you may note an error in a computer's configuration that, when fixed, eliminates the problem on the network as a whole. Otherwise, you may want to consider several specific problems, as described in the following sections.

No Servers Appear in Network Neighborhood

Complete failures of browsing are rare. As described in Chapter 11, NetBIOS networks automatically elect a master browser. This master browser maintains browse lists for the network, and clients can automatically locate their local master browsers. Once a client locates a local master browser, it can retrieve the browse list from the master browser, thus displaying computers in Network Neighborhood.

A complete failure to display computers in Network Neighborhood is usually caused by one of two mistakes:

Incorrect Network Binding   Samba operates using NetBIOS over TCP/IP (aka NBT), but some older clients use NetBEUI instead, and even modern Windows systems can be configured to use NetBEUI instead of NBT. Read "Checking SMB/CIFS Binding to TCP/IP," earlier, for a discussion of this issue.

Incorrect Workgroup Setting   Normally, all computers on a NetBIOS network belong to a single workgroup or domain. You set the workgroup of a Linux computer using the `workgroup` parameter. On Windows computers, you set the workgroup using the Identification tab of the Network dialog box (Figure 17.2). Even a one-character typo in these settings can remove a computer from the correct workgroup, so be careful!

Figure 17.2   An incorrect workgroup setting can isolate a Windows computer from others in its intended workgroup.

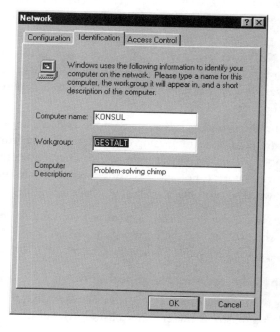

In addition to addressing these SMB/CIFS-specific configuration issues, be sure your client's basic networking functions are working correctly. Try using `ping` to and from the client to test network connectivity. You should also try some higher-level network protocol, such as a Web browser or Telnet, to verify that networking is functioning correctly.

Incomplete Browse Lists

One common and frustrating problem is that of incomplete browse lists—one or more computers appear in Network Neighborhood, but others don't. You should check the following factors if you're experiencing this discrepancy:

Check the domain and local master browsers.   If your network includes several subnets, you must either configure a domain master browser (on the same computer that functions as the PDC) or use Samba's `remote browse sync` parameter to synchronize browse lists among a workgroup's local master browsers. Failure to do this will result in incomplete browse lists on one or more subnets. Browsing is most likely to work smoothly if all the master browsers are of one type—all Samba or all Windows NT, for example.

Improve the stability of master browsers.   Whenever a master browser changes, there's a brief interruption to browsing on all systems on the subnet, and the new master browser's browse lists may be incomplete for a time afterward. You should therefore use the tricks discussed in Chapter 11 (particularly "Winning or Losing an Election") to configure one and only one Samba server to always be the master browser, or to have all the Samba servers step out of the way and let your highest-level Windows NT or 2000 system assume master browser duties. If a network contains multiple preferred master browsers, or if master browsers are frequently turned on and off, browse list stability will suffer.

Use `remote announce` where needed.   The Samba `remote announce` parameter allows an isolated server to announce its presence to a master browser on a distant subnet. If a server resides on a subnet apart from most of the workgroup or domain, and if the remote subnet doesn't have its own master browser that communicates with the other master browsers, it's imperative that you use this parameter if you want the server to appear on the workgroup or domain's browse list.

Samba's browsing options make for flexible configuration, but incorrect settings for options such as `preferred master` and `os level` can result in a chaotic and confusing network. As described in Chapter 11, be careful to configure precisely one computer as the domain master browser, and one computer per subnet as the preferred master browser. Take care that the preferred master browser has the credentials to win all browser elections. If your network uses Samba systems as master browsers on multiple subnets, using `remote browse sync` to synchronize these systems' browse lists is a good idea. Following these steps can eliminate many mysterious browse-list problems.

You should also remember that after a change in master browser, or when a computer appears on or disappears from a network, there may be a delay before the master browser's browse lists are updated. This is particularly true when subnets and multiple master browsers are involved. You may therefore see inconsistencies from one computer to another, but if there are no changes in your network's contents for a few minutes, these inconsistencies should disappear.

Inability to Browse to Shares on a Server

You may encounter a situation in which Network Neighborhood shows a server, but you can't access that server when you double-click it. There are many possible causes of such a difficulty, but they fall into two broad classes:

Network Access Issues The server may have crashed but its name hasn't yet been removed from the master browser's browse list, or there may be name resolution difficulties. Name resolution issues are discussed in more detail shortly, in "Name Resolution Problems."

Server Access Issues The server's shares may be off limits to the user for various reasons, described in "Problems Accessing Samba Shares."

In diagnosing share-browsing difficulties, you should check the server to be sure it's running, and try to access the server from a variety of clients. If the access problems vary from one host to another, check features such as the clients' network masks and whether the Samba server uses the `hosts allow` or `valid users` parameters (which can block access from specific clients or users).

Name Resolution Problems

As described in Chapter 9, SMB/CIFS networks can use any of several means of turning names (such as GRANDE) into IP addresses (such as 192.168.208.34). Depending upon the OSs involved, four methods may be used:

Broadcasts A computer knowing a name but not an address can send a *broadcast,* querying every computer on the network to find the needed computer. This machine should respond when its name is called.

NBNS Servers An NBNS server functions much like a TCP/IP network's DNS server, providing a clearinghouse for name resolution.

lmhosts A special file, called `lmhosts`, can provide a mapping of names to IP addresses on an individual computer.

DNS Resolution A computer can use TCP/IP name resolution systems—most notably DNS—to find a computer. This option is available for Samba, Windows NT, and Windows 2000, but not for Windows 9*x* (except indirectly, if a Samba system functions as an NBNS server that can fall back on DNS).

If name resolution fails, you won't be able to access a server by name. The server may appear in Network Neighborhood but be inaccessible, and if you type its name (as when using `smbclient` on Linux, or `NET USE` in Windows), the request won't work. There are several possible causes of name resolution failure:

Incorrect Node Type   The node type is a code for the order in which a computer uses various name resolution methods. Some node types exclude certain name resolution methods, and so can cause problems if the excluded methods are the ones that work. The section "Setting the Node Type" in Chapter 9 describes how to set the node type on a client or for a network.

Subnets with Broadcast Resolution   Unless you create clever configurations with the `wins proxy` parameter and network layouts, a network that uses two or more subnets cannot function using only broadcast name resolution. The best way to handle such a network is usually to configure an NBNS server, as described in Chapter 9.

Incorrect NBNS Server Address   If your network uses an NBNS server, every client must be told the correct NBNS server address. The easiest way to do this is by programming a DHCP server with the information and configuring your systems through DHCP. Samba can be given the address with the `wins server` parameter. If you don't use DHCP, Windows clients can be told the NBNS server's address as part of their TCP/IP configuration, as shown in Figure 17.3. You enter the NBNS server in the WINS Server Search Order field, click Add, and the IP address appears in the list.

Figure 17.3   You can configure Windows to *not* use NBNS, to use specified servers, or to acquire NBNS information from a DHCP server.

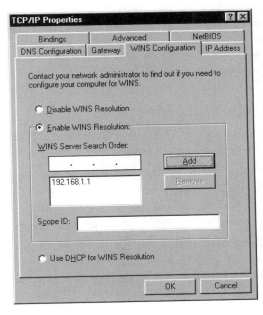

NBNS Server Failure   NBNS servers can and do fail—they can crash or contain incomplete information. If your NBNS server is a Samba system, you can tell it to use DNS lookups as a fallback position, by setting dns proxy = Yes. If this is set, and if your computers have the same NBNS and DNS names, an NBNS lookup through a Samba NBNS server will succeed as long as the target system's DNS entry is correct.

On most systems, you can force name lookup issues by creating an lmhosts file, which resides in a specific location depending on the OS. Typically, the lmhosts entries override other name lookup methods. Using this file isn't advisable except in special cases, however, because it can be difficult to maintain a separate lmhosts file on every computer.

Problems Accessing Samba Shares

Assuming you can see your Samba server in Network Neighborhood and can at least make initial SMB/CIFS connections, you can still run into trouble when it comes to accessing shares. You may have password problems, or the server may reject logon attempts from some machines but not others. Aside from issues relating to password encryption, these share-access problems are rare. That's because the Samba features likely to cause difficulty are optional extras, unlikely to be set unless you do so explicitly. Nonetheless, if you experiment with your configuration, you may unknowingly create access problems.

> **NOTE**   Some password-related troubles can occur even when you're establishing initial connections to the server. These problems are especially likely when using Windows NT or 2000 clients in a domain configuration. This arrangement requires client *trust accounts,* as described earlier in "Samba as a Domain Controller for Assorted Windows Versions."

Initial Troubleshooting Measures

Before digging through your smb.conf file to locate a problem parameter, there are some steps you can take to help isolate the source of trouble.

Connect from the server to itself.   You can use smbclient to connect from the server to itself—for instance, **smbclient //localhost/kohler** to connect to the [kohler] share. This action removes most potential network problems from the equation, letting you test the basic Samba configuration.

Use smbclient on another system.   Using smbclient rather than Windows's normal networking tools can be a useful debugging measure. smbclient sometimes returns more helpful error messages than do Windows networking clients, and you can check Samba's log files (on both client and server) for messages that may shed light on a networking problem.

Check log files.   Even when using a Windows client, you should check the server's log files for relevant information. You may want to increase the value of the debug level parameter in smb.conf to generate more information that may be valuable in debugging.

Verify a problem from multiple clients.   Find out if the problem occurs on more than one client. Errors isolated to just one client suggest that the client's networking configuration is incorrect in some way. It may have the wrong network mask or gateway specified, for instance.

It's possible that you'll uncover the source of the problem in performing these simple checks. If not, you'll at least get more data and may therefore be able to exclude possible causes.

Host-by-Host Security Features

As described in Chapter 14, Samba includes many security features that can result in denial of services to specific clients. The two most important of these are hosts allow and hosts deny, which set up lists of computers that are and are not, respectively, allowed to access the server. If you use hosts allow, *only* those hosts specified may use the system; if you use hosts deny, any computer *but* the ones specified may use the system. In case of conflict, hosts allow overrides hosts deny. Both parameters can be specified globally (in the [global] section of smb.conf) or for specific shares. You should therefore check both sections if you're having trouble accessing shares.

Many problems in the use of these two parameters stem from mistakes in the specification of computers. The "Restricting Access By Computer" section of Chapter 14 describes the rules for use of these parameters in detail. Likely culprits include the following:

Mistyped Names   A typo in a machine or network name can cause difficult-to-trace problems. These names are *not* case sensitive, though.

Omitted Periods   Periods (.) carry special meaning when they lead a name or trail a partial numeric IP address. In these contexts, periods specify network addresses. For example, .threeroomco.com specifies any computer in the threeroomco.com domain, such as chica.threeroomco.com or sultan.room3.threeroomco.com. In an IP address, the period comes at the end of the network portion, as in 192.168.104., which specifies the 192.168.104.0/24 network. Omitting a period, or adding one by mistake, can cause serious difficulties. If you omit the leading period in .threeroomco.com, for instance, Samba only matches a *single computer* called threeroomco.com, not the entire domain.

NetBIOS versus DNS Names   The hosts allow and hosts deny parameters require DNS names. If computers on your network have different DNS than Net-BIOS names, specifying the latter will not work correctly.

Network Name Search Scope   Samba uses normal DNS name-resolution proce-dures on names specified in the hosts allow and hosts deny parameters. It's there-fore susceptible to problems such as DNS server failures and peculiarities resulting from the list of domains to be searched in /etc/resolv.conf. For instance, suppose /etc/resolv.conf designates that the server is to search both room1.threeroomco.com and room2.threeroomco.com. If both these subdomains contain computers called grande, then specifying hosts deny = grande denies access to both comput-ers. If you only want to deny access to one system, use its complete domain name, such as grande.room2.threeroomco.com. If the computer's IP address is fixed, then using it rather than a host name can be safer still, because you'll avoid problems relating to the DNS server.

If you're using server- or domain-level security, it may also be smart to check the status of the allow trusted domains parameter. When set to Yes, this parameter allows Samba to accept logons from domains that are trusted by the domain controller. When set to No, logons are denied from any but the domain to which the server belongs. The default is Yes, but if you set this value to No, some clients may not be able to access the server's shares.

User-Based Security Features

As described in Chapter 14, Samba includes many access controls aimed at specific users. Of these, passwords are usually the most troublesome, because SMB/CIFS clients encode passwords in various ways. Other access restrictions, too, can be problematic from time to time, particularly if you're trying to create a complex security scheme on the server.

NOTE   In the vast majority of cases, your Samba server *must* have accounts for its users, even if you use some other authority (such as a domain controller) to authenticate users. If, say, gailet cannot access a server, you should first con-firm that she has an account on the server. The add user script parameter (Chapter 14) is a way around this requirement when the server is part of a domain. This parameter lets Samba add user accounts for users who have been approved by a domain controller. Guest access (Chapter 15) is another way to allow users access to a server without individual accounts.

Passwords

The single most trying password issue is that of encrypted versus cleartext passwords, as described in "Encrypted versus Cleartext Passwords" in Chapter 14. Since Windows 95 OSR2 and Windows NT 4.0 Service Pack 3, all versions of Windows send encrypted passwords by default and *do not* fall back to cleartext passwords. Therefore, if your Samba server lacks support for encrypted passwords, you won't be able to access its shares (indeed, you won't even be able to browse the shares). In Windows *9x*, the usual symptom of this problem is an error message that the IPC$ share is unavailable without a password. You may also see this message if the Samba server lacks an account for the username you've entered. In Windows NT, the error message is somewhat less cryptic but no more helpful; it refers to an incorrect password or unknown username and prompts you for a new username and password. Nothing you type will allow you access, though.

Chapter 14 describes how to configure Samba to accept encrypted passwords, or how to configure Windows to send cleartext passwords. Either method will overcome this password conflict, but the method you use will depend on your existing network configuration and needs, as described in Chapter 14.

By default, Samba employs user-level security, meaning that it authenticates users itself and grants access to shares based on this authentication. It's possible to pass this responsibility on to other computers, by setting the `security` parameter to `Server` or `Domain`. If you've done this, you should check to see that the user is a valid user on the password server (generally the domain controller).

Username Access Restrictions

You can use the Samba parameters `valid users` and `invalid users` to block specific users' access to a server or share. When these parameters are used in the [global] section, the result is effectively the same as removing the username from the server's list of users or from the smbpasswd file, depending upon your authentication method. When used in individual shares, however, these settings can make one share accessible but another inaccessible to any given user. Therefore, if a user has problems connecting to some shares but not others, look for these parameters to see that the user is *not* listed in the `invalid users` parameter, or to be sure that the user *is* included in the `valid users` list, if it's used.

Aside from basic share access, Samba's `read list` and `write list` parameters respectively grant specified users read-only access to otherwise read/write shares, and grant read/write access to otherwise read-only shares. If a user can't write to a share to which others can write, check to make sure there's not a `read list` parameter in use; or, if a `write list` parameter is in use, verify that the user's name appears on that list. (Permissions on a share's directory, as described just below in "Checking Permissions," can produce similar symptoms.)

Of course, entire shares can be rendered read-only or read/write. Samba's default is for shares to be read-only. To set a share to be read/write, you must specify any of several parameters (writeable = Yes, writable = Yes, write ok = Yes, or read only = No).

Problems Accessing Files

Even after you've gained access to a share, you may not have access to the files in that share. Such access barriers are particularly common on shares that service many users, because the files in the share typically have a host of owners and permissions. Other options, too, can cause problems—particularly Samba features related to the hiding of files and to filename translation.

Checking Permissions

The "Setting Ownership and Permissions" section of Chapter 5 explains Samba's permissions options in some detail. Following are the most important Samba options for forcing permissions:

force user This parameter makes Samba use the specified user's permissions for file access. Including this parameter can be helpful when a share is to be accessed by many users, in order to reduce the likelihood of ownership and permissions conflicts.

force group This parameter works just like force user except that it specifies the group ownership and permissions used in creating and accessing files.

create mask This parameter sets the maximum permissions allowed when creating ordinary files in a directory. create mask = 0600, for example, causes Samba to remove all permissions for everybody but the owner of the file.

directory mask This parameter works like create mask, but it applies to directories rather than ordinary files.

Chapter 5 describes these and related parameters in detail. They can be used to correct file access irregularities—but they can also *create* problems if used inappropriately. Some examples:

- If you use force user along with restrictive create mask and directory mask settings on a common-access share, and if a user creates a file using another server (such as Netatalk or NFS) or through a shell account, Samba users may be unable to modify the file that wasn't created through Samba. The best solution, if this sort of thing happens frequently, is to modify the system's umask or the other server's settings to ensure that the user specified by force user can modify the files.

- If you set tight `create mask` and `directory mask` permissions, non-Samba users other than the one who created the files may be unable to access them. This can be a positive or negative security feature, depending upon your needs. You can loosen the mask parameters if necessary.

- Local users, or those who use Windows NT clients, can modify the Samba permissions on files they own—for instance, changing 0644 permissions to 0600. It's a useful characteristic if your users understand the implications of these changes, but if they don't, they can inadvertently block other users' access to files. You can use the `force security mode` and `force directory security mode` parameters, described in Chapter 14, to stop Windows NT users from modifying specified Linux permissions bits.

In the end, the best way to configure permissions for file access is to examine the Linux permissions from Linux. Once you've spotted what makes troubled files different from the rest, try to figure out how those files were created or their permissions changed. You can then take steps to prevent the problem from recurring, or set Samba's security features to work around it.

File-Hiding Options

Samba can hide files from clients in either of two ways:

- By setting the SMB/CIFS *hidden bit*, which signals a request to the client OS to hide the file in directory listings. Assorted options on many clients, including Windows, can override this setting, however. Files remain accessible if a user takes steps to override the hidden bit in some way.

- By completely eliminating the file from the client's point of view. Any attempt to access the file, even if the user knows the exact filename, is refused. To the client, it's as if the file doesn't exist.

If your clients can't see particular files, first try to determine which of these two classes of hiding is involved. You can do this by following these steps in Windows:

1. Open a window onto a directory that's missing files, and Select View ➢ Folder Options or View ➢ Options. Windows displays a Folder Options or Options dialog box.

2. Select the View tab in the Folder Options or Options dialog box.

3. In Windows NT, select the Show All Files radio button under Hidden Files. In Windows 98, select the Show All Files radio button in the Advanced Settings area, as shown in Figure 17.4.

4. Click OK in the Options or Folder Options dialog box. Windows now shows all the hidden files in all windows.

Figure 17.4   If you select Show All Files, Windows disregards the hidden bit on files.

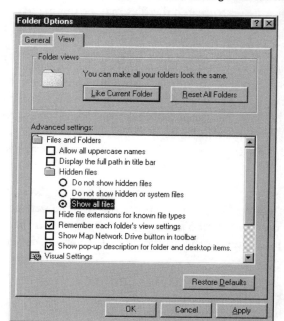

You can now look for whatever file was missing from your display. If it's still missing, chances are it's being hidden by the veto files parameter in smb.conf. This parameter, fully discussed in Chapter 5, is the one that causes Samba to completely ignore certain files. If the steps described just above cause the file to appear, then it's a *dot file* (its filename begins with a period); or it's being hidden by the hide files parameter; or its Linux world execute bit is set and Samba's map hidden parameter is set to Yes. If you want dot files to be visible on the clients, you can set hide dot files = No. This parameter affects *all* dot files, though, so if you only want one or two to be visible, this action may be too much.

> **TIP**   If you want easy access to just one or two dot files, consider creating links to those files under some other name. To get to .bashrc, for instance, you could log on using a shell account and type **ln -s .bashrc bashrc**, and then access .bashrc from Samba clients under the name bashrc.

Except for files that are hidden because of their world execute bits and map hidden = Yes, you can't adjust the hidden nature of files from the client OS. The default for map hidden is No, so your clients can normally see files that are executable in Linux. If a share has no need to hold Linux executable files, you can set map hidden = Yes and control the hidden bits of files from Windows, but this won't affect dot files or files hidden through hide files.

Filename Options

Linux's file-naming potential is, on the whole, more flexible than that of Windows and far more so than DOS. It's therefore possible for a legal Linux filename to be illegal in a client OS. Samba's usual response to this situation is to mangle or munge the filename into a format acceptable to the client. For example, Samba translates longfilename.txt into LONGF~A7.TXT for DOS clients, which can only accept names up to eight characters in length with an optional three-character extension (the so-called 8.3 filename limit).

One drawback to filename mangling is that a file's name may be mangled to something unintelligible and not what the user expects. Clients with differing capabilities may see the file under various names, making it hard to track files across clients. For instance, longfilename.txt is a perfectly legitimate name to Windows 9*x*, Windows NT, Windows 2000, OS/2, and Linux Samba clients; but DOS clients will see a mangled version of the filename. If there's also a file called longfaces.txt, a DOS user won't know which file is the desired one without checking both files' contents, because both filenames are mangled to the form LONGF~*??*.TXT.

> **NOTE** On very rare occasions, two long filenames may mangle to the same short filename. In such cases, one of the files will be inaccessible from clients that use the 8.3 mangled names. The only solution to this is to rename one of the long filenames.

The best way around long-filename problems is with user education. If your users will be using clients that can't cope with long filenames, such as DOS, tell them to use short 8.3 filenames even when using Windows or some other more sophisticated OS.

Samba includes a number of options that influence its handling of filename mangling. Some can make files disappear from at least some clients, so be cautious when using these options. If files with long filenames aren't present on some clients (particularly DOS clients), you might want to look into these parameters:

mangle case Normally, mangle case = No, which means that Samba doesn't try to mangle filenames that use mixed-case filenames but otherwise fit within the target OS's capabilities. If mangle case = Yes, Samba mangles more filenames, including some 8.3 filenames. This can make files more difficult to find, but it may be necessary for some clients or client programs that are picky about case in directory listings.

mangled names   When set to Yes (the default), this parameter causes Samba to mangle filenames. If set to No, Samba doesn't mangle names, which can make files with long names inaccessible to clients such as DOS that are unable to process those names.

mangled map   You can extend Samba's name-mangling capabilities by specifying pattern pairs for mangled name mapping. For instance, the parameter mangled map = (*.html *.htm) (*.jpeg *.jpg) replaces .html and .jpeg extensions with .htm and .jpg, respectively. This feature can improve name mangling in some cases, but it also produces problems if there's an error in the mangled map parameter specification. Consider mangled map = (*.html .htm). The omission of an asterisk on the mapped-to component results in all files ending in .html being mapped to the filename .htm, which is probably not what was intended and will make some files inaccessible.

If some files are mysteriously unavailable, particularly from DOS clients, you should review the settings of these parameters to see that they're not causing the trouble. If possible, create a small test share or a subdirectory in the main share, and try to reproduce the problem using as few files as possible. You can then experiment with the name-mangling options to see what happens.

In addition to name mangling, consider case sensitivity. Linux treats filesystems in a case-sensitive way, meaning that two filenames differing only in case are treated as unique. MIxeD.uP and mixed.up, for example, refer to two different files. Most SMB/CIFS clients, on the other hand, are either case-retentive or case-insensitive—they ignore case or convert all filenames to a single case in their filesystems. Samba tries to work around these differences by searching for files that match any variant in case when a client tries to open a file.

Problems may occur, however, particularly when users have access to the server from a Linux shell account or some other means, such as an NFS server. When this is true, users are allowed to create files that differ only in case. Samba users can still only access one file—only MIxeD.uP or mixed.up, not both. Setting case sensitive = Yes works around this by forcing Samba to operate in a case-sensitive manner. The disadvantage to this option is that some client programs may not work well with a case-sensitive server, because they alter filename case when opening files, resulting in "file not found" errors. If you're having difficulty accessing some files from certain clients or programs, check to see that this option is *not* set.

TIP   The include parameter, in conjunction with a variable to identify the client OS type, can be a useful tool. You can enter parameters such as case sensitive in OS-specific configuration files and call them using include. For example, include = smb.conf.%a will include smb.conf.win95 for Windows 9x clients, smb.conf.samba for Samba clients, and so on.

Problems with Printing

Printing problems are a bane to many Samba administrators. Although Samba is a very flexible print server—indeed, in part *because* of its flexibility—it's easy to misconfigure it so that print jobs vanish or become garbled. Before proceeding with explicit trouble-shooting, I recommend you read Chapter 6, which explains how to set up printer shares. Chapter 6 introduces many important concepts, such as the difference between a raw and a PostScript printer queue.

General Printer Troubleshooting Advice

Before proceeding to attack specific types of faults, you should engage in some general troubleshooting procedures to try to isolate the cause of the printing problem. What you believe to be a Samba glitch could in fact be something entirely different. It's important that you isolate the problem to as narrow a range of possibilities as you can. To this end, try the following:

Print PostScript locally.   If you can print PostScript files locally, using a command such as `lpr -Pbiglaser testfile.ps`, then you can be sure that a problem in a PostScript queue isn't due to fundamental problems in the Linux queue itself. Successful local printing means that the printer is working, Ghostscript is working, and so on. This test is only useful, of course, if your printer is a PostScript model or if you're printing to it through Ghostscript. If you're sharing a non-PostScript printer as a raw queue, this test will *not* work.

Print non-PostScript locally.   If you're trying to share a non-PostScript printer using a raw queue, try printing a non-PostScript file to it, using `lpr` or whatever command you specify with the `print command` parameter in `smb.conf`. There's a good chance that you'll only be able to print a simple text file in this way. If you *can* print the non-PostScript file, chances are the problem lies in Samba or the client.

Print from multiple clients.   Try printing from more than one client. If the error occurs on only one client, concentrate your troubleshooting on that system. If no clients can print, concentrate on the server. The Samba `smbclient` program is a useful tool, because you can control precisely what goes to the print server, and you can check Samba's log files on both the client and server.

Check log files.   As suggested for other problems, check Samba's log files for clues. If necessary, change the `debug level` parameter to a level as high as 3 to see what's going on.

"Print" to an interception queue.   You can use Samba's `print command` parameter to create a queue that does nothing but intercept the printer output, storing the file in some convenient location. For instance, `print command = mv %s %H/debug.prn` copies the print job to the user's home directory under the name

Maintaining a
Healthy System

PART 4

debug.prn. You can then try printing the file using lpr, viewing it with a Ghost-script-based PostScript viewer, examining it with a text editor, comparing it to the original file, or anything else you like. This process may uncover file corruption or a quirk in your Linux printer queue with respect to the file as delivered by the client.

Move the printer.   You may want to try connecting the printer directly to the client, and adjusting the client's printer queue appropriately to print directly. If the problem persists, then you know it's not Samba related. Otherwise, you can be fairly sure that the network link or Linux printer queue is causing the difficulty. This procedure will only work if the printer is a PostScript model or if you're serving it raw, however. If you're processing PostScript from the client through Ghostscript, moving the printer to the client won't be a useful diagnostic tool.

Vanishing Print Jobs

One particularly frustrating anomaly is when a print job just plain *vanishes*. Typically, you'll print from Windows and nothing will happen. Checking the print queues on both Windows and Linux shows nothing in the queue. There are several possible causes:

Misdirected Queue   The print queue may be misdirected in some way. You might be printing to a queue on another computer, for example, or you might have listed an incorrect queue in either the client printer definition or in the server's smb.conf printer definition.

Buggy Drivers or Incorrect Drivers   You may have selected the wrong drivers on the client side, or those drivers might have bugs.

Ghostscript Errors   Sometimes Ghostscript chokes on PostScript files that are mal-formed in one way or another. As described in Chapter 6, files that begin with a Ctrl+D character can cause problems—although this configuration usually produces print-outs of PostScript commands rather than the intended files, and not a failure to print at all. Nonetheless, you might try a different PostScript printer driver or an updated version of Ghostscript.

Incorrect Ghostscript Driver   Your Linux printer queue might be configured with the wrong Ghostscript driver—for instance, you might have configured the Linux queue for a Hewlett-Packard LaserJet 4 series, when in fact you've got a LaserJet IIP.

Mundane Printer Problems   Dozens of things can go wrong when printing, many of which seem obvious after they're corrected. Don't forget to verify that the printer is turned on, that its paper tray has paper, and so on.

In my experience, vanishing print jobs are most often caused by simple configuration problems—such as sending output to the wrong queue (while you pull your hair over lack of output, test printouts are piling up in another printer's output bin). Ghostscript configuration mistakes occasionally cause these irregularities, as well.

Garbled Output

One of the major sources of difficulty in using Linux as a print server comes when your printer spews gibberish. The usual cause of such garbled output is in mismatched drivers—if you try to use a driver for a Canon inkjet printer on an Epson inkjet, for instance, you're almost certain to get some awful output, if you get output at all. Your first step in diagnosing such errors should therefore always be to confirm that you're using the correct printer driver.

Another thing that can cause garbled output is a problem with Linux's handling of printer queues, or with Linux's ability to create either raw or Ghostscript-driven queues. Specifically:

- If a queue uses a smart filter, it might or might not be able to correctly interpret the contents of a print job destined for a non-PostScript printer. With luck, the smart filter will handle the job correctly. If you're a bit less lucky, the smart filter will discard the print job. If you're very unlucky, the smart filter will corrupt the print job, resulting in page after page of gibberish as a printout.

- If a queue uses a smart filter and you print using a PostScript driver in Windows, you might find yourself looking at raw PostScript code as output. You can usually correct this problem by setting `postscript = Yes` in the `smb.conf` file's entry for the share, or by configuring the Windows driver to *not* send a Ctrl+D at the start of the file, as described in Chapter 6's "Manual Driver Installation" section.

- If a Samba queue prints to a raw Linux queue, you shouldn't print using a PostScript driver in Windows unless the printer understands PostScript natively. Likewise, don't use the Samba `postscript = Yes` parameter on such a queue.

- If the Linux queue feeds results directly through Ghostscript, without using a smart filter, be sure to use that queue only with PostScript printer drivers on the client. Ghostscript will likely print an error message if it sees non-PostScript data coming its way.

Misconfiguring Samba, the Linux printer queue, or the client's printer queue so that a later queue's assumptions are violated by the input delivered by an earlier entity is the usual source of corruption problems. You must think through what each component (the Windows printer driver, Samba, the Linux smart filter, Ghostscript, and the printer) expects, what it receives from its predecessor, and what it produces as output.

Poor-Quality Printouts

Sometimes the result of printing is a legible printout, but one that's poor in quality. Text may look chunky, or colors on an inkjet printout may be poor. If you're using a raw printer queue, such problems are invariably the result of driver difficulties on the client, so you'll want to investigate your client's driver settings for things like resolution and color matching. If you're using a non-PostScript printer, a Windows PostScript driver, and Ghostscript on the server, however, the usual cause of such problems is poor configuration of the printer queue on Linux.

Here are several Linux printer-queue configuration issues you should investigate when debugging poor printout quality:

Check printer resolution settings.   Check your printer resolution settings, which you can usually set from Linux printer-queue configuration utilities or using the `-r` parameter to Ghostscript in a print filter.

Consider dithering options.   If your color printouts are of poor quality, investigate dithering options to Ghostscript. These options control how Ghostscript creates a given color from the half dozen or fewer colors available from most color printers. Some dithering options are superior to others. Unfortunately, these options vary substantially from one printer driver to another, so you'll need to research the options available for your particular printer. The Ghostscript documentation file `devices.txt` contains this information.

Try other Ghostscript drivers.   A few printers, such as the Epson Stylus Color line, work with more than one Ghostscript driver. Sometimes one of these drivers produces better results than does another.

Switch fonts.   Ghostscript versions later than 5.0 ship with a basic collection of PostScript-compatible fonts that are quite good, so you should get good print quality when using standard PostScript fonts. Earlier versions of Ghostscript often shipped with poor-quality bitmapped fonts, however, so these versions benefit from font upgrade packages, if not complete upgrades to more recent versions of Ghostscript. Print quality can also suffer from poor fonts on the client systems, especially when the font is converted to bitmaps of insufficient resolution. OS/2's PostScript drivers, for example, convert all fonts to bitmaps, so if OS/2's drivers are set for a resolution that's too low, text print quality will suffer.

Add fonts.   Ghostscript's collection of fonts is reasonably complete, but it can't cover every possibility. Some printers may come with fonts that aren't present in a standard Ghostscript installation, and if you use a driver for such a printer, you'll probably get Courier when you try to print using a font that's not loaded in Ghostscript. You should be able to add an appropriate font to Ghostscript (check its documentation for details), or switch to a printer driver that doesn't assume the font is built into the printer. If you do the latter and the font is installed on the client, it will print correctly, because the client will download it along with the print job.

If you're using a non-PostScript printer, it's useful to keep in mind that printouts using PostScript drivers and Ghostscript will not be identical to printouts using native drivers and a raw queue. Sometimes one solution produces superior quality, but other times another is better. It's best to experiment to determine which approach is best for your hardware and needs. Indeed, you may want to keep both types of printer queue, because one may be better for one purpose than the other. For instance, Ghostscript may yield better text quality, while a raw queue may do better with graphics.

Last-Page Difficulties

One final class of printing difficulties is problems with the last page of a printout. There are three common final-page problems:

Missing Final Page   If a final page doesn't print at all, or prints only partly, chances are the problem is a missing form feed at the end of that page. You can usually correct this problem by removing the `sf` option from the queue's `/etc/printcap` entry on the server system. Unfortunately, this may result in the opposite problem for local users of the printer. If so, you may be forced to use two queues, one for Samba and one for local users.

Extra Final Page   Sometimes print jobs appear correctly but are followed by a blank sheet. This sheet is usually caused by *lack of* the `sf` option in the Linux `/etc/printcap` entry for the printer. You can add this option to make the problem go away. Occasionally this results in a failure to eject the final page for local users; in that case you may need two print queues, one for local users and one for remote users.

Ghostscript Summary or Errors Printed on Final Page   Sometimes, Ghostscript prints an entire document correctly and then prints a summary or error message on the final page (or occasionally even on the *first* page). This unwanted page is likely to include messages like `%%[ LastPage ]%%`. This is caused by Windows printer drivers, which often try to include information about the progress of the print job, intended for display on the printer's small screen. When printing through Ghostscript, however, the information ends up printing on the last page. The fix is to locate the file that calls Ghostscript, and add `>/dev/null` to the `gs` command. In Red Hat and similar distributions, the file is `/usr/lib/rhs/rhs-printfilters/ps-to-printer.fpi`, and in Caldera the file is `/var/spool/lpd/`*queuename*`/printfilter` (where *queuename* is the printer queue name). You can also try another Windows printer driver.

Summary

The key to successful Samba troubleshooting lies in careful analysis of the irregularity. Using multiple clients, user accounts, and other variables, you can usually isolate a problem to a specific set of clients, usernames, or other important subsets of your network configuration. Doing this allows you to focus your efforts on aspects of your configuration that are most likely to be the source of the trouble, be they `smb.conf` parameters, client configuration, drivers, or something else.

As with other forms of problem solving, Samba troubleshooting requires a certain level of knowledge. This chapter refers to many of the earlier chapters in this book, because those chapters contain the information that's necessary for solving many problems. Indeed, each chapter was written with an eye toward alerting you to possible problems associated with various Samba features, so reading those chapters is sure to help you avoid encountering trouble in the first place.

Samba can be an extremely useful tool, either as a server for an all-Windows network or as one of several servers on a multiplatform network. Although configuring Samba can be difficult at times, and you may encounter problems doing it, the results can be very good. I hope you've found this book helpful in configuring your Samba server.

Appendices

- Configuration Reference Guide
- OS-Specific Issues
- The GNU GPL

Configuration Reference Guide

This appendix lists Samba's `smb.conf` file parameters. To learn how `smb.conf` is structured and used, consult Chapter 4, "GUI Configuration Tools and the `smb.conf` File."

Table A.1 `smb.conf` Configuration Options

Parameter	Scope	Values	Default	Description
add user script	Global	Command	(None)	Command Samba may run to dynamically add Linux accounts for authorized domain users.
admin users	Share	Usernames	(None)	Users given root privileges on the share.
allow hosts	Share	Hostnames	(None)	Synonym for hosts allow.
allow trusted domains	Global	Boolean	Yes	If Yes and if security is set to Server or Domain, Samba accepts logons from domains that are trusted by the domain controller. If No, Samba refuses such logons.

Table A.1 smb.conf Configuration Options *(continued)*

Parameter	Scope	Values	Default	Description
alternate permissions	Share	Boolean	No	Obsolete; has no effect in Samba 2.0 and later.
announce as	Global	NT, NT Server, NT Workstation, WfW, Win95	NT	The OS that Samba claims to be.
announce version	Global	Number	4.2	The OS version that Samba claims to be.
auto services	Global	Shares	(None)	Shares that always appear in browse lists. A synonym is preload.
available	Share	Boolean	Yes	Determines whether or not a share is accessible.
bind interfaces only	Global	Boolean	No	If set to Yes, Samba allows access only on the interfaces specified by the interfaces parameter.
blocking locks	Share	Boolean	Yes	If Yes, enables Samba to notify a client when a lock by another client is removed.
browsable	Share	Boolean	Yes	Synonym for browseable.
browse list	Global	Boolean	Yes	If Yes, Samba provides a list of shares to clients that request it.
browseable	Share	Boolean	Yes	Determines whether or not a share appears in browse lists. A synonym is browsable.

Table A.1   smb.conf Configuration Options *(continued)*

Parameter	Scope	Values	Default	Description
case sensitive	Global	Boolean	No	Determines whether Samba uses case in matching filenames.
casesignames	Global	Boolean	No	Synonym for case sensitive.
change notify timeout	Global	Positive number	60	Set the number of seconds between checks of changes to a directory.
character set	Global	ISO8859-1, ISO8859-2, ISO8859-5, ISO8859-7, KOI8-R	(None)	The Linux character set to which DOS filenames are translated.
client code page	Global	437, 737, 850, 852, 861, 866, 932, 936, 949, 950	850	The DOS code page that clients use.
coding system	Global	euc, cap, hex, hexN, sjis, j8bb, j8bj, jis8, j8bh, j8@b, j8@j, j8@h, j7bb, j7bj, jis7, j7bh, j7@b, j7@j, j7@h, jubb, jubj, junet, jubh, ju@b, ju@j, ju@h	(None)	The Kanji coding system used in conjunction with client code page = 932.

Appendices

Table A.1 smb.conf Configuration Options *(continued)*

Parameter	Scope	Values	Default	Description
comment	Share	Text	(None)	Sets a comment that's associated with a share in browse lists.
config file	Global	Filename	(None)	Load and use another configuration file, discarding the options in the current file.
copy	Share	Share name	(None)	Copies configuration parameters from another share.
create mask	Share	Octal value	0744	Sets maximum permissions on files created via a share.
create mode	Share	Octal value	0744	Synonym for create mask.
deadtime	Global	Minutes	0	How long Samba keeps an unused connection open. 0 means no time limit.
debug hires timestamp	Global	Boolean	No	If Yes, Samba stores debug timestamp information with millisecond precision; if No, timestamps are stored only to the nearest second.
debug level	Global	0–10	0	Amount of detail stored in Samba's log files. A synonym is log level.
debug pid	Global	Boolean	No	Stores the process ID of the program making an entry to debugging log file. debug timestamp must be Yes for this option to work.

Table A.1   smb.conf Configuration Options *(continued)*

Parameter	Scope	Values	Default	Description
debug uid	Global	Boolean	No	Stores the user ID and group ID under which a process runs, in debugging log file entries. debug time-stamp must be Yes for this option to work.
debug timestamp	Global	Boolean	Yes	If Yes, Samba stores times for all logged operations.
default	Global	Share name	(None)	Share used if the client doesn't specify one. A synonym is default service.
default case	Share	Lower, Upper	Lower	Case in which filenames are stored when preserve case = No.
default service	Global	Share name	(None)	Synonym for default.
delete readonly	Share	Boolean	No	If Yes, allows Samba to delete files that are marked read-only, which is normal for Linux, but not for DOS or Windows.
delete user script	Global	Command	(None)	If security = Domain, this parameter specifies a command that Samba runs if the domain controller reports that a user no longer exists.

Table A.1 smb.conf Configuration Options *(continued)*

Parameter	Scope	Values	Default	Description
delete veto files	Share	Boolean	No	If Yes, Samba deletes files the client can't access because of the veto files parameter, if the user deletes a directory containing those files.
deny hosts	Share	Hostnames	(None)	Synonym for hosts deny.
dfree command	Global	Shell command	(None)	Command run to determine free disk space. Not needed on Linux.
directory	Share	Pathname	/tmp	Directory to be shared. A synomym is path.
directory mask	Share	Octal value	0755	Maximum allowable permissions for directories created in a share.
directory mode	Share	Octal value	0755	Synonym for directory mask.
directory security mask	Share	Octal value	Same as directory mask	Linux permissions bits that Windows NT/2000 clients may modify if nt acl support = Yes.
domain logons	Global	Boolean	No	If Yes, Samba accepts domain logons.
domain master	Global	Boolean	No	If Yes, Samba tries to become the domain master browser.
dont descend	Share	Comma-separated directory list	(None)	A list of directories that aren't accessible from a share.

Table A.1   smb.conf Configuration Options *(continued)*

Parameter	Scope	Values	Default	Description
dos filetime resolution	Share	Boolean	No	If Yes, Samba rounds file creation times up to the next even second. Useful with some DOS and Windows software development tools.
dos filetimes	Share	Boolean	No	Allows nonowners to change a file's creation time.
encrypt passwords	Global	Boolean	No	If Yes, Samba accepts encrypted passwords, which are stored in the smbpasswd file.
exec	Share	Shell command	(None)	Synonym of preexec.
fake directory create times	Share	Boolean	No	If Yes, Samba sets all directory creation times to midnight, January 1, 1980, as a workaround for some Windows software development tools.
fake oplocks	Share	Boolean	No	Tells clients they can create oplocks, but doesn't create them.
follow symlinks	Share	Boolean	Yes	Controls whether or not Samba follows symbolic links.
force create mode	Share	Octal value	0000	Permissions bits that Samba forces on when creating files.

Appendices

Table A.1 smb.conf Configuration Options *(continued)*

Parameter	Scope	Values	Default	Description
force directory mode	Share	Octal value	0000	Permissions bits that Samba forces on when creating directories.
force directory security mode	Share	Octal value	Same as force directory mode	Permissions bits that Samba forces on when a user changes directory permissions from Windows NT/2000.
force group	Share	Linux group	User's normal group	Sets the group name Samba uses when accessing a share.
force security mode	Share	Octal value	Same as force create mode	Permissions bits that Samba forces on when a user changes permissions from Windows NT/2000.
force user	Share	Username	User's normal username	Sets the username Samba uses when accessing a share. In 2.0.5 and above, also sets the group Samba uses to be the user's primary group.
fstype	Share	String	NTFS	The filesystem type Samba reports it's using when a client asks.
getwd cache	Global	Boolean	No	If Yes, Samba caches the name of the current working directory.
group	Share	Linux group	(None)	Obsolete synonym for force group.

Table A.1 smb.conf Configuration Options *(continued)*

Parameter	Scope	Values	Default	Description
guest account	Share	Username	Compile-time option (usually nobody)	Linux account associated with SMB/CIFS guest account.
guest ok	Share	Boolean	No	Samba accepts guest logons (no password required).
guest only	Share	Boolean	No	Samba accepts only guest logons.
hide dot files	Share	Boolean	Yes	Sets the DOS hidden bit for files that begin with a dot (.).
hide files	Share	Slash-separated list	(None)	List of filenames that Samba hides by setting the DOS hidden bit.
homedir map	Global	Filename	auto.home	If nis homedir = Yes, Samba uses the NIS home directory specified by this parameter as the user's Samba home directory.
hosts allow	Share	Hostnames	(None)	List of machines that may access the share. If this and hosts deny are both unused, no computer is denied access. A synonym is allow hosts.
hosts deny	Share	Hostnames	(None)	List of machines that are denied access to the share. A synonym is deny hosts.

Table A.1 smb.conf Configuration Options *(continued)*

Parameter	Scope	Values	Default	Description
hosts equiv	Global	Filename	(None)	Specifies a file containing a list of machine names (with optional associated usernames) that are allowed access to shares without using passwords.
include	Share	Filename	(None)	Include the specified file in the main configuration file.
inherit permissions	Share	Boolean	No	If Yes, permissions on new files and directories are based on those of their owners. If No, Samba uses create mask and similar parameters to determine permissions on new files and directories.
interfaces	Global	Interface list	(None)	The interfaces to which Samba binds itself.
invalid users	Share	Usernames	(None)	List of users who are not allowed to access a share.
keepalive	Global	Seconds	0	Number of seconds between checks for a crashed client; 0 indicates no checks.
kernel oplocks	Global	Boolean	Automatic	Use the host's oplocks feature to implement Samba oplocks. Linux does not support oplocks in the 2.2.x kernel series.

Table A.1 smb.conf Configuration Options *(continued)*

Parameter	Scope	Values	Default	Description
ldap filter	Global	String	(None)	Username search string when Samba runs in conjunction with an LDAP password database.
ldap port	Global	Port number	389	The LDAP server's TCP/IP port number.
ldap root	Global	LDAP username	(None)	The LDAP username used by Samba for LDAP accesses.
ldap root password	Global	LDAP password	(None)	The LDAP password used by Samba for LDAP accesses.
ldap server	Global	Hostname	localhost	The DNS name of the LDAP server.
ldap suffix	Global	Name	(None)	The LDAP "distinguished name" used as a starting point for LDAP accesses.
level2 oplocks	Share	Boolean	No	Implements Level 2 (read-only) oplocks.
lm announce	Global	Auto, Yes, or No	Auto	If Yes, produces periodic browsing announcements required on OS/2 networks. Auto produces these broadcasts only if Samba detects them.
lm interval	Global	Seconds	60	Interval between lm announce broadcasts.

Table A.1 smb.conf Configuration Options *(continued)*

Parameter	Scope	Values	Default	Description
load printers	Global	Boolean	Yes	Loads printer names in /etc/printcap or equivalent file for generation of available printers in the [printers] share.
local master	Global	Boolean	Yes	If Yes, Samba participates in elections for the local master browser.
lock directory	Global	Pathname	Compile-time option	Directory in which Samba stores housekeeping files for file locking.
locking	Share	Boolean	Yes	If Yes, Samba performs file locking; if No, Samba accepts lock requests but doesn't act on them.
log file	Global	Filename	Compile-time option	File to which Samba logs important system events.
log level	Global	0–10	0	Synonym of debug level.
logon drive	Global	DOS drive letter	(None)	DOS-style drive letter to which Windows NT clients map the home share.
logon home	Global	UNC path	\\%N\%U	A user's domain home directory.
logon path	Global	UNC path	\\%N\%U \profile	The location of a user's domain profile. In Samba 2.0.6 and later, this doesn't work; instead, the profile directory in logon home is used.

Table A.1   smb.conf Configuration Options *(continued)*

Parameter	Scope	Values	Default	Description
logon script	Global	Filename	(None)	File in the [netlogon] service that's run when a client logs onto a Samba-controlled domain.
lppause command	Share	Command	Varies	Command Samba uses to pause a print job.
lpresume command	Share	Command	Varies	Command Samba uses to resume a paused print job.
lpq cache time	Global	Seconds	10	How long Samba caches the print queue status.
lprm command	Share	Command	Varies	Command Samba uses to delete a print job.
machine password timeout	Global	Seconds	604800	Number of seconds before Samba tries to change its NT domain password, if security = Domain.
magic output	Share	Filename	Script name, followed by .out	Output filename for the magic script parameter.
magic script	Share	Filename	(None)	File that's executed as a script whenever the client closes it.
mangle case	Share	Boolean	No	Adjust filenames to match case specified by default case.

Table A.1 smb.conf Configuration Options *(continued)*

Parameter	Scope	Values	Default	Description
mangle locks	Share	Boolean	Yes	Bug workaround for file lock requests from Windows NT clients to Samba running on 32-bit OSs (including Linux on x86 systems).
mangled map	Share	To-from pairs	(None)	Creates pairs of filename templates for filename mapping, as in (.jpeg .jpg).
mangled names	Share	Boolean	Yes	If Yes, Samba creates 8.3-conforming filenames for DOS clients and programs. These supplement but do not replace normal long filenames for clients able to use long filenames.
mangling char	Share	Character	~	Character used as part of name mangling.
mangled stack	Global	Number	50	Size of the cache used for name mangling.
map aliasname	Share	Filename	(None)	Synonym for map groupname.
map archive	Share	Boolean	Yes	If Yes, Samba uses the owner execute bit to store the DOS-style archive bit.
map hidden	Share	Boolean	No	If Yes, Samba uses the world execute bit to store the DOS-style hidden bit.

Table A.1   smb.conf Configuration Options *(continued)*

Parameter	Scope	Values	Default	Description
map groupname	Share	Filename	(None)	Points to a file containing associations between Linux groups and Windows NT groups.
map system	Share	Boolean	No	If Yes, Samba uses the group execute bit to store the DOS-style system bit.
map to guest	Global	Never, Bad User, Bad Password	Never	Specifies when to accept guest logons.
max connections	Share	Number	0	Specifies the maximum number of connections allowed to a share. 0 means there's no limit.
max disk size	Global	Megabytes	0	The upper limit for disk sizes returned to clients, some of whom don't work well with maximum disk sizes greater than 2048. 0 means no limit.
max log size	Global	Kilobytes	5000	The maximum size of log files, in kilobytes.
max mux	Global	Number	50	The maximum number of outstanding operations Samba accepts from a client.
max packet	Global	Number	(None)	Obsolete synonym for packet size.
max open files	Global	Number	10000	Maximum number of files Samba will try to open.

Appendices

Table A.1 smb.conf Configuration Options *(continued)*

Parameter	Scope	Values	Default	Description
max ttl	Global	Seconds	259200	Maximum time Samba stores NetBIOS names and associated IP addresses.
max wins ttl	Global	Seconds	518400	Maximum time a Samba NBNS server retains a NetBIOS name/IP address pair.
max xmit	Global	Bytes	65535	Maximum packet size negotiated by Samba.
message command	Global	Command	(None)	Sets the command the server runs if it receives a WinPopup command.
min print space	Share	Kilobytes	0	The minimum free space required before Samba accepts a print job.
min passwd length	Global	Number	5	Synonym for min password length.
min password length	Global	Number	5	The minimum password length Samba accepts when changing passwords.
min wins ttl	Global	Seconds	21600	Minimum time a Samba NBNS server retains a NetBIOS name/IP address pair.
name resolve order	Global	List of lmhosts, host, wins, bcast	lmhosts host wins bcast	Order of lookup to locate IP addresses given a NetBIOS name.

Table A.1 smb.conf Configuration Options *(continued)*

Parameter	Scope	Values	Default	Description
netbios aliases	Global	List of names	(None)	A list of NetBIOS names to which the server will respond, in addition to its main name (set from the hostname or netbios name parameter).
netbios name	Global	NetBIOS name	Hostname	NetBIOS name to which the computer responds; default is based on the system's TCP/IP hostname.
netbios scope	Global	String	(None)	Sets the NetBIOS scope for a system, potentially isolating it and others with the same scope, from other systems on your network.
networkstation user login	Global	Boolean	Yes	Obsolete workaround for Windows NT domain bug.
nis homedir	Global	Boolean	No	If Yes, then homedir map is used to look up the user's home directory.
nt acl support	Global	Boolean	Yes	If Yes, Samba maps Linux permissions and ownership onto Windows NT's ACL security model.
nt pipe support	Global	Boolean	Yes	Developer debugging option that allows Windows NT clients to connect to IPC$ pipes.
nt smb support	Global	Boolean	Yes	Allows enabling or disabling of NT-specific SMB/CIFS features.

Appendices

Table A.1   smb.conf Configuration Options *(continued)*

Parameter	Scope	Values	Default	Description
null passwords	Global	Boolean	No	If Yes, Samba allows users to access accounts that have null (empty) passwords.
ole locking compatibility	Share	Boolean	Yes	Allows Samba to handle peculiar locking mechanisms used by Windows OLE calls.
only guest	Share	Boolean	No	Synonym for guest only.
only user	Share	Boolean	No	If Yes, users of the share must be on a username list.
oplock break wait time	Global	Milliseconds	10	Delay before Samba responds to an oplock break request.
oplock contention limit	Share	Number	2	Number of oplocks allowed per file.
oplocks	Share	Boolean	Yes	Specifies whether Samba supports opportunistic locks (aka oplocks), which can improve performance.
os level	Global	Number	0 for Samba 2.0.5a and earlier; 20 for Samba 2.0.6–2.0.7; 32 for Samba TNG	Sets the OS level used in local master browser elections.

Table A.1   smb.conf Configuration Options *(continued)*

Parameter	Scope	Values	Default	Description
packet size	Global	Bytes	65535	Obsolete synonym for max packet.
panic action	Global	Command	(None)	Command Samba runs if either smbd or nmbd crashes.
passwd chat	Global	Command	Compile-time option	Command Samba runs whenever a user changes a password.
passwd chat debug	Global	Boolean	No	If Yes, Samba logs the entire password chat sequence when a user changes a password.
passwd program	Global	Program	/bin/ passwd	Program that Samba runs to change the Linux password for a user.
password level	Global	Number	0	Number of characters in a password Samba tries converting to uppercase in order to match a transmitted cleartext password to a local password.
password server	Global	NetBIOS name	(None)	NetBIOS name of the password server (typically the primary domain controller).
path	Share	Pathname	/tmp	Synonym for directory.
postexec	Share	Command	(None)	Command executed when a client closes a connection to a share.
postscript	Share	Boolean	No	If Yes, Samba prepends %! to print jobs, forcing smart filters to interpret the jobs as PostScript files.

Appendices

Table A.1 smb.conf Configuration Options *(continued)*

Parameter	Scope	Values	Default	Description
preexec	Share	Command	(None)	Command executed when a client opens a connection to a share. A synonym is exec.
preexec close	Share	Boolean	No	If Yes, a nonzero return from a preexec script (that is, an error) causes Samba to terminate the connection.
prefered master	Global	Boolean	No	Synonym for preferred master.
preferred master	Global	Boolean	No	If Yes, Samba forces a master browser election and has a small edge in winning it.
preload	Global	Shares	(None)	Synonym for auto services.
preserve case	Share	Boolean	Yes	If Yes, Samba preserves the case of filenames as specified by clients; if No, Samba converts filenames to the case specified by default case.
print command	Share	Command	Varies	Command used by Samba to print a print job.
print ok	Share	Boolean	No	Synonym for printable.
printable	Share	Boolean	No	Identifies a printer share.
printcap	Global	Filename	/etc/ printcap	Synonym for printcap name.

Table A.1   smb.conf Configuration Options *(continued)*

Parameter	Scope	Values	Default	Description
printcap name	Global	Filename	/etc/printcap	The complete path to the file that defines local printer queues.
printer	Share	String	Usually lp	The name of the Linux printer queue associated with a printer share. A synonym is printer name.
printer driver	Share	String	(None)	A string identifying the Windows printer driver to be used with a share.
printer driver file	Global	Filename	Compile-time option	File that contains information on printer driver files associated with a printer share.
printer driver location	Share	UNC path	(None)	Location of printer driver files, for clients wanting to set themselves up to use the share.
printer name	Share	String	Usually lp	Synonym for printer.
printing	Share	Bsd, Aix, Lprng, Plp, Sysv, Hpux, Qnx, Softq, Cups	Compile-time option	Host computer's printing system.
protocol	Global	NT1, CORE, COREPLUS, LANMAN1, LANMAN2	NT1	SMB/CIFS protocol version used by Samba.
public	Share	Boolean	No	Synonym for guest ok.

Appendices

Table A.1   smb.conf Configuration Options *(continued)*

Parameter	Scope	Values	Default	Description
queuepause command	Share	Command	Varies	Command Samba uses to pause printing all print jobs.
queueresume command	Share	Command	Varies	Command Samba uses to resume printing all print jobs.
read bmpx	Share	Boolean	No	Obsolete parameter enabling the SMB "read block multiplex" command.
read list	Share	Username list	(None)	List of users who are granted merely read-only access to an otherwise read/write share.
read only	Share	Boolean	Yes	If Yes, Samba grants only read access to the share. Antonym of write ok and writeable.
read prediction	Global	Boolean	No	Obsolete.
read raw	Global	Boolean	Yes	Allows fast 64KB reads over TCP/IP.
read size	Global	Bytes	16384	The number of bytes that must be received before Samba begins writing data to disk or sending it over the network.
remote announce	Global	Network addresses	(None)	Causes Samba to announce itself to the master browsers on the specified remote addresses.

Table A.1   smb.conf Configuration Options *(continued)*

Parameter	Scope	Values	Default	Description
remote browse sync	Global	Network addresses	(None)	Causes a Samba master browser to exchange browse lists with the specified remote addresses.
restrict anonymous	Global	Boolean	No	If Yes, Samba blocks all anonymous accesses. Windows NT clients sometimes use anonymous access to gather browse lists, so this parameter can cause problems on some networks.
revalidate	Share	Boolean	No	If Yes, Samba requires clients to send passwords for each share access, rather than just for the first one.
root	Global	Directory	(None)	Synonym for root directory.
root dir	Global	Directory	(None)	Synonym for root directory.
root directory	Global	Directory	(None)	Causes Samba to chroot() to the specified directory.
root postexec	Share	Command	(None)	Command Samba runs as root when a user disconnects from a share.
root preexec	Share	Command	(None)	Command Samba runs as root when a user connects to a share.

Appendices

Table A.1 smb.conf Configuration Options *(continued)*

Parameter	Scope	Values	Default	Description
root preexec close	Share	Boolean	No	If Yes, a nonzero return value from the root preexec script (that is, an error) causes Samba to close the connection.
security	Global	Share, User, Server, Domain	User	Sets the password security model.
security mask	Share	Octal value	Same as create mask	Sets the permission bits that Samba allows users to change from Windows NT/2000 clients.
server string	Global	String	Samba %v	A string that Samba associates with the server, for the benefit of browse lists.
set directory	Share	Boolean	No	Allows Digital Pathworks users to use the "set directory" command.
share modes	Share	Boolean	Yes	Enables use of certain DOS file open options. This parameter should never be set to No.
shared file entries	Global	Number	113	Obsolete.
shared mem size	Global	Bytes	1048576	Memory shared between smbd processes.

Table A.1   smb.conf Configuration Options *(continued)*

Parameter	Scope	Values	Default	Description
short preserve case	Global	Boolean	Yes	If Yes, Samba preserves the case of short (8.3) file-names; if No, Samba converts these to the case specified by default case.
smb passwd file	Global	Filename	Compile-time option	File in which Samba encrypted passwords are stored.
smbrun	Global	Command	Compile-time option	The path to the smbrun binary; you shouldn't need to change this.
socket address	Global	IP address	(None)	If set, this parameter tells Samba to listen for connections on only the interface associated with the specified address.
socket options	Global	Socket options	Compile-time option (usually None)	Sets TCP/IP socket options for Samba.
source environment	Global	Filename	(None)	File from which Samba reads environment variables.
ssl	Global	Boolean	No	If Yes, Samba accepts SSL-encrypted connections.
ssl ca certdir	Global	Pathname	(None)	Directory in which SSL CA server certificates are stored.
ssl ca certfile	Global	Filename	(None)	File in which SSL CA server certificates are stored.

Table A.1 smb.conf Configuration Options *(continued)*

Parameter	Scope	Values	Default	Description
ssl ciphers	Global	DEFAULT, DES-CFB-M1, NULL-MD5, RC4-MD5, EXP-RC4-MD5, RC2-CBC-MD5, EXP-RC2-CBC-MD5, IDEA-CBC-MD5, DES-CBC-MD5, DES-CBC-SHA, DES-CB3-MD5, DES-CB3-SHA, RC4-64-MD5, NULL	(None)	SSL ciphers that Samba will accept.
ssl client cert	Global	Filename	(None)	SSL client certificate used by smbclient.
ssl client key	Global	Filename	(None)	SSL client key used by smbclient.
ssl compatibility	Global	Boolean	No	Bug workaround for older versions of SSL.
ssl hosts	Global	Hostnames	(None)	Computers that are only allowed to connect via SSL. If unspecified and ssl = Yes, all computers must connect via SSL.
ssl hosts resign	Global	Hostnames	(None)	Computers that are not required to connect via SSL.
ssl require clientcert	Global	Boolean	No	Samba refuses an SSL connection if the client lacks a certificate.

Table A.1   smb.conf Configuration Options *(continued)*

Parameter	Scope	Values	Default	Description
ssl require servercert	Global	Boolean	No	smbclient refuses an SSL connection if the server lacks a certificate.
ssl server cert	Global	Filename	(None)	SSL server certificate used by Samba.
ssl server key	Global	Filename	(None)	SSL server key used by Samba.
ssl version	Global	ssl2or3, ssl2, ssl3, tls1	ssl2or3	SSL version used by Samba.
stat cache	Global	Boolean	Yes	If Yes, Samba uses a cache to speed up case-insensitive mappings.
stat cache size	Global	Number	50	The number of entries in the case-insensitive map cache.
status	Global	Boolean	Yes	If Yes, Samba logs connections to a file that smbstatus can read.
strict locking	Share	Boolean	No	If Yes, Samba checks every file access for file locks; if No, Samba only checks when the client asks for a check.
strict sync	Share	Boolean	No	If Yes, Samba syncs to disk whenever the client says to do so; if No, Samba syncs to disk whenever its buffers fill up.

Appendices

Table A.1   smb.conf Configuration Options *(continued)*

Parameter	Scope	Values	Default	Description
strip dot	Global	Boolean	No	If Yes, Samba strips trailing periods (.) from filenames.
sync always	Share	Boolean	No	If Yes, Samba syncs to disk whenever a write operation occurs.
syslog	Global	Number	1	Debugging level for messages sent to system log.
syslog only	Global	Boolean	No	If Yes, Samba sends its log messages only to the system log files; if No, Samba uses its own log files, in addition.
time offset	Global	Minutes	0	Sets minutes to add to system time calculations, to fix bugs in client daylight saving time.
time server	Global	Boolean	No	If Yes, nmbd provides time services to clients.
timestamp logs	Global	Boolean	Yes	Synonym for debug timestamp.
unix password sync	Global	Boolean	No	If Yes, Samba tries to change the Linux password whenever the Samba encrypted password is changed.

Table A.1   smb.conf Configuration Options *(continued)*

Parameter	Scope	Values	Default	Description
unix realname	Global	Boolean	No	If Yes, Samba provides the user's real name (from the /etc/passwd file) to the client when asked.
update encrypted	Global	Boolean	No	If Yes, Samba changes the encrypted password when a user logs on using a cleartext password, to aid in migrating a network from cleartext to encrypted passwords.
use rhosts	Share	Boolean	No	If Yes, Samba reads the user's ~/.rhosts file and allows access from listed hosts without the benefit of a password.
user	Share	Usernames	(None)	Synonym for username.
users	Share	Usernames	(None)	Synonym for username.
username	Share	Usernames	(None)	Samba tries each of the specified usernames if the client doesn't provide a username.
username level	Share	Number	0	The number of uppercase letter variants in a username Samba tries when a user logs on.
username map	Global	Filename	(None)	Specifies a file containing a mapping of Windows to Linux usernames.

Table A.1   smb.conf Configuration Options *(continued)*

Parameter	Scope	Values	Default	Description
valid chars	Share	Character list	(None)	Adds characters to the set of valid characters for use in filenames.
valid users	Share	Usernames	(None)	List of users authorized to use the share. If empty, all users who have provided valid usernames and passwords can use the share.
veto files	Share	Slash-separated list	(None)	Files that Samba makes disappear from the share, from the client's point of view.
veto oplock files	Share	Slash-separated list	(None)	Files for which Samba will not issue an oplock.
volume	Share	String	Share name	Sets the volume name for a share.
wide links	Share	Boolean	Yes	If Yes, Samba follows links outside of the share's directory tree.
wins hook	Global	Command	(None)	Command Samba runs whenever it changes its internal NBNS database, when Samba operates as an NBNS server.
wins proxy	Global	Boolean	No	If Yes, Samba responds to broadcast NetBIOS name resolution requests on behalf of systems located on remote network segments.

Table A.1   smb.conf Configuration Options *(continued)*

Parameter	Scope	Values	Default	Description
wins server	Global	Hostname	(None)	TCP/IP hostname or IP address of an NBNS server.
wins support	Global	Boolean	No	If Yes, Samba acts as an NBNS server.
workgroup	Global	Workgroup name	Compile-time option	The workgroup to which the server belongs; usually defaults to WORKGROUP.
writable	Share	Boolean	No	Synonym for writeable.
write cache size	Share	Bytes	0	Size of a write cache for oplocked files; new in Samba 2.0.7.
write list	Share	Comma-separated list	(None)	Users given write access to an otherwise read-only share.
write ok	Share	Boolean	No	Synonym for writeable.
write raw	Global	Boolean	Yes	Allows fast network writes, using 64KB buffers.
writeable	Share	Boolean	No	Allows users to write to a share. Synonyms are write ok and writable; antonym is read only.

B

OS-Specific Issues

Samba is most often used to serve files to Windows clients—and more precisely, Windows 95, 98, NT, and 2000 clients. Most of this book has emphasized the use of such clients, but there are other possible Samba clients.

DOS   The original OS for *x*86 computers ships with only the most minimal networking tools, but more sophisticated tools are available—including SMB/CIFS clients.

Windows 3.1   This old version of Windows is still in use in a few places, particularly where hardware is weak by today's standards. It's possible to use such systems on SMB/CIFS networks.

OS/2 Warp 4.0   IBM's OS/2 remains a viable OS and has a substantial installed base, although it's not making waves in the media in 2000. This OS includes SMB/CIFS functionality.

BeOS   Be's operating system has a small but growing following. BeOS's SMB/CIFS functionality is *very* new and consequently not as reliable as that of other OSs.

MacOS   The Macintosh's main operating system, MacOS, uses its own file- and printer-sharing protocol, AppleTalk; and there's a native Linux server for this protocol, known as Netatalk. You might want to use Samba for MacOS clients, though, particularly if your network is dominated by Windows systems. Fortunately, a MacOS SMB/CIFS client/server package is available, known as DAVE (http://www.thursby.com).

This appendix is devoted to using a Samba server with these alternative client OSs, including setup instructions and OS-specific filesystem quirks. It concludes with a look at configuring Samba when your network includes a variety of OSs with differing optimum requirements.

> **NOTE**   This appendix doesn't cover the use of Samba as a client. For information on this topic, consult Chapter 7, "Using Linux as an SMB/CIFS Client."

Samba and DOS

DOS was the operating system that IBM included with its original PC in 1984, and it remains available today. In fact, Windows 9*x* is built on a foundation composed of a modified version of DOS, so in some sense Windows 9*x* *is* DOS. Other versions of DOS include the following:

MS-DOS   Microsoft's DOS is no longer sold as a separate product, but millions of copies of MS-DOS are floating around. Some are gathering dust in closets, but others are still in use.

PC-DOS   IBM's variant of DOS is based on the same source code as MS-DOS. This product is still available, under the PC-DOS 2000 moniker.

DR-DOS   This DOS version has undergone several name changes (it's been known as DR-DOS, then OpenDOS, and now DR-DOS again). It's sold by Caldera's Lineo division (http://www.drdos.com).

FreeDOS   This is an open source clone of MS-DOS. It's available from http://www.freedos.org. At this writing, it's at version Beta-4, which means it's less than perfect.

DR-DOS includes Novell networking support, but the other versions of DOS don't have any networking support by default. Even DR-DOS's Novell networking support is useless for connecting DOS to a Samba server. You must therefore obtain and install a TCP/IP stack and SMB/CIFS client software to use DOS as a client to a Samba server.

Obtaining Software

Microsoft makes available the necessary networking software, including SMB/CIFS client tools, from its FTP site. Check ftp://ftp.microsoft.com/bussys/Clients/MSCLIENT/ for two files: DSK3-1.EXE and DSK3-2.EXE. If you have a Windows NT 4.0 Server installation CD-ROM, you can find these files in the CLIENTS\MSCLIENT\DISKS directory.

> **NOTE** In theory, Microsoft's SMB/CIFS client software can be used with any version of DOS. In writing this appendix, I've successfully tested it with both DR-DOS 7.03 and MS-DOS 6.0. FreeDOS Beta 4, however, failed because of what appeared to be FAT filesystem handling problems (partway through the installation process, the system started to believe that all disks were empty). Future versions of FreeDOS may fare better.

Once you've obtained them, the two .EXE files must be uncompressed. You can either run them as programs in DOS or Windows, or uncompress them in Linux using the unzip command that comes standard with most Linux distributions. Either way, I recommend uncompressing the files in an empty directory. The result is a large number of files you should then copy to two floppy disks, one for each of the two original files. These disks are the Microsoft Network Client disks.

In addition to the Microsoft Network Client disks, you'll probably need a DOS driver provided by your network adapter's manufacturer. The Microsoft Network Client disks include a limited number of network card drivers, but these drivers are for old equipment. If you can't find an appropriate driver, go ahead with the installation, and renew your search only if you don't see your card listed when it comes time to select your network adapter.

> **NOTE** Other SMB/CIFS clients for DOS are available. Most are limited in important ways, such as working with only a handful of network cards. You can find out more about these alternatives, as well as some tuning tips for Microsoft Network Client, at http://huizen.dds.nl/~jacco2/samba/dos.html.

Configuring Software

The Microsoft Network Client disks contain the software necessary to configure a DOS system as a client to a Samba server. To install the software, follow these steps:

1. Boot DOS.
2. Insert the Microsoft Network Client Disk 1 in your floppy disk.
3. Type **A:\SETUP** at the DOS prompt. This starts the Setup program, which displays an introductory screen informing you that the program installs the Microsoft Network Client software.
4. Press the Enter key to proceed into the Setup utility. The program asks for an installation location for the network software.

5. Press the Enter key to accept the default location of C:\NET, or type another location. The Setup utility now checks your basic configuration and displays a list of network adapters (Figure B.1).

Figure B.1 Microsoft includes drivers for several (mostly old) network cards with its SMB client package.

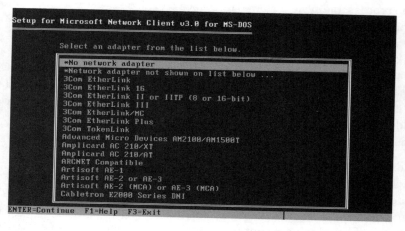

```
Setup for Microsoft Network Client v3.0 for MS-DOS

     Select an adapter from the list below.

   ┌──────────────────────────────────────────────┐
   │ *No network adapter                          │
   │ *Network adapter not shown on list below ... │
   │ 3Com EtherLink                               │
   │ 3Com EtherLink 16                            │
   │ 3Com EtherLink II or IITP (8 or 16-bit)      │
   │ 3Com EtherLink III                           │
   │ 3Com EtherLink/MC                            │
   │ 3Com EtherLink Plus                          │
   │ 3Com TokenLink                               │
   │ Advanced Micro Devices AM2100/AM1500T        │
   │ Amplicard AC 210/XT                          │
   │ Amplicard AC 210/AT                          │
   │ ARCNET Compatible                            │
   │ Artisoft AE-1                                │
   │ Artisoft AE-2 or AE-3                        │
   │ Artisoft AE-2 (MCA) or AE-3 (MCA)            │
   │ Cabletron E2000 Series DNI                   │
   └──────────────────────────────────────────────┘
ENTER=Continue  F1=Help  F3=Exit
```

6. If your network adapter is among those listed, select it. If not, choose the second entry, *Network adapter not shown on list below. Because most of the adapters on this list are quite old, the remaining instructions assume that you've made this selection. If the Microsoft Network Client disks include support for your network card, your installation will be slightly simpler.

7. The Setup program asks for the location of the original equipment manufacturer (OEM) driver disks for your network adapter. Type this location. When you've entered a correct driver location, the program responds by displaying the name of the device. (In some cases, you may get a choice of devices whose drivers are on the same disk.)

TIP The appropriate drivers for most network adapters are in a directory called NDIS or NDIS2 on their driver disks. If you're not sure what directory to use, try one that seems like a promising match. The installation won't proceed until you've entered a reasonable choice.

8. Select your driver and press the Enter key. The program informs you that the drivers allocate memory for network buffers, and that you may adjust these parameters for optimum performance.

9. If you like, you can press C to adjust your network buffer parameters. Pressing Enter results in default parameters, which work fine for most installations.

10. The program asks for a username. Type the Linux username used by the primary user of the computer, then press Enter.

11. The program now displays a summary screen like that in Figure B.2. Unfortunately, not all the default settings are reasonable, so you'll have to change a few items.

Figure B.2   Adjust defaults from the Microsoft Network Client main summary screen.

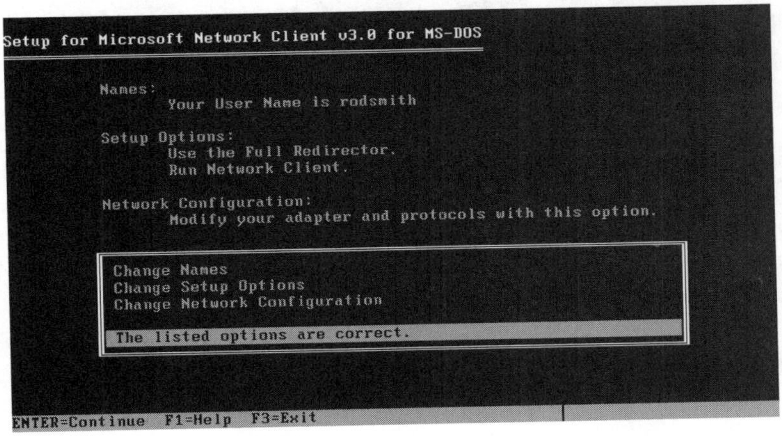

```
Setup for Microsoft Network Client v3.0 for MS-DOS

        Names:
                Your User Name is rodsmith

        Setup Options:
                Use the Full Redirector.
                Run Network Client.

        Network Configuration:
                Modify your adapter and protocols with this option.

        ┌─────────────────────────────────────────────────────────┐
        │ Change Names                                            │
        │ Change Setup Options                                    │
        │ Change Network Configuration                           │
        ├─────────────────────────────────────────────────────────┤
        │ The listed options are correct.                        │
        └─────────────────────────────────────────────────────────┘

ENTER=Continue   F1=Help   F3=Exit
```

12. Use the Up arrow key to select Change Names in the summary screen, and press Enter.

13. The installer displays name settings similar to those in Figure B.3. Use the Up and Down arrow keys to select the computer name, workgroup name, and domain name items, and change them as appropriate for your network. (You need change only one of the workgroup and domain name items, however.) When you're done, move the cursor to the line that says The listed names are correct, and press Enter. The program returns to the main summary screen (Figure B.2).

Appendices

Figure B.3   You'll probably have to change the default workgroup or domain name, as well as the computer name, for networking to function correctly.

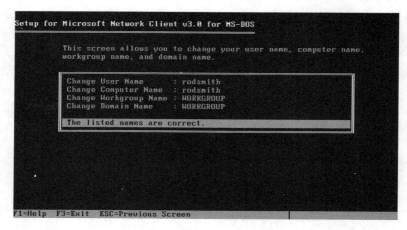

14. Select Change Setup Options. If you're using an 8088 or 8086 computer, you must change from the full redirector to the basic redirector. If you want your system to log on to a domain, you must change the logon validation option. When you're done with this screen, choose The listed options are correct. The program returns to the main summary screen (Figure B.2).

15. Select Change Network Configuration. The Setup utility displays a screen like that in Figure B.4.

Figure B.4   By default, Microsoft Network Client uses the IPX network stack, but Samba uses TCP/IP.

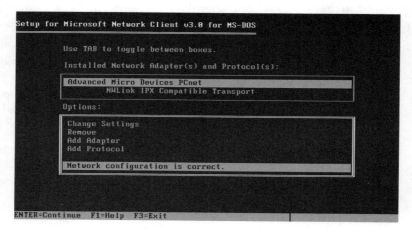

16. Press the Tab key to highlight the upper box, then press the Down arrow key to select NWLink IPX Compatible Transport. (Your configuration will show your network adapter's name rather than Advanced Micro Devices PCnet.)

17. Press the Tab key to highlight the lower box. Using the Up arrow key, select Remove and then press Enter. The program displays a list of possible protocol stacks.

18. Use the arrow keys to select Microsoft TCP/IP. Press Enter, and the program returns to the network adapters and protocols screen (Figure B.4). It should now display Microsoft TCP/IP rather than NWLink IPX Compatible Transport.

19. Be sure that Network configuration is correct is selected, and press Enter. The program returns to the main summary screen (Figure B.2).

20. Be sure that The listed options are correct is selected, and press Enter.

21. The program accesses your floppy disk. It may ask for several floppy-disk swaps. Change disks as directed.

> **TIP** The installer has a bug in its naming of disks. If it asks for the OEM driver disk and doesn't respond when you insert your network drivers disk, insert the Microsoft Network Client Disk 2.

22. When the program finishes, it prompts you to restart the computer. Press the Enter key to do so.

At this point, your system is configured with a simple TCP/IP stack and SMB/CIFS client software. The basic TCP/IP stack supplied with the Microsoft Network Client includes only the SMB/CIFS client; it doesn't include utilities such as a Telnet or FTP client.

> **NOTE** By default, Microsoft Network Client uses DHCP to acquire an IP address. If your network uses static IP addresses and has no DHCP server, you must edit the C:\NET\PROTOCOL.INI file. Locate the line that begins IPAddress0 and enter the computer's IP address, but substitute spaces for periods. Then change the line that reads DisableDHCP=0 to DisableDHCP=1.

Using Samba from DOS

Once you've restarted your DOS computer, you can use Samba shares by issuing the NET command. For example:

1. Type **NET USE** *N*: ***SERVER**SHARE***, where *N* is the drive letter you want to assign to the share, *SERVER* is the server's NetBIOS name, and *SHARE* is the share name.

2. DOS responds by asking if it's OK to start the workstation service. Respond **Y**.

3. You're prompted for both your username (with the default that you entered in step 10 in "Configuring Software") and password. Type these in.

DOS responds with a message such as `N: connected to \\SERVER\SHARE`. You can then access the server using normal DOS commands, such as `DIR` and `COPY`. You can also access server files using DOS programs such as WordPerfect for DOS.

The DOS `NET` command works much like the `NET` command in Windows 9x. To learn more about this command, type `NET /? | MORE`. The result is a list of subcommands and brief descriptions. You can get more information about specific subcommands by inserting the subcommand name between `NET` and `/?`, as in `NET USE /? | MORE`. Here are highlights of the available subcommands:

LOGOFF This subcommand disconnects all SMB/CIFS network connections.

PRINT \\SERVER\SHARE This command displays information about print jobs queued on `\\SERVER\SHARE`.

TIME [\\TSERVER] [/SET] [/YES] This command displays the time on the network time server, or on *TSERVER* if specified. If `/SET` is used, the time server's time is used to set the client's clock. `/YES` causes this to happen without further prompting.

USE [N:] [\\SERVER\SHARE] This subcommand maps a share onto a local drive letter. You can also use it in conjunction with a printer share to map the share onto a local pseudo-printer port, as in **NET USE PRN: \\SERVER\EPSON**, which maps the EPSON printer share onto the local `PRN:` printer port.

Once you've mapped shares onto the DOS system, you can use them almost as if they were local drives or printers. You can copy, delete, and otherwise access files and directories, and you can print files. The major restriction is that you can't format the remote drive from the client.

TIP Because DOS is such a small OS, it's possible to boot it entirely from a floppy disk. You can type **SYS A:** to create a bootable DOS floppy, and then copy modified versions of your `CONFIG.SYS` and `AUTOEXEC.BAT` files, along with core files from the `C:\NET` directory, to the floppy. The result is a bootable floppy that includes SMB/CIFS networking support. This disk can be very useful if you have a network of older computers that don't have hard disks; you can use a Samba server in place of hard disks for these computers.

Filename Options

In terms of Samba configuration, file-naming options are the main issues in dealing with DOS clients. The `smb.conf` parameters that are particularly important for DOS clients are as follows:

case sensitive   Because Linux uses case-sensitive filesystems, whereas DOS uses case-insensitive filesystems, Samba's default setting for this parameter is No. The result is that Samba tries to match a filename against all variants that differ only in case from the one provided by the client. Therefore, if a DOS client tells Samba to open MIXED.UP, Samba opens MIXED.UP, MiXEd.Up, mixed.up, or any other variant, if present. This behavior is highly desirable for DOS clients, so I recommend you leave it alone.

default case   This parameter's default value is Lower, which normally means nothing because this parameter is only meaningful if preserve case or short preserve case is set to No. In any event, the effect on DOS is nil. Rather, default case affects the way files created by a DOS client appear *in Linux* and *to non-DOS clients*. If you want your DOS-created files to appear as all-lowercase (such as mixed.up), leave this parameter alone. If you prefer DOS files to appear as they do in DOS, in all-uppercase (such as MIXED.UP), set this parameter to Upper.

preserve case   If set to No, this parameter causes all files created by all clients to be converted entirely to the case specified by default case. Most DOS programs provide all-uppercase filenames, so with the default settings (specifically, preserve case = Yes), those all-uppercase filenames are preserved by Samba. This may be objectionable on non-DOS clients. If so, setting preserve case = No corrects the problem, but at the cost of having *all* filenames converted to lowercase—even non-DOS filenames in which you might prefer to have mixed case.

short preserve case   Using this parameter is a way to preserve case on long file-names, while converting short filenames to the case specified by default case. This may be a convenient compromise in a mixed network where both DOS and non-DOS computers share the server. The default value is Yes.

mangled names   This parameter's default value is Yes, which causes Samba to provide 8.3 names for DOS clients, even when the original filename is longer. If your network includes a mix of DOS and non-DOS clients, or if users can create files in Samba shares using a Linux shell account, you should probably leave this parameter at its default. You can set it to No if you have only DOS clients on the network, but there's little advantage to doing so. If you want to be able to easily hide files from DOS clients by giving the files long names, you could set this parameter to No. (Setting mangled names = Yes does *not* impose truncated 8.3 filenames on non-DOS clients; rather, Samba provides *two* names for files with long names.)

Appendices

mangle case This parameter's default value is No, which means that Samba presents filenames to clients as is, even when the original filename is mixed case. When this parameter is set to Yes, Samba applies its name-mangling rules to short filenames that vary in case, such as MiXEd.Up. The result can be peculiar; for instance, MiXEd.Up might be changed to MIXED~AJ.UP. Leaving this parameter set to No seldom causes problems for DOS clients; indeed, many versions of DOS do their own case conversion, so that mixed-case names appear as all-uppercase in file listings.

mangled map Samba's normal name-mangling rules are very useful, but they sometimes produce undesirable results. For example, Samba might mangle short.html to SHORT~RH.HTM. Although the first part of the filename is less than eight characters, the .html extension causes Samba to mangle the filename. You can use the mangled map parameter to correct this problem if you regularly use filenames with long extensions, or other regularities you'd like compressed in a particular way. This parameter takes a series of match pairs in parentheses; for example:

```
mangled map = (*.html *.htm) (*.jpeg *.jpg)
```

This converts filenames ending in .html to equivalents ending in .htm, and likewise for .jpeg and .jpg. If this parameter is used, then short.html appears to DOS clients as SHORT.HTM.

mangled stack Samba stores recently mangled names in order to speed up accesses and improve the odds that a file-open request will return the correct file. By default, the size of this stack is 50, but you can reset this value with the mangled stack option. On a network that serves mostly DOS clients, you may want to increase the setting. Doing so, however, can slow down accesses on a network that uses mostly non-DOS clients.

WARNING Client programs sometimes save files by moving the original and then creating a fresh one in its place. This practice allows the program to keep a backup, and protects against power outages, system crashes, and similar problems during a file-save operation. If name mangling comes into play, though, the new file will have the mangled filename even on non-DOS clients. For instance, a Windows user might create short.html, but the file will be known as SHORT.HTM to DOS. If a DOS user edits the file, it may appear as SHORT.HTM even to Windows clients. Not all programs work this way, however; if you run into the problem, try using another editor.

On the whole, Samba's default filename-handling options are reasonable for both DOS and non-DOS clients. You might, however, want to set short preserve case = No, and perhaps set `mangled stack = 200` or so if your network serves mostly DOS clients. The `mangled map` parameter can be useful in some mixed environments, as well.

Samba and Windows 3.11

Windows 3.11 and earlier versions were technically not operating systems. Rather, they were graphical environments that ran atop DOS. Therefore, if you configure DOS to use a Samba server, as just described, Windows 3.11 and earlier can use the Samba server in the same way. The Windows File Manager application can be used to browse Samba shares, copy files, and so on. The trouble with this approach is that it relies on underlying DOS commands rather than the Windows GUI environment to initialize the connection. Many users prefer to use a GUI environment for entering passwords.

> **NOTE** Microsoft did market a version of Windows 3.11 that incorporated SMB/CIFS networking into the Windows environment. This version of Windows was known as Windows for Workgroups. It's similar to the Microsoft Network Client for MS-DOS in its capabilities, but uses GUI tools for configuration and entry of critical information such as usernames and passwords. In order to use Windows for Workgroups with Samba, you must download and install the freely available TCP/IP stack for this system (`ftp://ftp.microsoft.com/bussys/Clients/WFW/TCP32B.EXE`). Windows for Workgroups is no longer available as a new product; it was replaced by Windows 95, which has itself been supplanted by more recent versions of Windows. Because Windows 9x offers substantial user-interface and networking improvements over Windows for Workgroups 3.11, I recommend running Windows 9x rather than Windows for Workgroups 3.11 whenever possible.

Whether you access Samba shares through Windows with DOS running the Microsoft Network Client, or through Windows for Workgroups, Windows 3.11 and earlier versions all suffer from the same file-naming limitations as DOS. You should therefore configure your Samba server as if for DOS.

Samba and OS/2

OS/2 Warp 4.0, like all currently shipping versions of Windows, comes with SMB/CIFS network software. You can therefore use Samba to serve a network of OS/2 computers, or a network that includes OS/2 among other systems. As with most operating systems, OS/2 has a few quirks that should be considered when you configure Samba for an OS/2 client.

Configuring OS/2 for SMB/CIFS

OS/2 Warp 4.0 comes with SMB/CIFS support, but by default it's installed in a way that doesn't work with Samba, because OS/2 sets itself up to use NetBEUI rather than Net-BIOS. You must therefore do some minor reconfiguring of your OS/2 installation in order to use OS/2 with Samba. In the instructions that follow, it's assumed that you've installed OS/2 Warp 4.0 and its networking tools, and that your basic networking support is functioning (for instance, that you can ping other computers from OS/2).

> **NOTE** OS/2 Warp 3.0 and earlier didn't include the necessary SMB/CIFS soft-
> ware, but it is available from Microsoft at `ftp://ftp.microsoft.com/bussys/`
> `Clients/lanman.os2`. Obtain all four files in that directory and install them.
> Detailed instructions on use of this package can be found at `http://huizen`
> `.dds.nl/~jacco2/samba/lanman.html`.

To configure OS/2 to use SMB/CIFS over TCP/IP, follow these steps:

1. Open the OS/2 System Setup folder.
2. Double-click the MPTS Network Adapters and Protocol Services icon. The MPTS utility briefly displays a logo and then the main Multi-Protocol Transport Services dialog box (a simple dialog box that allows you to configure, install, or remove adapters and protocols).
3. Click the Configure button to display the Configure dialog box shown in Figure B.5.

Figure B.5   The Configure dialog box lets you choose MPTS options to adjust.

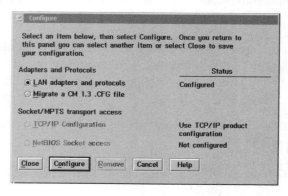

4. Be sure LAN Adapters and Protocols is selected, and click Configure. The MPTS utility displays the Adapter and Protocol Configuration dialog box (Figure B.6).

Figure B.6   Add, remove, and change the configuration of network adapters and protocols from the Adapter and Protocol Configuration dialog box.

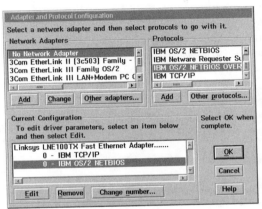

5. Under Current Configuration, select IBM OS/2 NETBIOS, and then click Remove.

6. In the Remove Protocol Driver confirmation dialog box, click Yes. The IBM OS/2 NETBIOS protocol disappears from the Current Configuration list.

7. In the Protocols section, select IBM OS/2 NETBIOS OVER TCP/IP (see Figure B.6).

8. Click Add. The MPTS utility adds the protocol to the Current Configuration list. This list now contains both IBM TCP/IP and IBM OS/2 NETBIOS OVER TCP/IP under your network adapter's name.

9. Some NetBIOS parameters can be fine-tuned, and I recommend you do so if you have an NBNS server on your network. (If you want to skip this, move ahead to step 18.) To do the adjustments now, select IBM OS/2 NETBIOS OVER TCP/IP and click Edit. The MPTS utility presents the NetBIOS Over TCP/IP options dialog box, which shows a list of three types of settings you can adjust.

10. Select Driver parameters and click Configure. The result is the Parameters for IBM OS/2 NetBIOS Over TCP/IP dialog box shown in Figure B.7.

Figure B.7 You can adjust many details of OS/2's SMB/CIFS operation.

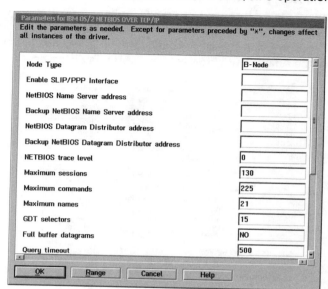

11. You'll most likely want to adjust the following NetBIOS parameters:

    • Node Type. You can set the node type (described in "Setting the Node Type" in Chapter 9) to B-Node, P-Node, or H-Node. If your network has an NBNS server, I recommend you use H-Node.

    • NetBIOS Name Server Address. Enter the name or IP address of the NetBIOS name server.

12. Click OK in the Parameters for IBM OS/2 NetBIOS Over TCP/IP dialog box. You should again see the NetBIOS Over TCP/IP options selection dialog box.

13. Select Names List and click Configure to set up a mapping of NetBIOS names to IP addresses (OS/2's equivalent of the lmhosts file). The MPTS utility displays the Names List dialog box (Figure B.8).

14. Click Add to add a machine name/IP address mapping. You'll see a dialog box with a field for the name and another for the IP address.

15. Enter the name and IP address and click OK. The pair are added to the list in the Names List dialog box.

Figure B.8   OS/2 provides a dialog box to manipulate its equivalent of the lmhosts file.

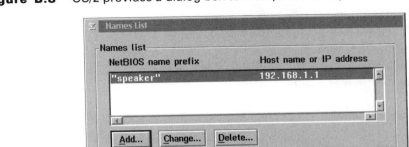

16. Repeat steps 14 and 15 for all the computers you want to add.

17. Click OK in the Names List dialog box, and then click Close in the NetBIOS Over TCP/IP dialog box.

18. Click OK in the Adapter and Protocol Configuration dialog box (Figure B.6), then Close in the Configure dialog box, and then Exit in the Multi-Protocol Transport Services dialog box. OS/2 may ask for confirmation to make the change to CONFIG.SYS, and it may ask for the installation CD-ROM.

19. MPTS informs you that you must restart the computer for the changes to take effect. Do so.

After rebooting, your OS/2 system should be configured for NetBIOS over TCP/IP networking. Unless you include an appropriate entry in your OS/2 Startup folder, however, OS/2 doesn't start NetBIOS networking automatically at startup; you must do this manually, as described in the next section.

> **NOTE** Normally, you specify the computer's NetBIOS name and workgroup or domain when you install the basic networking components. If you need to change those features, you can do so by editing the \IBMLAN\IBMLAN.INI file on the boot drive. Search this file for lines starting with Computername and Domain. Change the names that follow the equals signs (=) on these lines to change the NetBIOS name and workgroup/domain names, respectively.

Using Samba Shares from OS/2

OS/2's SMB/CIFS networking functions much like that of Windows, but many of the details differ. To use network resources from OS/2, follow these steps:

1. Open the Connections icon on the OS/2 desktop.

2. In the Connections window, double-click the Logons icon. The result is a list of several logon programs.

3. Double-click the File and Print Client Workstation Logon icon to log on to a workgroup, or the LAN Server Logon icon to log on to a domain. OS/2 displays the LAN Logon dialog box shown in Figure B.9. (If you're logging on to a workgroup, you won't see the Domain Name field.)

Figure B.9   OS/2's logon dialog box converts usernames to uppercase.

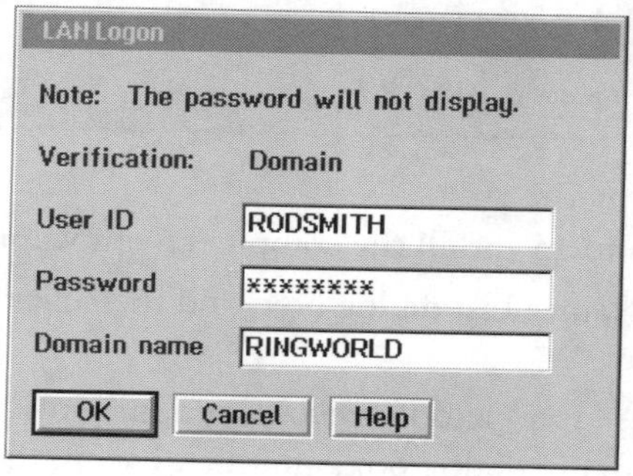

TIP   You can put a shadow of the File and Print Client Workstation Logon or the LAN Server Logon in the OS/2 Startup folder, to have OS/2 start the logon process when you boot the computer.

4. Type your username and password and click OK. After a few seconds' pause, OS/2 briefly displays the message "Logon was successful." In the case of a domain logon, you may also see an error message that OS/2 couldn't set up your home directory. You can ignore this message.

5. In the Connections window, expand or double-click the File and Print Client Resource Browser icon to see the computers available on your network.

NOTE   There may be a delay between logging on to the network and the appearance of servers in the browse list in OS/2. If you don't see all your servers immediately, wait a minute or two. If you still don't see the servers, read the section on browsing under "Understanding OS/2 SMB/CIFS Peculiarities."

Once you've logged on to the network, you can use network resources much as if they were local resources. File shares are easy to use; you can simply browse to them from the Connections desktop icon, much as you can browse to shares from Network Neighborhood in Windows. You can also use the NET command, which operates like the NET command in DOS or Windows. For instance, **NET USE** *N:* *//SERVER/SHARE* mounts the named share on the *N:* drive in OS/2.

Printer Sharing

Printer sharing isn't quite as simple as file sharing. In part this is because OS/2 requires printer drivers, and in part it's because of an incompatibility between Samba and OS/2's SMB/CIFS implementation. To use a printer shared through Samba on an OS/2 computer, follow these steps:

1. Create a batch file to link the remote printer to a local printer port, such as LPT1: or COM4:. Be sure to use a printer port that's not being used locally. Name this batch file something like LNKPRINT.CMD. It should contain a line similar to this:

   ```
   NET USE LPT1: //SERVER/PRINTER
   ```

2. Run the batch file.

3. Open the Templates folder in the OS/2 System folder. Among the WPS templates, find the one called Printer.

4. Right-click the Printer template and drag it to the WPS desktop. When you release the icon, OS/2 displays the Create a Printer dialog box shown in Figure B.10.

Figure B.10   You control creation of OS/2 printer queues in the Create a Printer dialog box.

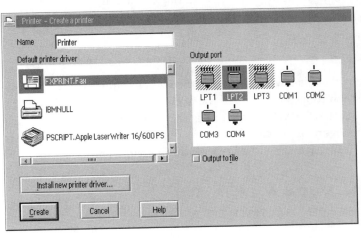

Appendices

5. Skip to step 7 if your printer driver is already present in the Default printer driver list. If you don't see an appropriate printer driver, click Install New Printer Driver. OS/2 presents a list of printer drivers available on its installation CD-ROM.

6. Locate an appropriate printer driver in the list. If you have drivers from the printer manufacturer, you can click Other OS/2 Printer Driver and type the path to the drivers in the Directory field. When you've located your drivers, click Install. OS/2 may ask for your installation CD-ROM and will install the drivers.

TIP   If you're setting up a queue for a Ghostscript-driven printer, the Apple LaserWriter 16/600 PS driver works well for most monochrome printers. For color printers, the QMS magicolor Laser Printer driver usually works well.

---

7. Select your driver from the Default Printer Driver field (Figure B.10). In the Output Port area, select the port you used in the script created in step 1.

8. If desired, you can change the printer name in the Name field near the top of the dialog box. This is the name by which your printer will be known to OS/2 programs.

9. Click the Create button.

OS/2 now creates a new WPS object for the printer queue. You can drag files to this object to print them, and the queue also appears in printer queue lists in OS/2 programs. You can also use the queue from DOS and Windows programs, by printing to the appropriate printer port. (You'll need to install Windows printer drivers to print from Windows programs running under OS/2.)

The foregoing procedure for printer sharing has a couple of drawbacks, unfortunately:

- You can only create as many printer objects as the Create a Printer dialog box has print destinations—seven, normally.

- You must remember to run the script you created in step 1 before you can print.

Fortunately, there is a workaround to the second requirement: You can add a call to the network logon tool to the *start* of the printer-mapping script. Normally, the logon tool is at *X*:\MUGLIB\LOGON.EXE, where *X* is the boot drive. Add a /v:local parameter for a workgroup logon, or /v:domain /d for a domain logon. You can then start your network services by using your modified initialization script. This script might resemble the following:

```
C:\MUGLIB\LOGON /v:domain /d
NET USE LPT1: //PSERVER/EPSON
```

In theory, you can create a link without taking over a local port by using the Network Printer template rather than the Printer template. Unfortunately, this procedure is buggy—it produces SYS0234 errors when used in conjunction with Samba servers, yielding unusable printer queues. It's possible that a future Samba release will work around this bug, or a future OS/2 FixPack or updated version of OS/2 will fix the problem. In the meantime, printing via a redirected local port works, and it has the advantage of working from DOS and Windows programs as well as from OS/2 programs.

Understanding OS/2 SMB/CIFS Peculiarities

OS/2, like most OSs, has some peculiarities with respect to SMB/CIFS networking. It's important that you understand these when you configure Samba and use OS/2 clients. Although the default Samba configuration options work well with OS/2, you should know what options *not* to change, and your users should know what to expect of Samba shares in OS/2.

Using Filenames and EAs in OS/2

OS/2 understands mixed-case long filenames. It handles these filenames in a case-retentive manner, just like Windows 9*x* and Windows NT/2000. This means OS/2 *displays* and *retains* uppercase and lowercase characters, but it treats them identically for purposes of file matching. OS/2 normally uses long filenames only on High-Performance Filesystem (HPFS) partitions, and those for which third-party filesystem drivers are available. Therefore, if an OS/2 HPFS partition has a file called MiXEd.Up, OS/2 will open that file if you type its name as MiXEd.Up, mixED.uP, or in any other form that differs only in case. Samba emulates this behavior with its default settings. A few OS/2 programs convert the case of filenames to all-uppercase or all-lowercase, so it's important that you leave the Samba case sensitive parameter at its default value of No.

OS/2 includes excellent DOS emulation support, and it can also run 16-bit Windows programs by running Windows 3.1 atop that DOS support. When run with a native HPFS partition, DOS and Windows programs see only files that conform to 8.3 filename limitations. This is because HPFS provides no support for storing 8.3-compliant filenames matched with the long filenames; nor does OS/2 dynamically generate 8.3 filenames. OS/2 users therefore frequently create short filenames even on HPFS partitions, so that DOS and Windows programs can access these files. Samba shares, however, include dynamically generated short filenames, and OS/2 makes these filenames available to its DOS and Windows subsystems. Therefore, OS/2 users can create long filenames on Samba shares using OS/2 programs but can still access those files from DOS and Windows programs run under OS/2, by using the Samba-created matching short filenames.

This practice does have certain drawbacks, however. The DOS or Windows program may end up permanently changing a filename to a mangled form, if that program saves changes by backing up the original and creating a new file under the original's name. Also, it may not always be obvious which short filename corresponds to a given long filename. These shortcomings are the same as those experienced under Windows when running 32-bit Windows programs along with DOS programs. Overall, the fact that DOS and Windows programs running in OS/2 can see files that were originally created with long filenames can be a boon to OS/2 users who are used to working with HPFS.

One peculiarity of OS/2 is that it uses Extended Attributes (EAs) to store certain types of information. OS/2 stores program icons, icon placement information, extended time-stamp information, and similar data in EAs. HPFS includes native support for EAs, and OS/2 stores EAs in a special file on FAT partitions. Unfortunately, SMB/CIFS doesn't support EAs, so OS/2 files stored on Samba servers lack EAs. This isn't a major problem for most applications, but it can be for some. If you use a Samba server to store graphics with customized "thumbnail" icons, for example, you'll lose those custom icons, which appear as EAs.

OS/2 creates a special file called `WP ROOT. SF` in the root directory of every drive. This file stores information about the preferred view mode for a drive and similar information (much like EAs for directories). You'll notice that this file appears in every read/write Samba share, once an OS/2 system has accessed it. You may want to use the Samba `hide files` parameter to hide this file (OS/2 can still access it once it's hidden).

Browsing

As described in Chapter 11, "Local and Routed Browsing," NetBIOS networks normally host a master browser computer that keeps track of the other systems on the network to facilitate browsing. When a client needs to display a browse list, the client contacts the master browser. OS/2 doesn't operate in quite the same way, however. Instead, it relies on every server to send a LAN Manager Announce (LM Announce) packet every few seconds (typically once a minute). Each OS/2 client then assembles its own browse list and removes computers from that list if they stop sending LM Announce packets. This approach is simpler in some ways than the master browser approach, but it generates a lot of fundamentally worthless network traffic, which can be a major problem on a large network.

Samba's `lm announce` and `lm interval` parameters (described in Chapter 11) are designed to address OS/2's need for LM Announce messages from servers. The defaults are `lm announce = Auto` and `lm interval = 60`, which work well for most networks; Samba sends LM Announce packets if and only if it detects them, as it will if an OS/2 client is on the network. You can force Samba to send LM Announce packets by setting `lm` announce = Yes, but this won't have much effect on a network with OS/2 systems. You should *not* set lm announce = No if you want your OS/2 systems to be able to see your Samba server in OS/2's Connections window.

Samba and BeOS

One of the newest major operating systems is BeOS, which is available for both Intel *x*86 and Motorola PowerPC (PPC) computers. Version 5.0 of this OS is available in a limited (but free) form from Be (`http://www.be.com`) and is also available on CD-ROM in a "Professional" edition. The latter includes SMB/CIFS client and server software called World O' Networking (WON), although WON is not installed by default. You can also obtain WON from `ftp://ftp.be.com/pub/experimental/r5/apps/WON/`. The rest of this section assumes that you're using the Professional version of BeOS 5.0.

> **WARNING** WON is considered *experimental* software. This means it's essentially beta- or even alpha-level in quality. It's not unusual for WON to work sluggishly or not at all. I strongly recommend that you back up any BeOS system prior to installing WON, and be prepared for some frustrating experiences.

Installing SMB/CIFS Support in BeOS

Unfortunately, WON is far from a polished product. On a fresh default installation of BeOS 5.0, the WON installer doesn't work correctly and leaves the system without networking support of any sort. The best way to get SMB/CIFS networking operating in BeOS is to start during system installation, thus:

1. Start the BeOS installation procedure.

2. Just after you accept the BeOS license terms, BeOS asks you to identify what partition it's to use. In this dialog box, click More Options. The result is a list of optional BeOS components.

3. Select the Experimental item, and continue with the installation.

4. After BeOS has installed, enable networking as described in Chapter 3 of the BeOS manual.

5. Run the WONSetup program; it's in the directory `/BeOS 5 Pro Edition/_packages_/Experimental/optional/experimental/World O' Networking`. (Your BeOS installation CD must be in the CD-ROM drive for this to work.) The result is the World O' Networking Setup dialog box shown in Figure B.11.

Appendices

Figure B.11   The BeOS WON Setup dialog box lets you enter the usual core SMB/CIFS parameters.

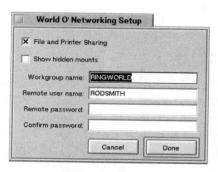

6. Type your domain or workgroup name, username, and password in this dialog box, then click Done. BeOS informs you that you must restart networking. Approve this action.

7. Copy the `Netscript.CIFS` file from the WON directory on the CD-ROM to the `/boot/beos/system/boot` directory, and rename it **Netscript**. (This action works around bugs in the `WONSetup` program.)

8. Restart BeOS.

With any luck, the result should be a working BeOS system, complete with a World O' Networking icon on the desktop. (This icon may take several seconds to appear after the rest of the OS has booted.) You can browse and use network resources using this icon, or you can use command-line tools to mount remote filesystems.

Using a Samba Server from BeOS

The easiest way to use a Samba server from BeOS is by using the World O' Networking icon. When double-clicked, this icon produces a network view that's similar to that of Windows's Network Neighborhood or OS/2's Connections. You can browse into work-groups, servers, and shares using this facility. Unlike DOS, Windows, and OS/2 clients, however, BeOS's World O' Networking does *not* acquire username and password information prior to displaying basic network information. This has two important consequences:

- You may be asked for a username and password more frequently than when using other clients, and at different times.

- Because there's no username to be associated with the client, you will *not* see a home directory with your username from World O' Networking. If you omit the `browseable = No` parameter in the [homes] share, however, you *will* see a share called Homes in the World O' Networking browse list.

If you prefer, you can use a command-line tool similar to the DOS, Windows, and OS/2 NET command, or Samba's smbmount. This command is called cifsmount, and its syntax is as follows:

```
cifsmount \\\\SERVER\\SHARE USERNAME PASSWORD mountpoint
```

> **TIP**   Be careful to type the correct number of backslashes (\ ) in the cifsmount command. If you omit one, you get a message relating the correct use of the program.

The meaning of the cifsmount parameters should be fairly self-evident. The *mountpoint* parameter works just like a Linux mount point—it must be a directory (typically an empty one) on the client's filesystem, such as /cifs/mystuff.

To use a Samba printer from BeOS, follow these instructions:

1. Select BeOS ➤ Preferences ➤ Printers from the Deskbar. This produces the Printers dialog box shown in Figure B.12 (although probably bereft of any entries in the Printers area).

Figure B.12   You can add and control printers from the BeOS Printers dialog box.

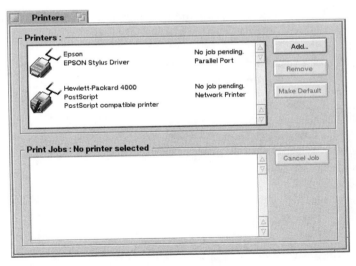

2. Click the Add button in the Printers dialog box. BeOS asks if you want to add a local or network printer.

3. Choose the network printer option and click Continue. BeOS displays the Add a Network Printer dialog box shown in Figure B.13.

Figure B.13 The Add a Network Printer dialog box allows you to specify a printer's name and network location.

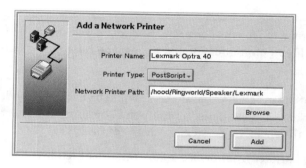

4. Type a printer name into the Printer Name field.

5. In the Printer Type selection box, select the general class of printer you're defining (PostScript, PCL, and so on). If you're planning to use a Ghostscript-driven printer, select PostScript.

6. Click the Browse button to locate the printer share. The result is the Open dialog box shown in Figure B.14.

Figure B.14 You can select either Samba or AppleTalk printers, if BeOS is configured with its AppleTalk printer support.

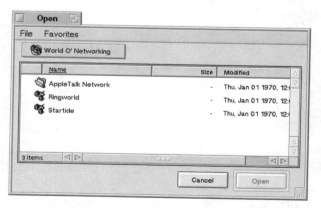

7. Browse through the networks and shares, find the printer, select it, and click the Open button. The printer's path appears in the Network Printer Path field of the Add a Network Printer dialog box (Figure B.13).

8. In the Add a Network Printer dialog box, click Add. BeOS now displays a list of printer manufacturers.

9. If you click a printer manufacturer, the list expands to include models by the manufacturers. Do this to locate an appropriate printer model, and click OK.

> **TIP** If you're using a Ghostscript-driven printer, an Apple LaserWriter series model is likely to work well.

10. BeOS now asks if you'd like to make the printer the default. Select Yes or No, as you see fit.

The printer will now appear in the list in the Printers dialog box (Figure B.12). I recommend that you test the configuration by trying to print a document from an application such as NetPositive (BeOS's Web browser). Chances are you'll be asked for a username and password when you do so.

BeOS Filesystem Quirks

Like all OSs, BeOS has its unique quirks with respect to filesystems. Unlike most SMB/CIFS clients, BeOS is case sensitive. In fact, many BeOS utilities, including its version of the bash shell, impose file-sensitive filename handling on Samba's normal case-insensitivity. To be sure you don't run into problems (say, by accidentally creating a "new" file over an existing one whose name differs only in case), you may want to set Samba's case sensitive = Yes parameter, which is not the default.

BeOS, like OS/2, uses extra filesystem information attached to ordinary files. OS/2 calls this information *extended attributes,* but BeOS uses the term *attributes.* Because SMB/CIFS makes no provision for such extra file data, this information can't be stored on a Samba server. You therefore lose BeOS attributes when you store a file on a Samba server. For many files, this loss is unimportant. Some BeOS-specific files, however, including BeOS's mail files, rely on attributes and so can be damaged by storage on a Samba server.

Like many OSs, BeOS implements a "trash can" for documents the user deletes. Unfortunately, this feature doesn't work on Samba shares. You therefore cannot delete files by moving them to the trash can. If you right-click a file and select Move to Trash from the pop-up menu, however, BeOS gives you the option of deleting the file directly. You can also delete files by using the rm command in the bash shell that comes with BeOS.

BeOS's native filesystem is more like that of Linux than like a traditional DOS, Windows, or OS/2 filesystem. Therefore, Samba settings for archive, system, and hidden bits are unimportant to a BeOS client. Although the BeOS filesystem includes support for Unix-style ownership and permissions, BeOS through version 5.0 doesn't implement this type of security. BeOS therefore doesn't try to use Windows NT–style ACLs to access Linux security features via Samba.

Samba and MacOS

Apple's MacOS has its own AppleTalk file- and printer-sharing protocol. Linux supports AppleTalk directly, through its Netatalk server. You might therefore prefer to use Netatalk to service Macintosh clients. You might want to use SMB/CIFS for Macintosh systems, though, when you want to

- Keep the number of servers on your Linux computer to a minimum.
- Use a peer-to-peer networking model with both Macintosh and *x*86 computers, in addition to Linux systems.
- Use a Macintosh to serve files that can be accessed from Linux (Netatalk supports accessing Macintosh printers from Linux, but not files).
- Use server features that are present in Samba but not Netatalk, such as automation tools (see Chapter 8, "Automation").

MacOS doesn't support SMB/CIFS directly, so you must obtain client software for it, as described in the upcoming section. Once this hurdle is overcome, using Samba from Macintoshes is a fairly straightforward task, but of course MacOS introduces its own peculiarities. The following discussion describes Samba used in conjunction with an SMB/CIFS client/server package called DAVE, version 2.5.

NOTE This appendix describes using Samba with MacOS 9 and earlier. (The system used as reference runs MacOS 8.6.) MacOS X, due out late in 2000, is based on Unix and so does not work with DAVE 2.5. Chances are that Samba will be quickly ported to MacOS X, however, so you'll be able to configure that system as a Samba client, or use NFS or some other file-sharing protocol. DAVE may also be ported to MacOS X.

Obtaining and Installing MacOS Client Software

DAVE is available from Thursby Software Systems (http://www.thursby.com). It's a commercial program, but a demo version is available from Thursby's Web site, so you can download it and try it out before buying it.

> **WARNING** Thursby also markets a product called MacSOHO. Like DAVE, Mac-SOHO uses SMB/CIFS networking; but MacSOHO relies exclusively upon Net-BEUI, rather than NetBIOS over TCP/IP, which Samba normally requires.

If you download DAVE from Thursby's Web site using a Macintosh tool such as Netscape Navigator or Internet Explorer, the Web browser should automatically expand the archive file. This produces a folder called DAVE Installation Folder, which in turn contains a DAVE 2.5.1 folder (or whatever version is current when you download the software). Open these folders and use the following instructions to install the software:

1. Exit from all other running programs.

2. Double-click the Install DAVE program icon. This launches the installer, which first displays a brief documentation file.

3. Click Continue when you've finished reading the instructions. The installer displays a license agreement.

4. If you agree to the license terms, click Continue. The program displays *another* dialog box asking if you agree with the license terms.

5. Click Agree. You'll be asked to indicate the disk where you want the software installed.

6. Choose a boot disk from the list and click Select. The installer now asks what type of installation it should perform—standard or customized. You can select the latter if you want to install only a subset of DAVE's components.

7. Click Start. The installer warns you that you'll have to restart the computer, and that it cannot run while other programs are running.

8. Click Continue to begin the installation. A progress bar displays the progress of the installation operation.

9. When the installation is finished, the installer prompts you to reboot the computer. Click Restart to do so.

Appendices

When the computer restarts, DAVE is installed but not configured. DAVE automatically launches its configuration utility to finish the job. Follow these steps to do so:

1. The first window displays introductory text. To work your way through the configuration utility, you'll click the right-arrow buttons in the lower-right corner of the window. Click the button now to continue.

2. The utility presents an option to configure TCP/IP for a home network or a corporate network. I assume you already have TCP/IP running, so select the TCP/IP Is Already Configured option. If you need to configure TCP/IP networking, however, select the appropriate option for your environment.

3. Click the right-arrow button; the "page count" jumps from 2 to 14 if you don't need to configure TCP/IP networking.

4. DAVE asks for your name, organization, and license code. If you downloaded DAVE, enter the demo license code that Thursby sent to you via e-mail; otherwise, enter the license code from the product packaging.

5. Next, DAVE asks if your network uses Windows NT servers. Because Samba emulates Windows NT rather than Windows 9x in most respects, I recommend that you respond Yes to this question.

6. In the next set of options, check the Use DHCP to Configure NetBIOS button if your network uses DHCP and your DHCP server includes configuration details for NetBIOS networking, as described in "Setting the Node Type" in Chapter 9.

7. DAVE now asks for the following information:

    -   A NetBIOS name

    -   A workgroup name

    -   A computer description (equivalent to the comment parameter in smb.conf)

8. DAVE gives you the option to log on to the network once at startup. Check this box or not, as you see fit.

9. Click the right-arrow button again, and DAVE summarizes your settings.

10. Continue the process, and DAVE gives you the option of sharing your local files via SMB/CIFS. If you elect to do so, DAVE asks additional questions about what volumes you want to share. For this procedure, I assume you do *not* want to share your Macintosh's files.

11. When the utility informs you that setup is complete, click OK. You're now returned to the Macintosh desktop.

Your Macintosh is now set up to participate in your NetBIOS network. Actual use of the system is discussed next.

Using Samba Resources from the Macintosh

DAVE follows the Macintosh networking model established by AppleTalk in its user interface. Using Samba resources should therefore be quite familiar to anybody who's used to AppleTalk networking. To use a Samba file share from a Macintosh, follow these steps:

1. From the Apple menu, open Chooser. You'll see the DAVE Client item, as shown in Figure B.15.

Figure B.15 DAVE Client coexists with AppleShare in Chooser.

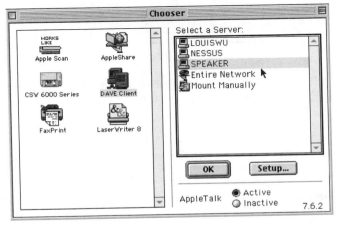

2. Click DAVE Client to see a list of servers in your workgroup or domain.

3. Click a server and then click OK. If you've not logged on to the server before, DAVE presents a username/password dialog box. Enter this information and click OK. DAVE now shows you the shares available on the server, as shown in Figure B.16.

4. Select a share and click OK. After a brief pause, a new icon for the share appears on the Macintosh's desktop.

5. If you want to mount more shares, select them from the Chooser as described in steps 3 and 4.

Appendices

Figure B.16   If you want to mount a Samba share whenever MacOS starts, check the box to
the right of the share name.

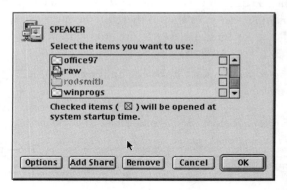

You can use Samba shares on the Macintosh much as you can use local disks or Apple-
Talk shares. There are, of course, some peculiarities, described in the upcoming section,
"Macintosh File Idiosyncrasies."

Configuring a printer is fairly straightforward if your Macintosh includes the LaserWriter 8
version 8.6.5 or later PostScript printer driver. To configure a printer, follow these steps:

1. Follow steps 1–3 in the file sharing instructions just above.

2. Select a PostScript or Ghostscript-driven printer share and click OK. DAVE informs
   you that it's creating a desktop printer.

3. Click Continue. The result is a new printer icon on your desktop.

> **NOTE**   DAVE includes another printing model that can be used with older ver-
> sions of the Apple LaserWriter driver. Consult the DAVE documentation for
> details on how to use this alternative printing system.

You can print to this printer much as you would any other—by drag-and-drop operations
or by selecting it from the Print dialog box in an application. Macintosh PostScript printer
definitions rely upon Printer Page Description (PPD) files. If you want to change the PPD
file used by your printer, you can select it and then choose Printing ➤ Change Setup from
the Finder's menu. You can then change to a new PPD file as you would for any other
printer.

DAVE is designed to print to PostScript printers. Few if any non-PostScript Macintosh
printer drivers will work with DAVE. You therefore *must* configure your Samba printer

share to handle PostScript input. If you're using a real PostScript printer, a raw queue will do well; otherwise, you must configure your queue to pass its data through Ghostscript, as described in Chapter 6, "Configuring Printer Sharing."

Macintosh File Idiosyncrasies

DAVE works quite well on most networks, but it's not without quirks. Keep them in mind when using the software and when configuring Samba for DAVE clients.

Filename Characteristics

MacOS is limited to 31-character filenames. Although not as severe a restriction as DOS's 8.3 limit, 31 characters is still fewer than Linux—or SMB/CIFS—permits. If you serve a Linux filesystem with Netatalk, the server drops all files whose names exceed 31 characters. With Samba and DAVE, by contrast, those filenames are mangled, assuming the `mangled names` parameter is set to `Yes` (the default). Unfortunately, such names are not mangled down to 31 characters, but to DOS-style 8.3 filenames. Typical name-mangling caveats apply to such files—if a Macintosh program saves changes by moving the original and creating a new file, the original long filename on the Samba server will be lost.

Macintosh users sometimes use peculiar characters, such as copyright symbols (©), in filenames. These usually don't translate properly to Windows clients, or to the underlying Linux server. The same is true of some characters from non-Roman alphabets.

Macintosh programs sometimes don't take well to having filenames changed unexpectedly. Therefore, you should leave `preserve case = Yes` and `short preserve case = Yes` (their defaults). Setting these to other values may result in filenames' case changing in peculiar ways.

Unlike most client OSs, MacOS is happy with either case-sensitive or case-retentive filesystems. You can therefore set `case sensitive = Yes` if you like, although the default `case sensitive = No` is more useful for most non-MacOS clients. Because MacOS can handle this setting just fine, you should probably leave it that way unless you have some compelling reason to do otherwise.

Resource Forks

Native MacOS filesystems support two forks for their files, a *data fork* and a *resource fork*. The data fork contains ordinary file data such as ASCII text, graphics file contents, and so on. The resource fork contains specialized Macintosh information, including custom file icons, program executable code, and so on. Probably the most important peculiarity when dealing with MacOS is the question of how to handle these resource forks.

In the case of Samba and DAVE, it's DAVE that does the work of storing resource forks. To do this, DAVE creates a special folder, `resource.frk`, in which it stores Macintosh resource forks. This folder's contents are *not* compatible with Netatalk's `.AppleDouble` folder, which serves the same function, but the two are conceptually the same.

TIP To avoid confusion in other OSs, you can add `resource.frk` to the `hide files` parameter for any share you expect to be used by Macintosh DAVE clients.

Macintoshes use a pair of four-byte codes to store information on the file type and creator. MacOS uses these codes to launch an appropriate program when you double-click on a data file. In most other OSs, the three- or four-character filename extension serves this function. DAVE therefore includes a mapping of common Windows filename extensions to equivalent Macintosh type codes. The result is that a Samba share appears to be populated by files with familiar icons—if the filename extensions appear in DAVE's list. DAVE stores appropriate codes with new files in the `resource.frk` directory. If your network uses both Windows and Macintosh clients, ask your Macintosh users to create files with filename extensions that are appropriate for Windows users.

Samba with Multiple Client OSs

On a network that contains multiple client OSs, you may need to create a Samba configuration that works equally well from OSs with differing needs. Linux and Unix Samba clients work best when `case sensitive = Yes`, for instance; but DOS and Windows clients work best when `case sensitive = No`. It can be a challenge to create a configuration that works equally well with multiple OSs. There are two basic approaches to this problem: Use the `include` parameter to create multiple variants, or create a "best compromise" configuration. Both possibilities are described here.

Using the *include* Parameter

The `include` parameter can be used to load an auxiliary configuration file that's used in conjunction with the original file. This parameter would be nearly useless except for one important fact: Filenames can include variables. Table B.1 summarizes the most important variables for use in an `include` parameter's value, for purposes of OS customization.

Table B.1   Variables Useful in an `include` Parameter's Value

Variable	Purpose
%a	The client's architecture code; may be Samba, WfWg, Win95, WinNT, Win2K, OS2, or UNKNOWN
%R	The negotiated protocol level; may be CORE, COREPLUS, LANMAN1, LANMAN2, or NT1
%m	The NetBIOS name of the client
%M	The TCP/IP name of the client
%I	The IP address of the client

> **WARNING**   Neither Samba's SWAT GUI configuration tool nor the `linuxconf` tool that ships with many distributions understands variables in conjunction with the `include` parameter. If you want to use the `include` parameter approach, therefore, you'll have to refrain from using these GUI configuration tools.

Most useful of all the parameters in Table B.1 is %a, which allows you to customize your configuration on a per-OS basis. For instance, you could use the parameter `include = smb.conf.%a` in the `[global]` section of your `smb.conf` file. This causes Samba to include, at that point in its configuration file, the contents of `smb.conf.Samba` for Samba clients, `smb.conf.Win95` for Windows 9*x* clients, and so on. Following are some possible options for each of these mini-configuration files:

`smb.conf.Samba`

```
case sensitive = Yes
hide dot files = No
strict sync = Yes
```

`smb.conf.WfWg`

```
preserve case = No
mangled map = (*.html *.htm) (*.jpeg *.jpg)
```

smb.conf.WinNT

```
dos filetime resolution = Yes
dos filetimes = Yes
```

These modifications achieve several important effects. Samba clients get case-sensitive filenames, and the burden of hiding dot files from the users is shifted to the client OS. The strict sync = Yes parameter isn't required but might produce a modest improvement in reliability. The smb.conf.WfWg file works with both DOS and Windows for Workgroups clients. It ensures that short filenames created by the client are converted to all-lowercase for the benefit of other users. It also sets up a name-mangling map for some common four-character filename extensions. The smb.conf.WinNT file includes a couple of Samba parameters that are useful for software developers—some development tools expect to be able to modify file creation times (dos filetimes = Yes), and they cope best when these file creation times have two-second resolution rather than Samba's default one-second resolution (dos filetime resolution = Yes).

Sometimes two OSs produce identical %a codes. (Table B.2 summarizes the OSs and the %a codes they produce.) When this happens, you may need to rely on some other means of distinguishing the OSs. The %R parameter may be useful in this regard. Failing that, you can use one of the codes relating to specific client computers—%m, %M, or %I—to create custom configurations on a per-machine basis. You can use links between groups of these files to allow for easy maintenance on a by-OS basis.

Table B.2   Operating Systems Associated with Specific %a Codes

%a Code	Operating Systems
OS2	IBM OS/2
Samba	Samba clients (smbclient, smbmount)
UNKNOWN	BeOS (WON), MacOS (DAVE)
WfWg	DOS (using the Microsoft Network Client software), Windows for Workgroups
Win2K	Windows 2000
Win95	Windows 95, Windows 98
WinNT	Windows NT 3.1–4.0

> **TIP** You can find out what code the %a variable produces with any given client OS by using the parameter postexec = touch %H/%a in a test share (substitute another variable for %a, if you like). After the user disconnects, the result is a file created in the user's home directory. This file has the name of the %a code, such as WfWg for DOS or Windows for Workgroups clients.

A single smb.conf file may host multiple include parameters. You can use this fact to incorporate multiple customizations, such as one on a per-machine basis and one on a per-user basis (using the %u or %U variables). You might also want to include separate customizations for the [global] section and for one or more individual shares.

Creating Compromise Configurations

A compromise configuration is just that—a compromise between two conflicting requirements. For example, you might prefer to use preserve case = No for DOS clients, so that DOS-created files all have a consistent case (determined by default case) as viewed in Linux or from other client OSs. This setting interferes with case retention in more advanced OSs, however. For case preservation, a compromise configuration is to use short preserve case = No, which applies a consistent case only to 8.3 filenames.

In most situations, compromise configurations are undesirable, because the include parameter allows you to get what you want for all OSs. Compromise configurations can be useful in quick setups, however, or if you want to use a GUI configuration tool like SWAT, which doesn't understand variables as part of include parameters. Some parameters, such as mangled stack, apply systemwide; it doesn't make sense to include these parameters in included configuration files.

Summary

Samba is often considered a tool for integrating Linux and Windows systems. It's much more than that, however. Although not ideal for all OSs, SMB/CIFS clients are available for DOS, Windows 3.1, OS/2, BeOS, and MacOS. Samba itself can be used as a client, although NFS is usually a better choice for file sharing with Unix or Linux computers.

Because every OS treats filesystems uniquely, it's important to know about the most important OS-specific quirks when configuring a Samba server. Although Samba's default settings work reasonably well with most OSs (and especially with Windows clients), you may want to adjust a handful of parameters if your network has non-Windows OSs. In a mixed environment, the include parameter can be extremely useful in allowing Samba to manage connections from clients in the ways that work best with each OS.

Appendices

The GNU GPL

Most software ships under the terms of one or another *license agreement*, which is a legal document detailing the rights granted the user by the software's copyright holder. This is true even of open source software. Unlike commercial licenses, however, open source licenses are designed to give the user unusually broad rights to use, modify, and copy the software. There are several open source licenses in common use today, and in fact all Linux distributions ship with software that's licensed under several different licenses. Samba and the Linux kernel are both covered by the terms of a license developed by the Free Software Foundation (FSF) for its GNU's Not Unix (GNU) project. This license is known as the GNU *General Public License (GPL)*, and it's reproduced here.

GNU General Public License

Version 2, June 1991

Copyright © 1989, 1991 Free Software Foundation, Inc.

59 Temple Place, Suite 330, Boston, MA 02111-1307 USA

Everyone is permitted to copy and distribute verbatim copies of this license document, but changing it is not allowed.

Preamble

The licenses for most software are designed to take away your freedom to share and change it. By contrast, the GNU General Public License is intended to guarantee your freedom to share and change free software--to make sure the software is free for all its users. This General Public License applies to most of the Free Software Foundation's software and to any other program whose authors commit to using it. (Some other Free Software Foundation software is covered by the GNU Library General Public License instead.) You can apply it to your programs, too.

When we speak of free software, we are referring to freedom, not price. Our General Public Licenses are designed to make sure that you have the freedom to distribute copies of free software (and charge for this service if you wish), that you receive source code or can get it if you want it, that you can change the software or use pieces of it in new free programs; and that you know you can do these things.

To protect your rights, we need to make restrictions that forbid anyone to deny you these rights or to ask you to surrender the rights. These restrictions translate to certain responsibilities for you if you distribute copies of the software, or if you modify it.

For example, if you distribute copies of such a program, whether gratis or for a fee, you must give the recipients all the rights that you have. You must make sure that they, too, receive or can get the source code. And you must show them these terms so they know their rights.

We protect your rights with two steps: (1) copyright the software, and (2) offer you this license which gives you legal permission to copy, distribute and/or modify the software.

Also, for each author's protection and ours, we want to make certain that everyone understands that there is no warranty for this free software. If the software is modified by someone else and passed on, we want its recipients to know that what they have is not the original, so that any problems introduced by others will not reflect on the original authors' reputations.

Finally, any free program is threatened constantly by software patents. We wish to avoid the danger that redistributors of a free program will individually obtain patent licenses, in effect making the program proprietary. To prevent this, we have made it clear that any patent must be licensed for everyone's free use or not licensed at all.

The precise terms and conditions for copying, distribution and modification follow.

GNU General Public License

Terms and Conditions for Copying, Distribution and Modification

0. This License applies to any program or other work which contains a notice placed by the copyright holder saying it may be distributed under the terms of this General Public License. The "Program", below, refers to any such program or work, and a "work based on the Program" means either the Program or any derivative work under copyright law: that is to say, a work containing the Program or a portion of it, either verbatim or with modifications and/or translated into another language. (Hereinafter, translation is included without limitation in the term "modification".) Each licensee is addressed as "you".

Activities other than copying, distribution and modification are not covered by this License; they are outside its scope. The act of running the Program is not restricted, and the output from the Program is covered only if its contents constitute a work based on the Program (independent of having been made by running the Program). Whether that is true depends on what the Program does.

1. You may copy and distribute verbatim copies of the Program's source code as you receive it, in any medium, provided that you conspicuously and appropriately publish on each copy an appropriate copyright notice and disclaimer of warranty; keep intact all the notices that refer to this License and to the absence of any warranty; and give any other recipients of the Program a copy of this License along with the Program.

You may charge a fee for the physical act of transferring a copy, and you may at your option offer warranty protection in exchange for a fee.

2. You may modify your copy or copies of the Program or any portion of it, thus forming a work based on the Program, and copy and distribute such modifications or work under the terms of Section 1 above, provided that you also meet all of these conditions:

a) You must cause the modified files to carry prominent notices stating that you changed the files and the date of any change.

b) You must cause any work that you distribute or publish, that in whole or in part contains or is derived from the Program or any part thereof, to be licensed as a whole at no charge to all third parties under the terms of this License.

c) If the modified program normally reads commands interactively when run, you must cause it, when started running for such interactive use in the most ordinary way, to print or display an announcement including an appropriate copyright notice and a notice that there is no warranty (or else, saying that you provide a warranty) and that users may redistribute the program under these conditions, and telling the user how to view a copy of this License. (Exception: if the Program itself is interactive but does not normally print such an announcement, your work based on the Program is not required to print an announcement.)

These requirements apply to the modified work as a whole. If identifiable sections of that work are not derived from the Program, and can be reasonably considered independent and separate works in themselves, then this License, and its terms, do not apply to those sections when you distribute them as separate works. But when you distribute the same sections as part of a whole which is a work based on the Program, the distribution of the whole must be on the terms of this License, whose permissions for other licensees extend to the entire whole, and thus to each and every part regardless of who wrote it.

Thus, it is not the intent of this section to claim rights or contest your rights to work written entirely by you; rather, the intent is to exercise the right to control the distribution of derivative or collective works based on the Program.

In addition, mere aggregation of another work not based on the Program with the Program (or with a work based on the Program) on a volume of a storage or distribution medium does not bring the other work under the scope of this License.

3. You may copy and distribute the Program (or a work based on it, under Section 2) in object code or executable form under the terms of Sections 1 and 2 above provided that you also do one of the following:

   a) Accompany it with the complete corresponding machine-readable source code, which must be distributed under the terms of Sections 1 and 2 above on a medium customarily used for software interchange; or,

   b) Accompany it with a written offer, valid for at least three years, to give any third party, for a charge no more than your cost of physically performing source distribution, a complete machine-readable copy of the corresponding source code, to be distributed under the terms of Sections 1 and 2 above on a medium customarily used for software interchange; or,

   c) Accompany it with the information you received as to the offer to distribute corresponding source code. (This alternative is allowed only for noncommercial distribution and only if you received the program in object code or executable form with such an offer, in accord with Subsection b above.)

The source code for a work means the preferred form of the work for making modifications to it. For an executable work, complete source code means all the source code for all modules it contains, plus any associated interface definition files, plus the scripts used to control compilation and installation of the executable. However, as a special exception, the source code distributed need not include anything that is normally distributed (in either source or binary form) with the major components (compiler, kernel, and so on) of the operating system on which the executable runs, unless that component itself accompanies the executable.

If distribution of executable or object code is made by offering access to copy from a designated place, then offering equivalent access to copy the source code from the same place counts as distribution of the source code, even though third parties are not compelled to copy the source along with the object code.

4. You may not copy, modify, sublicense, or distribute the Program except as expressly provided under this License. Any attempt otherwise to copy, modify, sublicense or distribute the Program is void, and will automatically terminate your rights under this License. However, parties who have received copies, or rights, from you under this License will not have their licenses terminated so long as such parties remain in full compliance.

5. You are not required to accept this License, since you have not signed it. However, nothing else grants you permission to modify or distribute the Program or its derivative works. These actions are prohibited by law if you do not accept this License. Therefore, by modifying or distributing the Program (or any work based on the Program), you indicate your acceptance of this License to do so, and all its terms and conditions for copying, distributing or modifying the Program or works based on it.

6. Each time you redistribute the Program (or any work based on the Program), the recipient automatically receives a license from the original licensor to copy, distribute or modify the Program subject to these terms and conditions. You may not impose any further restrictions on the recipients' exercise of the rights granted herein. You are not responsible for enforcing compliance by third parties to this License.

7. If, as a consequence of a court judgment or allegation of patent infringement or for any other reason (not limited to patent issues), conditions are imposed on you (whether by court order, agreement or otherwise) that contradict the conditions of this License, they do not excuse you from the conditions of this License. If you cannot distribute so as to satisfy simultaneously your obligations under this License and any other pertinent obligations, then as a consequence you may not distribute the Program at all. For example, if a patent license would not permit royalty-free redistribution of the Program by all those who receive copies directly or indirectly through you, then the only way you could satisfy both it and this License would be to refrain entirely from distribution of the Program.

If any portion of this section is held invalid or unenforceable under any particular circumstance, the balance of the section is intended to apply and the section as a whole is intended to apply in other circumstances.

It is not the purpose of this section to induce you to infringe any patents or other property right claims or to contest validity of any such claims; this section has the sole purpose of protecting the integrity of the free software distribution system, which is implemented by public license practices. Many people have made generous contributions to the wide range of software distributed through that system in reliance on consistent application of that system; it is up to the author/donor to decide if he or she is willing to distribute software through any other system and a licensee cannot impose that choice.

This section is intended to make thoroughly clear what is believed to be a consequence of the rest of this License.

8. If the distribution and/or use of the Program is restricted in certain countries either by patents or by copyrighted interfaces, the original copyright holder who places the Program under this License may add an explicit geographical distribution limitation excluding those countries, so that distribution is permitted only in or among countries not thus excluded. In such case, this License incorporates the limitation as if written in the body of this License.

9. The Free Software Foundation may publish revised and/or new versions of the General Public License from time to time. Such new versions will be similar in spirit to the present version, but may differ in detail to address new problems or concerns.

   Each version is given a distinguishing version number. If the Program specifies a version number of this License which applies to it and "any later version", you have the option of following the terms and conditions either of that version or of any later version published by the Free Software Foundation. If the Program does not specify a version number of this License, you may choose any version ever published by the Free Software Foundation.

10. If you wish to incorporate parts of the Program into other free programs whose distribution conditions are different, write to the author to ask for permission. For software which is copyrighted by the Free Software Foundation, write to the Free Software Foundation; we sometimes make exceptions for this. Our decision will be guided by the two goals of preserving the free status of all derivatives of our free software and of promoting the sharing and reuse of software generally.

NO WARRANTY

11. BECAUSE THE PROGRAM IS LICENSED FREE OF CHARGE, THERE IS NO WARRANTY FOR THE PROGRAM, TO THE EXTENT PERMITTED BY APPLICABLE LAW. EXCEPT WHEN OTHERWISE STATED IN WRITING THE COPYRIGHT HOLDERS AND/OR OTHER PARTIES PROVIDE THE PROGRAM "AS IS" WITHOUT WARRANTY OF ANY KIND, EITHER EXPRESSED OR IMPLIED, INCLUDING, BUT NOT LIMITED TO, THE IMPLIED WARRANTIES OF MERCHANTABILITY AND FITNESS FOR A PARTICULAR PURPOSE. THE ENTIRE RISK AS TO THE QUALITY AND PERFORMANCE OF THE PROGRAM IS WITH YOU. SHOULD THE PROGRAM PROVE DEFECTIVE, YOU ASSUME THE COST OF ALL NECESSARY SERVICING, REPAIR OR CORRECTION.

12. IN NO EVENT UNLESS REQUIRED BY APPLICABLE LAW OR AGREED TO IN WRITING WILL ANY COPYRIGHT HOLDER, OR ANY OTHER PARTY WHO MAY MODIFY AND/OR REDISTRIBUTE THE PROGRAM AS PERMITTED ABOVE, BE LIABLE TO YOU FOR DAMAGES, INCLUDING ANY GENERAL, SPECIAL, INCIDENTAL OR CONSEQUENTIAL DAMAGES ARISING OUT OF THE USE OR INABILITY TO USE THE PROGRAM (INCLUDING BUT NOT LIMITED TO LOSS OF DATA OR DATA BEING RENDERED INACCURATE OR LOSSES SUSTAINED BY YOU OR THIRD PARTIES OR A FAILURE OF THE PROGRAM TO OPERATE WITH ANY OTHER PROGRAMS), EVEN IF SUCH HOLDER OR OTHER PARTY HAS BEEN ADVISED OF THE POSSIBILITY OF SUCH DAMAGES.

END OF TERMS AND CONDITIONS

How to Apply These Terms to Your New Programs

If you develop a new program, and you want it to be of the greatest possible use to the public, the best way to achieve this is to make it free software which everyone can redistribute and change under these terms.

To do so, attach the following notices to the program. It is safest to attach them to the start of each source file to most effectively convey the exclusion of warranty; and each file should have at least the "copyright" line and a pointer to where the full notice is found.

<one line to give the program's name and a brief idea of what it does.>

Copyright (C) <year> <name of author>

This program is free software; you can redistribute it and/or modify it under the terms of the GNU General Public License as published by the Free Software Foundation; either version 2 of the License, or (at your option) any later version.

This program is distributed in the hope that it will be useful, but WITHOUT ANY WARRANTY; without even the implied warranty of MERCHANTABILITY or FITNESS FOR A PARTICULAR PURPOSE. See the GNU General Public License for more details.

You should have received a copy of the GNU General Public License along with this program; if not, write to the Free Software Foundation, Inc., 59 Temple Place, Suite 330, Boston, MA 02111-1307 USA

Also add information on how to contact you by electronic and paper mail.

If the program is interactive, make it output a short notice like this when it starts in an interactive mode:

Gnomovision version 69, Copyright (C) year name of author

Gnomovision comes with ABSOLUTELY NO WARRANTY; for details type 'show w'. This is free software, and you are welcome to redistribute it under certain conditions; type 'show c' for details.

The hypothetical commands 'show w' and 'show c' should show the appropriate parts of the General Public License. Of course, the commands you use may be called something other than 'show w' and 'show c'; they could even be mouse-clicks or menu items—whatever suits your program.

You should also get your employer (if you work as a programmer) or your school, if any, to sign a "copyright disclaimer" for the program, if necessary. Here is a sample; alter the names:

Yoyodyne, Inc., hereby disclaims all copyright interest in the program 'Gnomovision' (which makes passes at compilers) written by James Hacker.

<signature of Ty Coon>, 1 April 1989

Ty Coon, President of Vice

This General Public License does not permit incorporating your program into proprietary programs. If your program is a subroutine library, you may consider it more useful to permit linking proprietary applications with the library. If this is what you want to do, use the GNU Library General Public License instead of this License.

Index

Note to Reader: In this index, **boldfaced** page numbers refer to primary discussions of the topic; *italics* page numbers refer to figures.

Symbols & Numbers

Index

The Craig Hunt Linux Library

◆ Written under the direction of Craig Hunt, renowned Linux and TCP/IP guru
◆ Developed specifically for networking professionals working in Linux environments
◆ Offers the most advanced and focused coverage of key topics for Linux Administrators

Craig Hunt is a noted TCP/IP and Linux expert who lectures regularly on the topics at the NetWorld+Interop, ComNet, and other networking trade shows. His other books include the best-selling *Linux Network Servers 24seven* from Sybex®.

by Craig Hunt
0-7821-2736-3 • $39.99

by Charles Aulds
0-7821-2734-7 • $39.99

by Vicki Stanfield, etal
0-7821-2735-5 • $39.99

by Roderick W. Smith
0-7821-2740-1 • $39.99

by Craig Hunt
0-7821-2737-1 • $39.99
1st Quarter 2001

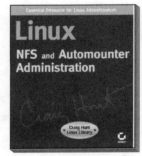

by Ranon J. Hontanon
0-7821-2739-8 • $39.99
Coming in 2001

Also Available: **Linux Security** by Ranon J. Hontanon • 0-7821-2739-8 • $39.99 • Coming in 2001

The Linux standard on your bookshelf.

www.sybex.com

Sample *smb.conf* File (cont.)

```
[netlogon]
        path = /home/samba/netlogon
        write list = isaac


[printer$]
        path = /home/samba/printer-files


[homes]
        comment = Home Directories
        writeable = Yes
        browseable = No

[shared]
        comment = Shared Windows Files
        path = /home/samba/shared
        writeable = Yes
        force user = nemo


[cd-create]
        path = /home/samba/cd-create
        writeable = Yes
        create mask = 0666
        directory mask = 0777
        max connections = 1
        hide dot files = No
        preexec = rm -r /home/samba/cd-create/*
        postexec = mkisofs -a -J -r -log-file %H/log-%d.txt↵
                     -o %H/image-%d.iso/home/samba/cd-create

[printers]
        path = /var/spool/samba
        printer driver = "Apple LaserWriter II NTX"
        printable = Yes
        browseable = No
        postscript = Yes

[epson-raw]
        comment = Epson inkjet
        path = /var/spool/samba
        printer driver = "Epson Stylus COLOR ESC/P 2"
        printable = Yes
        guest ok = Yes

[pdf-create]
        comment = Create a PDF file
        path = /var/spool/samba
        printer driver = "Apple LaserWriter II NTX"
        printable = Yes
        print command = gs -dNOPAUSE -sDEVICE=pdfwrite -q -dBATCH↵
                     -sOutputFile=%H/%s.pdf %s; rm %s
```